# How to Prepare and Present a Labor Arbitration Case

## Strategy and Tactics for Advocates

# How to Prepare and Present a Labor Arbitration Case

## Strategy and Tactics for Advocates

## Charles S. Loughran

The Bureau of National Affairs, Inc., Washington, D.C.

Copyright © 1996

The Bureau of National Affairs, Inc.

Second Printing, February 1997
Third Printing, April 1998
Fourth Printing, July 1999

**Library of Congress Cataloging-in-Publication Data**

Loughran, Charles S.
    How to prepare and present a labor arbitration case : strategy and
tactics for advocates / Charles S. Loughran.
        p.   cm.
    Includes index.
    ISBN 0-87179-887-5 (hc)
    1. Grievance arbitration--United States.  2. Grievance procedures-
-United States.  3. Arbitration, Industrial--United States.
I. Title.
KF3544.L68  1996
344.73'0189143--dc20
[347.304189143]                                              96-13105
                                                                CIP

Published by BNA Books
1250 23rd St. NW, Washington, DC 20037
International Standard Book Number: 0-87179-887-5
*Printed in the United States of America*

Dedicated to Jo
my wife, partner, and best friend

# Summary Table of Contents

## Part III. After the Hearing

# Detailed Table of Contents

## Part II. During the Hearing

### Part III. After the Hearing

# Preface

The following are just a few words to alert the reader about the type of book he or she is about to read and what, and what not, to expect from it.

Perhaps the closest analogy one might make between this volume and other types of books is to compare it to a cookbook. It attempts to lead the reader through each step of the labor arbitration process much as a cookbook is used to guide its reader through each step, for example, of baking a cake. For the novice advocate, a thorough reading of each and every chapter may be necessary just as the author (a *very* amateur cook) finds it absolutely essential to follow a cookbook's recipe and preparation instructions to the letter. An experienced advocate, however, may only need to refer to selected portions of the book much as a skilled cook might periodically check a cookbook merely to confirm the need for a particular ingredient and/or its quantity. In short, it is designed so that all advocates, novice and seasoned, will find value within its pages.

Arbitrators, too, might find it useful—particularly to see the arbitration process from the perspective of the advocate and to evaluate the strategies and tactics often employed by experienced advocates in case preparation and presentation. For these same reasons, students will hopefully find this to be an important resource in their studies of labor relations and advocacy.

This is a book essentially about *process*, not substantive labor arbitration principles. Many other well-written books cover arbitration principles in detail, most of which are included in the section entitled, "Other Readings on Labor Arbitration and Advocacy Skills" which can be found immediately following Appendix C. Although there are occassional references in the text and footnotes to substantive labor arbitration principles and issues, the intended scope of this volume is limited to the process of preparing and presenting a labor arbitration case.

Unlike my earlier work for BNA Books on labor contract negotiations (*Negotiating a Labor Contract; A Management Handbook, Second Ed.,* Washington, DC; BNA Books, 1992) this book is designed for union, as well as management, advocates. In virtually all aspects of case preparation and presentation, the tasks and skills of a union advocate are mirror images of those of his or her management counterpart, and vice versa. Although union advocates are almost always representing the party bringing the grievance or the "complainant," and the management advocates represent the employer defending the grievance, or "respondent," the specfic steps in handling the case are identical. In the many examples and practical tips found throughout the book, both union and management perspectives are reflected.

No attempt is made to distinguish between process and procedures used in the private versus the public sector, among differences within particular industries in the private sector, or among the variety of different procedures followed by various state and federal government employers. Admittedly, the terminology and examples used throughout the book focus primarily on the private sector, although the author believes that most, if not all, of the material in this book will be relevant and useful to advocates who operate in the public sector.

Despite the increasing prevalence of attorneys acting as labor arbitration advocates, particular care has been taken to avoid legalisms and technical jargon in presenting the material in this book. Notwithstanding, some readers may feel that the arbitration hearing procedures that are discussed in some chapters (particularly Chapter 10, Rules of Evidence, and Chapter 11, Making and Defending Against Objections) are more technical than necessary on the basis of their own experience. As explained in several chapters, the author appreciates the existence of a rather wide range of formality followed by different arbitrators. As a result, he has opted to include more technical advice and guidance on such matters as rules of evidence on the theory that the reader may encounter arbitrators who follow or apply litigation rules and procedures that are more common in court than in the traditional labor arbitration settings. The rationale underlying this approach is to forewarn and prepare the advocate to cope with such rules and procedures in the event that they are encountered. It is easier and more comforting to discard what is surplus than to be surprised and disadvantaged by new and unfamiliar procedures.

This book deals solely with *labor* arbitration, and no attempt has been made to address other types of arbitration such as non-collective bargaining employment disputes or commercial arbitration. It was felt that justice could not be done to other related fields of arbitration in the same book as labor arbitration, without critically sacrificing adequate treatment of the latter subject. Nevertheless, advocates finding themselves with a case in other related arenas, such as employment disputes in nonunion settings, may find relevant and useful information in a number of chapters in this book.

It also needs to be pointed out that this book addresses only *grievance* arbitration and not *interest* arbitration. Interest arbitration involves decision-making by an arbitrator of the terms and conditions of employment that unions and employers are going to incorporate into their labor agreement. Found most commonly in the public sector, it is typically an alternative to a strike at the expiration of a labor agreement. Most often the arbitrator is called upon to set the wages and benefits that will apply during the subsequent contract period. Grievance arbitration, on the other hand, requires the arbitrator to interpret the language of an existing labor agreement within the context of a particular set of facts brought forth by a grievance. Although hearing presentation is often very similar between the two types of arbitration, preparation and argumentation are normally quite different. Here again, however, the advocate approaching an interest arbitration may discover some useful guidance from this volume.

Having been a labor arbitration advocate in several hundred cases spanning a career of more than 25 years and having labored in the legal litigation arena for a portion of those years, the author is absolutely convinced that labor arbitration as it is commonly practiced in the United States is a far superior means of resolving labor agreement grievance disputes, and perhaps other labor disputes, than civil litigation. The speed, simplicity, economy, and finality of labor arbitration has allowed unions and employers in the United States, at least those with mature collective bargaining relationships, to co-exist, if not thrive, in a relatively stable and harmonious environment. Contrary to the European experience, strikes during the term of an existing labor agreement are extremely rare in this country. Moreover lawsuits about the meaning and application of existing labor agreements are few and far between. This is due almost exclusively to the wide acceptance and proven success of grievance arbitration. It is a process that has served unions and employers extremely well, and one about which the author is delighted to share his own lessons and experience and hopefully to which this book will make some lasting contribution.

C.L.S.

Oakland, CA
June, 1996

# Part I

# Before the Hearing

# 1

# Overview of the Labor Arbitration Process

A vital prerequisite to presenting a labor arbitration case is a thorough understanding of the procedure that will be followed during the hearing. Although different arbitrators follow somewhat different procedures, especially concerning the degree of formality required, most arbitrators adhere to processes that have been standardized sufficiently that it is possible to discuss them in one profile.

The principal purpose of this first chapter is to describe the structure of a typical arbitration hearing and the essential concepts that govern the sequence and conduct of the hearing. Also included in this chapter is a brief discussion of the application of the rules of evidence. Each of these subjects is covered in considerably more detail in succeeding chapters. The purpose of addressing them here is to give the reader an overview of the hearing process at the outset so that discussion of other subjects, such as preparing the case for hearing, covered in chapters 2 through 5, will have greater meaning and value.

Before launching into an overview of the hearing process it is useful to discuss the role of advocate and the person to whom that task should be assigned.

## SELECTING THE ADVOCATE

The initial reaction of the reader to the above heading is likely to be, "Why do we need to discuss this? *I'm* presenting the case." Indeed, this book is designed to be read by the employer or union representative who has been designated as the arbitration advocate. In most cases the selection of the advocate will already have been made. There may, however, be some readers who are not advocates, such as union officials or business managers, and who need to make that selection. Moreover, the designated advocate needs to consider whether he or she is in the best position to present a particular case, even though that person normally presents arbitration cases for his or her respective organization.

## Lawyers Versus Nonlawyers

The author has been an arbitration advocate before and after becoming a lawyer and therefore claims a certain amount of objectivity in addressing the question of whether arbitration cases are most effectively presented by lawyers or nonlawyers. In addition, the issue of practicality or cost effectiveness should be considered. Even though a lawyer might be more effective than a layperson, can the arbitrating party afford to pay for the services of a lawyer? There is usually a need to balance the desire for enhancing the chances of winning a case with the necessity of controlling expenses. Although this balancing act is typically more of a problem for unions than employers, it does affect both parties.

Because most arbitration hearings follow both the procedures of evidentiary hearings and, at least minimally, the rules of evidence, lawyers have a distinct advantage over nonlawyers when all else is equal. Typically, however, other things are not equal, and the native or acquired abilities of many lay advocates, coupled with their knowledge of the industry, bargaining history, work practices, and shop jargon frequently give them a distinct advantage over their legal counterparts. This disadvantage is minimized, however, if the lawyer is a regular representative of the union or employer organization being represented or is so frequently employed by that organization that he or she has command of the work place practices, jargon, and labor relations history.

### Cases with Significant Legal Aspects

Notwithstanding these individual differences, there are certain situations in which lawyers have an important advantage. Some cases are, by their subject matter or the type of evidence that is likely to be introduced, more "legalistic." For example, cases that raise possible civil or criminal claims such as racial or sex discrimination, embezzlement, fraud, and defamation are best handled by a lawyer. Similarly, where there is a pending court case on the same set of facts and where the evidence presented in arbitration is likely to be part of the court case, it is advisable to have an attorney conduct the arbitration (preferably the same one who will be handling the litigation). In arbitration hearings where key evidence is marginally admissible (e.g., double hearsay testimony or when the employer obtains the testimony of a terminated employee not offered as a witness by the union) it is often advisable to have a lawyer present the case to better argue the admissibility of key evidence.

## Lawyers Representing the Opposing Side

When one side has a lawyer presenting its case, it is often, but not always, advisable for the opposing party to have legal representation as well. This is not as important if the case is relatively simple and not legally complex and if the lay advocate is reasonably experienced. Nevertheless, the lawyer advocate is usually better trained to handle evidentiary issues, cross-examination of witnesses, and presentation of issues having to do with "external law" (i.e., legal issues outside the labor agreement).

If, after weighing the pros and cons, a party decides to use a lay advocate where a lawyer might be better suited, it is usually advisable for the lay advocate to at least consult with a labor lawyer before and during the preparation of the case. This will give the lay advocate the opportunity to anticipate the type of objections that are likely to be raised by the other side and to devise strategies to deal with them. Also, the lawyer can brief the lay advocate on the principal points of law that are essential to the case.

## Advocate's Testimony Is Essential to the Case

Another situation in which an advocate should consider whether he or she should present the case is where the advocate's own testimony is essential to proving key facts. Although arbitrators generally will permit advocates to testify[1], such testimony is apt to be given less weight by an arbitrator than it would if the witness were not an advocate in the case. The arbitrator is naturally inclined to presume that the advocate is biased

---

[1] Adolph Coors, 235 NLRB 271, 273, n.4, 98 LRRM 1539 (1978); Needham Packing Co., 44 LA 1057, 1088 (Davey, 1965); SCHOONHOVEN, FAIRWEATHER'S PRACTICE AND PROCEDURE IN LABOR ARBITRATION, 3d ed. (BNA Books, 1991).

toward his or her case and that the advocate-witness is likely to be careful about presenting any evidence that would be harmful to his or her case.

For many years labor arbitration has been an extremely effective means for resolving contract disputes where the majority of cases have been presented by laypersons. In more recent years there appears to be a distinct trend to use lawyers as arbitration advocates, particularly by employers. The author believes that most arbitration cases can be very effectively presented by nonlawyers and that, to a certain extent, the process works better for the long term union-management relationship because lay advocates are less likely to delay the proceedings or unduly complicate the hearing with technicalities and objections. A number of arbitrators have expressed this opinion to the author. It is a prudent union or management, however, that considers—before entering into a particular arbitration—whether the case in question is the type of case that should be presented by a lawyer.


# THE HEARING PROCESS

## Division between Evidence and Argument

One of most important distinctions that an advocate must keep in mind before, during, and after an arbitration hearing is the essential difference between evidence and argument. This difference is crucial to presenting an orderly and persuasive case, yet it is frequently misunderstood or misapplied by the inexperienced advocate. What makes it particularly difficult to apply is that fact and argument are invariably intertwined in a case, and it is often difficult to ascertain just where one ends and the other begins. The following example might be useful to illustrate this point.

A labor agreement provision limits an employer to promoting the employee with the most plant seniority who bids for a job vacancy unless another employee bids for the job and has "substantially greater qualifications" than the most senior employee. In this example Employee A has 15 years plant seniority and is judged by the employer to be reasonably capable, yet not exceptionally so, of performing the duties of the vacant position. Employee B has 6 years seniority, has previously performed the exact duties of the open position, and is judged by the employer to be especially well qualified for the open job. The employer selects Employee B for the position. Employee A files a grievance. In preparing for the case both union and employer advocates make lists of the points they wish to bring out in the hearing as follows:

- Union
    - Employee A has had an outstanding record of performance and attendance during his 15 years of service.
    - Employee A is fully capable of performing the job after a brief break-in period.
    - Employee B has less than half the length of service with the employer that Employee A has.
    - Employee B gained experience in performing the tasks in question while assigned to a temporary position that should have been, but was not, made available through the bid process.
    - Employee A has more education than Employee B.
    - The employer has never previously promoted a junior employee over a more senior employee where the difference in service between the competing employees was more than one year.

- Employer
    - Employee B would not need any training to perform fully the tasks of the vacant position.
    - Employee A produces a greater amount of waste or off-standard products than Employee B.
    - Employee B has a better safety record than Employee A.
    - The history of negotiations shows that the parties intended that the company would have the right to promote junior employees in this type of situation.
    - Employee B is a woman, and the employer is a government contractor with an affirmative action plan obligating it to increase opportunities for women and minorities.
    - The company is in a very competitive business and needs to maximize productivity. It should have the right to promote employees who are most likely to increase productivity, such as Employee B in this case.

The statements listed above are arguments that each side will present to the arbitrator. All of them are based on fact or at least on an alleged fact or group of facts. Some of the facts are easy to prove (Employee A has more than twice as much seniority as Employee B; Employee B is a woman and Employee A is a man). Other facts may be very difficult to prove (Employee B would not need any training to do the job; the negotiating parties intended to permit this type of promotion; Employee A has more production waste than Employee B). Whether the facts are difficult or easy to prove, it is important to distinguish between *facts*, which are *proven* by reliable and persuasive evidence, and *argu-*

*ment,* which is *supported* by facts but relies primarily on logic, reason, and common sense.

In this example the union's argument that Employee B gained her experience through a temporary assignment that was not filled through proper bidding procedures will be relatively easy to prove. But this is subject to the challenge by the employer of "So what?" because the question is whether Employee B has substantially greater qualifications than Employee A, not whether she acquired them in a proper fashion. Arbitrators are often influenced, however, by arguments based on equity, and this type of argument may carry some weight with the arbitrator if it can be shown that Employee B's temporary assignment was obtained in violation of the labor agreement.

Some arguments are based on very few facts or the factual content is almost taken for granted (e.g., the employer is in a very competitive business), and the basic thrust of the argument is therefore based on logic, principle, or rhetoric (e.g., the employer should be allowed to promote more productive employees over less productive ones in order to compete effectively in its industry). Most arbitrators will listen and give weight to such arguments but will not treat them as decisive unless the provisions of the labor agreement support such a result.

## Significance of the Evidence/Argument Distinction

It is important that the advocate keep the fact/argument distinction always in mind because, in preparing and presenting the case, he or she must always ask, "What facts and what supporting evidence are available to make this argument?" Those facts must be brought out and proven by evidence during the hearing. Because the argument phase of a labor arbitration hearing is frequently done through written briefs following the hearing, new or modified arguments can often be presented. This is not so with facts. If facts have not been presented to the arbitrator through admissible evidence in the hearing itself, the opportunity to bring them before the arbitrator is lost. Of course, new or changed arguments made in a brief will have little impact on an arbitrator if evidence to support those arguments was not presented in the hearing. It is common, however, that a certain body of evidence can support a number of different arguments. An advocate may come up with a new slant or concept in a brief, provided he or she has been careful to have entered into the record those documents or testimony that will support that argument.

Another important reason for keeping the fact/argument distinction in mind is in the proper conduct of the hearing. In certain parts of the hearing only the introduction of evidence is permitted, whereas in other parts argument is the essential element. In the opening statement and the closing argument (or written brief) arguments are permitted and frequently constitute the heart of the presentation, whereas in the central part of the hearing (i.e., case in chief and rebuttal) only the presentation of evidence is permitted.

As with all rules, there are some exceptions. In the course of presenting testimonial and documentary evidence, a certain amount of argument generally creeps in, and, unless it is too blatant, opposing counsel is apt to overlook or to tolerate it and therefore not object. Likewise, an arbitrator is likely to permit a certain amount of argument so long as it is intermingled with factual evidence. An advocate is apt to bring on the wrath of the arbitrator, however, by regularly making arguments during the portion of the hearing designed for presentation of evidence. A truly competent advocate makes a clear distinction in his or her mind as to the difference between fact and argument and presents them in those portions of the hearing in which they are appropriate.

### Marshaling the Facts and Evidence

Relating to the previous example of the case involving the promotion of a junior employee over a senior employee, an assemblage of evidence to support the union's version of the facts might look something like this.

- Record of Employee A's work performance during his career; testimony of coworkers or others about his good work record.
- Testimony by Employee A or others that Employee A has performed duties (in the same plant or elsewhere) similar to those in question and has done so proficiently. The advocate might offer evidence of Employee A's skills to perform that job by way of an actual demonstration.
- Seniority records reflecting Employee A's and Employee B's seniority dates; records and/or testimony concerning the levels of the two employee's education and training.
- Evidence of how Employee B improperly was assigned temporarily to the job in question and obtained experience on that job on which the employer is relying to promote outside seniority order.
- Records and testimony as to how the employer has adhered to seniority in the past in making promotions (i.e., past practice).

By gathering all of this evidence and presenting it to the arbitrator the union advocate is in a position to make the arguments listed previously.

## STRUCTURE OF THE HEARING

As stated earlier in this chapter, unless the controlling labor agreement spells out a distinct procedure for the conduct of arbitration hearings (and it is the very rare contract that does), the arbitrator is generally free to follow whatever procedure he or she believes to be fairest and most efficient. About the only limit on the arbitrator's authority in this regard is that the procedure provide for due process, meaning that the procedure must give each party a fair opportunity to present its side of the dispute. Other than that, the arbitrator has more or less free rein in determining how to conduct the hearing. Notwithstanding this broad latitude, most arbitrators follow more or less the same basic format (i.e., the general procedure followed in trials).

Perhaps the best way to visualize the course of the normal arbitration hearing is to view a typical contract interpretation grievance (i.e., not involving discipline or discharge of an employee) from a schematic or diagrammatic standpoint, as shown in fig. 1-1.

## PRELIMINARY MATTERS

There is no official portion of a hearing that is called "preliminary matters," but in virtually every hearing there are a number of matters that must be addressed before the actual hearing begins. These matters can range from identification of each party's advocate to the question of whether either party objects to publication of the decision and innumerable other questions. Depending on whether the arbitrator has heard other cases involving these same two parties, the preliminaries may be very brief or rather extended. Chapter 7 is devoted exclusively to this stage of the hearing. Issues raised in the preliminary stage are often off the record, that is, if there is a stenographic transcription being made of the case, the reporter does not record these discussions, and if no transcript is being made, the parties usually understand that these discussions are not part of the formal hearing. This is usually the best time for the advocates and the arbitrator to deal with any matters that could present problems later in the hearing.

### Determining the Issue

Fundamental to the hearing of any grievance arbitration is the identification and, it is hoped, agreement of the parties as to what issues

**Figure 1-1.**
**Schematic Diagram of a Labor Arbitration Hearing**
**(Labor Contract Interpretation Case)**

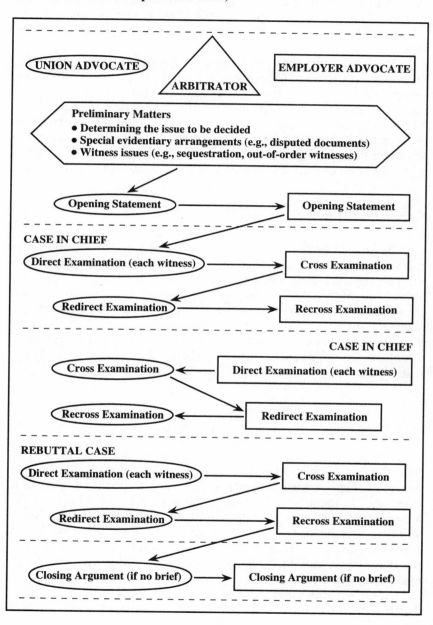

are to be decided by the arbitrator. Many arbitrators address this subject prior to opening the hearing. Others prefer to wait until the parties go on the record before addressing this question. In either case it is important that it not be delayed too long into the hearing, because questions of admissibility of evidence will turn on what issue(s) is to be decided in the case.

The issues will usually be framed in a general sense by the way the grievance was written. Grievants are not always precise in their language, however, and it is often difficult to formulate a cogent issue from the statement of the grievance. In cases where the parties are generally in agreement about the nature of the case but cannot reach a consensus on the exact phrasing of the issue, the parties will usually submit to the arbitrator their respective versions of the issue statement and agree to allow the arbitrator to fashion the exact statement of the issues.

## Other Preliminary Matters

Beyond identifying the issue to be decided by the arbitrator, the parties must usually address a number of other matters prior to opening the hearing, including whether there are any evidentiary issues that should be discussed, such as dealing with an unavailable witness; requested sequestration of witnesses (i.e., excluding witnesses from the hearing room); requests for unusual presentation of evidence such as videotaped evidence, telephonic testimony, or use of an interpreter; or any other matters that are best discussed before the hearing begins. These matters are discussed more fully in Chapter 7.

## OPENING STATEMENTS

The real start of most arbitration hearings is the presentation by both parties of their opening statements, that is, descriptions of what their cases are all about. This is usually the first real opportunity for the arbitrator to understand what the parties' dispute concerns, what issues will have to be decided, what the respective positions of the parties are on the issues, what evidence is likely to be introduced to support those positions, and other information that foreshadows what will occur in the evidentiary portion of the case.

Some advocates prefer to waive their opening statement. They feel that it is better to let their evidence come in without signaling their position to the other side too early in the case. Other advocates, particularly those representing the respondent party, i.e., defending side (generally the employer in contract interpretation cases and the union in discipline and discharge cases), prefer to postpone their opening statement until the other side has presented all its evidence. Chapter 8 discusses the strategy of these two approaches as well as other facets of opening statements. For now, it is sufficient to say that the opportunity is provided to both parties at the outset of the hearing to explain to the arbitrator how they see the case and how they intend to persuade the arbitrator of the correctness of their respective positions.

The opening statement can be, and normally should be, a mixture of fact and argument. In explaining the case the advocate should describe what his or her evidence will prove with regard to the facts and is free to put whatever gloss or spin on those facts that will best support his or her arguments. The factual context in which the arguments are placed must be that which the advocate will be able to produce in the hearing in order to be credible. Nevertheless, there is nothing that precludes the advocate from arguing the case to the arbitrator at this early stage of the procedure.

## THE CASE IN CHIEF

Once the preliminaries and opening statements are concluded, the evidentiary portion of the hearing may begin. The case in chief is simply the body of evidence that each party will present as its primary case. It is distinct from the rebuttal phase of the hearing, which consists of the body of evidence that is presented to refute or rebut the evidence presented by the other side during its case in chief.

The case in chief consists of each side's witnesses, documents, and other evidence necessary to prove its case. It should be sufficient to persuade an arbitrator to rule in its favor if no evidence is presented by the other side. Of course, there will virtually always be evidence from the other side, but the case in chief should be planned so that it would be strong enough to win the case if it were looked at in isolation. A party's case in chief begins when it calls its first witness and ends when its last witness (except for rebuttal witnesses) has completed his or her testimony, and all other evidence has been offered and received.

### Direct Examination

Direct examination is the portion of the case in chief in which advocates ask questions of their own witnesses. The questions should be designed to elicit facts that are essential to proving the case. These should be facts about which the witness is competent to testify (i.e., the witness has first-hand knowledge of the facts or reasonably reliable second-hand knowledge). In most instances documents and other evidence (e.g., physical evidence including tools, weapons, clothing, and models) are brought into evidence through the testimony of witnesses. To establish the identity and authenticity of a document or other piece of evidence, it is usually necessary for a witness to identify it and describe its origin, significance, and relevance to the case. Chapter 9 covers this process in considerable detail.

## Cross-Examination

Each party's witnesses are subject to questioning by the other side's advocate. This process is called cross-examination. Somewhat different guidelines apply to questions posed by the opposing party, and these are covered in detail in Chapter 11. This is one area that many advocates frequently neglect to cover sufficiently during their preparation of a case. They typically spend most of their available time on preparing the testimony of their own witnesses, but little or no time anticipating the testimony of the opposing side's witnesses and preparing questions to be asked of those witnesses. Although cases are not usually won or lost through cross-examination, effective questioning by the opposing side frequently aids in achieving a favorable result.

## Redirect and Recross-Examination

As the words connote, redirect examination (usually referred to simply as "redirect") and recross-examination (or simply "recross") are merely repetitions of direct examination and cross-examination in another round(s) of questions by the respective advocates. The general rule of civil trial procedure is that the only proper questions on redirect examination are ones directly related to the other party's questions asked on cross-examination (referred to as the "within the scope" rule). Under this rule, for example, the only proper questions on redirect examination are those concerning points that were brought up on cross-examination, and the only proper questions on recross-examination are those related to points brought out in the redirect examination.

Few labor arbitrators, however, are so locked into such formal procedures that they will limit the questioning in that manner, especially when the questions posed have the potential of eliciting useful and relevant information. As will be discussed throughout this book, the beauty of labor arbitration is that it enables the production of a great deal of evidence that might be excluded in formal civil or criminal trials and that often leads to well-reasoned and reasonably prompt decisions (at least when compared to trials). Adherence in labor arbitration to the rigid rules of trial procedure is a terrible mistake and does a disservice to the parties.

## REBUTTAL

Once both parties have presented all the witnesses and documents necessary to prove their case, they are then given the opportunity to present additional evidence through witnesses, documents, and other evidence to disprove or rebut the other side's case. For example, a grievant who was suspended for three days for unsafe operation of a forklift truck testifies that he was driving at a speed of only 15 miles per hour when an accident occurred. On rebuttal, the employer may offer testimony of another person who saw that the forklift truck was going at an estimated speed of 30 miles per hour just before the accident and that this was an unsafe speed under the conditions. The witness who testifies on behalf of the employer on that point is a rebuttal witness and is part of the employer's rebuttal case.

The same procedure of direct and cross-examination and redirect and recross-examination that was followed in the case in chief is followed in the rebuttal portion of the case. The only difference is that the scope of the evidence is supposed to be limited to that which disproves or rebuts evidence that was brought out earlier in the case by the other party. Again, however, most arbitrators will disregard that limitation unless it appears that the evidence is cumulative, meaning that it repeats what has already been presented.

## CLOSING ARGUMENTS AND POSTHEARING BRIEFS

The final stage of an arbitration hearing is the offering of closing arguments. This is the opportunity for the advocates to summarize the evidence and explain to the arbitrator the way in which the facts, coupled with the language of the labor agreement, past practice, bargaining history, and any other criteria should cause the arbitrator to rule in their favor. This is the ultimate confluence of fact and argument. It is similar in many respects to the opening statement, except that all the evidence is now before the arbitrator, whereas in the opening statement the evidence was completely prospective. At this final stage no argument should be withheld. In the opening statement an advocate might hold back one or more arguments until the evidence is produced so as not to tip off the other side or because of uncertainty as to whether the evidence would be sufficient to support that argument. Now that the entire body of evidence is before the arbitrator, there is no reason to hold back as long as the argument is a cogent one and is backed up by solid evidence.

A common feature of contemporary labor arbitration is the use of written posthearing briefs. To a large extent, this reflects the frequent presence of attorneys as arbitration advocates. Where written briefs are to be submitted, oral closing arguments are virtually always waived. The logic of this is simple. If both sides are going to make their arguments in writing after the hearing and after they have had a chance to review their notes or a verbatim transcript of the hearing, why go through the redundant process of making an oral argument as well? In addition, most trained advocates do not want to give the other side the benefit of hearing their arguments at the end of the hearing, thus enabling opposing advocates to be better prepared for writing their posthearing briefs.

The decision to make oral argument or file a brief and the techniques for accomplishing each are covered in chapters 14 and 15.

## THE BURDENS

A key element in any adversarial proceeding, including labor arbitration proceedings, is to identify which party has the burden of proof, the obligation of proving the issue in the case. For example, in the case of an employee discharged for excessive absenteeism, which party must prove that the employee was properly (or improperly) discharged? Or, in the case of an alleged assignment of overtime to the wrong employee, who has the burden of proving whether Employee A or Employee B was entitled to the overtime? The party having the obligation of proving the main element of the case is said to have the "burden of proof." In the example of the discharged employee the employer will normally carry the burden of proof that the employee was discharged for "just cause," and in the case of the overtime assignment dispute (i.e., a contract interpretation case) the union will usually carry the burden of proof that the assignment of overtime was in violation of the labor agreement.

Burden of proof has two facets: one is to initially present enough evidence to establish a plausible or prima facia case, that is, the "burden of going forward or the burden of production," and the other is to present enough evidence to persuade the arbitrator to rule in one's favor: the "burden of persuasion." In any case, therefore, there are two separate, but closely related, burdens.

## Burden of Production

The first of the two burdens, the burden of production, or, stated another way, the burden of going forward with the evidence, means that the party carrying the burden must present its evidence first. Although some arbitrators do not follow a hard-and-fast rule, the vast majority of arbitrators insist that in contract interpretation cases (all cases not involving discipline or discharge) the union has the burden of presenting its evidence first. The logic is that, because the union is claiming that the employer violated the labor agreement, it is the union that should initially present its evidence to show the alleged contract violation.

Conversely, in discharge or discipline cases it is the employer that takes action to discipline or terminate an employee, and most arbitrators will require the employer to present its evidence as to why the employee deserved such action first, before the union proceeds to present its case on the employee's behalf. Therefore, in discharge and discipline cases the employer has the burden of going forward with the evidence.

It should be noted that the burden of production or going forward with the evidence may be varied by the parties in a stipulated agreement (subject to the arbitrator's consent, which is normally given) or by a ruling from the arbitrator. Nevertheless, the prevailing practice in labor arbitration is so firmly grounded in this respect that most experienced advocates give little thought to this question and simply follow the rule outlined above.

## Burden of Persuasion

The second type of burden of proof is the burden of persuasion. This term refers to the obligation of ultimately persuading the arbitrator that the decision should be in a party's favor. From another perspective the question is: if the evidence on both sides is evenly balanced, which side should win? The answer is the side that does not bear the burden of persuasion. In other words, if the union has the burden of proving that the employer violated the labor contract by assigning certain work to a job classification that is not the normal job classification that performs such work and the evidence presented by both sides is evenly balanced to prove and disprove, respectively, that contention, the arbitrator should rule for the employer. In this situation the union had the burden of persuasion and failed to meet or carry its burden.

Fortunately, the rule on burden of persuasion in labor arbitration cases is generally the same as the rule for the burden of production. In contract interpretation cases the union has the burden of proving that a contract violation occurred. In discipline and discharge cases the employer has the burden of proving to the arbitrator that the action taken was proper (or, in the terminology of most labor agreements, there was "just cause" for the disciplinary action or discharge).[2]

## Quantum of Proof

Aside from the obligation of presenting one side's evidence first (the burden of going forward) and aside from proving one party's side of the case (the burden of persuasion), there is a third aspect of burden of proof usually referred to as "quantum of proof," which is simply the weight of the evidence. This concept addresses the question of how much evidence has to be shown to cause the arbitrator to rule for one side or the other. For example, is there enough evidence to prove that the contract was violated or that the grievant was discharged for just cause? There are different standards of proof for different kinds of cases, although differences in standards are generally significant only with respect to discharge cases.

The most common standards of quantum of proof applied in labor arbitration are as follows.

*Preponderance of the Evidence.* Which side has presented the most evidence to support its position?
*Clear and Convincing.* Has the side with the burden of proof shown by rather clear and persuasive evidence that its position should be upheld?

---

[2]Willamette Indus., 85-2 ARB ¶ 8396 (Fox, 1985); Southern Ohio Coal Co., 83 LA 523 (Feldman, 1984); Iowa-Illinois Gas & Elec., 86 LA 273 (Berger, 1986). An exception in contract interpretation cases is made by some arbitrators in a particular type of contract interpretation case by requiring the employer to assume the burden of proof in selecting a junior employee rather than a senior employee for promotion. Union Carbide Corp., 97 LA 771, 773 (Helburn, 1991).

*Proof beyond a Reasonable Doubt.* Is the evidence so strong that it cannot be reasonably concluded beyond a moral certainty that the evidence supports the position taken by the side that carries the burden of proof.

There is no clear consensus among arbitrators about which standard of proof relating to the weight of evidence applies in which types of cases. As a very broad generalization, preponderance of the evidence is usually applied in contract interpretation cases, whereas the clear and convincing standard is applied in discharge and disciplinary cases in which moral turpitude is not involved (e.g., absenteesim, negligence, and insubordination). Some, but not all, arbitrators apply the proof beyond a reasonable doubt standard in discharge cases involving moral turpitude (e.g., theft and sexual harassment).

## RULES OF EVIDENCE

One of the aspects of labor arbitration that is least well defined and most inconsistently applied is application of the rules of evidence. Because many labor arbitrators are not lawyers and because many arbitrators who are lawyers eschew technical procedures, the rules of evidence are often ignored or minimally applied. Other arbitrators, particularly lawyers with a litigation background, apply the rules of evidence so religiously that one might conclude the case is being heard in a court of law. This inconsistency causes a great deal of confusion and is especially troublesome to the lay advocate.

It is the author's firmly held opinion that a competent arbitration advocate should have a firm grasp of the basic rules of evidence, including such matters as the concept of relevant evidence, the "best evidence rule," establishing authenticity of documents, essential concepts of the "hearsay rule" and its major exceptions, admissibility of offers of compromise, and other such rules that are likely to arise in any arbitration hearing. If an arbitrator in a case is a layperson and does not apply the rules of evidence, the advocate need not use his or her knowledge and skills with evidentiary rules. If, however, the arbitrator is a stickler for applying the rules of evidence, an advocate unschooled in such rules is at a serious disadvantage. Not only is his or her case presentation disadvantaged, but the advocate is likely to be embarrassed and downgraded in the eyes of his or her client.

Chapter 10 is devoted solely to the subject of the rules of evidence and the strategy of their use. An advocate who has a firm grasp of the rules set out in that chapter will be well informed to the extent necessary to present a case effectively before most labor arbitrators. Knowing the rules is not enough, however—the effective advocate must learn how to use the rules in the hearing itself. This takes practice.

## FINALITY OF ARBITRATION

One of the most attractive features of labor arbitration is its finality. For the most part, arbitrators' decisions may not be appealed. The words "final and binding" are frequently found in the grievance/arbitration sections of labor agreements, and this concept is consistently used to describe the process of labor arbitration. The premise of labor arbitration is to have disputes heard and decided quickly and finally. These concepts are incorporated into the Labor Arbitration Rules of the American Arbitration Association, which is included as an appendix to this book.

It should be noted, however, that arbitration awards and decisions have been, and continue to be, overturned by the courts on occasion. The courts have set forth rather narrow grounds for overturning these decisions. Chapter 17 addresses challenges to arbitration awards. Notwithstanding the ability to negate awards, the fact remains that the vast majority of labor arbitration awards go unchallenged, or if challenged, are upheld by the courts. To the advocates and their principals or clients this means that the arbitrator's decision is usually final. This has a salutary effect on the decision of whether to go forward on a pending case and on consideration of possible settlement. Much, if not most, of the true value of arbitration would be negated if this characteristic of finality were to be lost.

# 2

# Reviewing Grievance History and Relevant Contract Provisions

Once it is known that a grievance has been appealed to arbitration, there are a number of steps that must be undertaken as part of the preparation. If the advocate who will present the case before the arbitrator has been involved in the processing of the grievance, the preparatory steps will be greatly reduced and simplified. In the interests of completeness and usefulness to all readers, this chapter as well as the entire book assumes that the advocate is new to the case and has no prior knowledge or involvement with the grievance. Where this is not the case, the steps that can be eliminated or shortened should be relatively apparent.

## PRELIMINARY REVIEW AND ANALYSIS OF THE GRIEVANCE

The first step in preparing for arbitration is to undertake a thorough review and analysis of the grievance. It is assumed that the grievance is in written form, since this is required by virtually all labor agreements. Grievances are generally written in simple, nontechnical language, and they are seldom models of clarity or specificity. In many cases they are poorly phrased and sometimes barely give a clue as to the actual complaint.

21

The union advocate who is presented with an imprecisely worded grievance has the advantage of being able to talk to the grievant to obtain more information. The employer advocate does not normally have that opportunity and must rely on the information obtained during earlier stages of the grievance procedure. Whether the union or the employer is reading the grievance for the first time, the grievance should be reviewed and analyzed from the standpoint of at least six different criteria: arbitrability, timeliness, standing, subject matter, facts, and contractual basis.

## Arbitrability

"Arbitrability" is the term used to describe the prerequisite that a grievance is one that an arbitrator can legitimately hear and decide. Phrased another way, is the question presented by the grievance and ultimately to be decided by the arbitrator one that is proper for an arbitrator to decide (regardless of which way the ruling goes)? For example, it is rather clear that it would not be appropriate for an arbitrator to decide whether an employer's corporate logo was a violation of the labor agreement. Similarly, the union could not normally contest the employer's choice of colors to paint its warehouse building. These matters are not within the confines of the labor agreement and therefore are not appropriate for an arbitrator to decide.

A closer, but not necessarily clear-cut, case is presented by a grievance challenging the employer's hiring of a nonunion supplier of raw materials used by the employer's unionized work force. In any of these cases the issue is whether the employer and the union have agreed to have disputes over such subjects submitted to an arbitrator.

Whether a grievance is arbitrable or not is a function of the subject matter of the grievance and the language of the labor agreement. Does the statement of the grievance, or the subject matter addressed directly or indirectly by the grievance, give rise to an issue that is reasonably addressed by the labor agreement? In some cases the matter complained of may not be directly addressed by the labor agreement, but the impact on employees or a resulting change in past practice is sufficiently significant in the lives of employees or the union that the grievance is arbitrable. For example, an employer reduces the size of the parking lot used by employees to such an extent that employees must park outside the plant confines and walk a much longer distance to work; or an employer reduces its subsidy for its employee cafeteria, causing a significant increase in prices. Are these grievances arbitrable? The answer depends on the language of the labor agreement. Assuming there is no direct reference in the labor agreement to the parking lot or the cafeteria, the advocate needs to examine the agreement carefully to see if there are any provisions that ensure that past practices will not be unilaterally changed and/or provisions that address the welfare of, and maintenance of good working conditions for, employees covered under that agreement. Often a mere thread of contract language is sufficient to support an arbitrable case, especially where there is a unilateral change by the employer of a long-standing practice or working condition.

Some grievances are based merely on a premise that what occurred ''wasn't fair,'' and the grievant believes that the employer should not be able to get away with such action, even though there is no specific contract provision that is alleged to have been violated. With the exception of discharge and disciplinary action by an employer where fairness, or more specifically, ''just cause'' (which is based on the concept of fairness and due process), is the standard, grievances grounded solely on lack of fairness without some contractual basis will be denied, usually on the grounds that they are not arbitrable.

A creative advocate can, however, sometimes find some contractual thread on which to string a successful case where the unfairness is patent and where the facts cry for relief. For example, an employer closes a facility because of equipment or process obsolescence and lack of profitability and declines to replace that facility. Nothing in the labor agreement covering the employees at the closed facility imposes an obligation on the employer relative to new operations. The union can, however, prove that the employer's vice president in charge of the closed facility gave assurances to union representatives that if the union cooperated in an orderly shutdown of the old facility and did not insist on exorbitant severance benefits, the employer would take such cooperation into account when it built a new facility to replace the one that was closed. The union's cooperation was secured by a promise (not in writing) of a future reward. Such a promise could constitute an ''implied contract,'' or binding obligation incurred by the reliance of one party to its detriment on a promise by another party. Such a theory may be sufficient for a union advocate to avoid a decision of nonarbitrability for lack of a contract violation.

Another type of case in which a serious arbitrability question arises is that which arguably is covered by some governmental law or regulation. A claim of discrimination, a dispute about safety, or an issue concerning pension benefits may be one that is covered by federal, state, or local law. Either the union or the employer, but most commonly the employer, may believe that the case should be heard by a judge or administrative agency rather than an arbitrator and will argue that the case is not arbitrable. In fact, the case may be one that can be heard (or, to use more technical language, "is cognizable") by an arbitrator and by a court of law or administrative agency. The appropriate forum for such a case may depend on how the grievance is phrased. Does the grievance allege that a particular contract provision has been violated, or is the complaint based on an allegation that the employer has not correctly applied the law in dealing with a particular matter? Sometimes both elements may be present. Normally, if the grievance claims a violation of a particular section of the labor agreement and there is at least one fact that would arguably support such an allegation, an arbitrator will be hard-pressed to refuse to hear the case on arbitrability grounds. On the other hand, if the grievance is based solely on an alleged violation of law or governmental regulation, a challenge based on the grievance not being arbitrable is likely to be upheld, unless the labor agreement has a provision that incorporates the law into the labor agreement.[1]

Many arbitrators are reluctant to dismiss a case on the basis of arbitrability since it means that the grievant and/or the union will not be able to put the "merits" (i.e., the substantive facts and arguments about the grievance) of the case before the arbitrator. In effect, the grievant and union are knocked out on a technicality. Employers, however, are loathe to have the facts and arguments placed before an arbitrator if the basis of the complaint is one about which the employer never entered into an agreement and never agreed to arbitrate.

Going back to the hypothetical case discussed earlier, of the employer that closed a plant, suppose that the situation has changed somewhat in that the employer builds a new plant to replace the one it closed, which was covered by a labor agreement. The new plant is to be located 30 miles from the old plant and will employ the same number of employees in the same occupations as the old plant. A grievance is filed contesting the employer's right to relocate the plant without union agreement. Nothing in the agreement addresses plant location or reloca-tion, but the agreement does say that "if the company changes any of its basic manufacturing processes or equipment that substantially affect conditions of employment, the company will meet with the union in advance to minimize the adverse impact on employees." Does this relocation amount to such a change, and did the failure of the employer to consult with the union in advance of the announced change amount to a contract violation? The employer is likely to be fearful of an arbitrator even hearing such a dispute because so much is at stake, whereas the

---

[1] Alpha Beta Co., 94 LA 477 (Gentile, 1989); George A. Hormel Co., 90 LA 1246, 1248 (Goodman, 1988); Owens-Illinois, 83 LA 1265, 1269 (Cantor, 1984). *But compare* Florida Power Corp. 87 LA 957, 960 (Wahl, 1986).

union will argue that the quoted language is sufficiently broad to encompass the relocation, at least to the extent that the arbitrator should not decline to hear the facts and arguments of the case, regardless of how he or she may rule on the merits.

### Determination of Arbitrability

Determinations in which a labor agreement is silent regarding arbitrability and in which the defense of nonarbitrability is that the subject matter is not appropriate for arbitration, or, "substantive arbitrability," are reserved for the courts.[2] As a practical matter, however, few employers or unions seek a court determination, and it is the norm (regardless of the language in the labor agreement) for arbitrators to decide most issues of arbitrability. In other words, in almost all cases the arbitrator determines his or her own jurisdiction. This is the same process as in the civil court system, except that arbitrators' decisions, unlike those of a trial judge, are not generally subject to appeal to a higher authority. Some labor agreements provide for a two-step, or bifurcated, process in which the issue of arbitrability is decided initially by the arbitrator. If, in the initial bifurcated hearing the arbitrator determines that the grievance is not arbitrable, there is no necessity to hold the second hearing on the merits of the case. If the party filing the grievance believes the arbitrator is in error in holding the grievance to not be arbitable, it may challenge that decision in court. Such bifurcated systems are, however, rather rare in labor agreements.

More is said in Chapter 8 about the strategy of handling arbitrability issues at the outset of a hearing. The coverage in the present chapter is to encourage the advocate to focus on this potential critical issue at the preliminary stage of preparation.

### Substantive Versus Procedural Arbitrability

The term "arbitrability" is often used to describe all types of issues that might arise in connection with the question of whether an arbitrator may properly decide the merits of a grievance. Besides addressing the question of whether the subject of the grievance is covered by the labor agreement, the term "arbitrability" is frequently used to describe the determination of whether a grievance was filed within the contractual time limits or filed by a person who is covered by the labor agreement. Such issues are, strictly speaking, ones of "timeliness" and "standing,"

---

[2]American Tel. & Tel. Co. v. Communications Workers, 475 U.S. 643, 121 LRRM 3329 (1986); Denver Public Schs.; 88 LA 507, 510 (Watkins, 1986); Bunn-O-Matic, 70 LA 34 (Talent, 1977).

although they clearly affect the jurisdiction of an arbitrator to hear the merits of a case. This illustrates the two aspects of the word arbitrability. In ''substantive arbitrability'' the question is whether the subject matter of the grievance or the issue it raises is appropriate for an arbitrator to decide under a particular contract. In ''procedural arbitrability'' the question is whether there is some technical or procedural flaw, such as the late filing of a grievance, that would cause an arbitrator to decline to hear the merits of a case.

Some practitioners prefer to call the latter type of arbitrability issues by their specific character, such as timeliness or standing, rather than referring to them as questions of arbitrability. Regardless of whether they are considered as arbitrablility or other issues, these are threshold questions that the advocate should consider at the outset of preparation. They are discussed in the subsequent sections under their own headings rather than as general arbitrability issues.

It should be noted that arbitrability issues are not all that common. The vast majority of cases are heard and decided without any question as to whether they are proper cases to be brought before an arbitrator. Nevertheless, the arbitrability of a grievance, when it arises, is potentially a decisive one, because if the grievance is not arbitrable, the merits of the case may never be heard by an arbitrator. A decision of nonarbitrability ends the case. Consequently, no advocate should ever overlook these issues as part of a preparation checklist.

## Timeliness of Grievance Filing and/or Processing

One of the simplest yet most frequently overlooked tasks in preparing for a grievance arbitration is to check to see whether the grievance was filed and/or processed within the time limits required by the labor agreement. Some agreements do not contain a limitations period for filing grievances, and in those cases it is not necessary to consider the filing date, unless the grievance filing was so tardy that an argument of ''laches'' might arise. Laches is a term describing an unusally long delay in the filing of a claim that can invalidate the claim.[3]

---

[3]Laches is a concept developed in the law of equity in the courts in which unreasonable delays in bringing a lawsuit would render it null and void. This concept has found favor in labor arbitration, usually with respect to labor agreements that do not have specific time periods within which a grievance must be filed or appealed to arbitration. In such cases arbitrators have held grievances to be not arbitrable where unreasonably long delays in filing or processing grievances have been encountered. Texstar Automotive Group, Inc., 81 LA 278 (Smith, 1983); Zia Co.; 81 LA 759 (Daughton, 1983); Keystone Consol. Indus., Inc., 71 LA 574 (Cohen, 1978).

Most agreements, however, do contain a limitations period of a specified number of days within which a grievance must be filed. Typical limitations periods range from a low of three days to a high of sixty days.

### When Must the Issue of Timeliness First Be Raised?

Assuming the grievance is filed by an employee or the union rather than the employer (which is true in virtually all cases), the employer advocate needs to check the timeliness of a grievance as part of the employer's effort to affirmatively defend against the grievance. The union advocate's purpose in checking timeliness is to be prepared to respond to any defense the employer may make based on timeliness. Of course, the first point at which timeliness should be considered by both parties, but especially by the employer, is when the grievance is initially filed. In the author's experience this important step is frequently over-looked by management representatives when they receive a grievance. Very often the grievance progresses through two or more grievance steps before anyone considers whether the grievance was filed on time. In some cases it is only when the employer's arbitration advocate is preparing the case for an arbitration hearing that this matter receives attention. Sometimes this is too late.

There is a divergence of opinion by arbitrators about the validity of an untimely filed grievance that is not challenged on that basis until the grievance reached the arbitration stage. Some arbitrators have ruled that the employer must challenge the grievance's untimely filing at one or more of the prearbitration grievance processing steps.[4] Their reasoning is that the employer's acceptance and consideration of the grievance, despite its untimely filing, constitutes a waiver of the defect and therefore legitimizes the grievance.

Other arbitrators have ruled that the defense of untimeliness may be raised at any time, even initially in arbitration, because it goes to the jurisdiction or authority of the arbitrator to hear the case.[5] Their reasoning is that, if the labor agreement requires a grievance to be filed within x days of the event giving rise to the grievance, then a grievance filed x + 3 days from the event is invalid, and the failure of the employer

---

[4]Westvaco Corp., 99 LA 513 (Dugan, 1992); Liquid Transp., 99 LA 217 (Witney, 1992); Teledyne Monarch Rubber Co., 97 LA 233 (Dworkin, 1991); PPG Indus., 90 LA 1033, 1034 (Edelman, 1988); Consolidated Coal Co., 91 LA 1011 (Stoltenberg, 1988).
[5]Mead Corp., 88 LA 540, 543 (Borland, 1986); Meridan Woodworking Co., 87 LA 645 (Howell, 1986); Murtis H. Taylor Multi-Serv. Ctr.; 83 LA 153 (Morgan, 1984); Western Elec. Co., 46 LA 1019, 1021 (Dugan, 1966).

to challenge it earlier in the grievance procedure does not convert an invalid grievance into a valid one.

### The Operative Dates for Determining a Timely Grievance

In order to assess timeliness one needs to ascertain the date on which the event causing the grievance occurred and the date on which the grievance was filed and compare those dates with the time limits in the labor agreement. It seems pretty simple. In practice it is not always as simple as it looks.

The event causing the grievance may not have occurred on just one date but may have continued for a period of time. For example, the employer may have been incorrectly computing vacation pay for a period of two years, but a grievance is not filed until the end of that two-year period. Is the grievance timely? In another situation the employer assigns overtime to a junior employee when a senior employee was entitled to it, but the senior employee files the grievance five days beyond the limitations period because he was unaware (through no fault of his own) of the erroneous overtime assignment until then. Is the grievance timely? In both of these cases the language of the labor agreement will control the result, although it is not unusual that the agreement does not provide a definitive answer.

### Continuing Violations

The wording in the following labor agreement provision of griev-ance-filing limitations is fairly common: "A grievance must be filed no later than ten (10) days following the occurrence which gives rise to that grievance."

Where, as in the previous example of the incorrectly computed vacation pay, there are multiple occurrences, arbitrators will normally look to the date of the last occurrence to measure timeliness. If the last occurrence of the alleged violation was still occurring within the limitations period of the labor agreement, a grievance based thereon will normally be considered timely. Nevertheless, if such a grievance is ultimately granted and back pay is awarded, the period for computing the back pay will usually be limited to a period commencing no earlier than the date on which the grievance was filed.[6] Such multiple occurrences are referred to as "continuing violations." In continuing violation cases arbitrators will usually examine the circumstances of the situation to

---

[6]C. Iber & Sons, Inc., 69 LA 697 (1977, Gibson), Maintenence Serv. Corp., 64 LA 978 (1975, Rauch); American Welding, 45 LA 812 (1965; Dworkin).

determine whether the grievant could reasonably have known of the violations while they were in progress in order to determine the extent of the back pay obligation.

In the other earlier scenario involving the assignment of overtime the grievant was unaware of the alleged overtime violation until after the filing deadline had passed. Although some agreements contain language that covers this situation (e.g., "the grievance must be filed within x days of the event giving rise to the grievance or within x days of reasonable first knowledge of it"), such language was not present in this hypothetical case. Perhaps not surprisingly, in cases where there is no "reasonable first knowledge" language in the applicable labor agreement, arbitrators nevertheless frequently follow the rationale contained in that language. They reason that if the employee did not know of the event in time to file the grievance before the deadline and if that lack of knowledge was not the employee's fault, it would be unfair to penalize the employee by ruling the grievance untimely.[7]

## Determining filing date

Just as the occurrence date of the alleged contract violation is important, so too is the filing date. Issues can and do arise as to when the grievance was effectively filed. Was it the date on which the employee first complained orally to his supervisor, the date on which the employee wrote out the grievance and signed and dated it, the date on which the written grievance was mailed, or the date on which the written grievance was received by the employer? As with most such questions in this book, the language of the agreement controls. Where, however, the language is not specific (and frequently it is not), the operative date for a filing of the grievance is usually the date on which the written grievance was received by the employer representative. Until that point the employer cannot be considered to have known of the specific grievance (even though it may have been discussed at the supervisory level) and to have acted on it. Careful parties date and initial on the grievance form or letter the receipt of grievances in order to establish an official filing date. Where the failure to file a grievance within the contractual time limits is simply a matter of days, arbitrators will often find some rationale to justify the late filing.[8]

---

[7]Mississippi Equip. Co., 87 LA 21, 25 (Penfield, 1986); Cities Serv. Co., 87 LA 1209, 1212 (Taylor, 1986); Sugardale Foods Inc., 87 LA 18 (DiLauro, 1986); Independent Stave Co., 82 LA 1170, 1171 (Herrick, 1984).
[8]Concrete Pipe Prods. Co., 87 LA 879 (Caraway, 1986); Silver Lake Bd. of Educ. and Nat'l Educ. Assn, 88 LA 885 (Madden, 1986).

*Past practice affecting timeliness.*

Time limits in a labor agreement can sometimes be voided when the parties have shown, by a consistent and mutually accepted pattern of behavior, that they have a history of not following them. Except where the language of the agreement regarding filing limits is so specific and unambiguous (e.g., "time limits for filing of grievances must be strictly adhered to, or the grievance is null and void") that no one could doubt the intent of the negotiating parties, a consistently followed practice of both parties of ignoring or tolerating exceptions to the filing limits can lead an arbitrator to conclude that the parties' true intent was to treat the filing period as advisory rather than mandatory.[9] The rationale is that permitting many grievances to be processed regardless of how late they were filed but denying a particular grievance because it was not filed on time would be an injustice, and therefore the late filing is not disqualifying.

### Timeliness Recap

Although issues of timeliness are often abhorred by those who believe that resolution of disputes should not be thwarted by technical rules, the fact remains that the parties have entered into a contract in which they established certain limitations periods for the filing of grievances. Whether the original negotiators of such periods intended them to be strictly enforced is seldom ascertainable, and therefore arbitrators must presume that the language of the agreement specifying limits for filing grievances was intended to nullify late-filed grievances. Consequently, it is vitally important for union and employer advocates to examine carefully the grievance being prepared for arbitration in order to determine whether any issue exists concerning the timely filing or processing of that grievance. If one exists, then the task is to investigate the facts to ascertain the reasons, if any, for the delay, whether the untimeliness was ever previously raised, and whether the parties have consistently adhered to the grievance time limits in the past. It may very well be that the case will stand or fall on this issue alone.

---

[9]Genesee Packaging Inc., 98 LA 777 (Ellman, 1992); Williams Air Force Base, 89 LA 370 (Smith, 1987); Sanford Corp., 81 LA 968 (Wies, 1987); CBS, Inc., 75 LA 789 (Roberts, 1980); Peru Foundry Co., 73 LA 959 (Sembower, 1979).

## Standing

The concept of "standing" is well known in civil litigation but is not frequently a factor in labor arbitration. It is based on the premise that the only persons who can legitimately make a claim are those who have been injured or otherwise adversely affected by an alleged contract violation. For example, if Employee A's pay is short by $50 and the employer denies that it is short, Employee A may file a grievance. However, Employee B normally cannot file a grievance protesting Employee A's inaccurate paycheck because the alleged violation did not adversely affect Employee B. Employee B does not "have standing" because Employee B has not been harmed.

As a practical matter, the issue of standing is seldom raised as a defense and rarely applied by arbitrators to deny grievances. The reason is that the employee who has been adversely affected by a contract violation is usually willing and available to file a grievance. Even if that employee is not, the union is normally prepared to file a grievance on his or her behalf. Issues of standing are most likely to occur where the grievant is a probationary employee or a retired employee.[10]

What is more common with regard to the issue of standing is the question of grievances filed by a union on behalf of one or more employees or of grievances filed for a group of employees ("group grievances") but signed by only one or some members of the group. It is not uncommon for grievances to be filed by the union, usually signed by a union official, alleging a contract violation that affects one or more union members. The employer may not believe that the employees on whose behalf the grievance has been filed have been harmed. The employer may also believe that such employees are not themselves protesting the validity of the grievance. Such employer defenses usually carry little weight. Most arbitrators hold that a contract violation, regardless of who and how many employees may be affected, may be grieved by the union because the union is the contracting party, and any violation of the contract may be challenged by that party.[11] The union has an obligation to "police" the contract (i.e., to see that it is followed), and filing grievances is a primary way of carrying out that obligation.

The question of group grievances is somewhat less clear. Can one or a few employees initiate a grievance on behalf of a larger group of employees? Is there such a thing as "class action grievances"? Although

---

[10]MJB Co., 77 LA 1294 (Burns, 1982); Veterans Admin. Medical Ctr., 77 LA 725 (Weiss, 1981); Reyco Indus., Inc., 74 LA 819 (Davidson, 1980).
[11]Duluth Community Action, 82 LA 426 (Boyer, 1984); Niagara Frontier Transp. Auth., 85 LA 229 (Lawson, 1985); A.E. Moore Co., 62 LA 153 (Green, 1974).

contract language can change the result, as a general proposition group grievances are permissible, especially when the identity of the individuals is shown on the grievance and/or when at least some of the individuals affected by the employer's action have signed the grievance.[12] Where, however, the grievance merely refers to "other employees" or alleges harm to an unspecified number of unidentified individuals, the group nature of the grievance, or at least a group remedy, is often voided.[13] Nevertheless, as long as at least one employee who was affected or one union official signs the grievance, it is not likely to be dismissed for lack of standing.

## Reviewing the Subject Matter of the Grievance Concerning Arbitrability

The initial review of a grievance should focus closely on the subject matter of the grievance, for example, whether it is a case about rates of pay, overtime assignment, promotion, layoff, scheduling of work, discipline or discharge, or one of the many other subjects that are encompassed in the labor agreement. The natural inclination is for the advocate to quickly read or hear the essential facts and immediately refer to the specific section of the labor agreement that addresses that subject. Before doing that, however, a thorough advocate should first ask several preliminary questions. First, "What is the basic claim being made here?" or "What action or inaction of the employer is being protested?" Second, "What harm or injury is alleged to have resulted from the action complained of?" Third, "According to the claim encompassed in the grievance, what does the grievant contend should have occurred instead of what actually occurred?" These questions are particularly important for the union advocate in order to ensure that all possible facts are considered, all viable contractual theories are explained, and all possible remedies are sought.

The employer advocate should likewise ask the same questions. The basic claim may be one that was the subject of another arbitration, albeit under different circumstances, and therefore the result may be obvious. The grievance may accurately allege a contract violation, but the violation may not have caused any tangible harm to the employee, thereby making the arbitration moot from a remedial standpoint. It is also

---

[12]Lake Erie Screw Corp., 90 LA 204, 206 (Coyne, 1987); Magic Chef, 88 LA 1046, 1049 (Caraway, 1987); Philadelphia Naval Shipyard, 85 LA 125, 132 (Seltzer, 1985).
[13]Gates Rubber Co., 90 LA 1045, 1048 (Cohen, 1988); Hillhaven Corp., 87 LA 360, 364 (Corbett, 1986); Compco Corp., 85 LA 725, 730 (Martin, 1985).

possible that the grievant may have alleged that certain actions should have been taken by the employer even though such actions were not possible. These and other conclusions will affect the employer's defense strategies and preparation.

## Importance of Reviewing the Entire Grievance File— The Facts

Frequently the grievance form or statement itself does not convey much information about the exact nature of the dispute. Employees who file grievances are not lawyers and are not schooled in the art of labor relations. Consequently, grievance statements often consist of several sentences that may suggest only in the vaguest of terms what claim is being made. In these cases, and even in situations where the grievance is more explicit, it is important for the advocate to review the entire grievance file to determine the full ramifications of the claim. What arguments were made by the grievant or union representatives at various stages of the grievance procedure prior to arbitration? What statements or notes are in the file that will fill in the facts and arguments concerning the grievance? What facts and defenses were supplied by employer representatives in connection with the case? The subject matter should become clear based on the documents in the file.

Because a grievance file contains documents relating to certain facts does not mean, however, that the actual facts are as they have been presented through those documents. The union and/or the employer may have missed the critical points in the case and may have been operating under erroneous or insufficient facts or relying on flimsy or invalid contractual theories. Not until a complete review of the relevant documents and interviews of the percipient witnesses are completed will it be possible to know the full and accurate scope of the case. In many instances, however, advocates may have to rely solely on the file documents for their initial preparation.

## The Labor Agreement— The Contractural Basis for Arbitration

Once the advocate has a grasp of the essential facts of the case, the basic claim being made, and the relief being sought by the grievant, the next step is to examine the labor agreement and other relevant binding provisions. The first rule that a competent advocate should follow is not to assume that the grievant, the union, or the employer has correctly or completely identified the relevant contract provisions. One of the most common mistakes made in labor arbitration is to base a case, offensive or defensive, on the wrong section of the contract or to overlook pertinent sections of the labor agreement. For example, work normally done by the employer's maintenance department is contracted to an outside firm that is nonunion. One of the employer's machinists files a grievance claiming that the labor agreement section on subcontracting was violated. Is that the correct section of the contract on which to rely? Probably. Is that the only relevant provision that might apply? Probably not. The union advocate will likely want to direct his or her attention to the seniority section of the labor agreement in which language giving preference to senior employees for work assignments might be found. Also, the union advocate should look to the section of the contract that addresses assignment of overtime. He or she may very well be able to argue that the work in question could have been performed on overtime and assigned in accordance with that provision. The union advocate may also find some support in general language that precludes the employer from changing past practices without union agreement.

From the employer's side of the case a management's rights clause can be particularly relevant to a contracting dispute. Also, labor agreements containing job descriptions that do not specifically mention the type of work that was contracted may be relied on by the employer to show that the parties did not intend to limit such work to bargaining unit employees. Of course, job descriptions that include such work will be sharp arrows in the union's quiver. The important point is that each advocate should take the most expansive view of the contract in relation to the grievance and the facts presented. It is simple enough to discard one or more of the contract provisions considered, but if they never have been considered, they will be unavailable to the advocate during the arbitration proceeding.

### Considering Sidebar Agreements

As any seasoned union or employer representative knows, the labor contract seldom contains all the agreements between the union and the employer. It is the rare collective bargaining relationship that does not have side letters, memoranda of agreement, letters of understanding, statements of mutual intent, departmental work practices, local rules, or other such supplemental agreements. Such documents typically expand on or make specific more general contract provisions. They may also address subjects that are not contained in the basic labor agreement. Occasionally, they conflict directly with one or more provisions of the basic labor agreement. One of the most difficult challenges to an arbitrator is to determine whether a provision contained in the basic labor agreement controls a given situation or whether a contradictory sidebar agreement should be followed. The ultimate question concerns which provision appears to best express the actual and most recent intent of the parties.

A related problem with sidebar agreements is determining whether they are authentic, valid, and binding on the parties. For example, consider a memo sent from a supervisor to a shop steward that explains how the department handles layoffs in a particular factual setting, ending with the words, "...if you agree, please sign and return." The shop steward does so, and the provisions of the memo are followed during the next layoff. Have the employer and the union entered into a side agreement that will bind the parties in the future? A key issue will be whether the agreement was entered into at about the same time as the labor agreement.[14] If the memo conflicts with a specific provision in the labor agreement, it is less likely that an arbitrator will rely on the sidebar agreement.[15] The reason is that likely neither the supervisor nor the shop steward have been authorized by their respective principals to bind their respective organizations. On the other hand, if the labor agreement is not specific as to how layoffs of this type are to be handled and if the side agreement appears to have been followed without dispute on a number of other occasions, an arbitrator will probably give it considerable weight in construing the labor agreement's seniority provisions in a case involving similar layoffs.

A related dilemma occurs when a side letter was signed long before the occurrence of the grievance in question and there is a dispute as to whether the letter is still binding. This sometimes occurs when one party is in possession of the letter and the other is not, and the party not having the letter was unaware of the provisions of the letter when it acted. The issue to be decided by the arbitrator is whether the parties in the negotiations and successive agreements following the letter intended to incorporate the letter into their agreements. If they have followed the provisions of the letter on those occasions when it would apply, it is likely that the arbitrator will rule that they so intended. If the parties have been careful in their negotiations to address the existence of and continued validity of such side agreements, the problem should not exist. This is sometimes accomplished by a "sunset clause," wherein previous agreements expire on a certain date (e.g., the expiration date of the labor agreement) unless they are specifically renewed. Another means is by the

---

[14]Trans World Airlines, 81 LA 524, 528 (Heinsz, 1983).
[15]Hoover Universal, Inc., 77 LA 107, 112 (Lipson, 1981).

inclusion of a "zipper clause,"[16] which declares null and void any agreement not included or specifically referenced in the labor agreement. Unfortunately, most labor agreements do not contain sunset or zipper clauses, and the thorny issue of sidebar agreements and their validity and continued viability often complicate grievance arbitration cases.

### Evaluating Prior Arbitration Decisions

Just as side agreements can govern the outcome of a case, so too can the results of previous arbitration cases determine the outcome of a particular grievance. Where an arbitrator has ruled in a particular way *under similar facts and under the same labor agreement and specific contract language,* that ruling will usually be binding on the parties in a subsequent case. While the legal principle of stare decisis (adherence to precedent) is not ingrained in arbitration to the same extent that it is in courts of law, nevertheless, arbitrators generally follow previous decisions where the facts and contract provisions are essentially the same.[17] Consequently, it is essential that advocates research all previous arbitration cases between the same parties that parallel the case being prepared to determine what potential impact they may have on an arbitrator's decision.

Arbitration decisions involving other parties and other contracts with distinct, though similar, language do not have the same binding effect. The use and impact of such decisions is discussed further in chapters 5 and 15.

### Considering Previous Grievance Settlements

Another category of provisions that can bind the employer and the union is the history of grievances that have involved the same or very similar facts. These are grievances that have been settled by the parties at some point in the past when the same contract provisions at issue in the current case were in effect. Similar to the analysis of previous arbitration decisions, the rationale is that when the same, or very similar, issue arose previously and both sides agreed as to the meaning and application of a

---

[16]Although the "zipper clause" referred to in this discussion applies to previous sidebar agreements, many zipper clauses have a much broader effect, often precluding the obligation of an employer to negotiate about any changes in working conditions not specifically covered by the labor agreement.

[17]Howard Paper Mills, 87 LA 863, 866 (Dworkin, 1986); Cone Mills Corp., 86 LA 992, 996 (Nolan, 1986); North Am. Coal Co., 84 LA 150 (Duda, 1985).

questionable contract provision, their determination—mutually and freely arrived at—should control the current dispute.[18]

Several exceptions to this principle are commonly applied. If the grievance settlement was made at the first or some other low level of consideration or if the settlement covered matters that were specifically reserved for the collective bargaining agreement, it is often held not to bind the employer or the union.[19] Their settlement is presumed to apply only to the grievance that they were dealing with at the time. If, however, higher level officials of the union and the employer have negotiated a grievance settlement that does not, by its terms, limit its application to the instant grievance and if it is not inconsistent with the collective bargaining agreement, it is likely to be held to bind the parties in future cases.[20]

Another factor that will make a grievance settlement inapplicable for future cases is an expressed intent of the parties to that effect. Experienced labor practitioners who do not want a grievance settlement to impact future cases know that they should include a statement such as the following in their agreement to settle such a grievance.

> This settlement applies only to grievance # _____ and is not intended to have any influence on any future case. Neither party may rely on, or argue the applicability of, this settlement to support its position in any future case.

The presence of such wording in a settlement will ensure that an arbitrator will not consider, or perhaps even allow into evidence, such a grievance settlement. The absence of such language leaves the door open for both parties to be bound by prior grievance settlements.

### Influence of Past Practice

Past practice is a pervasive issue in labor arbitration and should not be overlooked by the advocate in preparing a case. The rule of thumb is that arbitrators will consider past practice where they must interpret and apply contract language that is either ambiguous on its face or is subject to different meanings and applications. That rule is followed by the vast majority of arbitrators.[21]

---

[18]Scott & Fetzer Co., 79 LA 1091, 1093 (Sabghir, 1982); McDonnell Douglas Corp., 78 LA 401, 404 (Winston, 1982).
[19]General Motors, 92 LA 624, 629 (Kahn, 1988).
[20]Miller Brewing Co., 75 LA 1189 (Richman, 1980).
[21]Robertshaw Controls Co., 85 LA 538, 541 (Williams, 1985); Keystone Steel & Wire Co., 84 LA 369, 371 (Schwartz, 1985); Houston Publishers Ass'n., 83 LA 767, 776 (Milentz, 1984); City of Burlington, Iowa, 83 LA 973, 976 (Traynor, 1984).

However, *even when the contract language in question is rather clear and unambiguous, the author strongly recommends that evidence of past practice be accumulated and ultimately used if it supports the advocate's case.* There are several reasons for this admonition. First, clarity and lack of ambiguity often lie in the eyes of the beholder. What may seem to be clear to some may not be clear to others, or at least an adroit advocate can make a plausible argument that the language in question is subject to different interpretations. Second, even when the language is clear and without ambiguity, there is a chance that a long-standing and mutually accepted practice that contradicts or modifies the language in a labor agreement will be given some weight by an arbitrator. For example, a contract provision states, ''No employee may be granted a leave of absence without the written approval of the employee's immediate supervisor.'' The language appears to be rather clear and straightforward. If, however, the employer for the previous five years had consistently granted personal leaves of absence through its personnel department without any approval, written or oral, of employees' supervisors, a serious question will arise about the parties' real intent in negotiating such language. In this example, a grievance is filed by an employee who was denied a leave of absence because he did not receive his supervisor's written approval. Will the arbitrator accept evidence of the five-year past practice and will he or she base a decision, at least in part, on that evidence? The author believes that the arbitrator would not only receive such evidence, but would give it some weight. The lesson to be learned is that research and consideration of past practice in useful in virtually every case notwithstanding the fact that the contract language at issue appears to have only one meaning. Similarly, one should research past practice even where it might not support one's case simply to be prepared to defend against the other side's use of past practice.

It is one thing to want to use past practice and quite another to ascertain exactly what the past practice has been and how it can be proved or disproved. Many types of past practices, such as work assignments, temporary transfers, vacation scheduling arrangements, granting requests for time off, and so on are not always recorded, and therefore ascertaining and proving them may be very difficult, if not impossible. Searching the memories of supervisors and employees is often the only way to identify such practices. Memories are frequently dim, and recollections of past practices among different persons often conflict. The research task is likely to be formidable. Nevertheless, if past practice can possibly prove or disprove a substantial issue in the case, the research should always be undertaken.

## Researching Bargaining History

Just as past practice may be critical in determining the outcome of an arbitration case, so too is bargaining history likely to have a significant impact. Similarly, as with past practice, evidence of negotiations of previous labor contract negotiations is usually given weight by an arbitrator only where the contract is silent on the issue being arbitrated or where the language at issue is ambiguous or subject to varying interpretations.[22] Bargaining history is simply the record of bargaining proposals or testimony based on recollection of negotiations that led to the contractual language at issue in the case and that may shed light on the parties' original intent.

For example, in a case in which the employer and the union have a dispute over the meaning of the words "most qualified" as it applies in a promotional situation, one or both of the parties may produce evidence of the initial and subsequent proposals concerning the language, testimony of discussions at the bargaining table over that wording, examples used in negotiations of how the language was applied, and any other evidence that would suggest what the words were intended to mean and how they were to be applied. Notes of negotiations are often introduced in arbitration hearings to prove the position of one side or the other. Similarly, proposals made for contract wording changes that were either rejected or modified are frequently used to support an argument that the wording in the agreement does not mean what the other side says it means.

In the example above concerning promotion of a junior over a more senior employee, the employer justified its position on the basis that the junior employee was more qualified. If it can be shown that the union had proposed in an earlier labor contract negotiation that the word "most" be deleted from the seniority clause stating "most qualified" (resulting in the provision reading "promote the senior qualified employee"), and if such a proposal had been rejected by the employer, leaving the language unchanged, the union will have a difficult time convincing an arbitrator that a senior employee who is less qualified than a junior employee should be promoted simply because he or she meets the minimum qualifications of the position and has the most seniority. The employer's argument would be that the union's inability to gain such an advantage in negotiations (by removing the word "most") is strong evidence that the words "most qualified" mean that the employer is permitted to select a

---

[22]Firestone Synthetic Rubber & Latex Co., 76 LA 968, 973 (Williams, 1981); Bringham Apparel Corp., 52 LA 430, 431 (Andersen, 1969).

junior employee in preference to a senior employee, provided the employer is able to prove that the junior employee is more qualified. Evidence of rejected proposals are frequently relied on by arbitrators to interpret ambiguous contract language.[23]

More is said about bargaining history in Chapter 4 in terms of marshaling arguments to support a case. At this stage of the process the advocate should research bargaining history in order to evaluate the case and begin initial preparation.

## Ascertaining Previous Positions and Contractual Theories

An advocate does not start preparation of a labor arbitration case with a clean slate. The grievance has been heard at one, two, three, or perhaps even four earlier steps of the grievance procedure. Each side has produced evidence, argued the validity of its case, and has taken a position based on one or more theories of what it believes the contract means with respect to the facts thus far established. An advocate may assume, at least for the moment, that the opposing side will rely on the same arguments in arbitration that were taken by that party's representatives in the grievance procedure. The task at the outset is to understand the rationale of those theories, determine whether they are supported by the facts, and evaluate the strengths and weaknesses of the arguments based on the most current facts and on the advocate's assessment of the validity of those arguments.

It is not at all uncommon for an advocate to find that in preparing for an arbitration hearing certain facts relied on by one or both parties are not true or at least are not exactly as portrayed when the grievance was being processed. A more thorough review of documents and witnesses normally done in preparation for an arbitration hearing often reveals that factual discrepancies exist, differing from those facts known or believed at an earlier time. This clearly calls for a reevaluation of the case and sometimes suggests proposing a settlement or taking a different approach to the case than was taken during the grievance processing.

Even if the facts do not change from those existing during the earlier grievance processing, the advocate needs to access the validity and strength of the contractual theories advanced earlier by both sides. For example, just because the employer's representatives in the grievance process believed that the contract language covering holiday premium pay supported its position that employees who worked overtime on a

---

[23]FMC-Ordinance Div., 84 LA 163, 167 (Wyman, 1985); Transamerica Delaval, Inc., 84 LA 190, 194 (Brisco, 1985); Associated Elec. Coop., 84 LA 1020, 024 (Penfield, 1985).

holiday were entitled only to time-and-a-half does not mean that the argument will hold up in arbitration if there is conflicting language in the holiday section of the contract. Likewise, a discharge may have been challenged earlier in the grievance process by union representatives on the basis that the grievant's past work record was spotless. The union advocate may discover, however, that the grievant's record was not unblemished, and the advocate may have to find other grounds, such as disparate treatment (compared to other employees under similar circumstances) or lack of due process in order to challenge the discharge.

## Strategic Considerations

Although the tasks of gathering the facts and identifying applicable contract provisions are significant in and of themselves, there is more to an initial assessment of a case than what appears in the record. A resourceful advocate will begin to consider possible strategies that may be employed in presenting the case to an arbitrator. For example, a union may realize that the employer is very protective of its management rights and may be vulnerable to arguments challenging those rights. Such an employer may be inclined to settle a case involving one employee's claim for back pay rather than risk an adverse decision by an arbitrator that could weaken the employer's management rights. As another example, the union advocate may realize that the employer's case rests on the testimony of a supervisor who is not an effective witness. Such a weakness may also prompt the employer to settle short of arbitration. Conversely, an employer advocate may realize that documents in the employer's possession, not known to the union, make the case an almost certain winner, but such documents have not previously been disclosed out of concern for their confidentiality. The employer advocate needs to consider whether such documents should be disclosed to the union in advance of the hearing under an agreement of confidentiality in order to induce a settlement or whether they are best held back until the hearing for maximum impact.

Another strategic consideration in many arbitration cases is the effect that the arbitration of a claim is likely to have on the union-management relationship. Are there issues of trust involved? Are there larger and more important values that may be sacrificed by a particular case being argued before, and decided by, an arbitrator? These and many other strategic issues may present themselves. The most important strategic considerations, however, are assessments of the probabilities of winning and losing and the likely outcomes of each result.

### Evaluating Likely Outcome

It is never too early in the preparation process to make a preliminary estimate of the likely outcome of the arbitration hearing. In fact, for most advocates it is very difficult not to make such an evaluation as soon as they have reviewed the grievance file. Is the case a slam-dunk winner, a sure loser, or a close call? While it may be too early to come to any definitive judgment of a case that lies somewhere near the middle of the win-lose spectrum, if the case is clearly at one end of that spectrum (i.e., a sure winner or sure loser), then the prudent advocate may wish to consider proposing a settlement before more time passes. Investing time, energy, and money in a case that is almost certain to yield an unfavorable result does not serve the interests of either party. A prompt, negotiated settlement is advisable, provided satisfactory terms can be arranged.

However, when the facts are not fully ascertained or when there is some margin for differing results, the advocate should avoid a premature conclusion and perhaps an ill-advised settlement. There will be ample opportunity prior to the hearing to consider and explore settlement possibilities.

### Assessing Potential Liability and Remedies

Consistent with an early evaluation of the likely outcome of a case is an early assessment of the value of a case, regardless of whether it is considered to be a winner or a loser. For example, assuming that a union is successful in persuading an arbitrator that the contract has been violated, what is the most likely remedy the arbitrator will order? What is a range of probable outcomes? Is there potential for a substantial back-pay award, or is it a case in which no actual damages can be shown and the most that an arbitrator would decide is that the labor agreement had been violated? The reason for such an early assessment is probably obvious. If the damages are minimal or nonexistent and the case is evaluated as likely to favor a grievance violation, the employer may find it prudent to settle on the basis that it will change its practice and procedure in the future. Conversely, if the case has substantial back-pay liabilities, the likelihood of settlement may be diminished unless the employer and the union can agree on an acceptable amount.

In a case that has a very high value, either or both parties may wish to consider using additional and/or more experienced advocates. The union may want to minimize any risk of a claim by grievants that the union did not fairly represent them because it used an inexperienced advocate or nonprofessional in a high value case. The employer may likewise consider that it needs the most experienced and professional advocate possible if its financial exposure is very high. For at least these reasons, both advocates are well advised to include in their preliminary evaluations an estimate of the potential remedy an arbitrator might order in the case if the decision is that the contract was violated.

### Considering Relationship to Other Proceedings

One final step should be included in the advocates' initial preparation checklist. The question should be asked, "Is there any other proceeding that has taken place or is likely to take place involving the same party and the same or similar issues?" The types of proceedings referred to include unemployment and workers' compensation claims and hearings; civil and criminal litigation; and hearings of governmental agencies such as the National Labor Relations Board (NLRB), Occupational Safety and Health Administration (OSHA), Equal Employment Opportunity Commission (EEOC), and others. The significance of such proceedings is that they may yield critical evidence that could prove to be decisive in the grievance arbitration hearing; conversely, evidence produced in the grievance arbitration hearing may be subsequently used in one or more of the other proceedings. Use of evidence from the arbitration hearing in another forum is not the only consideration. Having the same basic case heard in multiple forums can result in different and possibly conflicting decisions. The advocate needs to evaluate how a possible conflicting decision could impact the case, possible remedies, and the work place environment.

Occasionally, the decision from another proceeding may be offered as evidence in arbitration to prove the correctness of a party's position. Most arbitrators will not accept such decisions as evidence or give them any weight in their decision making because they are based on criteria and standards that differ from the standard to be applied by the arbitrator, namely, whether there was a violation of the labor agreement.[24] The reverse may not be true. An unemployment compensation referee or a civil court judge may admit in evidence an arbitration decision or at least a portion of the evidence presented in an arbitration hearing. Here the advocate needs to evaluate whether the issues that will be decided by the arbitrator could overlap those in another forum and also what evidence may be adduced in the arbitration that could influence the decision maker in another forum. The results of those evaluations may suggest a different

[24]Aircraft Workers Alliance Inc., 99 LA 585 (Sharpe, 1992); American Fuel Cell & Coated Fabrics Co., 97 LA 1045 (Nicholas, 1991); Grinnell Corp., 92 LA 124 (Kilroy, 1989); Stokeley-Van Camp, Inc., 59 LA 655, 659 (Griffin, 1972); Wheeling Steel Corp., 25 LA 68, 73 (Shipman, 1955).

strategy than if no other proceeding were involved. Such a strategy may be to delay or accelerate the arbitration relative to the time of the other proceeding. It may also suggest that the advocate who is to represent the party in the other proceeding be the same one who handles the arbitration. It may also lead to the conclusion that a settlement of the arbitration may be advisable. In any event, the collateral proceeding should be taken into account.

There is an exception to the general rule that arbitration decisions are based on a standard (i.e., whether or not there is a contract violation) that is different from that applied in other forums. This exception occurs with respect to cases under the National Labor Relations Act (NLRA) in which unfair labor practices overlap labor contract violations. Under the *Collyer* doctrine a grievance that also involves alleged violations of the National Labor Relations Act may be deferred to arbitration.[25] Similarly, under the *Speilberg-Raytheon* doctrine the NLRB will give full weight to arbitration awards that dispose of unfair labor practice issues under certain circumstances.[26] The NLRB has established the following guidelines for determining when it will honor arbitration decisions that have been deferred from its jurisdiction.

1. The arbitration hearing appears to have been fairly and regularly handled by the arbitrator.
2. All parties involved with the subsequent unfair labor practice charge have agreed to be bound by the arbitration award.
3. The arbitration award disposes of the unfair labor practice aspects in a manner that is not clearly repugnant to the NLRB's policies.
4. The unfair labor practice aspects involved have been ''clearly decided'' by the arbitrator.
5. The issue decided by the arbitrator was ''within his competence.''[27]

---

[25]Collyer Insulated Wire, 192 NLRB 837, 77 LRRM (1971).
[26]Spielberg Mfg. Co., 112 NLRB 1080, 36 LRRM 1152 (1955); Raytheon Co., 140 NLRB 883, 52 LRRM 1129 (1963).
[27]For a thorough discussion of the application of the *Speilberg-Raytheon* and *Collyer* doctrines, see Hardin The Developing Labor Law, 3d ed. (BNA Books, 1992), 1008–1082.

# 3

# Selecting an Arbitrator and Arranging the Hearing

One of the distinct advantages of arbitration over litigation is that the parties to an arbitration case are able to select their own neutral arbitrator, whereas it is not possible for attorneys involved in a lawsuit, except perhaps in unusual situations, to select or influence the choice of the judge who will hear their case. This advantage places a serious responsibility on the advocates to make a good choice of arbitrators, however, because that choice can significantly influence the outcome of the case. Therefore, they need to devote considerable time and energy to ensure that their selection is as favorable as possible to the outcome of their case.

A common belief is that an arbitrator who is good for one party is likely to be bad for the other. This is based on the presumption that arbitrators generally tend to favor unions or employers. The belief that what is good for one side is bad for the other is not always true, however, because the selection of a truly competent and experienced arbitrator will benefit both sides. Similarly, the selection of an incompetent arbitrator will frequently disadvantage both parties. Nevertheless, even the most competent arbitrators often have certain leanings or tendencies that, although not necessarily favoring one party or the other, are likely to provide an advantage to one side, depending on the type of case involved. For example, an arbitrator may be a strict constructionist, meaning that he or she is inclined to interpret a contract just as it was written and therefore follows the letter of the contract. This tendency may favor either the union or the employer in a particular case, depending on which side is basing its position on the specific words in the labor agreement. By knowing an arbitrator's tendency in this regard, an advocate can make a better selection of an arbitrator for a case in which the strict application of the words of the labor agreement will be important.

## SINGLE ARBITRATOR VERSUS A BOARD OF ARBITRATION

Most labor agreements provide for a single arbitrator to hear and decide each case appealed to arbitration. A minority of contracts, however, provide for a board of arbitration, which typically consists of three members: one designated unilaterally by the union, one chosen unilaterally by the employer, and a third neutral member (the chair of the arbitration board) selected jointly by the parties. The existence of a board of arbitration, in contrast to a single arbitrator, does not change the essential task of selecting a neutral arbitrator. Whether the neutral arbitrator operates alone or in conjunction with other arbitrators designated by the parties, the function of the neutral arbitrator remains the same. He or she must conduct the hearing and must decide the merits of the case based on the evidence presented and the language of the labor agreement.

### Role of Partisan Arbitrators

In the vast majority of all cases heard by boards of arbitration, the arbitrators unilaterally selected by the parties (partisan arbitrators) vote in favor of the respective parties that selected them. These arbitrators are really not expected to be neutral. Consequently, the neutral arbitrator invariably winds up as a tiebreaker, casting the decisive vote. Moreover, the formal decision, or at least a draft of the decision, invariably is written by the neutral arbitrator and merely reviewed by, or perhaps amended slightly by, one or both of the partisan arbitrators. In most cases the partisan arbitrators are little more than window dressing. In some other cases, particularly those in which the issues or facts of the case may be technically specific to the industry or work activity involved, the partisan arbitrators can serve the very useful function of educating the neutral arbitrator about the industry, work activity, practices, jargon and other peculiarities that were not apparent from the presentation of the case.

## Selecting Partisan Arbitrators

Although the selection of a neutral arbitrator is not greatly influenced by whether the case is heard by a single arbitrator or a board of arbitration, there is an important selection decision involved for each party in selecting its partisan board member. Ideally the person selected should be someone who is quite familiar with the labor agreement, bargaining history, work environment, and work practices in the facility involved and knowledgeable in arbitration procedure. Arbitration board members normally are entitled to ask questions of witnesses and therefore can influence the evidence presented. They can also influence the neutral arbitrator, especially in executive sessions (the equivalent of caucuses or off-the-record meetings of the board members). Because board members can influence the hearing and the arbitrator, they should be intelligent, articulate, rational, and persuasive. Although the neutral arbitrator ultimately is going to make the decisive ruling in the case, and although the respective advocates will have made all (or almost all) the possible arguments, the partisan arbitrators can nevertheless influence to a limited degree the neutral arbitrator's final decision and the way the decision is written.

It is usually helpful to use partisan board members for a number of cases rather than different persons from one case to another. Inexperienced board members are not able to accumulate sufficient familiarity with arbitration proceedings and techniques to be truly effective. Hearing different types of cases presided over by different arbitrators provides valuable experience. Even when there is a sole permanent arbitrator who sits as the neutral member of the board of arbitrators, there is value in the continuity of the parties' representatives because trust and confidence between the neutral and the partisan arbitrators can build when the same partisan board member sits on a number of cases.

## Disadvantages of Tripartite Boards

Most advocates dislike tripartite boards of arbitration. One reason is that it adds an element of uncertainty. What influence might the other side's board member have on the arbitrator? Might the advocate's own board member speak inappropriately, and adversely influence the case? The normal uncertainty of how the neutral arbitrator will receive and weigh the evidence is enough of a challenge without having it multiplied by the presence of partisan arbitrators.

In addition, the participation of two additional arbitrators almost always increases the time necessary for a decision to be reached. Because neutral arbitrators usually circulate a draft decision to the other board members, and consider their suggestions, the award and decision are invariably issued later than they otherwise would be. Because the neutral arbitrator must spend more time on these matters, his or her fees will necessarily be higher (of course, the partisan arbitrators receive no fees for their services, although they are typically paid by the parties they represent).

For these reasons many advocates seek to avoid tripartite arbitration boards. Where the labor agreement provides for such boards, advocates can agree to waive the board, and have the case heard by a single neutral arbitrator. Unless a party has an excellent person to serve as an arbitration board member and feels that it achieves an advantage by having that person sit on the tripartite board, it is recommended that an attempt be made to reach agreement with the other party to waive the board.

## METHODS OF SELECTING AN ARBITRATOR

There are a number of methods of selecting an arbitrator, and it is likely that the language in the labor agreement will dictate the method used. Nevertheless, it is always possible for the parties, by mutual agreement, to vary the method of selection. Consequently, an advocate should not feel bound to follow the contractual method if a different approach may be more beneficial and if it is possible to reach an agreement with the opposing advocate to use a different method. Notwithstanding the opportunity to agree otherwise, the method normally used to select and appoint an arbitrator is the one set forth in the applicable labor agreement. The most common methods for arbitrator selection typically found in labor agreements are discussed in the following sections, although not necessarily in the order of their commonality.

### Sole Permanent Arbitrator

The simplest method for arbitrator selection is for the parties to select, during the negotiation of a contract, a single arbitrator to hear all arbitration cases between the parties during the term of that contract. The unions and employers who use this arrangement often employ the same person as their permanent arbitrator over a period of years spanning the terms of a number of labor agreements. Use of a single permanent arbitrator is, however, not very widespread in comparison with other methods of arbitrator selection. It has the advantage of simplicity, speed, efficiency, and certainty. The arbitrator is a known quantity, and that arbitrator's previous decisions involving these parties are known and readily available. Predictability is much greater with a permanent arbitrator than with any other method. The permanent arbitrator is much more likely to follow precedent (frequently his or her own previous decisions) than are other arbitrators. In addition, the single permanent arbitrator can become intimately familiar with the contract language, bargaining history, work processes and practices, the union's and employer's hierarchy and political situations, and key personalities from each side, especially the employer and union advocates.

This method is not, however, without significant disadvantages. The permanent arbitrator can fall into the trap of trying to balance the number of awards in favor of each side in order to remain as the permanent arbitrator. In addition, a long-term, permanent arbitrator sometimes assumes a proprietary role, believing that he or she is somehow in control of the union-management relationship, and is therefore providing not so much a decision-making service to the parties as he or she is trying to determine what is best for them, sometimes irrespective of what the parties have agreed on in the labor contract.

It is difficult for any arbitrator, no matter how competent, to retain the position of permanent arbitrator for an indefinite period of time. The necessity of deciding tough and important cases that go against one side, the possibility of issuing a series of decisions favoring one side (albeit legitimately based on the merits of those cases), and the operation of the adage ''familiarity breeds contempt'' make longevity in this role very difficult to achieve.

If an advocate is dealing with a labor agreement that provides for a sole permanent arbitrator there will be no opportunity to influence the selection of the arbitrator for a particular case and thereby influence the outcome of that case by careful research and selection. Nevertheless, the advocate can, and should, research the arbitrator's previous decisions (and, where necessary, the record in those cases) in the type of case that is to be heard. By knowing how the arbitrator has decided previous cases, revealed certain tendencies, ruled on evidentiary matters, and so forth, the advocate will be in a better position to plan strategy and achieve a favorable result.

## Preselected Panel

The arbitration section of some labor agreements contains a list of names of arbitrators selected by the parties to hear cases that arise during the term of the agreement. This list, or panel, typically comprises five to fifteen individuals with whom the parties have some experience or confidence. Normally, arbitrators on such panels are notified of their selection in advance of placement on the panel and must consent to serve on future cases subject to availability at the appropriate time. In some cases the names of the arbitrators are included in the contract. In others, the contract merely refers to a panel, and a separate agreement or letter of understanding contains the actual list of names. Some labor agreements provide for mutually agreed changes in the panel during the term of the agreement, whereas others lock in the same list of names for the duration of the labor agreement.

### Assigning from a Preselected Panel

The determination of which arbitrator from a preselected panel will hear a specific case varies from one contract to another, but the most common method appears to be the rotating panel, in which each case appealed to arbitration is assigned to a different arbitrator on the list in the order in which the name appears on the list. The first case that is appealed to arbitration during the term of a contract is assigned to the first name on the list, and so on. This rotational approach generally makes it difficult for either party to match up arbitrators who have specific tendencies (e.g., soft on discharges, strong on management rights) with cases in which those tendencies can affect the result. When the union can alter the order in which it appeals cases to arbitration, however, or when the company assumes the administrative function of matching up incoming cases with specific arbitrators, there may be some opportunity for influencing the assignment of arbitrators for strategic advantage.

Another method of using a preselected panel is to select the arbitrator for a particular case by alternately deleting or striking names from the list until only one name remains. The initial deletion is normally determined by chance (commonly by the toss of a coin). This process allows each party to reject, within limits, particular arbitrators for specific cases because of perceived tendencies that could unfavorably affect the result in those cases. Thus, for example, an arbitrator who favors expansive management's rights may be deleted from the list by the union advocate, or an arbitrator who insists on very serious grounds for sustaining a discharge may be deleted by the employer advocate.

The fact that both parties are able to delete names gives them some level of comfort that they can each eliminate one or more of those arbitrators on the panel who could render an adverse decision because of some preconceived bias or tendency as perceived by the advocate.

Nevertheless, that each party had initially agreed to all of the arbitrators on the panel when it was originally established goes a long way toward avoiding arbitrators with obvious biases. This safety factor does not exist when lists are provided for individual cases by the Federal Mediation and Conciliation Service (FMCS) or the American Arbitration Association (AAA), as discussed below.

Another method of using a preselected panel is to schedule particular arbitrators for a series of forthcoming dates and then to have them hear cases that happen to be ready for hearing during that time period. For example, Arbitrator X is scheduled months in advance for hearings to be held during the week of August 10–14. The cases heard by the arbitrator that week are the ones that are ready for hearing at that time. The opportunity for strategic matching of arbitrator and case under this system is usually more limited than with the method of selecting particular arbitrators for specific cases unless one party can pick and choose from a series of cases awaiting hearing.

## Advantages and Disadvantages of Preselected Panels

There are distinct advantages to using a preselected panel regardless of the method used to assign specific cases. First, it ensures that the only arbitrators who will hear cases are those whose records the parties know and who have been selected without the pressure of a particular case situation. Second, to the extent that the arbitrators on the panel are each able to hear a number of cases involving the same parties, they are better able to learn the intricacies of the business, trade, industry, and work environment and culture involved, as well as the union-management relationships and personalities. Third, the preselection of names affords greater efficiency and conservation of time than making an ad hoc selection for each case.

This method is not, however, without its own limitations. To the extent that the arbitrators on the list will be hearing a series of cases involving these same parties, there can be a tendency of arbitrators to keep both sides satisfied by splitting decisions (i.e., deciding some cases for the union and some for the employer), beyond what would be expected according to the merits of those cases. Although most arbitrators wish to retain their position on preselected panels, most, fortunately, do not let that desire influence their decisions.

Depending on the specific way in which the preselected panel operates to match arbitrator and case, the advocate may be able to gain some advantage from a good match. This is particularly true with the second variation discussed above (i.e., alternative deletion of names). It behooves the advocate to research the tendencies of each arbitrator on the preselected list to determine which is most likely to rule favorably in the type of case to be presented. (Specific techniques for this research are discussed later in the section titled "Researching Arbitrators.")

Tendencies other than just how an arbitrator rules on specific types of cases are also important. For example, where a piece of evidence critical to the case is marginally admissible, for example, hearsay testimony on a key event, an arbitrator's previously displayed willingness to admit hearsay evidence becomes a valuable piece of information. Similarly, some arbitrators will not require grievants in discharge cases (i.e., discharged employees) to be called as a witness by the employer (adopting the notion from constitutional law that a person need not testify against himself or herself). Where the testimony of a discharged grievant is vital to the employer's case, the union advocate will, of course, attempt to have such an arbitrator selected for that case.

## Federal Mediation and Conciliation Service (FMCS) Panel

Many collective bargaining agreements provide that when a case is appealed to arbitration, either party or both may request a list of arbitrators from the Federal Mediation and Conciliation Service (FMCS), a government agency that assists unions and employers in the selection of qualified arbitrators. Agreements specifying selection from a panel supplied by the FMCS typically provide that when the list of arbitrators is received, the parties are to select the specific arbitrator for the case by alternatively deleting names until only one name remains. The party designated to make the initial deletion is generally determined by chance, usually by the toss of a coin. This is the same method described above concerning the choice of specific arbitrators from a preselected panel. The only difference here is that the names on the panel are chosen by the government agency, or, more precisely, from the agency's computer data base on a random basis.

The request to the FMCS for the list of arbitrators may specify the arbitrator qualifications or geographical location of the arbitrators whose names should be included on the list. For example, the request may specify that only persons from Florida, Arkansas, Tennessee, and Louisiana should be on the list. Another request may specify that all arbitrators on the list be lawyers. Figure 3-1 is the form (FMCS Form R-43) used to request an arbitration panel from the FMCS. However, the FMCS will honor a letter as well.

**Figure 3-1.**
**FMCS Form R-43**

FMCS Form R-43
April 1994

**FEDERAL MEDIATION AND CONCILIATION SERVICE**
WASHINGTON, D.C. 20427

Form Approved
OMB NO. 23-R0007

**REQUEST FOR ARBITRATION PANEL**

To: Director, Arbitration Services
Federal Mediation and Conciliation Service
Washington, D.C. 20427

Date _____

**1.**

Name of Employer _____

Name and Address
of Representative
to Receive Panel

_____ (NAME)
_____ (STREET)
_____ (CITY, STATE, ZIP)

Telephone (include area code) _____

**2.**

Name of Union and Local No. _____

Name and Address
of Representative
to Receive Panel

_____ (NAME)
_____ (STREET)
_____ (CITY, STATE, ZIP)

Telephone (include area code) _____

**3.** Site of Dispute _____
(CITY, STATE, ZIP)

**4.** Type of Issue _____
(DISCHARGE, HOLIDAY PAY, SICK LEAVE, ETC.)

**5.** A panel of seven (7) names is usually provided; if you desire a different number, please indicate _____

**6.** Type of Industry

☐ Manufacturing
☐ Construction
☐ Mining, Agriculture and Finance
☐ Other (Specify) _____

☐ Federal Government
☐ State Government
☐ Local Government

☐ Public Utilities, Communications, Transportation (including trucking)
☐ Retail, Wholesale and Service Industries

**7.** Special Requirements _____
(SPECIAL ARBITRATOR QUALIFICATIONS, TIME LIMITATIONS ON HEARING OR DECISION, GEOGRAPHICAL RESTRICTIONS, ETC.)

**8.** Signatures

_____ (Employer)

_____ (UNION)

Although the FMCS prefers to act upon a joint request of the parties, a submission will be made based on the request of a single party. However, an submission of a panel should not be construed as anything more than compliance with a request and does not reflect on the substance or arbitrability of the issue in dispute.

The number of names to be provided may be specified in the labor agreement or, if not specified, the number may be designated by the parties in the written request to the FMCS. Because of the manner of selecting one name from a list, the number of names should be an uneven number. If no number is specified in the written request, the agency will supply seven names.

The persons whose names are on the roster of arbitrators maintained by the FMCS are private arbitrators in the sense that they are not in the employ of the government, nor do they represent the government in any way. The FMCS merely performs the function of screening arbitrators before placing them on the roster and providing their names to parties who request a panel. Along with the list the agency provides a short biography of each arbitrator indicating the person's work experience, education, industries in which he or she has arbitration experience, daily fee charged, and address and telephone number. Figure 3-2 is a sample of the information sheet provided on each arbitrator on the FMCS-provided panel.

Once the list is received, the parties make their selection in the manner of alternative deletions described earlier and then contact the arbitrator directly to notify him or her of the selection and to obtain a date or several dates when the arbitrator will be available to conduct the hearing. The FMCS requests that it be notified of the parties' selection from the list. There is no cost to the parties for using the FMCS arbitrator referral service.

## American Arbitration Association (AAA) Panel

In much the same manner as the FMCS, the American Arbitration Association (AAA) provides a service to unions and employers for selecting qualified labor arbitrators. This same service is provided by the AAA for disputes other than those involving labor and management. Disputes in the construction industry, lawyer-client disagreements, and real estate disputes are but a few of the types of cases for which the AAA provides panels of arbitrators.

There are some significant differences between the FMCS arbitrator referral service and that provided by the AAA. Although many of the names of arbitrators on the roster of AAA are the same as those on the FMCS roster, the experience requirements for inclusion on the FMCS roster are somewhat higher. Another difference is that the AAA charges a fee for its services whereas use of the FMCS is free. As of this writing the fee charged by the AAA is $300 per case, divided equally between the parties. However, the AAA supplies services in addition to that provided by the FMCS. The AAA maintains conference rooms in which arbitra-

**Figure 3-2.**
**Sample Arbitrator Information Sheet**

**MR JOE J DOE**          **FMCS-3900**

OCCUPATION: ARBITRATOR

ADDRESS
  (BUS):
    225 DOE AVENUE, SUITE 5400                          (HOME):
    DOETOWN, AL 22222
    (205) 222-2222

PROFESSIONAL AFFILIATIONS: NAA    AAA    IRRA

GENERAL EXPERIENCE:
    PROFESSOR    ANY COLLEGE 69 - PRESENT

  PERM PANEL:
    MIDGET FOODS/UFCW
    YOURTOWN HOSP/HEAR

ARBITRATION EXPERIENCE:

  ISSUES:
    ABSENTEEISM, ARBITRABILITY, BARG UNIT WORK, DEMOTION, DISCHARGE, DISCRIM, DRESS CODE
    ENV PAY, HEALTH & WELFARE, HOLIDAYS & HOL PAY, INCENTIVE RATES/STDS
    JOB POSTING & BIDDING, JURISDICTION, MGMT RTS, PAST PRACTICE, RATE OF PAY, RIF, SAFETY
    SCHED OF WORK, SENIORITY, SUBCONTR, TRANSF, UNION BUS, WORK PERF, WORK COND, OTHER
    COLA, CONTRACTING OUT, INSUBORDINATION, LEAVE OF ABSENCE, MERIT PAY, PROMOTIONS
    REASSIGNMENT, RED CIRCLE RATE, SHIFT HOURS, SICK LEAVE, WORK WEEK CHANGE
    SEXUAL HARASSMENT, GRIEVANCE MEDIATION, PENSION CLAIMS IN FED LAW, TRUSTEE DEADLOCKS

  INDUSTRIES:
    AEROSPACE, AIRLINES, BAKERY, CLOTHING, COAL, COMMUNICATIONS, DAIRY, ELEC COMMUNICATIONS
    ENT/ARTS, FOOD, GRAIN MILL, HEALTH CARE, HOTEL/RESTR, IRON, MANUF MISC, MARIT, MINING
    NUCLEAR ENERGY, PAINT & VARNISH, PETRO, PLBG, PRINT & PUBL, PUB SEC INT, REFR/AIR COND
    RETAIL STORES, RUBBER, SCIENTIFIC INSTRUMENTS, SHOE, STEEL, STONE, TEXTILE, TOBACCO
    TRANSPORTATION, TRUCK & STOR, UPHOL, UTILITIES, ELECTRICAL APPLIANCES, INSURANCE
    NONFERROUS METALS, RAILROADS, SPORTS, BANKING, REAL ESTATE

PUBLIC SECTOR AGENCY ROSTERS:
    AL PERB
    GA PERB
    TN PERB
    NMB

EDUCATION:
    BA     POLITICAL SCIENCE    UNIVERSITY OF DOETOWN   1964
    MA     EDUCATION    UNIVERSITY OF YOURTOWN    1970
    PHD    INDUSTRIAL RELATIONS    UNIVERSITY OF ANYWHERE    1974

CERTIFICATION:
    LAW    ALABAMA    75

PER DIEM FEE:  $400                    DATE OF BIRTH:  1940

950504

tion hearings may be held at no additional charge. In addition, AAA coordinates all the arrangements for the hearing among each party and the arbitrator, whereas with an FMCS-provided list of arbitrators the parties themselves make arrangements with the arbitrator for the time and location of the hearing. Some advocates prefer the savings in time and increased control of the direct method under FMCS. Other advocates, however, prefer to have the AAA spend the time and energy to make such arrangements. The procedural rules followed by the AAA are set forth in Appendix A.

Another distinction between the two services is the manner in which the arbitrator is selected from the panel submitted to the parties. With an FMCS list, the parties may use any method they choose to select a name although they commonly use the alternative name deletion method discussed above. With a list supplied by the AAA, the parties are instructed to delete the name of any arbitrator who is unacceptable, and to rank the rest in the order of most preferred. These rankings are returned to the AAA for an administrator to select the person most preferred by both parties. If no single name is acceptable to both parties, another list will be provided. Similarly, in scheduling a hearing date, calendars for upcoming months are provided to each party to mark available dates. The administrator then uses the calendars to coordinate with the arbitrator to select a date satisfactory to the parties and the arbitrator.

## Strategy of Selecting from a Panel

As discussed above, the advocates or other representatives of the union and employer normally select the specific arbitrator to hear a case by alternately deleting names. This need not be done, however. The parties may agree to simply select one of the persons on the list. This is most likely to happen when one of the persons listed is someone who is particularly familiar and acceptable to both sides. One of the difficulties with this approach is that if one of the advocates indicates a preference for a particular arbitrator on a list, the other side may conclude that this person is more favorable to the other party and therefore may be inclined to delete that name if and when the parties resort to the alternate striking method.

For example, the union suggests that both sides simply agree to use Ms. X to hear the case. The employer does not agree, and it becomes necessary to strike names. The employer is now more likely to strike the name of Ms. X because it believes that Ms. X is likely to favor the union, because the union was ready to select her above all the others on the list.

Assuming that the alternate striking method is used, one might question whether there is an advantage to making the first deletion. The answer is no. In fact, the exact opposite is true. The side that makes the initial deletion is at a disadvantage. An example illustrates the reason that deleting second rather than first is an advantage. If there is an uneven number of names on the list (as there invariably is) each side will get the same number of deletions. If there are five names on the list, each side will get the opportunity to delete two names; if there are seven names, each party is allowed three deletions, and so on.

The party that goes first (for example, the employer) makes the first and third deletions, and the union makes the second and fourth deletions. The union, by choosing second, has the advantage of knowing the employer's first deletion before making its first choice of which arbitrator to delete from the list. Similarly, the union advocate knows the employer's second deletion before making its second choice of whom to eliminate from the list. It is entirely possible that the union, had it had the first choice, would have deleted the same arbitrator as the one deleted by the employer. However, because that name was deleted by the employer, the union need not "waste" its choice to delete that person, and it can therefore go on to the next least desirable name. For this reason, the side that chooses second always has an advantage. To illustrate this point in a more concrete fashion, the example in Figure 3-3 shows how this might work in an actual situation.

In this example, the union rated Reed as its least preferred arbitrator. Because the employer deleted Reed's name first (because Reed was its least preferred arbitrator as well), the union was able to avoid using one of its strikes to delete Reed's name from the list. The union then was able to use its first strike to eliminate Smith (its fourth choice), who was the employer's second most preferred choice. Similarly, the employer deleting Wilson's name meant that the union did not have to use a strike to eliminate Wilson, its third least desirable selection. The union could then use its last strike to delete Jefferson, its second preferred choice, in order to leave Jones, its most preferred arbitrator. Although the order of striking names from the list may not always work out to give an advantage to the side that selects second, there is no case in which it is not preferable to choose second.

What does this mean to the advocate who wishes to have the advantage in his or her choice of arbitrators? Not winning the coin toss is

**Figure 3-3.**
**Example of Arbitrator Selection**

| Name | Panel of Arbitrators Employer's Preference * | Union's Preference* |
|------|-----------------------------------------------|---------------------|
| Smith | 2nd | 4th |
| Jones | 3rd | 1st |
| Wilson | 4th | 3rd |
| Reed | 5th | 5th |
| Jefferson | 1st | 2nd |

*In order of arbitrator most preferred that is, the 1st being the most desired arbitrator and the 5th being the least desirable. These preferences are not, of course, disclosed to the other side.

### Order of Deletions

| | |
|---|---|
| First deletion (by employer) | - Reed |
| Second deletion (by union) | - Smith |
| Third deletion (by employer) | - Wilson |
| Fourth deletion (by union) | - Jefferson |
| Remaining name-final selection | - Jones |

certainly one way, but this is not controllable. Another way of gaining this advantage is to offer the other side the opportunity to make the first deletion. Many advocates do not realize the disadvantage of selecting first and will accept a seemingly magnanimous offer to strike the first name from the list. Although the advantage of selecting second (and therefore last) does not ensure a better selection of an arbitrator, it does increase the odds of doing so.

Regardless of the exact method used to select a specific name from a panel of arbitrators, it is necessary for both advocates to make an evaluation of the relative merits and demerits of each name on the list in order to determine an order of preference. Unless all the names on the list are arbitrators with whom both parties have had considerable experience, such an evaluation and preparation of an order of preference requires some painstaking research and analysis. That process is outlined later in this chapter.

## Ad Hoc Selection of a Single Arbitrator

Some labor agreements explicitly provide the opportunity for the parties to mutually select an arbitrator for a particular case. Recognizing the possibility or even the likelihood that the parties may not agree on a single name, such agreements normally provide for a fail-safe procedure for selection, such as obtaining a panel from the FMCS or the AAA and eliminating all but one name by alternate deletions as described earlier. The initial option, selection of an arbitrator by mutual agreement, often serves the parties well and ensures that both sides will have the case heard by an arbitrator each has freely chosen. It also affords them the opportunity to select an arbitrator who may possess special skills or knowledge pertinent of their industry or the issue in their case, such as a lawyer when the case has statutory overtones, an engineer when there are technical or engineering issues, or an arbitrator with considerable experience in a particular industry when the issues in the case involve complex matters unique to that industry. Ad hoc selection by mutual agreement does not depend on the luck of the draw, whether that draw be the particular list of names submitted by the FMCS or the toss of a coin.

## RESEARCHING ARBITRATORS AND ANALYZING THEIR SUITABILITY FOR THE CASE

There are a number of sources of information about the expertise, rationality, judgment, and predispositions of arbitrators. No one source can provide all the information necessary to make a truly informed selection. A combination of methods is advised. Whatever methods are used, it is important to keep in mind that, unless the arbitrators available for selection are well known to the advocate, at least some research should be undertaken prior to selecting an arbitrator. To blindly choose an arbitrator without any research is akin to buying shares of stock without doing any research or analysis of the company whose shares are being purchased.

## Biographies and Resumes

Probably the most readily available, but one of the least helpful, sources of information about arbitrators is their biographical resumes. This information is provided by the FMCS and AAA when they submit panels of arbitrators. Resumes are also available in the labor arbitration reporting services published by the Bureau of National Affairs, Inc. (BNA), Commerce Clearing House (CCH), LRP Publications, and others. The detail provided in the resumes will vary somewhat from one source to another, and it is therefore often wise to review several sources.

As already indicated, the resume is of marginal value. It will indicate the general background of the arbitrator and reflect whether he or she has a management, union, academic, legal, or other specific background. It will indicate the level of education attained and at least a significant portion of the work experience achieved. It will often enable the advocate to estimate the arbitrator's age and years spent in arbitration. It also usually will state whether the arbitrator is a member of the National Academy of Arbitrators, a mark of experience and professionalism. What it will not reflect is the way in which the arbitrator conducts a hearing, how he or she generally rules on hearsay evidence, whether contract language is construed narrowly or broadly, what types of misconduct he or she usually holds to warrant discharge, and answers to the myriad other questions an advocate is likely to have. Fortunately, there are other means to answer at least some of these questions. These are discussed in the sections that follow.

When reviewing arbitrator biographies, an advocate should keep in mind at least one key principle: *just because an arbitrator has a background in either union or management work should not lead one to believe that the arbitrator is biased in that direction.* There is a tendency for inexperienced advocates (and even some experienced ones) to conclude that an arbitrator who has worked on one side is likely to favor that side's position. Such a conclusion is too simplistic. The author's experience and the experience of many advocates with whom the author has spoken do not bear out such a broad conclusion. Although it is true that some arbitrators are not able to shake off their union or management heritage, it is likewise true that such arbitrators are not, at least in the long run, often selected for cases. It takes both parties to select an arbitrator. If an arbitrator from a management background regularly favors employers in rendering decisions, unions will quickly learn that he or she is not a person to select. The arbitrator will soon be out of business or will operate with a minimal caseload. The same is true of arbitrators whose union backgrounds influence their decisions. An arbitrator with a distinct union or employer background being selected for a large number of cases by a wide range of unions and employers is a pretty good indication that the partisan orientation is not interfering with the arbitrator's ability to render unbiased and even-handed decisions.

## Reports from Colleagues and Other Advocates

One of the least scientific, yet perhaps most valuable, sources of arbitrator evaluations is that provided by colleagues and other advocates. These may be other union representatives, management personnel, lawyers, or others who have reason to know of the performance of arbitrators who are under active or potential consideration. The main reason this source is so valuable is that it usually is first-hand information from those who have presented cases before the particular arbitrators being considered. Second, the source can be advised of the particular nature of the case to be arbitrated and can frame the evaluation in terms of similar cases or issues. Third, there is an opportunity for the advocate to ask questions of the evaluator, to assess the evaluator's objectivity, and to pinpoint the particular attributes of the arbitrator that may be most crucial in the case to be arbitrated. Finally, one-on-one conversations between advocates (especially those who have a personal acquaintance and can speak with confidence) are apt to result in candid and open assessments.

The value of subjective evaluations obtained from colleagues and other advocates is directly proportional to the number of such evaluations obtained. One or even two evaluations may give a distorted picture, particularly if the persons providing the evaluations have had limited experience with the arbitrators under consideration. Four or five separate evaluations, however, are likely to provide a much clearer and more reliable picture. Similarly, the advocate must be careful to assess the objectivity and perceptiveness of the evaluator. For example, if the evaluator had only one case with an arbitrator under consideration—and the reporting advocate felt very strongly about the case being discussed—a single adverse decision by that arbitrator may be enough to cause the evaluator to provide a strongly negative report that is not justified by the arbitrator's overall record. Aside from simply indicating the winning side, the evaluation should take into consideration why the evaluator felt the arbitrator did not render a fair and competent decision. Did the arbitrator fail to admit all relevant evidence? Was insufficient weight given to a clear past practice? Were there statements or rulings made that showed an obvious bias or blind spot? These and other questions will help to elicit a more useful evaluation than simply whether or not the arbitrator ruled in favor of the evaluator's side.

Advocates who have been in the labor relations field for some time usually will have built a network of other practitioners from whom they can obtain candid evaluations. This is not generally true of recent entrants into the field or of those who have relocated to a new geographical area. Their access to information from other practitioners is more limited. Nevertheless, by contacting union advocates in sister unions or employer advocates with companies in the same industry, those without existing network contacts are often able to obtain useful information. Another means of making contacts and obtaining evaluations is through union coordinating bodies and employer associations. Some international unions maintain arbitrator rosters indicating acceptable and unacceptable ratings. Likewise, many employer associations keep information on arbitrators who hear cases in particular geographical areas or in specific industries. In addition to whatever formal rating or evaluation services may be available from union or employer coordinating bodies, such organizations are usually helpful in directing the inquiring advocate to other union or employer representatives who can provide arbitrator evaluations on a person-to-person basis.

## Reported Decisions

Another method of evaluating arbitrators is to review their previous decisions, particularly in cases involving issues similar to those in the case to be presented. Because the vast majority of arbitration cases are private (i.e., not part of a governmental or public process), there is no requirement for publication of such decisions. Decisions that are published are usually the result of specific agreements of the parties to the case being reported and the arbitrator rendering the decision. As a result, only a small fraction of all decisions issued by labor arbitrators are ever published. Nevertheless, some are, and, to the extent they are available in printed form, the careful advocate should not overlook this means of researching arbitrator performance. The principal publishers of labor arbitration cases are as follows.

The Bureau of National Affairs, Inc.
- *Labor Arbitration Reports*
- *Government Employee Relations Report*

Commerce Clearing House
- *Labor Arbitration Awards*

LRP Publications
- *Labor Arbitration Information Systems*
- *Federal Labor Relations Reporter*

American Arbitration Association
- *Summary of Labor Arbitration Awards*
- *Labor Arbitration in Government*
- *Arbitrations in the Schools*

Several of these services (at least the first two publishers) are usually available in most business, law, university and large public libraries. All of them are available through computerized subscription services, such as Lexis and Westlaw. Similarly, the Labor Arbitration Information System (LAIS) published by LRP Publications of Horsham, Pennsylvania, provides both a computerized system with indexed summaries and a looseleaf system. The LAIS service includes cases reported by each of the four publishers listed above. An example of the information in their reports is shown in Figure 3-4.

Reported decisions are most useful in gaining insight into the reasoning process employed by the arbitrators under consideration and are helpful in learning any tendencies exhibited that could influence the decision in the case to be presented. Reported decisions are less useful in compiling a scorecard of how a particular arbitrator ruled in a large number of cases. Because such a small percentage of all cases decided is reported, the scorecard approach is not useful and can be very misleading. Advocates should always keep in mind that a written arbitration decision does not always reflect all the facts and nuances that existed in a case. The arbitrator has sole discretion over what is included in the written decision, and some arbitrators are very selective in what they include in their written decisions to enhance the appearance of sound logic and convincing evidence. It is nevertheless true that reading the written opinion and decision of an arbitrator is one of the best ways of evaluating that arbitrator's competence, judgment, and standards of proof as an aid in making an intelligent selection of an arbitrator to hear the case at hand.

**Figure 3-4.**
**Sample LAIS Report**

**LRP Publications**
**747 Dresher Road**
**PO Box 980**
**Horsham PA 19044-0980**
**800-341-7874, Ext. 246**

Arbitrator: Wisdom, Solomon                    Arbitrator Number: 30
**DECISION SUMMARY**

|  | Total | M | U | S |
|---|---|---|---|---|
| All Cases | 70 | 32 | 14 | 24 |
| Percentage |  | 45.7 | 20.0 | 34.3 |
| Discipline Cases | 27 | 9 | 4 | 14 |
| Percentage |  | 33.3 | 14.8 | 51.9 |
| Nondiscipline Cases | 43 | 23 | 10 | 10 |

This table represents a statistical analysis of the total number of an arbitrator's cases on the database. The table divides the cases into categories representing the prevailing party as follows: M = management; U = union; and S = split.

**BIOGRAPHICAL INFORMATION**

| | |
|---|---|
| FULL NAME: | Solomon Wisdom |
| TITLE: | Labor Arbitrator |
| COMPANY: | Self-employed |
| ADDRESS1: | 1234 Main Street |
| ADDRESS2: | PO Box 567 |
| CITY STATE ZIP: | Anywhere, PA  19000 |
| BUS. PHONE: | (215) 555-1234 |
| BUS. FAX: | (215) 555-9876 |
| HOME ADDRESS: | Same as above |
| DATE OF BIRTH: | 11-05-35 |
| PLACE OF BIRTH: | Philadelphia, PA |
| OCCUPATION(S): | Arbitrator, Mediator |
| NATIONAL ACADEMY MEMBER: | Y |
| MEMBERSHIP ON PANELS: | AAA, FMCS... |
| CANCELLATION FEE/AMOUNT: | Y, $400 (Per Diem = $400) |
| CANCELLATION CIRCUMSTANCES: | W/in 14 days of hearing date |
| HEARING PROCEDURE: | Rely on personal notes |
| ARBITRATED ISSUES: | Ability; Absences; ... Disability; Discipline; ... |
| ARBITRATED INDUSTRIES: | Automobile; Bakery; Beverage; Cement; Chemicals;... Education; Electronics; ... |
| EDUCATION: | Ph.D.; Social History: Temple University |
| CERTIFICATION: | |
| EMPLOYMENT: | Self-employed |

**Wisdom, Solomon**
Cont'd

LABOR RELATIONS ACTIVITIES:                    Author, several books
                                               and approximately
                                               100 articles and
                                               monographs in the
                                               field of Industrial
                                               Relations
PROFESSIONAL MEMBERSHIPS:                       IRRA
AWARDS/HONORS:
PUBLICATIONS:                                   See Attached

### ARBITRATION RESEARCH
Case 1

ARBITRATOR:        Wisdom, Solomon
EMPLOYER:          Commonwealth Paper Co.
UNION:             USWA, Local 2564
AWARD DATE:        1/21/95
WINNER:            U
SUBJECT(S):        5.058 Grievance and Procedure
                   8.024 Evidence, Medical Opinions
                   17.151 Arbitrability, Timeliness
                   78.009 Work Rules...
CITE(S):           AAA 438-8; 22 LAIS 3771
SUMMARY:
The company violated regulations by refusing to allow the grievant to grow
a beard even though he proved...

Case 2

ARBITRATOR:        Wisdom, Solomon
EMPLOYER:          Mack's Groceries
UNION:             UFCW
AWARD DATE:        4/6/95
WINNER:            S
SUBJECT(S):        1.066 Authority of Arbitrator
                   37.060 Discipline, Incompetence...
CITE(S):           95 LA 1021;  18 LAIS 3339
SUMMARY:
The Employer placed the grievant, a frozen-food clerk, on indefinite
suspension while it investigated the alleged...

## Unreported Decisions

As mentioned above, most labor arbitration decisions are not published: it is estimated that less than three percent of all arbitration decisions are published. This does not mean that unpublished decisions are not available, however. Union and employer coordinating bodies (e.g., international unions and employer associations) often maintain files of unpublished arbitration decisions from member or affiliated unions and employers. In some cases, summaries of decisions are prepared and regularly disseminated to members or affiliates. The full decisions are usually available on request from those members or affiliates. Of course, as stated above, the individual unions and employers who were parties to the arbitration cases are sources of the unpublished decisions. To the extent that such cases have been decided by the arbitrator under consideration and involve the same or similar issues as the case at hand, they can be quite valuable.

## Published Arbitrator Evaluations

The author is aware of only one service that actually publishes evaluations of arbitrators. It is a subscription service, and subscribers are limited to employer representatives and advocates. It is *Arbitrator Qualification Reports (AQR),* published by R. C. Simpson Inc., of Charlotte, North Carolina. This service obtains qualitative reports on individual arbitrators from employers who have received arbitration decisions by those arbitrators. These reports reflect which side won the case, the subject matter of the case (e.g., discipline/discharge, seniority, vacation scheduling, contracting out), and a detailed report on the arbitrator's conduct of the hearing, the weight given to certain types of evidence, the regard given to management's rights, and a number of other factors. In addition, there is a compilation of reported and unreported decisions issued by the arbitrator.

The value of this service is open to debate. Many employers find it quite useful, especially because it includes citations to virtually all reported decisions by each arbitrator, broken down according to cases won by the employer and by the union. Other employers believe it is of little value. They believe that the employer advocates or employer representatives who rate the arbitrators are overly influenced by the win/loss result in each particular case (i.e., if the decision is in the employer's favor, the arbitrator did a good job and is given an excellent evaluation, whereas if the arbitrator ruled in the union's favor, he or she is given a low rating). Notwithstanding such deficiencies, the AQR reports are an additional piece of information, and, if they are not taken as being scientific but are viewed merely as the compilation of subjective judgments, they can be a useful addition to the other means of selecting an arbitrator.

## Weighing the Information and Making a Selection

After using one or more of the means discussed earlier for re-searching arbitrators and after analyzing that information, the advocate is likely to have conflicting reports and evaluations. That should not create undue concern. Most information about arbitrator performance is subjec-tive, and evaluators differ considerably in their fairness and percep-tiveness in evaluating arbitrators. Moreover, few arbitrators are com-pletely consistent in their decisionmaking. Even when they are generally consistent, small differences in facts, evidence, and contract language can produce significant differences in results. Often these small differ-ences are not obvious when one is reading and comparing decisions, and it is common for evaluators to overlook these differences in assessing arbitrator performance.

The advocate should keep in mind that it is highly unlikely that the ideal arbitrator can be selected for a case. First, such a person probably does not exist. Second, even if the ideal arbitrator did exist, it is not likely that two opposing advocates would join in selecting that person. Third, it is often difficult to predict with accuracy the exact key issues or points of fact on which the decision will turn. Consequently, the advocates should not be disturbed if the arbitrator who is selected was not their first or even second choice. Getting someone who appears to be reasonably compe-tent and fair is about all that one can expect in selecting an arbitrator. Nevertheless, careful and thorough research can improve the chances of making a good selection, and this step in preparing for arbitration should be given a very high priority.

## SCHEDULING THE HEARING

## Multiple Cases in a Single Hearing

In selecting an arbitrator and arranging a hearing, one of the procedural issues that sometimes arises is whether the arbitrator selected is going to hear a single case or several cases as part of one assignment. Some parties have a practice of scheduling several cases for a single day or series of days of hearings before the same arbitrator. More common, however, is the practice of scheduling one case for a single arbitrator in a single hearing (which may require one or more days to complete). The number of cases to be heard by a single arbitrator is a matter that the parties are free to establish by mutual agreement, and most arbitrators will comply with whatever protocol the parties mutually establish. A problem arises, however, when the labor agreement does not address the issue and when the parties disagree over whether multiple cases may be heard by a single arbitrator.

### Motives for Multiple Cases

It is not unusual for one party to seek to schedule several cases to be heard by a single arbitrator in one or more consecutive days of hearings, especially when there is a backlog of pending cases. More often than not, it is the union representative who advances this position. The motive is usually economic in that the arbitrator's fees, hearing room expenses and possible court reporter's fees can be spread over several cases rather than just one. Employers, on the other hand, are usually less concerned with costs and frequently do not want to make it easier or less expensive for unions to have grievances advanced to arbitration.

Another motive for seeking to have multiple cases heard by the same arbitrator is the feeling of some advocates that if several marginal cases are presented to a single arbitrator, the arbitrator is more likely to rule favorably in at least one of them than if the cases were heard separately. One of the major arguments against scheduling several cases back to back is the difficulty in adequately preparing several cases for a single set of hearings when one of the parties has only one advocate available to present arbitration cases.

### Means of Resolving Multiple Case Disputes

When a dispute exists over the issue of multiple cases to be heard by a single arbitrator, the issue will, if not resolved by the parties, typically wind up before an arbitrator. The arbitrator will first determine whether the labor agreement addresses the issue (normally it will not). Most labor agreements simply refer to "the grievance to be arbitrated" or "grievances to be arbitrated," and this may be construed as a reflection of the parties' intentions regarding the hearing of more than one grievance by a single arbitrator. Next, the arbitrator will look to past practice to see if the parties have scheduled multiple cases in the past, and, if so, how recently and frequently it has been done. Lastly, the arbitrator will look to arbitral precedent. While that precedent is not clear, the weight of authority seems to favor multiple cases.[1] The logic favoring this approach is efficiency and expeditious resolution of disputes.

Two of the key elements arbitrators look at in making decisions concerning the hearing of multiple cases by one arbitrator is how the case was appealed to arbitration and how the selection of the arbitrator was linked (or not linked) to the cases that are requested to be heard by a single arbitrator. For example, if a grievance concerning a rate of pay was appealed to arbitration as a single case and if an arbitrator was selected to hear that case, it will be difficult to sustain an argument that another grievance, for example, one concerning vacation scheduling, should be heard by the same arbitrator. If, however, both grievances were appealed to arbitration at the same time and if the selection of an arbitrator was not linked to a single specific case, a strong argument can be made that the arbitrator should hear and decide both cases as part of a single set of hearings. When the cases are factually or contractually related (e.g., the issue concerns the contractually required method for scheduling vacations and the appropriate rate of pay for those who perform the work of the vacationing employees), the justification for multiple cases is much stronger.

When the parties have a permanent arbitrator, the arguments favoring multiple cases in a single set of hearings is even stronger. Because the same arbitrator is going to hear all cases anyway, why not have him or her hear as many as possible as part of one set of hearings (one day or several consecutive days)? Some advocates believe that, even though the same person may ultimately decide all cases, there nevertheless should be some separation in the hearings and deliberations of those cases to avoid what might be an arbitrator's inclination to compromise decisions in an effort to placate one side or the other. Whether arbitrators have such an inclination or not is problematic. The author's view is that some arbitrators do harbor a concern that they not be perceived as favoring one side too consistently and that such concerns could influence their decisions, especially when two or more close cases are presented more or less simultaneously to them. However, if an arbitrator is inclined to compromise, it can be done over a period of time and in a series of cases, whether or not they are heard back to back. Consequently, it is recommended that permanent arbitrators hear cases

---

[1]ELKOURI AND ELKOURI, HOW ARBITRATION WORKS, 4th ed., (BNA Books, 1985), pp. 231–32.

in a fashion that best meets the practical needs of the parties (e.g., conservation of time and money and sufficient preparation time).

## Hearing Site and Room Arrangements

In most cases, the contracting parties have a standardized practice of determining where arbitration hearings take place. Usually, it is at the employer's facilities or at a neutral site such as a hotel conference room. Only rarely will hearings be held at the union's offices. Occasionally, disagreement may arise over the hearing site, such as when the employer operates out of a number of geographical locations and the grievant does not have a single work site (e.g., certain over-the-road truck drivers, movie actors, and specialized construction workers). Disagreement over the hearing site can also arise when there are a number of grievants from various locations who have joined together in a single grievance. When there is serious disagreement, practical considerations such as the location that will require the least amount of travel for the greatest number of necessary participants will usually prevail. Unresolved disagreements concerning hearing sites must ultimately be determined by an arbitrator. Fortunately, disagreements concerning arbitration hearing sites are relatively rare.

## Stenographic Record of the Hearing

Another issue concerning hearing arrangements is whether a verbatim transcript of the hearing should be taken. Public stenographers or so-called "court reporters" are often employed to record and prepare a transcript of the hearing. The common practice is for the parties to share the reporter's fees equally. Transcripts are more frequently taken when lawyers are serving as the advocates, when the advocates intend to file posthearing briefs, and when the issues in the case are likely to be the subject of disputes in other forums, such as before the Equal Employment Opportunity Commission or the National Labor Relations Board or in civil or criminal litigation.

Many arbitrators prefer to have a verbatim transcript because it reduces the need for them to take copious notes, although, many arbitrators take extensive notes whether or not the hearing is being transcribed. Arbitrators also favor hearing transcripts because they assist them in reviewing the case and in preparing a decision.

The cost of obtaining a verbatim transcript can easily amount to $500 to $1000 per full day of hearing (usually half paid by each party).

This works against the notion of economy, one of the main advantages of labor arbitration economy. Nevertheless, in cases involving discharge or significant contract interpretation issues, those in which there is likely to be substantial dispute concerning the facts and in which witness credibility may be decisive, or those in which the advocates plan to file posthearing briefs, a transcript is usually advisable. Traditional practices and the degree of formality with which the parties are accustomed will usually dictate whether a transcript is made. In a report issued by the FMCS for 1994, transcripts were taken in only nine percent of the cases decided.[2]

---

[2]Federal Mediation and Conciliation Service, Arbitration Statistics, Fiscal Year 1994.

# 4

# Assembling the Evidence

## IMPORTANCE OF THE EVIDENTIARY CASE

Although there are a number of ingredients that go into a successful arbitration result, there is nothing that is more likely to turn the tide in favor of one side or the other than having a good set of facts supported by solid evidence of those facts and capped with an effective presentation of that evidence. In cases of contract interpretation, no doubt contract language and/or past practice must support the position taken, but unless provable facts underlie the case, it will inevitably falter.

The vital importance of having a strong factual case means that the advocate must ensure that all relevant facts have been discovered and that the evidence of those facts is sufficiently established and persuasive. To reach this point, extensive preparation is usually required.

One might question whether the nuts-and-bolts preparation of a case should begin by focusing on evidence or whether it is preferable to concentrate initially on the contract language aspect of the case. Both are usually done simultaneously. It would be foolhardy to begin assembling evidence without having first reviewed the labor agreement and the pertinent sections of that agreement. Similarly, one cannot consider contract provisions without knowing the context in which those provisions may or may not apply. Once the cursory review of both facts and "law" (i.e., contract language, past practice and bargaining history) has been completed, however, the author's preferred order of actual case preparation is to begin by assembling the facts. This is the more time-consuming task and, generally, the one that the advocate has least control

71

over. Witnesses may not always be available, documents may be destroyed if they are not obtained promptly, data analysis may require considerable time to prepare, and other stumbling blocks may have to be overcome. The sooner the advocate focuses on the evidentiary case, the more likely it is that critical evidence will be available. This chapter deals with preparation of the factual or evidentiary case. The following chapter addresses preparation of the argumentation or contractual case.

## SUFFICIENCY OF THE RECORD TO DATE

Some advocates, especially less experienced ones, come to the preparation of a labor arbitration case with the notion that the facts are already well known and established because the grievance has been discussed, reviewed, and analyzed at least one and usually two to four steps earlier in the grievance procedure. The advocate (assuming he or she is not the same person who handled the case at earlier grievance steps) will be given a file that contains memoranda, notes, minutes, and documents that lay out the facts and the disposition of the grievance at the preliminary and intermediate grievance steps. The novice advocate is apt to assume that there is nothing more to be done than to prepare witnesses and to organize the documents for presentation to the arbitrator. This is seldom sufficient.

Invariably, there are significant gaps in the evidence necessary to prove the case: all potential witnesses may not have been interviewed, hearsay evidence may have been relied on when first-hand evidence was available, or witnesses' statements to prove past practice may have been relied on when irrefutable documentation can be obtained. Even where the evidence is complete, it may not be in the form that will be most persuasive to an arbitrator. A competent advocate should not assume that what is in the grievance file is going to be sufficient to prove the case. The better course is to look at the case from a fresh perspective and determine what will have to be presented to the arbitrator in order to prove the case. If that information is already in the file, the advocate may breathe a little easier, but where evidence is lacking, the advocate's task is to ferret out what is, or may be, available. A good arbitration advocate must have the instincts of an investigator, an analyst, a tactician, a producer, and a persuader.

# DEFINING THE ISSUES AND THE THEORY OF THE CASE

In order to put the meat (i.e., evidence of the facts) on the bones (i.e., contract language related to the case), the advocate should at an early stage define the issues in the case and what the theory(ies) behind the advocate's case will be. For example, a grievance being prepared for arbitration concerns an employer's assignment of maintenance work to a production employee under a labor agreement that does not contain any job descriptions or any specific language defining the scope of work jurisdiction.

## Focusing on the Issues

What are the issues? The specific issue to be presented to the arbitrator might be, "Did the employer violate the labor agreement by assigning the work of adjusting the upper gear arm of the unitizing machine to John Jones, a production worker, on July 22? If yes, what is the remedy?" This statement of the core issue does not, however, pinpoint the specific evidentiary matters necessary to prepare the advocate's case. A more detailed list of questions is necessary. Such a list might include the following:

1. Prior to this incident, who normally performed the work in question? If the practice was not consistent, was there any pattern or rationale to the manner in which it was normally done?
2. Was John Jones the operator of the machine on which the work was performed, and were the maintenance duties he performed part of his normal duties with respect to that machine?
3. Was a mechanic available to perform the work in question, and if so, why wasn't that person assigned to do the work?
4. How technical was the work that was performed, and is there a chance that a safety hazard might have been created by the work being done by someone other than a maintenance employee?
5. How extensive was the work that was performed? Was it a minor adjustment, or was it more significant? How long did it take, and what tools were used? What particular knowledge and skills were necessary to do the job?
6. Were there any discernable consequences (favorable or unfavorable) to production and/or safety because the work was done by Jones, the production worker, rather than a mechanic?

7. Had this type of assignment, or similar types of assignments, ever been done before by production workers, and if so, how frequently? If done, were any grievances filed, and if so, what were the results of the grievances?
8. Did the assignment of the work to a production worker cause the loss of work and pay to any mechanics? If the work had been done by a mechanic, who would have likely done the work? Would someone then at work have done the job, or would someone have to have been called in on an overtime basis to do the work?

The reader should note that the questions or issues posed apply equally for union and employer advocates. While both might quarrel with the framing of some of the questions, it is probable that an arbitrator would consider most, if not all, of them important in determining how to decide the case.

Defining the issues precisely, as illustrated above, helps the advocate to focus preparation of the case. It points toward the information that will be needed. A good deal of investigation will be needed into the type of equipment involved, the nature of John Jones's job and that of the mechanic, the detailed facts concerning the work performed on the day in question, the normal practices in that work area, and something of the grievance history concerning production workers performing maintenance work. These questions also help the advocate to develop a theory around which to build a case.

## Focusing on the Theory

Trial lawyers talking about their theory of a case set for trial sounds rather esoteric and sophisticated. In reality it is not so mysterious. The "theory" simply describes the underlying rationale for prosecuting or defending a legal action. For arbitration purposes the theory of a case is simply the approach or version of the case that the advocate will present to the arbitrator. In the example of the production-maintenance grievance discussed just above, the union's theory is likely to be that maintenance work "belongs" to maintenance employees, that the long-standing past practice in the shop supports such "ownership," and that it is very unsafe to have production workers trying to repair high-speed, intricate, and dangerous equipment. The employer advocate, conversely, is likely to develop a theory that production workers have an intimate knowledge of the equipment they operate, have made minor adjustments to their equipment in the past, that waiting for a mechanic to be summoned would be time consuming and costly, and that strict adherence to maintenance craft lines in cases such as this will preclude the employer from being truly competitive in its industry.

The theory or theories developed at the early stage of preparation should be considered as tentative. Flexibility at this point is paramount, because additional information will be needed to support initial theories, and such information may be lacking. Moreover, additional facts and arguments may present themselves, which will add to, modify, or replace earlier theories. At this early stage, however, it is important to have some structure or bones on which to hang the meat (i.e., evidence), and outlining issues and developing theories are good starting points.

## DETERMINING THE FACTS THAT NEED TO BE PROVEN

### Types of Facts

In most cases there are three categories of facts that the advocate needs to establish and therefore needs to prepare. They are: (1) background facts, (2) essential facts, and (3) rebuttal facts. The advocate should think of the overall presentation of the factual case as a story being told to the arbitrator. Most good stories do not start with the critical events in the first chapter. The author gives some background, so that when the action occurs, the reader can better understand the meaning of the action. So too in arbitration. The arbitrator will be in a much better position to appreciate the advocate's essential facts and subsequent arguments if he or she has a framework within which to fit those essential facts.

### *Background Facts*

Background facts are usually the least important of the three, but they serve a very useful purpose in putting the rest of the case in an understandable context for the arbitrator. Background facts include such matters as an overview of the employer's business and work activity, a description of the job or work environment in which the grievance occurred, identification of the key union and management decision makers, and perhaps information about their positions and career/ organizational history.

## Essential Facts

The second category, essential facts, must be given priority. If a union is presenting a grievance that the employer violated the labor agreement by the manner in which it laid off employees because of a curtailment of production, it must at least identify (1) who *was* laid off and their respective seniority dates; (2) which employees *should have been* laid off and their respective seniority dates; (3) the sequence of bumping that actually occurred and a description of the sequence the union argues should have been followed; and (4) the monetary and/or other consequences of the alleged contract violation.

Essential facts in a case of discharge for theft of the employer's property will be quite different. The employer will normally have to present facts showing that (1) the employer had a rule against the removal of company property and that the rule was adequately communicated; (2) that someone saw (or other evidence proving that) the grievant actually removed property belonging to the company from the company's premises; and, if available, (3) facts showing what disposition was made of the goods following their removal from the employer's premises. Each type of grievance has its own set of essential facts that need to be proven.

## Rebuttal Facts

The third type of facts that are usually required to be proven are those that will rebut the other side's evidence. For example, in the layoff situation referred to above, the employer defends the order of employees laid off on the basis that the employer had to disregard seniority in some cases in order to retain employees with certain skills critical to operate equipment under a labor agreement that permits exceptions to straight seniority layoffs in order to retain employees with essential skills. Anticipating this defense (probably because it was advanced at earlier stages of the grievance procedure), the union will need to develop facts showing that the skills the employer said it needed to have by retaining junior employees were not essential to the operations or that they were skills possessed by one or more senior employees who were laid off.

It is not always possible to anticipate arguments or facts that the opposing side will present. In some cases such facts and arguments may appear for the first time in the arbitration hearing. It simply may not have been possible to predict that the other side would come up with a surprise witness, a newly found document, or a different theory of the case than the one advanced in the earlier stages of the grievance procedure. These and other new developments can change the complexion of the case. Some arbitrators will, upon request, grant a continuance or postponement of the hearing to allow the party disadvantaged by important newly discovered evidence to obtain and prepare rebuttal evidence and arguments. Such continuances are, however, quite rare, and an advocate surprised by new evidence usually must make the most of what is available to rebut it. Where the surprise results simply from a new theory or set of arguments, continuances would not normally be granted. In the majority of cases the essential evidence to be produced in an arbitration hearing can be anticipated by both sides based on a thorough review of the evidence and arguments that were presented at earlier stages of the grievance procedure.

## Outlining the Facts and the Supporting Evidence

A valuable step in the preliminary stage of preparation is to determine which facts the advocate wants (and needs) to produce and how those facts will be proven by evidence. The list should include background, essential, and rebuttal facts. Figure 4-1 is an example of a list of facts that a union advocate might prepare in advance of a grievance

**Figure 4-1.**
**Facts and Evidence for Union Side in Arbitration of Subcontracting Grievance**

| FACTS | EVIDENCE |
|---|---|
| History of manufacturing sprocket gears | T-Pete Smith<br>T-Wally Price |
| Sprocket gear equipment, products and mfg. process, crewing, and work schedules | T-Pete Smith |
| Bargaining history—subcontracting language | T-Ben Tyson<br>D-negot. notes<br>('75,'89,'93) |
| Past grievances re subcontracting | T-Wally Price<br>T-Ben Tyson<br>D-griev. files |
| Productivity/cost of mfg. sprocket gears | T-Dr. Ann Hodge<br>D-Hodge's charts |
| Industry practice re subcontracting | T-Ben Tyson |

*Key*
T = Testimony   D = Documents

arbitration concerning subcontracting or out-sourcing by an employer. It is a simple outline of the major factual elements of the case that will need to be proved, with a corresponding list of persons, documents, and other types of evidence that will be used to prove those facts. The list might include subheadings that outline more precise facts that should be covered. Such a document serves as a checklist to ensure that the advocate does not overlook any key factual items in the case. It also is a useful way to identify any gaps that may exist in the grievance file that will need to be closed by additional investigation and research.

## Chronology

Another useful tool in preparing the factual case is a chronology of significant events. Except in the simplest of cases, there is usually a series of conversations, decisions, actions, agreements, and other occurrences that are relevant to the case. These events are often seen as isolated occurrences, and evidence related to them is located in diverse documents, records, and recollections of persons. It is frequently difficult to keep them straight without putting them into some kind of order. The order that usually makes the most sense is according to time, that is, chronological order. Figure 4-2 is an example of a chronological list of events related to the same subcontracting case referred to in the previous exhibit. Such chronologies are almost an absolute necessity in discharge cases in which an employee is being terminated for a succession of rule violations over a period of time. Chronologies may also be used as exhibits.

## Undisputed Facts—Stipulations

In preparing the factual case and in examining the elements of that case the advocate should evaluate each element on the basis of whether or not it is likely to be disputed by the other side. It is quite common that a number of facts in a case are clearly a matter of record or at least have not been disputed by either side. In fact, there are some cases in which there is no disagreement about any facts, and the case turns solely on the application of the labor agreement to those facts. In either of these cases a good deal of time for preparing and presenting the case can be saved by the parties entering into a stipulation.

A stipulation is nothing more than an agreement by both parties that certain facts are undisputed and can be taken as established facts in the

**Figure 4-2.**
**Chronology of Subcontracting Case**

| | |
|---|---|
| 1957 | Sprocket gears first manufactured in Tally, Neb., plant |
| 1962 | Second sprocket gear line added |
| 10/74 | Subassembly of gears contracted to Precision Instr. |
| 11/74 | Grievance 74-123-A filed re subcontracting |
| 2/75 | Grievance 74-123-A settled without precedent; subassembly work brought back to plant |
| 7/1/75 | Subcontracting language first negotiated into c/b/a |
| 1982 | Heavy maintenance of gear sprocket machine subcontracted |
| 1987 | Stem winder manufacture and assembly subcontracted |
| 7/1/89 | Change in subcontracting section negotiated |
| 4/15/92 | Stem winder assembly brought back to bargaining unit |
| 7/1/95 | Change in subcontracting section negotiated |
| 8/15/96 | Company informs union of planned subcontracting of all sprocket gear manufacture and assembly; union requests economic justification |
| 8/22/96 | Company refuses to provide economic data |
| 8/30/96 | Union files ULP |
| 10/5/96 | NLRB defers case to arbitration |
| 11/17/96 | Parties waive all grievance steps and agree to submit to Arbitrator Clarence Brown |

record without the parties having to enter evidence into the record with respect to those facts. Stipulations may also be used with respect to issues and interpretations of the labor agreement about which the parties do not disagree.

The only way an advocate can be sure that no dispute exists concerning certain facts and that the other side is willing to enter into a stipulation is to communicate with the opposing advocate in advance of the hearing. Although it may seem that the other side could not possibly disagree with a particular fact or set of facts and that a stipulation is the most practicable way to handle it, surprises can and do arise. Consequently, it is advisable to talk to the opposing advocate relatively well in advance of the hearing to see what factual disputes exist. Stipulations, if they are to be used, are best drafted and agreed on during the preparation stage in advance of the hearing. By doing so, the advocate can then be assured of not having to prepare evidence on those facts.

Occasionally, when both parties accept the same version of the facts and disagree only on whether or not those facts prove a violation of the labor agreement, a hearing can be avoided altogether. By both advocates stipulating the case, that is, entering into a stipulation as to what occurred, the issue the arbitrator is to decide, and perhaps any other aspects about which they agree (e.g., that specific sections of the labor agreement are the only ones that apply in the case), the case can be submitted to the arbitrator without a hearing. The advocates submit written stipulations to the arbitrator accompanied by their respective written arguments or briefs.

A more detailed discussion about stipulations and the strategy and tactics of using them is contained in Chapter 7.

## INTERVIEWING POTENTIAL WITNESSES

In the ordinary labor arbitration case, most of the evidence is provided by the testimony of witnesses. Even where there are a large number of documents introduced into evidence, there is normally considerable testimonial evidence to authenticate and explain the documents. The evidentiary case frequently stands or falls on the testimony of the witnesses. Beyond the value of the testimony of witnesses in the hearing is the importance of information that witnesses can provide to the advocate in preparing the case. Thorough interviewing of all potential witnesses is an absolute must.

### Timing

It is important to note that interviewing witnesses at this preliminary stage of case preparation is not usually for the purpose of preparing them to testify in the hearing, but rather to discover how much they know, what their personal knowledge of the facts is, how credible they will be as witnesses, and what information they have that could lead to additional evidence not yet discovered.

There are situations, however, where the time available to the advocate for preparation is so short that interviewing the witness and preparing him or her to testify must occur more or less simultaneously. This is usually not a problem with respect to minor witnesses, whose testimony is not crucial for the case. For significant witnesses, however, the author greatly prefers to have two meetings. The first meeting is an informal interview with exploratory questions aimed primarily at gathering information and assessing the suitability of the person to be a witness in the case. If the first meeting leads to a decision to use the person as a witness, a second meeting is held specifically to prepare the witness to testify.

The next sections of this chapter address the initial process of interviewing potential witnesses. Chapter 6 is devoted to the process of selecting and preparing witnesses to testify.

## Thoroughness

It is important that all persons who have any knowledge of the facts surrounding the grievance be interviewed. Even though it may seem quite unlikely that some persons would have enough information about a particular event or issue to enable them to testify, they should nevertheless be interviewed in order to determine just what they know and how good their recollection is of significant facts and events. In doing so the advocate is apt to find witnesses who can fill vital gaps in the evidence. In addition, several witnesses may have more or less the same knowledge and perception of certain facts. By interviewing all of them the advocate is able to select the one who will be most effective in testifying in the hearing. Beyond this the case may call for cumulative testimony on a critical fact where there is certain to be a conflict in testimony between employer and union witnesses. Multiple witnesses and/or rebuttal witnesses on that point may be needed. For these reasons all persons who conceivably can provide useful information should be interviewed.

## Individual Versus Group Interviews

There are several schools of thought as to whether witnesses or potential witnesses should be interviewed (and/or prepared to give testimony) individually or in a group. Some would argue that it is improper to use the group method, at least where those in the group were witnesses to a single event, because witnesses are likely to be unduly influenced by the recollections and descriptions of the other witnesses, resulting in their testimony consisting at least in part of the recollections of others rather than their own.[1] Others contend that the group method is an effective means to gather all the facts.[2]

---

[1]See HILL AND SINICROPI, EVIDENCE IN ARBITRATION, 2d ed. (BNA Books, 1987) 70.
[2]ZIMMY, DOLSON, AND BARRECA, LABOR ARBITRATION, A PRACTICAL GUIDE FOR ADVOCATES, (BNA Books, 1990), 150

As with most procedural admonitions, it is difficult to say that one method is always the best. In general, however, the author prefers the group method for interviewing witnesses, assuming: (1) that the number in the group is not too large, (2) that the potential witnesses are not likely to be unduly influenced or intimidated by the others, and (3) that the information possessed by some of the potential witnesses is likely to refresh or trigger some additional or clearer recollections by the others.

When it comes to preparing witnesses to testify at the hearing, however, the author prefers separate meetings with each witness. The reason for the difference is that the interviewing process is aimed primarily at gathering facts and developing the strategy for preparing and presenting the case. The more facts, the better, and information from one witness is likely to produce more and better information from the others. When it comes to formulating the exact testimony of witnesses, however, it is best that the witnesses tell their own stories in their own ways without the influence of other witnesses' testimony.

## Questioning Format

At the outset of interviews prospective witnesses should be given a brief overview of the case, unless they are already familiar with it, although, it is usually advisable not to get into the specifics of what facts are already established. It is best to allow the prospective witnesses the widest latitude to provide their information without constraints that might be self-imposed after hearing of "established facts" from the advocate. Similarly, the advocate should open the meeting with the suggestion that each person should feel free to give information, recollections, perceptions, and so on without regard as to whether they appear to help or hurt the case. The advocate needs to know all facts concerning the case in order to fully prepare for the hearing; therefore, at this point the advocate wants all available information. A later decision can be made as to whether that evidence will be used in the hearing, and if so, how it will be used.

The persons being interviewed usually should not be referred to as "prospective witnesses" at this stage of preparation, because they are only providing information. Perhaps only a few of those interviewed will ultimately testify. To treat them as witnesses at this point could be inhibiting to some who are reluctant to be witnesses, possibly restraining them from providing as much information as possible. For those who are eager to testify, the suggestion that they will be witnesses (albeit prospective), only to not be selected later, could alienate them. For the moment it is preferable to treat all persons simply as sources of information rather than as prospective witnesses.

Each person to be interviewed should be asked to bring to the interview all documents, data, and other tangible items that are in any way relevant to the case. Where this information may be too voluminous to transport, the interview is best conducted near the information storage location. Sufficient time, privacy, and freedom from interruptions should be ensured. The location of the interview should be one that is most conducive to the sharing and free flow of information. This may be in an office, a home, a hotel room, or any other site that is most comfortable to the persons being interviewed, yet practical for the advocate.

## Questioning Techniques

In order to put an interviewee's information in context it is helpful to know the person's background. After some small talk to put the person at ease, the initial questioning should focus on such fundamental information as the job he or she holds, length of time in that job, the duties of the job, previous jobs held with the current employer, union positions held (where applicable), employment history with other employers, special experiences or responsibilities, and so forth.

Because the object of the interview is to gather facts, it is important that interviewees feel that they can provide information without adverse consequences. In cases in which the advocate anticipates some reluctance on the part of a witness to tell the truth or relate all of the facts, an opening comment such as the following can be helpful.

> At this stage of preparing our case, I need to know everything about this case, and I need your help in doing so. I want you to feel free to tell me everything you know about it. Don't worry about whether it helps or hurts our case at this point. What you think may be harmful could turn out to help our case. If you think something is confidential or shouldn't be known by others, you should nevertheless tell me about it. We can talk about it, and if I think it's necessary for the case, we'll see if there's a way to do it without destroying any confidences or rules. If we can't, and if you're not in agreement with disclosing it at the hearing, I'll respect your wishes. It's also important for you to tell me everything in the most accurate way. If you feel that something might sound better if you tell it one way rather than another, that won't help me or you if it's not one hundred percent true. I need to hear everything just the way it happened. If I know the complete truth I can help to put it in its best light. But if I don't, it's going to come back to haunt us in the hearing. In other words, Tell it like it is, and we'll be able to deal with it. Fair enough?

Questioning is best initiated with open-ended inquiries, for example, "Tell me what you remember about what happened the morning of the accident.'' As the interview progresses, the questions should become more pointed and precise, for example, '' Where were you standing at the time the lever struck the attendant?'' Only after most of the facts have been elicited should the more sensitive questions be asked, such as, ''Why didn't you sound the alarm earlier?'' In many cases the challenge for the advocate is to obtain as much information as possible without putting the interviewee on the defensive.

The advocate must always keep in mind that the person being interviewed is likely to be a witness, and the good will and cooperation of that person will probably be vital to obtaining helpful testimony. The advocate's manner should be cordial, nonthreatening, and non-judgmental. Obtaining the truth is extremely important, but obtaining the full and voluntary cooperation of the witness is equally important. The manner of interviewing the prospective witness should assist in eliciting the full cooperation of the interviewee.

## Refreshing Recollections

Another difficult area in questioning prospective witnesses is the person whose recollection of events is hazy or insufficiently specific: the spirit may be willing, but the memory is weak. This requires careful and sympathetic assistance. Sometimes the rephrasing or reorientation of a question may aid recollection, for example, ''Did you prepare a system report last year?'' after the person was unable to answer the question, ''When did you last file a system report?'' Getting good information may require preparing a chronological list of events, a sketch, or some other visual aid to give the witness a context for recollecting what was seen or experienced.

In other cases records, reports, or documents may help to refresh a recollection. Hearing information from others may serve to jog the memory. This is where group interviews are valuable. It may be necessary to have the witness close his or her eyes and slowly talk through the sequence of events in order to search the mind as much as possible. Some people need to visualize a scene in order to capture lost perceptions. Gentle, yet persistent probing by the advocate can be helpful. Another technique that sometimes works is to excuse the interviewee and request that he or she prepare a written statement of everything that can be remembered about the facts relevant to the case. Some persons can remember more when they are alone in a non-pressurized situation and can put their recollections on a piece of paper.

In the final analysis a prospective witness's recollection may be too sketchy or imprecise to enable him or her to testify effectively. Before conceding that, however, the advocate should explore all possible means of refreshing the witness's recollection. After doing so, and after interviewing all other possible witnesses, a decision can be made as to whether or not to use this person's testimony.

Credibility of the witness is absolutely vital, not only to the testimony of that witness, but to the entire case being presented by the advocate. If an arbitrator believes that a witness is lying or has been pressured to recollect facts that were not truthful, that impression will almost certainly influence the arbitrator's judgment of the entire case of the side offering that witness.


## EVALUATING WITNESSES

After interviewing all prospective witnesses the advocate needs to decide which ones should testify. This requires an evaluation of a number of factors. The following questions will help to take them into account.

1. What is the substance of the person's knowledge and recollections, and how does it tie into the case?
2. How vivid and consistent are this person's recollections.
3. Is the substance of the prospective witness's testimony available from any other source, and if so, which source is superior?
4. Can the information provided by this person be entered into the record through stipulation? Is the person's testimony or a stipulation apt to be more effective or more reliable?
5. How effective is the prospective witness likely to be in the hearing itself? Will this person be capable of withstanding a tough cross-examination?
6. Are there likely to be any adverse (or favorable) consequences outside the hearing if the prospective witness testifies (e.g., employee testifying against discharged coworker)?
7. How appealing and sympathetic would this person be as a witness? Is an arbitrator likely to receive this person's testimony favorably?

As a general rule, if someone is not needed to testify (e.g., because the information is not really needed to prove the case), it is best not to call that person as a witness. Because witnesses are always subject to cross-examination, there is the possibility of a slip of the tongue that could damage the advocate's case. It is also possible for witnesses to change their testimony or fail to recollect some part of their testimony, thus weakening the case.

# Characteristics of Marginal Witnesses

Where a person's information is essential to the case, should that person be called if he or she would not be an effective witness? Evaluating whether a witness should testify or not is a crucial issue, because cases typically stand or fall on the evidence supplied by witnesses. Many people simply do not make good witnesses. The following discusses certain characteristics of witnesses that usually result in ineffective or harmful testimony.

### Eager or Incredible

There are persons who initially appear to have valuable testimony to offer and are eager to contribute it, but who lack direct observation or participation and are merely speculating, guessing, or fabricating the facts. This type of person may simply be seeking the role of a star witness, or may have some personal motivation to influence the outcome of the case.

### Inarticulate

Some persons do not have a facility with words. They may be reasonably intelligent but have difficulty putting ideas into words. Such persons seldom make good witnesses because they are not effective in describing what they have seen or experienced. Similarly, when confronted with cleverly worded questions on cross examination, they are apt to be fooled into giving unhelpful answers.

### Easily Led

This characteristic finds the witness agreeing with much of what is asked on cross-examination because the questions are asked in a leading fashion, for example "You didn't check the oil before starting the fork lift did you?" or "You felt pretty good about the result, right?" Persons who display this characteristic tend to be unduly cooperative with others and can do great damage to the advocate's case.

### Explosive or Argumentative

This is the tendency to become angry or argumentative when asked pointed or accusatory questions. When emotion takes over, reason goes out the door. Once this happens, the testimony that follows is likely to be harmful to the case.

### *Garrulous*

Some persons are not satisfied with simple answers and like to elaborate. In doing so, they often open areas that are not helpful to their side's case. Although some persons can effectively be counseled to avoid rambling, others are so instinctively drawn to it that no amount of coaching will restrain them.

### *Inconsistent or Forgetful*

Preparing a witness for giving testimony involves developing a set of specific questions followed by a set of corresponding answers. Some people have a difficult time following the script. They either want to be original or simply can't remember the wording of the answer they were supposed to give. Whatever the reason, they wind up giving answers that can surprise and dismay the advocate.

### *Unpersuasive*

No matter how truthful some people are when answering questions, they leave the impression that they are just the opposite. Whether it is the tone of voice, the focus of the eyes, or an appearance of discomfort, they do not convey an impression of credibility or conviction.

### *Excessively Protective or Defensive*

These witnesses are so intent on doing a good job for their side that they refuse to provide any answer that could be helpful to the other side. In so doing, they refuse to make any concessions, no matter how true or obvious. Such witnesses soon lose credibility with the arbitrator—and for the side for which they are testifying.

These and other characteristics can be frustrating and disastrous to an advocate who is trying to put a case together. The author's experience is that only about half of the persons who are prospective witnesses are truly effective. The rest display one or more of the characteristics noted above or other unfavorable traits. Nevertheless, the advocate often has to play the hand that was dealt and use the witnesses that are available and necessary.

## Adapting to Marginal Witnesses

In some cases it is possible to overcome or adapt to witnesses' weaknesses. In attempting to do so the advocate should consider the following possible options.

1. Use another witness who is slated to testify about another matter and attempt to add the information possessed by the weak witness, perhaps even through hearsay, if necessary.
2. If possible, use documents or other forms of evidence to supply the facts to be delivered by the weak witness.
3. Obtain the necessary evidence through cross-examination of one of the other side's witnesses.
4. Prepare the weak witness to testify but hold back that testimony until as late as possible in the hearing on the possibility that the information could come in from some other source, perhaps the other side.
5. Seek a stipulation from the other side on the information to be supplied by the weak witness.
6. In the ostensible (yet still true) interests of conserving the time and expense of the parties, prepare to make an offer of proof as to what the witness would testify about. An offer of proof is a statement by the advocate as to what a witness would testify to if called as a witness. More specific information about offers of proof is contained in Chapter 10.

Notwithstanding the above possibilities, there will be situations where the evidence to be supplied by a weak witness is so important to the case, with no alternate means of presenting the evidence available, that the advocate will have to call that person as a witness. In those cases the challenge will be to do a careful and thorough job of preparing the witness to give testimony in the hearing. The techniques for doing this are discussed in detail in Chapter 6.

## The Unavailable or Uncooperative Witness

It has been assumed that the witnesses who are being interviewed and prepared to testify are willing to testify, and will cooperate with the advocate in such testimony. There are situations, however, where this is not true, and it is necessary for the advocate to subpoena them to give testimony in the hearing. In other cases, persons may be willing to testify, but wish to be subpoenaed in order to be excused from their place of employment or to give the appearance that they did not volunteer to testify (e.g., an employee from the bargaining unit who is asked to testify about the misconduct of another employee).

If the witness is truly uncooperative and will only appear if forced by a subpoena, the advocate will not have an opportunity to do any preparation in advance of the hearing. In fact, the testimony of the uncooperative witness may be of little value, and the advocate may wish to reconsider the efforts to force an appearance. Where, however, the source of the uncooperativeness or unavailability is unrelated to the merits of the case (as in the co-worker's testimony described above), the advocate may be able to do some preparation of the witness in advance of the hearing.

The advocate should prepare a subpoena for signature by the arbitrator (or the AAA, which is authorized to issue subpoenas), and have it personally served on the person whose testimony is needed. It should be served sufficiently in advance of the hearing so that the witness can make the necessary personal arrangements to attend the hearing. A form of subpoena is shown in Figure 4-3.

## GATHERING AND PREPARING DOCUMENTARY EVIDENCE

In most cases, next in order of importance after the testimony of witnesses is evidence contained in documents. Because so much of what happens in businesses, public institutions, or other organizations results in a paper transaction, documentary evidence is vitally important in most arbitration cases. In preparing the case for arbitration the advocate needs to locate all relevant documents and determine whether they can and should be used in the case.

### Relevancy and Authenticity

During the preparation stage the advocate is simply gathering information that may or may not become evidence in the case. Much of the information gathered may not even be helpful to the case. Consequently, at this point advocates need not make a conclusive determination as to whether available documents being accumulated are admissible in evidence. Nevertheless, it is useful to keep in mind the potential use of the documents as evidence and consider the basic evidentiary requirements for admission of documents into evidence. Two essential elements concerning the admissibility of documents are relevancy and authenticity.

A document, or any other type of evidence, is admissible only if it is relevant, that is, it helps to prove or disprove any fact or issue in the case. For example, in a case where the issue is whether overtime should have

**Figure 4-3.**
**Sample Subpoena Form**

# The Arbitration Tribunals of the
# American Arbitration Association

In the Matter of the Arbitration between

} Subpoena

FROM THE PEOPLE OF THE STATE OF

to

GREETING:

WE COMMAND YOU that, all business and excuses being laid aside, you and each of you appear and attend before

, arbitrators(s)

acting under the arbitration law of this state, at

_____

(address)

on the                day of                        , 19        , at              o'clock, to testify and give evidence in a certain arbitration, then and there to be held between the above entitled parties.

Signed: _____

Signed: _____
                              Arbitrator(s)

Request by: _____

_____
           Name of Representative

_____
           Address              ZIP Code

_____
           Telephone

Dated: _____                    Form G9–11/89

been assigned to an employee on the second shift as opposed to the third shift on a particular day, a series of reports that show the total amount of overtime worked in the plant during the previous year will normally be irrelevant. Sometimes this type of information is offered for the purpose of providing background to the arbitrator, but most arbitrators do not need or want general background information that is unrelated to the immediate issues to be decided. If the evidence is not particularly harmful to the other side, it may not raise an objection and may therefore be admitted; however, an advocate wastes time and distracts the arbitrator's focus by introducing irrelevant information.

Authenticity with respect to documents means that the document actually is what it is purported to be. For example, each of an employer's supervisors keeps a daily log of all complaints received from customers. At the end of each week a summary is prepared from all the supervisors' logs and sent throughout the company. In a case involving an employee being disciplined as a result of a customer's complaint, the weekly summary is not the authentic or actual record of the complaint. The supervisor's log or a customer's letter would be the authentic document that contains the complaint. The weekly summary is a secondhand document and may likely be ruled inadmissible either because it is not authentic or because it is a form of hearsay containing secondary rather than primary evidence.

In gathering documents for possible use in an arbitration hearing the advocate should attempt as much as possible to obtain documents that are relevant and authentic. This means getting originals of the documents rather than copies and getting actual records rather than summaries. Although copies may be the ones taken into evidence, having the original in the hearing to permit inspection and verification of authenticity is usually important if not absolutely essential.

## Types of Documentary Evidence

There is an almost infinite number of types of documents that are introduced into evidence in arbitration hearings. Business records (including payroll computer runs, time cards, work schedules, production records, safety reports, invoices, etc.), letters, grievances, minutes of meetings, union records, reports, brochures, newspaper articles or advertisements, handwritten notes, and numerous other types of documents may be relevant depending on the issues and facts in the case. These pieces of paper are created in the normal functioning of organizations or in the interrelationship of individuals in the case. They are not pieces of paper created specifically for the arbitration and they were in existence at or before the time the grievance was appealed to arbitration. This documentary evidence is distinguished from documents that are created specifically as exhibits for the arbitration hearing—a type of evidence that will be discussed later in this chapter.

### Notes and Logs Prepared by Supervisors and Others

A frequent area of dispute in arbitration hearings is the admissibility of notes and logs of supervisors, particularly those relating to specific individuals and to any disciplinary action taken against those individuals. The common problem with such notes is that employees are seldom privy to the information in the notes and even less often given a copy of them. In some cases the disciplinary notations summarize a discussion or interaction with an employee and in other cases they simply contain supervisor's observations about employee conduct without the employee having been informed of the supervisor's displeasure. Where the displeasure was never brought to the employee's attention, arbitrators will usually exclude such notations from evidence. They do so on the basis that if the observed behavior was part of the foundation for subsequent disciplinary action, the employee should have been so informed in order to have an opportunity to modify his or her conduct.

While many arbitrators will not admit into evidence supervisors' notes of employee misconduct where there was no notice to the employee, they may permit some testimony by a supervisor about an employee's improper conduct where it can be shown that the employee had reason to know that the conduct was improper. Admitting the evidence does not necessarily mean, however, that the arbitrator will rule that it was permissible to base later disciplinary action on the earlier misconduct under the principle of progressive discipline. If no discipline was meted out in the earlier misconduct, it is not usually considered to be part of the disciplinary record.

Supervisor's notes on other matters such as production interruptions, grievance discussions, safety violations, work assignments, and so on are usually admissible, particularly where the supervisor is a witness and is able to explain the circumstances under which the notes were prepared and what they mean to the case, as well as to answer questions on cross-examination. Such notes can be particularly useful in pinpointing dates, times, locations, statements, and other details that are often forgotten.

The same treatment is usually given to notes prepared by employees and union representatives. While such notes are not as common as those prepared by supervisors, they are nevertheless entitled to the same treatment, provided they were prepared at or shortly after the time of the situation they describe.

In some cases notes made by supervisors or others contain some information that is helpful to the case as well as some comments that are harmful. If the notes that contain information harmful to the case are introduced into evidence, the case may be weaker than it would otherwise be. In such situations the advocate may simply use the notes to aid the witness in preparing to testify, provided the witness's recollection of events is sufficiently clear so that he or she can testify without the notes in the hearing.

There is nothing unethical in declining to use such notes in the hearing. There are no rules of ethics or proper arbitration procedure that would require an advocate to use evidence that is not helpful to his or her case, so long as there is no improper destruction of records or documents. At the same time, if a witness who had prepared notes of an event or situation is asked in the hearing on cross-examination whether any notes were prepared, he or she should answer truthfully that they were but that they were not brought to the hearing.

## Obtaining Documents in the Other Party's Possession

Often documents and other types of evidence that are important in a case are not available to an advocate, but are in the possession or under the control of the other party. The same problem may exist with respect to a witness (e.g., the identity of an informant whose information resulted in the discharge of a co-worker may be known only to the employer). In civil litigation the process of discovery has been established to enable each side in a lawsuit to obtain extensive information possessed by the other party about the case. Such techniques as written interrogatories, depositions, and requests for the production of documents are tools that are available to attorneys in lawsuits. Discovery, as such, is not generally available in labor arbitration, unless the labor agreement specifically provides for it, and such provisions in labor agreements are quite rare.

Difficulty in obtaining evidence from the other party is a problem for union advocates more frequently than for employer advocates because the employer normally has considerably more evidence at its disposal than the union does. A similar situation exists when the advocate does not know that a specific document exists but presumes or believes that it does and that it is likely to be in the possession of the other side. Examples of these are production records, safety reports, disciplinary notes, correspondence, medical reports, performance evaluations, and supervisor's logs. Even though formal discovery does not exist in arbitration, there are several means available to uncover such evidence.

### Written Request

The first and most obvious step that a party should take in seeking evidence from the other side is to make a written request for the evidence sought. As a courtesy, an oral request might precede, or be made simultaneously with, the written request. The request should be as specific as possible about the evidence sought. In addition, if it is not obvious why the information is needed by the requesting party, the request should also include an explanation as to the relevance of the evidence to the case and any other information that would substantiate the need for that evidence. Some labor agreements contain language that, on its face or by reasonable interpretation, compels disclosure of relevant information to the other side. In such cases an oral or written request should be sufficient to elicit the needed evidence. If such contract language is not available, the written request nevertheless serves as a preliminary to alternate means that can be used.

If the written request is denied, the requesting party should obtain the specific reasons for the denial. If the denial is based on policy grounds (i.e., there is no contractual obligation to provide it), the stage is set to pursue more aggressive means. If the denial is because of more pragmatic considerations (e.g., the information is confidential or obtaining it would be unduly burdensome), then the next step would normally be to explore ways to overcome the proffered difficulty. If the problem is confidentiality, an offer to limit the number of persons who would have access to the evidence or to exclude or redact the truly confidential portions of the evidence while still providing less sensitive relevant portions may solve the problem. If the difficulty is the burdensomeness of providing the information, offering assistance in searching records or agreeing to pay for additional help to do so may overcome the denial. Before going to a higher authority both parties (and certainly the requesting party) should explore all possible ways to circumvent perceived problems in disclosing requested evidence.

### Subpoena or Motion to Produce

If, despite one party's extended efforts to obtain the evidence voluntarily, the party in possession continues to withhold the needed evidence, the next logical step is to petition the arbitrator to issue a *subpoena duces tecum* or to file a motion to produce evidence with the arbitrator. A number of states either have statutes that grant an arbitrator the right to issue subpoenas or have adopted the Uniform Arbitration Act, which provides for issuance of subpoenas.[3] In addition, some arbitrators and courts have held that the U.S. Arbitration Act empowers arbitrators to issue subpoenas.[4]

Although the forms of subpoena and motions may differ from state to state, the cautious advocate is best advised to include with the documents submitted to the arbitrator a statement as to why the request is being made, the relevance of the evidence to the case, and the inability to obtain the necessary information from any other source or by any other means. Examples of the form of subpoena to produce documents are shown in Figure 4-4.

### Unfair Labor Practice Charge

Sections 8(a)(5) and 8(b)(3) of the National Labor Relations Act, as amended, make it an unfair labor practice (ULP) for employers and unions respectively to refuse to bargain in good faith. These provisions have long been held to require both parties to provide the other with information that is necessary to carry out collective bargaining functions. One of the critical collective bargaining functions is to ensure that the labor agreement is being properly enforced and that grievances can be processed without interference. Consequently, it is well established that each side has an obligation to provide the other with evidence in its possession that is necessary for the other side to properly process and arbitrate grievances.[5]

---

[3]7 UNIFORM LAWS ANNOTATED. (Master Ed. 1985 & Supp. 1989). The states in which arbitrators may grant subpoenas are: Alaska, Arizona, Arkansas, Colorado, Delaware, Idaho, Illinois, Indiana, Iowa, Kansas, Maine, Maryland, Massachusetts, Michigan, Minnesota, Missouri, Montana, Nebraska, Nevada, New Mexico, North Carolina, North Dakota, Oklahoma, Pennsylvania, South Carolina, South Dakota, Tennessee, Texas, Utah, Vermont, Virginia, and Wyoming. SCHOONHOVEN FAIRWEATHER'S PRACTICE AND PROCEDURE IN LABOR ARBITRATION, 3d ed. (BNA Books, 1991), 129.
[4]Great Scott Supermarkets v. Teamsters Local 337, 363 F. Supp. 1351, 84 LRRM 2514 (E.D. Mich., 1973); Machinists Local Lodge 1746 v. Pratt & Whitney Div. of United Aircraft Corp., 329 F. Supp. 283, 77 LRRM 2596 (D. Conn. 1971).
[5]Steelworkers v. American Mfg. Co., 363 U.S. 564, 46 LRRM 2414 (1960); Steelworkers v. Warrior & Gulf Navigation Co., 363 U.S. 574, 46 LRRM 2416 (1960); Steelworkers v. Enterprise Wheel & Car Corp., 363 U.S. 593, 46 LRRM 2423 (1969); Montgomery Ward & Co., 234 NLRB 588, 98 LRRM 1022 (1978); Kroger Co., 226 NLRB 512, 93 NLRB 1315 (1976).

**Figure 4-4.**
**Sample Subpoena to Produce Documents**

# The Arbitration Tribunals of the
# American Arbitration Association

**In the Matter of the Arbitration between**

**Subpoena Duces Tecum
(Documents)**

FROM THE PEOPLE OF THE STATE OF

to

GREETING:

WE COMMAND YOU that, all business and excuses being laid aside, you and each of you appear and attend before

, arbitrators(s)

acting under the arbitration law of this state, at

_____
(address)

on the          day of                    , 19     , at          o'clock,
to testify and give evidence in a certain arbitration, then and there to be held between the above entitled parties, and that you bring with you and produce certain

now in your custody.

Request by: _____     Signed: _____

_____                 Signed: _____
Name of Representative                               Arbitrator(s)

_____
Address          ZIP Code

_____
Telephone

Dated: _____                    Form G10–11/89

The NLRB has established guidelines for determining what must be provided. It requires (1) that the party seeking the information make a request or demand to the other side, (2) that the information sought be relevant or necessary, and (3) that the party seeking the information not have previously waived its right to obtain it.[6] If a bona fide request is denied, the party requesting the information must file a ULP charge with a regional office of the NLRB. The charge will be investigated, and, if the regional director finds that there are reasonable grounds to believe an unfair labor practice has been committed, a complaint is issued and the matter is set for a hearing before an administrative law judge (ALJ). A decision by an ALJ is reviewable by the NLRB, and its decisions are appealable to U.S. Courts of Appeals and finally to the U.S. Supreme Court. An unfair labor practice charge, carried to its ultimate appeal, can easily take three or more years to reach a final decision. Even obtaining a decision from the NLRB can require several years. As a result of this cumbersome and time-consuming process, a ULP charge is often not a very practicable means of seeking evidence for arbitration if the party in possession of the evidence is intent on not producing it.

Nevertheless, realization by the party withholding the evidence that the NLRB is likely or certain to rule in favor of the requesting party is often sufficient to induce the party possessing the evidence to turn it over. Sometimes the legal costs of defending a ULP will far exceed the cost of arbitration and any monetary award the arbitrator may issue. Resisting the request for evidence may not be worth the costs of defense, depending on the issues and the financial liability at stake in the arbitration case.

### Other Means of Obtaining Evidence

If the information sought is likely to be contained in an employee's personnel file, it is possible that it may be obtained by virtue of a request or demand made pursuant to a state statute requiring the revelation of contents of a personnel file to the employee to whom the file pertains. For example, California has a labor code provision that states:

> Every employer shall at reasonable times, and at reasonable intervals as determined by the Labor Commissioner, upon the request of an employee, permit that employee to inspect such personnel files which are used or have been used to determine that employee's qualifications for employment, promotion, additional compensation, or termination or other disciplinary action. . . .[7]

---

[6]HARDIN, THE DEVELOPING LABOR LAW, 3d ed. (BNA Books, 1992), 657–72.
[7]California Labor Code § 1198.5.

A number of other states have similar provisions.[8] Although state laws do not always make reference to union representatives having the same access to personnel files as employees have, it is easy enough for the employee to search the file and provide copies of the contents to his or her union representative or to have the union representative accompany the employee when viewing the file.

If the employer in the arbitration case is a governmental agency, there is the possibility of obtaining the desired information through the Freedom of Information Act (FOIA), which applies to federal agencies, or through state freedom of information statutes if the employer is a state agency. Access to documents through freedom of information statutes is not, however, without its limits. Exceptions exist for a variety of reasons, and these should be reviewed prior to making a formal request.[9] For example, the federal FOIA makes exceptions for ''matters related solely to the internal personal rules and practices of an agency'' and for ''personnel and medical files, the disclosure of which would constitute a clearly unwarranted invasion of personal privacy.''[10] These exceptions, on their face, would appear to exclude many documents that would be relevant to an arbitration case, but numerous court cases have modified the literal interpretation of the exceptions, and research of those cases should be undertaken if it anticipated that one of the exceptions is likely to be invoked by the agency involved.


## PREPARING EXHIBITS


An ancient proverb states, ''A picture is worth a thousand words,'' and the wisdom of that statement is never more true than in an evidentiary hearing such as labor arbitration. The picture need not be a photograph or other traditional graphic representation, but may be a blueprint, map, diagram, chart, computer simulation, or other means of depicting objects, facts, places, and other factors critical to the case. An arbitrator

---

[8]The states that have some law or regulation mandating employee access to personnel files are Alaska (Alas S Sec. 23.10.430), California (Labor Code Sec. 1198.5),Connecticut (GS Sec. 31-128a), Deleware (19 Del C Sec. 732-734), Illinois (820 Il cs Sec. 40/2-3), Iowa (Iowa CA Sec. 91B), Maine (26 Me RSA Sec. 631), Massachusetts (Mass ALM c 149 Sec. 52C), Michigan (Mich LA Sec. 423.503-507), Minnesota (Minn SA 181.960-961), Nevada (Nev RS 613.075), New Hampshire (NH RSA 275:56), Oregon (Ore RS 652.750), Pennsylvania (43 P Pa SA Sec. 1322-1323), Rhode Island (RI GS Sec. 28-6.4-1), Washington (RC Wash 49.12-240-260), and Wisconsin (Wis SA 101-103).
[9]5 U.S.C. § 522(b) (1986).
[10]5 U.S.C. § 522(b)(2) and (6).

decides a labor arbitration case much as a jury issues a verdict in a lawsuit. Although an arbitrator is more experienced and sophisticated in evaluating evidence and applying labor agreement provisions to the facts, he or she is still a human being and is likely to be persuaded more easily by facts that are presented in a simple, interesting, graphic, and comprehensible fashion. Well-conceived and well-prepared exhibits substantially enhance the chances of winning the case.

## Charts and Graphs

In cases in which a significant amount of numerical data is presented, the advocate should strongly consider organizing the data in chart or graph form. Many pages of numbers, unless well organized, are apt to confuse, if not bore, the arbitrator. More important, the major conclusions to be drawn from the data are apt to be lost, or at least blunted, by a mode of presentation that is random or obtuse. Consider a case in which the union is arguing that the employer has not been following seniority in awarding overtime. The labor agreement provides that employees will be offered overtime in seniority order within each department without regard to job classification. The only data available to the union is a computer report provided by the employer that shows overtime offered and overtime worked by employees listed in alphabetical order with seniority dates of each employee shown on the report. It will be a challenge for the union advocate to make a persuasive argument based on such a report.

It may be possible for the union to request that the report be sorted by department and by seniority so that comparisons are facilitated. The union advocate's argument is much more persuasive when the data are represented in graph form. Data should often be presented in two or more forms so that the graphic representation is supported by the raw data.

Even when the graph or chart does not make such a telling case, the advocate needs to consider summarizing voluminous data. If an arbitrator is given dozens of pages of computer reports to sort through, he or she is likely to get confused, bored, or simply weary of sifting through the maze in order to come to the conclusion that the advocate is advancing. The advocate needs to make it easy for the arbitrator to draw the "right" conclusion. Thus, in a dispute over work schedules introduction of dozens of pages of schedules without analysis or summarization is likely to be ineffective. If, however, the main points are summarized and tallied, with the results being highlighted or graphed, the points are much more likely to be understood and accepted.

## Photographs, Videotapes, and Computer Graphics

Seldom is it possible to explain an object, a process, a setting, or many other physical situations as clearly through spoken or written words as it is through visual impressions. Whether it be a damaged piece of equipment, employees picketing at a customer's facility, a poorly maintained lunch room, or the relative positions of machinery at a work station, a picture certainly is worth a thousand words. Advocates need only place themselves in the shoes of the arbitrator. How easy or difficult will it be for the arbitrator to envision the object, place, or situation that is important in the case and about which witnesses will be testifying? How much more persuasive will the advocate's arguments be if the arbitrator can view the critical scenes or objects? Advocates should be creative in utilizing technology to enhance their case.

### Still Photos Versus Videos

Still photographs have the advantage of being easier to display in a hearing. Unlike videotape, no equipment is necessary and the arbitrator and witnesses can see the subject of the photograph while testimony about that subject is being given. Attention can be focused on details of the photo over and over. Moreover, photographs can be easily entered into the record. On the other hand photographs do not usually depict the overall scope of a setting the way a videotape can, nor can they capture action as well. For example, if the advocate wishes to show the arbitrator the work requirements of a warehouse worker, the video camera can follow the worker throughout a day, capturing shots of each element of the job. The tape can later be edited to remove irrelevant matters, and in the space of perhaps five to ten minutes an arbitrator can see just what the worker does during the course of an entire work shift. In addition, video carries sound, which can be important in conveying the noise level in a work place, a narrator's description of what the viewers are seeing, or the many other sounds that make the viewed place, object, or person more real.

### Computer Graphics

Computer graphics or computer-generated recreations are constantly being refined and have become mainstays of civil and criminal trials. Their application to labor arbitration is no less useful. From diagrams of facilities to simulated recreations of events (e.g., accidents, altercations, and work processes), computers can be of great assistance to the advocate in presenting evidence. A certain degree of imagination may be called for in identifying the type of information or situation that calls for computer assistance. A number of consultants have developed successful businesses assisting attorneys in preparing for trial. The wise labor arbitration advocate needs to keep abreast of what such consultants can deliver and how this can be used in the arbitration forum.

### Integrity of Graphics

Regardless of the technology employed, the advocate must be careful to fairly depict the subjects of the photos, videos, or computer graphics. They should not be applied in such a way as to distort size, perspective, or reality. Records should be made of the date, time, and location when visuals were taken, and, if there is likely to be a dispute over them, the person who took the photos or tapes should be available to testify. This is especially important when the visuals are used to depict conditions before and after a particular event or change in those conditions. Similarly, the person who prepared the computer graphics should be available to testify if questions are likely to be raised about the reality of the information conveyed in the graphics.

### Other Practical Issues Regarding Graphics

The advocate should attempt to have three copies of each photograph or graphic—one for the arbitrator (the one entered into the record), one for the opposing advocate, and one for the advocate who is offering the evidence. Additional copies of videotapes should be available to give to the arbitrator and the opposing advocate for viewing following the hearing. Photocopies of photographs are often accepted, especially where precise details of the photograph are not critical, but it is usually preferable to have process copies of photographs to provide to the arbitrator and opposing counsel as well as for retention by the offering advocate.

In some cases the photos and videos are not critical as evidence but are used primarily as background to give the arbitrator a better perspective of the matters about which testimony is being given. In such cases the visuals may not need to be introduced into evidence but can nevertheless be made available to the arbitrator for viewing following the hearing. For such purposes copies are not necessary.

## Diagrams, Blueprints, and Other Graphic Representations

In some cases even photos and videos do not convey the full scope, complexity, or interrelationship of people, places, and objects. While a video might be used to show the complete method of manufacturing a particular product and the various jobs required to complete the production cycle, it may not be completely clear how each step of the process fits in with the others. A schematic diagram may be more useful for this purpose. Similarly, videos or photographs might be used to show various sites in a building where key events occurred, but a blueprint or diagram of the facility may be more useful to show the movement from one place to another and the juxtaposition of those places to each other.

Diagrams, maps, and other graphics (including computer-generated ones) printed on paper have the advantage of allowing contradictory witnesses to testify as to what, where, and when certain things happened and to mark locations and times on the map or diagram. This allows the arbitrator to better follow the testimony of witnesses while comparing and contrasting differences in testimony among various witnesses.

## Multiple Visuals

In spite of the advantages and disadvantages of various forms of presenting evidence, they are not mutually exclusive—they can be used in tandem. A videotape of a manufacturing plant can be supplemented with a blueprint of the facility layout and a schematic diagram of the manufacturing process. Still photographs of individual operations or work stations can also be introduced. One must always be wary of possible excessive use of exhibits; only when visuals or other exhibits enhance the presentation should they be used. Nevertheless, the advocate can significantly enhance, if not dramatically improve, the presentation of a case by developing effective visual exhibits.

## OBTAINING REAL EVIDENCE

In preparing evidence for a hearing, the advocate is naturally inclined to think of documentary evidence and seek to obtain such documents. One's attention is not, however, quite so naturally drawn to the use of real or physical evidence. In many cases physical evidence may be much more telling than documentary evidence or even the testimony of witnesses. In a case of discharge for theft producing the stolen articles is usually crucial to the case. When an employee has been demoted for poor production, introduction of the poorly produced products could be quite significant. The introduction of a sharp carving tool would be very important where the arbitration concerns discharge for an employee's attack on a coworker with a lethal weapon. A claim that a dress code required by an employer is unreasonable would be considerably enhanced by having an employee appear at the hearing wearing the clothing to which the union is objecting.

In some cases physical evidence may not be crucial for deciding the case but may be quite helpful as background evidence. For example, in a case involving the subcontracting of machine parts to a specialized outside vendor because of the intricacy of the machining work, viewing the parts being contracted out could be helpful to one side or the other. A job evaluation case might be clarified for the arbitrator if he or she can examine some of the physical elements (e.g., tools, materials, products) of the job.

In some cases the physical object may be entered into evidence, such as the weapon used by the grievant in the attack on a coworker, whereas in other cases the physical goods (e.g., machine parts contracted out) may be viewed by the arbitrator during the hearing but not become part of the formal record as exhibits. In many cases photographs may be substituted for, or provided in addition to, the physical evidence. For example, in the case of the challenged dress code, an employee may appear at the hearing in the objectionable clothing, with the union advocate offering in evidence a photograph of the employee in the same clothing. The advantage of the physical evidence and the photograph is twofold. First, the arbitrator has the opportunity to see the object in its true form and examine it, while at the same time having a representation of it to view at a later time during the decision-making phase. Second, if only a photograph is offered, the opposing advocate may argue that the photograph is not an authentic representation of the actual object (e.g., stolen goods), was not photographed under the same conditions as when the grievance arose (e.g., machined parts), or in some other way is not reliable evidence.

Sometimes, producing physical evidence may be hindered by the difficulty in obtaining it. If the difficulty lies in obtaining it from the opposing side, the procedures outlined in the preceding section concerning obtaining documents from the other side apply. If the objects are in the possession or under the control of a third party, resorting to a subpoena from the arbitrator is advised.

## Site Visitations

Another form of evidence, although a type that does not lend itself to admission into the record is observation by the arbitrator, in the presence of parties' representatives, of a site where relevant actions occur or occurred or where relevant objects and/or people can be viewed. The range of possible sites is almost limitless. Frequently, the workplace where the grievant is or was working is relevant to the case. When discharge or discipline is involved, the site of the action that triggered the discharge is often significant. Observation of equipment, work processes, and training facilities may be important.

Strictly speaking, the observation is not evidence because there is usually no record made of what was seen, but the observations are in the mind of the arbitrator, and the impact of the place, things, and persons seen at the site may be much more determinative of the outcome than exhibits in the record. As with photographs of physical evidence, it is possible to provide the arbitrator with a videotape or photograph of the observations and to offer them in evidence. If the conditions at the site are not the same as when events relevant to the case occurred, there are grounds for objection by the other side. Similarly, if the videotape or photograph does not accurately represent the relevant objects or people (e.g., long and barely visible shots of items important to the other side, but clear close-up shots to the side offering the videotape), the tape is apt to be rejected by the arbitrator.

Advocates should make sure that any site visitation accomplishes the purpose for which it is intended. Is the timing such that the right objects, actions and people will be present? Are the conditions the same as during the relevant period? Is it possible that the arbitrator viewing the site might come to a different conclusion than that planned by the offering advocate? Will the viewing produce better perceptions and conclusions by the arbitrator than relying on the other evidence available? The advocate should be conservative in answering these questions. A site visitation offered by an advocate should never have the possibility of making the case presentation weaker than it would otherwise be.

The following general guidelines should be taken into consideration in planning any site visitation.

1. The visit should be accomplished with relative ease and without expending too much time, however, the more critical the viewing is to the case, the greater the latitude for time and convenience.
2. Plans should be made for who will accompany the arbitrator. Generally, only two or three persons from each side should be permitted. The advocates should be among those accompanying the arbitrator. These arrangements should be worked out between the advocates in advance of the hearing.
3. At least one of the two or three persons from each side accompanying the arbitrator should be personally familiar with the site,

know what occurs or occurred there, understand why it is important to the case, and be able to answer detailed questions by the arbitrator.

4. Where possible, the site should be checked out just prior to the visitation to ensure that it is available for viewing, that no critical elements have been changed, and that what is significant to the offering advocate will be observable by the arbitrator.

5. Consider supplementing the site visitation with other documents or other evidence to support and/or reinforce the visitation. In addition to videotape, consider photographs, diagrams, and brochures.

6. Be cognizant of the fact that things may be told to an arbitrator in the course of a site visitation that are not consistent with testimony or other evidence in the record. Communications made during the visitation are generally not part of the record and are not subject to cross-examination. This can work to the advantage or disadvantage of either party, depending on the nature of the communication. It is not unusual for one or both parties (usually not the advocates themselves) to argue their case during these site visitations.

Whether an arbitrator will assent to a site visitation is completely within his or her discretion. When both parties make the request, it is virtually certain that the arbitrator will accede to the request. Even when one party makes the request, the arbitrator is likely to assent unless there is some reason to believe that it would be prejudicial or unfair to the other side or would require too much time and effort when weighed against the potential value to the arbitrator in understanding the evidence and deciding the case.

## Demonstrative Evidence

Another type of evidence that can occasionally be employed to advantage is demonstrative evidence. This is evidence that is usually some form of a re-creation or replication of an event or situation that is relevant to the case. Some years ago the author was representing an employer involving the disqualification of an employee for insufficient skills to perform his job of maintenance mechanic. In order to demonstrate the employee's skills, both parties and the arbitrator agreed to have the employee participate in a trial repair of an engine. The employee had to troubleshoot a malfunction in the engine and make the repair. The employee was given access to the tools and manuals necessary to complete the work, and his work activity could be viewed periodically during the day by the arbitrator. At the end of the trial the arbitrator took testimony from the parties relative to how well or how poorly the job was done.

When a witness contends that something happened to explain an event (e.g., that several windows of a bus were broken because of the normal movement of that bus on a bumpy road rather than being caused by the negligent driving of the driver), the parties might recreate the situation to prove that it could or could not occur in the manner alleged (e.g., drive the bus over the same road in a normal manner under the same or similar conditions as when the damage occurred). Where one side contends that something could or could not be seen from a particular site (i.e., because of obstructions) or at a particular time of day (e.g., because of darkness), a re-creation of the situation may be attempted to show the conditions of visibility.

Arbitrators and opposing advocates are usually quite wary of demonstrative evidence. The fear is that the conditions that existed at the time of the relevant event cannot be completely replicated. Are weather, light, temperature, time of day, persons, equipment, and so on exactly the same as they were on the day in question? If not, could they have a significant effect on the outcome of the demonstration? Of course, it is completely within the discretion of the arbitrator to allow the demonstration, and the offering advocate must lay a solid foundation as to the relevance of the evidence and the consistency of the conditions of the demonstration relative to the conditions of the actual event.

The advocate considering the use of demonstrative evidence should be as certain as possible that the result of the demonstration will prove what is intended. When possible, the demonstration should be repeated a number of times in advance of the hearing in order to ensure that it goes as planned. In some cases it may be possible to videotape a trial demonstration and offer the videotape in evidence. If this is done, precautions should be taken to show each step of setting up the demonstration, each element in the event itself, and close-up shots of the results.

# USE OF EXPERT WITNESSES

## Appropriateness

The use of expert witnesses has become routine in civil and criminal litigation. Trial lawyers are wary of entering a courtroom without one or more experts to testify in their case. The use of experts in labor arbitration is considerably less frequent. Nevertheless, in certain situations experts can be helpful in proving critical points. One of the more common uses of experts involves medical issues, especially those concerning the ability and inability of employees to return to work following an illness or injury. Often, the physician who has been treating the employee testifies on behalf of the union (employee) or the employer and describes the employee's condition and ability to work based on examinations and tests. At the same time the physician is usually qualified as an expert, enabling him or her to give an opinion as part of the testimony. The opposing side may offer a physician to counter that testimony, with the second physician also being qualified as an expert.

Other examples of witnesses and the types of cases in which they are called to testify include:

1. Safety engineers and industrial hygienists—Workplace safety and health issues
2. Pension actuaries and benefit specialists—Cases involving pension, health care, and other benefits
3. Accountants and financial advisors—Issues of plant closures, relocations, and subcontracting
4. Forensic pathologists—Cases involving drug and alcohol tests
5. Industrial engineers—Incentive and gain-sharing plans, job evaluation disputes, and grievances concerning work loads.

Whether an expert witness is appropriate in a particular case depends primarily on two factors: first, whether the subjects about which the expert is going to testify are outside the knowledge and experience of the arbitrator, and, second, whether it will be necessary for the expert to render an informed opinion about an issue important in the case. For example, labor arbitrators are quite familiar with layoff and recall procedures governed by seniority rules. It is normally not necessary or appropriate to call an expert to explain such procedures or give an opinion about them. On the other hand, for example, a case involving discharge for excessive absenteeism of an employee who suffers from Epstein-Barr syndrome would easily call for a doctor to testify as to the nature of the disease, the recommended treatment, and an opinion as to the likelihood that an employee who has such a disease could, given proper treatment, maintain a regular work schedule.

The advocate contemplating use of an expert should make sure that the person is truly an expert in the field about which he or she will be expected to testify. Even though a physician may have treated several persons with Epstein-Barr syndrome, that experience might not be sufficient to qualify that doctor as an expert without any other particular experience or training specific to that disease. Because standards for qualifying as an expert in arbitration are not especially stringent and not as formalized as they are in litigation, it may be possible to have the physician's testimony admitted as expert testimony, but great damage can be done on cross-examination by a seasoned advocate who asks a number of probing questions, such as, "Have you ever participated in any specialized training concerning this syndrome?" or "Have you ever done any research or written any articles on this subject?"

Consequently, the careful advocate should obtain a CV (curriculum vitae) or resume of the expert well in advance of the hearing and interview that person (in person or on the telephone) to determine whether the expertise has been sufficiently established. In addition, the advocate should ask enough questions to make at least a preliminary judgment as to how effective the expert's testimony is likely to be. Does the expert know about the basic facts in this case? Has the expert previously dealt with similar situations? What is the expert's initial view of the situation, and is he or she likely to give favorable testimony? How good a witness is the expert likely to be—articulation, clarity, responsiveness to questions, knowledge of subject, ability to withstand tough cross-examination, and so on? Has this person previously testified as an expert in any other cases, and, if so, what were the cases about and before whom was the testimony given?

Details concerning the expert's availability on the day of the hearing, fees charged, potential for conflict of interest (expert witness for other side in a previous case on the same issue) or claimed bias (e.g., retained by the employer on other matters) should be addressed early in the relationship. Much time and energy can be expended only to discover that there is some impediment that would make the expert's testimony infeasible.

The process of preparing expert witnesses to testify is discussed in Chapter 6. At this stage of preparation the advocate simply wants to determine whether an expert witness is appropriate and necessary for the case, and, if so, who that expert should be. As described in the section that follows, it may not be necessary to go very far afield.

## Use of Fact Witnesses as Expert Witnesses

Because the standards for expert testimony in labor arbitration cases are relatively loose, it is sometimes possible to qualify fact witnesses (i.e., those who are testifying about facts in the case) as expert witnesses. The employer's chief chemist, who is called to testify about changes made in the manufacturing process requiring less skill and effort on the part of machine operators, may also be qualified as an expert and render an opinion as to whether the chemical process used involves any safety risk to employees working with it. The union's witness who is a lead maintenance technician may have sufficient training and experience to be qualified as an expert to testify as to the feasibility of the employer to maintain certain machinery with the currently available tools and personnel rather than to subcontract the work outside the bargaining unit. Even if the testimony given following the qualification of the fact witness as an expert does not require an opinion to be given, the process of qualifying regular witnesses as experts adds to the credibility and impact of their testimony.

## ORGANIZING EXHIBITS AND OTHER MATERIALS

Much of the time and energy devoted to gathering and developing evidence can be for naught if the advocate does not properly summarize and organize the materials. In many cases there are many dozens of documents and other pieces of evidence. In addition, there may be a large number of witnesses, whose testimony must be integrated with the other evidence. Without a systematic method for organizing the materials, some important items may be overlooked, introduced out of logical sequence and/or presented in a fashion that does not reflect professionalism or adequate preparation.

There is no single best way for organizing materials. Each advocate has his or her own preferred style. The author prefers to work with a "hearing notebook" consisting of a three-ring binder with tabbed dividers organized as follows.

1. **Miscellaneous Notes**—General notes that do not fit elsewhere
2. **Own Opening Statement**—Advocate's side (verbatim notes or outline)
3. **Opposing Opening Statement**—Other side (notes made during hearing)
4. **Witness List**—Names and titles of each witness for the advocate's side and the points each will cover
5. **Witnesses' testimony**—Separate divided section for each of the advocate's witnesses, with the questions and answers to be posed to each witness; a copy of each exhibit to be introduced through that witness to be included at the appropriate section of the questions and answers when the exhibit will be introduced.

6. **Cross-examination**—Separate divided section for each anticipated witness for the opposing side with questions prepared in
advance to pose to that witness. Also, notes of the direct
testimony of that witness during the hearing.
7. **Exhibits**—Separate section for each side containing a copy of
each exhibit introduced and admitted for each party.
8. **Closing Statement**—Verbatim notes or outline (if no brief is to
be filed)

In addition to the notebook the author prefers to have a file folder for
each exhibit to be introduced. The file is marked with a short description
of the documents contained in the file (e.g., "grievance," "letter 3/11 to
Gen.Mgr.") but no exhibit number. Because it is often not possible to
know the number that will be assigned to each document, it is preferable
to leave the exhibits unnumbered until they are admitted into evidence.
There should be four copies of each document in the file. One, usually the
original, is to be offered into evidence and made a part of the record and
will be available to the arbitrator during the hearing. The second is for the
advocate for the other side, and the third is to hand to the witness to
identify and use while testifying. The advocate has a fourth copy in the
notebook at the proper place with the questions and answers related to
that exhibit.

The advantages of the notebook are that it allows the advocate to
proceed through the hearing in an organized and systematic fashion. The
presentation is smoother and more professional than if papers are scat-
tered on the conference table. This level of organization impresses not
only the arbitrator but also the opposing advocate. It also allows the
advocate to focus on the key points in the hearing rather than being
distracted by trying to find documents or notes concerning a witness's
testimony. In addition, it keeps all pertinent papers in one well-organized
place, which is quite helpful if and when the advocate proceeds to write a
posthearing brief.

# 5

# Researching Authorities and Formulating Arguments

The evidentiary case discussed in the previous chapter might be compared to the bullets fired from a gun to hit a target. They are absolutely necessary in order to hit the bull's-eye, but without a gun they are of little value. In this somewhat strained analogy the gun is the argument aspect of the case, which consists of supporting contract language, rational arguments and previous arbitration and legal authorities. Only with an effective gun will the bullets be projected in the direction of the intended target. That gun, that is, arguments and authorities, forms a framework within which the evidentiary case is developed. A strong set of facts without supporting contract language and effective arguments will not win the day. Similarly, strong arguments and favorable contract language without good facts fare no better. Each depends on the other. In preparing the case for presentation the advocate needs to focus on both of these aspects.

For example, because of a reduction in force, an employer lays off an employee with ten years seniority while retaining another who has only four years seniority. Both of them hold the same job classification. Does the laid-off employee, who has six year's more seniority, have a valid grievance? There will be no question that the union will be able to gather the essential facts to show that the senior employee was laid off while an employee with six years less service was retained, but was this a violation of the labor agreement? That question will turn on the language of the labor agreement regarding the application of seniority during layoffs.

Assume that the contract in this case contains a clause that says, "In reducing the work force the employer shall follow seniority, insofar as practicable, in determining the order in which employees will be laid off." The employer argues that the employee with four years service can perform certain essential procedures involving the finishing of widgets that the ten-year employee is unable to do, and therefore it is impracticable to lay off the four-year employee, since essential work will not get done. The union counters that the ten-year employee can perform the work in question, although not as proficiently as the four-year employee, and that he can raise his proficiency with some additional training. The union also argues that work assignments within the department can be modified and certain tasks shifted to several other employees in the department, so that it is practicable to lay off the junior employee. Although an issue of fact exists with respect to the relative skills of the two individuals, the key issue for the arbitrator will be to determine just what the word "practicable" means in this situation. This will necessarily lead each side to marshal arguments and supporting authorities in order to prove its own interpretation of what that key word means when applied to the facts in this case.

Because the argument phase of a labor arbitration hearing follows the evidentiary phase, there is sometimes a tendency to follow the same order in preparing a case, that is, to prepare the evidence first and address the arguments later. The problem with delaying the preparation of arguments is that fact and argument are inextricably intertwined. The articulation of arguments invariably leads to facts that must be established to support those arguments. Similarly, facts must be matched with arguments that will lead an arbitrator to rule in the advocate's favor. Consequently, when a case is being prepared, neither part of the case—facts nor argument—should be neglected, nor should either one be made subservient to the other. They are both important and should be addressed simultaneously when the case is being prepared.

## FRAMING THE ARGUMENTS

By the time the essential facts have become known to the advocate, most of the arguments linked to those facts will also have become apparent. The experienced advocate will have made mental notes of each argument as the facts became known. There is a real value, however, in going beyond mental notes and reducing the arguments to writing. As with many ideas, forcing them into words and sentences helps to spot errors in logic, identify need for additional facts, avoid redundancies, and enhance the persuasiveness of the argument. It is strongly recommended, therefore, that the advocate list each argument for his or her side of the case in simple yet convincing language.

## Arguments—Employer's Side

Returning to the hypothetical layoff situation discussed above, the following are arguments that the employer's advocate might frame in preparing the case.

1. The labor agreement requires that seniority be followed for layoffs only where it is *practicable* to do so.
2. The junior employee in this case has demonstrated over a period of time that he is fully qualified to process widgets through the finishing machine efficiently and without producing any significant waste or defective widgets.
3. The senior employee in this case is not qualified to process widgets through the finishing machine, which is an essential function in Department A. The senior employee has processed widgets only twice before, and on both occasions he caused machine breakdowns and a large number of defective widgets.
4. The word "practicable" means "capable of being effected, done or executed; feasible" ( *The American Heritage Dictionary of the English Language).* It is not feasible to retain an employee who cannot perform essential work while laying off another who can.
5. In a prior arbitration decision under this same labor agreement (although involving a different job) the arbitrator ruled that the employer did not have to follow straight seniority for layoffs where it was vital to the employer's business that essential skills be retained.
6. The history of negotiations of the language in question shows that the parties intended to permit the employer to do just what it did in this case.

By putting into words the essential arguments supporting the employer's case, the key evidentiary elements of its case have been identified. The gun has identified the bullets it needs to hit the target. The employer will need to prove the widget-finishing capabilities of the four-year employee while proving the deficiencies of the ten-year employee.

It will also be important to show the critical importance of the finishing function. Testimony of supervisors and engineers, and perhaps production records, will be the evidence to prove those facts. A copy of the previous arbitration decision and perhaps the transcript of the hearing in that case will need to be entered into evidence. A copy of contract language concerning seniority during layoffs from prior labor agreements will be necessary to show negotiating history, supplemented perhaps by the testimony of employer negotiators who developed the labor agreement language at issue in this case.

## Arguments—Union's Side

Just as the employer advocate marshals arguments to support the employer's version of the case, so too should the union advocate be framing the arguments that will form the basis of the union's case. They might look something like the following.

1. Seniority is an essential part of a labor agreement and it should not be disregarded except where the facts strongly support an exception.
2. "Practicable" does not mean convenient or easy. It means that there is a feasible way to continue to operate the plant if seniority order is followed in carrying out the layoff. Laying off an employee with four years service will not jeopardize the operation of the plant.
3. If the ten-year employee is given sufficient training, he will be able to finish widgets efficiently. That was not done in the previous two instances when he was assigned this work.
4. Even if the ten-year employee cannot learn to finish widgets, it is still practicable to lay off the four-year employee. There are two other employees in the department who can finish widgets, so the work can be shifted in such a way as to relieve the ten-year employee of having to finish widgets. That is a practicable solution.
5. The previous arbitration decision relied on by the employer dealt with a very different set of facts and therefore does not apply in this case.
6. The development through successive negotiations of the labor agreement language at issue in this case does not show that the employer can disregard seniority under the set of facts that exist in this situation.

Some of the arguments used by the union advocate (e.g., numbers 5 and 6 above) are simply responsive to arguments posed by the employer advocate. It is possible that the union advocate will not know of or be able to anticipate all the employer advocate's arguments and will therefore not be in a position to frame these responsive arguments prior to the hearing. That is not a common phenomenon, however, because most arguments surface at one time or another in the earlier stages of the grievance procedure.

## Anticipating the Other Side's Arguments

The preceding sections contain sample lists of arguments prepared respectively by employer and union advocates. Where a thorough job of preparation is being done, *both advocates should prepare arguments to counter the points anticipated from the other side.* In other words, each advocate should not only prepare the arguments that he or she will use, but should also anticipate and formulate the arguments that the other side is likely to use. Too often, advocates become enamored with the logic and persuasiveness of their case before hearing the other side's arguments. Only by anticipating the positions that the other side will put forward and by articulating the arguments the opposing side will likely produce will an advocate be completely prepared to address all the issues and to present all the evidence that will be necessary to win the case.

## LINKING ARGUMENTS AND EVIDENCE

The time at which the arguments are being formulated is an ideal time to focus on the pieces of evidence that will support each argument. By listing each evidentiary point alongside each argument, the advocate is less likely to overlook any evidence that is apt to help the case. This list will also be useful as a checklist when witnesses and other evidence are being assembled for the hearing. Figure 5-1 is a useful format to ensure that arguments and evidence are properly linked.

## ANALYZING LABOR AGREEMENT LANGUAGE

The heart of any argument in a labor arbitration case involving contract interpretation (i.e., a case other than discipline or discharge) is

**Figure 5-1.**
**Linking Arguments and Evidence**

| ARGUMENTS | SUPPORTING EVIDENCE |
|---|---|
| Seniority only where practicable | CBA—Art. III, Sec. C |
| Junior employee is fully qualified | Testimony of Chester Morris |
| | Testimony of Edith Murray |
| Senior employee is not qualified | Testimony of Walter Haas |
| | Production Records |
| Bargaining history supports employer | Testimony of Bob Gray |

the operative language of the labor agreement. That language may be in one or more sections of the labor agreement or may be in a side letter of agreement. That is the starting point and the point to which the advocate should return continually during the preparation phase.

The operative language is so important to the outcome of the case that the advocate should spend time focusing on nothing but the language, turning the words over in his or her mind, developing alternative possible meanings of the words, looking in the dictionary for different possible meanings of key words, and applying the words in different contexts. It is surprising how a sentence or paragraph that seems relatively simple on its face can have different meanings or different applications in diverse factual situations. For example, a labor contract provision in a newly negotiated labor agreement reads as follows:

> Employees who have completed ninety (90) days of active employment and who have worked the last workday prior to the holiday and the first workday following the holiday will be entitled to eight (8) hours pay for each holiday not worked.

A grievance is filed by an employee who was laid off one week prior to a holiday and who was denied holiday pay. The employee had regular attendance up to the time of the layoff. Is the employee entitled to holiday pay while on layoff? At first glance it may appear that there is no entitlement, but if the word ''workday'' means the last day on which the employee was scheduled and expected to be at work, then there is entitlement because the employee reported for work on the last day work was scheduled to be performed by that employee. On the other hand, if ''workday'' means the last day on which the plant operated prior to the holiday, and other employees were working in the plant on the day prior to the holiday, there is no entitlement. What difference might it make if the layoff occurred only one day prior to the holiday? What if it was three months? What if the employee was not at work because of a serious automobile accident on the way to work? What is the purpose of the language in the first place? Is it to minimize the employer's holiday costs by excluding as many persons as possible, or is it to deter employees from absenting themselves from work by extending their holiday period? These and other questions might be raised in analyzing the language at issue.

## Review All Possible Provisions

The analysis just described should include every section and paragraph of the labor agreement that could possibly bear on the subject. For this reason the agreement should be reviewed cover to cover to ensure that all language in the agreement that is relevant to the case is considered. This review should include all side letters of agreement.

## Analyze Rationale of the Relevant Provisions

As suggested in the last example, the analysis of the language should include the questions, "What is the purpose of this language? Why was it included in the labor agreement?" Too often, it is easy to focus on the meaning of the words and fail to consider the intent and rationale behind the words. Admittedly, some language finds its way into a labor contract without much rhyme or reason. It may have been adopted from some other contract, or it may have been the pet project of some ancient negotiator whose reasons, if there were any, are now unfathomable.

Normally, however, it is possible to research the parties' intents in negotiating certain provisions or to reason their intention by analyzing the words and the context of the provision at issue. In the holiday pay example just above it is rather clear that the requirement to work before and after a holiday was intended to dissuade employees from taking unauthorized time off in connection with a holiday in order to make a holiday break longer than it would otherwise be. Applying this rationale, an employee on layoff is not taking unauthorized time off, nor is an employee who is injured on the way to work just prior to a holiday. Consequently, a strong argument can be made that an employee on layoff prior to a holiday was not absent on a "workday," that is, a day on which he or she was scheduled or expected to be at work, and is therefore eligible for holiday pay.

# RESEARCHING AUTHORITY UNDER
# THE LABOR AGREEMENT

Unless the labor agreement under which the grievance was filed is a brand-new agreement, there is likely to be some history that will provide guidance and direction to an arbitrator as to how the case should be decided. This history may consist of prior arbitration awards, grievance settlements, past practices, and bargaining history. The task of the advocate is to unearth all relevant information that will help to persuade the arbitrator of the correctness of the advocate's position. There are a number of sources to be researched.

## Previous Similar or Analogous Cases

A common and well-established method for determining the proper interpretation of disputed contract language or the appropriate amount of discipline in a particular case is to ascertain what has been done in previous similar cases. While the previous disposition does not necessarily control what is to be done in the instant case, it does provide some guidance as to what the appropriate result should be. The level at which the issue was resolved or decided will usually determine how influential the previous result will be in the case at hand. The following discussion covers the categories of dispositions from the most to the least binding.

### Arbitration Awards

It is generally held that previous arbitration awards are binding on the parties in future cases in which the same issue, contract language, and factual setting were involved.[1] In legal terminology the principle of such precedent setting is "stare decisis." In such situations the previous arbitration award generally sets a precedent for the subsequent case. For example, if an arbitrator interprets the word "days" in the grievance section of a labor agreement to mean calendar days rather than work days for purposes of reckoning time for filing grievances and appealing decisions, that interpretation will apply in all future cases just as if it had been written into the agreement. Of course, if the parties agree to change the words in the agreement on which the decision was based, the precedent would no longer be binding.

---

[1]North Star Steel Co., 87 LA 40, 44 (Miller, 1986); Cone Mills Corp., 86 LA 992, 996 (Nolan, 1986).

Some arbitrators have gone so far as to hold that if a previous arbitrator had decided a case based on the very same contract language and the same or virtually the same set of facts, the grievance is not arbitrable because it had already been decided, that is, in the language of the law it is "res judicata."[2]

The difficulty often encountered in relying on prior arbitration awards to provide a definitive answer is that the factual settings in which the previous cases occurred are often different than those in the case at hand. When trying to use earlier cases as a precedent, the advocate must show that the circumstances under which the language was applied were the same or very similar to the instant case. When faced with different facts than the earlier case, however, a resourceful advocate will argue that the factual differences are not significant and that the same result should apply, notwithstanding the changed circumstances.

Advocates should also be attentive to any changes that have been made in the disputed contract language since the precedent-setting arbitration decision was issued. Not only should attention be paid to the provisions directly at issue, but also to changes in other sections of the contract or laws that could bear on the issue at hand. Assume, for example, that an arbitrator ruled in a 1987 case that an employer did not have any obligation under the contract to put an employee returning from a disability leave on "light duty" (i.e., work less strenuous than the normal job) when the employee was not physically capable of returning to his normal job. The labor agreement's provisions concerning such a return had not changed since that decision, but the agreement did have a provision that "rights and obligations provided by state and federal law are incorporated into this agreement." The passage of the Americans with Disabilities Act of 1990 (ADA), combined with the contract language quoted above, imposes a duty of "reasonable accommodation" on the employer that did not previously exist. Consequently, the previous arbitration decision that did not require light duty or modified work assignments is likely to have lost its precedential value for the employer, because of a change in the law, in the current case.

## Grievance Settlements

Another type of potentially precedent-setting situation is the settlement of one or more previous cases involving the same or similar facts

---

[2]Armstrong World Indus., 75 LA 720 (Johnston, 1980); Webster Cent. Sch. Distr., 80 L.A. 1138 (Brand, 1983); Hill and Sinicropi, *Evidence in Arbitration*, 390–95, (BNA Books, 1987); Schoonhoven, *Fairweather's Practice and Procedure in Labor Arbitration*, 460–61 (BNA Books, 1991).

and contract language. Although not as persuasive as an arbitration decision, the logic is similar. If the parties resolved a previous dispute in a certain way, why would the same resolution not be applicable in the instant case, provided the same circumstances exist? If the parties' representatives were foresighted, they would have envisioned future cases arising that would present the same issue and would have addressed it in the settlement agreement. It is not unusual, for example, for one party or both to insist on some type of restrictive language in their agreement to settle a grievance to preclude its application in other cases. Sometimes the simple words ''settled without precedent'' are used. Other parties prefer to use more formal or legalistic language such as the following:

> The Company and the Union agree that the settlement of this case is strictly limited to grievance # _____. Neither party shall be bound by this settlement in any future case, nor may either party rely on this settlement, or introduce it in evidence in any hearing, to support its position in any future case.

Such language places a protective shield or fence around the settlement in order to avoid it binding either party in the future. Without such language it is probable that one side or the other will seek to use it as a precedent-setting settlement to apply to all future similar cases.

Consequently, in preparing for arbitration advocates should review files to determine whether any such settlement agreements exist, determine whether they contain any restrictions on future reliance, and ascertain whether the facts and circumstances were sufficiently similar for them to be presently applicable.

### *Informal Grievance Dispositions*

Sometimes grievances are settled or simply granted without any written explanation as to the rationale behind the disposition. The most common situation is one in which a grievance is filed by an employee and the employee's supervisor grants the grievance along, perhaps, with some grant of back pay. There may be no written record, or there may be a simple written notation, ''granted,'' on the grievance form. Similarly, grievances may be dropped (or not appealed to the next higher level) at the first or second step of the grievance procedure with no evidence given of why they were not pursued.

Grievances granted by the employer and grievances dropped by the union create a presumption concerning the merits of the claim.[3] If the employer granted the grievance, it is presumed that it must have been a valid claim. If the grievant or the union dropped the grievance prior to

---

[3]Virginia Pocahontas Mining Co., 95 LA 1271, 1276 (Roberts, 1990)

arbitration, the presumption is that it must have lacked merit. Neither of these presumptions may be true. The supervisor who granted the grievance may have simply felt that the time and energy required to contest a grievance that had some merit were simply not worth the cost of defending it and may have decided to settle for that reason. The employee who agreed to have his grievance dropped may have had a change of circumstances (e.g., was transferred to another department), which made the claim unimportant to that employee, who decided not to pursue it further. Nevertheless, such dispositions can favor one side or the other, the degree of value in the arbitration hearing depending largely on the weight given to them by different arbitrators.

There is a range of opinion held by arbitrators as to the weight that should be given to informal grievance dispositions. In general, they are not given a great deal of weight when the disposition was made at a relatively low level of the grievance procedure (e.g., shop foreman and employee) or when it appears that the disposition was not based on a conscious decision of the management and union hierarchies concerning the meaning of certain provisions of the labor agreement.[4]

Because the grievance procedure is often regarded as an extension of the contract negotiating process, changes in the meaning and application of the labor agreement are thought to be reserved to representatives of the parties who entered into that agreement, not to lower level persons in the respective organizations. The logic is that the parties themselves should not be bound in future cases by possible misinterpretations by persons not in a position to know the true meaning and application of certain contract provisions. Having said that, it is nevertheless prudent for unions and employers to caution their representatives not to grant or drop grievances without some effort to protect against adverse inferences that may be drawn from such actions in future cases. Adding the words "without precedent" to the words "grievance granted" or "grievance dropped" will usually be sufficient to avoid any later contentions of an intention to impact future cases.[5]

Some parties protect against the possibility of such future impacts by including in their labor agreements language that precludes any grievance disposition or settlement from affecting any future cases unless the parties specifically agree in writing for it to set a precedent. This is probably a positive step for union-management relationships in that it provides greater latitude for settlement of grievances at lower

---

[4]James River Corp., 92 LA 533, 540 (Neas, 1989); General Motors, 92 LA 624, 629 (Kahn, 1988).
[5]Exide Corp., 98 LA 626 (Daly, 1992).

levels (e.g., employee, shop steward, and first-line supervisor) without concern as to how it will affect other cases.

## Past Practice

Although not usually considered to be authority for deciding labor arbitration cases, one of the most persuasive methods of proving the intended application of a labor agreement provision is to show a past practice of such application. Labor arbitration principles establish that a regular practice or custom for certain activities, known to both parties, and carried out more or less consistently over a significant period of time, can establish a binding precedent on the parties involved, at least where the provisions of the labor agreement on that point are silent or ambiguous.

For example, a labor agreement provision states that vacation pay shall be paid on the basis of forty hours pay per week of vacation at the employee's "regular rate of pay." For many years the employer has computed vacation pay by taking total straight time wages, dividing that by the total number of straight time hours worked, computing an average of each employee's hourly rate, and multiplying that average rate by forty hours to arrive at each employee's weekly vacation pay. Mary Jones has a "regular job" (i.e., the one on which she holds a job bid) that pays fifteen percent more than the job on which she has worked for most of the last six months. She claims that she should receive forty hours pay at the rate of her bid job, rather than at the average rate based on earnings as computed by the employer. Without anything more than the contract language quoted above and the evidence of past practice, an arbitrator is likely to rule that vacation pay is to be paid on the basis of the employee's straight time earnings rather than at the rate of the employee's regular job, even though a literal reading of the contract provision would lead to a different conclusion. The logic is that if the parties had intended something different, they would not have continued the vacation pay practice for such a long period of time without correcting it or without the employer receiving opposition from the union or employees.

### When Past Practice Applies

In relying on past practice to support a case it is not sufficient to simply show that a practice has existed. Arbitrators have established over many years of decisions certain rules or standards against which the past practice must be evaluated. Far and away the most essential rule concerning the application of past practice is that it may only be relied on when the contract language at issue is ambiguous or subject to more than one interpretation.[6] When the contract language is clear on its face and when the words can have no other plausible meaning than what they say, past practice is irrelevant. For example, a labor contract provides that an employee's pension shall be based on "the employee's years of credited service excluding all time off due to personal leaves of absence." For six years the employer's benefits department has calculated pension benefits based on all periods when employees were on the employee roster, *including personal leaves of absence.* In year seven the calculation is changed to exclude such leave periods, and a grievance is filed. What result?

Most likely, the employer will win the case, because the language is unambiguous. While the arbitrator is apt to preclude the employer from reducing the benefits of those already retired, those retiring in year seven and beyond will likely be subject to the literal meaning of the labor agreement provision. Of course, it is not always as easy as in the example just cited to determine when contract language is as unambiguous, and resourceful advocates can often find ambiguities where others might not.

Other standards have been developed by arbitrators for applying past practice. The most common ones are as follows:

- The practice must be unequivocal and consistent, that is, it must be shown that the practice was consistently followed.[7]
- The practice must have been apparent to the parties and at least tacitly accepted by them. When the practice has not generally been known or when disputes have arisen over the practice, the practice cannot be held to have been accepted.[8]
- The practice must have existed over a reasonably long period of time and with sufficient frequency in order to consider it a "practice." No precise time periods or frequencies have been established.[9]

[6]Ashland Oil, Inc., 100 L.A. 480, 482 (Feldman, 1993); Ashland Petroleum Co., 94 LA 271, 276 (Shanker, 1990).
[7]Reyco Indus., Inc., 85 LA 1034 (Newmark, 1985), Zack & Block, *Labor Agreement in Negotiation and Arbitration,* 10 (BNA Books, 1983).
[8]Intek Weatherseal Products Inc. and Electrical Workers, IBEW. Local 2047, 96 LA 64 (Berquist, 1990); Standard Products Co. and Steelworkers, Local 3568, 88 LA 1164 (Richard, 1987).
[9]Farrell Lines Inc. and Longshoremen, ILA, Local 333, 86 LA 36, (Hockenberry, 1986); Klickitat County, Washington and State, County & Municipal Employees, Local 1533, 86 LA 283 (Smith, 1985); Reyco Industries Inc. and Molders, Local 296, 85 LA 1034, (Newmark, 1985).

*Proving Past Practice*

It is one thing to know that a past practice exists and quite another to prove it sufficiently to meet the standards necessary to make it a binding past practice. In many cases the practice is one that is never recorded. For example, employees in a particular department of the employer's facility have, over a period of time, left their work areas ten to fifteen minutes early in order to wash up. If they perform fairly autonomous jobs (e.g., field maintenance work), the only persons who may be aware of the practice are the employees themselves. Their testimony will normally be sufficient to prove the existence of the practice, but there may be some difficulty on the part of the union in establishing the practice as binding if there is no proof that management knew of the practice. Assuming, as in this case, that it is the union that is trying to prove the past practice, it will be the task of the union advocate to show that supervisors and/or managers knew or should be presumed to have known of the practice, thereby establishing the employer's tacit acceptance of the practice. This may be done through the testimony of employee witnesses, supervisors or former supervisors, or perhaps third parties.

Another difficulty in proving past practice is encountered when there are exceptions to the past practice, that is, instances in which the past practice was not followed. Even though one of the standards of proving past practice is that the practice was consistently followed, it does not follow that it must always have been followed. Some exceptions may be tolerated without disproving the practice, but the exceptions normally must be based on unusual circumstances or an understanding between the parties to deviate from the normally accepted practice.[10]

# BARGAINING HISTORY

When the meaning or application of a provision of the labor contract is in question, arbitrators often search for evidence that will point to the meaning that the parties intended to give the words in dispute. Searching for the negotiators' intentions is a difficult task, especially because both parties do not always intend the same thing or, more frequently, the parties did not, in formulating their labor agreement, envision the type of situation to which the language must later be applied. Nevertheless, the search should always be undertaken. One of the most common methods

---

[10]Commercial Filters Div. and Clothing & Textile Workers, Local 1749, 91 LA 25 (Bethel, 1988); Intek Weatherseal Products Inc. and Electrical Workers, IBEW, Local 2047, 96 LA 64 (Berquist, 1990); Dole Can Plant and Longshoremen & Warehousemen, ILWU, Local 142 (Tsukiyama, 1984).

of uncovering the parties' intent in agreeing to certain contract provisions is to research the history of how the language came into being, how it evolved over time, what circumstances preceded its introduction or change, and what was said by the negotiators at or about the time the agreement was being negotiated. Each of these elements comes under the heading of "bargaining history." The advocate's task in preparing the case is to research the history surrounding the negotiations that resulted in the specific provisions that are at issue in the case.

## Evolution of Contract Clauses

It is often useful to determine when the provision in question first appeared in the labor agreement and to trace its evolution over time. Frequently, the language at issue initially came into being in an earlier labor agreement in other than its current form and was modified one or more times in subsequent contract negotiations to meet the demands or needs of one or both parties. Tracing the development of a clause over a succession of labor agreements often provides insight as to the parties' intent—especially when there is some bargaining history to supplement that evolution. An example of such tracing is shown in Figure 5-2.

---

**Figure 5-2**
**Development of Seniority Clause re Temporary Assignments**

**1975–1988**

Section 2-B (4). When a job is anticipated to last for less than thirty (30) days, the employer may fill it without respect to the seniority provisions of this agreement.

**1989–1995**

Section 2-B (5). When a job is anticipated to continue for no more than forty-five (45) days, and the job carries a classification less than Grade 10, the employer may fill it without using the bid system, provided, however, that the employee who fills that position shall not accrue any seniority in the position nor have any preference for filling that position on a permanent basis.

**1996–present**

Section 2-C (1). All positions are subject to the bidding procedure except temporary vacancies occurring because of the illness or injury of an employee when such absence is not reasonably anticipated to continue for more than sixty (60) days. In filling such temporary vacancies the employer shall award the position to the senior qualified employee who does not hold a permanent bid at the time the temporary period of the assignment begins.

---

## Analyzing Proposals and Counterproposals

Another key step in the advocate's research should be a review of the initial proposal and the corresponding counterproposals that culminated in the language finally adopted by the parties. Analysis of the phrasing of the alternative proposals often provides telling evidence of what each side was attempting to accomplish and how successful they were in doing so. An example of such an analysis is shown in Figure 5-3. Arbitrators are generally quite sophisticated in deciphering the intent of

---

**Figure 5-3**
**Negotiating Development of a Contract Provision**

### Employer Proposal 9/2/93 (opening agenda)

Item C-32. There shall be no limitations on the right of the company to subcontract work as long as there is an economic basis for the decision.

### Union Counterproposal 9/24/93

Item C-32. The employer may subcontract work of the machine shop, billet processing, and weld shop, provided the following conditions are met:

1. No employees lose work as a result of the subcontracting.
2. The work has been subcontracted at some time prior to 1993.
3. The company can demonstrate to the union that there is at least a twenty percent savings to the company and that the union has an opportunity to propose an alternative method of achieving those savings.

### Employer Counterproposal 9/26/93

Item C-32. The employer may subcontract all work except that of Departments 3 and 6, provided that the employer can achieve a cost savings of at least ten percent and that the union is given an opportunity prior to the subcontracting to eliminate that differential.

### Final Agreement 11/15/93

Item C-32. Any subcontracting not in effect as of August 15, 1993, may not be subcontracted unless (a) no employees are laid off as a result of the subcontracting and (b) the employer can demonstrate conclusively to the union that there is at least a savings of twenty percent in labor and transportation costs and that the union is notified at least thirty days prior to the subcontracting and given a reasonable opportunity to propose modifications in wages, hours, and/or working conditions to reduce the differential to no more than five percent.

---

the respective negotiators by the way the proposals where made, rejected, modified, and finally accepted. This process of proof is made more feasible if the proposals and counterproposals were made in writing. Unfortunately, that is not always the case, and often to prove such development the advocates must rely on the testimony of the negotiators to the extent that it is available. In such cases ascertaining the true intent of the parties becomes an extremely difficult process for the arbitrator.

## Contemporaneous Circumstances

Another facet of researching the ambiguous provision is to examine circumstances that may have preceded, or occurred approximately at the time of, the introduction or change in the language at issue. For example, if there were significant layoffs and numerous grievances concerning such layoffs preceding a change in the seniority section of the labor agreement, it may be inferred that the new language was an attempt to correct some of the unfavorable impacts of those layoffs. Similarly, if one side or the other obtains a favorable decision in a major arbitration case prior to negotiations and the side that lost the case proposes changing the language on which the decision was based, a negotiated change in that provision may be presumed to have been intended to change the interpretation of the labor agreement that was decided by the arbitrator. Behind most new or changed provisions in a labor contract there is a story. The task of the advocate is to discover that story in order to determine whether it can be used in some way to support the advocate's case.

## The Unaccepted Change

An important factor considered by arbitrators in construing the meaning of a labor agreement provision within the context of bargaining history is the attempt by one party to change the wording of a provision without being successful in obtaining the agreement of the other party. If the provision in question is subject to several interpretations, most arbitrators are likely to rule in favor of the party that did not agree to change that provision.

For example, a labor agreement stated, ''In the event of a need to change production line speeds, the company and the union will meet to determine all matters concerning such changes.'' The employer announced an increase in production line speeds and offered to meet with the union to discuss the changes and their impacts on the work force but not to seek the union's agreement. The union protested the increased speeds and argued that the contract required the union's agreement before any changes in line speeds could be implemented. The dispute was referred to arbitration.

In the hearing the union offered evidence of the employer's opening proposals in a previous contract negotiation that showed that the employer had proposed that the sentence in question be changed to read, " . . . the company and the union will meet to address any problems resulting from the line speed changes." This proposal was not accepted by the union, and the language remained unchanged. Because the employer's proposed language was very similar to the interpretation the employer now urges the arbitrator to adopt and because that proposal was not agreed to by the union, the arbitrator is likely to rule in favor of the union unless there are other factors that strongly weigh in the opposite direction.

When, however, the facts indicate that the party proposing the change was not attempting to change the meaning or application of the provision in question but was merely attempting to clarify an ambiguous clause, the above rationale would not normally apply. Unless the proposal, when it was advanced in negotiations, included some reference to "clarification" or "no intent to change meaning and application of language," it will be very difficult to prove that the proposed change was not intended by the proposing party to change the meaning and application of the provision.

## Communications during Negotiations

Besides examining the wording of proposals and counterproposals themselves, much information can be gleaned from the explanations, questions and answers, documents exchanged, data presented, and statements made during the negotiations that resulted in the language at issue. When legislators pass a new law, the debate on that bill prior to its passage becomes part of its legislative history. Courts often cite legislative speeches and debates in analyzing the meaning of statutes. Although there is not normally a formal record of labor negotiations, each party usually keeps its own notes of what transpired before, during, and after the adoption of new or changed contract language. These notes or records become a part of the bargaining history that can later be used to interpret questionable provisions. Similarly, such notes and records can often be introduced into evidence in arbitration hearings.

Generally speaking, notes of labor contract negotiations standing alone without the testimony of the note taker are either inadmissible or are given little weight if admitted. The reason is that they are hearsay and are not subject to cross-examination. They are similar to a written statement or affidavit of a person who is not called as a witness. Consequently, all notes should be signed or initialed by the note taker. If they are subsequently typed by another person, the original notes should be retained, or at least the note taker should sign or initial the typed transcription of the written notes.

In proving this type of bargaining history the advocate should attempt to have his or her side's chief spokesperson testify as to what was said in negotiations. If the chief spokesperson was also the note taker, the notes and related testimony can be presented simultaneously. If the note taker was another person, that person should normally follow the spokesperson on the stand to relate his or her recollection of the statements made in the negotiating meetings with the notes being offered into evidence to substantiate the testimony. If there were other participants in the negotiations, they also can testify as to their recollections, also supported by any notes or records they kept.

## OUTSIDE AUTHORITIES

In addition to research concerning the various facets of bargaining history, past practice, and other aspects of the arbitrating parties' relationship as it bears on the grievance being arbitrated, it is also useful to see how grievances of the same type have been handled in previous labor arbitration cases involving other parties. Although there is no such thing as arbitration precedent as there is in the law, it is nevertheless true that arbitrators can be influenced by decisions issued by other arbitrators under other contracts. The manner in which arbitrators have reasoned through similar cases can be influential in causing an arbitrator to apply the same rationale in the case at hand.

Additionally, when a large number of arbitrators have accepted the validity of a particular principle (e.g., requiring progressive discipline as a condition for sustaining discharges for less grievous offenses), an arbitrator is quite likely to adopt the same principle. In the parlance of the law, arbitration decisions from other contracts and other parties on issues similar to that involved in a particular case can be "persuasive authority" but not "precedential authority"—in other words, an arbitrator is in no way obligated to follow the earlier decision but may be influenced by it in formulating his or her own decision.

## Published Arbitration Decisions

A number of publishing organizations issue reports of arbitration decisions and awards. They include The Bureau of National Affairs' *Labor Arbitration Reports* and *Government Employee Relations Report*; Commerce Clearing House's *Labor Arbitration Awards*; the American Arbitration Association's *Summary of Labor Arbitration Awards*, *Arbitrations in the Schools*, and *Labor Arbitration in Government*; and LRP Publications' *Labor Arbitration Information System* and *Federal Labor Relations Reporter*. These services publish decisions and awards periodically that can be accessed via computer and are available in print. They are all thoroughly indexed by subject matter, by names of arbitrator, employer, and union, and sometimes by other criteria. They are available on a subscription basis from each of the publishers and are sometimes available in general libraries and usually in law libraries.

It should always be kept in mind that the number of reported decisions represents but a small fraction of all decisions issued by labor arbitrators, so, simply by reading reported decisions, one cannot claim that most arbitrators have ruled in a particular way; but if a large number of reported decisions on a particular issue appear to reach the same result, there is some basis for claiming a majority or predominant point of view held by arbitrators. This leads to the question of how much weight is given by arbitrators to these reported decisions.

### *Influence of Decisions Involving Other Parties*

An arbitrator's decision and award concerning parties and a labor contract other than the ones involved in the case at hand certainly does not set a precedent for that case and may even be disregarded. At most, arbitration decisions and awards involving other parties under a different labor agreement are persuasive or instructive as to what a reasonable decision in a similar case might be. They are merely reference points against which the facts and contract language in the present case can be evaluated.

Notwithstanding the limitation just described, it is nevertheless quite helpful to examine and use for argument purposes other arbitration decisions to glean insights as to what factors arbitrators rely on when deciding the same type of case. Moreover, to the extent that the facts and contract language in a prior case are the same or very similar to the one at hand, the decision in the prior case may be very persuasive to an arbitrator, especially if the prior case was well reasoned or if the person who decided the prior case is a well-known and well-respected arbitrator.

Another factor that can enhance the persuasiveness of a prior decision and award is whether it involves the same parent union or employer or comes from the same industry as the case at hand. In other words, the more links that can be drawn between the earlier reported decision and the instant case, the greater the chances are that it will influence the decision in the present case.

## *Value of Reported Decisions in Preparing a Case*

The use of arbitration decisions involving other parties for purposes of argument will be discussed in greater detail in Chapter 13. These decisions, however, have real value as a preparation tool. First, they often help advocates to focus on the key elements necessary in a particular type of case. Second, they frequently provide useful ideas or insights as to how to approach a case that differ from the way the case was addressed in the prior grievance steps or from the way the advocate would otherwise have approached the case. Third, they may point to other helpful cases or legal authorities of which the advocate was unaware. Consequently, a portion of the advocate's preparation time should be devoted to researching published arbitration decisions and awards on the specific issues involved in the case being prepared.

## Unpublished Arbitration Decisions

Because such a small percentage of all arbitration decisions are published, there is a large reservoir of unpublished decisions that are likely to deal with the same issues that are involved in the instant case, but accessing these decisions is not an easy task. Because they are not published, they are often difficult to locate. In addition, parties to an unpublished decision may not have granted approval for it to be seen or used by others. Because labor arbitration is a private adjudication process, decisions resulting from this process are not a matter of public record unless one or both of the parties are public entities. As a result, parties to arbitration decisions are entitled to keep their decisions to themselves. It is not unusual, though, for such private decisions to be circulated among other employers and unions, especially when there are networks or associations of employers and unions that have an interest in such decisions. These networks and associations can facilitate locating and obtaining copies of unpublished decisions. Without such networks it is very difficult for union and employer advocates to know what is available and how to obtain copies of decisions.

Once in hand, the unpublished decision can usually be used much like a published decision, whether for preparation or for supporting arguments before the arbitrator. As with reported decisions, unpublished decisions generally are accepted only for their persuasive value rather than for any precedential effect. One of the differences between published and unpublished decisions is that the latter are more likely to come from an industry or collective bargaining relationship that is similar to the one involved in the advocate's case (because it is more likely to have been obtained from an employer or union source similar to the one represented by the searching advocate). In fact, the arbitrator who decided the unreported decision may be the same one who is scheduled to hear the case at hand, and there is a possibility that the wording of the contract language is similar or even identical. In such cases the unreported decision will be more persuasive than the normal reported decision involving other parties and other language.

## External Law

The guiding duty of arbitrators is to decide grievances according to the terms of the applicable labor agreement. From time to time cases arise that bring into play what is referred to as external law, that is, legal authority outside the specific terms of the labor agreement. Such external law may be federal or state statues, cases decided by the NLRB, EEOC or various state administrative agencies, or decisions of other forums. Examples of the types of grievance arbitrations cases that are likely to involve external law are as follows.

- Alleged racial, gender, age, handicap, or other invidious discrimination.
- Disputes involving hours of work, workers' compensation, and safety that overlap state laws on these subjects.
- Claims for pension and other benefits addressed by state and/or federal benefit legislation, for example, the Employee Retirement Security Act (ERISA).
- Contentions of unilateral changes in terms and conditions of employment and claims of discrimination caused by union activity that are raised under the National Labor Relations Act (NLRA).
- Issues of seniority and benefit entitlements of employees returning from military service, where the federal law imposes certain beneficial provisions.

External law does not usually supplant the terms of the labor agreement but is more often looked to as a guide or standard for applying the terms of an agreement. For example, a particular labor agreement may provide that sexual harassment is grounds for disciplinary action. A case involving certain suggestive remarks by one employee to another provokes disciplinary action by the employer, over which the disciplined employee files a grievance claiming that the remarks did not constitute sexual harassment. Cases arising under federal and state discrimination statutes may very well come into play as a means of determining the parameters of sexual harassment for deciding the case at hand.

Occasionally, external law can also come into play to supersede labor contract provisions. Most labor agreements contain a savings clause that allows state or federal law to supersede contract terms, while preserving or saving the balance of the contract from being null and void. The language allowing the law to supersede the contract terms is usually conditioned on the contract terms being in violation of the law. In such cases external law becomes the controlling factor. Grievances under these conditions require the arbitrator to apply, or at least consider, such external law in order to render a decision.

In both of the above-described situations it is incumbent on the advocate to research applicable law and/or to obtain a legal opinion as to what, if any, impact external law might have on the case being prepared.

## Scholarly Texts, Conference Reports, and so Forth

Usually less influential than arbitration decisions, but nevertheless sometimes persuasive, are books, journal articles, reports of conferences and symposia, and other written material that address issues arising in labor arbitration cases. Frequently, such writings summarize or synthesize numerous arbitration or legal decisions and therefore carry some of the same persuasive qualities as the decisions themselves. Examples of such writings are as follows.

- Elkouri and Elkouri, *How Arbitration Works* (BNA Books, 1985).
- Schoonhaven, *Fairweather's Practice and Procedure in Labor Arbitration* (BNA Books, 1991).
- Reports of the National Academy of Labor Arbitrators.

## Industry Practices

Earlier in this chapter the importance of researching past practice was discussed. The practices that were referred to in that discussion were those involving the same parties operating under the same labor agreement. Related somewhat to those past practices are industry practices that reflect customs and standards in a particular industry or field of work. For example, a person employed as a newspaper reporter is terminated for not maintaining a sufficiently high level of professional journalism, and the termination is appealed to arbitration. The principal issue in the case is likely to center around what constitutes professional journalism. Practices and standards of performance in the newspaper industry are apt to be as important, if not more important, than the customs and practices at the individual newspaper where the terminated reporter was employed.

Evidence of industry practices may be difficult to obtain and in most cases must come from the testimony of witnesses outside the organization that are parties to the arbitration. There may be some rare instances when trade publications, scholarly journals, or other written materials may be used to prove industry practices. One of the key factors in utilizing this type of evidence is the similarity of the conditions within which the industry practices exist as compared with those of the employer and workplace situation in the case to be heard.

## PREHEARING BRIEFS

Advocates who have done trial work and argued certain types of cases before administrative agencies may be accustomed to writing a pretrial or prehearing brief. Such documents usually summarize the evidence to be presented, make the legal arguments that will be advanced to the judge or jury and cite legal authority to support the arguments.

Prehearing briefs are not common in labor arbitration. Because the process is usually much more informal and the matters at stake are frequently less crucial than those in most trials and many administrative hearings, advocates are not as likely to undertake the demanding task of preparing a prehearing brief. There are, however, more compelling reasons for not doing so. Principal among these is the fact that the prehearing brief reveals to the other side arguments that the advocate plans to make long before the arguments actually have to be made. In addition, the evidence that results from the hearing may differ significantly from that summarized in the prehearing brief, requiring the advocate to explain and rationalize the differences. For these reasons, unless the labor agreement requires a prehearing brief (which is very unusual) or unless there is a well-established practice of doing so, the author recommends not presenting a brief to the arbitrator or the opposing advocate before or during the hearing.

If the advocate feels more confident and better prepared in having the evidence summarized and the arguments set forth in a formal context prior to the hearing, a brief may be prepared for use only by the advocate. It may also be used as a prototype or draft for a posthearing brief following the closing of the record. Seldom, however, will the value of a prehearing brief outweigh the time and effort spent in preparing it. The advocate's limited time to prepare the case is better invested in the other steps discussed in chapters 2 through 6 of this book.

# 6

# Selecting and Preparing Witnesses

The advocate's job of preparing a case for presentation to an arbitrator might be compared to that of a theatrical director preparing a play. Under this analogy selecting and preparing witnesses is like the director's job of selecting the cast and rehearsing the actors in the play. If the performance is to be a convincing one, each part must be played with skill and ease. The roles must be understood by the actors who play them, and the lines (testimony) need to be delivered flawlessly. The purpose in arbitration is not entertainment, however, but persuasion, and the roles and lines are real, not the creation of a playwright. Nevertheless, the advocate should view his or her task much as a director does—to select the right people, prepare them to give an effective presentation, and make sure that all parts fit together for an effective performance.

## SELECTION OF WITNESSES

In Chapter 4 considerable attention was devoted to interviewing and evaluating witnesses. That process should produce a rather accurate picture of the potential witnesses, the extent of the information they will provide, and how effective they are likely to be in advancing the presentation of the case. Nevertheless, until all the evidence is assembled it is often difficult to determine for certain whether a person should be a

137

witness or not. For this reason the author prefers to advise most witnesses during the initial interviews, and frequently even during the preparation of their testimony, that it is not certain that they will actually testify (unless it is quite clear that their testimony will be vital to the case). This gives the advocate more leeway in deciding how to put the evidentiary pieces together without embarrassment or discomfort to witnesses ultimately not selected to testify.

In some cases the final decision on whether or not to use a particular witness may not be made until the hearing is in progress. For example, some witnesses are selected to serve solely as rebuttal witnesses, meaning that their testimony is designed to rebut or refute evidence expected to be presented by the other side. If the expected evidence does not materialize, the rebuttal witness is not necessary. In other cases the testimony of particular witnesses may be designed to support or amplify other testimony. If such other testimony turns out to be sufficient by itself, the advocate may decide to rely solely on the other testimony and not to use the supporting witness. The selection of witnesses and the decision as to the scope of their testimony is a judgment call on the part of the advocate. The greater the advocate's experience, the more effective that judgment is likely to be.

## PREPARING WITNESSES TO TESTIFY

One of the most crucial aspects of preparing for an arbitration hearing is the preparation of witnesses. Contrary to what is believed by some laypersons, there is absolutely nothing improper about an advocate going over, in advance of the hearing, the questions to be asked of a witness and assisting the witness in framing answers that will be as effective as possible in the hearing. In fact, an advocate who does not prepare witnesses to give testimony is negligent. Not only will such cases suffer from lack of preparation, but witnesses will suffer from apprehension and unpreparedness at having to provide testimony without knowing in advance the questions to be asked by the witness's advocate and without having been prepared to respond to the questions likely to be asked by the opposing advocate.

### Timing

If a potential witness is initially interviewed in a thorough manner well in advance of the hearing, as was suggested in Chapter 4, then the preparation of that witness to give testimony is best accomplished shortly before the hearing. It is usually ideal to prepare witnesses to testify a day or two before the hearing. There are several reasons for this. The objective is to have the witness give concise, well-articulated, and accurate answers. If the preparation of the witness to give testimony is done too far in advance of the hearing, the witness is likely to forget all or some parts of the answers that have been worked out with the advocate. Key witnesses in important cases or persons who, because of hazy recollection, lack of confidence, or other weaknesses, will need special preparation. Several meetings may be necessary to prepare them. In these cases the last preparatory meeting should usually be held within 24 hours of the hearing.

Another advantage of preparing shortly before the hearing is that new evidence or new theories about the case may have developed during other preparatory steps of the case, and such new evidence or theories will be available to the witnesses as they are being finally prepared to give testimony.

In those instances when it is not possible to interview the prospective witnesses in advance of preparing them to testify and when interviewing and preparation must be accomplished in the same conference, it is usually advisable to schedule such a session at least several days in advance of the hearing. The reason for this is that the interview of the prospective witness may reveal that there is other supporting evidence, such as documents or other witnesses, that need to be obtained for the hearing. If the combined interview and preparation for testimony are done just before the hearing, there may not be enough time available to obtain the additional evidence.

## Efficient Use of Time

In most cases an advocate will have at least two, and perhaps as many as six or seven, witnesses to prepare for testifying. If only a limited amount of time is available, it is important that the preparation be done as efficiently as possible. This usually means scheduling the witnesses in blocks of time so that each is given sufficient time and attention to be fully prepared to testify.

When the basic facts and the advocate's theory of the case are not well known by all the witnesses, it will be advisable to brief them on these matters at the outset of the preparation. If this initial briefing will take more than a few minutes and if there are a number of witnesses to testify, all of whom are available in one location, it may be advisable to schedule an initial meeting with all the witnesses at the outset of the preparation to give them a group briefing, thereby obviating the need to continually repeat the briefing to each one of them. The matters to be covered in such a meeting (or individually with each witness if a group meeting is not feasible) are reviewed in the next section.

## Initial Briefing of Witnesses

Prior to going through the actual questions and answers to be used in the hearing, it is helpful to give all witnesses an initial briefing about the case and about the arbitration process. This permits each witness to understand the case in its entirety and to see how his or her testimony fits into the whole. In addition, it helps the witness from being blind-sided on cross-examination concerning possible conflicts in testimony given by other witnesses. Having an understanding of the format of the hearing and the rationale underlying the arbitration process, the witnesses will feel more confident about testifying. As discussed above, this briefing can be done in a group meeting when a number of witnesses are present at the same time. Whether the briefing is done in a group setting or individually, the important point is that it be done.

The principal items to be covered in an initial briefing of a witness are as follows.

1. The issues to be decided by the arbitrator.
2. The key unrebutted facts.
3. The contested facts in the case and each side's evidence as to those contested facts, including a description of the anticipated testimony of each side's key witnesses.
4. The advocate's theory of the case and the key contractual provisions that will be relied on.
5. An explanation to each witness of the significance of his or her testimony and how it relates to the rest of the case.
6. How an arbitration hearing proceeds, the physical setting, the persons participating, the order of events, the function of the arbitrator, and so on. It is sometimes feasible to cover the "Witnesses' Dos and Don'ts" at this stage, although it is usually preferable to cover these points during the question and answer phase of the preparation.

## Putting Witnesses at Ease

Inexperienced advocates, and even many experienced ones, have little appreciation for the apprehension and anxiety felt by most persons who are required to testify. For most people testifying in a hearing is a very stressful and unnatural experience. Even those who appear to be at ease with the idea of testifying often feel anxious about taking the witness chair, especially as the time for testifying grows nearer. Persons who testify usually take their responsibilities very seriously and feel that their own credibility and their stature in their respective organizations (union or management) are at risk. As a result of this stress, the quality of their testimony may be affected. The advocate should therefore make a special effort to minimize the apprehension likely to be felt by witnesses.

The means of doing this will depend on the style of the advocate, the personality of the witness, the degree of apprehension exhibited by the witness, and the nature of the case. As discussed above, a description of the arbitration process will usually help to alleviate some concerns. Other techniques that are sometimes used include putting the case into its proper perspective (e.g., "This is not a Supreme Court case"); describing comments made by other apprehensive witnesses in prior cases about how easy testifing was; assuring them that simply telling the facts as they know them makes it a painless process; and explaining how well prepared they will be, after going over the questions and answers that will be asked, to anticipate questions on cross-examination from the other side.

## Refreshing Recollections

A common problem with witnesses is remembering details of events or situations that are essential parts of the case. Whether the problem is initial poor perception, weak memory, or perhaps confusion, the lack of good recollection and the ability to testify with a reasonable degree of certainty can seriously impair the value of a witness. In some cases the recollection may be somewhat vague but nevertheless sufficient to use even if it cannot be enhanced. In other cases it may be so imprecise that unless the recollection can be improved, the testimony is worthless. In either event the advocate needs to devote some time and effort to refreshing the witness's recollection.

There are a number of techniques that can be employed to refresh a witness's recollections, among which are the following.

1. Have the witness review notes, records, transcripts of previous testimony, or other documents relating to the poorly recollected event or situation.
2. Show the witness photographs, videotapes, or other graphic representations. Accompany the witness to the scene of the event to be recollected and walk through the sequence of occurrences.

3. Have the witness discuss the matter with others who were present at or have knowledge about the event or situation.
4. Instruct the witness to take ample time free of distractions to write out a complete description of the poorly recollected matter.
5. Have the witness relax, close his or her eyes, and attempt to visualize the situation. The advocate can ask questions, suggest alternatives, and attempt to draw out the witness on uncertainties.
6. Ask the witness about the matter in different ways, using different words and different perspectives.

In attempting to enhance the recollections of a witness, the advocate should be careful to avoid putting too much pressure on the witness to remember something that is not in the witness's memory and to avoid prompting recollections in the witness's mind that have never been there. Witnesses are normally predisposed to help their side of the case, and they want to assist the advocate who is representing their side in every way possible. Starting with such a cooperative orientation, many witnesses are susceptible to influences that will fill in memory gaps in order to help their side's case. It is unethical for an advocate to knowingly induce the filling of gaps where the witness does not have a bona fide recollection.

## Preparing Direct Examination

The central aspect of preparing a witness to testify is to develop the questions and answers that will constitute direct examination of the witness. The witness needs to know exactly what questions will be asked by the advocate who presents him or her as a witness and what answers to those questions will be most effective.

### Outline of Witnesses and Points to be Covered

In Chapter 4 it was suggested that an outline be prepared containing the facts to be proved and the corresponding evidence (testimonial, documentary, and other) to prove each fact. Relying on that chart (Figure 4-1) and any other information that has come to light, the advocate should make a corresponding list of each witness and the facts to be established by each. The list need not be detailed, but should be helpful in ensuring that nothing is forgotten as each witness's testimony is being prepared. An example of such a list is shown in Figure 6-1.

**Figure 6-1.**
**List of Witnesses and the Facts to be Proved by Each**

| Witness | Facts |
|---|---|
| Pete Smith | - History of mfg. of sprocket gears<br>- Background—crewing, schedules, etc.<br>- Statements by crew foremen |
| Wally Price | - History of mfg. of sprocket gears<br>- Previous grievances—gear mfg.<br>- Testimony of plant mgr.—1988 case |
| Ben Tyson | - Bargaining history re subcontr.<br>- Previous grievances—subcontr.<br>- Industry practices—subcontr. |
| Dr. Ann Hodge | - Productivity/Cost Analysis |

## *Method of Recording Questions and Answers*

Advocates use different techniques for ensuring that the questions and answers developed by the advocate in cooperation with the witness in the process of preparing the testimony are the ones used in the hearing. Some advocates have the exact text of the questions and answers typewritten and give a copy to the witness. Others prefer to use simply an outline or rough notes to prompt the advocate in asking the witness questions during the hearing. The author's preference is to have the specific wording of questions and answers developed during the preparation in handwritten form but for the advocate alone to use them. The reasons for this are several.

First, it is important that the specific wording and sequence of the questions be the same in the hearing as mutually worked out during preparation. If the wording and/or the order of questions asked of the witness in the hearing differs from that developed during preparation, the witness may become confused and provide incorrect answers. Second, it is useful to leave the questions in handwritten form as they are developed in the preparation. If they are in typewritten form and seen by the arbitrator in the hearing (which they are likely to be), it could convey the sense that a script has been prepared and that the witness is merely reciting the lines of that script. Third, it is, in the author's opinion, generally not a good idea to give the witness a copy of the questions and answers. The witness should *know* the answers to the questions, and the answers should be given in as natural a way as possible, with the witness's own words coming directly from the witness's memory. If the specific answers are given to the witness in writing, there is a distinct possibility that the witness will memorize or try to memorize the exact words of the answer. If that is done, the answers given in the hearing are apt to sound rehearsed and unnatural. This will detract from the witness's credibility. Moreover, if the witness recites the answers because they were on a sheet of paper rather than because they came from his or her recollections, he or she is less likely to respond effectively to questions on cross-examination.

## Reviewing the Background of the Witness

It is customary to begin the questioning of a witness on direct examination by identifying the witness and reviewing his or her status with respect to the collective bargaining relationship and the matters at issue in the case. A typical set of preliminary questions from a union negotiator would be as follows.

*Q.* What is your name?
*A.* Ben Tyson.

*Q.* What is your position with the union?
*A.* President of Local 77.

*Q.* How long have you held that position?
*A.* Six and a half years.

*Q.* Prior to that office, did you hold any other positions with the union?
*A.* Yes, previously I was secretary-treasurer of Local 77 for five years, and before that I was a shop steward for thirteen years.

*Q.* Are you employed by XYZ Corporation?
*A.* Yes.

*Q.* In what capacity and for how long?
*A.* I am a maintenance electrician, and have held that position for twenty-five years since I was hired by XYZ.

*Q.* Have you ever negotiated a labor contract on behalf of Local 77?
*A.* Yes, I was chief spokesperson for Local 77 for the last three labor agreements, and before that I served as a member of Local 77's bargaining committee for five contracts.

*Q.* Were you the union's chief spokesperson for the labor agreement under which the grievance in this case is being arbitrated?
*A.* Yes, I was.

Although leading questions (i.e., questions that suggest the answer sought by the questioner) are generally not permitted on direct examination, and compound questions (i.e., several inquiries contained in a single question) are frowned upon, most arbitrators will permit leading and compound questions on such preliminary matters as those covered just above in order to quickly cover noncontroversial background information. The above information could be elicited somewhat more efficiently as follows.

*Q.* Your name and position with the union, please?
*A.* Ben Tyson, president of Local 77.

*Q.* Is it true that you were president of Local 77 for six and a half years, and before that secretary-treasurer for five years, and prior to that a shop steward for thirteen years?
*A.* Yes.

*Q.* Have you been employed by XYZ Corporation as a maintenance electrician?
*A.* Yes.

   . . . etc.

It is not suggested that the advocate use the second and somewhat more expeditious approach. There are, in fact, some good reasons for avoiding it. First, it does not save all that much time. Second, it can give the appearance that the witness is not very bright or does not have a good recollection because he or she must be led in the questioning. Consequently, the advocate is usually better advised to utilize conventional questions to elicit even preliminary matters on direct examination. Leading questions are, however, very valuable on cross-examination, and these are discussed later in this chapter and in Chapter 11.

Although it is helpful to establish the background of a witness to put the testimony in better perspective, the advocate should be careful not to overdo these questions. The arbitrator does not need, and likely does not want to know, the life history or even the work history of every witness. What the arbitrator needs and wants to know about the witness is the experience and institutional history that the witness brings to his or her testimony in cases in which that experience and history gives credence to the matters to which the testimony is directed. Thus, if the dispute concerns the parties' intent concerning ambiguous contract language, a witness's history in negotiations is important to know. If, however, a witness is going to testify simply about the time of day when he or she saw the grievant report to a work site, for example, it is not necessary to cover much, if any, of the witness's background.

## Order of Questions

Usually, it is important not only to ask the right questions, but to ask them in the order that is easiest for the witness to remember and that will be easiest for the arbitrator to follow.

### Laying a Foundation

As a general rule, it is usually necessary to have the witness explain how it is that he or she has the knowledge or perception of the matters contained in the testimony, that is, to lay a foundation for a witness to testify about a particular matter. Thus, if a witness is going to testify about events that occurred just prior to an accident in a plant, it must be shown that the witness was at or around the location where the events occurred and was in a position to observe what happened; or if a witness is going to testify about how customers are served by sales clerks, the witness must show that he or she has worked as a sales clerk or is otherwise knowledgeable about how that service is delivered. In other words, the witness must usually provide testimony that will show the arbitrator that the witness has first-hand knowledge of the facts about which he or she is testifying.

In some cases the preliminary questions about the job or status of a witness will automatically reveal the foundation for the testimony. For example, if the witness has been identified as a plant manager and is asked to describe the process of manufacturing widgets, it will generally be accepted that the plant manager has sufficient knowledge with which to describe the process, but simply identifying a witness as a plant guard will not automatically establish a foundation that the witness observed a person leave through the plant gate on a particular day.

Generally, the foundation should be laid just prior to the questions relating to the matters requiring a foundation, but it is often possible to lay a foundation for all matters by covering the witness's background and perceptions at one time. Thus, if a witness is going to testify about several separate matters, for example, the plant manager in the grievance above concerning sprocket gears, it may be possible to provide a comprehensive description of his or her previous experiences at the outset of the testimony to show that the witness has sufficient knowledge and perception of the facts about which he or she is going to testify. The plant guard who is going to testify as to observations of employees entering and exiting through the plant gate over the course of several weeks, however, will need to testify as to his or her presence and ability to observe the subject of the testimony on each of the days that the testimony is concerned with.

### Chronological Order

Once a proper foundation has been laid, there are no hard and fast rules about the order in which questions should be asked. What is important is that the questioning follow a more or less logical or rational sequence. The advocate should always be conscious of the arbitrator and the arbitrator's need to follow the testimony. The order of questions should not confuse or mislead the arbitrator. The advocate should always keep in mind that a story is being told and that the events and characters in the story should be introduced in a sequence that best relates the story and in a way that presents the advocate's case in its most persuasive light.

A common and usually preferable order of questioning is a chronological one. This is especially true for testimony concerning past events or occurrences. If a witness is going to testify about an event or series of events, it makes sense to begin with the earliest one and proceed to the most recent one. In some cases the time sequence best follows a reverse chronological order, that is, beginning with the most recent event and proceeding to the earlier ones. For example, in the case of an employee being discharged for absenteeism following previous warnings for excessive absences, it would be appropriate to begin with the final absence from work that was the cause of the discharge and proceed to the earlier instances of absenteeism that formed part of the justification for the termination.

### Order of Importance of Other Factors

In some cases chronological order in presenting evidence may not be especially significant. A series of events, decisions, or conditions may need to be introduced, but what is most significant about them is not when they occurred, but how and/or why they occurred. Forcing them into a chronological sequence may be artificial or may obscure the main import of the evidence. For example, the employer may have instituted a series of changes in work procedures that caused a job to carry much more responsibility than when the wage rate for that job was originally negotiated, thereby entitling incumbents in that job to higher rates of pay. The union wants to introduce evidence of the job changes and wants to emphasize the nature of the changes, how they relate to one another, and how they have made the job requirements much more demanding. The specific periods of time in which the changes were made may be rather incidental, and following a chronological sequence may even be confusing. The advocate in such a case should not feel bound to follow a time sequence if some other order makes more sense.

When there is doubt about which order to follow, the advocate should ask, ''What are the most important facts that support my case?''

Frequently, this will point up the best order to follow. Leading from strength is always a good rule of thumb, and there is a risk of losing the impact of persuasive evidence by not getting it before the arbitrator as soon as possible in the case. In fact, waiting to introduce key evidence may give the impression that the evidence is not as important as argued by the advocate. Therefore, if the story can be told more simply and convincingly by following an order of questions other than a chronological one, it should be done.

## Molding the Questions and Answers

There are innumerable ways to present testimony, some of which will be more persuasive than others. One mark of an effective advocate is shaping the questions and answers in such a way as to achieve maximum persuasion and clarity.

### *Framing Questions*

The advocate should always be sensitive to the various ways in which questions can be asked of each witness. The same body of information can be elicited in many ways. Various forms of questions may all seek the same information, but the specificity and the phrasing of each form, as well as the tone in which the question is delivered, may differ significantly. The following comparisons illustrate this point.

A. *Q1.* Were you at work on Saturday?
   *Q2.* Were you on duty in the finishing department between the hours of 4 and 6 P.M. on Saturday, November 5?

B. *Q1.* How did the crew feel about the change in work schedules?
   *Q2.* Did *any* members of the crew express to you their reaction about the company's change in work schedules? [follow-up question] If so, what was said and by whom?

C. *Q1.* Why were you late for work that day?
   *Q2.* Was there anything that prevented you from reporting to work at your regular reporting time on Tuesday, February 18?

D. *Q1.* What has been your previous experience with work done by Mr. Smith?
   *Q2.* Have there been any previous occasions on which Mr. Smith's work performance was not satisfactory? [follow-up question] If so, please identify and describe each such instance.

Note that the differences in the framing of these question are not dramatic and some require a follow-up question to elicit the desired information. Nevertheless, the second question in each of the four examples is more likely to lead to precise and helpful answers. The second alternative in set A pins down the information to the specific time and place about which the advocate is going to inquire. The first question in set B is likely to be objectionable in that it calls the witness to probe into the psyche of each of the crew members to ascertain their feelings. The alternative, however, merely asks the witness to relate what the crew members actually said about the schedule change. The first question in set C puts the witness somewhat on the defensive, whereas the second choice implies that there was some presumably outside cause that precluded a timely reporting to work. The first question in set D appears to ask the witness for all of his or her experiences with Mr. Smith's work, whereas the second seeks only the unsatisfactory aspects of that work.

Advocates seldom have the time or inclination to analyze in minute detail each and every question that will be asked of each witness. Normally, such attention to detail is neither necessary nor practicable. Nevertheless, the advocate should be careful in framing those questions that are critical to the case and in formulating questions that may, during preparation, be giving the witness problems in answering appropriately. If a witness repeatedly hesitates or stumbles over an answer during preparation, it may be a sign that the question is not well framed, at least for this particular witness. The advocate should try to rephrase the question, break it into several parts, or perhaps transfer it to a different part of the witness's testimony. In a different context of questions it may be easier for the witness to remember and phrase a good answer. Sometimes when preparing a witness it is helpful to simply let the witness take a few minutes to explain in his or her own words the substance and the background of the information to be elicited. This background and additional information may better enable the advocate to frame the question in a form more comfortable to the witness.

### Structuring Answers

Even more important than the wording of questions is the framing of answers. Beginning with the premise that the advocate's own witnesses will give only truthful answers, one of the most important tasks in preparing a witness to testify is to ensure that each answer puts the truthful information in its most favorable light. This means that each answer contains only truthful information but is presented in a form that makes it most believable, reasonable, and persuasive. This is sometimes a challenging task but is one that can vitally affect the credibility and the impact of testimony.

As an initial guiding principle, a witness's natural answers should not be modified unless it is really necessary to do so. Witnesses will be much more credible and consistent if they answer questions in their own words. This is particularly true when the witness is testifying on cross-examination. In cross-examination the same question may be asked in several forms and contexts. A witness is more likely to withstand grueling cross-examination and do so credibly if he or she is relating back to answers given under direct examination if those answers came naturally rather than having been shaped and molded during the preparation stage.

Nevertheless, there will be times when the witness's automatic and natural answers to a question will not help the case and may do significant damage. In such cases modifications of answers are necessary. For example, an employee has been discharged for sleeping on the job. The employee's supervisor previously claimed, and is expected to testify in the hearing, that he saw the employee sitting in a chair with his eyes closed and was sleeping and that the employee remained in that position for five minutes, after which the supervisor shook the employee awake. In interviewing the employee initially the union advocate asks the employee if he was sleeping, and the answer is, "Yes, I suppose I was." The advocate asks the employee how he knows he was sleeping, and the employee replies, "I don't remember seeing the supervisor in front of me, but I do remember him telling me to wake up." How does an advocate handle such a problem? First, it is important to instruct the witness that only the truth should be told and that there is to be no misstating the facts. Second, it is helpful to explain to the witness that an honest, yet understandable, explanation of the facts may lead the arbitrator to mitigate the penalty of discharge. The following testimony can put the facts in their best possible light.

> *Q.* Were you in the control room on the graveyard shift on Monday, April 3?
>
> *A.* Yes.
>
> *Q.* Where were you located in that room between 1:00 and 1:30 A.M.?
>
> *A.* I was seated in the swivel chair in the center, front part of the room.
>
> *Q.* What were you doing while you were seated in the chair?
>
> *A.* I was monitoring the gauges on the control panel.
>
> *Q.* Did you see Supervisor Harry Range between 1:15 and 1:30 that morning?

*A.* Yes, I did.

*Q.* Where was he?

*A.* He was standing to my left, and he had his hand on my arm.

*Q.* Did he say anything?

*A.* Yes, he said, "Wake up, Pete."

*Q.* Did he say that more than once?

*A.* Yes, I believe that he said it twice.

*Q.* Were you sleeping on the job?

*A.* I honestly can't say for sure. I know I had no intention of sleeping, but it is possible that I dozed off for a few minutes when Harry was in the control room.

*Q.* Why do you think that you dozed off?

*A.* I know Harry was in the Control Room when he talked to me, but I wasn't aware of his presence in the room until he spoke to me.

*Q.* Is there any reason why you might have dozed off?

*A.* Yes, my youngest son was taken to the hospital with a case of ptomaine poisoning the day before, and my wife and I were at the hospital for twenty-four straight hours. I only had about two hours sleep in the forty-eight hours before the shift in question.

*Q.* Why didn't you call in to be excused?

*A.* I knew the relief control room operator was on vacation that week and that if I didn't show up the company would really be in a bind.

*Q.* Did you intend to sleep on the job that night?

*A.* No, in fact I took two caffeine tablets about an hour before going on shift in order to stay awake.

*Q.* If you had intended to go to sleep while on duty, was there some place you could have done so with less chance of being caught?

*A.* Yes. Some other employees have told me that they have occasionally been able to get some sleep in the men's room or in the supply room in the basement and that no one ever bothered them.

*Q.* Have you ever slept or even dozed off on the job in your previous fifteen years with the company?

*A.* No.

Many labor arbitrators have refused to uphold discharges for sleeping on the job when it appears that it was unintentional and there are extenuating circumstances. By being honest, yet emphasizing the inadvertent and exceptional reasons explaining the employee's condition, there is a good chance of avoiding the discharge. It may be necessary, however, as in the above example, to mold the employee's testimony in order to put the infraction in its most favorable light.

In modifying testimony to present the best perspective it is incumbent on the advocate to thoroughly prepare the witness for cross-examination. The fact that the natural responses to questions are being altered may present the witness with some difficulty in handling cleverly formulated questions on cross-examination. Preparing witnesses for cross-examination is discussed later in this chapter.

## INSTRUCTIONS TO WITNESSES

Regardless of the type of case or the personality of the witness, some general guidelines should be given to witnesses to help them deliver more effective testimony. Sometimes in the rush to prepare a case, the advocate neglects to pass on these guidelines to witnesses. For this reason, a list of instructions has been prepared for the advocate to use in preparing the witness, or at least to give to the witness in advance of the hearing. That list of instructions is contained in Figure 6-2. The list contains all of the items to be discussed in this section.

**Figure 6-2.**
**Checklist**

---

### *CHECKLIST—INSTRUCTIONS TO WITNESSES*

Your participation as a witness is important to the case, and your testimony will be much more effective if you observe the following instructions.

1. **First Rule.** The most important thing to remember is to tell *the truth*. You may give your answers in a way that puts your testimony in its most favorable light, but in doing so do not vary from what is truthful.
2. **Dress.** Please wear neat, clean, and conservative clothes. You do not need to wear formal clothes, but you should appear businesslike. When in doubt, wear the type of clothes that you might wear to a business meeting, church gathering, or professional performance.
3. **Grooming.** Hair should be at a reasonable length and neatly trimmed and combed. Men should be clean-shaven, or if they have facial hair, it should be neatly trimmed. Women should appear with an appropriate amount of cosmetics, avoiding excessive makeup and jewelry. You will be judged not only by what you say, but how you look.

4. **Demeanor.** This simply refers to how you conduct yourself—your facial expressions, your body language, and the kind of image you present. Avoid aggressive, hostile, evasive, and uncooperative conduct. You want to appear to be a reasonable, believable, and thoroughly honest person. Whether you are inside or outside the hearing room, men should conduct themselves as gentlemen and women as ladies. No foul or loud language should be used. When the other side's witnesses are testifying, do not make facial expressions of disbelief or say anything (or make any sounds) to contradict or put down their testimony.

5. **On the witness stand.** Focus your primary attention on the person asking you the questions. Make eye contact with him or her. This will help you to understand all the questions asked you, and will make you more believable. Occasionally, you may want to look at the arbitrator and address your answer to him or her. Sit erect while you are testifying, be polite and serious (without being somber). An occasional smile helps. Speak clearly and with enough volume so that everyone in the hearing room can hear you.

6. **Understanding each question.** Do not attempt to answer any question unless you understand what is being asked. If you did not hear the question or are not sure what has been asked, ask the questioner to repeat or rephrase the question. If you want to clarify a question, you may ask the questioner, "Are you asking if . . .". In order to make sure you understand the specific question being asked, focus on the key questioning word, such as "who," "what," and "when."

7. **Be natural—don't memorize.** Your testimony will be much more effective if you come across as natural—not artificial. Therefore, the more relaxed, open, and forthcoming you appear, the more believable you will be. Do not try to memorize your testimony, because it will not appear as your words. Keep in mind the main points and put them into your own words (as you have reviewed them with your advocate in advance of the hearing).

8. **Be alert for the opposing advocate.** No matter how friendly and accommodating the advocate for the other side appears, make no mistake that he or she is trying to get you to testify to something that will help their case. This does not mean that you should not give truthful answers, but rather that you should be on your guard, and attempt to put your answers in the light that is most favorable to the side for which you are testifying.

9. **Leading Questions.** During cross-examination you can expect the opposing advocate to ask you leading questions. These are questions that point you in the direction of the answer, such as "It's true isn't it that . . .?", "So you then decided to . . .didn't you?" "It's fair to say, isn't it, that . . . .?". These questions are designed to have you give the testimony desired by the other side. If the answer they point to is the

correct and *the best* answer you can give, go ahead and give it. If, however, the answer called for by the leading question makes you uncomfortable, is not completely true or accurate, or casts a misleading light on the truth, you should give the answer that is truthful, accurate, and most enlightening.

10. **Control your emotions.** Regardless of how hostile or demanding the opposing advocate is to you, do not lose your temper or self control. By doing so, you will simply look less believable to the arbitrator, and you may accidentally say something that is not true or helpful to your testimony.

11. **Answer only the question that is asked.** It is especially important that you *answer only the question that is asked.* If you can answer with a simple yes or no (and feel comfortable with your answer), *STOP* after you've given the simple answer. Do not feel that you have to offer more explanation. If the advocate for your side feels that you left out something important, he or she will give you an opportunity later in the hearing to explain it more fully. However, many witnesses get themselves (and their side of the case) into trouble by offering additional information beyond that called for by the question.

12. **Do not guess at an answer.** If you're not sure of the answer to a question, *do not guess.* You should (assuming you understand the question being asked) either say "I don't know" or "I don't recall." It is important to understand the difference between these two phrases. "I don't know" means that you never (now or in the past) had the knowledge to answer the question. "I don't recall" means that at some point in the past you knew the answer to the question, but at the present time you don't remember. If you know the answer to part of a question, but not all of it, answer the part you know and explain the part that you don't know or don't recall. If you have a recollection of something, but are not absolutely sure, you may answer, "to the best of my recollection." However, don't use that phrase if you are very sure of your answer, or if you are very unsure. If you are very certain of your answer, simply say, "I saw," "I heard," etc. If you are very unsure, say "I don't recall" or "I don't know."

13. **Mistakes.** Everyone makes mistakes from time to time, and if you discover that you have made a mistake in your testimony, the best thing to do is to admit it, and, if possible, explain what caused you to make the mistake ("I forgot about . . ."). In some cases you may do this while you are in the midst of testifying. In other cases, it is better to wait until you have completed your testimony, and explain the mistake to your advocate. He or she will then assess how the mistake can best be corrected. If you correct the mistake, do not say "I lied," but simply say, "I made a mistake when I said. . .".

14. **Objections.** If your advocate or the advocate for the other side makes an objection, stop your testimony and wait for the arbitrator to rule on

the objection. The arbitrator will rule on the objection by saying, "overruled," which means you will answer the question, or, "sustained," which means that you will not answer the question. Listen carefully to the objection and the arguments being made by both advocates concerning the objection. Sometimes the things they say can help you to provide a better answer to the question if you eventually have to answer it.

15. **When not testifying.** You will spend most of your time in the hearing listening to the advocates and the testimony of other witnesses. You should be attentive to everything that is going on—especially the testimony of the other side's witnesses. Have a note pad and pencil or pen to write down anything that you think is not truthful, accurate, or that should otherwise be brought to the attention of your advocate. He or she will be too busy during the questioning of the other witnesses to discuss these matters with you. Make a note of the important points and discuss them with your advocate at a recess or other appropriate time.

## Dress, Decorum, and Demeanor

Appearances and manner are important factors affecting our relationships with others. They are no less important in an arbitration hearing. Arbitrators can be significantly influenced, favorably or unfavorably, by the way witnesses appear and act. These factors may seem to be superficial matters, but they convey impressions that will influence the arbitrator's perception of the evidence.

### Clothing and Grooming

It is important for witnesses to be appropriately dressed for the hearing. This does not mean that a witness needs to wear his best suit or her best dress or be "fancy" in any way. In fact, overly formal or ostentatious dress is likely to convey the wrong message. Clothing should be neat and clean and should be appropriate for the witness. A male office worker or supervisor might be expected to wear a suit or sport coat with a dress shirt and tie if that clothing is normally worn on the job. A female service worker may be expected to wear a skirt or slacks with a color-coordinated blouse. Employees who wear uniforms at work may appear in the hearing in uniform if there is a logical reason for doing so (e.g., just finished or just ready to start work). The important thing is that the witness appear neat and clean and have a businesslike appearance. When in doubt, dress up.

Grooming is likewise important. Hair should be at a reasonable length and have a neat, well-trimmed appearance. Men should be clean-shaven, unless they normally wear a moustache or beard, in which case the facial hair should be neatly trimmed. Women should avoid excessive makeup and ostentatious jewelry. When in doubt, witnesses should be conservatively groomed.

### Decorum

Without being unnatural, witnesses should conduct themselves in as professional a manner as possible at all times in the hearing room and in adjacent areas where they can be seen by the arbitrator. This means avoiding loud talk, foul or crude language, overly casual posture and positions (e.g., slouching or putting one's feet on a chair or table), arguing with others, and inappropriate gestures or facial expressions (e.g., frowning or shaking one's head or rolling one's eyes while an opposing witness is testifying). Other things being equal, arbitrators are more inclined to rule in favor of the side that presents courteous, well-mannered witnesses than one whose witnesses are an embarrassment.

### Demeanor

It is a well-accepted concept in the law that judges and juries decide the truthfulness and reasonableness of testimony in part based on the demeanor of the witness, that is, the way the witness looks and speaks while testifying. This concept is no less significant in labor arbitration. The way a witness appears during questioning impacts the way the testimony is received. Thus, a witness who looks the interrogating advocate in the eye while the question is being asked and looks at the arbitrator (at least periodically) while giving the answers is apt to be more believed than one who looks away or otherwise fails to make eye contact. The witness who gives straightforward answers without undue pauses, stammering, and contradictions is much more believable than one that has to think about the questions and answers for long periods of time and who gives answers that appear to be uncertain and devised solely for the hearing. The witness who waits until the question is asked before answering and who remains silent while an objection is being resolved is given more credence than one who interrupts or insists on speaking even though his or her advocate is registering an objection. The witness who sits erect in the witness stand, smiles occasionally, and avoids hostility toward the opposing advocate is going to be more effective than one who does the opposite. Finally, the witness who is polite (without being unnaturally solicitous) and serious (without being somber) will make a stronger impression than one who is discourteous and unduly casual.

### Decorum and Demeanor When Not Testifying

The advice given above concerning decorum and demeanor is applicable not just when the witness is testifying, but at all times throughout the course of the hearing—inside and outside the hearing room. Witnesses should be reminded that arbitrators are always looking for clues to the character and credibility of witnesses, and that search begins from the moment the arbitrator walks into the building in which the hearing is conducted. Facial expressions, statements, posture, and overall conduct of witnesses throughout the period preceding, during, and following the hearing can influence the arbitrator. A witness who grimaces at the testimony of the other side's witnesses, sighs during extended examination or cross-examination, uses profanity in the hallway outside the hearing room during breaks, and engages in similar conduct will weaken the quality of his or her testimony. Advocates should caution each witness to act with propriety at all times, and advocates should monitor the conduct of their witnesses throughout the hearing.

### Focusing on the Questions

As the preparation of witnesses proceeds, the advocate should concentrate more and more on how questions are framed and what answers are elicited from the questions. The advocate's ear needs to be tuned to how the questions and answers sound and how they are likely to be perceived by the arbitrator.

*Nonresponsive Answers.* Witnesses need to be constantly reminded to listen to each question and to answer only the question that is asked. A common failing of witnesses is paying insufficient attention to the questions being asked and providing answers that are not truly responsive to the questions posed. For example:

Q. Where did you get the tools to do the job?
A. From the supply room.
Q. Was there anyone there with you?
A. I always go in there by myself.

or

Q. Why weren't you at your regular work station at the time?
A. I was in the personnel office.

Of course, with careful preparation of the direct examination such nonresponsive answers can usually be avoided, but not all questions that are asked on cross-examination can be anticipated, and an effective witness needs to concentrate on each of the questions being asked in order to avoid giving a nonresponsive or incorrect answer. Obviously, some witnesses are naturally more precise and responsive than others in answering questions. For witnesses who have difficulty in providing precise answers, the following suggestions may prove helpful.

- Listen carefully to each question. If you have any doubt about what information is being sought, ask the questioner to repeat or rephrase the question.
- Prior to answering a difficult question, repeat the question silently to yourself before answering.
- Focus primarily on the key questioning word (who? what? where? when? why?) to determine what is being sought.

The problem with a witness who is prone to giving nonresponsive answers is not usually disastrous on direct examination, however, because it can normally be cured by repeating or rephrasing the question and focusing the witness's attention on the key information being sought, for example, "But, *what was the reason* that you weren't at your work station?" A related and potentially more serious problem, however, is the witness who provides more information than is sought by the question.

*Volunteering Information.* Some witnesses motivated by a desire to be helpful, to be complete, or simply because of carelessness or garrulousness have a tendency to provide answers that go beyond the range of the question. For example:

*Q.* Who did you see when you turned the corner?

*A.* Jim was there. He had just gone into the lunch room. I knew that he and Mary were going to be there, because they told me they would be having lunch around noon.

In this example the appropriate answer is a very simple one, "I saw Jim." Instead, the witness ventured far beyond the scope of the question and supplied information that was at best unnecessary and at worst potentially harmful. Volunteering information may or may not hurt the witness's testimony, but it constitutes an unnecessary risk because it provides information that goes beyond that sought by the examiner and opens up areas of inquiry that could later be damaging to the witness's case. Identifying the problem, however, is considerably easier than curing it, because witnesses who volunteer are not easily converted into witnesses who provide more limited and structured answers.

The advocate will need to take some time during preparation to address the problem of witnesses who habitually provide answers that extend beyond the questions asked. First, the witness should be given a thorough explanation of the harm created by the practice. The advocate should make it clear that the witness helps only the other side when he or she gives answers that extend beyond the question. The opposing advocate is given information that he or she likely would not have obtained any other way. Another disadvantage is that the witness is likely to be in the witness chair longer by extending the answers. This is not solely because the extended answers take longer, but also because the extra information may trigger additional questions on cross-examination, many of which will be more difficult to answer than the original question asked. Moreover, it often makes the witness appear naive or even stupid, because he or she is unable to provide simple, straightforward answers to questions.

Sometimes merely explaining the problem to the volunteering witness is not enough. Some witnesses need to be shown. One helpful way is for the advocate to relate an anecdote or example from an actual case in which a witness's volunteering got him or her into trouble. If the advocate cannot think of such an anecdote, the following may prove useful.

> In a case in which a grievant had been terminated for insubordination in telling a supervisor that he would not perform a particular assigned task, the supervisor was being interrogated by his own counsel. Counsel asked, "Was there any basis for Mr. Smith (the grievant) to refuse the assignment?" The appropriate answer was "no." However, the supervisor responded, "No, this was his work to do, and *just because some of the other guys turned it down* didn't mean that he could." Needless to say, the emphasized portion of the answer caused the advocate for the other side to ask a number of pointed questions of the supervisor when it was time for cross-examination.

Beyond impressing the witness with the importance of answering only the question asked, the advocate should coach the witness on how that can be accomplished. This can be done by using a simple exercise as the witness is being prepared to testify. Whenever the witness goes beyond the simple answer that is responsive to the question, the advocate should stop and ask the witness to repeat the question that was asked. When the witness responds, the advocate should then say, "What's the simple answer to that?" The witness will then usually provide the limited answer. The advocate then asks the witness to repeat the expanded answer he or she originally gave. The witness will usually realize the error before finishing the end of that answer and will come to appreciate the difference between simple answers that respond to the questions presented compared to expanded answers that go beyond the question. Every time the witness volunteers information, the advocate should repeat the exercise described above. It should not take more than a few repetitions of the exercise before the witness learns the lesson that the only information to be supplied is that which is directly responsive to the question asked.

*Answering Confusing, Unclear, or Imprecise Questions.* It is not at all uncommon for witnesses to be presented with questions that they do not understand or that are otherwise confusing to them. The fault may lie with the interrogator (either one of the advocates or the arbitrator) or with the witness. The question may be poorly phrased, out of context, vague, or subject to varying interpretations. Even if the question is a good one, the witness may not have heard it, may have had a lapse of concentration, or may have misunderstood the meaning or intent of the question. For whatever reason the witness is faced with the task of answering a question that he or she is unprepared to answer.

In such situations the worst course of action is for the witness to guess or surmise the information that is being sought by the question and to provide an answer without indicating his or her uncertainty about the question.

For example, in the context of a series of questions about a mechanical malfunction at the beginning of the witness's work shift, the witness is asked, "When did it start?" The witness presumes that the question refers to the time the work shift began, whereas the interrogator meant to inquire about when the malfunction first occurred. The likelihood for an incorrect answer is very high unless the witness clarifies the question. The witness might ask, "When did what start?" Of course, the advocate asking this question on direct examination should avoid or correct such imprecise wording during the preparation of the witness's direct testimony. If the question is posed on cross-examination, the witness's advocate should spot the vague wording and object ("Objection, question is vague and ambiguous") or merely request that the ambiguity be removed ("Mr./Ms. Arbitrator, we request that the question be clarified to specify what is being referred to by the word 'it' in the question"). The times that an advocate can caution a witness are limited, however, and witnesses need to be schooled to protect themselves.

The critical lesson for the witness to learn in these situations is, *if you don't understand exactly what is being asked for in a question, don't guess. Get the questioner to clarify the question.* This is easily done by simply requesting that the interrogator clarify the question or pose a specific inquiry concerning what is being asked, for example, "Do you mean what time did the shift start or are you asking what time did the malfunction start?" If the witness is relatively sure of the area of inquiry but has a marginal doubt, this problem can be handled with a specific answer, for example, '' The shift started at 8:00 A.M.'' or ''Assuming you mean the shift starting time, it was 8:00 A.M.''

*Answering Questions without Knowing the Answer.* It would seem very obvious that witnesses should not answer questions when they simply do not know the answers. Unfortunately, many witnesses do so. The reasons for this are many. Some witnesses do not want to admit that they lack certain knowledge or information that they would be expected to have, and they therefore provide an answer that they think fits. Others believe that the information they have about related matters can be extrapolated to apply to the immediate question, the answer to which they do not know. Others want to be cooperative with the interrogator and/or help their case and are ready to provide an answer they think the interrogator wants to hear, even though they do not know the answer from their own knowledge. The lesson for the witness in these cases is, do not answer a question unless you know the answer. Witnesses need to understand that it is okay to say, ''I don't know'' or ''I don't remember.'' Unless the information is something that the witness must surely know or remember, an arbitrator will understand the lack of knowledge or recollection.

In some cases the witness may not know the precise answer to a question but can give a fairly accurate approximation. Approximations may be much more helpful to the case than simple ''I don't know'' or ''I'm not sure'' answers. In such cases the witness should be instructed to come as close as possible to an accurate answer. For example:

*Q.* When did you first learn of the new procedure?

*A.* I can't say for certain, but I know it was after I had completed my probationary period in June, but before my first anniversary with the company, which was in late September.

or

*Q.* How far away were you from the two waiters when the argument started?

*A.* I can't give you a precise answer, but I estimate I was between ten and fifteen feet away from them. It was close enough that I could hear their voices quite clearly.

*Differences between Knowledge and Recollection.* Many witnesses confuse knowledge and recollection. They answer ''I don't know'' when they should say ''I don't recall'' and vice versa. Either way, they are unable to answer the question, but the reason they give for their inability to answer can have an impact on their credibility with the arbitrator. For example:

> *Q.* When were you promoted to foreman?
> *A.* I don't know. [Does not know? More likely, does not remember.]

or

> *Q.* Was there some reason why he might have "had it in for you?"
> *A.* I don't recall. [Surely, one would recall such a matter, if one knew in the first place, although one might not know the reason why someone felt a particular way.]

Witnesses should be cautioned about the distinctions between these two responses and instructed to use them appropriately. "I don't know" means the witness does not know the answer and never did know it. "I don't recall" means the witness knew the answer at some earlier time but cannot recollect it at the present time. In the preparation stage the advocate should be sensitive to information that cannot be recalled that would be helpful to the case and attempt to refresh or otherwise assist the witness to recollect the missing information. This may mean finding documents, persons, or other things that would help the witness to remember. Inevitably, though, there will be some information that a witness simply will not remember either because of the passage of time or the faintness of original perception or knowledge. What is stressed here is that the witness understand and convey his or her lack of recollection when the memory fails and lack of knowledge when the answer to the question was never within the witness's knowledge.

*Answers With "To the Best of My Recollection."* Another related and common mistake made by witnesses is to answer questions with the tag "to the best of my recollection" when it is not appropriate and to fail to add these words when it is appropriate. Some witnesses qualify their answers with the "best recollection" phrase when, in fact, their recollection is quite good and they have little or no doubt about their answer. Such witnesses are possibly motivated by the desire not to be too positive lest they be caught up later in an inconsistency. In other cases they may simply be parroting the phrase heard so commonly in trials on television and in films. Whatever the cause, witnesses should understand that the "best recollection" tag does indeed qualify their answer and therefore weakens it. An arbitrator will reasonably conclude that a witness who testifies to a fact based on his or her best recollection is admitting to less than a strong recollection and is conceding that the recollection may be inaccurate. Moreover, when juxtaposed with conflicting testimony without such a qualifier, "best recollection" testimony will come out second best. The lesson for the witness, therefore, is unless you are unsure of your recollection, do not use the words "to the best of my recollection."

This is not to say that the "best recollection" qualifier should not be used at all. On the contrary, there are many times when it should be used and it is not. Witnesses who might otherwise testify "I don't recall" might be able to relate certain facts or perceptions "to the best of my recollection" where their memory is sufficiently strong to extract key facets of the information or event. What the words mean is, "I don't have absolute recollection of these matters, but my memory of them is good enough that I feel I can honestly testify about them to the extent that I have." This allows the production of evidence that might otherwise be lost.

Another important reason for using the "best recollection" qualifier is to avoid being tripped up or discredited by conflicting evidence. The witness who testifies with certainty about a particular matter only to be contradicted later in the hearing by unimpeachable evidence to the contrary is likely to have suffered a mortal wound that will adversely impact all aspects of that witness's testimony. For this reason the witness who is not quite sure about the quality of his or her recollection should feel free to use it when it is appropriate. Too frequent use of it, however, will adversely impact the witness's testimony because it will appear that the witness's remembrance of a number of things in the past is not very good and therefore cannot be relied on.

Where the degree of recollection of particular aspects of facts or events varies, the witness should explain those items of which his or her recollection is strong and those of which it is weak. For example,

Q. What were the weather conditions on the day of the incident?
A. I don't remember exactly what the temperature was, although I would estimate it was between 50 and 60 degrees. I do recall specifically, however, that it rained most of the afternoon. There was also heavy fog in the area of the incident throughout the morning—I remember that well.

A witness can enhance credibility with the arbitrator by differentiating the degrees of recollection, particularly when such recollection is critical to the decision and the witness makes clear that he or she is cautious about potentially decisive testimony that depends on the quality of recollection.

## Manner and Style of Testifying

Witnesses are most effective when they are natural (not artificial), confident (not timid or arrogant), and straightforward (not confused, uncertain, or evasive). Although these characteristics are naturally present or lacking in a witness's manner, there are some techniques that a witness can utilize that will enhance credibility and persuasiveness.

## *Vocabulary*

The words used in hearing testimony should be those normally used by the witness (absent, of course, profanity or crude words) in normal daily use. The witness should not attempt to adopt a pseudo-sophisticated manner of speaking to impress an arbitrator. In addition, the witness should be careful to explain any jargon or special terminology that would be foreign to the arbitrator. Technical terminology ("biosensory stagnates"), acronyms ("ARCNET"), industry slang ("head rig"), and other such words or phrases should be explained in advance of, or simultaneously with, their use by the witness. Here the advocate must play a leading role. The advocate is more likely to be sensitive to the use of terminology that would be unfamiliar to the arbitrator and should make it a point during preparation to have the witness explain such terminology at the time it is used. If the witness finds it awkward or forgets to do so, the advocate should include appropriate questions during the direct examination to ensure that the arbitrator is not confused.

## *Addressing the Arbitrator and the Advocates*

Although witnesses do not frequently need to address the arbitrator, when they do it should generally be, "Mister Arbitrator" or "Madam Arbitrator." In more casual environments last names may be appropriate, for example, "Mr. Jones" or "Ms. Smith." Usually, witnesses do not directly address the advocates by name, but the author has seen it used with good effect by some witnesses. It is especially effective in referring to the advocate for the other side. For example (on cross-examination):

*Q.* Isn't it true that you lied to your supervisor?
*A.* No, Ms. Brown, it isn't true. I never lied to my supervisor.

If a witness is going to address an advocate by name, the last name should always be used, except in those rare situations where the parties have developed such a familiarity and informal procedure that to use last names would be artificial.

## *Articulation*

It is not usually feasible to change the style of a witness who has a tendency to speak unclearly or too rapidly. Most people cannot change their style of speaking beyond a few brief moments, after which they forget their instructions and revert to normal patterns of speech. Nevertheless, the advocate should work with witnesses who have such difficulties to attempt to clear up any major problems with speech and articulation. Asking a witness during preparation of the witness's testimony to repeat certain words, to speak louder, to slow down, and so on may help somewhat to overcome weaknesses in delivery that could seriously detract from the witness's testimony. More likely, the advocate will have to note these weaknesses in his or her hearing notebook (see Chapter 4) next to the questions and answers planned for the witness with articulation problems. During the witness's testimony the advocate can then ask the witness to repeat unintelligible words, speak more slowly or loudly, and so forth. Of course, if the problems are major and results do not improve after repeated attempts during hearing preparation, the decision to use such witnesses should be reconsidered by measuring the value of their testimony against the difficulties of comprehension.

## Significance of Word Selection in Answers

Earlier in this section the use of the words "to the best of my recollection" were discussed in terms of how they qualify (and usually weaken) a witness's testimony. There are a number of other qualifiers that can have the same effect. Use of the phrase "I believe so" is considerably weaker than "Yes." "You could be right" is considerably less positive than "Absolutely." Of course, the tone, inflection, and volume of the response will also make responses either more or less positive. Consider the following choices of responses to a question given by a supervisor as to whether she instructed a subordinate in the proper procedures for handling a detailed work task.

- "I think I did."
- "Yes."
- "Yes, I'm sure I did."
- "Absolutely, I gave her those instructions."

Many witnesses do not hear themselves, and do not fully appreciate the impression they give when they are testifying. With such witnesses the advocate must practice creative and sensitive coaching. Making a timid witness more forceful and an arrogant one milder requires real skill. It requires a perceptive eye and knowing ear for what is credible and persuasive. Moreover, it requires the greatest sensitivity for the ego and personality of the witness in order to motivate change and enlist cooperation without creating ill will or deflating the witness's self-image.

A good coach/advocate will use such phrases as "How would it sound if you said ...''; "Perhaps you might emphasize the word _____ a little more"; "I think the arbitrator will be more impressed if you say, _____.'' The advocate should not be shy about molding the testimony of the witness as long as the facts and statements are not falsified.

It is not practical to tailor the entire testimony of a witness to fit the most persuasive and credible style possible. In most cases there are, however, critical portions of a witness's testimony that can make or break a case. It is in these parts that the advocate needs to devote the greatest time and energy to enhance the witness's presentation.

### *Eye Contact*

Most witnesses are uncertain on whom they should focus their attention while answering questions. Although seasoned advocates will sometimes give contrary advice on this question, the author favors the style in which the witness looks directly at the inquiring advocate while the question is being asked and when the answer is being given. Occasionally, the witnesses should direct his or her attention to the arbitrator while delivering answers, particularly answers to critical questions. The reason for this suggested approach is that the witness should hear and understand each question as fully as possible. Focusing on the questioning advocate while the question is being asked is an important aid to understanding. Since the advocate asked the question, he or she is entitled to the witness's attention while the answer is being given. Moreover, such attention will allow the witness to detect the questioning advocate's facial expressions in the event the witness answers the wrong question or is otherwise inaccurate. In addition, the witness should periodically make eye contact with the arbitrator while testifying in order to acknowledge the authority and importance of the arbitrator and also to ensure that the arbitrator is following the train of the testimony.

## Correcting Errors in Testimony

Witnesses should be instructed to correct errors in their testimony as soon as they realize an error has been made. Although such errors are more likely to occur during cross-examination or during questioning by the arbitrator, they sometimes occur during direct examination as well. No one is perfect, and it is not unusual for a witness to misspeak, forget, or otherwise provide an incorrect or inaccurate answer. In order to avoid possible impeachment by the opposing advocate, the witness should acknowledge the error at the earliest possible time. For example, a witness earlier in her testimony had testified that the color of the customer's suit was gray and that his hair was brown. Later, realizing that an error was made, the witness should correct the erroneous testimony along the following lines.

> Mr. Reynolds, a few questions back you asked me to describe the customer who was in the store at the time of the incident. I said that he was about six feet tall, had brown hair, and was wearing a gray suit. I was partly wrong in that description. In fact, he had gray hair and was wearing a brown suit. I'm afraid I got a little mixed up with my colors.

Techniques that can be employed by the advocate to assist witnesses in correcting errors in their testimony that they fail to discover themselves are covered in Chapter 9.

## Assisting the Advocate When Not Testifying

Witnesses help their side's case when they provide credible, persuasive, and consistent testimony. They can also be of assistance when they are not testifying. Witnesses should be instructed that when they are not testifying, they should listen to the testimony of the other witnesses (especially those from the other side) and make notes of any portions of that testimony that are inconsistent with the facts as known by the witness. Some witnesses make the mistake of whispering in the ear of the advocate while the hearing is in progress in order to bring to the advocate's attention some aspect of testimony that they know to be false or inconsistent with other testimony. The problem with this approach is that the advocate is listening intently to the testimony and cannot afford to be interrupted by his or her own witnesses. By making notes of the items in question, the witnesses can bring those matters to the advocate's attention at the conclusion of direct examination or at some other timely break in the testimony.

## SPECIAL INSTRUCTIONS TO WITNESSES REGARDING CROSS-EXAMINATION

Most of the instructions outlined in the above section apply to cross-examination as well as to direct examination. There are some additional pointers, though, that advocates should impart to their witnesses that apply primarily, if not exclusively, to cross-examination.

168 How to Prepare and Present a Labor Arbitration Case

### Controlling One's Temper

Cross-examination can be a trying and sometimes traumatic experience for a witness. The opposing advocate may use tactics designed to trick the witness into giving inconsistent testimony, make the witness appear foolish or ill-prepared, or insinuate that the witness is not being truthful. Despite such tactics the witness must keep cool and respond truthfully to all questions. Losing one's temper or arguing with the opposing advocate simply plays into the hands of that advocate and can make the witness appear less credible or rational to the arbitrator. If the other side's advocate becomes too hostile or badgering, the advocate who offered the witness must come to the witness's aid with objections aimed at stopping such attacks (see Chapter 10 for ways that this can be done). Arbitrators who sense that a cross-examination is getting out of line will sometimes admonish the cross-examining advocate to back away from undue hostility. With or without such aid the witness must always maintain composure.

### Dealing with Leading Questions

Leading questions are those framed in such a way that the question suggests the answer sought by the questioner. Examples of leading questions are as follows.

Q. You shouted at her, didn't you?

Q. You're saying then that you were driving at about 60 miles per hour at the time?

Q. It's a fact, is it not, that prior to being hired at XYZ Corporation, you worked for ABC Enterprises and were fired by that company?

Q. No one told you to go to the rear entrance, did they?

Leading questions often make witnesses uncomfortable because they feel they are being forced into a corner with little room to move. Witnesses need to be cautioned about leading questions and about the fact that such questions are permitted on cross-examination. To minimize witnesses' discomfort and vulnerability, they should be instructed to focus on the substance of the question and provide the correct answer just as they would if the question were asked in an objective, nonleading fashion. Leading questions can be effectively blunted with straightforward answers; thus, the questions posed above may be answered as follows.

A. No, I did not shout at her.

A. No, I would not say that I was driving at about 60 miles per hour. I was driving at a speed no greater than 45 miles per hour.

A. It is a fact that I worked for ABC Enterprises before joining XYZ, but it is not true that I was fired by them. I left voluntarily.

A. No one specifically told me to go to the rear entrance.

## Stopping for Objections

When preparing the witness to testify, advocates should explain to witnesses that during the course of the hearing both of the advocates will likely be making objections. The purpose of objections is to cause the arbitrator to prohibit certain types of questions from being asked, to change the form of a question, or to keep out certain types of evidence. Witnesses should be instructed to stop testifying when an objection has been made. Because objections are designed to keep witnesses from answering particular questions, a witness should refrain from answering a question to which an objection has been raised until a ruling on the objection has been made. Otherwise, the witness may provide an answer that under the rules of evidence is not admissible evidence and that is harmful to the witness's testimony.

After the advocates and the arbitrator complete their discussion of the objection the arbitrator will rule on the objection, and the witness will be advised (by the arbitrator or the questioning advocate) whether the question must be answered. If the objection is sustained (the question is disallowed), the inquiring advocate will proceed to another question. If the objection is overruled (the question is permissible), the witness will be instructed to answer the question previously posed and must comply.

Because arguments concerning an objection often take a little while before the arbitrator rules on the objection, witnesses are likely to forget the specific question posed. It is usually wise, therefore, for the witness to request that the question be repeated, so that the proper answer is given.

## Listening to Objections

If a witness is bright or has previous experience in the witness chair, it is usually advisable to instruct him or her to listen carefully to the arguments of the advocates about the objection in order to be better prepared to answer the question. This is especially the case concerning questions posed on cross-examination. These questions are posed by the opposing advocate and objected to by the witness's advocate. By focusing on the arguments being made by the advocate for his or her side the witness can sometimes discover pitfalls in the question and perhaps realize the best way to frame the answer. For example:

> *Employer Advocate:* (on cross-examination) Ms. Glass, why do you think your relief, Mr. Branch, didn't report for work on time that day?
>
> *Union Advocate:* (whose witness is testifying) Objection, Mr. Arbitrator, the question calls for speculation, in that the witness cannot know what was in the mind of Mr. Branch, and besides, she previously testified that she had not talked to Mr. Branch for at least forty-eight hours before the time period in question.
>
> *Employer Advocate:* Mr. Arbitrator, the question is permissible, in that the witness does not need to speculate. She may have independent evidence as to the reason for Mr. Branch's failure to report.
>
> *Arbitrator:* I am going to overrule the objection. Ms. Glass, you may answer the question.
>
> *Witness:* I have no idea why Mr. Branch didn't report.

In this sequence the objection by the witness's advocate called the witness's attention to the fact that she should not guess the reason for her relief worker's failure to report. Without such an objection the witness may have speculated about, and advanced a reason why, she thought her coworker did not report, an answer that might have harmed her side's case. By listening to the objection the witness was indirectly cautioned by the advocate on her side not to speculate.

## ADDITIONAL WAYS TO ENHANCE THE TESTIMONY OF WITNESSES

Depending on the nature and gravity of the case, the importance of the witnesses in proving critical elements of the case, and the level of experience and competence of the witnesses, there are some additional ways of improving the witnesses' testimony. If the case is a particularly important one, the testimony of the witnesses is critical to a successful outcome, and the witnesses are neither very experienced nor competent, one or more of the following techniques may be advisable.

### Role Play Cross-Examination

In almost any type of case it is advisable to have the witness go through a simulated cross-examination. After adequate time has been spent going over the questions to be asked on direct examination, it is helpful to put the witness through a mock or simulated cross-examination. The advocate takes the role of the opposing advocate and asks the witness questions that are likely to be posed on cross-examination, trying to cover the substantive areas likely to be part of the cross-examination, and asking the questions in the same manner as would be expected from the opposing advocate. This means that a number of leading questions should be included, and the thrust of the questioning should be to attack the points made on direct examination.

While the questions in the simulated cross-examination are being answered, the advocate should evaluate the accuracy, credibility, and persuasiveness of the answers, especially focusing on the substance and tone of the answers as they are likely to be perceived by the arbitrator. The advocate should point out to the witness those answers that are not likely to be effective and suggest alternative phrasing, syntax, and emphasis. As long as the advocate does not encourage the witness to testify to anything other than what the witness knows or believes to be true, there is nothing unethical about assisting the witness in this regard.

### Questioning by a Different Advocate

One method of improving the realism of the cross-examination role play is to have a person other than the advocate who is preparing the witness for direct examination play the role of the opposing advocate. In other words, have a new face play the role of the opposing advocate. By doing so, the witness is more inclined to treat the simulation as a real cross-examination. In the arbitration hearing itself the witness will be confronted by an advocate different (and unquestionably less accommodating) from the one on his or her side who will be asking questions on direct. The closer the preparation is to reality, the better the witness will be able to handle the real cross-examination. Enlisting the assistance of another person to conduct the simulated cross-examination will bring the preparation much closer to reality.

### Prepare in the Actual Hearing Room

For much the same reason as using a different advocate to prepare for cross-examination, it is sometimes useful to do the actual preparation (direct and cross-examination) in the very room in which the hearing is to be held to make the simulation as realistic as possible.

In a large number of cases access to the actual hearing room will not be possible. If, however, the hearing room is at all unique (e.g., a court room or cramped quarters), if the witness is likely to be nervous or disoriented, and if the hearing room is easily accessible, this option may prove to be beneficial.

### Videotape the Witness's Testimony

Some persons have no idea how they come across as witnesses. This is especially true of those who have done little or no public speaking. Frequently, witnesses will mumble, speak very softly, look away from the interrogator, make distracting facial or hand gestures, or conduct themselves in other ways that distract or are otherwise not helpful to their testimony. Simply telling them about the negative tendency may not be sufficient to change their habits. Seeing themselves on video is likely to be a much more effective teacher to them and may provide some motivation to change.

In addition, videotaping the practice testimony allows the advocate and witness alike (and perhaps others assisting in the preparation) to evaluate the effectiveness of the testimony in general and the selection of questions and answers in particular. It is the closest thing possible to a dry run of the hearing.

# 7

# Preliminary Matters

The events covered in this chapter usually occur in advance of the hearing, some as much as weeks before the hearing day, and others only minutes in advance or even at the beginning of the hearing. Some matters, such as settlement and stipulations, often occur well in advance of the hearing, whereas others, such as exclusion and swearing of witnesses, are more likely to occur immediately prior to, or coincident with, commencement of the hearing. In any event, the well-prepared advocate should take them into consideration during the preparation phase to ensure that the case is ready for presentation when the hearing begins.

## COMPLIANCE WITH REQUESTS FOR PRODUCTION OF EVIDENCE

The term ''discovery'' relates to the procedures followed in civil and criminal litigation wherein each side has an opportunity to uncover the facts and arguments that the opposing side intends to use at trial. Included within the term are depositions (recorded testimony of potential witnesses), written interrogatories (written questions posed by one side and corresponding written answers provided by the other), and requests for documents relevant to the case.

## Applicability of Discovery to Labor Arbitration

Absent specific language in the controlling labor agreement or unless there are governmental regulations (in the case of public sector arbitration) that so provide, there is no general right to discovery in labor arbitration. In fact, one of the reasons for the simplicity, speed, and economy of arbitration, especially compared to civil litigation, is that there is no right to discovery (at least as that concept exists in state or federal litigation). In civil litigation hundreds, sometimes thousands, of hours are commonly spent and thousands of pages of documents are routinely provided in a single lawsuit to comply with discovery requests.

Notwithstanding the general unavailability of discovery in arbitration, advocates should not conclude that they are unable to obtain documents or information from the other side in order to prepare adequately for their cases, nor should they conclude that they are immune from having to provide such documents or information to the other side. The discussion in Chapter 4 outlines the types of information that may be obtained in advance of the hearing and the ways in which the advocate may proceed to obtain it.

## Compliance with Information Requests or Orders

Although requests for information typically precede the hearing by weeks or months, issues relating to the compliance with such requests may not present themselves (at least to the arbitrator) until the outset of the hearing. If either party has failed to comply with a requirement to produce documents or make available a witness who has been subpoenaed, the party making the request may seek a ruling by the arbitrator that the other side be sanctioned in some way that will remedy any unfairness created by the noncompliance. For example, if the union subpoenaed a company supervisor to testify about what occurred on the job on a particular day and the company refused to release the supervisor from duty to attend the hearing, the union might seek a ruling from the arbitrator to prohibit the employer from calling any other witnesses concerning such occurrences. If the employer had made it impossible for the supervisor to testify, the arbitrator might very well restrict the employer in the manner sought by the union.

The prudent advocate should therefore determine in advance of the hearing whether there are any information requests that the other side has not complied with. It is important that any such issues be dealt with before the hearing commences. Once the hearing has started, it may be too late to fully address the matter. Although certain witnesses and documents may be objected to by an advocate and excluded by the arbitrator at the time they are offered in evidence, unless some sanction is imposed by the arbitrator prior to the hearing reference to such evidence may be included in the opposing advocate's opening statement or referred to obliquely in other testimony, so that the damage cannot be undone.

## SETTLEMENT

Many long-time observers of the arbitration process insist that the best arbitration decisions are the ones that are never issued—because they are settled before being heard or before a ruling is issued. The author supports that point of view. In a grievance resolution agreed on by the parties both sides have an opportunity to consider all options and arrive at a compromise that each finds acceptable or at least believes is the best result that can be achieved, considering all factors. An arbitrator's decision, on the other hand, may not satisfy either party. An arbitrator must make a decision based on the evidence and the contract language presented in the case. Even if the decision is well reasoned and consistent with the evidence presented, it may not meet the needs of the parties.

It is not unusual for an arbitrator to rule in favor of one side but include language in the decision that works against the winning side's long-term interests. In such cases neither side is satisfied. Similarly, an arbitrator may rule in favor of the grieving party, usually the union, but refuse to grant any specific monetary relief. This likewise may not satisfy either party. Justice is often blind to the true needs and desires of the parties, many of which are political or institutional. As a result of these factors (to say nothing of the savings in time, energy, expense, and avoidance of possible damage to the collective bargaining relationship), a negotiated settlement is invariably preferable to an arbitrator's decision.

### Evaluating Settlement Possibilities

The essential question posed to each side in considering a settlement is usually a rather simple one: "Are the chances of success sufficiently high, measured against the costs of losing, to justify the risk of trying the case, recognizing the tangible and intangible costs of having the case heard and decided by an arbitrator?'' Within the framework of that question the subissues that need to be evaluated are as follows.

1. What are the odds of winning the case?
2. What is the benefit/cost likely to be if we win/lose the case?
3. Is there a significant issue concerning the meaning or application of contract language that needs to be resolved for future cases? Are the parties likely to find such a resolution through a negotiated settlement, or is it necessary to have an arbitrator do so?
4. Is there a significant matter of principle involved in the case, making the cost/benefit determination unimportant or less important?
5. What impact is an adverse decision likely to have on future cases? What future impact is a settlement likely to produce?
6. What are the political pressures/factors that affect each side and need to be considered?
7. How much will the arbitration cost each side, and how does that amount relate to the value of the issues in the case? What are the intangible costs/benefits of having the case decided by an arbitrator?

In order to get a better idea of how these factors influence a decision, let us evaluate a hypothetical case. The employer is a parcel delivery company, the employees of which are represented by the Teamsters Union. An employee truck driver with fifteen years service and an unblemished work record is involved in an accident in which the passenger of the other vehicle is seriously but not critically injured. The company's truck is badly damaged, requiring more than $15,000 in repairs. Following the accident, the driver is given a urinalysis and tests positive for alcohol. The driver is terminated in accordance with a written rule that says that any employee ''working under the influence of alcohol'' will be terminated. The employee claims that he drank only one bottle of beer and was not affected by the alcohol in any way. Further, the union challenges the validity of the company's testing on the basis that the test does not accurately measure the amount of alcohol in the employee's body, and there is therefore no evidence that the employee was impaired. The union also alleges that the employer's managers have known of several previous cases of employees being under the influence of alcohol while at work and did not terminate those employees.

The employer evaluates the case as follows.

1. The employer's advocate estimates that there is a fifty-five to sixty-five percent chance of winning the case, with the principal issues being the degree of accuracy of the tests in measuring the

driver's extent of impairment, the driver's long and spotless record, and the fact that the employer previously allowed another employee (not a driver) to return to work after a lengthy suspension for working under the influence of alcohol.

2. The cost of losing the case would be possible full back pay for a period of five months, benefits for that period, and reinstatement with full seniority. Aside from the costs of the arbitration hearing itself, the estimated cost of losing is approximately $15,000. There is no calculable monetary benefit to winning.

3. While no contract language is at issue, the meaning of "under the influence" in the employer's rule is at stake. The employer wants the arbitrator to rule that any amount of alcohol in an employee's system influences that employee's work activity. It is possible that as part of a settlement the union and the employer could agree on a suitable standard for determining alcohol influence.

4. There is a very strong matter of principle at stake. The employer sends its drivers on public streets every day, and the sobriety of its drivers is vital to the success of its business. This issue far overrides the monetary value of the case.

5. An adverse decision would seriously weaken the employer's disciplinary rules, especially its drug and alcohol policies. A settlement that results in the reinstatement of the employee could have much the same result.

6. The employer's president is adamant that the drug and alcohol policy be strictly enforced. The union will strenuously support the employee, especially in view of his long service and spotless record.

7. The arbitration hearing will cost the employer approximately $4,000. The intangible costs relate primarily to the possible damage to the reputation of the company as a safe, reliable delivery company.

The union evaluates the case as follows.

1. The union advocate estimates the chances of the employee being reinstated at forty to fifty percent, but estimates the chances of winning back pay at only about twenty percent.

2. The benefit of winning will be to save the job of a good employee/union member and perhaps nullify the employer's harsh drug and alcohol program. The cost of losing is just the reverse.

3. Major issues of principle are involved. The employer should not be terminating employees solely on the proof of a chemical test

(e.g., urinanalysis). This is especially true of long-time employees. Moreover, the employer's drug and alcohol policies were never negotiated with the union. A settlement of the grievance could possibly be linked to a new policy with which the union could agree.

4. If the employer is successful in discharging this employee, there is little to stop it from unfairly terminating employees when the adverse consequences of the drinking are not so great, giving the employer a blank check. A settlement with a more reasonable approach to drug and alcohol could avoid this result.

5. The parent union's policy is to ensure that all workplace drug and alcohol policies are part of the collective bargaining process—not unilateral policies. The employer's management is adamant in maintaining that it has the right to establish these policies on its own.

6. The union estimates its cost of presenting the grievant's case in arbitration to be $6,000 to $7,000 because it will hire an outside attorney to handle the case. There would be a real intangible benefit to the union to settle the case on favorable terms, because such a settlement could be used as a model for other employers, at least in this industry.

In virtually all arbitration cases the merits of the particular case have been considered previously by the parties, usually at two or three lower levels. The fact that the case remains in dispute despite such prior consideration usually reflects that there is no simple solution. Nevertheless, as the case approaches arbitration, both parties are forced to take a more realistic view of their chances of winning and losing and the consequences of those risks. It is not a matter of coincidence that a large number of disputes are settled "on the courthouse steps." In addition, as the parties prepare their evidence, gather documents, interview and prepare witnesses to testify, and so on, they gain a better insight into the strengths and weaknesses of their respective cases. This adds greater impetus to settle.

In the example given above of discharge for work under the influence of alcohol and a coincident accident, there are significant strengths and weaknesses on both sides. The employer will stress the clarity of its rule and the fact that being "under the influence" does not require proof of any given level of alcohol in the system. The employer will stress the necessity to its business of enforcing a strong policy against drugs and alcohol. Further, it will point to the severe consequences that resulted in this case from the driver's use of alcohol. The union will argue that urinalysis is not a reliable indicator of any impairment caused by the presence of alcohol and that "under the influence'' means that the driver was impaired from driving safely, that the employer's policies were not negotiated with the union, and that the employee had a long and spotless record. As in so many cases, the issues at stake go beyond the immediate incident and the particular employees involved.

The reader will have to evaluate the hypothetical situation outlined above to determine whether a settlement is advisable in this case, and, if so, what type of settlement would be reasonable to each party. One possible compromise would be to reinstate the employee with partial or no back pay, require that he complete a program of alcohol rehabilitation, and negotiate a drug and alcohol policy that clarifies the level of alcohol presence that is sufficient to justify termination and how that presence will be determined (perhaps by a blood sample taken as part of a postaccident test). Such a settlement would deal not only with the employee's disciplinary action, but would also address how future cases would be handled. This latter element would not automatically emerge from an arbitrator's decision.

The issues presented to the arbitrator in this hypothetical case would normally be, "Was [*name of employee*] discharged for just cause? If not, what remedy is appropriate?" In answering those questions the arbitrator would be required to determine whether this case met the proper just-cause standard. If the arbitrator found that just cause did not exist, he or she would not be charged with the responsibility of developing a policy and procedure that would meet the standards. While the decision might contain some direction and guidelines as to what such a policy might look like, the arbitrator is not empowered in grievance arbitration to rewrite the parties' labor agreement.[1]

## Avoiding Precedent-Setting Settlements

In the hypothetical discharge case outlined above, in which the parties are trying to fashion a compromise, they seek to establish a standard that can be applied to future cases. This is not always the intent of parties trying to settle an arbitration case. Frequently, one or both of the parties simply want to dispose of the immediate dispute without having it influence other cases in any way. Under somewhat different circumstances this might have been true with the hypothetical alcohol

---

[1]In interest arbitration arbitrators are given much greater latitude and in effect make decisions as to what the parties' labor agreement will encompass with respect to the matters submitted for decision. In grievance arbitration, however, the arbitrator is limited solely to deciding the meaning and interpretation of the contract provisions on which the parties have already reached agreement and that are included in the labor agreement.

case described above. The employer may have been satisfied with its drug and alcohol policies but afraid to have them challenged in a case involving a long-time employee with a perfect work record. Similarly, the union may have been so intent on saving the discharged employee's job that it would put off for another day any attack on the employer's policies.

It is not unusual for parties to a labor agreement to want to settle an individual case without addressing broader or longer term issues. For one thing, the situation may be unique and unlikely to reoccur. For another, the parties may have plans to renegotiate the contract language at issue in the case the next time the labor contract is up for renewal, and they see no need to have an arbitrator interpret language that they intend to change through their own efforts. Alternatively, the matters at issue and the monetary cost involved in a particular case may be so small that neither party wishes to spend the amount of money necessary to have the dispute arbitrated. In these and other situations the parties need a settlement that does not set a precedent for future cases. The solution is a simple one. The written agreement that resolves the grievance and avoids arbitration should contain a phrase or paragraph that establishes that the resolution will have no future effect.

In settling cases in such a way some parties merely use the words "Settled without precedent" or "Settled without prejudice." The author prefers a somewhat more specific statement along the lines of the following:

> The undersigned parties agree that this settlement will not set a precedent for any future case, nor will either party refer to this case or this settlement to support its position in any future matter.

Some unions and employers wish, as an ongoing practice, to encourage settlements of grievances at lower steps of the grievance procedure to avoid arbitration and do so by ensuring that such settlements do not set precedents for other cases. Wording such as the following is therefore inserted into their agreement.

> Any grievances settled, paid, withdrawn, or otherwise disposed of at Steps 1-4 of the grievance procedure will not set a precedent for, or in any way affect, any other case unless the parties to this labor contract agree in writing that the settlement or other disposition of a grievance shall have such future effect.

Whether the protective language is set forth in the labor agreement or is inserted into specific grievance settlements as they are negotiated, it is prudent for union and management representatives to carefully consider the impact of their settlements on future cases, and, unless they are willing to treat future similar cases in the same manner, they should use protective language such as in the examples above.

## Resolving Difficult Discharge Cases

Discharge cases often present the most difficult challenges to advocates and arbitrators alike. In many cases the arbitrator can decide only all or nothing—either the employee was discharged for just cause or not. The options open to the arbitrator are to sustain the discharge or to return the employee to work with full, partial, or no back pay. Some cases cry out for another alternative, but it is one that is outside the range of options available to the arbitrator.

An example will be used to illustrate the dilemma. An employee with a record of numerous rule infractions is discharged for theft. Most factors indicate that the employee committed the theft, but the arbitrator cannot sustain the discharge because of some fatal flaw in the employer's evidence proving the theft. The union advocate believes the employee stole the property involved but cannot drop the case because of the union's duty to fairly represent the employee. The employer may feel that it can still win the case by the weight of circumstantial evidence, notwithstanding the major flaw in its case, but would prefer not to risk losing the case and possibly be faced with the return of the terminated employee to the work force, perhaps with back pay. The union is likewise uncertain of its case but feels it must do the best job possible of giving the employee his or her "day in court." The employee may fear that the arbitrator will rule in the employer's favor and does not want to lose employment, especially with the stigma of having been discharged for theft.

One solution to these dilemmas used successfully by a number of employers and unions is to convert the discharge to a voluntary resignation, sometimes providing the employee with a severance allowance. The employee is satisfied in that he or she leaves the employer with a clean record and with a sum of money to assist in transitioning to a new job. The employer's need to keep the rule-breaking employee off the payroll is met, and the union's need to fairly represent the interests of the employee are met by a settlement that is satisfactory to the employee. Many employers would object to paying off an employee who has stolen from it, but without sufficient evidence to prove the theft, the discharged employee may eventually be paid off (i.e., awarded back pay by an arbitrator) while also being reinstated to employment.

## Rejected Offers of Settlement

Some employer and union representatives may be reluctant to make an offer of settlement for fear that if it does not result in a settlement, it could be used against them by the other side as evidence of the lack of merit in their case. Such fears are unfounded. It is a well-established principle in labor arbitration (as it is in civil and criminal litigation) that offers of compromise are not admissible in evidence. The reason for the rule is obvious. The framers of the rule did not want anything to discourage parties from settling cases on their own. If either side feared that a settlement offer (ultimately rejected and therefore not ending the case) could be made known to the arbitrator, it would be reluctant to make such an offer. Consequently, arbitrators invariably reject the introduction of, or reference to, evidence of an unsuccessful offer of settlement. The rule on which arbitrators rely in rejecting such evidence is covered in Chapter 10.

## STIPULATIONS

Although arbitration is a means of resolving a disagreement or dispute between the parties, it does not mean that the parties disagree on all aspects of a case. In fact, there are usually a number of matters on which they agree. The ability to identify and articulate those areas of agreement goes a long way in saving the time and cost of arbitration and may greatly assist the arbitrator in issuing a wise decision. Those items relevant to the case on which the parties agree and are willing to state to the arbitrator are called ''stipulations'' or are sometimes referred to simply as ''stips.'' Although stipulations may be oral or written, the stipulations that are agreed on by the parties prior to the hearing are best put in writing.

### Matters Suitable for Stipulation

Although virtually any aspect of an arbitration can be made the subject of a stipulation, there are certain matters to which advocates commonly stipulate.

#### Issue(s) To Be Decided by the Arbitrator

The most critical matter to which advocates stipulate is the issue(s) to be decided by the arbitrator. This establishes the framework for the case and sets the limits of the arbitrator's authority. Frequently, each party attempts to frame the issue in such a manner as to favor its side. For example, the employer advocate may try to limit a contract interpretation dispute to one section of the contract by stating the issue as follows:

"Was there a violation of Article XX, paragraph 6, when Mary Wagner, not Harold James, was promoted to the position of crew chief?"

The union, on the other hand, will want the arbitrator to have as much latitude as possible in order to find a contract violation. It therefore might propose the following statement: "Was the promotion of Mary Wagner to crew chief in violation of the labor contract, side agreements, or past practices, or was it otherwise unfair or inequitable?"

Neither of the proposed versions is likely to be acceptable to the other side. A more evenhanded statement of the issue would be as follows: "Did the employer violate the labor agreement when it promoted Mary Wagner to the position of crew chief? If not, what remedy is appropriate?"

As a general rule, contract interpretation issues can usually be fairly stated by beginning the question with the words, "Did the employer violate the labor agreement by . . . " followed by a short statement of the action taken by the employer. That should be followed by the stock question, "If not, what is the appropriate remedy?" In this manner the arbitrator is directed to interpret the labor agreement (which includes any agreement amendments and past practices where appropriate) within the framework of the specific facts of the case. In addition, the arbitrator is given the authority by the parties to fashion an appropriate remedy if a violation is found. The issues in a discharge or discipline case can usually be fairly stated, "Was the grievant discharged (suspended or reprimanded) for just cause? If not, what remedy is appropriate?"

One of the common problems encountered by both sides in trying to reach agreement on a statement of the issue is the scope of the original grievance. If the grievance was stated very narrowly, the employer may attempt to limit the extent to which the arbitrator may consider facts, contract provisions, and arguments that go beyond the original grievance. On the other hand, the union will normally argue that the grievance is merely a notice to the employer of a contract violation and is not intended to be a legal document that limits the full range of matters that may be decided by the arbitrator. A key factor in trying to sort through such a disagreement will be the issues, facts, contract provisions and arguments that were discussed by the parties at earlier steps of the grievance procedure. Even if the grievance did not refer to certain matters, the parties' discussion and consideration of them in connection with the processing of the grievance or other type of advance notice is likely to make them germane as viewed by the arbitrator.[2]

---

[2]St. Louis Post Dispatch and Newspaper Guild, Local 47, 97 LA 1136 (Heinsz, 1991); Ryder Truck Rental Inc. and Teamsters, Local 284, 96 LA 1080 (Gibson, 1991).

It is traditional in labor arbitration that if the parties cannot agree to a common statement of the issue, they will stipulate on the record that the arbitrator has the authority to frame the issue after considering the respective versions advanced by the advocates, after hearing all the evidence presented by the parties and after receiving their oral arguments or written briefs. This usually results in a satisfactory statement developed by the arbitrator. Nevertheless, the author highly recommends that advocates work diligently to agree on a mutually acceptable statement of the issue. One can never be completely certain that a statement of the issues framed by the arbitrator will ultimately be satisfactory.

## Facts

It is not unusual, particularly in a contract interpretation case, for the facts to be relatively undisputed. The time and date when certain events occurred, the relative seniority dates of employees involved in the grievance, the date the grievance was filed, the grievance meetings that were held, and many other facts are frequently not in contention. Even more extensive matters such as the nature and sequence of events and past practices relevant to the grievance being arbitrated may be agreed on by the parties, obviating the need to present evidence of these subjects. The more matters that can be stipulated, the faster and easier the arbitration hearing will go.

The best way to proceed to obtain useful stipulations is for one or both of the advocates to prepare a list of proposed stipulations and to deliver them to the opposing advocate as much in advance of the hearing as possible. Unfortunately, this does not often occur, and delivery frequently does not take place until the day of the hearing after both sides have prepared their witnesses. Such a delay is unfortunate, because once the advocates have prepared their evidence, including preparing their witnesses, the motivation to enter into stipulations of the facts is seriously reduced, if not completely lost.

## Applicable Agreement Provisions and Limits on the Arbitrator's Authority

There are cases in which both sides agree on the specific contract provisions that should govern the outcome. They may have some concern, however, that the arbitrator may disregard those provisions and stray into other parts of the contract that they know should not be controlling in the case. In these instances they may elect to establish one or more stipulations that limit the arbitrator to deciding the case based on the provisions they identify. Such a stipulation would read as follows.

The parties stipulate that Article XXIV, subparagraphs A and C, are the only relevant sections of the contract that apply in this case and that the arbitrator's decision is to be based on the arbitrator's interpretation and application solely of those provisions as they apply to the facts in the case.

A variation on this type of stipulation occurs when the parties have a common understanding of some relevant contract provision but cannot agree on how it applies in a particular case. Here again, a simple stipulation will aid the parties and the arbitrator. For example:

The Company and the Union stipulate that the words "insofar as practicable" as used in Section 10, paragraph C, do not apply to outsourcing of welding work that has been done on a regular basis within the Eastbank Plant.

There are other situations in which the parties may have resolved some aspects of the case and have reserved the unresolved portion for the arbitrator. They need to set limits on the arbitrator's authority in order to guard against any disruption of what they have resolved. In these cases a stipulation such as the following would be appropriate.

The parties stipulate that the layoff that was effective on November 1 was pursuant to a special agreement by the Union and the Company. The parties now recognize that the procedure set forth in that agreement was not consistent with the labor agreement or past practice, and therefore it must be modified. The arbitrator in this case is authorized to determine which employees should be on layoff status and which employees should be in active employment. Any changes in employment status resulting from the arbitrator's award will be effective two weeks following the date of receipt of the award. The arbitrator is precluded from changing any employee's established job classification and from granting any back pay or other monetary award.

## Documents and Other Evidence

Time and energy in the hearing can be conserved if the parties have reviewed documents and other evidence in advance of the hearing and determined which items they agree on as relevant, authentic, and otherwise admissible. In most cases these same documents and evidence were produced and discussed in the earlier steps of the grievance procedure and therefore should not surprise either party. Occasionally, however, new evidence may develop during preparation for the hearing and may not be known by the other side. To protect against charges of unfair surprise or "sandbagging," the party in possession of the new evidence should make the evidence available to the other side and seek a stipulation as to its admissibility. This is a voluntary matter, however, since there is no entitlement to production or notice of newly discovered evidence unless the labor agreement or other side agreement mandates it.

When the parties agree on the admissibility of documents or other tangible evidence that does not favor one side to the disadvantage of the other, it is common practice to identify those documents as joint exhibits. Examples of documents commonly designated as joint exhibits are the applicable labor agreement, seniority lists, minutes of meetings, and correspondence between the parties.

## Other Matters Suitable for Stipulations

There is virtually nothing about which the parties may not stipulate, although certain other subjects (not previously discussed) are more logical than others for stipulations. They include:

1. *Applicability or Nonapplicability of External Law.* External law consists of federal, state, or local laws or regulations that may bear on the issues being arbitrated. The parties may agree, and therefore stipulate, on the degree to which such laws should be applied to the case at hand.
2. *Past Practice and Bargaining History.* Where both sides have the same view as to the relevance of past practice and bargaining history, they may stipulate what that practice or history is and to what extent it should be taken into account by the arbitrator.
3. *Arbitrability.* If neither party raises a question about the arbitrability of a grievance, it is presumed that it is arbitrable. Nevertheless, to remove any doubt about the suitability of a case for hearing and decision by an arbitrator, the parties may elect to stipulate that the grievance is arbitrable.
4. *Filing of Briefs or Other Argument.* The way in which a case will be argued is often determined during the hearing after all evidence has been presented, but when both parties have a preference for the same manner of arguing their case (e.g., posthearing briefs with opening and reply briefs at specific time intervals), they may wish to enter into a stipulation to ensure that this occurs. When the filing of briefs is arranged during the hearing, arbitrators will sometimes exert pressure on advocates to meet the arbitrator's desires rather than those of the advocates. A written stipulation prior to the hearing should preclude that from happening.

## Stipulations during the Hearing

Stipulations have thus far been discussed in the context of prehearing agreements. In addition, stipulations may be made in the course of the hearing. During cross-examination, for example, an advocate may be probing into an area that the opposing advocate does not intend on to rely to support his or her case. Further exploration into that subject is not only a waste of time, but may also expose the witness to some other damaging testimony. Consequently, the advocate whose witness is being questioned may propose a stipulation that takes the subject out of controversy. This is done in the following manner:

> Madam Arbitrator, the employer will stipulate that its supervisor failed to post schedules two weeks in advance as required by the labor agreement, and we will further stipulate that we have never contended that they were posted within that time period.

Numerous other opportunities typically present themselves for stipulations during the hearing, and occasionally an arbitrator may propose a stipulation when it appears that there is agreement by the parties on an evidentiary or contractual matter and when a stipulation on that point will preclude one or both sides from spending time and energy on a matter that is not contested. Stipulations made during a hearing are not usually written or signed by the parties, but are made a part of the record either by being transcribed by a court reporter, recorded by a tape recorder, or simply included in the notes being made by the arbitrator.

### Caveats Concerning Stipulations

Despite the many advantages of stipulations discussed above, advocates and arbitrators alike should be aware that they have their drawbacks. Reaching agreement on stipulations may require a considerable amount of time, and the time necessary to frame a stipulation satisfactory to both sides may be greater than if the matter had been covered in a normal fashion through testimony and documents. This is particularly true with respect to stipulations of fact. Some hearings in which the author has been involved have been delayed considerably by the advocates' attempts to frame stipulations concerning matters that could have been presented in much less time in the hearing.

In addition, despite the fact that the parties have entered into a stipulation on a particular factual point, one side or both will sometimes offer evidence on the same point in order to give the arbitrator a more complete picture of the factual setting. It is difficult to write a stipulation in such a complete fashion that it encompasses all relevant facts and captures the full impact of an event or situation. For this reason live testimony is often preferable to a written account of such facts, especially where motivations and nuances are involved. Moreover, stipulations cannot be cross-examined. Consequently, advocates should carefully

weigh the usefulness of stipulations against both the time and effort
likely to be necessary to achieve agreement on them and the loss of
perhaps a fuller and more persuasive presentation of those facts from a
live witness.

## SPECIAL ARRANGEMENTS
## CONCERNING WITNESSES

In some cases it will be necessary to make special arrangements
having to do with the manner and timing in which witnesses will testify.
Usually, it is advisable to address such issues in advance of the hearing.
The most common of these arrangements are discussed below.

### Witnesses Unavailable to Testify in Person

There are a myriad of reasons why a witness may not be available to
testify on the day of the hearing. The witness may be ill, called out of
town on an emergency, or stranded in a distant city because of weather
problems. Depending on the importance of the witness to the advocate's
case, a decision needs to be made as to how to obtain the necessary
testimony. Subject to the arbitrator's approval, the following options are
generally available.

1. Postpone the hearing.
2. Allow the witness to testify by telephone.
3. Schedule a "mini-hearing" at a different time with just the
   advocates and the arbitrator to take the witness's testimony.
4. Schedule a deposition with just the advocates and a court
   reporter, and have the transcript of the deposition made a part of
   the record of the case.
5. Allow the witness to submit a sworn statement.
6. Allow the advocate offering the witness to make an offer of
   proof as to the matters to which the witness would have testified.
7. Abandon the testimony of the absent witness, and seek to supply
   the evidence through another witness or other means.

Option 1 (postponing the hearing) is obviously the most drastic and
would be done only if a witness was absolutely critical to the case. Option
2 (telephonic testimony) allows the witness's testimony to be heard but
not seen. Most important, it does not allow the arbitrator to observe the
demeanor of the witness to evaluate credibility. Furthermore, if this type

of testimony is sought from a witness against a grievant who was discharged, it does not afford the grievant the opportunity to face his accusers, which is a common principle to which arbitrators usually adhere.[3] Option 3 (mini-hearing) overcomes some of the deficit of option 2 in that there is face-to-face testimony, but it is not completely satisfactory if there is likely to be rebuttal testimony by other witnesses to refute the statements of the absent witness. Option 4 (deposition without the presence of the arbitrator) has many of the same advantages and disadvantages as option 3 but does not permit the arbitrator to observe or hear the witness during the testimony. The main advantage of option 4 is practicability, in that the arbitrator's availability and certain logistical problems may make a mini-hearing (option 3) difficult to schedule. Options 5 (sworn statement) and 6 (offer of proof) are unlikely to be permitted by the arbitrator if the opposing advocate objects, which is highly probable. Neither a sworn statement nor an offer of proof allow for cross-examination or observation of the witness. If the testimony of the witness is not critical and not likely to be in conflict with that of other witnesses, the opposing advocate may waive his or her objections, particularly if there is some offsetting compromise favoring the other side. Option 7 (omitting the witness's testimony) is probably the least favorable one, but if the witness's testimony is sufficiently innocuous to allow either options 5 or 6 to be acceptable to the other side, it is probable that the evidence can be supplied by some other means.

Before an advocate raises a problem of witness availability with the arbitrator, it is advisable for him or her to discuss it privately with the opposing advocate to determine that advocate's position on the matter. Any arrangements that can be worked out with the other party will virtually always be acceptable to the arbitrator. If a resolution cannot be worked out in that manner, it will be up to the arbitrator to determine what, if any, option will be approved.

## Witness Testifying Out of Order

A difficulty similar to, but much less serious than, the one discussed just above is that of the witness who is available to testify on the day of the hearing, but not at a time that naturally fits into the proper order of presenting evidence. For example, an arbitration hearing of a contract interpretation case is scheduled to begin at 9:00 A.M., and the union's

---

[3]Rhor Indus., 93 LA 145, 156 (Goulet, 1989); Snapper Power Equip., 89 LA 501, 505 (Weston, 1987); Air France, 71 LA 1113 (Turkus, 1978); *but see* Veterans Admin. Medical Cent., 87 LA 405, 407 (Yarowsky, 1986).

evidentiary case is estimated to last two to three hours, ending around the noon lunch break. The employer is expected to begin its case at 1:30 P.M. and finish before the end of the day. One of the union's witnesses is not available until the afternoon, after the union has completed its case in chief. If the union's witness testifies in the afternoon, it would be in the middle of the employer's case in chief or during rebuttal testimony, which normally would be inappropriate and objectionable.

The problem is not an uncommon one and is routinely handled by allowing the witness to testify out of order, that is, out of the normal order in which the witness would testify. Usually, there is no objection from the opposing advocate, unless by having the witness testify at a different time the other side would be prejudiced in some way (e.g., one of the other side's witnesses might not, because of that witness's own schedule conflict, be in the hearing room to hear the testimony of the out-of-order witness, thereby precluding effective rebuttal testimony). The need to call witnesses out of order seems to occur most frequently with expert witnesses, such as doctors, engineers, consultants, and other professionals whose work or travel schedules limit their availability. Raising this matter with the opposing advocate and the arbitrator at the earliest possible time will normally result in a satisfactory schedule to allow the witness to testify at a time that accommodates the witness's availability.

## Sequestering Witnesses

The normal procedure in labor arbitration hearings is to have all participants, including all witnesses, in the hearing room for the duration of the hearing. There are cases, however, in which the facts are clearly in conflict and there is a possibility that the testimony of one or more witnesses could alter or affect the testimony of others. For example, a witness for the employer may have testimony concerning his observation of events that occurred at the scene of a critical incident in the case. A union witness may have testimony concerning the same incident. If both witnesses are in the room at the same time, hearing the testimony of the union's witness could color the testimony of the employer's witness and vice versa (for example, by hearing details recalled by the other side's witness, a witness could make his or her recitation of the event more credible by confirming or elaborating on those details). In such cases it may be advisable for the advocates to request that the arbitrator sequester, or exclude from the hearing room, all witnesses in the case except when they are testifying. Unless it can be shown that sequestration of witnesses will prejudice the other party, arbitrators will, except for the situations discussed in the next section, generally grant a party's request if there is reason to believe that the presence of witnesses throughout the hearing could influence their testimony.

## Rules Concerning Sequestration

There are certain practices followed by most arbitrators in carrying out a sequestration request. First, all witnesses, except the specific exclusions discussed in the next two paragraphs, are to be sequestered. Even though some witnesses are expected to present noncontroversial testimony, they will be excluded from the hearing room as well.

Second, the grievant in a discharge or disciplinary case is always permitted to remain in the hearing room regardless of whether he or she is going to testify. The underlying concept, premised on constitutional principles, is that all persons who are accused are entitled to face their accusers.

Third, each party is entitled to have one person in the hearing room to assist the advocate in the presentation of the case, even if that person is scheduled to testify. For example, the union may have its business agent present to assist the union advocate, and the employer may do likewise with its labor relations manager, both of whom may testify as witnesses in the case. The logic for this is that each advocate may need to have someone who is familiar with the local work environment to assist in the presentation of the case and to provide background to the advocate in making an effective presentation, even though that person is also a witness in the case.

Fourth, each witness and each observer in the hearing, including the advocates, are prohibited from discussing their testimony or the testimony of any witnesses with any of the sequestered witnesses. The reason is obvious. The purpose of sequestration is to prevent any witness's testimony from influencing that of another witness. That purpose is thwarted whether the testimony is heard directly or through another person. The arbitrator has an obligation to instruct each participant in the hearing, prior to the witnesses leaving the hearing room, that there is to be no discussion about the testimony of any witness with any other witness.

## Strategy of Requesting Sequestration

An advocate should consider carefully the decision whether or not to request that witnesses be sequestered. Even though the testimony of some witnesses may influence others, the key question is, ''Whose testimony is likely to influence which witnesses, and if that occurs, which side is likely to benefit or be harmed by that influence?'' It is entirely possible that such influence will work to one side's favor, thus making a sequestration request by that party unwise. This is particularly true when one side's witnesses are stronger, have better recollection, or are more credible. These attributes will often enable those witnesses to capitalize on the weakness displayed by the other side's witnesses.

It should also be kept in mind that the sequestration process will normally prevent the witnesses from hearing the opening statements of both parties if the sequestration is requested prior to going on the record in the hearing. In many cases, one side's opening statement is designed to affect the testimony of the other side's witnesses (see the discussion of this point in the next chapter). Consequently, if an advocate wishes to have the other side's witnesses hear his or her opening statement, the request for sequestering witnesses should not be made until the opening statements are completed.

## Swearing of Witnesses

The rules of the American Arbitration Association provide that the arbitrator may require witnesses to testify under oath if it is required by law or requested by any party (see Appendix A). There is no legal obligation for witnesses to be sworn in labor arbitration cases, although the labor agreement may contain such a requirement, but labor arbitrators will generally comply with a request or a motion from either or both advocates that witnesses be sworn.

Swearing of witnesses is particularly appropriate when the facts are in dispute and when the credibility of witnesses is important. Some advocates automatically ask that witnesses be sworn, because they cannot predict the full extent of the testimony that will eventually be offered. The author's experience is that witnesses who are prone to be untruthful or shade their testimony are seldom discouraged from doing so by taking an oath. Nevertheless, there is no harm or downside risk of having witnesses sworn, particularly if an advocate is confident of the veracity of his or her own witnesses. It is generally advisable to have witnesses sworn as a routine matter.

It rarely, if ever, happens that a witness is charged with perjury for giving false testimony under oath in a labor arbitration case. Consequently, the swearing of witnesses is more of a psychological than real inducement for witnesses to tell the truth. Few witnesses, however, are likely to be aware of this fact, and at least some witnesses, therefore, are likely to be influenced to tell the truth by taking an oath, especially if they have a religious or moral background that places importance on the taking of an oath. The oath may be administered by the arbitrator or by a stenographic reporter if the case is being transcribed.

## Use of Interpreters

The increasing number of non-English speaking immigrants in recent years has resulted in the need for more interpreters in court and arbitration proceedings, although the presence of an interpreter in labor arbitration hearings is still relatively rare.

In court proceedings it is common to use certified interpreters for translating the testimony of witnesses. For many languages, however, there is no certification process. With respect to labor arbitration, there are no hard and fast rules as to the qualifications required of interpreters. Regardless of certification, the key ingredients for qualifying as an interpreter are competency in the language involved and objectivity. The person should have sufficient command of English and the second language, as well as a facility for quickly translating both languages clearly and accurately. Equally important, if not more so, is objectivity and disinterest of the interpreter with respect to the persons and issues in the case. If both of these criteria are satisfied, certification is not essential. Although objectivity may be ascertained without great difficulty (particularly when the interpreter has performed this work in a number of other cases), competency in both languages and in translating skills may be more difficult to evaluate. An advocate who intends to use an interpreter is best advised to hire a professional who has been employed as a qualified interpreter in previous cases.

## Failure of a Subpoenaed Witness to Appear

In Chapter 4 the need and procedure for subpoenaing a witness was discussed. If, notwithstanding proper service of the subpoena, the witness fails to appear, the advocate who obtained the subpoena has the option of either seeking a postponement of the hearing until court enforcement of the subpoena can be effected or proceeding with the hearing with the agreement of the arbitrator and the opposing advocate to utilize options 3 or 4 (subsequent mini-hearing or deposition) outlined earlier in this chapter in the section *Unavailable Witnesses*. Of course, the advocate always has the option of proceeding without the witness and with the expectation or hope of getting the facts into evidence in some other manner.

The advocate should evaluate the value of testimony that ultimately might be given by a witness who is so reluctant to testify that he or she does not honor a subpoena. The author once needed the testimony of a young man who had been working as an employee of a contractor in the plant of the author's employer. An employee in the plant, considerably larger than the contractor's employee, had threatened the young man with great bodily harm. The young man was so intimidated that he refused to testify voluntarily. In addition to having the witness subpoenaed, the author had to make continued appeals to the young man's integrity and manhood to persuade him to appear in the hearing of the employee's discharge. Although the subpoena was honored, the young man's reluctance to testify about the threat was so great that his testimony was virtually worthless. A witness who does not honor a subpoena is almost certain to be a reluctant, if not totally uncooperative, witness.

# PROCEDURAL MATTERS

## Arbitrability and Timeliness

In Chapter 2 the reader's attention was drawn to the importance of reviewing and analyzing the grievance in order to determine whether any arbitrability or timeliness issues existed. If they do, the best time to raise these matters is in advance of going on record in the hearing. In most cases the arbitrability or timeliness question would have been addressed in earlier steps of the grievance procedure. If it was not, the side raising the issue (usually the employer) should, in advance of the hearing, bring such issues to the attention of the other side's advocate.

In preparing the stipulations of the issues to be decided by the arbitrator, arbitrability and/or timeliness should be included as issues. They can be easily phrased as follows: Is the grievance arbitrable? Was the grievance filed within the time limits set forth in the labor agreement? Was the grievance appealed to arbitration in a timely manner in accordance with the labor agreement?

## Collateral Proceedings

Occasionally, the facts and issues in a labor arbitration case are the subject of a complaint, charge, or action in another forum. An employer's scheduling of lunch and work breaks may be under investigation by a state labor agency, the discharge of an employee who is a member of a minority group may be the subject of a discrimination charge filed with the EEOC, or the unilateral relocation of work to another facility of the employer may be scheduled for a hearing by the NLRB. Although the collateral proceeding may be completely independent of the grievance in form, the substance of the issues may be identical.

The advocate needs to determine in advance of the hearing what, if any, action can be taken to avoid duplicate hearings, conflicting results, inconsistent evidentiary records, multiple damages, and other adverse consequences. In some cases, especially NLRB unfair labor practice cases alleging violations of Sections 8(a)(3) and (5) (i.e., discrimination for union activity and refusal to bargain), the administrative agency will defer or follow the decision of the arbitrator, at least where the arbitrator's decision is not contrary to the policy of the agency.[4] In other cases, such as unemployment compensation hearings, the issues (usually discharge) involved are nearly identical in both forums, but the standards applied are often different. In general, unemployment compensation judges or referees may consider, but are not bound by, arbitration decisions in evaluating the evidence for benefit eligibility, whereas labor arbitrators will not usually admit evidence of a determination for unemployment compensation. In either forum transcribed testimony from one hearing is usually admissible in evidence in the hearing of the other forum for purposes of impeachment (i.e. showing that a witness testified differently from one hearing to another).

Whatever the forum involved and whatever the impact of one proceeding on another, the advocate should consider and raise such matters, where appropriate, with the arbitrator prior to the hearing. The advocate may wish to bring the arbitrator's attention to the collateral proceeding or seek to have it kept completely out of the record. Conversely, the advocate may seek a continuance (postponement) of the arbitration hearing to enable the other forum to issue a decision, which may make the arbitration hearing moot. The specific action or inaction will depend on too many factors to address in this volume, but the existence and impact of collateral proceedings should not be overlooked.

---

[4]Collyer Insulated Wire, 192 NLRB 837, 77 LRRM 1931 (1971); Spielberg Mfg. Co., 112 NLRB 1080, 36 LRRM 1152 (1955); Raytheon Co., 140 NLRB 883, 52 LRRM 1129 (1963).

## Site Visitation

Although perhaps not strictly a procedural matter, the issue of having the arbitrator visit a site outside the hearing room to observe places, things, or events relevant to the case should be raised prior to the commencement of the hearing. Examples of the types of sites that may be involved include the scene of an incident, accident, or altercation; the site of a critical piece of equipment; the view from a particular observation point; or the physical environment in which employees work. While photographs and videos may be used to give the arbitrator the flavor of a particular site, nothing quite matches the impressions and observations that are possible by actually being at the site of a particular event or object.

The advocate who desires an arbitrator to visit a site should carefully consider the following questions with respect to the site.

1. Why is it important for the arbitrator to visit the site, and what arguments can be used to persuade the arbitrator to do so if there is any objection to the visit?
2. When is the best time for the visit? Is it before the hearing begins, during the course of the hearing, or after the presentation of all other evidence? (Consider the impact the visit is likely to have on the overall case presentation and how it relates to the rest of the evidence.)
3. How will the visit be conducted? Who will accompany the arbitrator? Who will lead the visitation? Who will explain to the arbitrator what is being seen and how it relates to the case? What will be said?
4. If the case is being reported by a stenographic reporter, will the reporter accompany the arbitrator to record what is said during the visit? (It is unusual to do so.)
5. Is there any chance that the visit may not be successful (or possibly be harmful to the case) because of unfavorable climate, lighting or operational conditions? How can these risks be eliminated or minimized? Is the risk so great that the visit should be reevaluated?

Depending on the remoteness of the site, the visit may have to be made on a different day than that of the hearing. This may require a different schedule for the arbitrator than if no visit was involved. Consequently, consideration of a site visit should be done early in the preparation process, and it should be arranged well in advance to avoid any scheduling problems. The arbitrator is not required to visit a site unless he or she believes it will aid in the consideration of the case. The advocate should therefore be prepared with a number of arguments as to why the visit is important to the full consideration of the case—not just why it will be useful to understand one party's version of the case. Furthermore, the advocate should attempt to enlist the opposing advocate to join in the request or to sign a stipulation stating that a site visitation would be valuable to the arbitrator in deciding the case.

## Bifurcation of the Hearing

When there are multiple issues (and especially when there is an issue of arbitrability or timeliness), multiple-fact situations, or complex remedy issues, it may be advisable to divide the hearing into two or more parts. For example, if there is a question of arbitrability concerning whether the employer is subject to a labor agreement negotiated by an employers' association, the issue of the arbitrator's authority is at stake. If the employer was not a member of the association or had withdrawn before the contract was negotiated, the employer is not bound by the contract, and an arbitrator's decision based on that contract is of no effect. Rather than spending the time and money to hear the evidence on arbitrability, as well as the evidence on the merits of the case, one or both parties may seek to have the hearing bifurcated, or separated into two parts. The first hearing and determination may be on the issue of whether the employer is bound by the contract and therefore whether the grievance is arbitrable. The second part deals with the issue of a possible contract violation (i.e., the merits of the case) and would occur only if the arbitrator found the case to be arbitrable based on the first part of the bifurcated hearing. Some labor agreements specify that issues dealing with arbitrability must be heard and decided before any hearing on the merits of the grievance. These agreements incorporate bifurcation into the arbitration process without any need for the arbitrator to approve the bifurcation.

The issue of bifurcation may also arise when there are multiple grievants, distinct fact patterns, and divergent issues. While this type of bifurcation is less common, it may be advisable when multiple locations and diverse witnesses are involved. In most grievances the concept of remedy is virtually always an issue (e.g., "If a contract violation occurred, what remedy?") and frequently the remedy sought is back pay. The calculation of back pay amounts is sometimes a complex process and an unnecessary one if no contract violation is found. Consequently, the question of remedy can often be set aside for a separate hearing if necessary. More often than not, an arbitrator's award finding a contract violation will remand the case to the parties to determine whether they can agree on the back pay amounts or other remedy. If they cannot, the arbitrator retains jurisdiction to determine back pay through evidence submitted by the parties to the arbitrator or by holding another hearing limited to the issue of the appropriate remedy. Thus the merits of the case (i.e., did a contract violation occur?) is separated from the issue of remedy, and the case has been bifurcated.

The advocate who seeks a bifurcation should discuss it in advance with the opposing advocate and, if agreement is reached, enter into a stipulation. If no agreement is reached, a motion or request for bifurcation should be submitted to the arbitrator before the hearing commences.

## Continuance

From time to time an unforseen event may make it difficult, impossible, or inadvisable for an advocate to properly present his or her case. The discovery of new and critical evidence just before the hearing, the sudden unavailability of a key witness, or the illness or injury of the advocate are events that may justify a continuance or postponement of the hearing. The advocate seeking the continuance should notify the arbitrator and the opposing advocate of the continuance request at the earliest possible time. As a matter of courtesy, the opposing advocate should be contacted first, if possible, to see whether the other party will join in the request for the continuance or at least not oppose it.

A continuance should not be sought for a frivolous reason. It should be a matter that could change the outcome of the case, and the period requested for the continuance should be no longer than absolutely necessary. A key factor that will influence the length of any continuance that is granted is the arbitrator's availability. Arbitrator's schedules are usually very crowded, and the length of the continuance will likely be based on open dates in that schedule.

## Expedited or "Bench" Decision

Some cases involve matters for which there are compelling reasons for an immediate decision. Discharges of employees in critical job categories and contract interpretation cases on which daily procedures or urgent and critical decisions depend are but two examples of such cases

The need for an immediate decision can be met by a bench decision, whereby the arbitrator issues a decision and award immediately following the close of the hearing, that is, from the bench. Obviously, the decision is an oral one and may be followed by a written decision at a later date.

Arbitrators are generally reluctant, and justifiably so, to issue bench awards. Little time is available to study the record, check reported decisions in comparable cases, or give the time and thought to the case that is usually necessary for a wise decision—the amount of time that is available in the normal arbitration procedure. When, however, both advocates find it in their best interests to risk a hasty decision in order to obtain a prompt result, arbitrators will usually comply or at least agree to a decision within a very short period of time. A stipulation signed, or at least affirmed orally, by both parties is the ordinary method of obtaining the arbitrator's approval to issue a bench decision.

A close and generally preferable alternative to a pure bench decision is a decision issued by the arbitrator within twenty-four, forty-eight, or perhaps seventy-two hours after the close of the hearing. Such promptness usually will suffice to meet the immediate needs of the parties, while giving the arbitrator some time to weigh the evidence and issue a thoughtful decision.

## ISSUES RELATED TO THE ARBITRATOR

Because the advocates selected the arbitrator who will hear the case, it is presumed that they are confident of the arbitrator's competency and objectivity. This presumption is generally valid, although it does not ensure that some matters relating to the qualifications of an arbitrator to hear a case may not arise. Moreover, it does not mean that the arbitrator may not have to be limited in some respects, based on the nature of the case and the contract language involved.

## Arbitrator's Impartiality and Suitability to Hear a Case

Although rare, there are cases in which an apparently well-qualified and impartial arbitrator has been selected but is later discovered to have some defect that could render him or her unqualified to hear a particular case. The advocate needs to carefully investigate any possible basis for disqualification that comes to his or her attention, and to determine whether it is appropriate to challenge the arbitrator. The following reasons could be grounds for a challenge.

### Undisclosed Relationship with the Other Party

An arbitrator selected to hear a case has an obligation to disclose, prior to accepting an appointment, any current or previous employment, consultantcy, or other business relationship with any party to the case.[5] Such a relationship could also include stock ownership in a corporation that is a party in the case or the receipt of payments from one of the parties for anything other than serving as an arbitrator. Following selection of the arbitrator, the advocate may discover that such a relationship exists or did exist and that the arbitrator has failed to disclose it. The failure to disclose may not be caused by any intent to deceive. For example, the arbitrator may have provided consulting services for a division or subsidiary of the parent corporation that is a party to the case but was unaware of the corporate connection with the division or subsidiary. Likewise, the arbitrator may have worked on a research project for a union (and was paid for such work by the union) many years in the past and simply forgot about the assignment. The advocate needs to make an evaluation as to whether such a relationship is likely to interfere with the arbitrator's impartiality in judging the present case.

## Personal Relationship with a Party's Principal or Representative

Just as a business relationship can affect an arbitrator's impartiality, so too can a personal relationship with a principal or representative of one of the parties tend to influence an arbitrator's judgement of a case. Given the fact that professionals in the labor relations field have frequent contact and often belong to the same professional organizations, the categories of personal relationships that could prompt a challenge should not be drawn too narrowly.

When, however, the relationship deviates from a professional one and is more personal in nature, the concern for impartiality is more justified. For example, if an advocate and an arbitrator occasionally have lunch together (and especially if they share the cost), nothing untoward normally would be presumed. If the relationship involves shared family

---

[5]Code of Professional Responsibility for Arbitrators of Labor-Management Disputes, II. B. "Required Disclosures," adopted by the National Academy of Arbitrators, the American Arbitration Association, and the Federal Mediation and Conciliation Service.

vacations, relatively frequent presence in reciprocal home social gatherings, or any type of a romantic relationship, though, the impartiality of the arbitrator would certainly be called into question. At a minimum, the arbitrator has a duty to disclose the nature of a social or personal relationship to the noninvolved party before the appointment is made.

## Ex-Parte Communications between a Party and the Arbitrator About the Case at Hand

It is assumed that an arbitrator comes to a hearing with a clean slate, knowing little or nothing about the case to be presented and at least having no preconceptions about the merits of the case. There will be some situations in which the arbitrator may be advised of certain aspects of a case in connection with the issuance of a subpoena or some prehearing procedural determination, but, as a general rule, the arbitrator is normally unaware of any specifics concerning a case set for hearing except the general subject matter (e.g., discharge for absenteeism, grievance concerning the application of seniority, etc.).

A problem arises when one party has communicated with the arbitrator concerning a case without the knowledge and/or approval of the other (ex-parte communication). Such communications open the door to the formation of possible preconceptions or predispositions in the mind of the arbitrator that could influence the outcome of the case. Although experienced arbitrators are usually capable of discounting information they learn from one of the parties prior to the hearing, one can never be absolutely certain that an ex-parte communication has had no influence on the arbitrator. Consequently, the arbitrator should decline to hear or receive any such communications or, if they have already been received, should disclose them to the other party.

## Decision and Procedure to Challenge an Arbitrator

If an advocate becomes aware of a business or personal relationship or an ex-parte communication between the arbitrator and the other party, the advocate needs to decide whether the relationship or communication is likely to have an influence on the arbitrator's decision in or handling of the case. If the arbitrator has not previously disclosed the connection but admits to it prior to or during the hearing, the advocate usually is best advised to challenge the arbitrator, unless the connection is so tenuous and remote that the failure to disclose is easily explained. If the connection is disclosed by the arbitrator or the other party and if it appears to be relatively innocuous, the advocate may choose to withhold any challenge. When there is a significant doubt about the arbitrator's ability to be objective because of the relationship or communication, the advocate is probably wise to challenge the arbitrator. The decision to challenge an arbitrator, however, should not be made lightly.

Once the decision to challenge has been made, it must be registered. This may be done informally prior to going on the record and is best done in a private meeting with the arbitrator and the opposing advocate. The advocate should explain that he or she must represent the best interests of the advocate's principals, and, although the arbitrator may not be influenced by the relationship or communication, the potential for influence exists, and the mere appearance of influence is sufficient to raise concerns on the part of the client. The likelihood is that the arbitrator will choose to remove himself or herself. If that is not the case, the advocate will have to register the challenge on the record at the outset of the hearing. The advocate then has the following three options.

1. Refuse to proceed with the hearing.
2. Ask for a continuance to allow for time to seek a judicial determination of the arbitrator's qualifications (i.e., impartiality) to hear and decide the case.
3. Proceed with the hearing, being prepared to appeal an unsatisfactory result to court on the basis of the lack of arbitrator impartiality.

Option 1 is strongly discouraged. The arbitrator may very well proceed to hear the case on an ex-parte basis (i.e., with only one party presenting its case), and the result is almost certain to go in favor of the other side. Option 2 is probably the best alternative, depending on the law in the particular jurisdiction on arbitrator disqualification. Option 3 has the advantage of conserving legal expenses, with the possibility that the case can be won. Certainly, the arbitrator is apt to be somewhat more cautious in handling the case after a challenge to impartiality has been registered, but the decision to proceed with the hearing, notwithstanding the objection to the arbitrator, may be later construed as a waiver of the challenge.

## Publication of Decision and Award

Arbitration hearings, decisions, and awards are private proceedings and documents and are not available to the public unless one of the parties is a public entity and subject to public disclosure laws or regulations or unless the parties agree to publicly disclose one or more aspects of the case. The most common type of disclosure is the publication of the arbitrator's decision and award in one of the reporting services (see Chapter 3 in the section *Reported Decisions*).

The responsibility of submitting the decision and award to the reporting organization lies with the arbitrator, but the authority to submit them must come from the parties. Some arbitrators routinely refrain from reporting any of their decisions. Others report their decisions, particularly when they feel the subject matter or nature of the decision may be helpful to other arbitrators or advocates in future cases. Arbitrators who wish to submit cases for publication will usually ask the advocates prior to going on the record, or at least at the outset of the hearing, whether they have any objection to publication of the decision and award. If either party objects, no publication is authorized. Even if neither party objects, the arbitrator may subsequently elect not to submit the case for publication.

Whether an advocate should agree (i.e., refrain from objecting) to publication is a judgment call for the advocate and the advocate's principals. The argument in favor of publication is that it advances the knowledge of arbitration and arbitrators' reasoning in general, and that of the individual arbitrator in particular, to the labor relations community, presumably adding value to the advocates themselves in the long run. The argument against publication is that it exposes the parties' dirty linen to the public and could embarrass the losing party and its advocate. Neither argument is an especially compelling one, and the personal views of the respective parties are likely to control the decision. The nature of the case and how the position of the advocate's party is likely to be perceived by those reading the case should be taken into consideration in making that decision.

# Part II

# During the Hearing

# 8

# Opening Statements

After much preparation and after disposing of preliminary matters, it is time to begin the hearing. The first formal phase of the hearing is the delivery of opening statements by each side. This is normally the first opportunity each side has to acquaint the arbitrator with the basic facts in the case and with the labor agreement provisions address those facts.

Opening statements can have a significant impact on the outcome. In the court system, studies of jury verdicts have shown that as many as eighty percent of jurors made up their minds on cases immediately following the opening statements.[1] Arbitrators are not jurors, however, and it should not be expected that an arbitrator will reach any conclusions as a result of hearing opening statements. Nevertheless, arbitrators can establish tentative leanings or predispositions based on what the advocates say in their opening statements.

## PURPOSES OF AN OPENING STATEMENT

Although the principal purpose of an opening statement is rather obvious, that is, to explain to the arbitrator what the case is about and what the advocate's evidence will prove, there are some additional and somewhat more subtle functions that the opening statement can fulfill. These will be explored in this section.

---

[1]Decof, *Art of Advocacy: Opening Statement,* § 1.01 at 1-4 (1983).

## Orienting the Arbitrator

The first and foremost reason for making an opening statement is to give the arbitrator an overview of the case that highlights the evidence that will be presented. As indicated in the last chapter, prior to the beginning of the hearing (or prior to the prehearing preliminary matters) arbitrators usually have little or no knowledge of the case they are about to hear and the issues they will have to decide. Consequently, most often they are in the dark as to what the case is all about and what it is that the respective advocates will be trying to prove. The opening statement is the initial opportunity to orient the arbitrator. The orientation should include not just the major facts of the case, but also how those facts relate to the relevant provisions of the labor contract and how together they address the issues being presented to the arbitrator for decision.

## Influencing the Arbitrator

An effective opening statement does not stop at orienting the arbitrator. It includes elements designed to influence the arbitrator in a favorable way toward the party delivering the opening statement. This influence does not go as far as attempting to convince the arbitrator of the correctness of the delivering advocate's position, because few arbitrators are open to such ultimate persuasion prior to hearing any evidence. The influence ideally sought to be established is a favorable disposition of the arbitrator to consider the evidence and arguments to be presented by the advocate as the hearing progresses.

The elements of the advocate's case that should be highlighted in the opening statement are reasonableness, rationality, and respect (for the labor agreement, the collective bargaining relationship and, the arbitration process). Ideally, the arbitrator should come away from an advocate's opening statement not only having a good idea of what the case is all about, but also believing that the advocate's principals have acted in a reasonable manner and have taken a reasonable and rational position with respect to the grievance. Moreover, an effective opening statement should cause the arbitrator to believe that the side making the opening statement wants to respect and abide by the labor agreement, wants to preserve a positive collective bargaining relationship with the other side, values the arbitration process, and will cooperate in seeing that the arbitration hearing is fairly conducted.

An effective opening statement will contain some elements of argument of the case, but not the type of comprehensive or aggressive argument that will be made at the conclusion of the hearing. The arguments in the opening statement are more subtle and should be almost imperceptibly intertwined with the statement of facts. For example,

> On July 20, just prior to the opening of the new department, the Company posted for bid all jobs in that department in strict compliance with the provisions of Article IX, Sections 7 and 8. Twenty-two new positions were filled in this manner.

Here the employer advocate is explaining that the new jobs were open to bid and does so by mentioning that his principals followed the labor agreement in doing so.

The union's opening statement on this same point might well be as follows:

> Following the employer's decision to open a new department (a decision that was not discussed or agreed on with the union in advance), the employer decided to post the jobs in that department for bid. Unfortunately, the bids were posted only in Departments 2 and 4, which was contrary to the labor agreement and past practice. Without all employees in the plant being given an opportunity to bid on these positions, the employer filled all positions from employees in Departments 2 and 4 to the disadvantage of all other employees in the bargaining unit.

## Influencing the Witnesses

Most advocates present their opening statement in order to influence the arbitrator, often overlooking how the statement may impact the witnesses—especially the witnesses to be called by the other side. Most witnesses know what the case is about, but they know it in relation to the testimony they will be delivering. It is likely they do not have a good understanding of the overall case, and it is even more likely that they do not have a good grasp of the other side's case. For a witness to hear the other side's case outlined in a clear, organized, and persuasive fashion is to raise a question in the witness's mind that his or her side of the case may not be the correct one. If the opening statement does not accomplish quite that much, it is nevertheless possible to at least plant some seeds of doubt that could later affect the certainty with which witnesses testify.

Some witnesses are under the mistaken impression that the opening statement is evidence and that the way the advocate portrays the facts will necessarily be supported by the advocate's evidence. Consequently, an advocate who explains the facts in a way that persuasively supports his or her case has a chance to create in the minds of witnesses the belief that it is the true version. The author has seen witnesses in the course of their testimony refer to passages in the opening statement of their side's advocate or the advocate for the other party as if those passages had been testimony or other evidence already admitted into the record.

Of course, an advocate should explain to his or her witnesses in advance of the hearing that the opposing advocate's opening statement is simply that advocate's version of the facts and does not have to be supported by the facts. Nevertheless, the witness should listen attentively to both side's opening statements in order to understand the positions being taken by each party and what the major points in dispute are in the case.

Just as an advocate's opening statement, if truly effective, is likely to have an impact on the other side's witnesses, so too may it favorably influence the advocate's own witnesses. A logical, persuasive, and cogent opening statement can lead the advocate's own witnesses to feel confident about their testimony and reassured that their testimony is corroborated by other evidence in the case. If an opening statement has a favorable influence on the other side's witnesses, it is almost certain to have a positive impact on one's own witnesses.

## KEY ELEMENTS OF AN EFFECTIVE
## OPENING STATEMENT

Opening statements vary with the advocates who deliver them. It is not possible to say which elements of an opening statement are absolutely necessary and which are a matter of style and discretion. That must be left to the individual advocate. Nevertheless, the following elements of opening statements have proven useful to a number of successful labor arbitration advocates.

### Theme

In Chapter 4 the value of developing a theory for the case was discussed. A theory of a case is a line of reasoning that forms the basis for the position being taken in the case. Closely allied to the theory of a case is a theme for the case, a short group of words or phrases that summarizes the essence of the case as seen by the party advancing the theme. The first time that the theme should appear in the case is during the opening statement. In fact, it is often most effectively placed at the very beginning of the opening statement. The following are a few examples of case themes.

- Mr./Ms. Arbitrator, this case is about careless and uncaring supervision.
- If one wanted to summarize the essence of this case, the phrase ''penny wise and pound foolish'' would best characterize what was going on here.
- Seldom have the facts in a case made such a convincing case for the removal of an employee who represented a danger to himself and his coworkers. His presence on the job was truly an accident waiting to happen.

The value of the theme is that it gives the arbitrator a hook onto which he or she can hang the body of evidence and an abbreviated phrase or conceptual framework to identify the case and to distinguish it from others he or she has heard in the recent past. As the evidence is later presented, it can be tied with words or implications to the original theme. For example,

Q. So, would you say, Ms. Jones, that the company was being penny wise with respect to the policy on uniforms?

A. Yes, I think pound foolish as well, since the overall cost was far in excess of what was possible.

Although some cases do not always lend themselves to such short, pithy summarizations, it is surprising how easy it is to translate a complex set of facts and contractual arguments into one or several short sayings or characterizations.

## Summarization of Facts

It is highly desirable that the arbitrator have a reasonably firm grasp of the essential facts in a case by the time the opening statements have been completed. This allows him or her to place the subsequent testimony into a proper contextual framework. Unfortunately, a clear summary of the facts is not always provided, especially in contract interpretation cases. Too frequently, the advocates are so focused on arguing their respective interpretations of disputed contract language that they neglect to lay out the key facts in a logical and understandable way. This is a serious mistake, because the party that best explains the factual setting in a clear and objective fashion is likely to gain an advantage with the arbitrator because it shows the arbitrator that its side understands what the case is all about and wants the arbitrator to share in that understanding.

Whether the facts are given in a chronological order or some other logical sequence, it is important to place them before the arbitrator in a comprehensible fashion. The facts presented should not simply be those that support the advocate's own case, but all the facts that are particularly relevant to the case. By presenting an even-handed description of the facts the advocate demonstrates to the arbitrator that he or she is not afraid that the arbitrator will consider facts that support both sides. It heightens credibility. Moreover, if unfavorable facts are delivered first by the side that is disadvantaged by such facts, such disclosure steals the thunder of the other party, which likely hoped to gain an advantage by highlighting them. The following is an example of a presentation of the facts that indicates evidence supporting both sides' cases.

> Madam Arbitrator, we will show, through the eyewitness testimony of Bob Wall and Anne Edwards, that the shipment arrived shortly after noon on Thursday, July 16, and that it was placed in the storage bin within 30 minutes following its arrival. The company is expected to offer evidence that the shipment did not arrive until 4:00 P.M. on the 16th. We believe the company's evidence on this point is unreliable. In any event, the exact arrival time of the shipment is one of the key factual determinations that you will have to make in this case.

It should be kept in mind that the normal length of an opening statement does not usually allow for a recitation of each and every fact in the case. Even if time did permit, such a recitation would likely result in the arbitrator losing interest. The opening statement should include only the salient or most important facts that will be necessary to enable the arbitrator to make a decision.

In preparing the factual summary the advocate may find it useful to review the five Ws (i.e., who, what, where, when, and why) as was done in the preparation of the case. This should help in making sure that no key facts are omitted.

## Principal Persons Involved

Many cases involve the activities of a relatively large number of persons and their interactions with each other. In such cases arbitrators typically have some difficulty in remembering all of the names and activities of each, at least in the early part of the hearing. The advocates are so familiar with the identity and roles of each of these persons that they frequently do not appreciate the difficulty arbitrators have in keeping the names and roles straight. An advocate can greatly assist the arbitrator in acquiring a grasp of the case by introducing the cast of characters. The following excerpt of an opening statement demonstrates this technique.

Mr./Ms. Arbitrator, this case involves the actions of five key persons who are employed in the company's East St. Louis warehouse. First, there is the grievant, Sol Timmons, who is a forklift operator and who was suspended for gross negligence and insubordination. Then there is Sol's supervisor, Helen Gonzales, who is in charge of the shipping department and the person who suspended Mr. Timmons. The next person involved is Michael Chin, warehouse general manager, who is Helen Gonzales's boss and who has overall management responsibility for the warehouse. Mr. Chin heard the grievance at the third step and affirmed the suspension. Two other important persons in this case are Philip Cartwright and Sue Allotti, who are shipping clerks and who were witnesses to the incidents that are the subject of today's case.

## Technical Terminology and Technical Processes

Some cases require that the arbitrator understand technical terminology and/or technical processes. Such matters as manufacturing equipment and processes, medical terms and procedures, industry jargon, work procedures, and so on are frequently critical to a full understanding of a case. When this is true, it is usually helpful to the arbitrator to have such key technical points explained in the opening statement. The following is an example of this type of explanation.

An important element in this case has to do with the way in which nurses must treat patients with bronchial pneumonia. First, they must understand the functioning of the ventilator equipment, often called "the vent." In particular, they must be careful to ensure that the regulator is properly adjusted in accordance with the doctor's orders. Second, they must. . . .

If the explanation is likely to be too long and detailed, it may be best to simply outline the general subject matter and rely on a witness to present the technical information. The advantage, however, of presenting the information in the opening statement is that it gives the arbitrator an advance view of the critical information before any evidence is introduced. Moreover, the party that first presents the technical information gains an advantage of appearing to have special technical expertise in the matters presented, assuming, of course, that the information is presented in a correct, logical, and understandable manner. Likewise, the advocate who first delivers a clear, precise, and complete description of the technical information is likely to have a favorable impact on witnesses, demonstrating that the advocate has command of the relevant technical information.

When technical jargon is lengthy and important in a case, it may be useful to prepare a glossary or list of terms and definitions to aid the arbitrator, rather than trying to explain all the terms in the opening statement. This list can be presented through a witness who has the technical expertise to validate the information in the glossary.

## Relevant Contract Provisions

It is extremely important in the opening statement to direct the arbitrator's attention to those parts of the labor agreement that are relevant to the case being heard. Because the arbitrator's principal task in the case is to decide what the labor agreement means in the context of the facts presented, the arbitrator should know at the outset of the hearing what contract provisions bear on the case and what position each side takes with respect to those provisions. An example of this aspect of the opening statement follows.

> Mr. Arbitrator, there are three contract provisions that bear directly on this case. First is Section 2, paragraph A, found on page 3 of the agreement. This is the management rights clause. Your attention is drawn to the last sentence of that paragraph, which states, "Nothing in this labor agreement is intended to limit the company's right to operate in a cost-effective manner, provided such operation does not violate any provision of this labor agreement." The company's reliance on the management's rights clause, according to this provision, cannot be exercised in disregard of specific sections of the agreement. The next relevant part of the labor agreement is Section 7, paragraphs C and D on page ten of the agreement, which spell out the procedures for filling newly created positions. The union will present evidence to show that these procedures were not followed in the instant case. Last, you should consider Section 16, paragraph 2-C, on page twenty-three of the labor agreement, which lists all job classifications in the plant. Nowhere will you find the classification of press room expediter, which the company unilaterally established and filled in this case in violation of the labor agreement.

Note that in this example the union advocate not only highlighted the key contractual provisions and the specific pages of the labor agreement on which they could be found, but used the opportunity to state how each supported the union's case.

If there are pertinent provisions contained in a side letter of agreement, and/or supported by past practice, or bargaining history, these should likewise be mentioned, along with the advocate's explanation of how those matters support the advocate's position.

## Remedy Sought

The party filing the grievance (usually the union) should not neglect in the opening statement to tell the arbitrator what relief is being sought.

While such information will usually be surmised by the arbitrator, the advocate should leave no doubt in the arbitrator's mind as to exactly what the grieving party is seeking from the case. For example,

> The union in this case seeks a cancellation of the layoffs of Ms. Smith and Mr. Green, reinstatement to the positions they held prior to the layoff, full back pay, restoration of benefits, and reinstatement of full seniority. We also seek reimbursement to them for any personal expenses they incurred as a result of the layoff and lack of company-provided benefits. Lastly, the union seeks a declaration from the arbitrator that any future layoffs that result from departmental closures are to be accomplished according to job seniority.

By knowing the remedy sought by the union on behalf of the grievant at the outset of the case, the arbitrator is better able to evaluate the subsequent evidence and arguments.

## STRATEGIC ISSUES

### When to Make the Opening Statement

Most arbitrators seem to prefer that both parties make their opening statements at the beginning of the hearing. In this way both sides' versions of the facts and positions can be known at the outset and can be compared. The differences in the case can be spotted early, and the arbitrator can then focus his or her attention on the key areas of difference.

Some advocates, however, do not like to reveal their case until they are ready to present their evidence. Their purpose is to deny the other side the opportunity of knowing what facts and arguments they are going to rely on to prove their case. Thus, for example, the union in a discharge or discipline case may postpone its opening statement until the employer has presented its evidence, and an employer in a contract interpretation case may refrain from making an opening statement until the union has put on its witnesses and evidence. The proper way to advise the arbitrator of this option is as follows: "The union reserves making its opening statement until the employer has completed its case in chief."

The advocate needs to evaluate whether the advantages of this strategy outweigh its disadvantages. The advantage of reserving the opening statement until later in the hearing is, of course, that it precludes the other side from knowing for certain just what evidence is going to be stressed and what contractual arguments will be raised. In postponing the opening statement, however, the postponing party misses the opportunity to focus the arbitrator's attention on the salient facts as seen by it, to influence the arbitrator's judgment at an early stage of the process, and to influence the witnesses as described above.

Other things being equal, the author favors giving an opening statement at the outset of the hearing. Because the case being presented will invariably have been discussed at one or more earlier steps of the grievance procedure, most of what will be presented in the arbitration hearing has already been covered by the parties. It is the exceptional case in which completely new evidence or arguments are advanced, hence, there is little to be gained by holding back on the opening statement.

When, however, a party does have new evidence, different contractual theories, and/or a different approach to the case than was taken at earlier stages of the grievance procedure, the advocate may achieve some strategic advantage by reserving the opening statement until the other side has presented all of its evidence. A party that does hold back its position and evidence in such a manner risks a hostile reaction from the other party for playing games, being less than open and forthright, and other such allegations. There is also a risk that the arbitrator may agree with such allegations, resulting in an advantage to the other side.

### Waiving the Opening Statement

A step more drastic than reserving the opening statement is to waive it completely. The logic for doing so would be that the facts and positions are so simple and straightforward that they will come out in a satisfactory way through the evidence. This is a rather weak rationale, however, because no matter how simple the facts and arguments, each side's case presentation can always be enhanced by an effective opening statement. In virtually all cases an advocate does his or her principals a disservice by waiving the opening statement.

### Substituting a Written Opening Statement or Prehearing Brief for an Oral Opening Statement

Prehearing briefs are seldom used in labor arbitration cases. One does see them more frequently when an advocate is a trial attorney who is unfamiliar with labor arbitration practice or when the controlling labor agreement provides for them (which is rather unusual).

A major problem with prehearing briefs is that the arbitrator seldom has an opportunity to read the brief prior to the beginning of the hearing.

Therefore, the principal value of the brief, that is, to orient and influence the arbitrator prior to the introduction of evidence, is lost. If the arbitrator does not read the brief until the case has been presented, the material can be better presented in a posthearing brief, which is a commonly used tool in labor arbitration cases.

In rare instances a prehearing brief may be useful—in major cases where the matters at stake are quite large and the evidence and contractual arguments are complex and voluminous. When a hearing is expected to run for days or weeks and the exhibits and testimony are expected to run to hundreds or thousands of pages, an oral opening statement may be insufficient to properly direct the arbitrator to all the critical parts of the case. In such cases a well-organized prehearing brief can be helpful, and perhaps persuasive, to the arbitrator.

## Revealing Weaknesses in the Advocate's Evidence or Arguments

An interesting strategic issue arises when an advocate has a weakness in his or her case that is known by the other side. The question is whether that advocate should reveal the weakness to the arbitrator first or wait for the other side to bring it up. For example, in discharging an employee for gross negligence, the supervisor neglected to give the employee an opportunity to explain his actions prior to being discharged. Although there is ample evidence of the employee's negligence, there was a lack of due process in the employer's termination process in not allowing the employee to present his version of the facts before the action was taken. Should the employer's advocate in the opening statement disclose, and try to explain, this failure, or should the advocate ignore it until the union raises it?

The author's view on this point is to reveal a weakness in one's own case at the earliest possible time, provided it is a significant weakness and definitely known by the other party. By identifying the problem first, the advocate can avoid the appearance of trying to hide something from the arbitrator and can put the weakness in the best possible light. For example, the following is one way in which the employer's advocate in the discharge case just discussed may disclose the weakness in the employer's case.

> Following the grievant's failure to lubricate the machine and following his complete inattention to the high-pitched noise coming from the unlubricated bearings, the supervisor called the grievant into the office and told him he was being terminated. The supervisor did not ask the grievant what had happened, because the supervisor had previously been informed

of the grievant's negligence by two eyewitnesses and because the supervisor had to attend immediately to the smoking bearing before a fire broke out.

Although the advocate's early admission of a weakness will not nullify the damage to the case, it can soften the impact it has on the arbitrator, and it will defuse somewhat the other side's highlighting of this damaging evidence. The advocate contemplating such a disclosure should be certain that the weakness is truly a weakness and should be quite certain that the other side intends to raise it. A review of the processing of the grievance at earlier stages of the grievance procedure will usually indicate whether the other side knows of the weakness and is likely to use it in the arbitration hearing.

# FORM AND MANNER OF PRESENTATION

## Length

There are no hard and fast rules as to how long an opening statement should be. Obviously, the nature and complexity of the case will influence how long the statement should be. As a rule of thumb, an opening statement of about three to seven minutes is appropriate, but if the evidence and contractual theories warrant, an advocate should not hesitate to make a longer statement.

## Prepared Statement Versus Notes

Whether an advocate should have the opening statement written in advance to read at the hearing or whether it should be delivered from notes or an outline is a matter of individual style and capabilities. Most statements that are read verbatim have a canned quality and often lack emotion or enthusiasm. Some advocates, however, are skilled at reading a prepared text in a way that sounds extemporaneous. By having a prepared script they can be sure that carefully constructed phrasing is used. Maintaining regular eye contact with the arbitrator while reading from a script is a bit difficult, however, and it is usually more difficult to capture the full attention of the arbitrator when reading a prepared statement.

The author prefers opening statements that are delivered simply with the aid of notes. In this way the presentation can achieve freshness and spontaneity that is difficult, if not impossible, to achieve by reading a prepared statement. If the advocate feels it is important to state certain matters in an exact, verbatim way, the statements themselves can be written in the notes, allowing a more free-flowing style for less critical parts. The advocate should have sufficient familiarity with the material so that extensive reference to the notes is not necessary. Some advocates feel that they have a sufficient grasp of the case to deliver an opening statement without notes. That is usually a mistake. It is simply too easy to overlook some critical points if one relies solely on memory. Nevertheless, the more the advocate can appear to be speaking extemporaneously, the more effective the presentation will be.

In order to ensure a more effective presentation the advocate is advised to rehearse the statement, preferably before one or more colleagues or persons assisting in the case. Unclear or inappropriate passages are more easily spotted in such a dry run.

## Style

The components of a good general speaking style apply to the delivery of an opening statement. Eye contact with the arbitrator is absolutely vital. A calm, deliberate, and reasonably slow pace enhances comprehension. Some variation in pace, tone, and voice volume will heighten interest. Depending on the nature of the case, some emotion (indignation, surprise, pity) may be appropriate, although it must be carefully controlled and used sparingly. The opening statement is not designed to persuade the arbitrator about the final outcome of the case, but to set the scene for favorable reception of evidence. Consequently, the tone of the statement should be less of a hard sell than the closing argument. Nevertheless, the advocate should leave no doubt in the mind of the arbitrator of the advocate's determination, sincerity, and confidence.

The advocate should be careful in an opening statement to avoid overstating the weight of evidence or the contractual underpinnings of his or her case. Credibility is vital, and by promising more conclusive evidence than one can deliver or by making a contract provision appear to say more than it can reasonably be interpreted to mean is to jeopardize the advocate's (and his or her party's) credibility with the arbitrator.

Gestures can enhance a presentation. They should be appropriate to the matters being discussed and should not be so frequent or elaborate as to distract from the presentation.

Because one of the goals of the opening statement is to capture and hold the arbitrator's attention to the case in general, and in particular to the delivering advocate's case, it is sometimes useful to pique the arbitrator's interest with an element of suggestion or mystery. Rather than describe certain pieces of evidence in detail, the advocate may simply allude to the evidence in a way that sparks interest. For example,

- We will hear the testimony of Ms. Pimental, who will describe just what she saw when she entered the locker room on the day in question.
- The company's history of dealing with alcohol and drug abuse will be shown through a series of witnesses and documents. It will be very enlightening and perhaps a bit surprising to see how that history has evolved.

The advocate should be careful in how such techniques are employed, however, lest there be an appearance of being cute or clever or trying to manipulate the arbitrator. Moreover, such a teasing statement should never promise more than can be delivered. Nevertheless, arbitration cases are sometimes dull affairs, and an attempt to raise the interest level will usually be appreciated by the arbitrator. More importantly, the arbitrator, after hearing such an introduction, is likely to be anticipating and focusing on the evidence much more than if no element of surprise or mystery was involved.

## SAMPLE OPENING STATEMENTS

The following examples of employer and union opening statements illustrate the points discussed in this chapter. The hypothetical case involves the discharge of a hotel desk clerk for rudeness to a guest.

### Sample Employer Opening Statement

This case involves the discharge of Ms. Wilma Banky for an act that strikes at the very heart of the employer's business-customer service. The Rincon Hotel, one of a chain of ten hotels operated by the Fidelity Group throughout the United States, provides hotel rooms, meeting rooms, and food and beverage service to its guests. But essentially it provides only one unique product—customer service. The hospitality industry is an extremely competitive one. In this city alone there are twelve first-class hotels. During the current year, the occupancy rate has been only sixty-five percent. Each hotel is scrambling for a piece of a shrinking pie. The Rincon relies on its employees to deliver the type of service that will allow the hotel to continue to compete in this extremely competitive market.

The employer's evidence will show that on September 23, Ms. Banky was handling the checkout of one of the hotel's most influential guests, Mr.

Robert Burns, who is president of World Wide Travel, a travel agency with 250 offices throughout the United States and Europe. The way in which Ms. Banky talked to Mr. Burns and the manner in which she handled his account were so offensive to Mr. Burns that he later advised the hotel that he would never stay in another hotel operated by the Fidelity Group and that in his next newsletter to his 250 offices, he would alert them to the insulting behavior he experienced at the Rincon. Mr. Burns's letter to Fidelity's president will be introduced in evidence.

Beyond the incident on September 23, the grievant, Ms. Banky, has been involved in several previous occurrences that demonstrate her unwillingness or inability to follow the rules established by the hotel. Her previous record of excessive absenteeism and her failure to follow policies concerning proper grooming and uniform appearance led to a written reprimand and a suspension, both within the last two years. Although the hotel did commend her several times for her good service at the front desk, such commendations cannot erase the other negative aspects of her record nor her most serious behavior on September 23.

We anticipate the union will attempt to defend Ms. Banky's activities on September 23 by the words and behavior of Mr. Burns. Because there were no witnesses other than Ms. Banky and Mr. Burns, the union cannot prove from an objective standpoint the truth of her allegations. Ms. Banky certainly has a motive to cast Mr. Burns as a villain in this case in order to save her own job.

The employer will prove that procedures concerning customer service and treatment of guests were well publicized and that employees were given substantial training in these matters. In fact, Ms. Banky attended a training course on this subject only six months prior to the incident. She knew what was expected of her, and she failed to live up to that expectation.

## Sample Union Opening Statement

It is ironic that a company that places such a high value on thoughtful and caring treatment to its guests places such a low value on caring treatment of its employees. This company discharged an employee with eight years of excellent service for one, single, solitary incident involving an arrogant, abusive, and totally insensitive bully.

The union's evidence will show without a doubt that the interchange between Ms. Wilma Banky and Mr. Burns on September 23 was (1) caused by the abusive words of Mr. Burns, (2) a totally understandable reaction to debasing and inflammatory words used by Mr. Burns, and (3) not nearly as serious as the conduct of many other employees of the Rincon Hotel, none of which have received any more serious disciplinary action than a written reprimand.

Our evidence will show that at 6:30 A.M., Mr. Burns was checking out of the Rincon. Ms. Banky, weary after working seven hours in the middle of the night, was preparing Mr. Burns's bill. She will testify that Burns, without provocation, called her names, including ''dumb broad'' and ''surly bitch,'' and that he threatened to have her fired. Ms. Banky will credibly testify that she did everything in her power to meet the guest's needs and offered to have someone else help him. It was only after a long and blistering harangue by Burns that she could not control her emotions and said "Go fuck yourself." The union does not condone that type of language and recognizes that perhaps some disciplinary action might have been appropriate, but at the same time it points out that all persons have a breaking point and that a long-time, faithful employee should not lose her job for one error in judgment.

The union will prove that Wilma Banky was one of the Rincon's best desk clerks and one of its employees who was most attentive to guests' needs and that on no less than four occasions her supervisors found her work so outstanding that they awarded her written letters of commendation. Those letters will be entered into evidence.

The union will offer the testimony of Mr. Manual Hernandez, another desk clerk with the Rincon who will testify to an incident that he had with Mr. Burns several months prior to September 23, in which Mr. Burns displayed his coarse and abusive style toward Mr. Hernandez in much the same manner as he did with Ms. Banky. The company never bothered to investigate this case enough to learn from Mr. Hernandez just what type of guest this Mr. Burns really was. Fortunately, the arbitrator will have that opportunity.

# 9

# Presenting the Case in Chief

Most arbitration cases are won (or lost) on the strength (or weakness) of the parties' cases in chief. This is especially true in those cases where there is a dispute as to the facts in the case, as opposed to those cases involving merely a disagreement as to how the labor agreement applies to facts that are relatively undisputed. There are, of course, exceptions to this general proposition, such as when a blistering cross-examination destroys a key witness or an exceptionally strong final argument or brief carries the day, but most often it is the excellent witnesses and other superior evidence presented by the winning party during its case in chief that accounts for a successful result. Therefore, it behooves the advocate to focus on this aspect of the case more than on any other.

## ORDER OF PRESENTATION

### Burden of Going Forward

As discussed in Chapter 1, labor arbitration practice generally assigns the task of proceeding first with the evidence (i.e., the "burden of going forward") according to the nature of the case being heard. If the case involves discipline or discharge, the employer generally has the obligation of presenting its evidence first. If the case is anything other than discipline or discharge, that is, a contract interpretation dispute, the

223

union typically must present its case first. While there are exceptional cases in which this order is not followed, the exceptions are rare.

# Sequencing the Evidence

Having prepared the witnesses and other evidence for the hearing, each advocate needs to determine the order in which it will present that evidence. There are a number of considerations.

## *Leading from Strength*

Many experienced advocates prefer to begin their case with the strongest witness and proceed to the weakest, provided that the order is not likely to confuse the arbitrator. The rationale is that first impressions are lasting and that the arbitrator is likely to form an early impression of the merits of the case based on the testimony of the witnesses heard early in the case. Moreover, the opposing advocate and the other side's witnesses are likely to be influenced, perhaps even demoralized, by persuasive initial witnesses from the other side. Strong witnesses are those who speak with confidence and certainty (but not cockiness or arrogance), who are articulate and have good recollection, who are intelligent and persuasive, who are credible, and who can respond promptly and effectively to rigorous cross-examination.

Another facet of leading from strength has to do with the value of giving support to subsequent witnesses who do not have strong recollections or who are not articulate in testifying about their recollections. When an advocate leads off with a strong witness and has one or more weaker witnesses to the same events or situations, the advocate may be able to ''piggyback'' a weaker witness onto the stronger one. For example, in a case involving discipline of an employee (Helen Smith) for insubordination toward her supervisor, there is another employee witness who can substantiate Smith's testimony but who is not able to articulate the details very well on his own. By presenting the testimony of Ms. Smith first, the advocate can then offer the testimony of the other employee witness and begin his testimony as follows.

> *Q.* Mr. Lightweight, you have heard, have you not, the testimony of Ms. Smith concerning the events of February 22 in the Malibu store?
>
> *A.* Yes.
>
> *Q.* Would you say that her testimony was accurate as far as what you yourself saw and heard?

*A.* Yes.

In this way the testimony of the weaker witnesses can be introduced without having the witness independently recall all the details of the incident. Of course, the witness is subject to cross-examination on the specifics of the incident, and he or she will have to testify as to his or her own recollection. The employer advocate may, however, be reluctant to probe this witness's recollection too much for fear of merely implanting the union's version of the facts even more deeply in the arbitrator's mind. In this case the advocate offering a weak witness must be careful that the witness does indeed have a personal recollection of having seen and heard the matters about which the testimony is given and can recount those recollections on cross-examination if required to do so.

### Chronological or Other Logical Order

Another major consideration in determining the best order of presenting evidence is that it follow a logical order of events. If the case is about the proper rate of pay established for a new job classification, the union would not present a witness to testify about the computation of damages, no matter how effective that witness would be. The union's advocate would need to put on a witness who could testify about the composition and duties of the position and relate them to other job classifications or to criteria established for measuring job worth. In other words, the order of witnesses should follow a logical development of the case.

The most common logical development of a case is a chronological order. If a case concerns the subcontracting or outsourcing of bargaining unit work, a logical first witness for the union would be someone who could testify about the history of the work having been done by bargaining unit personnel. Sometimes the more logical order is reverse chronological order, that is, beginning with the most recent event and progressing to earlier ones. In a discharge for repeated absenteeism, for example, the employer advocate may present a witness who would testify about the last absence—the one resulting in discharge—and then present other witnesses or documentary evidence establishing previous incidents of absenteeism.

When bargaining history and past practice must be proven, evidence of these will typically follow evidence concerning the action that caused the grievance. For example, in a grievance concerning the propriety of a new work schedule unilaterally established by the employer, the union's case in chief would usually lead off with evidence as to what the actual work schedule change was and how it affected the employees involved. Only after these were established would the advocate proceed to show how the change deviated from past practice or was inconsistent with the intent of the parties who negotiated the contract language at issue.

More often than not, the testimony of one witness will be interrelated with that of another, or the testimony of one will necessarily precede that of another, and the advocate must be aware of which elements of the case need to be established in which order. For example, a union's case in which the grievance was based on the failure of the employer to post a job opening announcement prior to filling a position would logically begin with a witness or other evidence that a job opening actually existed and that it was filled by someone other than the grievant, before introducing evidence concerning the employer's failure to formally announce the job vacancy or post it for employees to bid.

In determining the order of evidence, the advocate should place himself or herself in the shoes of the arbitrator and ask, "What information would I want to know and in which sequence would I want to hear it in order to fully grasp the facts?"

### Meshing Testimony with Other Evidence

Not only should the advocate consider the logical order of witnesses, but also the proper sequence of documentary or other evidence. When a party's case rests on violation of plant rules or violation of a procedure, evidence of the rules or procedure should normally be entered into evidence early in the case in chief. Sometimes, the other party will stipulate to the admission of the rule or procedure, but if this does not occur, the party relying on the document will need a witness to authenticate or lay a foundation for introduction of the document.

When the arbitrator is to view the site of an incident in order to fully comprehend the evidence in the case, a visit to the site in advance may be advised. Similarly, diagrams, photographs, and videos should be introduced early enough in the case to enable the arbitrator to fully appreciate the testimony of witnesses who describe them.

### Maintaining Arbitrator Interest

Advocates should never forget that an arbitrator who loses interest in a case is likely to overlook or otherwise fail to fully appreciate evidence. A successful advocate presents evidence in a way that helps the arbitrator to retain interest in, and curiosity about, the case. This may mean that two witnesses who are going to testify about the technical aspects of a machine or process or any other uninteresting topic should be separated by a witness with more interesting testimony to deliver. Perhaps the testimony of the two technical witnesses can be combined into one. Although this is not usually a matter of great concern, because most arbitrators are able to wade through a good deal of boring evidence, advocates can improve their presentation's effectiveness by being sensitive to the arbitrator's interest and attention level.

# EXAMINING WITNESSES

The initial portions of this section address the types of evidence that are admissible in labor arbitration hearings. Coverage of this subject now is designed to provide the reader with a general background as a prelude to discussing the process of examining witnesses and introducing other evidence in the hearing. A more detailed explanation of the rules of evidence, including the procedures for making and opposing objections, is contained in the next chapter and Chapter 11. This chapter touches on some of the same topics as discussed in Chapter 6 concerning the selection and preparation of witnesses. Chapter 6, however, focused on the preparation of individual witnesses, whereas this section deals with the overall presentation of evidence and how the array of witnesses and other evidence should be integrated.

## Admissible Evidence

The first and primary rule with respect to evidence in almost any evidentiary hearing is that only *material, relevant, and competent evidence* is admissible. This rule applies to trials and other evidentiary hearings and is generally followed in labor arbitration hearings as well, although arbitrators generally interpret the standards for admissibility much more broadly than do judges in a court of law.[1]

Material evidence is that which is directly connected with the matters at issue in the case. If an arbitration case concerns the discharge of an employee for poor work performance, the fact that the employee

---

[1]Lever Bros. Co., 82 LA 164 (Stix, 1983); Hill and Sinicropi, *Evidence in Arbitration,* (BNA Books, 1987), 14–18; Roberts, *Memory and Searching for the Truth: II. Evidence: Taking It for What It's Worth, Arbitration 1987: The Academy at Forty,* Proceedings of the 40th Annual Meeting, National Academy of Arbitrators, G.D. Gruenberg, ed. (BNA Books, 1988), 112–13.

had been convicted of a felony for conduct off the job would not be admissible unless the employer could show that there was a direct connection between the felonious conduct and the poor work performance.

Relevant evidence is evidence that has a tendency to prove or disprove any fact that is necessary to be proven in the case. In a discharge case for the use of alcohol on the job the grievant's unwillingness to have company officials search his or her locker for the presence of a bottle of an alcoholic beverage would be relevant to the fact of actual usage (although it would not be conclusive evidence).

Competent evidence is evidence given by a person who has sufficient knowledge and perception of the matters contained in the testimony to be able to competently testify about them. In a case involving the promotion of a junior employee in preference to a senior employee based on the employer's evaluation of the junior employee's superior skills, the testimony of a department head from a different department than the one in which the two employees worked would not be competent, unless it could be shown that such a person had personally observed the work of both individuals and was in a position to evaluate their relative capabilities. Competency also must exist with respect to documentary or other evidence. A quality control report prepared by someone who had never reviewed the data on which it was based would not normally be competent evidence.

## Procedure for Offering a Witness

Labor arbitration hearings are not usually formal proceedings, and strict rules of procedure are not typically enforced with great zeal. Nevertheless, it is desirable that advocates act as professional as possible in presenting their case. In offering a witnesses to give testimony, the following phrases and statements are typically used:

*Advocate*—Mr./Madam Arbitrator, the union calls Mr. Thomas Rothenberg as its first witness.

*Arbitrator*—Mr. Rothenberg, would you please take the witness chair (witness is sworn at this time, if witnesses are being sworn).

*Advocate*—Would you please state your full name for the record.

*Witness*—Thomas A. Rothenberg.

*Advocate*—What is your position with the union?

*Witness*—I am the secretary-treasurer for IBEW Local 602.

## Facts Versus Opinion and Argument

One of the most common difficulties encountered by inexperienced lay (i.e., nonlawyer) advocates is to distinguish between evidence that is factual and "evidence" that is opinion or argument. The purpose of the evidentiary portion of a hearing is to establish the facts in the case. The testimony of witnesses and other evidence are used to bring out the facts, not to argue the case. For this reason the following types of questions are neither appropriate nor admissible in a labor arbitration hearing.

*Q.* Do you think the company was right in doing what it did?

*Q.* In your mind what does Article XX, Section 3, mean?

*Q.* Did you feel that Ms. Jones's grievance was justified?

Some labor arbitrators will allow testimony on the questions listed above, even though it is not admissible by the ordinary rules of evidentiary hearings. Nevertheless, advocates should be aware of these rules in order to be prepared for arbitrators who are more rigid in their application of them.

The types of questions that are appropriate with respect to presenting factual evidence are illustrated as follows.

*Q.* When was the first time you observed the customer in the store?

*Q.* When you filed the grievance, did your supervisor say anything to you?

*Q.* What did the chief spokesperson of the union bargaining committee say when the new language for Section 7 was initially proposed in the 1990 negotiations?

This last group of questions asks about observations of actions or objects, statements heard, and motivations. They require the witness to respond with factual statements. They do not invite the witnesses to argue their cases or to render opinions.

## Opinion Testimony

Although it is not admissible evidence for a witness to give an opinion as to why a grievance is justified or for a supervisor to give an opinion as to the meaning of a section of the contract, witnesses are permitted to give opinion testimony under certain limited conditions. The conditions under which opinion testimony will generally be admitted in labor arbitration cases are as follows.

1. When a person has special knowledge, expertise, or familiarity with the subject of the testimony;
2. When the subject is one not within the normal experience or competence of most people; and/or
3. When the subject about which the opinion is requested is not the issue submitted to the arbitrator for decision (e.g., the meaning of a particular contract provision is for the arbitrator to decide and therefore an opinion on that exact point would not be an appropriate subject for a witness to address).

In courts of law, opinion testimony can be given only by an expert witness who has met certain requirements (i.e., has been qualified) for being an expert. For example, physicians who specialize in orthopedic medicine may testify as to the likelihood of a person recovering the use of his or her legs following a serious auto accident.

Opinion testimony in labor arbitration does not require that the person offering the testimony meet the strict tests that an expert witness would have to meet in a court of law.[2] Arbitrators will usually allow opinion testimony if the person offering it appears to have a good background and knowledge of the matters on which the testimony is centered. An employee driver who has driven a particular type of truck for more than twenty years and who presents testimony about the possible causes of a steering problem on that same type of truck will usually be heard. Similarly, a production supervisor who has worked and supervised in plastics extrusion plants for twenty-five years would likely be permitted by an arbitrator to answer questions about the low probability of an extruder malfunction caused by a power failure. Of course, the party not offering the witness may, prior to the witness being allowed to give opinion testimony, attempt to challenge the witness's expertise and may ask questions of the witness, using the process called voir dire to test the level of the witness's expertise. (Voir dire is discussed in detail in Chapter 11.) Similarly, the arbitrator may ask the witness questions to ensure that the witness is truly competent to render opinions on the matters being inquired about.

Such opinion testimony must be limited to those matters that are outside the knowledge and purview of the arbitrator who is to decide the case. In an arbitration hearing concerning a contract interpretation dispute, a question put to a witness about the meaning and effect of the particular contract provision at issue in the case is not normally admissible opinion testimony, because it is the arbitrator's function to interpret

---

[2]S. Calif. Rapid Transit Dist., 96 LA 20, 23 (Gentile, 1990); Hosp. Employees, 77-2 ARB 8554 (Handsaker, 1979).

the contract, not the witness's, no matter how experienced or knowledgeable the witness may be with the labor contract involved. Such a question is the ultimate question, the one that finally has to be decided by the arbitrator. Similarly, an opinion sought from a witness as to the justification of an employee being late for work three days in a row as a result of a faulty alarm clock is not normally admissible because it is an opinion that could not be rendered by any nonexpert, unless the witness has some special expertise in the operation of alarm clocks.

Later in this chapter is a detailed discussion concerning the ways to introduce opinion testimony. The purpose of addressing opinion testimony at this point is to assist the advocate in avoiding having his or her own witnesses giving opinion testimony where it is not appropriate and to spot it in the testimony of the other side's witnesses as a prelude to registering an objection.

## Properly Framed Questions

### *Clarity*

Regardless of the subject matter of a question, it is important that each question be clear to the witness and to the arbitrator. Unclear or poorly phrased questions are likely to confuse witnesses and, even if answered correctly, may prove to be of little value to the case because the arbitrator does not understand the importance of what was asked and answered. The following are examples of the type of questions that should be avoided.

Q. When they were beginning the new process on your side of the trench did the others say anything about them not knowing how to work both sides together so that they could see what they were doing?

Q. You told us about how you went to work and that you completed three jobs, A, B, and C. When was that?

Q. Of all the times you supervised Crew A between September and January, how many people worked?

A careful witness would almost certainly have to ask for a clarification of each of these questions in order to provide correct answers. Even if the witness were able to answer without clarification, an attentive arbitrator would almost certainly have to ask the witness to clarify the answer. Either way, the advocate is asking for problems. Sometimes a poorly phrased question can only be improved by breaking the question into several parts. In other cases, a complete rephrasing of the question will permit the same information to be elicited with just one question. The examples listed above might be improved as follows.

Q. You testified about the new process being done on your side of the trench, while the other crew was working on their side. During this time, did anyone ask how the job could be done by both crews working together? [answer] [If answer is yes] Who made the statement and what did he or she say?

Q. What time did you finish Job A? What time for Job B? What time for Job C?

Q. During the period from September to January when you supervised Crew A, what was the average [normal] number of employees on your crew each day?

## Questions Calling for Narrative Answers

A major differentiation between types of questions is the distinction between questions that can be answered by a simple yes or no and questions that call for the witness to give a narrative reply. The following are examples of each.

Q. Were you displeased with the results of the test? [answer: yes or no]

Q. How would you describe your feelings about the test results? [answer: narrative answer]

Generally, a number of questions calling for yes/no answers are necessary to elicit the same information that results from one question calling for a narrative answer. For example:

*Yes/No*
Did you go to the locker room at the end of your shift?
Was Jim Smith in the locker room at the time?
What, if anything, did you say to Mr. Smith?

*Narrative*
Describe what happened in the locker room when you went there after your shift ended.

There is no formula to guide an advocate as to which of these two types of questions to use and when to use them. There are several guidelines, however, that may prove helpful in making good selections. Questions that call for narrative answers work better for witnesses who are articulate and have a good recollection of the details that need to be brought out in an answer. Questions calling for yes/no answers are generally more helpful at critical parts of testimony when essential facts are being elicited. Questions calling for narrative answers are good for covering background information. When it is crucial that specific words be used as part of an answer, questions calling for a yes/no answer are generally preferable. It is usually a good idea to use a mixture of these types of questions when interrogating any one witness. For example:

*Q.* Ms. Oakes, how long have you been a waitress?
*A.* Ten years.

*Q.* Has this been with the same employer?
*A.* Yes.

*Q.* When did you last work for this employer?
*A.* June 30 of this year.

*Q.* Please describe the circumstances that caused you to leave this work.
*A.* I was continually being asked by my supervisor to date him after I finished work. He started to pressure me.

*Q.* Would you have left but for his conduct in this regard?
*A.* No.

The advantages of a mixture of questions are that it relieves the witness of the burden of remembering too many narrative answers and it helps to keep the interrogation interesting to the arbitrator by varying the pace and the form of questions.

### Leading Versus Open-Ended Questions

Very closely related to the distinction between questions calling for yes/no or narrative answers is the distinction between leading questions and open-ended questions. Leading questions are those that suggest the answer sought by the interrogator or that lead the witness to the desired answer. The following are examples of leading questions.

*Q.* You were very tired by that time, weren't you?

*Q.* She didn't answer your question, did she?

*Q.* Wasn't that the last document you placed in that box?

The reader will note that the answers not only call for a simple yes or no answer, but that the witness is encouraged or suggested to select only one of those two options. If the witness had any doubt about the "correct" answer to the question (i.e., the one sought by the interrogator), that doubt is removed by the manner in which the question is framed.

The rule followed by most arbitrators is that *leading questions may not be asked on direct examination.*[3] In other words, an advocate may not ask his or her own witness a leading question. The reason should be rather obvious. When questions are asked that lead the witness to the answer suggested by the interrogator, the resulting testimony becomes that of the advocate instead of the witness's. For this reason, arbitrators usually sustain objections from the opposing side that the advocate is leading the witness. The objection does not mean that the question cannot be asked at all, but merely that it must be rephrased in a nonleading fashion. For example, the above examples of leading questions could have been framed in a nonleading manner as follows.

*Q.* How did you feel by that time?

*Q.* Did she answer your question or not?

*Q.* What was the last document you placed in the box?

Leading questions are sometimes permitted on direct examination for preliminary or background matters when there is no dispute about the facts. For example, in having the witness outline his or her background and experience with the employer or union, advocates may ask leading questions. Once the questions go to facts that are essential to proving the case, however, the leading nature of the questions must stop. As discussed in Chapter 6, the author does not recommend leading questions even for this limited purpose because little is gained by way of time conservation and the witness can be made to appear inadequate by having to be led on matters that should be known and recollected naturally.

### Use of Notes by Witnesses

It is expected that witnesses will testify as to their experiences and perceptions based on their own recollections. Consequently, the general rule is that a witness's testimony should not normally rely on notes or other documents. Some witnesses do not feel confident about testifying in a hearing without the benefit of notes. Unless the arbitrator is one who does not follow the general rules of evidence, the witness will simply have to overcome that reluctance and testify from recollection.

Despite the general rule against the use of notes to aid testimony, there are several exceptions. First, if a witness is testifying about a particular document or other piece of evidence, the document may be given to the witness at the time the testimony is being given. Generally,

---

[3]"Problems of Proof in the Arbitration Process: Report of the Chicago Area Tripartite Committee," in *Problems of Proof in Arbitration,* Proceedings of the 19th Annual Meeting, National Academy of Arbitrators, 86 (BNA Books, 1967) 101–102.

the document itself is entered into the record just before or after the testimony related to that document. This process is discussed in greater detail later in this chapter under the heading "Introducing Documents and Other Exhibits."

## Refreshing the Recollection of a Witness

Another exception to the general rule of a witness not relying on notes to testify occurs when a witness is testifying concerning a particular subject or event about which the witness previously made notes, but the details of which the witness cannot remember without referring to the notes. In such cases the notes or other documents may be used to refresh the witness's recollection. These notes, however, must have been prepared at or around the time of the event or situation reported in the notes. If the notes were prepared in advance of the hearing simply to assist the witness in testifying, they will not generally be permitted by the arbitrator to refresh the witness's recollection. The proper manner for refreshing the witness's recollection is to establish that the witness did observe or experience the situation or event but is unable to recall at the time of testifying just what occurred without the aid of the notes or some document. The following interchange would be an appropriate way to accomplish this.

Q. Did you take a reading of the pressure and temperature of the boiler before you took your lunch break?

A. Yes.

Q. What were they?

A. I don't specifically recall.

Q. Is there anything that would help you to recall?

A. Yes, I made a note in my personal log of the boiler pressure and temperature?

Q. Is this the log to which you refer? [Advocate shows the log to the witness.]

[At this point, the examining advocate should pass the log to the opposing advocate for his or her inspection, and if there is no objection or questions of the witness by the opposing advocate, the log may be given to the witness.]

Q. Would you take a look at the log and tell us whether it helps to refresh your recollection?

A. Yes, it does.

Q. What were the pressure and temperature readings?

*A.* The pressure was 275 psi and the temperature was 130 degrees Fahrenheit.

[At this point the log, or a copy, may be offered into evidence, but it is not necessary to do so. It is usually preferable to do so, however, since evidence in writing supporting oral testimony usually is more persuasive than oral testimony alone.]

## Defining Transitions

The testimony of most witnesses consists of information about a series of matters. The first part usually consists of background information about the witness and his or her connection with the issues in the case. Subsequent parts of the testimony convey recollections of events or incidents, conversations, participation in meetings, past practices, and so on. For the benefit of the arbitrator and frequently for the witness as well, it is sometimes helpful to separate subject areas of the testimony with statements denoting a transition from one subject to another. For example,

Now, Ms. Peterson, I am going to ask you some questions about your tenure in the accounts receivable department and your experience in working under the supervision of Mr. Swayze, the manager of that department.

Such a demarcation alerts the witness to shift focus and to be ready for questions on a new subject. It also signals the arbitrator that a new subject is being opened up, identifies the subject of the subsequent testimony, and may even heighten the arbitrator's interest in the testimony to come.

## Ensuring That the Record Reflects Nonverbal Testimony

It is rather common for witnesses to use their heads, hands, or other parts of the body to express themselves during their testimony. Gestures such as shrugging the shoulders, spreading the hands apart to indicate the length of an object, or raising the eyebrows are natural ways that individuals use to intensify the meaning of their spoken words. Unfortunately, when a verbatim transcript of the hearing is being taken, the reporter will seldom note the gesture in the transcript (or, if it is noted, it is usually only a cryptic reference, "gesturing"). If an advocate wants the gesture to be included in the record, the advocate must articulate the movements so that they will be reflected in the record. The proper means for doing so are as follows.

[Immediately following a gesture by a witness]

*Advocate:* Madam Arbitrator, may the record reflect that the witness just raised his hands to his face and covered his face with the hands in a cupped posture.

*Arbitrator:* The record shall so reflect.

When the witness is indicating distance with the use of the hands or fingers, the advocate may make a similar statement estimating the actual distance shown by the witness's gesture. The advocate may say, "Mr. Arbitrator, may the record reflect that the witness is holding her index fingers apart with approximately six inches between the two fingers."

In some cases the advocate may elect to characterize the gesture in a more descriptive way, such as the following: "Madam Arbitrator, may the record reflect that the witness raised his eyebrows in a fashion reflecting surprise or astonishment."

What is important is that the gesture and its elaboration of the witness's testimony not get lost in the record of the case simply because the reporter could not, or did not, put the gestures into words.

## Revealing Weaknesses

In Chapter 8, "Opening Statements," it was recommended that weaknesses in one side's case that are known to the other side should generally be revealed for the record in the opening statement. The same recommendation is made with respect to weaknesses in a witness's testimony. When a witness has not previously been forthright, when a grievant's previous work record has serious blemishes, or when a supervisor's treatment of employees has been seriously called into question, it is generally advisable to bring out such vulnerabilities on direct examination if it is anticipated that the other side will do so on cross-examination.

By raising the weaknesses on direct examination the matter can be put in its most favorable light by the way the question is posed and by the manner in which the prepared answer is delivered. In addition, the witness's and advocate's credibility with the arbitrator is usually enhanced by the revelation of a fact that is harmful to their side's case. The following is an example of how this can be accomplished.

*Q.* Ms. Taylor, your grievance states that you worked overtime for four hours on December 24, is that what it says?

A. Yes.

Q. Was that the actual number of hours you worked that day?

A. No, I actually worked two hours.

Q. How do you account for the discrepancy?

A. When I filed the grievance I was thinking of the number of hours pay I was entitled to rather than the number of hours I actually worked. Christmas Eve overtime is paid at double time.

Q. When did you realize your mistake?

A. Not until the third-step grievance meeting in which this error was brought to my attention.

If weaknesses are initially brought out on cross-examination rather than on direct examination, it can often appear as though the witness or the advocate for the witness's side was trying to hide the weakness. Moreover, the questions posed by the opposing advocate are likely to be more accusatory than those posed by the advocate for the witness's side.

This recommendation to reveal a weakness in one's own case or in one's own witness is made, however, only for those situations in which the weakness is clearly known by the other side and is certain to be raised by the other side if not brought out on direct examination. Even though it is brought out on direct examination, it can be anticipated that the other side will pursue it on cross-examination. Nevertheless, by that time it will be old news, and hopefully most of the sting will be out of it by then.

## Assisting or Rehabilitating the Forgetful or Misspeaking Witness

Notwithstanding extensive preparation, witnesses can always surprise the advocate who prepared them. One of the most difficult situations an advocate can encounter in the examination of a witness is to have that witness give incorrect testimony, forget an answer, give an unexpected damaging answer, or contradict earlier testimony. In essence, the wandering witness does not follow the script. The solutions are not the same for each type of problem nor for each witness. The advocate has to make a quick evaluation as to how to proceed in any given situation. At most, the author can provide only general guidelines.

### The Forgetful Witness

Perhaps the easiest of wandering witnesses to deal with is the one who merely forgets an answer. At least no harmful testimony has yet been given. Most arbitrators are sympathetic with persons who forget and are willing to grant some leeway to the advocate to assist the witness in remembering. The advocate's challenge is to get the witness's mind back on the subject at hand in order to remember the correct answer. There are several ways to this.

The most obvious solution is to repeat the question slowly to the witness, perhaps emphasizing one or two key words of the question. If that does not work, the question might be rephrased to make it more understandable or to focus the witness's attention on the correct answer. If that does not help, the advocate should evaluate just how important the testimony is to the overall case. If it is not essential or if the information can be provided by another witness, it may be advisable to drop the question altogether. If, however, that is not the case, the advocate should proceed with an attempt to jog the witness's memory. One approach is to take the witness back to the preparation of testimony and to draw out the lost answer. The following is an example of this approach.

> *Q.* Mr. Lighthead, do you recall that when you and I were preparing your testimony two days ago, you described to me the incident involving the cleanup assignment given to you and Ms. Herald in October of last year?
>
> *A.* Yes.
>
> *Q.* Who did you tell me gave you that assignment?
>
> *A.* The catering department supervisor, whose name I don't remember.
>
> *Q.* Ok. Now, what did you tell me that the supervisor told you and Ms. Herald just before assigning you the work?
>
> *A.* I don't exactly remember.
>
> *Q.* Did you tell me something about the places the supervisor wanted you to work?
>
> *A.* Yes, I did.
>
> *Q.* Where were those places?
>
> ... etc.

This can be an agonizing process akin to pulling teeth, and it may very well draw an objection from the other side that the witness is being coached or led into giving the answers that the advocate wants the witness to provide. The counterargument to the arbitrator is that the witness has simply forgotten the answer and that the advocate is merely trying to refresh the witness's recollection. Most arbitrators will allow some efforts to help the witness, at least up to the point where it appears that the information is coming from the advocate and not the witness.

Another method of assisting a forgetful witness is the one described earlier in the chapter, that is, using notes or other documents to refresh the witness's recollection, provided the notes were not prepared just in advance of the hearing to assist the witness in testifying.

## The Misspeaking Witness

A more serious problem occurs when a witness gives testimony that goes beyond that which was prepared to be given or which is simply erroneous. In such a case, potentially damaging evidence is in the record, and the advocate needs to determine what, if any, effective action needs to be taken.

### Volunteered Truthful Information

One situation involving a misspeaking witness is one in which the witness provides more information than is called for by the question or more than what he or she had been prepared to respond. An example of this type of problem is as follows.

Q. Where did you work prior to joining XYZ Corp.?
A. I worked for ABC Corp., but I quit because I thought they were going to fire me.

Obviously, the advocate asked only the name of the prior employer and did not ask the witness the reason for leaving the prior company. The witness foolishly offered the damaging information. Although the advocate might ask that the last portion of the answer be struck "because it was not responsive to the question," such a request would not usually be granted, and the mere attempt to do so would make the information appear even more harmful than it otherwise would be. If the information volunteered is truthful, there is little that the inquiring advocate can do to repair the damage. To the extent that the advocate was previously unaware of the damaging information, the advocate cannot safely ask other questions at the time to repair or modify the damaging information. Further questions about the witness's experience at ABC Corp. to offset the negative impression can be very dangerous without advance discussion, because the advocate may simply make the situation worse.

The advocate may request a brief recess to confer with the witness, or, if there is a break in the witness's testimony or if the witness is later recalled, there may be an opportunity to repair the damage if there are some facts that could be effective in mitigating the harmful effects. For example:

Q. When you testified previously, you said you were afraid of being fired from your job at ABC. Why were you afraid?

A. They were firing a lot of people who didn't have college degrees.

Q. Did you have a good record at ABC?

A. Yes, I did.

When it is not feasible to improve the situation as illustrated above, the best course of action is to let the volunteered information lie and attempt to minimize its significance in the closing argument or posthearing brief.

*Erroneous Answer*

Another harmful situation occurs when the witness gives the wrong answer to a question. The error may be caused by a misunderstanding of the question, an error in recollection, or some confusion in the witness's mind that results in giving the wrong answer. If the cause is a misunderstanding of the question, the problem can usually be solved by simply repeating the question, perhaps more slowly. If the error is because of poor recollection or confusion, curing the problem will be more difficult.

If the error is on a minor point, it may sometimes be advisable to ignore the error and simply proceed, but, the witness's credibility can be injured even on a minor point if reliable contrary evidence is received that shows the witness to be wrong. Consequently, it is usually preferable to try to correct the witness even on minor points. One way to do this is to suggest the correct answer to the witness, as illustrated in the following example.

Q. Ms. Plum, how long have you worked for XYZ Corp.?

A. Six months.

Q. You mean six years?

A. Oh yes, six years.

This technique may also be attempted on errors of greater moment, although with some risk of being accused of leading or coaching the witness. The following is an example:

Q. Ms. Plum, did your supervisor, Alice Jones, ever tell you that when you registered late-arriving guests you should mark the register with a blue pencil?

A. No.

Q. Are you sure she didn't instruct you to use a blue pencil when you checked in a guest who was later than the scheduled arrival time?

A. Oh yes, I think I misunderstood you at first. She did tell me to use the blue pencil when that happened.

Another method of attempting to correct the witness is to rephrase the question, as follows.

*Q.* Ms. Plum, did your supervisor, Alice Jones, ever tell you that under certain circumstances you should mark the register with a blue pencil?

*A.* No.

*Q.* Let me rephrase that question because it may not have been completely clear to you. Did Alice Jones at one time or another instruct you that you should use a blue pencil when you registered guests who had arrived later than they were scheduled to check in?

*A.* Oh yes, she told me that guests who checked in after 6 P.M. were to be registered with a blue pencil.

The use of the statement, "Let me rephrase..." sends a signal to the witness that a mistake has been made. Hopefully, that introduction plus the actual rephrasing of the question will be sufficient to get the witness to correct the answer. That is not always true, however, when the witness simply forgets or is otherwise confused about the correct answer. The problem with trying to rehabilitate a witness is that one or more unsuccessful attempts will inevitably be perceived as efforts to manipulate or control the witness's testimony and, if objected to, are likely to draw the ire of the arbitrator. Nevertheless, when the point of error is crucial to the case, the advocate cannot remain passive with a witness who is giving erroneous testimony.

### *Delayed Rehabilitation*

In the above examples the advocate attempts to correct the witness's testimony immediately after the erroneous information is given. This is the ideal time, because if the witness can correct the error right away, less attention will be drawn to the error and subsequent related testimony will not be premised on erroneous information. It is sometimes not feasible, though, to alert the witness that an error has been made, and efforts at correction may simply reinforce the error. Too much damage may be done that cannot later be undone. Consequently, the advocate needs to assess just how confused the witness is and determine whether the correction can be made immediately or whether the witness needs to be counseled during a break in the hearing.

If the witness, despite the advocate's attempt to correct, appears to be convinced that the erroneous testimony is accurate, the advocate should try to pass over the point, counsel the witness at a later time in a private conversation, and bring the witness back to testify in order to correct the problem. The following example shows how this might be accomplished.

   *Q.* Mr. Harriman, about what time of the day did you discuss with Ms. Peterson the need to restock the tote bags?

   *A.* It was about 3 P.M.

   *Q.* Based on your earlier testimony, are you certain that it was 3:00 in the afternoon of October 27 when you told Ms. Peterson to replenish the tote bags?

   *A.* Yes.

   *Q.* Let me pass this subject and ask you some questions about the incident concerning the claim checks. . . .

[After Mr. Harriman completes his testimony, the advocate asks the arbitrator for a five-minute break to consult with his witness. During that consultation the advocate reminds the witness that in their initial interview and during the preparation of his testimony, Harriman had said that he told Ms. Peterson to restock the tote bags at 10:00 A.M. on the morning of October 27. Harriman explains that he simply got mixed up and provides the advocate with the probable reason for the confusion.]

*Advocate:* Mr. Arbitrator, I wish to have Mr. Harriman resume the witness chair for a few more questions. [Arbitrator grants request.]

   *Q.* Mr. Harriman, in your earlier testimony you stated that you told Ms. Peterson to restock the tote bags at 3 P.M. on October 27. Do you still believe that time to be correct.

   *A.* No, I talked to her about the tote bags at approximately 10:00 A.M. that day.

   *Q.* Are you certain of that time?

   *A.* Yes, I am certain because I was out of the store on that day from 1:30 P.M. to 4:00 P.M. and could not have spoken with her then. Also, I distinctly remember talking to her about the bags just after her morning coffee break, which ends at 10 A.M.

   *Q.* Can you explain why you said in your earlier testimony that it was 3 P.M.?

   *A.* I confused this discussion with one I had with her the week before when I asked her to do a price check on some new merchandise. That conversation took place in midafternoon.

During the course of this process the advocate should expect serious objections to be registered by the opposing advocate. In reply, the advocate can only explain to the arbitrator that the witness was confused,

244 How to Prepare and Present a Labor Arbitration Case

that his initial testimony varied from that which was conveyed to the advocate on two earlier occasions, and that the advocate felt an obligation to assist the witness in eliminating the confusion.

Regardless of the means used to induce a witness to correct erroneous testimony, the impact of the error cannot be completely undone. The witness's overall credibility will have been reduced as a result of the error and the attempts to correct it. On balance, however, it is usually preferable to have the testimony corrected for the record even at the cost of diminished credibility.

## The Hostile Witness

There is another category of erroneous testimony that occurs, usually not because of a simple mistake or confusion by the witness, but because of an intentional change in the witness's version of the facts from those related earlier to the advocate. In other words, when the witness was being interviewed and prepared by the advocate, he or she gave one story, but when questioned by the same advocate in the hearing, he or she intentionally gives another story. This phenomenon sometimes occurs when the witness is an employee from the bargaining unit who testifies on behalf of the employer, the witness is a third party unaffiliated with either the employer or the union (e.g., a customer or bystander), or the witness is initially reluctant to testify but subsequently agrees to do so under some duress.

### Strategic Considerations

The advocate faced with a witness who is intentionally not following the testimony that was outlined in the preparation must quickly assess the situation and select from among the options that are available, none of which are very appealing. The options are:

1. Try, with followup questions, to correct or modify the witness's testimony on the premise that the witness has misunderstood the questions or is otherwise confused.
2. Without further questioning excuse the witness in the hope that not too much damage has been done and out of fear that further questioning may only make matters worse.
3. Attempt to impeach the witness by identifying him or her as a hostile witness.

There are no easy guidelines that will make the choice of options a simple one. Much will depend on the advocate's assessment of the witness and the witness's good faith. If it appears that the witness simply intended all along to trick the advocate and is trying to damage the advocate's case, there is little room for anything other than option three, i.e., trying to impeach the witness by treating him or her as hostile. If, however, the witness appears to be acting in good faith and has simply come to realize that the planned testimony was erroneous, it may be preferable to excuse the witness with the fervent hope that irreparable damage has not been done and that perhaps other possible evidence can outweigh or mitigate the harmful testimony. Of course, if the witness is merely confused and gave the harmful testimony in error, additional questioning should be sufficient to bring the witness back on track.

When the advocate feels that the only real recourse is to challenge the witness's integrity, that is, go for option 3 above, the advocate should then request that the arbitrator declare the witness a hostile witness thereby enabling the advocate to use leading questions for the balance of that witness's testimony.

The theory behind this rule of allowing leading questions of one's own witness is that the party that calls the witness vouches for the truthfulness of that witness. When, however, that witness surprises the inquiring advocate by giving adverse testimony, the advocate is no longer bound by the testimony and may ask leading questions just as if the witness were testifying as a witness for the other side.

It is essential that the advocate wishing to convert the witness to a hostile witness announce to the arbitrator that he or she has been surprised. This may be done by explaining to the arbitrator, and/or showing notes to prove, that the witness's testimony in the hearing differs from that given to the advocate prior to the hearing. Upon a proper showing, the arbitrator will declare the witness as hostile to the side calling him or her and will allow the questioning to continue in the manner of cross-examination.

## INTRODUCING DOCUMENTS AND OTHER EXHIBITS

Chapter 4 covered in some detail the types of documentary and other evidence that need to be obtained and prepared for the hearing. The following sections address the process of getting those materials admitted into evidence. As with so many other aspects of an arbitration hearing, the degree of formality followed by arbitrators with respect to the introduction of exhibits varies considerably. Most arbitrators are willing to forgo formal hearing procedures, at least for lay advocates, so long as the evidence appears to be relevant and authentic. Nevertheless, the quality of the advocate's presentation of the case will be more effective, professional, and persuasive if the advocate follows, as much as possible, the accepted formalities of an evidentiary hearing. The following sections outline the standard procedures followed in more formal labor arbitration administrative hearings.

## Steps in Introducing Exhibits

There are essentially five steps to be taken in order to get an exhibit admitted into evidence.

1. Have the exhibit marked for identification and present the original to the arbitrator.
2. Present a copy of the exhibit to the opposing advocate.
3. Show the exhibit to the witness or present the witness with a copy of the exhibit.
4. Ask the witness sufficient questions to lay a foundation for admission of the exhibit.
5. Offer the exhibit in evidence or make a motion that the exhibit be admitted into evidence.

Each of these steps will be discussed separately.

### *Step 1—Have the Exhibit Marked for Identification*

As suggested in Chapter 4, there normally should be four copies of each exhibit. The first copy, usually the original (although some arbitrators are satisfied with a copy if there is no dispute concerning the authenticity of the document), should be given to the arbitrator and will become part of the official record. The second copy is to be given to the opposing advocate. The third should be handed to the witness to be used to aid his or her testimony concerning the exhibit. The fourth is for the examining advocate and is part of the advocate's hearing notebook. If the case is being heard by a board of arbitration, there should be an additional copy for each board member besides the neutral arbitrator.

### *When to Mark Exhibits*

Although some advocates mark their exhibits in advance of the hearing, the author prefers to delay marking them for identification until they are produced in the hearing. There are several reasons for this suggestion. First, there may be one or more exhibits that the advocate feels are marginal and that may never be used. If exhibits are premarked but not offered in evidence, there will be an obvious gap in the numbering sequence. Second, sometimes the order in which the advocate offers exhibits varies from the preparation stage to the actual hearing (e.g., one witness testifies before another because of a scheduling problem), and, if exhibits are premarked, they will be entered into the record out of numerical order or will have to be remarked. Consequently, it is usually best to leave exhibits unmarked until the hearing is in progress.

## How to Mark Exhibits

The designations for marking exhibits varies somewhat from region to region and arbitrator to arbitrator, but the one that appears to be most common is a simple arabic numeral system with separate, sequentially numbered employer exhibits, union exhibits, and joint exhibits. For example, the first exhibit entered by the employer is designated Employer Exhibit 1 and the fourth exhibit entered into evidence by the union is Union Exhibit 4. When single documents have multiple pages, the separate pages are sometimes given alphabetical markings, so that a union bulletin consisting of six pages would be marked union exhibit 3 A–F or union exhibits 3A through 3F.

Joint exhibits are used for evidence that is produced by both parties or that is accepted by both parties as their own. The applicable labor agreement is typically a joint exhibit and is commonly marked Joint Exhibit 1. Minutes of grievance meetings that have previously been distributed to and/or signed by both parties are often designated as joint exhibits. The willingness of a party to have an exhibit marked as a joint exhibit usually means that the party has no objection to its introduction even though the other party may have produced it.

## Marked Exhibits Are Not Neccessarily Admitted

Some lay and/or novice advocates are under the impression that once an exhibit has been marked for identification it has therefore been admitted into evidence and is thereafter part of the record. That is not true. The exhibit has to be offered in evidence, an opportunity must be provided for the opposing advocate to register an objection, and, finally, the exhibit must be admitted before it is part of the record. Some arbitrators prefer a nontechnical approach to evidence and will treat exhibits marked for identification as having been admitted into evidence unless the other party raises an objection, but, whenever this procedure is to be used, the arbitrator should specifically advise the parties of this informal handling lest they miss an opportunity to object to the introduction of an exhibit before it becomes part of the record.

*Who Marks Exhibits*

There is no hard and fast rule as to who physically marks the exhibits. The most common practice seems to be that the arbitrator marks the original or the copy that will be part of the record, and the advocates each mark their own copies. When a verbatim transcript of the hearing is being taken, the reporter will often mark exhibits. It is not at all unusual, however, for the advocate offering an exhibit to mark the original and each copy.

The correct procedure for having an exhibit marked for identification and subsequent introduction is as follows: "M/Ms. Arbitrator, we ask that this document be marked for identification as Union Exhibit 3" [while handing the original document to the arbitrator].

Once the original document and the copies have been marked, the advocate proceeds to step two.

### Step 2—Present a Copy of the Exhibit to the Opposing Advocate

Simultaneously with, or immediately after, giving the original of the exhibit to the arbitrator, the offering advocate should present a copy thereof to the opposing advocate for examination and retention (some advocates pass a copy to the opposing advocate first as a matter of courtesy, although this is not required). This allows the opposing advocate time to make a determination as to whether to register an objection to the document when the document is offered into evidence. It also allows the opposing advocate to determine whether he or she wishes to ask the witness any questions about the exhibit on voir dire before registering any objection (this type of voir dire questioning is discussed in detail later in this chapter and in Chapter 11).

### Step 3—Present a Copy of the Exhibit to the Witness

Because the witness will be asked to identify the exhibit and also perhaps asked other questions about the exhibit, it is necessary for him or her to see it. Some advocates merely show the exhibit to the witness, withdraw it, and begin asking questions. Others give a copy of the exhibit to the witness to retain while the questions are being asked. The author prefers the latter method, especially if the witness will be asked any detailed questions concerning the contents of the exhibit. For example, if the witness is given a copy of an accounting report and asked to identify it and to explain the meaning of some of the columnar headings, it will be easier for the witness to have a copy of the report to refer to as the questions are being asked and answered.

Once the exhibit has been identified and entered into evidence and the witness has answered all the offering advocate's questions about the exhibit, it is advisable for the advocate to take the exhibit back from the witness. The reason is that unless it is at the end of his or her testimony, the witness will be asked about other matters and perhaps other exhibits, and it is preferable that he or she not be distracted or confused by several exhibits. If there are questions about the exhibit by the opposing advocate on cross-examination, the exhibit can be returned to the witness when those questions are posed.

### Step 4—Ask the Witness Sufficient Questions about the Exhibit in Order to Lay a Foundation for its Introduction

In order for evidence to be admissible, it must be shown that the evidence is authentic (it is what it purports to be) and relevant (it will prove or tend to prove a fact that directly or indirectly bears on an issue in the case). Because most exhibits must be introduced through witnesses in order to establish their identity and authenticity, it must also be shown that the witness who qualifies the exhibit is competent to establish the nature and source of the document. Sufficient questions must be posed and corresponding answers given to accomplish these elements. For example, in offering a letter into evidence, the advocate may proceed as follows.

> *Q.* Ms. Jones, I am handing you a letter dated March 1, 1995 addressed to you and printed on the letterhead of the Minimax Company. Do you recognize it?
> *A.* Yes, it is a letter from my files. I recall receiving it sometime within the first week in March.
>
> *Q.* Do you recognize the signature of the person signing the letter?
> *A.* Yes, it is the signature of Anne Clarke, director of industrial relations of Minimax Company.

If an exhibit consists of payroll records, the advocate might lay a foundation for its admission in the following manner.

> *Q.* Mr. Smith, what is your position with XYZ Corporation?
> *A.* I am the payroll supervisor.
>
> *Q.* Is one of your duties to oversee the preparation of all pay to employees of XYZ corporation and to monitor all payroll records?
> *A.* Yes, it is.

*Q.* I am handing you a series of documents that have been identified as Employer Exhibit 9a through 9f. Can you identify these documents?

*A.* Yes, these are payroll records for all full-time employees in our company's customer service department for the months of July and August of last year.

*Q.* Were these records prepared under your supervision and control?

*A.* Yes.

*Q.* Are they maintained in the normal course of business of the XYZ Corporation?

*A.* Yes, they are.

The somewhat longer process involving the payroll records is used in order to head off any objection that the records might be hearsay evidence. The advocate avoids any such objection by establishing that these are business records that are an exception to the hearsay rule. The next chapter discusses in some detail the rules of evidence, including the hearsay rule and its exceptions.

In order to make sure that a sufficient foundation has been laid for the admission of an exhibit, the advocate needs to ask himself or herself, "What do I need to show the arbitrator about this piece of evidence to establish that it is what we say it is and that the person who identifies the exhibit knows enough about it to establish its authenticity and genuineness?" When documents have been part of previous grievance meetings and when both parties have accepted the documents as being real and relevant to the grievance, little time need be spent in laying a foundation for their admission in the arbitration hearing. When, however, the exhibit is new or at all controversial, the advocate offering the exhibit should spend time preparing a solid foundation through carefully prepared questions of the witness.

## Exhibits Prepared Specifically for the Arbitration Hearing

Exhibits prepared especially for the arbitration hearing (contrasted with exhibits that were in existence during the grievance processing phase) such as photographs, diagrams, or charts often require special attention in order to lay a sufficient foundation. For example, a photograph taken of a store checkout stand several weeks prior to the arbitration hearing, but several months following the filing of a grievance concerning that checkout stand, may require a foundation along the following lines.

*Q.* Ms. Maple, I am showing you a photograph of what looks like a checkout stand in a grocery store. Can you identify the photo?

*A.* Yes, it is a picture of checkstand number 3 of the Minimax store located at 4th and Broad Streets.

*Q.* Who took the photograph?

*A.* I did.

*Q.* When was it taken?

*A.* On Tuesday, April 23, 1996.

*Q.* Is this the same checkstand at which you were working on the day the grievance occurred?

*A.* Yes, it is.

*Q.* Has the checkstand been physically altered or changed in any way from the day of the grievance until the day you took the photograph?

*A.* No.

*Q.* Is there anything different about the checkstand in the photograph and the checkstand that existed on the day the grievance occurred?

*A.* The only thing that is different is that I was standing behind the checkstand on the day of the grievance, but I am not shown in the photograph.

## Step 5—*Offer the Exhibit in Evidence*

Once a sufficient foundation has been laid for the admission of an exhibit, the exhibit may be offered in evidence. Some advocates prefer to proceed with their interrogation of the witness about the exhibit before they offer the exhibit in evidence. This has the advantage of making it clear to the arbitrator and opposing advocate the relevance of the exhibit to the case, but it has the disadvantage of delaying the admission, with the possibility that the advocate may proceed to other matters, forgetting to offer the exhibit for admission. In general, it is better form for the advocate to offer the exhibit immediately following the laying of the foundation. In most cases the relevancy of the exhibit will be obvious upon its presentation. If it is not, the offering advocate can explain the relevance of the exhibit at the time it is offered.

The words used to enter an exhibit in evidence are simple and straightforward, although there are several variations that may be employed. The following are the common phrases used.

- Mr./Madam Arbitrator, we offer Union Exhibit 8 in evidence.
- Mr./Madam Arbitrator, we offer the photograph of checkstand number 3 in evidence as Union Exhibit 8.
- I move for the admission of Union Exhibit 8 into the record.

Unless the opposing advocate registers an objection to the admission of the exhibit or offers the words "no objection," the arbitrator will normally ask the opposing advocate, "Any objections to this exhibit?" If the opposing advocate has an objection to the admission of the exhibit, it must be raised at this time with the reasons for the objection. The basis and process for making objections is covered in detail in Chapter 11.


## Voir Dire

If an opposing advocate wants to object or is considering an objection to the admission of an exhibit but does not have sufficient information on which to base an objection, the process of voir dire may be employed. This is a procedure available to the opposing side to ask questions of the witness concerning an exhibit and the witness's knowledge of the exhibit. The purpose of the questioning is to establish facts that could discredit the foundation or otherwise attack the admissibility of an exhibit. Returning to the example of the grocery checkstand, the following voir dire might take place.

Q. Ms. Maple, how many checkstands are there in the Minimax store at 4th and Broad Streets?

A. I believe there are eight.

Q. Are they all the same? By that I mean, are they all the same size, shape, and configuration?

A. Not exactly, the three at the far end of the lineup are the old style, which does not have an automatic conveyor in advance of the register.

Q. Do you usually work at the same checkstand every day or even every hour within a day?

A. No, I am the relief checker and therefore rotate among most of the stands on any one day.

Q. Is that what occurred on the day of the grievance?

A. Yes.

The opposing advocate is intending to attack the foundation of the photograph on the basis that the witness may not have taken a picture of the same checkstand as the one at which she was working at the crucial time on the day of the grievance. If the questions can cast doubt on whether the photograph depicts the actual relevant conditions that relate to the grievance, the arbitrator may refuse to admit the exhibit. Alternately, the arbitrator may defer ruling on the admission of the exhibit until additional evidence can show whether the correct checkstand is shown on the photograph or whether the difference in checkstands will impact the photograph's relevance and usefulness to the case.

An important point for the advocate offering an exhibit to keep in mind is that the opposing advocate can interrogate a witness whose testimony lays the foundation for the introduction of an exhibit prior to the admission of the exhibit (and, of course, in advance of cross-examination) and can do enough damage to the witness and/or the exhibit to preclude or delay the admission of the exhibit, as well as challenge the credibility of the witness. For this reason the advocate offering an exhibit should make sure that the witness is fully knowledgeable about the exhibit and can verify and authenticate it sufficiently to withstand a strong challenge. To have an exhibit rejected for lack of a foundation is a serious setback and can do great damage to the advocate's credibility and case even before the other side has put on its evidence.

An advocate's professionalism and experience (or lack thereof) in hearing procedures are clearly revealed by the way in which exhibits are presented and offered. A union or employer representative aspiring to be a skilled advocate should memorize the five steps described above and rehearse their use in order to carry them out smoothly and effectively in the hearing.

## USE OF EXHIBITS IN DIRECT EXAMINATION

Some exhibits need only be identified and verified by the witness and need no further examination or elaboration. Such documents as letters, grievances, and notices often speak for themselves, that is, a simple reading of the document by the arbitrator reveals its relevance and significance to the case without any need for explanation. Other exhibits require more information and elaboration before they are useful to the side presenting them and to the arbitrator. Such exhibits as charts, diagrams, photographs, and so on usually require the witness to explain what the exhibits depict and their significance to the case. These types of exhibits are often critical elements in proving one's case, and the way in which the witness describes the key aspects of the exhibit will determine how valuable the exhibit will be in the overall presentation of the case.

## Marking Key Aspects of Exhibits

If the witness is going to describe particular features of an exhibit, he or she should retain a copy of it to look at as the advocate's questions are posed. In some cases, especially with diagrams and sketches, it is helpful to have the witness mark particular portions of the exhibit, indicating aspects that are of special importance, for example, where events occurred, where people were situated, or structural changes were made. When the witness is going to mark the exhibit, it is usually preferable to use the arbitrator's copy (i.e., the official or original exhibit). For example, in a case of discharge for fighting the union may present a diagram of the site where the altercation occurred and have a witness describe and mark locations on the diagram where key actions took place. Figure 9-1 shows a diagram of a construction project where a fight occurred. The purpose of the diagram is to depict the scene of the fight and allow the arbitrator to follow the testimony of an eyewitness to the fight. The eyewitness is a coworker of the grievant, whose defense to the employer's discharge action is self-defense. The questioning and use of the diagram might proceed as follows.

*Q.* Mr. Witnowski, where were you present at the job site when the altercation between Mr. Agrezzor and Mr. Difindir (grievant) took place?

*A.* I was standing next to the large pillar on the northwest corner of the first floor. I was on the east side of the pillar.

*Q.* Looking at Union Exhibit 5, which is a diagram of the first floor of the Dallas Technical Institute job site would you please put a "W" at the spot where you were located.

*A.* Yes, I was standing here [places a "W" as shown on Figure 9-1].

*Q.* What time was that?

*A.* It was just after the morning break, I would say at 10:05 A.M.

*Q.* Where was Mr. Agrezzor located at that time?

*A.* He was standing on the west side of the northeast pillar several feet away from the pillar.

*Q.* Would you please mark the diagram with an "A" showing where Mr. Agrezzor was located? [witness marks exhibit]...

*Q.* After you heard Mr. Agrezzor say "Come over here, you son of a bitch," where was Mr. Difindir located?

*A.* He was standing about fifteen to twenty feet away from me at the northeast pillar.

**Figure 9–1.**
**Example of Exhibit Marked to Depict Key Aspect(s) of Evidence**

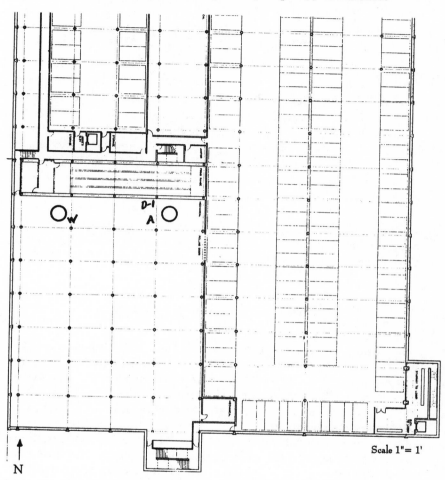

Scale 1"= 1'

N

DIAGRAM OF FIRST FLOOR OF DALLAS TECHNICAL INSTITUTE

*Q.* Please mark the place on Union Exhibit 5 with a "D-1" to show where Mr. Difindir was located at that time [witness marks exhibit as instructed].

In having the diagram marked in this fashion, the arbitrator not only can follow the action more clearly during the interrogation, but has a permanent graphic record to refer to in preparing the decision and award.

Additional markings, such as dotted lines to reflect routes of travel and Xs to denote significant points (e.g., where Mr. Agrezzor struck Mr. Difindir) can be helpful. Different colored pens or pencils can be used to distinguish markings made by different witnesses, although it must be kept in mind that if photocopies are to be made, they will not normally reflect the different colors unless a color copier is available. If several witnesses will be testifying with the same diagram, it may be more practical to use different copies of the same exhibit or transparencies overlaid on the same exhibit. When conflicting testimony is anticipated and/or witnesses to the same event have been sequestered, separate copies of the diagram should be used for each witness in order to avoid having one witness's markings affect another's.

## EXAMINING EXPERT WITNESSES

The use of expert witnesses in labor arbitration hearings is considerably less common than it is in civil and criminal trials. There are, however, a number of types of cases in which experts are quite useful. This is especially true in cases with issues involving medical matters (e.g., physical condition of an employee, qualifications of employees in the health care industry, etc.), safety (e.g., condition of equipment, cause of accident, etc.), technical business (e.g., plant closure and relocation), and other such specialized fields. Considering the potentially high cost of hiring an expert witness and the potential impact the testimony of an expert witness can have on a case, it is important that an advocate who uses an expert as a witness do a competent job in examining that person.

### Establishing Qualifications

The initial phase of examining an expert witness should be devoted to establishing the witness's qualifications. Ideally, the witness will have a typed resume or curriculum vitae (CV), which forms the basis for the initial questions to be asked. It is usually more effective, however, that the qualifications be presented through questions posed to and answered by the witness, rather than by simply entering the resume into the record. Consequently, the witness should be examined about his or her qualifications first, before producing the resume. Only after those qualifications are described by the witness should the resume be shown and offered in evidence. The following example (involving the examination of a pension actuary in a case concerning the funding and benefit levels of a pension plan) is a normal method for establishing qualifications.

*Q.* Ms. Stipple, by whom are you employed?
*A.* Morgan and Norman, Consulting Actuaries.

*Q.* What is your position with that firm?
*A.* I am a partner and group leader.

Q. Are you a pension actuary?
*A.* Yes, I am an enrolled pension actuary, and a member of the National Academy of Actuarial Science.

*Q.* How long have you been in this field?
*A.* Twenty-five years.

*Q.* Would you please tell us what education you have completed to prepare you for this work?
*A.* Yes, I have a B.S. in mathematics from Princeton University and an M.S. in actuarial science from the Wharton School of Business, University of Pennsylvania. In addition, I have completed a number of professional actuarial seminars and workshops in my field.

*Q.* Have you written any papers or materials in your field of specialization that have been published?
*A.* Yes, I have had several articles published in the *Journal of Actuarial Science*, and I am the author of the chapter entitled, "Funding Assumptions for Defined Benefit Plans" in the leading text, *Handbook of Pensions and Annuities*, published by John Wiley and Sons.

*Q.* Do you have any other credentials in your field?
*A.* I am on the adjunct faculty of the University of Central Illinois, where I teach graduate level courses in pensions and deferred compensation programs. I have also presented workshops and seminars to professionals in my field of specialization.

The obvious purpose of this series of questions and answers is to impress the arbitrator (and perhaps the other side and its witnesses) with the expertise of the witness. Sometimes the opposing advocate will offer to stipulate to the qualifications of the witness to testify as an expert. Such an offer should be refused, because it would preclude the type of full and impressive presentation of the witness's expertise illustrated above.

# Vulnerabilities of the Expert Witness

An opposing advocate may attempt to discredit the expert witness in several ways.

## *Possible Bias*

One such way is an attempt to show bias, that is, that the witness has some personal reason to give favorable testimony on behalf of the side calling that witness other than that which would be explained by the merits of matter. An example might be a physician who is called to testify and render an opinion as to the physical capabilities of an employee and who is also on a regular retainer with that employer to do pre-employment physical examinations. The opposing advocate may very well delve into the financial arrangements between the employer and the physician to show that the doctor would be inclined to testify favorably for the employer in order to avoid jeopardizing the income earned from providing physical exams.

## *Remuneration for Testimony*

In a similar vein expert witnesses are often asked by the opposing advocate about the compensation to be received by the expert for the testimony given. The idea here is to impress the arbitrator with the high amount of compensation to suggest that the witness will be less than completely objective because of the income earned from testifying in a favorable way for the side paying the bill. Such tactics are usually more effective in jury trials than in arbitration. Arbitrators are more aware than lay persons of customary hourly billing rates of professionals and, unless the payment is completely out of line, most arbitrators will not infer bias because of high billing rates. If, however, the billing rate charged by the expert for testifying is significantly higher than that charged for other services provided by the expert, then the expert may be vulnerable to attack by the other side. When an expert is to be retained, the advocate should inquire about the fees the expert will charge for giving testimony in the case and determine how that rate compares with fees charged for other services delivered by that witness and how the expert's fees for testifying relate to those charged by comparable expert witnesses for testifying in evidentiary hearings.

### Previous Writings and Testimony

Experts can sometimes be tripped up or embarrassed by something they have previously written or said (that has been quoted or otherwise recorded) that conflicts with their testimony in the hearing. This may include testimony in prior evidentiary hearings. Consequently, it is important for the advocate calling an expert witness to review, or at least have the witness review, all relatively recent writings by or about the witness that may bear in some way on the matters about which the witness is testifying. If there appears to be some conflict, the advocate and the expert need to develop a rationale for reconciling the conflict. If the conflict is so serious as to jeopardize the credibility of the expert, it may be necessary to excuse or dismiss the expert prior to the hearing and locate one who does not bring such baggage to the case.

Sometimes the expert's previous writings or statements do not bear directly on the subject of the testimony but are embarrassing or open to question for some other reason. For example, an economist may be testifying about the viability of a particular plant that is slated for closure. If that economist had recently made an economic prediction that was patently off base (e.g., prediction of an economic depression that never occurred), the opposing side may use such material to discredit the expertise of the witness. Consequently, the advocate may wish to ask the expert to bring a copy of all writings produced within the last three to five years so that they can be reviewed by the advocate prior to the hearing. For most experts used in labor arbitration cases, however, such precautions are seldom necessary. Because it is not necessary to disclose to the opposing party in advance of the hearing that an expert witness will be called and because discovery is generally not available in labor arbitration, it is unlikely that the other side will have had a chance to research the writings of the expert or be able to locate inconsistencies that could be used to impeach the credibility or expertise of the witness.

## Eliciting Opinion Testimony from the Expert Witness

The principal function of an expert witness is to give an opinion on a critical element in the case. Experts' opinions may range from a physician's opinion as to whether an employee is physically capable of returning to a specific job, a journalism professor's opinion as to whether a newspaper reporter's copy meets a professional standard of quality, or an industrial hygienist's opinion as to whether the air quality in a particular workplace is safe.

The opinion should be within the scope of the witness's expertise and should not be on the specific issue that the arbitrator is to decide. If the case concerns the filling of a job by a newly hired employee rather than an employee who has ten years experience with the employer, the expert witness should not render an opinion as to whether or not the selection procedure violated the labor agreement. That is the arbitrator's task. Conversely, in a case involving a change in a production incentive plan, an expert who is an industrial engineer might render an opinion as to whether the time values established for different work processes are valid from an engineering standpoint. That expert should not, however, attempt to give an opinion as to whether a change in the incentive plan violated the labor agreement. In short, an expert may give an opinion on a technical matter within his or her field of expertise as long as it is not the ultimate question that is to be decided by the arbitrator.

## Testifying from Personal Observations

In most cases the expert will, prior to testifying, have examined documents, objects, sites, or other aspects of evidence that will form the basis of the expert testimony to be given. The physician will usually have examined the grievant prior to the physician's testimony concerning the grievant's ability to return to work, the journalism professor would have read articles written by the newspaper reporter, and the industrial hygienist would have conducted certain tests before testifying about the air quality in a workplace. The expert's observations and analysis must be reviewed in the testimony before an opinion based on these matters is given. The following is an example of how this can be done.

*Q.* Ms. Green, following your retention by IMB Local 33, did you take air samples of the environment within the Miller Brothers plastics plant in Evergreen, New Hampshire?

*A.* Yes, I did.

*Q.* Will you please tell us the number, type, and origin of the samples you took and when they were obtained?

*A.* Yes, I took a total of thirty-five samples from five locations from July, 1995 through February, 1996. . . .

*Q.* After you obtained the samples, what did you do with them?

*A.* I put each sample through three distinct tests. The first I performed was the. . . .

*Q.* What were the results of the tests you ran?

*A.* If you will look at Union Exhibit 14, I will explain the results. The result of the thin layer test was as follows: . . .

Q. Ms. Green, based on the samples that you took and the tests that you conducted within the Miller Brothers plant in Evergreen, do you have an opinion concerning the safety of employees working within that plant insofar as air quality is concerned?

A. Yes, I do.

Q. Would you please tell us what that opinion is.

A. Yes, it is my opinion that. . . .


## Testifying from Information Supplied by Others

In some cases the expert will not have made personal observations or examinations of the phenomenon about which the testimony is given, but is instead relying on information gathered by others. In such cases the expert will usually have reviewed documents prepared by others and may even have talked to the persons who obtained the information. In these types of cases it is usually sufficient that the expert have read and analyzed the information on which the opinion is based. While personal observations are generally preferable, they are not absolutely necessary. An example of how such testimony may be elicited is as follows.

Q. Dr. Saunders, have you reviewed any data or other information concerning the quality of air in the Miller Brothers plant in Evergreen, New Hampshire?

A. Yes, I reviewed the reports prepared by Ms. Thelma Green, field technologist for the firm of Walters and Brown, that were dated June 15 and July 7 of this year.

Q. Besides reviewing those reports, did you have any other sources of information on which your testimony today is based?

A. Yes, I spoke with Ms. Green on the telephone two or perhaps three times about her reports and about the conditions at the Miller Brothers plant. In addition, I reviewed the results of the periodic air quality audits conducted of the Miller Brothers plant that were performed by the New Hampshire Air Quality Resources Board. In particular, I reviewed results from four separate audits [specifies the dates of the audits] of that plant done over the last six years.

Q. Based on all the information at your disposal and on your analysis of that information, have you come to a conclusion concerning the quality of air within Miller Brothers' Evergreen plant?

A. Yes, it is my conclusion that. . . .

## Hypothetical Questions

A traditional means for eliciting opinion testimony from expert witnesses has been the hypothetical question. Although not used extensively in current labor arbitration practice, it remains a useful tool for obtaining opinion testimony when the facts in a case are not as well established as they would need to be for more direct opinion testimony.

For example, in a case involving the discharge of an employee for an accident causing serious injury to a coworker and resulting in considerable damage to the employer's property, an expert witness may be called by the union to prove that the accident was not the fault of the employee, but rather the malfunctioning of the equipment being operated by the grievant. Not all of the necessary evidence of defective equipment may have been established, but enough circumstantial evidence has been produced to form the basis for an effective hypothetical question such as the following (asked of a professor of mechanical engineering who has testified as an expert witness in a number of civil trials involving accidents).

*Q.* Dr. Silver, I am going to ask you a question based on an assumed set of facts, and then I will ask your opinion based on those facts. Assume the following:

1. The operator of an overhead crane, the grievant in this case, is a male, forty-seven years of age and in good health, who has six and one half years experience in operating overhead cranes.

2. This same operator has an unblemished safety record except for one minor accident that occurred two years prior to the incident in question.

3. Immediately following the incident, the operator was given a urinanalysis for the presence of drugs and alcohol, with the tests being reported as negative.

4. On the day in question the crane operated by the grievant was traveling in the northerly direction as shown on Union Exhibit 9. The crane was carrying a steel girder weighing approximately 7.8 tons. The load was being carried at a position. . . .

5. While the crane was about to stop at point S on Union Exhibit 9, the cable released and allowed the piece of steel to fall onto a hydraulic press, injuring the operator of the press and destroying the machine.

6. The crane was seven years old, manufactured by Townsend Industrial Equipment Corp., had a rated capacity of two hundred tons, and had most recently been inspected and certified six months prior to the incident in question.

7. Following the incident, the crane was inspected by the union's safety engineer, who reported that the main interlock was out of its normal position and was in the location shown in the diagram that is Union Exhibit 11. The safety engineer reported that the housing for the interlock showed signs of stress.

8. In the normal weekly maintenance of that crane, which was performed three days prior to the accident, the mechanic performing routine lubrication made a note in his report that the interlock housing and trigger arm should be replaced at the next major overhaul of the crane.

*Q.* Dr. Silver, based on these facts, do you have an opinion, to a reasonable degree of certainty, as to what caused the load to drop from the crane on the day in question?
*A.* Yes, I have.
*Q.* What is that opinion?
*A.* [Professor gives opinion].
*Q.* What is the reason for your opinion?
*A.* [Professor explains why].

Although each of the factual elements of the question are "assumed," they nevertheless must be reasonably established through the evidence in the case. If one or more elements is not proven, the expert's opinion is open to attack because the premises on which the opinion is based have been eroded.

## EXAMINING ADVERSE WITNESSES

An adverse witness is one whose interests and/or position are contrary to the party calling that witness to testify. Thus, a supervisory or management employee called by the union to testify would be an adverse witness. Similarly, a union business agent called by the employer to testify would be an adverse witness. The principal consequences of a witness being characterized as adverse are twofold. First, the party calling the witness may ask leading questions, which it would not otherwise be permitted to do. Second, the party calling an adverse witness is not bound by the answers provided, whereas it would be for other witnesses it calls. Being bound by the answers means that the testimony provided would be considered by the arbitrator as being established as fact, thus the party calling the witness would be stuck with the answers given.

By identifying a witness as adverse, the party calling that witness will not be saddled with adverse inferences that flow from that witness's testimony. For example, if a union calls a supervisor as an adverse witness and as part of the examination the supervisor testifies that he saw the grievant violating a rule established by the employer, the arbitrator will not consider that such testimony came from a union witness and will not hold the union bound by that testimony.

## Strategy of Calling Adverse Witnesses

Whether a witness whose interests are aligned with the opposing side should be called is a key strategic decision. Even though the party calling that witness will not, from a technical standpoint, be bound by the answers provided, nevertheless, if testimony adverse to an advocate's case results from the adverse witness, it will damage that advocate's case. In order for an adverse witness to be called to testify, there must be a reasonable expectation that some favorable testimony can be elicited from an adverse witness in order to justify calling that person. For example, it may be anticipated that a particular witness will tell the truth regardless of who it helps or hurts, or it may be that a witness whose position and ostensible interests would be allied with one side is really motivated to assist the other side (a supervisor who wants the union to win a grievance because it would make the supervisor's job easier). Another possible rationale for calling an adverse witness is that by effective questioning the witness may reveal information that he or she would have preferred not to reveal.

Notwithstanding such reasonable expectations, the advocate contemplating calling an adverse witness needs to carefully weigh the likely benefits along with the likely costs of the gambit before deciding to call that witness. When it is decided that the potential benefits of the adverse witness's testimony outweigh the potential harm, it is recommended that the adverse witness be asked only those questions that are essential to meeting the objectives of the testimony. If the adverse witness is asked additional questions, he or she may attempt to offset the impact of the earlier testimony and weaken the case of the advocate calling that witness. In most cases it is advisable to excuse the witness as soon as possible after getting the essential information.

## Calling the Grievant as an Adverse Witness

Perhaps the most sensitive situation regarding use of adverse witnesses is the one in which the grievant is called by the employer as an adverse witness. The sensitivity is increased in discharge cases in which the discharged employee is the grievant. Many arbitrators will not permit the employer advocate to call a discharged employee as an adverse witness on the theory that it violates the precepts of freedom from self-incrimination, while other arbitrators do not hold to such constitutional limitations and will permit the discharged grievant to be called by the employer.[4] It appears from a survey of labor arbitrators that a majority of neutrals would permit the discharged employee to be called by the employer.[5]

There also appears to be a distinction applied by some arbitrators between calling the grievant as the employer's first witness and calling the grievant later in the case after the employer has established a prima facie case to support the discharge.[6] If the union is going to call the grievant as its own witness, there would not appear to be significant need for the employer to call the grievant as an adverse witness, as opposed to waiting until the union calls the grievant and relying on cross-examination to ask the pertinent questions.

## Method for Establishing a Witness as Adverse

In order to receive the benefits described above (i.e., use of leading questions and not being bound by answers), the party calling an adverse witness must bring that matter to the attention of the arbitrator prior to beginning the direct examination. The normal method for doing so is as follows.

---

[4]Rohm & Haas Texas, Inc., 91 LA 339, 343 (McDermott, 1988); City of San Antonio, 90 LA 159, 162 (Williams, 1987).
[5] *Report of AAA Survey of Labor Arbitrators,* 1984 Daily Labor Report (BNA) 234: E-1, E-7.
[6]Teamsters Local 560 v. Eazor Express, 230 A.2d 521, 65 LRRM 2647 (N.J. Super., 1967).

E.A.:    Madam Arbitrator, as the employer's next witness, I wish to call Mr. Henry Hyde. Mr. Hyde is a shop steward for Local 23, and we therefore request that he be designated as an adverse witness.

A.    Your request is granted. The employer advocate may ask Mr. Hyde leading questions, and the employer will not be bound by his answers. You may proceed with your examination.

## THE ADVOCATE AS A WITNESS

From time to time in labor arbitration cases, the advocate presenting a case may have been a participant in matters directly related to the case and may wish to testify to such matters in order to help prove the case. This occurs most frequently when union representatives or employer labor relations managers are the advocates in cases involving matters with which they previously dealt, for example, a union business agent who investigated the grievance or a labor relations manager who negotiated the contract. Such testimony is entirely proper, provided there is adequate opportunity for the opposing side to register objections during the testimony and to cross-examine the witness/advocate.

There are two methods that can be used by the advocate who is going to be a witness. The first is to use the same question and answer technique as is used for all other witnesses (except, of course, that the person asking the questions and the one providing the answers are one and the same). The second method is for the advocate to give narrative testimony. Having been a witness and an advocate in a number of cases, the author strongly prefers the latter method. The question and answer method appears, and is, awkward for the advocate. It gives the testimony an air of artificiality that is not helpful to the case. The narrative style allows the advocate to relate the facts in a smooth, unbroken manner in a more or less conversational mode.

The major difficulty with the narrative style from the opposition standpoint is that it is often difficult to detect objectional testimony and register an objection before the words are actually spoken and heard by the arbitrator. For example, if the witness is testifying about discussions at the bargaining table when disputed contract language was originally negotiated and proceeds to describe second- or third-hand statements made by others as reported by the negotiators, objectionable hearsay testimony may be completed before the other side can object. If the testimony had been elicited through the normal question and answer method, it would have been much easier for the opposing advocate to anticipate the ensuing hearsay and object to it before it had been uttered. One solution for this problem is for the opposing advocate to request prior to the beginning of the testimony that the arbitrator instruct the witness/advocate to speak slowly while giving his or her testimony so that timely objections can be registered. Of course, the witness/advocate is subject to cross-examination in the same manner as all other witnesses.

# CALLING WITNESSES OUT OF ORDER

A procedural issue sometimes occurs when a party wishes to call a witness to testify at a time that is inconsistent with the normal sequence of evidence production. For example, in a case involving a contract interpretation dispute wherein the union has the burden of producing its evidence first, the employer may wish to have its general manager testify as the first or second witness of the hearing because he or she needs to catch a midday flight to attend to important out-of-town company business. In such a case the employer advocate would ask the arbitrator for permission to call the witness out of order. Similar requests are often made when doctors or other professionals are scheduled to testify. Because their time is limited and costly, advocates calling them as witnesses will usually try to accommodate the professionals' schedules by having them testify at a time convenient for them and out of the normal sequence of evidence presentation.

Advocates should make the request for out of order witnesses as early as the need is known to the advocate. Usually, an informal conversation with the opposing advocate prior to the hearing or during the hearing will result in an agreement or stipulation to be submitted to the arbitrator that a witness may be called out of order. Arbitrators will invariably accept such stipulations and will normally grant unilateral requests for witnesses to testify out of order when there are reasonable grounds for doing so.

# EXAMINATION BY THE ARBITRATOR

In addition to examination of witnesses by both advocates, many witnesses may be required to answer questions posed by the arbitrator. The right of an arbitrator to ask questions of a witness is well established in arbitration practice and procedure.[7] Many arbitrators make it a practice to refrain from asking questions of witnesses, believing that the advocates are responsible for putting on their cases and should be expected to cover all necessary points. These arbitrators often feel that any questions posed by arbitrators are necessarily going to favor one side or the other. Other arbitrators take the opposite position. They believe that the purpose of arbitration is to get to the truth and that if their questions can reveal truth that has not been uncovered by the advocates, they are duty bound to ask questions of witnesses. Arbitrators who choose to examine witnesses usually do so after all direct and cross-examination has been completed. Advocates should advise their witnesses during the preparation of their testimony that the arbitrator may ask questions of them and that they should answer them with the same truthfulness and clarity that they answer questions posed by the advocates.

A dilemma is faced by advocates when an arbitrator asks a question that the advocate believes is objectionable. For example, in a case involving the ability of an employee to return to work following a disabling accident occurring off the job, an arbitrator may ask the witness about his or her discussion with the treating physician about his or her physical condition. The content of the communication is likely to be safeguarded under physician-patient privilege. If the question were to be asked by the opposing advocate and an objection registered, it would normally be sustained by an arbitrator as coming within that privilege. Where the question is posed by the arbitrator, however, most advocates are reluctant, if not completely unwilling, to state an objection. They fear that such an objection would incur the arbitrator's displeasure and perhaps cause the arbitrator to draw adverse inferences from the objection and thereby possibly jeopardize the entire case.

When the arbitrator's question is likely to elicit testimony that could seriously injure the advocate's case, the advocate is advised to make the objection in a manner that is as unobtrusive as possible. For example,

> Mr./Madam Arbitrator, I respectively enter an objection to the question just posed. I believe that the communication between Ms. Brown and her doctor is a privileged communication and is therefore not a valid area of inquiry. Moreover, it interferes with Ms. Brown's privacy.

Notwithstanding the above advice, unless the answer likely to be elicited by an arbitrator's question would significantly harm the advocate's case, it is recommended that no objections be made. It must be recognized that the arbitrator will be ruling on his or her own question and that the arbitrator may be embarrassed by being accused of asking an

---

[7]Elkouri and Elkouri, *How Arbitration Works*, (BNA Books, 1985) 264; Hill and Sinicropi, *Evidence in Arbitration*, (BNA Books, 1987) 95.

improper question. Even if the objection is sustained, winning the battle may be at the expense of losing the war.

# SITE VISITATION BY THE ARBITRATOR

In Chapter 7 the reader was advised to consider the advisability of having the arbitrator visit one or more sites that are relevant to the case and it was suggested that arrangements for any such visit be worked out in advance of the hearing. The actual site visit becomes part of a party's case in chief, even though no testimony or other evidence is entered into the record.

The advocate needs to keep in mind that the arbitrator's viewing of the site is only one aspect of the impact likely to be produced by such a visit. During the visit those who accompany the arbitrator will undoubtedly make statements that will have some influence on the arbitrator. Likewise, there may be other persons in the vicinity who will say or do something that could sway the arbitrator. It is important for the advocate to orchestrate the visitation as much as possible so as to achieve the maximum favorable impact. This means assigning the most knowledgeable, persuasive persons possible to accompany the arbitrator; having the visit conducted at a time that will best reveal the important aspects of the site from the advocate's perspective; arranging supporting and reinforcing evidence such as videos, photographs, diagrams, descriptive and informative data, or other materials; and planning details of the visit as much as possible, including the sequence of places to visit, length of viewing times, and all other aspects of the visit.

# 10

# Rules of Evidence

As explained in the foreword to this book and in several earlier chapters, the degree of formality with which labor arbitration hearings are conducted varies enormously from one hearing to another. Some hearings are extremely informal with the advocates mixing fact and argument, interspersing witnesses' testimony with advocate's commentary, and appearing more like a debate than an evidentiary hearing. At the other end of the spectrum are hearings conducted with such formality that they might be mistaken for civil trials conducted before a judge in a courtroom. Of course, there are various shades of formality between these two extremes.

Nowhere is the spread in degrees of formalism more apparent than in the application of the rules of evidence. When both advocates and the arbitrator are nonlawyers, evidentiary rules are usually applied sporadically, if at all. When the advocates and the arbitrator are lawyers, hearings are often rife with objections based on rules of evidence. One of the major difficulties in writing a book to assist advocates in preparing and presenting a labor arbitration case is selecting the most appropriate degree of formalism that is likely to prevail in the broad range of cases.

In this chapter and in parts of several others the author has elected to assume that the advocate is likely, at some point in his or her experience with labor arbitration, to encounter a hearing in which the rules of evidence are rather rigidly applied. Consequently, the material in this chapter regarding rules of evidence goes into more detail and evidentiary technicalities than would be encountered in the typical labor arbitration hearing. The rationale is that if the advocate is able to handle a formal hearing, he or she will be able to perform that much better in an informal one. Moreover, the increasing use of lawyers to present labor arbitration cases in recent years indicates that, in general, hearings are becoming more and more technical. Therefore, advocates who become competent in knowing and applying rules of evidence will be better prepared to cope with the increasing legalism with which labor arbitration proceedings are being conducted.

All advocates, lay and lawyer alike, should keep in mind that having a command of the rules of evidence does not mean that they must necessarily be used. Many arbitrators who are very knowledgeable in the rules of evidence dislike and discourage their frequent use in labor arbitration. They realize that a great number of these rules were created to protect juries from hearing testimony that might prejudice or unduly influence them. When the trier of fact (i.e., the person who is responsible for making decisions on disputes over issues of fact) is a judge or an arbitrator, the protections afforded by application of the rules of evidence are not as necessary as when a jury determines the factual findings. Strict application of rules of evidence often keeps legitimate and useful information from being introduced. For this reason labor arbitration, and other forms of arbitration, lean heavily in the direction of informality and minimal application of the rules of evidence.

The successful advocate is one who is sensitive to the orientation of the arbitrator with respect to rules of evidence and other hearing formalities. Taking into account the arbitrator's background (i.e., legal versus nonlegal), information received from other advocates about the arbitrator's style, and the arbitrator's actions during the early part of the hearing (and, in particular, the way in which initial objections are handled), the thoughtful advocate should be able to assess early in the proceedings the arbitrator's general philosophy and practice with regard to enforcing the rules of evidence. These perceptions and assessments should guide the advocate for the balance of the hearing.

## ADMISSIBILITY BASED ON SUBSTANCE VERSUS FORM

### Substantive Rules of Evidence

The rules of evidence are used to determine what kind of evidence may be entered into the record and how that is to be accomplished. Certain rules absolutely prohibit certain kinds of evidence. For example, the rule barring evidence of offers of compromise and settlement is designed to keep out any testimony, documents, and other evidence that one side or the other has made to compromise its position in order to settle the case. The party offering such evidence is motivated by a desire to show that the other side's case is flawed—"If they had a strong case, why would they be willing to compromise?" goes the argument. The rationale for the rule to exclude such evidence is that if it were allowed in evidence, in the future it would discourage parties from exploring possible settlements. Labor arbitration principles seek to encourage, not discourage, voluntary settlements. Consequently, the rule prohibiting introduction of offers of compromise is intended to completely exclude such evidence, regardless of the manner in which it may be introduced. For this reason this is a "substantive rule of evidence."

## Admissibility Based on Form

Contrasted with substantive rules of evidence are rules based on the form in which an advocate seeks to introduce the evidence. For example, it is a long established rule of evidence that information sought by an advocate from his or her own witness may not be obtained by means of leading questions. A leading question is one in which the answer sought by the questioner is suggested by the form of the question. For example, if an advocate wishes to have his or her witness describe which of two fighting employees precipitated the altercation, the advocate is not permitted to do so in the following fashion.

> *Q.* Mr. Witness, you saw, didn't you, that Pete Piper punched Sam Spade in the stomach when they were in the lunchroom.

Although testimony from the witness about the altercation he saw is permissible, it may not be elicited by the advocate who called the witness to testify in a manner that suggests the desired answer. Nevertheless, the same information can be placed in evidence if it is elicited by a question that is framed in an objective, nonleading way. For example:

> *Q.* Mr. Witness, what did you see when Sam Spade entered the lunchroom on the day in question?

Thus, a simple change in the form of the question permits evidence to come into the case that was inadmissible in another form. For this reason advocates should understand not just the rules of evidence, but how to differentiate which rules relate to substance and which are based on form. If inadmissibility of certain evidence is based on the substance of the information sought to be produced and an objection to the introduction of that evidence is sustained by the arbitrator, it is unlikely, if not impossible, that the evidence can be admitted regardless of how the question is framed or altered. If, however, the inadmissibility is based on form alone, the advocate normally will have an opportunity to reframe the question in order to elicit the desired evidence.

This chapter reviews rules of evidence, focusing first on those rules that relate to substantive admissibility, followed by a listing of rules that are based on form. The discussion of each rule will follow the following format.

First      The rule will be stated.
Second     The rationale for the rule will be explained.
Third      One, and in some cases two, examples will be given to
           show how the rule would be applied in a hearing.
Fourth     There will be a discussion of the application of the rule
           in arbitration hearings, exceptions that may apply, ways
           to circumvent the rule's harsh effects, and other facets of
           the rule.

## SUBSTANTIVE ADMISSIBILITY

### Rationale Underlying Substantive Rules of Evidence

Generally speaking, the rules of evidence that are intended to block evidence regardless of the form of the question, that is, substantive inadmissibility, are based on policies or rationales that are designed to keep out evidence that is inherently unreliable or to preclude evidence that, if permitted to be introduced, would interfere with efficient and beneficial means of carrying out collective bargaining, business, and legal affairs, that is, policy reasons. An example of a rule based on the first rationale is the hearsay rule. It is designed to preclude evidence that is thought to be unreliable, that is, testimony of a witness relating what someone else said outside the hearing room. The underlying notion, albeit frequently criticized, is that a second-hand report of a statement of a person who is not present in the hearing and not subject to being examined about the truth of the statement is unreliable.

The second rationale for substantive inadmissibility is that the admission of such evidence would have an adverse impact on the way unions and employers deal with one another, the way people lead their daily lives, the way in which business and/or other activities of the employer's enterprise are conducted, and/or the process by which positive and important activities in our society are carried out. For example, certain private communications between particular individuals are considered private, or privileged, and are not subject to inquiry in a hearing. Communications between a doctor and a patient are considered privileged, as are communications between a lawyer and the lawyer's client in anticipation of, or in the course of, litigation. The reasons for these rules are relatively simple. If a patient cannot communicate freely and openly with a doctor without fear of having the conservation publicly disclosed in a hearing, it would impede the free flow of information between them and likely reduce the effectiveness of medical treatment rendered by physicians to patients. Moreover, the subjects discussed in such communications are apt to be of such a personal and sensitive nature that they should not, out of respect to individuals' privacy, be divulged to others. The rule applying to communications between lawyers and their clients during, or in anticipation of, litigation is designed to remove any inhibitions to these parties exploring a wide range of legal defenses, attacks, and other strategies. For these policy reasons such communications are not admissible in evidence, unless the persons they are designed to protect (e.g., the doctor and the patient) waive such protection and privilege.

## RULES OF EVIDENCE BASED ON SUBSTANTIVE ADMISSIBILITY

### Relevancy

#### *Statement of the Rule*

Evidence is admissible only when it will tend to make the existence of a fact that is of some consequence in the case more or less probable than it would be without the evidence.[1]

---

[1]Whether the fact to be proved bears on an issue in the case is really a question of "materiality." Although traditional rules of evidence distinguished between relevancy and materiality, the most recent formulation of the Federal Rules of Evidence combine the two concepts into one rule. *Federal Rules of Evidence,* Rule 401, 28 U.S.C.

## Rationale

Hearings should not be burdened by evidence that either does not have anything to do with the case or that fails to prove a fact that bears on some issue in the case. Irrelevant evidence is not only unrelated to any issue in the case, but may also be prejudicial to one side or the other. For this added reason the evidence may be inadmissible.

*Example A.* [In a case involving seniority rights under a labor contract between XYZ Corporation and the Meatcutters Union]

> *EA:*[2]  Ms. Jones, when you were the director of industrial relations for ABC Corporation, did you utilize plant seniority or department seniority in effectuating layoffs under your contract with the Boilermakers Union?
>
> *UA:*  Objection. It's irrelevant. Those layoffs were under a different contract with a different union and have no bearing on the case before us.
>
> *A:*  Objection sustained.

The arbitrator sustained the objection because what ABC Corporation and the Meatcutters Union did under a separate labor agreement will not *normally* have any influence on what the language means in the labor agreement between XYZ Corporation and the Boilermakers Union. The word "normally" is emphasized because there are some circumstances in which such an agreement might be relevant. If the language in both agreements is identical and if the employer advocate can show that both parties intended to have their seniority provision applied in the same way as under the ABC/Meatcutter contract, an arbitrator would be inclined to admit the evidence and to give it significant weight. Absent such supporting evidence, however, an objection to that type of evidence will be sustained on the grounds that it is irrelevant.

*Example B.* [In a case involving discharge for an employee's insubordination toward her supervisor]

> *EA:*  Mr. Tompkins [employer's personnel manager], would you please review for the arbitrator the record of absenteeism of Ms. Phillips [the discharged employee] during the last six months prior to her discharge?

---

[2]Throughout this chapter and in subsequent chapters, EA means employer advocate, UA means union advocate, A means arbitrator, and W means witness.

*UA:* Objection on grounds of relevancy. Ms. Phillips was discharged solely for insubordination. Nothing in the discharge notice referred to absenteeism.

*A:* The objection is sustained.

A common error made by novice employer advocates in discharge cases is to try to show that the employee is a bad person, and to attempt to introduce evidence of almost any type of prior misconduct or rule infractions by the employee, no matter how remote from the real reason for the discharge. When the discharge is for a specific rule violation, for example, insubordination toward a supervisor, it is usually not relevant that the employee had a history of excessive absenteeism. The absenteeism may very well have been grounds for independent disciplinary action, but if that action was not taken or if the employer did not (prior to the discharge for insubordination) make some link between the two distinct types of misconduct, the grievant's record of absenteeism will be irrelevant and an objection on that basis sustained.

### Discussion

#### Lenient Application

Labor arbitrators are generally very lenient with respect to applying the rule of relevancy. There is good reason for this. This rule was designed to prevent juries from hearing evidence that was possibly prejudicial unless it clearly bore on an issue in the case. Arbitrators are much less likely to be influenced by potentially prejudicial evidence than are juries, and, when the evidence is marginally relevant (i.e. it might have some connection to the case, although one that is not immediately apparent), arbitrators are much more likely to admit evidence than are judges in civil or criminal trials.

As with judges, however, arbitrators faced with borderline relevant evidence must weigh the possible harm of such evidence against the potential benefit it might add. Because arbitrators are much less susceptible to prejudicial influence, the harm caused by admitting possibly irrelevant evidence is usually less than the disadvantage of excluding evidence that may have a bearing on the outcome of a case. When marginally relevant evidence is admitted, arbitrators commonly qualify the admission with the phrase, "Admitted subject to weight" or "I'll admit it for whatever it's worth," meaning that although the evidence may be introduced, it is not likely to be given full consideration by the arbitrator.

In contract interpretation cases relevancy issues sometimes arise when one or both of the parties attempts to introduce evidence of what their negotiators intended the language to mean. A troublesome issue arises when the evidence of intent consists of what the negotiators thought the words meant, rather than what was actually said or agreed on in the course of negotiations. The opportunity for mischief in allowing such evidence is patent. Anyone can testify that they understood certain words and phrases to have a particular meaning when the agreement was reached. There is virtually no way to disprove such thoughts. If, however, the testimony is about what was said during the negotiations of such language, the other party can respond. Notwithstanding the potential for abuse, arbitrators frequently permit such testimony of one or both parties' intentions or understandings during labor negotiations, recognizing that they will give little or no weight to that testimony when deciding the case.

Even arbitrators who are very accommodating with respect to allowing marginally relevant evidence into cases have some limits. This is especially true if it appears that the production of such evidence will consume a considerable amount of time in the hearing. An advocate who attempts to introduce marginally relevant evidence (to which an objection has been made by the opposing side) may increase the chances of admission if he or she assures the arbitrator that the time needed to produce the evidence is short. For example, ''Mr. Arbitrator, I have just a couple of questions of the witness on this point. I can assure you this testimony will not unduly delay the hearing.'' The advocate who makes such assurances is well advised not to disappoint the arbitrator.

### Linking Up

In some instances the relevancy of one witness's testimony depends on other evidence. For example, the testimony of a maintenance mechanic about the functioning of a door in a case of discharge for theft might appear to be irrelevant, unless it is shown that the article alleged to have been stolen (a computer) could not have been removed through the door in question without an alarm sounding. At the time the witness begins his or her testimony, the connection between that testimony and the issue in the case may not be apparent, causing the other side to object on grounds of relevancy.

One way to show the relevancy is to explain to the arbitrator just how the proffered evidence relates to the issue in the case (e.g., the door in question is the only one from which the grievant could have exited the facility, and, if a computer had been removed by the grievant, movement of the door would have sounded an alarm). The advocate offering the evidence may not, however, wish to lay out the whole theory of his or her case early in the hearing. To do so may tip off the opposing side, enabling them to change their approach to the case. Thus, the advocate offering the challenged testimony may have to beg the indulgence of the arbitrator by promising that subsequent evidence will make the relevancy obvious. For example, "Madam Arbitrator, we will link up this testimony with other evidence shortly in order to establish the clear relevancy of this line of questioning. We ask that you give us a little leeway at this point." Most arbitrators will be sympathetic with this approach, provided the testimony does not require a great deal of time and that the linking evidence comes into the case not too long after the disputed testimony.

## Opinion Testimony

### *Statement of the Rule*

Unless a witness has been qualified as having special expertise in a particular subject, he or she will not be permitted to give testimony as to his or her opinion about a subject in the case.

### *Rationale*

The purpose of evidence is to prove facts that will enable an arbitrator to make a decision. An opinion is not a fact, and, therefore, many opinions are not useful in deciding a case. When, however, proof that a fact may be more or less probable can reasonably be based on the opinion of a person with special knowledge, skill, education, and/or experience in a subject closely related to the fact to be proven, such opinion testimony is admissible.

*Example A.* [In a case involving the promotion by an employer of a junior lathe operator to a tool and die maker that is challenged by a more senior lathe operator]

> EA: Mr. Ruggles [Plant Manager], in making your decision to promote Ms. Junior over Mr. Senior, what was your opinion of Ms. Junior's qualifications to do the tool and die making work relative to Mr. Senior's qualifications?

> UA: Objection. The question calls for an opinion.

> A: Mr. Ruggles, what experience do you have performing tool and die work or in directly supervising tool and die work?

*W.* I have no specific experience in that regard.

*A.* Objection sustained.

The arbitrator in this case disallowed the testimony of the plant manager because the question called for an opinion about a technical matter, that is, tool and die work performance requirements, without any showing that the witness had the knowledge or experience to evaluate such requirements. Since the plant manager was not knowledgeable about the technical requirements of the job in question, it is likely that he relied on some other facts in order to make his decision. If he did, they could be brought out in another way without relying on opinion testimony. The following example shows how this might be done in an unobjectionable manner.

*Example A-1.*

*EA:* Mr. Ruggles, in deciding to promote Ms. Junior over Mr. Senior, what factors did you take into consideration?

*W.* I considered the relative qualifications of each person, the seniority of each employee, their respective employment records including safety, attendance, and discipline, and the number of excellent performance ratings each one had received in the last five years.

*EA:* With respect to their relative qualifications, what information did you rely on?

*W.* I spoke to each of their supervisors about the quality and quantity of their work. I examined production records to gauge their productivity and percentage of off-standard work. I also reviewed their training records and their performance on tests administered by our training department.

*EA:* Based on that information, what conclusion did you reach?

*W.* I concluded that Ms. Junior was more qualified to perform the work of a tool and die maker than was Mr. Senior.

*Example B.* [In a case involving the request of an employee to return to her former position following a work-incurred injury, wherein an employer-appointed physician is testifying about the employee's physical abilities]

*EA:* Dr. Welbing, based on all the information at your disposal that you have described, do you have an opinion as to whether Ms. Hurt can safely resume the position of a forklift operator in the plant?

*UA:* Objection. There is no showing that Dr. Welbing is qualified to render an opinion about the capabilities of Ms. Hurt's knee, since he is not an orthopedic specialist.

*EA:* Mr. Arbitrator, Dr. Welbing has previously testified that in addition to examining Ms. Hurt's knee and examining current X rays of her knee, he discussed her condition with Dr. Philip Joint, who performed the surgery on Ms. Hurt's knee.

*A.* Objection overruled. Doctor, you may answer the question.

Although the objection was overruled, the example points out the importance of ensuring that the expert really has the knowledge and experience in the area specifically related to the matter on which the opinion testimony is being given. A mechanical engineer may not have had any actual experience with the type of machinery about which he is asked to render an opinion. A professor of chemistry may have conducted extensive research and written a large number of books and articles in scholarly journals, but if the scholarship is not in the area in which the opinion is being given, it is subject to attack.

*Example C.* [In a case involving the suspension of an employee for unsafe operation of a mobile crane]

*UA:* Mr. Smith, as you were observing the operation of the crane by Ms. Whooping, what is your opinion as to how far away the boom was from the side of the building?

*EA:* Objection. Calls for an opinion.

*UA:* Madam Arbitrator, this question merely calls for the witness to estimate a distance. The witness has already testified that he could see the crane and the building very clearly from where he was standing. This type of estimate is within the competence of most persons and is not objectionable opinion testimony.

*A.* Objection overruled.

It is generally held that opinions, or, more appropriately, estimates, as to such matters as time of day, distances, visibility conditions, and so on, are within the competence of most persons, and testimony about them does not require a showing of any special expertise. Of course, the opposing advocate is free to challenge the estimating capability of the witness through cross-examination (e.g., "Mr. Witness, could you give us your estimate of the length and width of the room in which you and I are now sitting?").

## Discussion

The rule concerning opinion testimony is sometimes explained on the basis that someone other than an expert witness cannot render an opinion about an issue to be decided in the case. While this explanation is essentially accurate, the reason it is not permitted is not that the opinion was rendered by a nonexpert, but rather because it is an opinion that is reserved for the arbitrator alone to decide, that is, it is the ultimate question. Thus, in a discharge case an expert witness (no matter how learned) may not give an opinion as to whether or not the grievant was discharged for good cause. That is the sole province of the arbitrator. Nevertheless, an expert may render an opinion concerning a matter that is a threshold issue to the one that the arbitrator must decide. For example, if an employee who is a truck driver is discharged for driving under the influence of alcohol, an expert (e.g., an operator of a breath analysis machine) may testify as to the blood-alcohol content of the driver and render an opinion as to whether the driver was under the influence of alcohol at the time he was driving. Nevertheless, the issue to be decided by the arbitrator is whether the discharge was for just cause. Neither an expert nor a layperson can render an opinion as to whether or not there was just cause, although the expert's opinion as to whether the discharged employee was under the influence of alcohol will help the arbitrator to determine whether there was or was not just cause.

## Best Evidence Rule

### Statement of Rule

In order to prove the terms of a document, the document itself (usually the original, not a copy) must be produced unless it can be shown that the original is not available.

### Rationale

The actual document is the only truly reliable evidence of what a document proves. Summaries, recapitulations, or copies are subject to interpretation and alteration, which may not reflect the true meaning of the original document.

*Example.* [In a case in which the employer is attempting to show a practice of employees of punching time clocks as much as twenty to thirty minutes prior to the beginning of their scheduled shifts]

*EA:* Ms. Smith, can you please identify the document that has been marked as Employer Exhibit 3?

*W.* Yes, it is a computer printout of entries on time cards of all employees in Department A for a two-year period, showing the times when they punched the time clock before starting work and after finishing their work for the day.

*EA:* We offer Employer Exhibit 3.

*UA:* Objection, inadmissible on the basis of the best evidence rule. The actual documents on which start and stop times were recorded are the time cards themselves. This computer print-out is merely a transcription and is subject to error on the part of the data entry clerk in reading the time card accurately and in transferring the information into the computer. If the advocate for the company wishes to prove what the start and stop times were for the period in question, she could introduce the actual time cards.

*EA:* Mr. Arbitrator, the time cards have been destroyed in accordance with the employer's document destruction policy. The computer printouts are the only evidence available. They are accurate records, and the advocate for the union may cross-examine our witness to verify the manner in which the computer records were prepared.

*A.* Objection overruled. Employer Exhibit 3 is admitted.

### Discussion

The best evidence rule is seldom raised in labor arbitration hearings. Because copies of documents are so commonly used and are generally accurate, copies are routinely accepted as originals without objection. Occasionally, the rule will be raised with regard to summaries and computer records as in the above example. Unless it can be shown, however, that the records were not prepared by a competent person in the normal course of business, any objection is likely to be overruled. Even if there is some question as to the regularity of preparation of such summaries or records, or a question as to whether the source document is or is not available, the secondary document or record is likely to be admitted. If, however, the advocate opposing the introduction of the document can show some error or irregularity in the summary or computer record, it may be possible to keep the document from being admitted into evidence.

## Parol Evidence Rule

### Statement of Rule

Evidence of a written or oral agreement outside the contract itself to prove the meaning or interpretation of that contract is not admissible. The meaning is to be drawn from the words of the contract itself.

### Rationale

When parties enter into a contract, they are expected to incorporate their entire agreement into the contract document. Collateral evidence as to the meaning and intent of the contract should not be admitted to alter the terms of the contract as written.

*Example.* [In a case involving a dispute over the reimbursement employees are to receive for the purchase of safety shoes, where the contract specifies a maximum reimbursement of $100 per year]

   *UA:* Mr. Rubersole, did you have a discussion with Mr. Honcho, the plant manager, about how much you could spend for safety shoes each year?

   *W.* Yes.

   *UA:* When was that discussion?

   *W.* It was at our annual union-management meeting in January.

   *UA:* What did he say about how much you could spend?

   *EA:* Objection, parol evidence rule. The question calls for testimony that would vary the specific terms of a written contract.

   *A.* I will permit the witness to answer, but I must advise the union advocate that I will be very skeptical of the evidence unless there is some showing that Mr. Honcho had the authority and intent to modify the labor agreement. The objection is overruled.

   *W.* He said that if safety shoes from the approved vendor cost more than $100, he would see that the company made up the difference.

### Discussion

Strictly speaking, the parol evidence rule is not a rule of evidence, but a rule of contract construction. It is used to determine the way in which written contracts are to be interpreted. In its proper application it should not be used to exclude evidence, but should be applied by the arbitrator to decide whether the offered evidence would influence the meaning and interpretation of the contract.

## Parol Evidence Frequently Admitted

Parol evidence is, in fact, quite commonly introduced in labor arbitration hearings. Evidence of past practice, discussions between union and management representatives when agreements were reached, side letters of understanding, and previous grievance settlements are all routinely admitted to prove what specific agreements mean, notwithstanding the fact that they arguably constitute parol evidence. The key point that should be kept in mind is that such evidence will be admitted and given weight by an arbitrator if there is some ambiguity in the language of the contract. If the language is clear on its face and not reasonably subject to an interpretation other than what the words say, such parol evidence, although admitted, will not normally be accorded much weight.

Relating back to the example above, suppose the language of the agreement read, "Unless otherwise provided by practices within a department or special agreement, employees shall be entitled to a maximum annual allowance of $100 per year for the purpose of purchasing safety shoes." There the words "unless otherwise provided by . . . special agreement" could conceivably include permission by the plant manager to an employee to spend more, and evidence of the employee's conversation with the plant manager could not only be admitted, but might also be seriously considered by the arbitrator depending on the circumstances of the conversation (e.g., whether said in passing, in exchange for a concession, in jest, coupled with the words "I promise," etc.).

If, however, the contract provision read, "The annual safety shoe allowance is $100," it could hardly be said that an ambiguity existed, and application of the parol evidence rule would normally apply and little or no weight would be given to the conversation at the meeting. As indicated earlier, however it is applied, the parol evidence rule should be employed for construing the contract language and rendering a decision, not for the purpose of excluding the evidence completely.

## Foreclosing Parol Evidence in Advance

One way in which contract negotiators can protect against collateral discussions, letters of understanding, and past practices being brought into evidence to modify the clear meaning of labor contract language is to incorporate a ''zipper clause'' into their labor agreements. This type of clause provides that the written agreement is to be considered as the entire agreement between the parties, and nothing outside that written document should be used to modify it in any way. Such a clause typically reads as follows.

> This labor agreement contains the complete and exclusive agreement between the parties on all issues of collective bargaining. Nothing outside this contract document shall be used to modify, expand, or limit the terms of the agreement.

Parties should not casually enter into such agreements because they can preclude reliance on past practices and customs that can benefit either side in any particular case.

## Privileged Communications

### *Statement of the Rule*

Oral and written communications between certain parties who have a confidential relationship are inadmissible and therefore protected from unwanted disclosure in the hearing, provided such confidentiality has not been otherwise voluntarily disclosed or otherwise waived.

### *Rationale*

Rules of evidence developed for trials established protections against the introduction of evidence of confidential communications between certain parties. Rules applied in labor arbitration have more or less followed suit. To allow such communications to be open to examination in a hearing would have the effect of inhibiting open communications in such confidential relationships. For this reason confidential communications between certain persons are considered privileged and are therefore inadmissible. The most common relationships covered under this rule in trial settings are as follows.

Doctor-Patient
Psychotherapist-Patient
Lawyer-Client
Husband-Wife
Clergyperson-Religious Adherent (sometimes ''penitent'')

*Example.* [Case involving an employee being discharged for fraudently claiming an industrial injury]

*EA:* Mr. Payne, prior to filing your claim for workers' compensation, did you visit a Dr. Wellbing, who was your personal physician?

*W.* Yes, I did.

*EA:* When was that?

*W.* About a year ago, last June.

*EA:* What did you tell Dr. Wellbing?

*UA:* Objection, Madam Arbitrator, that was a privileged communication.

*A.* Objection sustained.

### *Discussion*

With the exception of the doctor-patient and lawyer-client privileges the traditional confidential relationships that come under the rule of privileged communications found in the courts (i.e., those listed above under "rationale") are seldom encountered in labor arbitration. There are, however, some additional categories of confidential communications not found in legal proceedings that can raise serious evidentiary issues in labor arbitration hearings. For example, are communications between union representatives and union members in private discussions subject to the privilege? The same question applies to such discussions among employer representatives. Likewise, discussions by negotiators from one side or the other with a mediator in the course of labor contract negotiations raise issues of privilege.

While there are no firmly established rules governing these types of communications, it would seem that when the same policy reasons (i.e., the importance of free and open communications) exist in a labor-management context for maintaining confidentiality of a relationship as exist in traditional legal forums, the privilege should apply in labor arbitration. Thus, where a union representative must represent a union member much as a lawyer would represent a client, the privilege should apply. Similarly, the importance of union and employer representatives being able to explore freely and without fear of disclosure alternative bargaining strategies in their respective caucuses is reason enough for extending the privilege against unwanted disclosure in an arbitration hearing. This rationale also applies to discussions between union or employer negotiators with a mediator. In fact, the Federal Mediation and Conciliation Service (FMCS) has a rule that its mediators are not permitted to disclose any information acquired in the course of their mediation work or to testify on behalf of any party without the approval of the director of the FMCS.[3]

The opportunity to claim a privilege may be lost if any one of the parties to a confidential communication reveals the substance of the communication to one or more other parties. In so doing, that party is considered to have waived the privilege by disregarding the confidentiality of the communication. Thus, a grievant who reveals to an employer representative that she had previously admitted to her union representative that she had been untruthful about the reasons for not reporting to work as scheduled may not later claim a privilege if asked what she told her union representative about the reason for her being absent from work. Telling another of the substance of a confidential communication constitutes a waiver of the privilege.

It must always be remembered that for a privilege to be effective it must be claimed. Thus, if a witness is asked to reveal the substance of a conversation with his or her physician and no objection is registered, the question must be answered. Failure to register an objection to a question calling for revelation of a privileged communication constitutes a waiver of the privilege.

The privileged communications objection is designed to protect the persons who participated in the communication. If those persons choose to reveal the communication and have it admitted into evidence, the opposing side may not object to such admission on the basis of privilege. For example, if an employee testifies about her conversations with her physician, the employer advocate does not have a valid objection to the admission of that testimony. The employer is not protected by the privilege, and therefore may not claim it to exclude evidence.

## Offers of Compromise and Settlement

### Statement of the Rule

Evidence that one of the parties in a labor arbitration has made an offer of compromise as a means to achieve a settlement of the case is inadmissible.

### Rationale

Settlements of disputes are to be encouraged. If evidence of unsuccessful attempts to settle cases were to be admissible in arbitration cases, it would seriously inhibit attempts to reach settlements.

---

[3]29 C.F.R. § 1401.2(b) (1979).

*Example.* [In a case involving a grievance over the right of an employer to unilaterally change work schedules]

> *UA:* Following the fourth-step grievance meeting on this grievance, did the company offer to reinstate the previous work schedule if you would drop the grievance?

> *EA:* Objection. Calls for testimony concerning an alleged offer of settlement.

> *A.* Objection sustained.

### Discussion

Perhaps no rule of evidence in legal proceedings or labor arbitration is so firmly entrenched and uniformly enforced than the rule prohibiting the admission of evidence of offers of settlement. In fact, even if the other side does not register an objection, many arbitrators will interrupt the testimony and refuse to hear it. This is based on the universally held premise that voluntary settlements of disputes should be encouraged to the greatest extent possible.

In virtually every case the party that receives the settlement offer is the one that seeks to have the offer entered into the record (in order to show that the other party does not have a strong position or it would not have offered to compromise it). An interesting variation exists when the party making the offer of settlement seeks to have evidence of the offer entered into the record. When this occurs (and it is extremely rare), it is usually because the offering party wishes to show that it was reasonable and that it made a reasonable offer to settle the case short of the arbitration hearing. While there is no clear precedent controlling such an issue based on the policy underlying the rule (i.e., to encourage the free exploration of settlements without fear of such exploration being raised in the arbitration hearing), it would seem that regardless of which side attempts to enter into evidence the offer of settlement, it should be ruled inadmissible.

## Beyond the Scope of Direct Examination

### Statement of the Rule

Interrogation of a witness on cross-examination about matters not covered in the direct examination are subject to objection.

## Rationale

Witnesses are prepared to testify about certain matters. They should not be required to testify about other matters on cross-examination (when leading questions can be asked) for which they are not prepared to testify. If the cross-examining advocate needed to ask questions of this witness to prove his or her own case, the advocate should have arranged to call that person as his or her own witness.

*Example.* [In a case involving a grievance over a work assignment given to an employee in a department other than the one in which the work is normally assigned. The union shop steward is testifying on cross-examination.]

> *EA:* Mr. Stuart, isn't it true that the union proposed in the last labor contract negotiations to include in the labor agreement language that would have prevented the company from making the very type of assignment that was made in this case and that the company refused to agree to the language proposed by the union?
>
> *UA:* Objection. There was no testimony by Mr. Stuart concerning labor contract negotiations. This question goes beyond the scope of direct.
>
> *A.* Sustained. If you wish to inquire into such matters, you may call Mr. Stuart as your own witness.

## Discussion

The scope of direct rule is one that may have a place in court proceedings, but in the opinion of the author it is misplaced in labor arbitration. The purpose of labor arbitration is to get to the facts in the simplest and most forthright manner possible. To go through the formality of excusing a witness from answering a question on direct, only to be able to recall the witness as the advocate's own and ask the very same question appears to place form over substance. The rationale is that because the witness can be asked leading questions on cross-examination, he or she should not be required during cross-examination to answer such questions unless they were the subject of the direct examination. This rationale overlooks the ability of the inquiring advocate to call the witness as an adverse witness and utilize leading questions. With that option it makes no difference whether the witness is being interrogated on direct or cross-examination.

## Hearsay Rule

### *Statement of the Rule*

Evidence of an oral or written statement made outside the hearing by anyone other than the witness who is testifying that is offered to prove the truth of the matters asserted in the statement is inadmissible.

### *Rationale*

Reports of statements by persons other than the witness made outside the hearing are considered to be unreliable. The person who made the statement (the declarant) is not testifying in the hearing and is not subject to cross-examination. In addition, and perhaps most important, the arbitrator is not able to observe and hear the declarant nor make an assessment of the declarant's credibility. All the arbitrator has to go on is the second-hand report of what was said by the absent declarant. For all of these reasons arbitrators are justifiably cautious in accepting a second-hand account of what was allegedly said outside the hearing.

*Example A.* [In a case involving the discharge of an employee/grievant (Mr. Jenks) for theft, where the witness is a coworker of a third employee, Ms. Hamilton (declarant), who allegedly saw the grievant leave work on the day in question]

> *EA:* Did you speak with Ms. Hamilton later that day?
> *W.* Yes.
> *EA:* Did she tell you she saw Mr. Jenks put something in his duffel bag just before he left the store?
> *UA:* Objection. The question calls for hearsay testimony.
> *A.* Mr. Employer Advocate, do you intend to call Ms. Hamilton as a witness?
> *EA:* No, Madam Arbitrator, Ms. Hamilton unfortunately no longer works for the employer and is unavailable to testify.
> *A.* I agree that the question calls for hearsay. Nevertheless, I will permit the question subject to weight.

*Example B.* [In the same factual case as above, where the employer is attempting to introduce the affidavit of Ms. Hamilton to prove that Mr. Jenks took goods belonging to the employer]

> *EA:* Madam Arbitrator, we wish to offer in evidence the affidavit of Ms. Hamilton, a former employee in the children's clothing

department of the employer's store, who observed Mr. Jenks leaving the store on the day in question. This is a three-page affidavit signed and sworn before a notary public of this state. We offer this affidavit as Employer Exhibit 6.

*UA:* We object, Madam Arbitrator, the affidavit is clearly hearsay. Ms. Hamilton is not a witness in this arbitration. I do not have the opportunity to cross-examine Ms. Hamilton, and you, Madam Arbitrator, do not have the opportunity to observe the demeanor of the declarant and evaluate her credibility. If the employer was able to have Ms. Hamilton provide an affidavit, it certainly could have her testify here today so that we all might hear her version of what occurred in her own words. We strongly object to the admission of this affidavit.

*A.* My general practice is to preclude affidavits unless the offering advocate can show that it was not possible to produce the witness to testify in the hearing. Can you make such a showing?

*EA:* Madam Arbitrator, on two separate occasions we requested Ms. Hamilton to appear at this hearing to testify, but she declined to do so.

*A.* Did you seek a subpoena to require Ms. Hamilton to appear?

*EA:* No, we did not.

*A.* I am not persuaded. You could have subpoenaed her but did not. The objection to the proffered affidavit is sustained.

### Discussion

No rule of evidence, as it applies in arbitration or in the courts, presents so many difficulties in application and is so riddled with exceptions as the hearsay rule. Designed to exclude unreliable testimony, when applied in its strict sense it serves little more than to keep out valuable or at least potentially valuable evidence. Fortunately for labor arbitration advocates, it is seldom applied in its strict sense to completely exclude evidence.

### Admitting ''For What It's Worth''

The practice followed by a majority of labor arbitrators is to permit most types of hearsay evidence but to condition its admission on the basis that it will not be given the weight or credence it would if it were direct evidence. The arbitrator will, as in the first example just above, state that the evidence will be admitted ''subject to weight'' or ''for whatever it is worth." This means that the arbitrator will consider the circumstances under which the statement was made, the credibility of the witness who is testifying about the hearsay statement, how trustworthy the hearsay statement appears to be, and whether there is corroborating evidence.

## Written Hearsay

Written hearsay, often in the form of an affidavit or written statement, as in example B, is often no more or less unreliable than an oral account of the declarant's statement, but arbitrators are generally more reluctant to admit such written statements than they are to admit the same information in the form of oral testimony. The reasons are fairly obvious. First, the normal weaknesses of hearsay are present: the declarant is not in the hearing, cannot be cross-examined, and cannot be evaluated by the arbitrator with respect to credibility. Second, even a witness giving hearsay testimony can be questioned about the circumstances under which the hearsay was communicated. In the first example given above, the witness could have at least been questioned about the way in which the message from Ms. Hamilton was conveyed to the witness and what the witness knows about the reliability of Ms. Hamilton. In the second example—of written hearsay in the form of an affidavit—there is usually no one present who can relate the circumstances under which the affidavit was obtained, except perhaps the advocate offering the document, to test or attack the veracity, accuracy of perception, and powers of recollection of the declarant. All that is available is a document, which, of course, cannot respond to questions. Consequently, most arbitrators are inclined to exclude written hearsay, such as that in the form of affidavits or written statements, when the declarant is not present to testify.[4]

## Reliability of Hearsay

Many types of hearsay evidence are quite reliable. Testimony by persons who have no interest in the case concerning statements by an out-of-hearing declarant are often very reliable. Likewise, a statement made outside the hearing when the declarant has no personal interest at stake in the outcome of the case may be quite reliable, particularly if the witness who is relating the hearsay statement appears to be perceptive and

---

[4]Beverly Enterprises d/b/a Metro Care & Rehabilitation Center and Food & Commercial Workers, Local 653, 100 LA 522 (Berquist, 1993); J & L Specialty Products Corp.and Steelworkers, 94 LA 600 (Duda, 1990); Armstrong Cork Co., 53 LA 1112 (Williams, 1969). However, Rule 29 of the Rules of the American Arbitration Association provides that, "The Arbitrator may receive and consider the evidence of witnesses by affidavit, giving it only such weight as seems proper after consideration of any objections to its admission."(See Appendix A).

unbiased and possesses a good recollection on other matters about which he or she is testifying. Also, when the hearsay statement is consistent with one or more other pieces of evidence in the case, there is more reason for admitting and crediting the hearsay evidence.

If, as discussed above, hearsay evidence is generally admitted in labor arbitration hearings, one may question how necessary it is for the labor arbitration advocate to understand the hearsay rule and its exceptions. The answer is that it is quite necessary. There are several reasons. First, if there is no understanding of the hearsay rule, the advocate may not register an objection to hearsay, allowing it to be admitted with no limitations or realization that hearsay testimony is being given. Second, an advocate who is attempting to have his or her witness give hearsay testimony may be faced with an objection from the other side. The arbitrator may admit such testimony, subject to diminished credibility or weight unless the offering advocate can demonstrate that the evidence is not truly hearsay evidence because it comes within one or more of the many exceptions to the hearsay rule. For this reason considerable attention will be devoted in the following pages to discussing the exceptions to the hearsay rule.

## Nonhearsay Versus Exceptions to the Hearsay Rule

As discussed earlier, the definition of hearsay evidence is an oral or written statement made outside the hearing by someone other than the presently testifying witness and *offered to prove the truth of the matter(s) asserted in the statement.* Most lay persons, many lawyers, some labor arbitrators, and even a few judges usually focus on the first part of the definition (i.e., the statement was made outside of the hearing) and overlook the second part (i.e., the statement is offered to prove the truth of the subject matter of the statement).

Thus, if a witness testifies about something he heard another person say (e.g., "I'm sick and tired of this job"), but the purpose of the statement is to show the state of mind of the declarant (e.g., that he is frustrated) rather than the truth of the words (i.e., that the declarant was actually intending to quit), the testimony is not truly hearsay even though it is a statement made outside the hearing by someone other than the witness. The reason is that it is not being offered to prove the truth of the matters asserted therein (i.e., an intention to quit), but rather what the declarant was thinking and believing at the time the statement was made. Similarly, if a witness testifies that a declarant said, "You're crazy" to his supervisor, it is not really hearsay because the statement is not offered to prove the truth of the matter asserted (i.e., that the supervisor was really crazy), but rather the employee's disagreement or exasperation with his or her supervisor.

Such examples of nonhearsay are commonly referred to, even by many lawyers, as exceptions to the hearsay rule, whereas they are not really hearsay evidence at all. While distinctions between nonhearsay and exceptions to the hearsay rule are of particular interest to judges and law professors, they need not particularly concern labor arbitration advocates, because the difference between an out of hearing statement that is admissible because it is nonhearsay (not offered to prove the truth of the matters asserted) or an exception to the hearsay rule makes little difference—either way, the testimony or written document is admissible.

The following section discusses exceptions to the hearsay rule. Included among these exceptions will be types of nonhearsay that do not fall within the exclusionary hearsay rule because they are not offered to prove the truth of the statements. If an advocate argues to an arbitrator that particular testimony is admissible, notwithstanding its apparent hearsay character, it will most likely make no difference whether the advocate asserts that the statement is admissible because it is not really hearsay or because it is an exception to the hearsay rule. The arbitrator is not likely to know the distinction, or if he or she does, it is one that is not likely to make any difference with regard to the decision to admit the evidence. Whichever it is, the evidence should be admitted for its full value, and not simply subject to weight.

## Exceptions to the Hearsay Rule

### Declaration or Admission against Interest

#### Statement of the Exception to the Rule

A statement by an out-of-hearing declarant that is contrary to the interests of the declarant (including one of the parties in the case with which the declarant is allied) is admissible as an exception to the hearsay rule.

#### Rationale

The normal unreliability of an out-of-hearing statement is diminished substantially when the identity of the declarant and the content of the hearsay statement are contrary to the interests of the declarant (i.e., they are unlikely to have been motivated by a desire to influence the case and are more likely to be truthful).

*Example.* [In a case involving the discharge of an employee, Mr. Jones, for excessive absenteeism and for misrepresenting the reasons for being absent from work; a coworker is testifying]

*EA:* Did Mr. Jones tell you where he was on July 5?

*W.* Yes.

*EA:* What did he say?

*W.* He said he was fishing in Canada with several friends.

*UA:* Objection, move to strike the answer on the basis that it was hearsay.

*EA:* Mr. Arbitrator, this testimony comes within an exception to the hearsay rule. It is an admission against interest by the grievant, Mr. Jones. In addition, Mr. Jones is here as a witness and is capable of refuting the testimony if that is possible.

*A.* Objection overruled. You may answer the question.

## Discussion

The reliability of hearsay is based not only on the integrity and recollection of the witness, it is influenced as well by the identity and circumstances of the declarant. When a statement is made by someone under circumstances in which no reasonable person would have a motive to make such a statement, the hearsay statement is thought to be sufficiently reliable to be admitted into evidence. Whether or not this is true in the real world, for purposes of applying the rules of evidence, it is an important exception to the hearsay rule.

## Spontaneous or Excited Utterance

### Statement of the Exception to the Rule

When a hearsay statement is made by a declarant under circumstances of surprise and/or excitement such that the statement appears to be spontaneous or uncontrolled, the statement is admissible.

### Rationale

The trustworthiness of an out-of-hearing statement is greatly enhanced when circumstances surrounding the making of the statement indicate that the declarant did not premeditate or plan the statement, resulting in a spontaneous, and presumably candid, declaration.

*Example.* [In a case in which a machine operator files a grievance protesting a reprimand he received from his supervisor, Mr. Boss, for unsafe operation of a cutting machine, which caused an accident]

> *UA:* At the time when the cutting machine went off the track, causing the accident, did you hear your supervisor, Mr. Boss, say anything?
>
> *W.* Yes.
>
> *UA:* What did he say?
>
> *EA:* Objection, calls for hearsay.
>
> *UA:* Mr. Arbitrator, while Mr. Boss's statement might otherwise be considered hearsay, the circumstances here indicate that it was made under stressful and unexpected circumstances. It therefore is an exception to the hearsay rule under the spontaneous declaration exception.
>
> *A.* I'll allow the question. The witness may answer.
>
> *W.* He said, "There goes that damn machine again."

## Discussion

The theory of this exception is that someone who is in an unpredictable situation and who, in a condition of surprise or stress, utters a spontaneous statement is likely to be telling the truth, and therefore the resulting statement should be admitted into evidence despite the fact that it is hearsay. The rationale is that persons who speak off the cuff or under conditions that indicate they did not calculate the effect of their words are likely to be telling the truth.

## Past Recollection Recorded

### Statement of the Exception to the Rule

Testimony concerning a hearsay statement about which the witness does not have a current and complete recollection, but about which a written record or memorandum was made about the time the statement was uttered that would refresh the witness's recollection, may be admitted.

298 How to Prepare and Present a Labor Arbitration Case

The reliability of hearsay is significantly increased when the witness who is providing the hearsay testimony made a written record at the time of or soon after the occurrence of the out-of-hearing statement.

*Example.* [In a case of suspension of an employee, Ms. Hazel Nutt, for leaving work early without authorization]

> *UA:* Ms. Smith, do you recall what Hazel Nutt said to you at approximately 3:00 P.M. on the day in question?
>
> *W.* Well, she told me that she had to leave work early that day.
>
> *UA:* Did she say why she was leaving?
>
> *W.* Yes, she did say something about that, but I don't remember just what she said.
>
> *UA:* Do you have anything that would refresh your recollection?
>
> *W.* Yes, I made a short note in a log book that I kept at my desk.
>
> *UA:* I'm showing you a log book from your department. Based on the note on page 18, can you tell us what Hazel said to you?
>
> *EA:* Objection, calls for hearsay.
>
> *UA:* Mr. Arbitrator, this is admissible under the past recollection recorded exception to the hearsay rule.
>
> *A.* Ms. Smith, when did you make that note?
>
> *W.* Within a few minutes after she spoke with me.
>
> *A.* [To the witness] You may answer the question posed by the union advocate.

*Discussion*

The past recollection recorded exception to the hearsay rule is rather artificial. If a witness has his or her recollection refreshed by examining a document at the hearing, what is to prevent the witness from viewing the document in advance of the hearing and simply testifying based on the refreshed recollection without any reference to the document that enabled the recollection? In most labor arbitration cases that is exactly what occurs. The advocate who is preparing the witness shows the document to the witness (or the witness produces the document), and the advocate uses it in preparing the witness to testify.

An anomaly resulting from strict application of this rule of evidence is that the document that is used to refresh the witness's recollection is normally not admissible in evidence, even though the testimony that is refreshed by that document is admissible. In most labor arbitration cases, however, both the testimony and the document will be admitted by the arbitrator. The advocate who invokes the past recollection recorded exception to the hearsay rule will be at an advantage in having the arbitrator give full credence to the document as well as the testimony.

### Business and Public Records

*Statement of the Exception to the Rule*

Evidence in the form of a business or public record that is kept in the normal course of business or the administration of the public agency is admissible even though it would otherwise be objectionable as hearsay evidence.

*Rationale*

Where business or public entities maintain records, reports, and so on as part of their normal functioning, such records or other documents are unlikely to be subject to fabrication, manipulation, tampering, or other actions that are intended to make such documents untruthful. For this reason they are usually reliable and therefore admissible.

*Example.* [In a case involving the suspension of a truck driver because of an excessive number of motor vehicle violations]

EA: Have you obtained the driving record of Mr. Mack from the state department of motor vehicles?

W. Yes.

EA: How did you obtain it?

W. I mailed a written request to that agency and asked for a copy of Mr. Mack's driving record that would reflect any citations received by him within the last three years. It was mailed to me, and I received it on August 9 of this year.

EA: What did it indicate?

UA: Objection, this calls for hearsay evidence. The union cannot cross-examine the highway patrol officers who allegedly issued the tickets referred to nor can it question the employees of the department of motor vehicles who maintain the records.

EA: Madam Arbitrator, this evidence falls within the business and public records exception to the hearsay rule. These records are maintained in the normal course of business of that department.

A. Objection overruled.

## Discussion

Documents, and particularly records of businesses and public agencies, are seldom thought of as hearsay evidence. Nevertheless, they constitute statements, albeit written statements, made outside the hearing that are offered to prove the truth of the matters asserted, for example, that the truck driver grievant had an excessive number of traffic citations, which violated the employer's rules concerning safe driving. There are few labor arbitration cases in which an arbitrator would not admit such documents, provided the records or other documents are shown to be authentic. When there is a question as to the authenticity or whether the records are kept in the normal course of business, the custodian or keeper of the records may need to be called as a witness. More often, however, the appearance of the record on its face and testimony about how it was obtained will reflect its authenticity and will be sufficient to support admission into evidence.

## State of Mind

### Statement of the Exception to the Rule

Evidence of an oral or written statement that was made outside the hearing and that is offered for the purpose of showing the state of mind of the declarant (rather than the truth of the matters asserted in the statement) is not actually hearsay evidence and is therefore admissible.

### Rationale

Evidence reflecting a declarant's state of mind at the time that an out-of-hearing statement was made is admissible because it is not offered to prove the truth of the matters asserted. Consequently, it is not actually hearsay and is therefore admissible.

*Example.* [In a grievance by an employee, Mr. Jones, protesting that he was not assigned overtime by his supervisor, overtime to which he contends he was entitled]

UA: What did your supervisor say when you overheard him speaking in the men's room at lunchtime that day?

EA: Objection. The question asks for hearsay testimony.

*UA:* Mr. Arbitrator, the witness is being asked to state what he heard his supervisor say. We are offering his testimony on this point not for the purpose of proving the truth of what the supervisor said, but merely to show the supervisor's state of mind at that time.

*A.* I will permit the witness to answer the question, but I will consider the answer solely for the purpose of reflecting the declarant's state of mind at the time the statement was made. The witness may answer the question.

*W.* I heard him say, "Jones isn't worth a damn, I won't give him the overtime no matter what the contract says."

## Discussion

The distinction between the state of mind of the declarant and the assertion of the truth of the matters contained in the hearsay statement is indeed a fine one. Once the arbitrator has heard the statement, it is difficult to conceive that he or she will be able to limit the meaning or interpretation of the statement to one narrow concept, that is, what was in the mind of the person who made the original statement. Nevertheless, this is the rationale behind the state of mind exception to the hearsay rule, and it is helpful for advocates to understand it.

### Prior Testimony

#### Statement of the Exception to the Rule

Testimony that was given in a prior hearing, trial, or deposition is admissible when the circumstances surrounding the taking of the testimony and the opportunity to cross-examine the declarant were such as to render the hearsay statements reasonably reliable.

#### Rationale

When a person testifies in an adversary proceeding, particularly under oath and when a verbatim recording has been made, the statements are likely to be reliable, particularly when the same or similar parties and issues were involved and when there was an opportunity for the witness to be cross-examined by a competent advocate.

*Example.* [In an arbitration where the grievant was discharged for falsification of an employment application, the grievant had previously filed an unemployment compensation claim, which resulted in an unemployment hearing prior to the arbitration hearing. In the unemployment hearing, the grievant's supervisor had testified about the reason for the discharge. The grievant's union representative is testifying.]

> UA: Did you attend the unemployment compensation hearing concerning Mr. Wax?
>
> W. Yes, I did.
>
> UA: Did you obtain a copy of the transcript of that hearing?
>
> W. Yes, I did.
>
> UA: In that hearing did Mr. Wax's supervisor say what his reason was for the discharge?
>
> EA: Objection, this question calls for hearsay.
>
> UA: We can produce the transcript of the hearing to substantiate the witness's testimony. While admittedly hearsay, it comes within the hearsay exception of recorded testimony and is therefore admissible.
>
> A. I will overrule the objection and permit the witness to answer.
>
> W. Mr. Wax's supervisor said that he discharged Wax because he had a bad attitude.

*Discussion*

In most adversary hearings and in all trials, witnesses are sworn to tell the truth. When the testimony of a witness has been given in such a proceeding and when a record of that testimony has been kept, evidence in the form of testimony or a transcript containing such prior testimony will be admitted. Even if it does not prove the truth of the matters asserted (e.g., that an employee was fired for a bad attitude), it may be used to attack the credibility of the declarant (e.g., that the supervisor fired an employee for reasons other than those used to justify the discharge in arbitration, i.e., on a pretext).

## Statements Having Independent Legal Significance

*Statement of the Exception to the Rule*

Testimony or documentary evidence of statements made outside the hearing that have a legal significance irrespective of the truth of the matters contained in the statement are admissible. In a labor arbitration context statements made by parties to a labor agreement leading up to their agreement are generally admissible for the purpose of proving the meaning of language in that agreement. Because they have such independent legal significance, they are not truly hearsay, inasmuch as they are not offered to prove the truth of the matters asserted.[5]

*Rationale*

This exception is based on the notion that certain words have legal consequences, that is, they create legal rights and obligations. Because a labor agreement is considered to embody the intentions of the parties expressed in the making of that agreement, the discussions have independent legal significance and are therefore admissible.

*Example.* [In a case in which the union and employer contest whether the seniority clause modified in recent negotiations was intended to change the way employees were recalled from layoff]

UA: Mr. Green, did you participate in labor negotiations as a union representative in the last contract negotiations?

W. Yes.

UA: Were you in attendance on July 30 when Section 17 was finally agreed on.

W. Yes.

UA: What, if anything, did the employer's spokesman, Mr. Blue, say that day about the wording changes being made in Section 17?

EA: Objection. Calls for hearsay testimony.

UA: Madam Arbitrator, this testimony is admissible. Mr. Blue's statements have an independent legal significance and are not precluded by the hearsay rule.

A. Objection overruled. The witness may answer.

W. He said, "Don't worry about this change in wording. This is simply to clarify the meaning of this section, not to change the layoff procedures."

*Discussion*

Most labor arbitrators will give short shrift to any objections concerning statements made at the bargaining table that will shed light on

---

[5]Lilly, *An Introduction to the Law of Evidence,* (West Publishing, 1987) p.190; Hill and Sinicropi, *Evidence in Arbitration,* (BNA Books, 1987) p.148.

the meaning of disputed or ambiguous contract language. Unless the language of an agreement is absolutely clear on its face and not subject to multiple meanings (and completely clear language is relatively rare in labor contracts), such evidence is usually instructive as to the parties' intentions concerning the language. Moreover, unless the negotiations in which the statements were made occurred a long time prior to the hearing, the other side would normally have ample opportunity to rebut the claimed hearsay evidence.

### Prior Inconsistent Statement

#### Statement of the Exception to the Rule

When a witness provides testimony that a declarant made a state-ment outside the hearing that is inconsistent with a statement or position taken in the case by the declarant (or a party with which the declarant is allied), the hearsay testimony is admissible.

#### Rationale

As with the state of mind exception discussed above, evidence of a prior inconsistent statement made by a witness or a principal party in the case is often nonhearsay in that it is used to impeach the declarant and may or may not be used to prove the truth of the matters asserted.

*Example.* [In a case involving the denial of a requested transfer of a grievant from one department to another when the supervisor in charge has testified in the arbitration that it was because he believed the grievant was unqualified to do the work in the other department]

UA: Mr. Stuart, as the union representative for the grievant, did you attend the second-step hearing of this grievance?

W. Yes, I did.

UA: Was Mr. Boss present?

W. Yes.

UA: What did Mr. Boss say was the reason for denying the grievant the opportunity to transfer into a new department.

EA: Objection, calls for hearsay.

UA: Mr. Arbitrator, we submit that this evidence will show that Mr. Boss took a position and made a statement that were contrary to that which he has testified to today, and it therefore falls within the prior inconsistent statement exception to the hearsay rule.

*A.* Objection overruled. I believe the exception applies. Additionally, Mr. Boss is present in the hearing room and will have an opportunity to refute the evidence if that is appropriate.

*W.* He said, "Peters is not loyal to the company."

## Discussion

Whether inconsistent statements made outside the arbitration hearing are justified as an exception to the hearsay rule or as nonhearsay for the purpose of impeachment, such inconsistent statements are admissible. Moreover, the subject of the prior inconsistent statement need not even concern a matter involved in the case. As long as it shows the declarant to be inconsistent (and presumably untruthful), it is relevant to the case and therefore admissible.

## Other Hearsay Exceptions

The exceptions discussed above are the principal exceptions to the hearsay rule that have been traditionally accepted by the courts and to some degree in labor arbitration. There are some others that are less frequently recognized but in many cases no less significant to labor arbitration advocates. These will be reviewed in a more summary fashion.

## Present Sense Impression

When a declarant describes his or her observation or impression about a condition at or soon after an operative event or condition, the statement repeated by a witness in a hearing may be admitted as an exception to the hearsay rule. For example, a witness testifies that she overheard her supervisor state during the morning coffee break, "I'm sick of this place." This exception is somewhat similar to the spontaneous or excited utterance, although the element of surprise is not required.

## Present Physical Condition

When the hearsay testimony consists of a statement made by a person who is describing his or her physical condition at the time of the statement, the testimony relating such a statement is admissible as an exception to the hearsay rule. For example, an employee who testifies that a coworker said, "I have a splitting headache," before the coworker went home early has given admissible evidence under this exception to the hearsay rule.

### Surveys and Polls

Evidence of the results of an opinion survey or poll is a result of statements made to poll takers and is ostensibly hearsay but is admissible as an exception. In some cases the evidence may be considered under another label, such a state of mind or present sense impression, but may also be admitted for its own sake.

### Concluding Note Concerning Hearsay Exceptions

It bears repeating that hearsay evidence is usually admissible in labor arbitration, provided the evidence is relevant. Advocates need not normally rely on exceptions to the hearsay rule for the purpose of having evidence entered into the record, but such exceptions can be helpful in persuading the arbitrator that the alleged evidence is either not hearsay (because it is not offered to prove the truth of the matters asserted, but for some other purpose, such as the state of mind of the declarant) or is clearly admissible under the hearsay rule because it constitutes an exception. The main purpose of arguing the exceptions to the hearsay rule is to have the arbitrator accept the evidence and give full weight to its significance, rather than to have it admitted for whatever weight it deserves. Nevertheless, advocates should not be overly concerned if they do not fully understand or feel comfortable with the hearsay rule and/or its exceptions. Lack of understanding or facility with the hearsay rule is seldom a serious liability in labor arbitration. It is one that is often shared with the arbitrator.

## RULES OF EVIDENCE BASED ON FORM OF QUESTIONS

The rules of evidence discussed thus far in this chapter are designed to exclude evidence that is considered to be unreliable or that should be rejected for policy reasons. Thus, where the rule applies, the evidence will not be admitted into the record. When applied less strictly—hearsay, for example—it may be admitted but given diminished weight or significance.

Other rules of evidence, those regarding form, are based on the notion that the way in which information is sought from a witness, that is, the phrasing of questions, can unfairly influence the reliability and veracity of the resulting evidence and therefore should not be admitted unless the questions are reframed in such a way as to eliminate the defect that creates the unreliability or lack of veracity. The thrust of these rules is not so much to exclude the evidence, but to require that it be elicited in a different way. Thus, in most cases a competent advocate will be able to overcome an objection to the form of a question simply by rephrasing the question.

In contrast to many of the traditional exclusionary rules (especially the rules concerning hearsay, opinion, best evidence, and parol evidence) discussed above, labor arbitrators are often likely to sustain objections based on the form of the question. The reason is that the effect need not be to exclude the proffered evidence, but merely to modify the way in which the evidence is produced. Some lay and/or inexperienced advocates encounter difficulty with objections as to form. Unless the advocate understands the basic rule on which the objection is based and the rationale underlying that rule, it is often difficult to rephrase the question to remove the troublesome aspect of the question. Consequently, all labor arbitration advocates are well advised to learn and become familiar with rules of evidence based on the form of questions.

## Lack of Foundation—Lack of Competency

### Statement of the Rule

In order for evidence to be admissible it must be shown that the person providing the testimony or explaining documentary or other tangible evidence is someone who has sufficient knowledge, familiarity, and perception of the evidence being offered to be a competent witness.

### Rationale

The value and reliability of evidence is based on the ability of the witness to know about, perceive, or otherwise be capable of presenting evidence on a particular subject. The arbitrator and the opposing side should have, in advance of the pertinent questions being posed, sufficient preliminary information about the witness's connection to the evidence to determine that the witness has such qualifications.

*Example.* [In a case in which a supervisor is testifying about a warehouse in which the grievance arose and is offering a photograph of one portion of the warehouse]

> *EA:* [Questioning immediately after swearing in the witness] Ms. Bliss, I'm showing you a photograph of the ABC warehouse and asking you if you could tell us where the grievant was seen removing the articles on the day in question.
>
> *UA:* Objection, lack of foundation. We know nothing of the competency of this witness to testify as to these matters, nor of the circumstances under which this photograph was taken.
>
> *A.* Sustained. Would the advocate please lay a foundation for this witness's testimony, as well as for the introduction of the photograph.
>
> *EA:* I'm sorry, Madam Arbitrator. Let me go back. Ms. Bliss, what is your position with the employer?
>
> *W.* I'm the warehouse supervisor on the day shift. The grievant worked under my direction.
>
> *EA:* Did you take the photograph that has been marked as Employer Exhibit 6?
>
> *W.* Yes, I did.
>
> *EA:* When did you take the photograph?
>
> *W.* One week after the incident.
>
> *EA:* Was there anything different about the warehouse on the day you took the photo than on the day in question?
>
> *W.* No.
>
> [The employer advocate should continue to lay a foundation to show that the witness was in a position to observe critical events related to the incident at issue and is otherwise knowledgeable about what the testimony will concern]

### Discussion

The rule concerning foundation is, strictly speaking, a substantive rule of evidence, because if a proper foundation cannot be laid, the evidence to be offered by the witness will be excluded. More often, however, the rule regarding foundation is really one of form, because the advocate is usually able (as in the example above) to go back and have the witness provide the necessary information to satisfy the requirements of a proper foundation.

Novice advocates sometimes run afoul of the foundation rule, because they are so familiar with the facts in the case and the competency of the witnesses to testify that they overlook the fact that the opposing advocate and the arbitrator are not as enmeshed in the case, its facts, and witnesses and cannot as easily understand why the witness is able to provide the offered evidence. In some other situations, particularly after the hearing is well under way and after a number of witnesses have testified, foundations may be less necessary since in the course of the case presentation, the basis for some witnesses' testimony and related exhibits will be obvious from evidence previously received. Nevertheless, it is better for the advocate to be overly cautious to ensure that a proper foundation has been laid for each witness and each piece of evidence. Not only will it avoid embarrassing sustained objections, but it will also enhance the quality and credibility of the evidence being presented.

## Leading Questions

### Statement of the Rule

An advocate may not, except for preliminary noncritical matters, ask a question of his or her own witness if the form of the question suggests the answer desired by the advocate posing the question.

### Rationale

It is assumed that there is a friendly relationship between an advocate and the advocate's own witness, that the witness wishes to assist the advocate who calls that witness, and that they have spent some time in advance of the hearing preparing the witness's testimony. With that background there is no justification for questions to be framed in such a way as to suggest the desired answer. It is the truthful testimony of the witness that is desired, not the ideas and words of the advocate.

*Example.* [On direct examination]

EA: During the time you were in charge of the processing department, you told your subordinates many times, didn't you, that they were never to remove any of the tape files from the computer room?

UA: Objection. That is a leading question.

A. Sustained. Would you please rephrase the question in a nonleading form.

   *EA:* What, if anything, did you tell employees in your department concerning the subject of removal of tapes from the computer room?

## Discussion

   Leading questions are prohibited on direct examination except for preliminary or inconsequential matters. As a practical matter, many leading questions asked during direct examination are never objected to, because they either are not detected or are asked with respect to matters that are noncontroversial or when the impact of the answer is insignificant. Leading questions, even when objections to them are sustained, can be used to signal a witness as to the correct answer. As in the above example, the witness surely knows that the correct answer to the question is that employees were frequently told not to remove tapes from the computer room. An advocate who continues to use leading questions, despite having objections to them sustained, is subject to reprimand from the arbitrator and is likely to lose credibility. A great deal more is said about leading questions in Chapter 12, Cross-Examination.

## Assumes Facts Not in Evidence; Misquotes Testimony

### Statement of the Rule

   A question that assumes facts that are not in evidence, that incorrectly quotes testimony of a witness, or that misstates evidence in the case is improper, and evidence resulting from such a question is inadmissible.

### Rationale

   When the predicate to a question is other evidence in the case, it is improper to base the question on matters not actually entered into evidence in the case or on an inaccurate representation of evidence that has been introduced. Testimony based on nonexistent or inaccurate evidence is almost certain to be inaccurate itself. Moreover, merely asking a question that presumes matters not in evidence taints the record by attempting to get matters into evidence through the back door.

*Example.*

> *EA:* Ms. Oaknoll, do you agree with Ms. Tepid's testimony that all the work was completed in satisfactory fashion by 8:15 P.M. that day?
>
> *UA:* Objection. The question misstates the testimony of Ms. Tepid. She did not testify that the work was satisfactory.
>
> *A.* Sustained. I believe that question does not properly characterize Ms. Tepid's testimony.
>
> *EA:* Do you agree, Ms. Oaknoll, that the work was completed by 8:15 P.M. that evening?
>
> *W.* Yes, it was completed by that time.

### Discussion

Many advocates like to piggyback the testimony of one witness onto that of another, especially when the second person is not a particularly strong witness, and it is easier to feed the witness prior testimony and merely have the second witness affirm it. When this is done, it is important that the testimony of the first witness not be misrepresented in any way. In most cases it is preferable to quote the first witness's actual testimony. By using that witness's exact words there is no opportunity for the opposing advocate to challenge the question.

In the example just above, the objection was based on a misstatement of the evidence. The objection might just as well have been phrased, ''Assumes facts not in evidence.'' Since Ms. Tepid did not testify that the work had been done satisfactorily, a question premised on that fact assumed a fact that was not in evidence.

## Hypothetical Questions

### Statement of the Rule

Questions based on hypothetical facts are not admissible, unless the witness to whom they are posed has been qualified as an expert witness.

### Rationale

If a question contains certain facts that have not been established and is based on hypothetical or presumed facts or situations, any answer to such a question will be based on conjecture and surmise and is therefore not reliable. When such a question is asked of a witness who has been qualified as an expert, and the facts presumed in the question parallel those in the case, opinion testimony based on those hypothetical facts is admissible.

*Example A.*

UA: Dr. Wallenburg, you have described your broad background in mechanical engineering. You have also heard the previous testimony about the failure of the thrust hammer and its piston to function properly on the day in question. If the grievant had correctly operated the thrust hammer that day, is there any way the accident could have occurred for some other reason?

EA: Objection. The question is based on a hypothetical premise that has not been proven. We will show that the grievant did not operate the machine properly.

A. Objection overruled. While you may offer evidence concerning the manner in which the grievant operated the machine, Dr. Wallenburg has been qualified as an expert and may render an opinion based on a hypothetical question. I recognize that the premise of the question has not yet been established, and I will keep that in mind.

W. I believe that the sink shaft on the throttle could, and very likely did in this case, cause the throttle to malfunction.

*Example B.*

UA: If Ms. Robinson, your supervisor, had not directed you to continue working at the end of your shift, would you have nevertheless stayed on the job until the emergency was over?

EA: Objection. It's a hypothetical question. Her supervisor did direct her to work over.

A. It is a hypothetical question, but I will allow the witness to answer.

W. Yes, I would have stayed. I have done so several times in the past under similar circumstances.

*Discussion*

Traditionally, hypothetical questions were used to elicit opinions of expert witnesses. Under the current federal rules of evidence, that is not necessary. Hypothetical questions may be used for ordinary fact witnesses to show state of mind, motivation, and patterns of conduct. Unless the hypothetical question is too absurd and too unlikely to have occurred, arbitrators will usually permit such questions. In the second example, the employer advocate might also have based the objection on the rule discussed just above (i.e., that questions based on facts not in evidence are not admissible). There is no assurance that the arbitrator would have been any more sympathetic to that objection, but it would have added a little more ammunition in attempting to avoid having the witness speculate as to what she would have done.

## Compound Questions

### *Statement of the Rule*

Except for preliminary or noncontroversial matters, questions are to be phrased in such a way that they only ask for information on one point at a time.

### *Rationale*

When a question inquires about several matters in one interrogatory, it is difficult to determine to which of the questions the answer is directed. Moreover, one of the questions may seek testimony that is admissible, while the other seeks inadmissible evidence and is therefore objectionable. By merging the two questions, registering a proper objection is made more difficult.

### *Example.*

UA: Is it true that you punched out before Fred, and that Fred went home about 6:00 A.M.?

EA: Objection. Compound question.

A. Sustained. Please break the question apart.

UA: Did you punch out on the time clock before Fred that day?

W. Yes.

UA: Did Fred go home about 6:00 A.M. that day?

W. I don't know for sure. I never saw him leave, but he was there when I left.

## Discussion

When the matters being inquired about are not controverted or not critical to the case, the opposing advocate is not likely to object to a compound question, and if he or she does, the arbitrator is not likely to sustain the objection. When, however, the matters are essential to the case and there is a probability that the answers to the two parts of the question will be different, the inquiring advocate should be careful to ask only one question at a time.

## Questions Calling for Speculation

### Statement of the Rule

A question is improper if it calls for the witness to speculate or to otherwise testify about matters that the witness is not capable of knowing first-hand.

### Rationale

Witnesses are to testify about matters they know from their own knowledge, perception, or experience. They should not be asked questions attempting to elicit information that goes beyond those factors. The resulting testimony is unreliable.

### Example A.

*UA:* Mr. Dixon, what do you think was on Art Park's mind when you told him to start the motor?

*EA:* Objection. Calls for speculation. Mr. Dixon could not know what Mr. Park was thinking.

*A.* Sustained.

*UA:* Mr. Dixon, did Mr. Park say or do anything at the time you told him to start the motor?

*W.* He said, "I was waiting for Joe to tell me to start."

### Example B.

*EA:* Ms. Sampson, what's your guess as to why there were so few customers in the store that day?

*UA:* Objection. Calls for speculation.

A. Sustained, unless there is some foundation laid for the witness's ability to have that knowledge.

*EA:* Ms. Sampson, did you have any information available to you that would indicate why there were so few customers in the store that day?

W. I saw an ad in the local newspaper the previous day saying that our major competitor, Gumps, was having a half-off sale that day.

*EA:* Do you believe that was the cause of the light turnout of customers at your store that day?

W. Yes.

### Discussion

Labor arbitrators are usually willing to allow lay witnesses to speculate and give opinions, at least when the matters the testimony concern fall within their normal work or experience competencies. Thus, in the second example above, had it been established earlier that Ms. Sampson had worked in the store for some time and had some understanding of the business, the arbitrator would likely have permitted the initial question concerning the lack of customers over the objection of the union advocate. When, however, the question calls for a witness to speculate about matters that seem to be outside the reasonable knowledge or perception of the witness (e.g., inquiring about what someone else was thinking, as in the first example), an objection is likely to be sustained.

## Ambiguous, Vague, Misleading, and Unintelligible Questions

### Statement of the Rule

A question that is so ambiguous, vague, misleading, or unintelligible that a reasonable person would not understand, or would at least be confused about, the information being sought is an improper question.

### Rationale

If a reasonable person cannot understand what information is being sought from a question or is uncertain as to exactly what matters are being referred to in a question, there is a likelihood that the witness may provide an erroneous answer. If no objection is raised and if the witness does not ask for a clarification, there is a strong chance that erroneous information may be placed in the record despite the witness's intention to be truthful.

*Example A.*

> *EA:* Would you tell us whatever it was that you thought someone said that might have caused you or the rest of the crew to believe that there was something that the company should have done that would have prevented the grievance about which we are arbitrating today?
>
> *UA:* Objection. Ambiguous and confusing.
>
> *A.* Sustained. Would you please rephrase the question.
>
> *EA:* Was there anything you heard that day that led you to believe that the company was at fault in the way the work was assigned to your crew?

*Example B.*

> *EA:* Ms. Combs, you previously testified that you worked overtime on November 22 with Juanita Gonzalez. You also testified that you found out that night that your supervisor, Stella Dallas, came in later that night to check inventory. When did she leave?
>
> *UA:* Objection. Ambiguous. It's not clear who "she" refers to.
>
> *A.* I agree. Would you please clarify the question.
>
> *EA:* When, if you know, did Stella Dallas leave the store?

### Discussion

More often than not, this objection is unnecessary, in that a truly ambiguous, vague, or confusing question will usually prompt the witness to ask for a clarification or a rephrasing of the question. Some questions, however, may be interpreted by a witness in such a way that the confusion or ambiguity in the question is not apparent to them, and, unless the advocate points out the problem, the witness may answer the question incorrectly based on the misinterpretation. Moreover, if an arbitrator is confused by a question, he or she will usually want it clarified so that the record (especially when a verbatim transcript is being made) is clear.

# Argumentative or Badgering Questions

## *Statement of the Rule*

Questions that do not ask for information but are posed merely for the purpose of expressing an argument or characterizing testimony are improper and therefore objectionable. Similarly, questions that are designed to harass or intimidate a witness, rather than obtain information, are objectionable.

## *Rationale*

The purpose of examining witnesses is to elicit information or challenge credibility. Questions that go beyond these limits are improper. Argumentation is to be reserved until after all evidence has been received. It is not to be advanced during the evidentiary portion of the case in the form of questions or in any other form. Similarly, witnesses should not be required to undergo badgering or intimidating questions out of deference to their dignity and out of concern that they might be intimidated from giving accurate testimony in order to bring an end to the harassment.

*Example A.*

> *UA:* Mr. Stuart, why did you assign the cleanup work to the maintenance technician?
>
> *W.* Because he was the only one available at that time, and because he had no other pressing duties to perform just then.
>
> *UA:* Isn't it a fact that you did it just to embarrass him?
>
> *EA:* Objection. The question is argumentative.
>
> *A.* Sustained.

*Example B.*

> *EA:* Would you tell us why you filed a grievance about the work assignment?
>
> *W.* I thought it was in violation of the contract.
>
> *EA:* Did you *really* think that?
>
> *W.* Yes, I did.
>
> *EA:* The fact is that you had it in for your supervisor, and you just wanted to make his life more difficult. Correct?
>
> *UA:* I object. He is badgering the witness.
>
> *A.* Sustained.

## Discussion

Argumentative questions are frequently posed by inexperienced advocates who do not always understand the distinction between the evidentiary portion of a hearing and the argumentation phase. They are not usually trying to take advantage of the witness, but are anxious to make their arguments to the arbitrator. In other cases such questions are posed simply out of frustration that the witness is not providing the answers that the advocate wants and believes are the truthful ones.

Badgering, in contrast, usually involves more malice on the part of the interrogator. The challenging or accusatory content of the words is usually matched with a loud or sarcastic tone. Almost always used on cross-examination, this type of questioning is usually employed to degrade or embarrass a witness to try to show that the witness is not being truthful or unbiased. There is no clear line dividing merely aggressive questioning and badgering. Often it is a question of frequency. One or two rough questions may be permitted before an arbitrator will sustain an objection for badgering. An effective advocate will not permit his or her witness to be badgered without vehemently objecting to the arbitrator.

## Questions Calling for a Conclusion

### Statement of the Rule

A question is objectionable when it calls for a witness to draw a conclusion from a set of facts and when the conclusion has a determinative effect on the case and would be expected to be drawn by the arbitrator.

### Rationale

Witnesses are to testify as to facts and not invade the province of the arbitrator by making conclusions that are judgmental and essential to deciding the case.

### Example.

> UA: Ms. Jones, what happened when you finished that particular job?
>
> W. Our supervisor sent us home, less than halfway through our shift.
>
> UA: And was that a violation of the labor agreement?

*EA:* Objection. Calls for a conclusion.

*A.* Sustained. I believe I will have to make that determination.

## Discussion

This rule, developed for civil and criminal trials, particularly jury trials, is not commonly followed in labor arbitration. Arbitrators are used to ignoring or discounting such conclusions and commonly permit witnesses to draw conclusions as long as these occurrences do not become frequent in a hearing.

## Questions Calling for Explanation or Interpretation of a Document

### Statement of the Rule

Questions that require a witness to explain or interpret the meaning of a document that is clear, or relatively clear, on its face are objectionable.

### Rationale

A document that has significance in the final determination of a case will be read and interpreted by the arbitrator. Unless there is some arcane or technical language used in the document, no elaboration is necessary. The language in the document "speaks for itself," and no amount of embellishment by a witness can add or subtract from the meaning of the document.

### Example.

*EA:* I'm handing the witness a copy of Employer Exhibit 14, which has previously been identified as a letter you sent to the union vice president. Would you tell us what this letter means?

*UA:* Objection. The document speaks for itself.

*A.* I agree. I'll sustain the objection.

*EA:* Can you tell us what prompted you to send the letter?

*W.* Yes, it was in response to a discussion we had earlier that day.

## Discussion

A common failing of novice advocates is to have their witness explain documents and to try to use that explanation to argue the case. This often occurs with respect to agreements and correspondence. When an objection is made, and often sustained, the novice advocate may be puzzled. This is another example of a misunderstanding of the difference between the evidentiary and argumentation phases of the hearing. It is also a misunderstanding of the role of the arbitrator. The arbitrator is charged with the responsibility of interpreting agreements and drawing the significance from letters, memos, and other communications. For a witness to try to explain what the words mean or were intended to mean, is but another form of the objectionable testimony discussed just above, that is, drawing conclusions. Nevertheless, a great many arbitrators permit such questions.

## Questions Previously Asked and Answered

### Statement of the Rule

When a question has been asked and answered by an advocate, that same advocate asking the same or virtually the same question is objectionable.

### Rationale

Permitting the same questions to be asked and answered prolongs hearings. Repetition of the same questions does nothing to enhance the production of facts on which a decision can be based.

*Example.*

> *EA:* Did you wait on the customer, a Ms. Lane Bryant, who later complained to the store manager?
>
> *W.* Yes.
>
> *EA:* Did you observe her complaining to the manager?
>
> *W.* Yes, I did.
>
> *EA:* Was it actually Ms. Bryant who you waited on?
>
> *W.* Objection. Asked and answered.
>
> *EA:* Sustained. I believe the witness just testified to that fact.

## Discussion

Advocates who repeat questions previously asked and answered by a witness do so primarily for two reasons. First, when there is a separation of some interval between the two questions, the advocate may have forgotten that the question was already asked. Second, on cross-examination the inquiring advocate will try to have the witness contradict his or her earlier testimony. Arbitrators are often willing to permit repetition of questions when different words are used to phrase the question and when it appears that the advocate is trying to test the accuracy of the witness' recollection or the witness' credibility. Thus, when the advocate uses the preamble, ''Are you absolutely sure . . . '', it is likely that the question will survive an objection. If, however, the same question is later repeated, an objection is likely to be sustained.

# Cumulative Testimony

## Statement of the Rule

When a question calls for a witness to testify about facts that have already been established through one or more witnesses and/or other evidence and there is little or no rebuttal evidence, the question is likely to be objectionable.

## Rationale

Hearings will be unduly prolonged by repetition of evidence when there is little or no contrary evidence. It merely accumulates more facts, without adding anything new on which a decision may be based.

## Example.

    *EA:* Mr. Largent, you heard the testimony of Peter Graves, Silas Marner, Juanita Rosales, and Charles Choy. Do you agree that the procedure followed was the way they said it was?

    *W.* Yes.

    *EA:* Would you please describe it in your own words.

    *UA:* Objection. This evidence is simply cumulative.

    *A.* Mr. Largent, do you have any facts that will vary from or add to those provided by the other witnesses mentioned.

    *W.* No, I don't.

    *A.* I will sustain the objection.

### Discussion

The rule concerning cumulative evidence is not a cut-and-dried one. In some cases the weight of evidence will be an important factor for the determination of the case. If four or five persons saw an event in the same way, an arbitrator is likely to give significant credence to their testimony. Arbitrators are wary of cutting off such testimony. If, however, the facts about which the cumulative evidence centers are largely undisputed by the other side, additional witnesses are of little value. One witness's testimony that is unrebutted will be accepted by the arbitrator, unless the witness and the witness's testimony are very incredible.

## Questions That Call for a Narrative Answer

### Statement of the Rule

Questions that are very broad and general and call for the witness to give a long, narrative answer are objectionable.

### Rationale

When a witness is called to provide a long and expansive answer, the opposing advocate is precluded from reasonably registering an objection, because the witness is simply speaking in a manner and about subjects that he or she has chosen. Thus, inadmissible evidence may be included in the statement without the opposing counsel being able to foresee what is about to be said and without a reasonable opportunity to register an objection.

### Example.

> UA: Ms. Blake, would you please tell us what you can recall about your employment with Minamax Corporation?
>
> EA: Objection, calls for a narrative answer.
>
> A. Could you please break your question down so that it does not cover such a broad range of subjects?

### Discussion

This is another objection that is made more frequently in courts than in labor arbitration. Nevertheless, advocates are well advised to try to prevent witnesses from rambling on in their testimony without intervening questions. Skillful witnesses may present a great deal of testimony, with hearsay and opinion testimony woven in among otherwise nonobjectionable factual testimony, but may do it so rapidly and smoothly as to preclude an opposing advocate from objecting in a timely manner. If the arbitrator does not sustain the objection and permits the witness to give a narrative answer, the advocate is advised to request that the arbitrator instruct the witness to speak slowly so that the opposing advocate may object if and when he or she feels it necessary.

# SPECIAL EVIDENTIARY ISSUES

Most of the rules of evidence fall into relatively neat categories, substantive exclusionary rules contrasted with rules related to form. There are, however, some additional principles of evidence that do not fall neatly into such categories.

## Nonresponsive or Volunteered Testimony

### Statement of the Rule

An answer to a question that does not directly respond to or answer the question asked, or testimony that is offered despite the absence of any question soliciting such testimony, is objectionable.

### Rationale

Evidentiary hearings are meant to be orderly, with the respective advocates controlling the production of evidence, subject to rulings by the arbitrator. Consequently, answers that do not respond to the question posed by either advocate, and testimony that is volunteered (i.e., information presented by the witness that was not asked for by either advocate) should not be admitted into evidence.

*Example A.*

    *UA:* Ms. Singelton, what did Mr. Gomes say then?

      *W.* I knew that he was just going to give us more of his b.s., and I was sick and tired of everything he said. He has never told us the truth ever since he got here.

    *EA:* Objection. Nonresponsive. Move to strike the answer.

A. The objection is sustained, and the answer will be struck. Ms. Singelton, would you please answer the question that was asked of you, which was what Mr. Gomes said just then.

*Example B.*

UA: When did you first realize that your paycheck did not reflect the overtime hours you had worked?

W. It was about the first payday in August. Besides, I had talked to my buddy, Jake, and he told me that the payroll department was really screwed up. He said that a year or so ago, they. . . .

EA: Objection. The answer is nonresponsive and is volunteered testimony, at least regarding all testimony following the reference to when he says he first noticed a change in his paycheck.

A. Objection sustained. Please just answer the question asked.

### Discussion

In the first example the witness completely ignored the question and said what she wanted to say. The objection of nonresponsive testimony was appropriate. In the second example the witness answered the question asked but then proceeded to volunteer additional testimony that was not at all called for in the question. The objection of nonresponsive was accurate concerning the second part of the testimony, and it is accurate that the second part of the answer was volunteered and not responsive to the question asked. Arbitrators may not be too concerned about such additional testimony, because they can usually block such nonresponsive testimony from their minds and from further consideration. Nevertheless, the advocate must always remember that the arbitrator is a human being and is subject to the same type of stimuli and influences that affect persons who sit on juries. Consequently, witnesses should not, without objection, be permitted to launch into independent monologues about anything that strikes their fancies.

## Judicial (Arbitral) Notice

### Statement of the Rule

Facts that are known to the public at large or that are available in public documents and that are not in serious dispute among learned and rational persons may be recognized as if they were evidence (i.e., judicial or arbitral notice will be taken of them), despite the absence of testimonial or other evidence establishing such facts.

## Rationale

Established facts in the realm of history, science, human nature, mathematics, medicine, weather, geography, and other such areas of knowledge need not be proven by specific introduction of evidence. The matters offered are so well understood and established in the body of common knowledge that no reasonable person could dispute them. Similarly, information contained in public documents (e.g., tide tables, census information, official maps) is admissible without further foundational evidence. Therefore, the sponsoring party need not produce specific evidence to establish them.

*Example.*

> *EA:* When did you call Ms. Jones in her office in Honolulu?
> *W.* At 3:00 P.M. in New York City.
> *EA:* What time was that in Honolulu?
> *W.* I'm not sure.
> *EA:* We would ask the arbitrator to take notice of the fact that Hawaii is in the Hawaiian time zone, which is five hours earlier than Eastern Standard Time, meaning that Ms. Jones received the call at 10:00 A.M. in Honolulu.
> *A.* Unless the union advocate has other information, I will take notice of that fact.
> *UA:* We do not dispute that fact.

## Discussion

Judicial notice is seldom invoked in labor arbitration. Facts that would be proposed for judicial notice in a trial setting are frequently accepted by arbitrators without the formality of judicial notice. Nevertheless, there are cases that involve matters that might not be easily or economically proved through witnesses (especially scientific or technical matters), but that can be established through judicial notice. The advocate may need to substantiate the noncontroversial aspect of the facts offered for judicial notice through the presentation of learned treatises, encyclopedias, or other generally recognized texts. Matters suitable for judicial notice include such facts as that darkness does not immediately follow sunset (i.e., there is twilight), California is west of

Arizona, things dropped from the sky fall to the ground (gravity), and water on a smooth surface creates a slippery condition. Such commonplace matters could take some time to prove in a traditional evidentiary mode. Since they are so well understood, it is usually easier to ask the arbitrator to take judicial or arbitral notice of them.

## Offers of Proof

### *Statement of the Rule*

When an advocate seeks to introduce evidence into the case, but that evidence has not been admitted because of an objection, the advocate who is propounding the evidence may make an offer of proof by describing what the witness would have testified about or what the other evidence would have shown, so as to have some record of the evidence that was rejected.

### *Rationale*

Developed for traditional court trials, the offer of proof was a way to preserve the record (i.e., have some record of what evidence was excluded and how that evidence might have influenced the case) for a possible appeal. In arbitration it can serve the same function if one of the parties later attempts to vacate an award. It may also have some value with respect to collateral proceedings (e.g., an NLRB hearing), where the same evidence may be involved.

*Example.* [In a case of discharge for theft of drugs from a hospital; the witness, Ms. Alred, is a former union steward who was recently promoted to a supervisory position]

> EA: Ms. Alred, what did Mr. Peterson say to you that led you to believe he had taken hospital property?
>
> UA: Objection. Hearsay. Moreover, it was a privileged communication. At the time of the alleged discussion Mr. Peterson was a union member and Ms. Alred was a union steward and therefore the communications between them were privileged.
>
> A. I will sustain the objection. The employer will have to prove its case on this critical issue with direct evidence.
>
> EA: Mr. Arbitrator, we adamantly oppose this ruling. This is testimony that is critical to our case, and Ms. Alred is a credible

witness with no reason to fabricate. Although technically hearsay, it is an admission against interest. The privilege does not apply because Ms. Alred was not acting in the capacity of a union steward when the communication took place.

*A.* I hear you, but do not agree. The objection is sustained.

*EA:* We wish to make an offer of proof.

*A.* You may proceed.

*EA:* If Ms. Alred were permitted to continue her testimony, she would testify that Mr. Peterson described in detail how he was able to enter the medications room and remove three boxes of narcotics, and she would relate how he described to her the method he used to remove them from the hospital.

*A.* It is noted for the record.


## Discussion

The importance of offers of proof in labor arbitration is not great. Because the avenue of appeal is so narrow, virtually no cases are taken to a higher authority (at least based on an evidentiary ruling), and the value of having a record of excluded evidence is negligible. Nevertheless, many advocates (primarily lawyers) like to have the record (when a transcript is being taken) reflect the evidence they tried to get into the case. In the small number of cases that are appealed to the courts, such offers of proof may have some limited value, especially if the arbitrator has excluded crucial evidence in the case. Some advocates also believe that making an offer of proof is a signal to the arbitrator that adverse rulings on important matters will not be easily accepted, suggesting that the arbitrator should be very careful in making future similar rulings.

Another advantage of offers of proof is that they are a way of getting the information to the arbitrator. Although the offer is not in evidence (in fact, just the opposite: it has been rejected, and the offer is simply a way of recording what was excluded from the case), the arbitrator cannot ignore what he or she has heard, and therefore some of the value of the evidence has been realized. Although the arbitrator will state that it has no effect on the decision, no one can say for certain that it did not have some influence on the arbitrator's evaluation of the case.

There is a possibility that making an offer of proof will tend to irritate the arbitrator and work against the offering advocate. While that possibility certainly exists, if the offer is made in a deferential way, with little or no fanfare, no offense is likely to be taken by the arbitrator.

## UNDERSTANDING AND USING
## THE RULES OF EVIDENCE

Some advocates see the rules of evidence as a tool of gamesmanship, relying on them to thwart the other side's attempts to introduce evidence. Indeed, they can be used in that manner, but such tactics will usually be detected by the arbitrator and will ultimately hurt the case of the advocate who uses them simply for tactical reasons. Moveover, opposing advocates will soon learn that the game-playing advocate is not to be trusted and is only trying to gain an advantage, rather than getting the facts before the arbitrator.

The rules of evidence are not usually strictly applied in labor arbitration, and the advocate who relies on them needs to justify their use on the basis of the unfairness that results from evidence that does not comport with the rules. An arbitrator needs to be shown that evidence objected to would be unreliable or prejudicial to the fair presentation of facts. Reliance on mere technicalities usually will not win the day.

Not only should the labor arbitration advocate understand the rules of evidence, but it is vital that he or she knows how and when to use them. Application of the rules of evidence through the making of objections and the defense against such objections is the subject of the next chapter.

# 11

# Making and Defending Against Objections

In the previous chapter considerable attention was devoted to reviewing the rules of evidence. Except under unusual circumstances, those rules have significance only when objections are made. If no objection is raised to a question, the witness will proceed to answer the question or the documentary or other offered evidence will come into the case. Except in the rarest of cases, arbitrators will not inject themselves into the hearing to preclude evidence to which no objection has been raised. It is vital, therefore, that effective advocates know how and when to make proper objections. Moreover, it is important for advocates to know how and when to defend against objections made by the other side (e.g., to protect the evidence that the advocate is trying to introduce from being excluded because of an objection from the other side).

This chapter covers the procedure by which objections are properly made and the means by which they can be rebutted. First, however, some attention will be devoted to the strategies and tactics underlying their use.

## PURPOSES OF MAKING OBJECTIONS

In this chapter, the reader is exposed to some tactical weapons used by experienced advocates. The reader may view some of the tactics as unethical. The author makes no value judgments as to whether or not they

329

are proper. They are in use, and the reader is entitled to learn of them and know how and when they are used.

## Excluding and Diminishing the Impact of Evidence

The principal and most obvious reason for making an objection is to exclude evidence. The objecting advocate wishes to keep testimony or some other form of evidence from entering the case and from having an effect on the arbitrator's decision that is adverse to the advocate's case. Closely allied with that rationale is the desire to diminish or blunt the impact of the evidence even if it is admitted.

An advocate may know from experience that a particular arbitrator regularly admits hearsay evidence. Nevertheless, the advocate may raise a hearsay objection, not in the expectation of having it sustained, but to have the arbitrator realize the defect in the testimony, downgrade its importance, and admit it only for whatever it is worth.

Of course, when an objection is being formulated in the mind of the objecting advocate, it is not always clear to that advocate whether the purpose of the objection is to exclude or merely to diminish the impact of the evidence. It makes little difference. Framing the objection and using supporting arguments to justify the objection is the same regardless of which objective is sought.

## Protecting the Record

In trials one of the principal reasons for making an objection is to protect the record or, more precisely, protect the record for appeal. In civil and criminal procedure an error in the admission of evidence is not generally appealable unless a proper and timely objection has been registered and reflected in the record (i.e., the transcript of the case).

Arbitration differs markedly from trials in that the range of cases that may be reversed on appeal (i.e., a legal action to vacate an award) is extremely narrow, so narrow, in fact, that little thought is normally given to appealing an adverse arbitration award. The opportunities for vacating arbitration awards are discussed in some detail in Chapter 17. Despite the very narrow window of reversing labor arbitration decisions, there are nevertheless some cases that can be challenged, and for this reason there is some, albeit small, value to protecting the record by making objections to inadmissible evidence. In making such objections it is important that the advocate not only register an objection, but also state the reason for the objection.

## Interrupting the Flow of Testimony

There are occasions when a witness for the opposing side is testifying with such ease, clarity, and effectiveness that an advocate feels the need to slow down or impede the course of the other side's examination. As do trial lawyers, arbitration advocates occasionally utilize one or more tactically placed objections to interrupt the flow of testimony.

The same rationale (although in reverse) applies when an advocate's own witness is testifying, that is, if the advocate's own witness is testifying very poorly on cross-examination, some assistance in the form of an objection may be in order. The witness may be barraged with question after question to the figurative point of drowning. A life preserver appears to be needed. In such cases properly timed questions may give the witness some respite and an opportunity to collect his or her thoughts. Moreover, it may be a signal of support for the witness, that he or she is not totally alone in trying to withstand the barrage of the cross-examiner.

It is important that either one of such tactically motivated objections not be baseless. In other words, there should be some grounds for the objection, however remote, based on the rules of evidence. Otherwise, the purpose of the objection will be obvious, and the objecting advocate (and his or her case) will be damaged in the eyes of the arbitrator. Obviously, such objections should be used only rarely and with extreme discretion.

## Signaling or Instructing the Witness

From time to time an advocate's witness, while being interrogated on cross-examination, becomes confused or is in dangerous territory, that is, about to give damaging testimony that is not completely accurate. The advocate's natural instincts are to ask the arbitrator for a recess and to confer with the witness in order to remove the confusion from the witness's mind or explain the pitfall that is at hand. Such recesses are not well received, however, and are not normally granted by arbitrators. In addition, any request for a recess is likely to be attacked by the other side as merely an attempt to alter the witness's testimony (which it, of course, is). In such situations experienced advocates sometimes interpose an objection to a question for the purpose of clearing up the confusion in the witness's mind or of tipping the witness off to the dangerous ground on which he or she is about to tread. As with the tactic of interrupting the flow of testimony as described just above, there should be some plausible grounds for making an objection other than to signal or instruct a witness. Further discussion of tactical objections can be found later in this chapter.

## DECIDING TO OBJECT

The fact that the opposing advocate has asked a question calling for inadmissible testimony or is attempting to introduce other evidence that is inadmissible does not mean that an objection should necessarily be made. The advocate considering an objection should evaluate whether the inadmissible evidence will adversely impact his or her case. If the evidence does no harm to the advocate's own case and does not significantly benefit the other side, it is usually preferable to waive the objection by remaining silent. To paraphrase a maxim from the sport of basketball, "No harm, no objection."

In almost any case there is a great amount of evidence that is merely background to the key issues. Such evidence may be sought through questions that are improperly phrased (e.g., leading questions, questions calling for a conclusion, etc.) and therefore technically objectionable. Making an objection to such evidence accomplishes very little and often does more harm than good. If the evidence does not significantly impact either party's case, there is no benefit to the opposing advocate in attempting to stop the evidence or to have the improperly phrased question reworded. Moreover, the arbitrator's patience is apt to be tried by such objections. An attentive arbitrator will realize that the evidence will have little or no influence on the case and is likely to look unfavorably on objections to inconsequential matters. Advocates should reserve their objections to those matters that can have a significant impact on the outcome of the case. When such matters are sought to be introduced in violation of the rules of evidence, objections should be registered. Otherwise, they should be ignored.

## TIMING OF OBJECTIONS

It is vitally important that objections to testimony be made before the witness has answered the question. Ideally, the objection should be registered *before the witness has begun to answer the question.* Once an improper question has been fully answered, it is almost always too late to have the objection sustained. Even if it is sustained, the arbitrator has heard the answer, and much of the damage is irreparable.

Similarly, it is essential to make objections to other types of evidence such as documents or real evidence before the arbitrator has admitted them. The timing of objections as to evidence is not as serious a problem as with testimony, however, because most arbitrators will, prior to admitting the evidence, give the opposing advocate an opportunity to make an objection. The opposing advocate usually has a few moments to contemplate the possible bases of objection before having to register an objection on documentary or other nontestimonial evidence, whereas the time available with testimonial evidence is usually only a split second.

Just as it is important to make an objection before the witness has begun to answer, it is also important to wait until the question has been completed before making an objection. Even though a question may appear to be objectionable from the initial phrasing, it may be corrected by the inquiring advocate before it is completed. It is a matter of procedural etiquette to allow the opposing advocate to finish a question before raising an objection. In addition, the interval between the moment when the objecting advocate first realizes that an improper question is being asked to the point when the question is completed usually affords the objecting advocate an opportunity to frame a better objection to the question.

There will be times where the objectionable nature of a question and its resulting testimony is not apparent to the opposing advocate until the question has been answered or at least partially answered. There will also be times when the witness begins an answer before the question is completed, leaving insufficient time for the opposing advocate to register an objection. In either case the objecting advocate should make the objection as soon as he or she realizes that the matter is objectionable, even if the witness has already begun, or even completed, the answer. If the witness has partially or fully completed the answer, the advocate should nevertheless make the objection, state the reasons therefor, and ask that the answer be struck from the record. Of course, by that time the arbitrator has heard the witness's response, and a good deal of the damage has already been done. Nevertheless, if the question clearly called for inadmissible evidence, there is at least some chance that the objection will be sustained and the evidence struck from the record. The advocate can only hope that the arbitrator will make a good faith effort to give the information no consideration when the final decision in the case is being formulated.

While such tardy objections may be sustained by the arbitrator, it is unlikely that this will be done very often. Advocates are expected to make their objections promptly following the end of an objectionable question. More important, late-registered objections will be sustained only if the objection has been made immediately following the answer. If another question has been posed, it will almost certainly be too late to have the objection sustained and the answer stricken.

## MANNER OF MAKING OBJECTIONS

Although the informality of labor arbitration permits a good deal of leeway in the conduct of hearings, and especially in the way the rules of evidence are applied, there is nevertheless a preferred manner of making objections.

First, the words, "Objection," "I object," or "I object to the question" should be stated clearly and with sufficient volume that the arbitrator, the opposing advocate, and, most important, the witness can hear. It is usually a good idea for the objecting advocate to raise his or her voice above the normal volume used in the hearing, but well short of shouting. The reason is that a witness is more likely to refrain from answering the question when the opposing advocate has been emphatic in making the objection.

Once an objection has been registered, it is advisable for the advocate to immediately state the reason for the objection. For example, "Objection, the question calls for speculation," "I object on grounds of relevancy," "I object; that is a leading question." There may be questions that are so obviously objectionable that the grounds do not need to be stated (e.g., a question calling for evidence concerning an offer of compromise to settle the case). Nevertheless, it is better practice to state the basis for an objection every time one is made. It is important that the declaration of the objection precede the explanation of the reasons for the objection. Some advocates interrupt the interrogation explaining the reasons for the interruption ("the witness is giving testimony that appears . . . ") without making it clear that an objection is being registered. That is bad form.

In some cases it is advisable not only to state the basis for an objection, but to elaborate on the way the objection addresses the question asked as well as the testimony or evidence sought to be introduced. For example,

> *UA:* Ms. Chin, based on the testimony of Mr. Brooks that he did not consult the labor agreement before making the assignment, do you still believe the assignment was proper?

*EA:* I object. The question assumes facts not in evidence. Mr. Brooks testified that he talked to his labor relations manager, who advised him that the assignment was OK under the contract. He did consult the agreement through another person, a specialist in labor matters.

In the above example the objection takes somewhat the form of argumentation, but it is a valid objection. If the objecting advocate did not explain the rationale for objection of assuming facts not in evidence, it might not have been clear to the arbitrator how that objection fit the phrasing of the question.

The need or advisablilty of elaborating on the basis for an objection also applies with respect to objections to the introduction of evidence other than oral testimony. For example, in a case in which an advocate offers a diagram of the layout of an office where a particular incident took place, the following means for registering an objection would be appropriate.

*EA:* Madam Arbitrator, we offer the diagram of the third floor of the building as Employer Exhibit 3.

*UA:* Objection. Lack of foundation. There has been no evidence as to how the diagram was prepared, whether it was drawn to scale, or whether it represents the configuration of the floor eight months ago when the grievance occurred.

*A:* The union advocate's points are well taken. We will need some foundational testimony as to the preparation of this exhibit.

## Sensing When Objectionable Questions Are Being Asked

It is one thing to understand the rules of evidence and when an objection is called for. It is quite another matter to be able to recognize instantaneously an objectionable question, identify the rule of evidence that it violates, and interject the appropriate objection before the witness begins to answer the question. The ability to do this in a timely fashion is largely a matter of experience. In addition, however, there are some tricks of the trade that assist in developing this skill.

Experienced trial lawyers and arbitration advocates learn and become sensitive to certain buzz words that signal objectionable questions so that they are able to anticipate the improper question before it is finished and make the objection in a timely manner. Questions that begin with the words, ''Isn't it a fact that . . . '' or ''Would you agree that . . . '' invariably are objectionable as leading questions if asked on direct examination. Questions that begin with "Is it possible . . . " or "Do you think . . . " are usually objectionable on the basis of calling for speculation or an opinion. Labor arbitration advocates need to be attentive to the way in which questions are phrased so as to be able to recognize objectionable questions before the question is completed in order to identify the rule of evidence that applies and determine how to phrase the objection.

## DEALING WITH OVERRULED OBJECTIONS

Once an objection has been made and is overruled by the arbitrator, it is usually advisable to accept the ruling gracefully and proceed to ask other questions. As with any rule of thumb, however, there are exceptions.

### Pursuing the Objection

There are situations in which a ruling is so clearly erroneous or will improperly permit the admission of such damaging evidence that the objecting advocate should pursue the objection. The advocate must search for all possible reasons why the objection should be sustained. For example:

*EA:* And then while you were in your bargaining committee caucus, what strategy did the union's spokesman tell his committee he was going to pursue to try to force the company to settle the matter?

*UA:* Objection. The question calls for hearsay.

*A:* Overruled. Hearsay is admissible in labor arbitration.

*UA:* Mr. Arbitrator, this is not only hearsay, but it is a privileged communication. It calls for testimony about what a union spokesman said to his bargaining committee concerning the strategy of negotiations. If either the union or the company cannot conduct its committee caucuses and develop its negotiations strategy in privacy, without the fear of having such discussions revealed in arbitrations, it will inhibit the free exploration of options and do violence to the proper functioning of the collective bargaining process. In fact, it will adversely influence the bargaining relationships of these parties for many years to come. We renew the objection and ask you to sustain our objection to this very improper testimony.

A: Your point is well taken. Unless the employer can show that the information sought by the question was otherwise revealed by the union to a third party, which would amount to a waiver of the privilege, I will sustain the objection.

In the above example the objection had two separate grounds for being found inadmissible. In most cases there will be only one basis for making an objection. The advocate will have to marshal all the rational, and even emotional, arguments to persuade the arbitrator to reverse his or her initial ruling. Generally, that will be extremely difficult, because arbitrators are like baseball umpires: once the play is called, they refuse to reverse their call. Moreover, the concept of arbitration is to allow as much evidence as possible into the record, recognizing that the arbitrator will be astute enough to sort out reliable from unreliable evidence.

If, however, strong and very persuasive arguments are made, it is sometimes possible to convince arbitrators to reverse their decisions regarding admission of evidence. Sometimes a heavy price is paid for such reversals in that the arbitrator who has reversed himself or herself on an evidentiary point is not likely to do so again, absent extremely compelling reasons. Considering all these factors, an appeal to an arbitrator to reverse an initial ruling to admit evidence should be carefully evaluated. Only when the evidence is especially damaging to a case should further appeals and arguments be employed.

## Excepting to an Adverse Ruling and Registering a Continuing Objection

In court trials, where the potential for appeal exists, it is, as explained earlier in this chapter, common to object in order to protect the record by preserving the objection for appeal. This is done by the attorney noting that the evidentiary ruling is not satisfactory and that continuing objections are made to the same or similar evidence. Although the opportunity to appeal an adverse arbitration decision is extremely limited, it is sometimes advisable to treat an adverse evidentiary ruling in arbitration as one would in a full-blown trial.

If an objection is overruled, the objecting advocate may note his or her disagreement with the ruling by saying, "We take exception to the ruling." Although it is understood that an advocate who makes an objection that is overruled does not agree with the ruling and that mere silence is not a waiver of the right to contest the ruling, it is nevertheless useful in some cases to put the arbitrator on notice that the advocate is not willing to simply sit back and accept the defeat. By taking exception to a ruling the advocate has, in effect, said to the arbitrator, "I think that was a bad call on your part, and if you decide the case against us, and if, by chance, we attempt to vacate your award in a court of law, we want it clearly noted in the record that we strongly opposed your ruling on allowing the admission of this evidence.''

When an arbitrator has overruled an objection and has permitted evidence to come into the record and when additional evidence of the same character is sought to be introduced, the objecting advocate may say, ''We make a continuing objection to this line of testimony.'' This signals the arbitrator that the objecting advocate will not lie down after the adverse evidentiary ruling and will persist in challenging the questionable evidence. Caution should be exercised in this approach.

## Strategy of Challenging Adverse Evidentiary Rulings

As discussed above, persistence in trying to change the mind of an arbitrator with respect to an adverse evidentiary ruling risks the wrath of the arbitrator. At the same time it may cause the arbitrator to be more cautious in ruling on future objections made by the persistent advocate.

Many years ago, a very successful baseball field manager of the Brooklyn Dodgers, Leo Durocher, was famous for arguing with baseball umpires for calls against his team with which he did not agree. He would invariably run out of the dugout, confront the umpire face to face, and scream obscenities and any other words that came to his mind in addition to kicking dirt, waving his arms, and using unmentionable gestures. Without exception, he was unsuccessful in changing the umpire's mind and quite often was ejected from the game. A newspaper reporter once asked Durocher, ''Why do you argue with the umpires? They never change their calls.'' His answer was that he didn't expect them to reverse that call, but that he was working on the next close play. He reasoned that the more grief he caused them on a close call, the less anxious they would be to rule against his team the next time a close play developed. Some might call this intimidation, which it no doubt was. Nevertheless, that rationale underlies the vigorous pursuit by some advocates of their disagreements with evidentiary rulings.

## DEFENDING AGAINST AND DEFEATING OBJECTIONS

When an advocate is examining a witness (on direct or cross-examination) or is offering other nontestimonial evidence and an objection is made, it is usually advisable for the inquiring advocate to support the admissibility of the evidence by defending the question or the offer of evidence before the arbitrator has ruled on the objection. Without such a defense the arbitrator may sustain the objection without knowing all the reasons why the evidence is reliable or admissible under the rules of evidence. For example [in a case of discharge of an employee for sexual harassment]:

> *UA:* Did you, Ms. Evans, after the day when the alleged sexual harassment took place, tell Mr. Peterson that you would join him for a drink after work?

> *EA:* Objection. The question is irrelevant. Anything that occurred after the grievant's harassment is irrelevant.

> *UA:* Madam Arbitrator, we recognize that in most cases activities following the critical incident or after the grievance was filed are irrelevant. Here, however, the actions of which we inquire reflect the relationship of the grievant with the woman who claims to have been harassed. They are so closely related to the conduct for which the grievant was terminated that to exclude the testimony would do a grave injustice to the grievant. We submit that it is admissible evidence.

> *A:* Objection overruled. The witness may answer.

A large percentage of arbitrators will, immediately following the making of an objection, look to the advocate offering the challenged testimony or other offered evidence with an inquiring glance seeking some response (to justify the admissibility of their evidence). In some cases the arbitrator will extend an invitation to the advocate offering the evidence to respond to the objection (''Counsel, your position?''). Without question, the advocate needs to respond to such covert, as well as overt, invitations. Even when an invitation is not extended, the advocate offering evidence to which an objection has been made should unhesitatingly defend the admissibility of the evidence.

## BASES FOR RESPONDING TO SUSTAINED OBJECTIONS

Not only must an advocate determine when to resist an adverse ruling on an objection, but he or she must also quickly assess the basis on which to ground such resistance. The chances of success will depend on how persuasive the arguments in support of the resistance are, and the persuasiveness of the arguments will usually depend on the grounds on which they are based.

## Substantive Grounds

The ideal way to resist an objection is to show that it is unfounded on the basis of the rules of evidence, that is, that the evidence is admissible in the form in which it is sought to be introduced. This requires that the advocate defending against an objection have command of the rules of evidence and be able to show the arbitrator why the objection is without merit. For example [in a case of suspension for failing to report as scheduled and for misrepresentation of the reasons for the absence]:

> *EA:* Ms. Graceland, what was your opinion about the truth of Mr. Loomis's excuse for not being at work that day?
>
> *UA:* Objection. Calls for opinion testimony. The witness is not an expert and is not entitled to render an opinion.
>
> *EA:* Madam Arbitrator, the question calls for the witness to relate her state of mind at the time of the incident. In essence, we have asked her to explain her state of mind at the time and the rationale that prompted her to take the disciplinary action. We are not asking for expert opinion in any sense.
>
> *A:* I will allow the witness to explain her perception of the matter and the reasons that caused her to suspend Mr. Loomis. The witness may answer.

The reader should note that the use of the word ''opinion'' was the red flag that triggered the objection. If the advocate had asked the witness, ''Did you believe Mr. Loomis when he explained why he did not report for work?'' there likely would have been no objection registered by the opposing advocate. Just as it is important for an advocate to identify such red flags for purposes of making objections, it is equally important to recognize the red flags to avoid when asking questions.

# Common Sense, Fairness, and Reliability of Evidence

Many lawyers and others familiar with the rules of evidence are often dismayed by the amount of useful and generally reliable evidence that is excluded by strict interpretation of the rules of evidence. A statement made by an individual in an open room with thirty persons in attendance, about which the testimony of such thirty listeners is offered can technically be excluded from evidence if the hearsay rule is strictly applied. Numerous other examples exist. Sometimes rules of evidence can exclude evidence that is much more reliable than other evidence that is admissible under the same rules. Likewise, evidentiary rulings that favor the other side may not be evenhandedly applied to the advocate's side. This disparity can sometimes successfully (if tactfully) be pointed out to persuade the arbitrator to change his or her mind.

The advocate who is astute and persistent can often cut through the rules of evidence to show the arbitrator that certain evidence should be admitted, notwithstanding the fact that it would not past muster under the traditional rules of evidence. For example:

*UA:* What did Mr. Smith say about resolving the matter?

*EA:* Objection, calls for evidence regarding an offer of compromise.

*UA:* Madam Arbitrator, that objection is completely without merit. First, when Mr. Smith offered to settle the dispute, no grievance had even been filed. Second, we're trying to get to the facts in this case, and the other side is trying to exclude evidence that will shed light on what was actually going on. If, after you hear the facts, you decide that the evidence is improper, you can give no weight to the evidence and/or strike the evidence.

*A:* Objection overruled.

In another example [where the employer is attempting to call the grievant as a witness in a discharge case]:

*EA:* The employer calls the grievant, Steve Versteeg, as its next witness.

*UA:* Objection. It is a violation of the grievant's right against self-incrimination to be called to testify in his own case.

*EA:* Mr. Arbitrator, the union called the employer's plant manager as its witness. We see no reason why the grievant in this case should not testify. This is not a criminal trial. The fifth amendment does not apply.

## Rephrasing the Question

When an objection to a question based on the form of the question has been sustained, the advocate posing the question has an opportunity to rephrase the question in a form that will not be objectionable. Successful advocates never hesitate to reformulate their questions one or more times in order to get the desired testimony into evidence. For example [in a case involving the suspension of an employee for punching the time card of another employee]:

*EA:* Mr. Waldorf, would you tell us why you punched the time card of Ms. Hillier on the day in question?

W: I thought it was my card.

*EA:* Now, Mr. Waldorf, you don't really expect us to believe that you actually thought her card was yours, do you?

*UA:* I object. The question is argumentative!

 *A:* Sustained. I think you are arguing with the witness.

*EA:* Mr. Waldorf, what exactly was it that led you to believe that the card you inserted into the time clock on the day in question was yours?

In virtually all questions that are objectionable on the basis of form, the wording of the question can be reformulated in such a way as to make it permissible. Again, a good foundation in the rules of evidence will be of enormous help in avoiding objectionable questions as well as detecting them when they are posed by the other side; most certainly, the knowledge of the rules of evidence can aid immeasurably in reformulating objectionable questions.

## Offer of Proof

There will be occasions when it is simply impossible to change an arbitrator's mind about an evidentiary ruling, and the evidence sought to be admitted will be excluded from the case. In such situations the advocate may wish to make an offer of proof. This is a technique whereby the advocate who has unsuccessfully offered evidence in a case tells the arbitrator of his or her intention to make a record of the nature of the evidence that would have been admitted into the case if the witness had been permitted to testify or if the proffered documentary or other nontestimonial evidence had been admitted.

Usually, the advocate explains in a narrative form the evidence sought to be introduced. For example:

*UA:* Would you please tell us all that you heard about how your department was to be scheduled that afternoon.

*EA:* Objection. Calls for hearsay. In fact it is double hearsay, because the witness was not at the scene when the schedule was decided and announced.

 *A:* Objection is sustained.

*UA:* Madam Arbitrator, this is reliable evidence. Hearsay is admissible in labor arbitration, and, furthermore, the declarants are here in this room and able to refute the testimony if they feel it is inaccurate.

*A:* The objection is still sustained.

*UA:* Madam Arbitrator, we wish to make an offer of proof.

*A:* Proceed.

*UA:* If permitted to testify, the witness would relate a conversation he had with Sylvia Sims and Peter Nero on June 1 of this year in which they told him that the schedule that was implemented was announced by the department manager as "the best he could come up with, and that he didn't give a damn if it violated the contract or not." The witness would further testify that he made notes of the conversation and that he talked to two other employees who heard the same remarks.

Although the offer of proof has only minimal value for a possible attempt to vacate an adverse award, its principal value is in alerting the arbitrator that such exclusions of evidence will not be accepted without protest and that the arbitrator may later be called to account for erroneous decisions. It is another example of the Leo Durocher (intimidation) rationale for pursuing protests of excluded evidence.

## Pursuing the Adverse Evidentiary Ruling in Final Arguments

Having made every attempt to persuade the arbitrator to admit the evidence to which an objection has been sustained and having been unsuccessful in doing so, the only recourse left to the offering advocate is to spotlight the proffered evidence in the closing argument or in a written brief filed following the hearing. It is more than a long-shot attempt to have the evidence considered by the arbitrator in making a decision, but it is nevertheless a way to emphasize important evidence in the case that has been excluded because of application of the rules of evidence.

Only when the proffered evidence is especially important to winning the case should this tactic be utilized. Because the evidence was never entered in the case, technically it cannot be relied on in argument. If, however, it was a reasonably close call in deciding to exclude the evidence, the offering advocate may wish to dangle the evidence once more in front of the arbitrator as a way of supporting other evidence in the case. The arbitrator will not be able to officially recognize such previously rejected evidence, but it is possible that it could influence him or her in some way. This is especially true if there was an offer of proof that described in some detail what would have come into the record if the objection had been overruled.

# 12

# Conducting
# Cross-Examination

The aspect of a labor arbitration hearing that requires the greatest skill and experience on the advocates' part is unquestionably cross-examination. The ability to elicit evidence favorable to one's side through the testimony of the other party's witnesses is a skill not easily mastered. This ability is not acquired through reading books, although the concepts underlying effective cross-examination may be gleaned from reading, by being taught, and by observing skilled advocates. The skill itself, however, is acquired only through practice—by examining adverse witnesses in case after case and by learning what works (and what does not) through trial and error. The most that a book such as this can do is to focus the reader's attention on basic principles and certain time-tested techniques that have proven successful for others. The key to becoming a successful cross-examiner is to put the principles and techniques into practice and to learn from successes and failures those techniques that work best for the individual advocate.

Most laypersons, many inexperienced advocates, and even some experienced advocates place inordinate expectations on the results of cross-examination. The stereotypical image of witnesses being brought to their knees by a blistering cross-examination has been fostered by fiction in books and films and on television. Jurors in trials and observers of other hearings such as labor arbitration disputes are often disappointed when the cross-examiner fails to turn around the testimony of a witness through razor-sharp questioning. In the real world it is a distinct minority of cases that are won or lost by virtue of cross-examination. To be sure,

345

effective cross-examination can go a long way toward achieving a favorable decision and occasionally may be the decisive factor in winning a case, but an advocate, and an advocate's client (the party being represented), should not be disappointed if a cross-examination fails to cause the witness to contradict his or her direct testimony or to otherwise fail to testify in a way that hurts that witness's own case. A well-prepared witness who is testifying in a truthful manner should be expected to be consistent and credible. No amount of skillful cross-examining will change that fact.

It should be pointed out that there is a wide difference between the value of a well-prepared, effectively executed cross-examination and one in which the advocate flies by the seat of the pants and merely takes the witness back through the subjects covered in the direct examination. One need only watch a successful veteran trial lawyer with dozens, or perhaps hundreds, of trials under his or her belt compared to a novice attorney trying his or her first case in order to appreciate the dramatic range in quality of cross-examinations. Such differences in experience manifest themselves in all aspects of the case, but nowhere is it as apparent than in cross-examination.

In reading the balance of this chapter the reader is counseled to keep in mind that, regardless of the principles and techniques of effective cross-examination, each advocate must develop his or her own style. The order of questioning, the manner of phrasing questions, the tone and inflection of the voice, and all other facets of cross-examination must be honed by the advocate to agree with the advocate's own personality. While a certain amount of acting may occasionally be necessary in presenting a case, each advocate must, in the final analysis, do what comes naturally. Within that context this chapter lays out some substantive principles and stylistic techniques that the advocate may wish to incorporate into his or her own repertoire, keeping in mind that the personality and style of the advocate should always come across as genuine and authentic.

# OBJECTIVES OF CROSS-EXAMINATION

There are at least five separate, although interrelated, objectives of cross-examination, discussed here in order of importance.

## Attack the Credibility of a Witness

The most confrontational objective of cross-examination, and the most difficult one to achieve, is to show that the witness is not, or has not been, truthful and is therefore not to be believed. In most cases it is not necessary to demonstrate that a witness is completely untruthful, but merely that he or she has inaccurately perceived or recollected a statement or an event and has therefore provided testimony that cannot be relied on. There are situations, however, in which the witness's testimony on cross-examination is so directly contrary to what that witness testified to on direct examination or to what other credible witnesses testified to that the witness's veracity is directly called into question.

When a witness is shown to be incredible, not only has major damage been done to that witness, but often the entire case being presented by that witness's side has been seriously impaired. In such situations the advocate shares with the witness in the disapprobation of the arbitrator. The thinking goes, ''How could an advocate with integrity present a witness who is so untruthful, and therefore how could the witness's side have any legitimacy?'' Such conclusions are not always valid, but they nevertheless are natural ones to draw. For this reason a successful attack of a single witness's credibility can sometimes be the sole decisive factor in winning a case.

## Attack the Credibility of a Portion of a Witness's Testimony

More common than a complete discrediting of a witness, a successful cross-examination will show that one or several aspects of a witness's testimony are not true. Such an accomplishment may be possible even with a witness who has no intention to prevaricate. For example, a skillful cross-examiner may show that the witness was not in a good position to make an accurate observation of the situation to which the testimony relates or that the witness has a poor recollection of the events about which the testimony concerns, even though the witness believes that the events occurred as he or she has testified. In other words, the advocate's purpose is not to destroy the witness, but merely to show that the witness is deficient with respect to perception or recollection—not necessarily veracity. In many cases it is sufficient to prove that some aspect of a witness's testimony is not true.

## Elicit Favorable Testimony

The general notion of effective cross-examination is that its sole purpose is to show that the witness is lying or giving inaccurate testimony. Some, or perhaps all, of the other party's witnesses, however, may not be impeachable. Such witnesses may nevertheless be helpful to the cross-examining side by testifying about aspects of the case that favor the cross-examining advocate's position. These aspects may or may not be disputed in that case, but when an adverse witness testifies to matters that favor the other side, such testimony carries much more weight than if the same evidence had been provided by a witness of the party favored by the evidence. The presumption is that since neither the witness nor the witness's side of the case has anything to gain from testimony favorable to the other party, the matters related by such witnesses are likely to be truthful.

For this reason advocates should not overlook the opportunity to elicit testimony from an adverse witness that favors the advocate's case. Of course, a wise advocate will not rely solely on an adverse witness to provide necessary evidence. Sometimes the witness will disappoint the advocate. A backup (and friendly) witness should always be available to provide essential evidence. Nevertheless, bringing the desired evidence into the record through the other side's witness is ideal.

## Elicit Contradictory Testimony

Another way to gain an advantage from a witness on cross-examination is to have him or her contradict the testimony of another witness from the same side. In so doing the credibility of both witnesses is damaged.

It is often difficult get such contradictory testimony in labor arbitration hearings because all of the witnesses are usually in the hearing room at the same time and are therefore able to hear the testimony of the other witnesses on their side (and the other side as well). If the advocate believes that the testimony of one or more witnesses from the other side is likely to influence the testimony of the opposing party's other witnesses, the advocate is advised to request, or move, that the arbitrator sequester, or exclude, witnesses who are not testifying at the time. The chances of eliciting contradictory testimony from opposing witnesses on cross-examination is greatly enhanced when such witnesses do not hear the testimony of their party's other witnesses.

## Elicit Foundational Testimony

Occasionally the testimony of the opposing party's witness will be necessary to lay a foundation for other evidence (e.g., documents or other tangible evidence). Such evidence as records, reports, equipment, and photographs is sometimes created and/or used exclusively by persons representing the opposing party (more often than not, the employer). It may be somewhat difficult to get such evidence admitted into the record (and its accuracy verified) without some foundational testimony. When only a person affiliated with the opposing party can provide the essential foundation for this evidence, the advocate desiring to rely on this evidence is left with cross-examination to do this (or perhaps calling the witness from the other side as one's own witness). As indicated earlier in this chapter with respect to eliciting favorable testimony, the weight given to such foundational evidence is much greater when it comes from a witness whose side gains nothing (and perhaps is disadvantaged) by the introduction of such evidence.

# PREPARATION

As with all other aspects of an arbitration hearing, careful and thorough preparation for cross-examination is absolutely essential. Unfortunately, it is an aspect of case preparation that is often neglected by advocates. Even though the advocate cannot normally predict precisely what an opposing side's witness will say on direct examination, the opportunities for improving the quality of a cross-examination are so significantly enhanced by anticipating such testimony and framing appropriate questions that any advocate is foolish indeed not to undertake advance preparation. Cross-examination is no place to wing it.

## Research Witnesses

Although there is no requirement (or even a practice) in labor arbitration for exchanging lists of witnesses with the other side as there is in criminal and civil trials, there is usually a good opportunity to learn the identity of the other side's witnesses. A review of the grievance file, a discussion with the key witnesses for the advocate's side, and an informal discussion with the opposing advocate in advance of the hearing will usually reveal most, if not all, of the names of the opposing side's witnesses.

In addition to the information possessed by the other side's witnesses, it should be understood that all witnesses have individual life experiences, background, and biases (however mild) that are likely to influence their testimony. The task of the opposing advocate is to ascertain what substantive evidence the witness is likely to possess and to testify about in the hearing. The record of grievance processing at earlier stages of the grievance procedure is usually the best source of such information. The second chore is to determine just what the witness's background is and what his or her biases are likely to be. Does the witness have a reputation for truthfulness? Has the witness had a grievance similar to the one at issue in this case? Has the witness testified in a prior case on issues similar to those at issue in this case? Has the witness taken a position in an earlier case or discussion that is contrary to the one anticipated in this case? Answers to these and similar questions are usually best obtained from others on the union or employer team who are likely to be familiar with the witness. Occasionally, such information may be gleaned from files and transcripts of previous arbitrations or grievances.

By knowing those subjects about which the witness is likely to testify and by ascertaining the witness's biases and perspectives, the opposing advocate is in a much better position to conduct an effective cross-examination.

## Anticipating the Witness's Testimony

Beyond assessing the witness's background, biases, previous testimony, and so on, the resourceful advocate should take some time to plan the anticipated testimony of key adverse witnesses. Statements of such witnesses in earlier steps of the grievance procedure yield many clues as to what their testimony is likely to be in the arbitration hearing. To the extent that it differs in the hearing itself, ample opportunities are available to the cross-examining advocate to impeach the witness.

One useful way to anticipate the testimony of opposing witnesses is to role play the testimony. By selecting someone who is familiar with the case and the testimony likely to be given by the witness and by having that person assume the persona of the witness, the advocate can simulate the testimony of that witness on direct examination. Following this process, the same advocate can then adopt the mantle of the opposing advocate and question the same witness on cross-examination. This process allows the advocate to anticipate the obstacles to piercing the veneer of the witness and prepares the advocate to wrestle with the witness's determination to avoid contradiction and impeachment.

This practice cross-examination is likely to reveal those particular aspects of the witness's testimony that are most vulnerable to attack. In the course of this exercise, or immediately following it, the cross-examining advocate's questions can be framed and reframed to elicit the most desired responses. Available time is seldom sufficient to permit such an extensive preparation for cross-examination of all the opposing side's anticipated witnesses, but when the testimony of a witness is especially crucial and when the witness is potentially vulnerable to incisive cross-examination, the investment of time is usually worth it.

## Script the Cross-Examination of Key Witnesses

Just as it is well worth the time to role play critical cross-examination, it is also productive to script, that is, write out the questions in sequence for, the cross-examination of key witnesses. A careful advocate writes down the questions, in the most effective order, that he or she may want to pose to key witnesses offered by the opposing side. This process is made infinitely easier if the role play suggested in the preceding section has been done. Having gone through a mock cross-examination, the advocate is able to visualize the witness and the context of the interrogation as a prelude to composing the questions and arranging the order of the questions to have the most favorable impact during cross-examination.

Having done so, the advocate should not feel bound in the hearing itself to follow the order or wording of the prearranged questions. The context, pace, and momentum of the hearing and, most importantly, the information resulting from the direct examination of witnesses will signal the advocate about whether it is advisable to stay with the script or to depart from it. The ability to adapt the script to the witness is often the difference between the average advocate and the one who wins case after case. Having a plan of questions for an adverse witness, but being flexible and creative enough to vary from that plan, is essential to achieving consistently favorable results in labor arbitration.

# VOIR DIRE VERSUS CROSS-EXAMINATION

Periodically, there are opportunities for an advocate to question a witness from the opposing side prior to the end of the direct examination and prior to the beginning of the cross-examination. Those opportunities present themselves when the opposing side seeks to introduce evidence, testimonial or otherwise, that has a questionable foundation. The process is called voir dire (pronounced ''vwor dear'' and is literally translated from French as "to say the truth"). This process allows the advocate from the side opposing the witness to ask questions of the witness that seek to establish whether the witness is competent to testify about certain matters and whether other evidence, such as documents, photographs, objects, and so on are objectionable.

## Strategic Value

Voir dire is not cross-examination, but in many cases it may be used for the same effect as cross-examination, that is, to impeach the credibility of witnesses or to attack the authenticity or persuasiveness of other evidence. Its actual or ostensible purpose is to obtain information that may allow the opposing advocate to make an objection to the introduction of the evidence. As it is sometimes phrased, voir dire is used in aid of objection. The reason for discussing voir dire in this chapter is to see its potential use as an alternative to cross-examination.

In a number of situations the advocate may not believe that he or she can prevent the introduction of certain evidence (i.e., because it meets the technical rules of evidence for admissibility) but nevertheless believes that the evidence is deficient in one respect or another and is vulnerable to attack. The advocate may not be content to wait until cross-examination to launch an attack on the evidence. By asking questions before the witness begins to testify or before the evidence has been admitted, the opposing advocate makes a preemptive attack on the evidence and may plant seeds of doubt in the mind of the arbitrator about the credibility or persuasiveness of the evidence before it is even heard. Thus, the impact of the challenging questions may be greater than if they were asked on cross-examination.

## Prelude to Objecting to Testimony

As indicated, questions asked during voir dire invariably are aimed at challenging the competency of the witness to testify concerning certain matters or at challenging the evidence sought to be introduced through a particular witness. The following is an example of voir dire being used to prevent the testimony of a person claimed to be an expert witness.

> [A medical doctor has been called as an expert witness by the employer to testify about whether an employee (grievant) is able to return to his regular position following a stroke. The

employer has already asked the doctor a number of questions about his education and medical experience relative to stroke in order to establish his expertise to testify as an expert witness. Before beginning the doctor's substantive testimony, the union advocate asks the arbitrator if she may ask the doctor some questions on voir dire. The arbitrator says yes.]

*UA:* Dr. Smith, as I understand it, you are here to testify as an expert witness concerning the ability of the grievant, Mr. Golf, to return to work, considering the effects of his stroke on his capacity to perform the physical aspects of his job. Is that correct?

*W:* Yes.

*UA:* Dr. Smith, have you taken any specialized courses, given by an accredited medical university, on the specific subject of stroke?

*W:* No, I have not.

*UA:* Are you certified by the Board of Medical Examiners of this state to engage in the specialized practice of brain disfunction?

*W:* No.

*UA:* Have you written any articles that have been published in scholarly journals on the subject of stroke?

*W:* No.

*UA:* Aside from any records of the grievant's medical condition that you may have reviewed, have you personally examined the grievant?

*W:* No, I have not.

*UA:* Madam Arbitrator, we object to any testimony that Dr. Smith may provide as an expert witness in this case. We believe he is not qualified to testify about the matters for which he is being called to testify.

If the employer advocate had previously established a reasonably solid basis of expertise possessed by Dr. Smith, it is unlikely that the arbitrator would disqualify Dr. Smith from testifying. Nevertheless, the union advocate has done an effective job in breaking down the aura of expertise that the employer advocate had built up. Moreover, this was accomplished prior to Dr. Smith testifying, and therefore the arbitrator is likely to be more skeptical of what Dr. Smith says than if the same questions had been asked on cross-examination.

The use of voir dire to challenge the testimony of a witness may be used not only with expert witnesses, but also with other types of witnesses. For example, a witness may be called to give testimony about an event that she did not personally observe, that is, to give hearsay testimony. The opposing advocate could challenge the hearsay testimony on cross-examination or could seek to ask questions on voir dire in aid of objection in an ostensible attempt to preclude the witness's testimony, but more realistically to weaken the credibility of the witness before the testimony is delivered.

## Prelude to Objecting to Other Evidence

Because arbitrators are quite lenient about the use of expert witnesses and about other types of testimony, such as hearsay, the use of voir dire to challenge the testimony of a witness is used less frequently for that purpose than it is to challenge the admission of other evidence, such as documents. The following is an example of this use:

> [The union is seeking to have admitted a hand-drawn diagram of a work site to assist a witness in testifying about the events at that site on a particular day. The union advocate has asked several foundational questions about the drawing—what it depicts and how it was prepared. The advocate then offers it in evidence. The employer advocate decides to try to challenge the diagram.]

*EA:* Madam Arbitrator, may I ask several questions on voir dire?

 *A:* Yes, proceed.

*EA:* Mr. Pimental, you say that the drawing was sketched by your sales supervisor last week, is that correct?

 *W:* Yes.

*EA:* Now, the events that are in issue in this case occurred more than ten months ago. Isn't it true that you have had one or more rearrangements of store displays at that site in the last ten months?

 *W:* Yes, two, I think.

*EA:* But the diagram depicts the floor arrangement the way it was last week, not ten months ago, isn't that correct?

 *W:* Yes, but it's not all that different.

*EA:* But, it is different, isn't it?

 *W:* Yes.

*EA:* Also, isn't it a fact that your sales supervisor didn't take measurements of the floor dimensions or the proximity of objects to one another, and therefore this drawing isn't at all to scale?

*W:* I don't know if she took measurements or not, I wasn't there myself.

*EA:* So you can't represent to us, or to the arbitrator, that the diagram is to scale, and you can't testify as to any other aspect of its accuracy because you didn't prepare it yourself, and you weren't there when it was prepared?

*W:* Well, not exactly, but it looks very accurate to me.

*EA:* Madam Arbitrator, we object to the admission of Union Exhibit 12 for the reasons made obvious from the witness's answers on voir dire.

Whether the arbitrator will admit the diagram will be based on the arbitrator's overall assessment of the accuracy of the drawing based on what was elicited on the foundational questions on direct examination and on the testimony presented just above. Even if the diagram is admitted, however, the employer advocate has likely raised some doubts in the arbitrator's mind about the accuracy of the drawing and the arbitrator is apt to view somewhat skeptically any evidence based on the diagram.

## Reasons for Deferring to Cross-Examination

Notwithstanding the apparent tactical advantage of using voir dire for a preemptive strike, there are cogent reasons for not employing this technique. By saving impeaching and/or challenging questions for cross-examination, the opposing advocate may be able to rattle, confuse, or demoralize a witness to the point of opening up other areas of attack that would not be possible on voir dire. By deferring to cross-examination, the penetrating questions may be a starting point for a frontal attack on a witness. Voir dire can be very useful for planting seeds of doubt, but it is not a practical base for developing momentum for a full-scale attack, because the voir dire may only proceed on the specific points related to a possible objection. Because it will be followed by the direct examination of the witness, the witness has time and the assistance of his or her own advocate to recover and perhaps regain lost composure and momentum.

These are rather fine distinctions, and intelligent choices between using voir dire and cross-examination to challenge a witness can usually be made only after experience in a number of arbitration or other evidentiary hearings, but if the purpose of the examination is to prevent the opposing party from introducing the evidence at all, there is no choice to be made. Voir dire is the only means to develop additional information with which to support an objection to the introduction of the evidence.

## TRACKING DIRECT EXAMINATION TO PREPARE FOR CROSS-EXAMINATION

Earlier in this chapter it was recommended that an advocate who prepares for cross-examination in advance of the hearing should compile a list of questions to pose to the witness to be cross-examined. As useful as such advance preparation may be, it can never substitute for careful observation of direct examination of the witness and an almost instantaneous analysis of the significance and potential vulnerability of that testimony. The effective cross-examiner must master the skills of listening, observing, and recording the key points of a witness's testimony and quickly formulating questions that will be responsive to that testimony. Each element of tracking the testimony of a witness and using it to cross-examine the witness is discussed below in order.

### Careful Listening and Observation

The starting point for tracking a witness's testimony is carefully listening to and observing the witness. Of course, the information contained in the answers is the most significant aspect of the testimony. Careful attention to the words used, the meaning conveyed, and the way in which the information meshes (or does not mesh) with other evidence in the case is vital. The advocate needs to concentrate intently on the witness, the interchange between the examining advocate and the witness, and the impact the witness is having on the arbitrator. In so doing, the advocate should also be attentive to observable aspects of the witness during testimony, such as eye movement and focus, facial expressions, gestures, and body language. These mannerisms often reflect the witness's veracity, the degree to which the witness has been rehearsed, and other aspects that may assist the cross-examining advocate to frame effective questions. Based on the substance of the testimony and the observable demeanor of the witness, the advocate about to cross-examine can make a reasonable assessment as to whether the witness is testifying from his or her own knowledge, whether the witness is credible, and whether the witness can be impeached on cross-examination.

In addition to observing the witness the opposing advocate should periodically glance at the arbitrator in an effort to detect any clues as to how he or she is perceiving the witness's testimony. Most experienced arbitrators will not change expressions from witness to witness, regardless of how they perceive them. Occasionally, however, slight variations of eye and facial features will provide some insight as to how the arbitrator is receiving and evaluating the witness's testimony.

## Note Taking

During the direct examination of a witness, the opposing advocate needs to make notes of the testimony (or at least key aspects thereof) to assist during cross-examination. Even if someone else is available to assist the advocate and takes detailed notes of the direct examination, the limited time normally available between direct and cross-examination precludes total reliance on someone else's notes. Invariably, the advocate will require his or her own notes in order to cross-examine effectively.

Although advocates each have their own style of taking notes, many advocates prefer to utilize the split-page approach, recording on the left side of the page the questions asked by the opposing advocate and on the right side of the page the responses thereto. Figure 12-1 is an example of this style.

**Exhibit 12-1.**
**Taking Notes During Direct Examination**

|  | Witness—M. Mead |
| --- | --- |
| Questions | Answers |
| *Arrive at plant* | *7:45 AM* |
| *Punch in* | *yes* |
| *What seen* | *foreman at time clock* |
| *Who* | *Joe Roberts* |
| *Say anything* | *"Don't bother to punch in—no work today"* |
| *Ask ?* | *yes, why* |
| *Reply* | *union has called strike—"no work today"* |
| *What then* | *went home* |
| *Did you go on strike* | *no* |
| *Why didn't work* | *wasn't allowed to* |
| *When did you next report to plant* | *Tues 8/15* |
| *Why* | *called by foreman* |

## Input from Others on the Advocate's Team

During direct examination the opposing advocate who will soon be cross-examining the witness must focus his or her complete attention on the inquiring advocate, the witness, and the arbitrator. The advocate cannot afford to discuss anything with his or her own witnesses or others on the arbitration team while the direct (or redirect) examination is in progress. Otherwise, some vital aspect of the testimony may be missed. For this reason the author always instructs his witnesses in the hearing room and others on his team who are observing the hearing to take notes of key points of the direct examination in order to be able to bring them to the advocate's attention following the direct examination.

When the direct examination is completed, the advocate should take a few minutes (after asking for and receiving permission from the arbitrator for such a pause or recess) in order to consult with his or her own witnesses or others on the team to see whether there is anything that should be covered on cross-examination that the advocate did not already plan to cover. Usually, the points of apparent conflict or incredibility resulting from the direct examination noted by others on the team will coincide with those picked up by the advocate. Occasionally, however, a witness or other person will catch something in the witness's testimony that provides new insight, a different slant on the case, or an avenue of attack that was not apparent to the advocate. These should be incorporated into the advocate's notes for cross-examination.

From time to time a natural break will occur in a hearing (e.g., lunchtime or the end of a normal work day) more or less at the end of direct examination. The resourceful advocate will suggest the break be taken immediately following the direct examination in order to afford more time to closely examine his or her notes of direct examination, consult with others about the testimony, and prepare better questions and strategy for cross-examination.

# DECIDING WHETHER TO CROSS-EXAMINE A PARTICULAR WITNESS

The fact that the opposing side has presented a person to testify and has examined that witness on a range of topics does not automatically mean that the witness should be cross-examined. The advocate approaching cross-examination needs to carefully, albeit quickly, determine whether he or she should cross-examine that witness. Based on such a determination, the advocate may elect to waive cross-examination or perhaps conduct the interrogation in a somewhat different manner than is normally done. If, as suggested just above, a longer than normal lunch break or an end-of-day recess can be taken, the time for such a determination will be conveniently increased. In making the decision as to whether to cross-examine, several factors should be considered.

## Damage Report

The single most important factor in deciding whether to cross-examine a witness is whether the witness on direct examination did any harm or damage to the opposing side's case. Many witnesses simply provide foundational or background testimony for the introduction of other evidence later in the case. Others may provide more substantive testimony that will, however, often make little difference in the outcome of the case. In these situations it is not usually productive to cross-examine such a witness.

After each witness for the other side has completed testimony on direct examination the opposing advocate should ask himself or herself, "What harm did this witness do to my case?" If the answer is "Little or None," cross-examination should be avoided (unless the witness can provide foundational testimony not otherwise available from the cross-examining advocate's own witnesses, contradict the testimony of others of the opposing side's witnesses, or otherwise provide favorable testimony to the cross-examiner's side).

## Assessing the Strength of the Witness

During and immediately following the direct examination, the advocate should size up the witness's strength, that is, assess just how confident, articulate, truthful, calm, assertive, precise, and intelligent the person is as a witness and just how good the witness's recollection is of the matters being testified about. The range in strength of witnesses can be dramatic. Some witnesses have an excellent recollection of the matters about which they are testifying and are well in control of themselves to the point where it is very difficult to diminish their testimony. In fact, cross-examination of such witnesses may only enhance their credibility. A prudent advocate will be very cautious in deciding to cross-examine such a witness.

Other witnesses, on the other hand, may not have a solid grasp of their facts and may be very inexperienced and/or uneasy about testifying.

To add to their vulnerability, they may be somewhat imprecise in their use of words or estimates of time, distance, and so on. Moreover, the time spent on preparing their testimony may have been insufficient. Such witnesses, even though truthfully stating the facts as they understand them, may be damaged by effective cross-examination.

Advocates should not take undue advantage of such witnesses simply to win a case when the witness is obviously telling the truth in an accurate fashion. Not only is this unethical, but a perceptive arbitrator will spot the disadvantage and discount the points scored by the cross-examining advocate, likely causing the arbitrator to mentally penalize the side whose advocate engaged in such sharp practice. When, however, the witness's weaknesses go to the quality of the testimony and present an inaccurate reflection of the facts, an aggressive, incisive cross-examination is entirely proper and advisable.

In making a damage report of a witness's testimony to decide whether to cross-examine, the advocate is advised to factor in the strength of the witness with the evidence produced by that witness. If the damage caused by the testimony has been only marginal and if the person is strong in the witness chair, the advocate is probably wise to waive cross-examination. If the witness is weak, however, cross-examination may be advisable even when the damage done by that witness on direct examination was minimal. The advocate may not only be able to capitalize on the minimal damage done by the witness, but may be able to make some valuable points for his or her side through a less than effective witness.

## The Nominal or Superficial Cross-Examination

Occasionally, a strong witness may testify truthfully about certain matters that may not have a great impact on the case. The opposing advocate, however, is reluctant to waive cross-examination for fear of conveying to the arbitrator, and to a lesser extent to the opposing advocate and other side's witnesses, that full credit should be given to the witness. A simple waiver of cross-examination may be interpreted to mean that the witness was completely truthful and accurate or that the cross-examining advocate is afraid to challenge such an effective witness. To avoid such conclusions being drawn, the advocate may wish to conduct some cross-examination in order to show his or her principal or client that the advocate is conducting a vigorous case and is not afraid to cross-examine a strong witness.

In such cases the advocate should proceed with a nominal or superficial cross-examination that does not challenge the overall credibility of the witness or the witness's testimony (because it was concluded by the advocate that this was not possible). The advocate may, however, seek to make one or two minor points that could prove helpful. Such a cross-examination is intended simply to avoid conveying any advantage to the other side that might be perceived by the arbitrator or the other side if the right to cross-examine were waived. The following are examples of the type of questions that can be asked during such nominal or superficial cross-examinations.

*Q.* Who asked you to testify in this case?

*Q.* You did not have to be subpoenaed to appear, did you?

*Q.* Therefore, your testimony in this case is completely voluntary on your part, is that correct? You thought you could help the grievant, is that true?

*Q.* Did the advocate who just asked you questions rehearse those questions with you before today?

*Q.* Did you attend any meetings in preparation for this case where other witnesses were present? [If yes:] You learned what the other witnesses were going to testify about, didn't you?

*Q.* Did you make any notes of the events about which you have just testified? [If yes:] Do you have them with you today? [If yes and if the witness doesn't have them with him or her:] Why didn't you bring them with you? [If no notes were made:] Then you have nothing to rely on to verify the accuracy of your memory, do you?

*Q.* It's fair to say, isn't it, that it would be beneficial to you personally if the grievant were to win this arbitration?

*Q.* Did your supervisor instruct you to testify in this case today? You didn't have any choice whether or not to be a witness in this case, did you?

*Q.* You've testified in previous arbitration hearings, haven't you? [If yes:] In each case you have testified for the employer [union], haven't you?

None of these questions goes to the heart of a witness's testimony but may elicit some answers that are disadvantageous to the witness's testimony. Even if none hit the mark, no significant harm has been done, and the inquiring advocate has avoided waiving cross-examination completely and has avoided giving any psychological advantage to the other side.

## Opening New Areas of Inquiry

Although a witness may not have done any significant harm to the opposing side, there may nevertheless be some merit in proceeding with cross-examination if there is some relevant area about which the witness has knowledge and about which his or her testimony could possibly help the opposing side. This opportunity is available only when the arbitrator does not enforce the technical "scope of direct rule" of evidence. As discussed in Chapter 10, a standard rule in court proceedings is that a cross-examiner may not inquire about matters that the witness did not address on direct examination. A question about some other subject is not considered to be within the scope of direct examination and is therefore inadmissible. This rule, however, is not generally followed by most labor arbitrators, and, therefore, advocates may usually open up new subjects with a witness on cross-examination.

The new subject may prove helpful to the advocate's case, although there is usually uncertainty as to what the witness will say because the matter was not covered on direct. Sometimes, however, witnesses make statements or take positions during the grievance procedure or at some other time prior to the arbitration that may lead to explorations in other subject areas helpful to the cross-examining advocate's case. Consequently, opening such subjects on cross-examination may be safe, because failure of the witness to confirm could lead to impeachment. Even when such a prior statement or position is not known, there are times when broaching new subjects is advisable simply in the hope of scoring some necessary points if the case appears to be going badly.

## STYLE OF CONDUCTING CROSS-EXAMINATION

As indicated earlier, each advocate must develop his or her own style of cross-examining witnesses. What works for some will not work for others. Most importantly, advocates must be natural, that is, must be themselves. An advocate cannot effectively play a role as cross-examiner that is inconsistent with his or her manner in other parts of the case without some loss of credibility with the arbitrator. Within that limitation, however, advocates can adopt certain stylistic approaches that may enhance their performance in cross-examination. Several of these approaches are presented below for the reader's consideration.

## A Gracious and Respectful Manner

Invariably, witnesses facing a cross-examiner are tense, on guard, and anticipating the worst. They see the cross-examining advocate as an enemy out to destroy them, and they steel themselves to prevent that from happening. A witness's defensive posture can be somewhat disarmed by a manner that is nonconfrontational, cordial, and perhaps even friendly. Although most witnesses will not be easily lulled into a sense of security simply by a gracious manner, a pleasant, nonhostile approach is likely to relax witnesses and lead to more cooperation than if the cross-examiner conveys a tone of combativeness from the outset. What does this mean in practical terms?

The cross-examining advocate should treat the witnesses with respect, usually addressing them with the appropriate "Mr./Mrs./Ms." before their last name. This may sometimes be inappropriate when the relationship between the cross-examiner and the witness is a personal one or when the tone of the parties' arbitration hearings is rather informal. Nonetheless, most witness will feel honored if addressed in a formal, respectful way. In certain hearings it also a useful practice for the advocate to introduce herself or himself to the witness before proceeding with the questioning. For example, "Mr. Smith, my name is Harriet Robbins and I represent the union in this case. I have some questions I would like to ask you." Occasionally, this introduction may be followed by some helpful tips such as, "If you don't understand any of my questions, please feel free to ask me to repeat or rephrase them. We want you to understand all the questions that you are expected to answer."

Such suggestions will usually be taken by the witness to be helpful, and, as a result, all but the most cynical witnesses are likely to regard the cross-examiner as someone who wants to be fair with them (even though retaining much of their initial fear and trepidation of the cross-examiner). If these suggestions are given to the first witness to be cross-examined while other witnesses from the same side are in the hearing room and hear the instructions, it will not be necessary to repeat the admonitions (in fact, repetition will likely create the appearance of disingenuousness). Some opposing advocates may object to such instructions, but there is nothing improper about them, and most arbitrators will permit them.

## Noting Transition Points

Some cross-examiners like to signal the witness and the arbitrator when forthcoming questions are going to focus on a new subject area. For example: "Ms. Wharton, I am now going to ask you some questions about the events of January 25, the day on which you learned of the reduction in force. Can you tell us, ..."

One might question the wisdom of such signaling to a witness, the argument being, "Why help witnesses to see that the topic is changing and give them an opportunity to adjust their thinking and get ready for the new topic?" The technique is primarily for the benefit of, and the effect on, the arbitrator. Some arbitrators can become confused and/or lose concentration, especially after many hours of listening to, and perhaps taking notes of, testimony. Such arbitrators appreciate an advocate's demarcation of new subject matter. Additionally, arbitrators are likely to see the advocate as someone who is quite organized and who is being fair to the witness in giving notice of the forthcoming areas of inquiry.

## SEQUENCING QUESTIONS

In discussing the order of direct examination in Chapter 9, it was suggested that the order of questions follow a chronological and/or a logical sequence, so that the witness is essentially telling a story. Not so with cross-examination. The order should be one that is best suited to the objectives and strategy of the cross-examiner.

### Easing into the Critical Areas

Although some cross-examiners prefer to proceed promptly to the areas of the witness's testimony wherein the witness is most vulnerable, the author prefers a strategy in which the cross-examiner commences the interrogation with relatively innocuous or background questioning and then advances to the areas that are more crucial to the case. As indicated just above, most witnesses are afraid and wary of a cross-examining advocate. If an advocate moves directly to the tough questioning, the witness may never have a chance to relax and develop any sense of trust in the cross-examiner.

Throwing out easy questions at the outset will not cause most witnesses to completely let their guards down, but at least they are apt to be less suspicious of the cross-examiner's intentions if the initial questions are relatively easy and nonthreatening. For example:

> *UA:*  Ms. Jones, you have been an employee of XYZ Corporation for nearly fifteen years, haven't you?

*W:* Yes.

*UA:* And you have been a supervisor for nearly six of those fifteen years, correct?

*W:* That's right.

*UA:* Would you say you have learned a lot about the widget manufacturing business in those fifteen years?

*W:* Oh yes, I have.

*UA:* And how would you describe the relationship you have had in the last six years with representatives of Widget Manufacturing Employees Local 196?

*W:* I think it has been a very good relationship.

These are types of questions that can be answered rather easily, and they allow the witness to relax somewhat and get used to the manner of the cross-examiner's interrogation. There is ample time for the tough questions later in the witness's testimony. The initial questions should aid the cross-examiner in putting the witness at ease and perhaps persuading the witness to believe that the cross-examination will not be as challenging as originally anticipated.

The initial questions on cross-examination are often useful in obtaining testimony that corroborates the testimony of one or more of the cross-examiner's witnesses. When it is clear that the witness will not be disputing certain matters to which the cross-examiner's witnesses have testified or will be testifying, it is advantageous to utilize the initial questioning to nail down such corroboration. For example:

*EA:* Mr. Phillips, you heard, didn't you, the testimony of Ms. Jenkins earlier in this hearing concerning what took place in the reception area that day?

*W:* Yes, I did.

*EA:* Would you say that her testimony was accurate?

*W:* Yes, I would.

*EA:* And you heard her testimony about what took place two hours later in the warehouse, didn't you?

*W:* Yes.

*EA:* And would you say that was accurate as well?

*W:* Yes, I think it was.

Although no points are necessarily scored by this line of interrogation, the cross-examiner is easing into the cross-examination and putting the witness at ease, while at the same time strengthening the credibility of his or her own witnesses by gaining corroboration for their testimony.

### Following a Circuitous Path

Most witnesses are prepared by their advocates to respond to questions in a particular order (i.e., the order followed on direct examination). In so doing, they comprehend certain phases of their testimony in relation to other phases by the order in which the questions are asked. Some witnesses can be thrown off guard by changing the order of the questions, perhaps by starting at the end of the testimony, moving to the beginning phases of that testimony, and ending with the subjects covered in the middle of the direct examination.

Despite such rearrangement of subject matter, a truthful and articulate witness with a good recollection of the facts will be able to adhere to the testimony given on direct examination, whereas a witness who required careful preparation to tell a coherent story or who does not have a solid recollection of the facts may have great difficulty in sticking with the testimony delivered on direct.

In jumping from one topic to another the cross-examiner should not be so haphazard as to confuse the arbitrator or cause the arbitrator to believe that the cross-examiner is simply trying to trick the witness in order to elicit testimony favorable to the cross-examiner's case.

## DOS AND DON'TS OF CROSS-EXAMINATION

Numerous authorative texts over the years have provided advice about cross-examination.[1] Most, if not all, contain homilies about how to and how not to conduct an effective cross-examination. Many suggest absolute rules, the violation of which are said to be disastrous to an advocate's case. The author's point of view is that such homilies have value but should not be followed blindly or religiously. There are few, if any, rules that do not have exceptions. This is as true in cross-examination as it is in English grammar. Nevertheless, this section sets forth most of the traditional, and some not-so-traditional, rules, concerning cross-

---

[1]WELLMAN, FRANCIS L., THE ART OF CROSS-EXAMINATION, 4th ed. (New York, Collier, 1962); ARON, DUFFY & ROSNER, CROSS-EXAMINATION OF WITNESSES: THE LITIGATOR'S PUZZLE (Sheppards/McGraw-Hill, 1989); MAUET, FUNDAMENTALS OF TRIAL TECHNIQUES, 3rd ed., Chapter VI (Little, Brown and Company, 1992).

examination. The reader is advised to consider them carefully and, through the process of trial and error in actual hearings, determine those that work and those that do not. No book in the world can convey the lessons that only experience can teach.

## DO: Use Leading Questions

No admonition should be followed more closely than that most questions on cross-examination should be leading questions. As explained earlier in several other chapters, a leading question is one that suggests its own answer. Such questions can normally be answered with a simple yes or no. In effect, the witness is led directly to the answer sought by the interrogator. Leading questions usually contain phrases such as the following.

- "It's a fact, isn't it, that ...?"
- "You were the one, weren't you, who ...?"
- " [statement], correct?
- "Is it fair to say that ...?"
- "Would you say that ...?"
- " [statement]. You would agree with that, wouldn't you?"

Leading questions can often put a witness on guard, because the form of the question makes it apparent what answer the cross-examiner is seeking. When leading questions are used only occasionally during cross-examination, the witness is more likely to be sensitive to their presence and consequently to be on guard against delivering an answer that is harmful to his or her side. For example:

*EA:* What part of the hospital did you go to at the beginning of your work shift?

*W:* To the maternity ward.

*EA:* How did you decide to start there?

*W:* I knew that it needed to be serviced because of a note that was left by the previous custodian on duty.

*EA:* Where did you see the note?

*W:* On the work assignment bulletin board.

*EA:* So if you looked at the bulletin board, you also must have seen the note saying, "Custodian—report to respiratory unit *immediately*," correct?

*W:* [spotting the leading question]. I don't recall what else I saw on the board.

The key to a successful cross-examination is to use leading questions so repetitively that the witness becomes accustomed to them and finds it more or less natural to be answering leading questions. For example:

EA: You reported to the maternity ward at the beginning of your work shift, correct?

W: Yes.

EA: And was that because you read or were told about what needed to be done there?

W: I read a note, yes.

EA: The note was on the work assignment bulletin board, wasn't it?

W: That's correct.

EA: And so before you went to the maternity ward you looked at the bulletin board?

W: Sure.

EA: There were other notes on the bulletin board, weren't there?

W: Yes, I'm sure there were.

EA: And it's your responsibility to look at all notes that pertain to your job, isn't it?

W: Yes, I suppose it is.

EA: You didn't respond, did you, to the note that said to report to the respiratory unit immediately?

W: No, I didn't.

Another variation on the use of leading questions is to make a statement and then ask the witness to agree with it. The following are examples of these types of questions.

Q: Nurses are among the most important care-givers in a hospital, wouldn't you say?

Q: Union members are bound to follow the union's regulations and by-laws, aren't they?

Q: Labor contracts are supposed to be followed by both sides, aren't they?

Still another variation is to have a witness adopt the testimony of another witness as a basis for further cross-examination. For example:

UA: You heard the testimony of Robert Quartermaine, didn't you, concerning the sequence of events just before the accident?

W: Yes.

> *UA:* You would agree, wouldn't you, that his testimony was an accurate account of what happened that day?
>
> *W:* Yes, I think it was.

Although it is wise practice to use leading questions exclusively on cross-examination, there are some who suggest that an occasional harmless nonleading question should be included to break the pattern of monotonous leading questions. For example:

> *EA:* You were used to seeing the work schedule posted on the bulletin board, weren't you? [leading]
>
> *W:* Yes.
>
> *EA:* And is that because you had been instructed early in your employment to do so? [leading]
>
> *W:* That's true.
>
> *EA:* All employees in the unit are required to check the bulletin board, aren't they? [leading]
>
> *W:* Yes, every day at the beginning of the shift.
>
> *EA:* By the way, what is the size of the bulletin board? [nonleading]
>
> *W:* I'd say about 4 feet wide and 2 feet high.

If the cross-examining advocate uses nonleading questions periodically, it is important to remember to use them only on tangential or innocuous subjects. Because they give the witness a more or less free reign to respond, they can result in unpredictable and sometimes disadvantageous answers.

The routine use of leading questions is not something that comes naturally to most persons. For this reason the advocate who aspires to be an excellent cross-examiner should practice using leading questions over and over. Whether in mock cross-examination or in daily conversations, it is very useful to develop a wide range of leading phrases and words that can be drawn on in actual cross-examination. Such practice will help the advocate to feel very natural in using them and to make them part of his or her repertoire.

## DON'T: Ask Open-Ended Questions or Questions that Ask "Why?"

The corollary to the previous admonition to use leading questions is that of not using open-ended questions. Such questions give the witness an open field within which to score valuable points for the other side. The following are some examples.

- How did you feel when he called you on the phone?
- What was your opinion of the instructions you were given?
- What's been your experience with that process?
- How would you characterize the work he performed in your department?
- Why did you take that course of action?

Each of these questions invites the witness to provide a narrative answer of his or her own choosing, often an answer that will be self-serving. Perhaps the worst of the open-ended questions is the one that asks "Why?" or "What was the reason for...?" These not only allow the witness to provide a self-serving narrative, but also invite a rationalization that should simply not be made available to a witness on cross-examination. An example of the adverse consequences of such questions is as follows:

> *EA:* So after looking at the bulletin board, you went to the maternity ward rather than the respiratory unit, correct?
>
> *W:* Yes.
>
> *EA:* Why did you do that?
>
> *W:* Wilma Bankey had just told me that she was going to cover that assignment and that she could handle it herself. I knew from experience that the maternity ward was understaffed on the graveyard shift and that they would need help.

## DO: Ask Short, Direct, and Clear Questions

An effective cross-examiner wants the witness to understand his or her questions and to give relatively quick and responsive answers. For this to happen, the questions put to the witness should be as short, direct, and clear as possible. Lengthy questions consisting of complex words or phrases are likely to confuse the witness and cause him or her to ask for an explanation or repetition. Such interruptions in the flow of interrogation are apt to work against the cross-examiner. The following is an example of such an inadvisable question:

> Would you say that the contract section concerning layoffs, and in particular the clauses having to do with bumping from one job to another in different departments within the same division (which you will find on page 33 of the labor contract, which is Joint Exhibit 1 in this case), was one of the last ones you and your bargaining committee negotiated in the labor contract negotiations that took place two years ago?

Instead the advocate could use short, direct, and clear questions to receive the desired answers.

*UA:* You're familiar, aren't you, with Section 10, articles a, b, and c, which applies in a layoff situation?

*W:* Yes, I am.

*UA:* And that language deals with bumping from one department to another in the same division, right?

*W:* Yes, that's right.

*UA:* That language was negotiated into the agreement in the last labor contract negotiations two years ago, wasn't it?

*W:* Yes.

*UA:* And you recall, don't you, that the negotiations that year ended on the day before Labor Day?

*W:* I believe that's correct.

*UA:* It's true, isn't it, that the articles on bumping we just referred to were agreed upon at the very end of negotiations?

*W:* Yes, that's my recollection.

Although the number of questions that need to be asked using this technique is greater, the speed of the questioning and the ability to have the witness answer in rapid, logical sequence is valuable not only to the comprehension of the arbitrator, but also to the record (where the hearing is being transcribed).

The ability to pose such short, direct, and clear questions is greatly enhanced by preparation. By preparing questions in advance the advocate is able to delete irrelevant, unnecessary, and confusing words and phrases. If, however, the cross-examiner has to formulate all or most of the questions extemporaneously following direct examination, the probability of having long, confusing, and convoluted questions is greatly increased.

## DON'T: Ask Questions Whose Answers You Do Not Know

A traditional axiom in the field of trial advocacy is that a cross-examiner should never ask a question unless he or she knows what the witness's answer will be. In other words, don't go fishing. The reason is that witnesses may provide testimony that could surprise and be very damaging to the cross-examiner's case. The following is an example.

*EA:* Did you finish the job before 5 P.M.?

*W:* Yes.

*EA:* Were there other jobs to do at the site?

*W:* Yes.

*EA:* But you didn't do them, did you?

*W:* No.

*EA:* Why did you leave early? [advocate does not know the answer]

*W:* It started to thunder and lighting, and I knew from our safety training that it would be dangerous to stay on the job.

Notwithstanding the admonition of not asking questions to which the answer is not known, there are times when the advocate must seek evidence from an opposing side's witness, even though it is not clear that a favorable reply will be forthcoming. The following are some instances where careful "fishing" may be advisable:

1. When the other side's witness is the only witness to an event, it may be necessary to ask questions when there is a reasonable expectation of eliciting favorable testimony.
2. When the cross-examining advocate's case is weak on the facts, it may be worth risking an unfavorable answer or two in order to obtain some favorable ones.
3. When it appears that the advocate for the opposing side has deliberately avoided certain subjects on direct examination that normally would have been asked, it may be safe to conclude that there is some weakness in the witness's knowledge or experience that could be exploited.
4. When the witness appears to be tentative or not confident about certain subjects, probing such areas could elicit valuable evidence. By inquiring about details of the subject, it may be possible to show that the witness's perception or recollection is so weak that the earlier testimony on that subject was deficient.

## DO: Control the Witness

Some persons who testify on cross-examination will do almost anything to avoid giving answers that are adverse to their side. By avoiding questions, by adding self-serving explanations, or by volunteering information they will try to maneuver the testimony to support their case. The cross-examiner must control these witnesses in order to preclude them from avoiding the truth. There are several techniques that can be used for this purpose. One is to cut off nonresponsive answers. For example:

*UA:* Mr. Smith, to the best of your knowledge, weren't you the only person who claims to have seen the broken pipe that day?

*W:* Well, I'm not sure, but I know that everyone in the shop from time to time. . . .

*UA:* [interrupting] Mr. Smith, you are not responding to my question. I simply asked you if you, to the best of your knowledge, were or were not the only person who claimed to see the broken pipe. Please just answer yes or no, or if you don't know, just say you don't know.

If a witness persists in avoiding directly answering questions on cross-examination, the advocate may ask the arbitrator to instruct the witness to refrain from such evasive testimony. For example:

*EA:* Is it true that you received a vacation check for the week of August 9 through 16?

*W:* There were a couple of times last year when I wasn't allowed to take my vacation. . . .

*EA:* [interrupting] Madam Arbitrator, we ask that you instruct the witness to answer the question asked. This is the third time in his testimony that he has given nonresponsive answers to my questions.

*A:* Mr. Laidlaw, please listen closely to the questions that are being asked and answer them directly. The last question was, "Did you receive a vacation check for the week of August 9 through 16?"

*W:* Yes, I did.

In some cases the witness may not be as obvious about evading the question, but nevertheless does not directly answer the question posed. Unless the advocate is very attentive, such minor diversions may go unnoticed. The cross-examiner should not let such witnesses off the hook easily. For example:

*EA:* When the letter was completed, what did you do with it?

*W:* I removed it from the printer and put in the folder for signature.

*EA:* Is that the normal office practice?

*W:* Sometimes the copies are made first, and then put into the folder for signatures.

In a long and active hearing the last answer may appear to be responsive, that is, that the normal office practice is to put one copy of a letter in a folder for signature, but occasionally it is normal to make multiple copies and then put the original and the copies in the folder for signature. That is not, however, what the witness testified. The witness did not say what the normal office practice was, but only that sometimes copies were made first. The cross-examiner needs to pin down the witness. The following is one way to do it.

> [Continuing the cross-examination from above].
>
> *EA:* So, is it your testimony that the normal office practice is to make one copy of a letter, put it in the folder for signature, and after the letter is signed, make the necessary number of copies?
>
> *W:* Yes.
>
> *EA:* And is it also your testimony that you do not always follow the normal office procedure and that you sometimes make the copies before the correspondence is signed? Is that correct?
>
> *W:* Yes.
>
> *EA:* In terms of the overall word processing of letters that you do, approximately what percentage of the time do you make the copies first?
>
> *W:* Oh, I'd say about one out of four or five.

By following up on the somewhat evasive answer, the cross-examiner was able to determine what the normal office procedure was, and that the witness periodically did not follow the normal office procedure.

## DON'T: Ask More Questions Than Necessary

Another traditional rule in cross-examination is that the cross-examiner should not ask any more questions than are necessary to discredit some aspect of the witness's testimony. Going beyond the point of scoring some valuable points in an attempt to totally destroy the witness or to gain additional ground may jeopardize what has already been accomplished. In simple terms, don't be greedy.

An old vignette is told about the "one too many questions" problem. It goes like this.

> [In a criminal case in which the defendant is accused of biting off a man's finger, a bystander who witnessed the event is called by the defending attorney and is being cross-examined as follows.]
>
> *Defense Counsel:* And what were you doing at the exact time the two men were fighting (the time the biting allegedly took place)?
>
> *Witness:* I was taking a suitcase out of my car.

*Defense Counsel:* And isn't it true, therefore, that you did not actually see the defendant bite off the finger of the complaining party?

*Witness:* Well, yes—that's true. [valuable evidence has been obtained, yet the cross-examiner proceeds]

*Defense Counsel:* And therefore you have no way of knowing that my client actually bit off his adversary's finger, do you? [the "one too many question"]

*Witness:* Well, I saw him spit it out.

While this story is undoubtedly fictional, it well illustrates the pitfalls of going too far with a cross-examination. Striking a significant blow to the opposing side's witness so that his or her credibility is called into question should usually be welcomed by the cross-examiner without attempting to completely devastate the witness. By forcing the witness completely into a corner the advocate may simply cause the witness to conjure up an explanation sufficient to erode the gains made. The following example in an arbitration setting illustrates the point.

> [The witness, Ms. O'Hara, is a coworker of the grievant and has testified on direct examination favorably for the grievant. The employer advocate is cross-examining the witness, trying to show a predisposition to favor the grievant.]

EA: Ms. O'Hara, you work with Ms. Peters, don't you?

W: Yes, I do.

EA: And you have worked in the same department as she has for more than ten years, haven't you?

W: That's correct.

EA: And isn't it a fact that you went to high school with her and that you both belonged to the same sorority?

W: Yes. [sufficient facts have been elicited to show a presumption of bias]

EA: And you and Ms. Peters are very good friends, and you would like to help her in this case, wouldn't you? [the "one too many question"]

W: No, we aren't friends now. We had a falling out, and haven't spoken to each other in more than six months.

Of course, it must be recognized that if a witness has facts that can override damaging testimony elicited on cross-examination, the advocate who examined the witness on direct examination is likely to bring out such facts on redirect examination. Nevertheless, it cannot be assumed that will happen. Moreover, the stinging impact of the impeachment will remain in the mind of the arbitrator until the redirect, and the advocate asking questions on redirect will clearly be at a disadvantage in trying to regain the lost ground. Rehabilitating a discredited witness on redirect examination is nowhere nearly as satisfactory as having the witness rehabilitate himself or herself with an answer on cross-examination that salvages the witness's credibility.

## DON'T: Argue with a Witness

An unmistakable sign of an inexperienced cross-examiner is the practice of arguing with a witness, that is, not accepting the answers given by a witness and trying to change the witness's testimony through repeated questions seeking to elicit the answer sought by the questioner. The following is an example of a cross-examiner arguing with a witness.

*EA:* Ms. Hernandez, it's a fact, isn't it, that you punched the time card of Mr. Agee on the morning of November 24?

*W:* No, it's not a fact.

*EA:* Do you mean to tell us that you punched only your own card that day?

*W:* That's correct.

*EA:* How can you deny that you punched his card when we have a witness who saw you doing it?

*W:* I don't care how many witnesses you have, I didn't do it.

*EA:* So it's your testimony, today, that you never punched his time card on November 24?

*UA:* Objection. The question is argumentative. Also the question has been asked and answered—twice.

*A:* Objection sustained.

Novice advocates become frustrated when witnesses do not provide answers the advocate believes are called for by the question. They believe the witness is lying (which may very well be the case) and think that by repeating more or less the same questions the witness will change the testimony and provide truthful answers. In fact, that hardly ever happens, and the cross-examining advocate merely winds up appearing amateurish, frustrated, and helpless.

While impeachment of an incredible witness is often possible, it is usually accomplished only with contradictory or inconsistent evidence from other sources, and only rarely by forcing the witness to change his or her testimony. More is said later in this chapter about impeaching witnesses.

## DO: Test the Witness's Powers of Perception, Recollection, and Estimation

A considerable proportion of testimony that is crucial in arbitration cases is based on the accuracy of witnesses' perceptions, recollections, and/or estimates of time, distance, or other quantitative factors. In such instances it is often useful to put the witness to a test to demonstrate his or her powers of perception, recollection, and estimation (or, hopefully, the lack thereof). With respect to perception and/or recollection it is often helpful to probe other aspects of the event or situation about which the witness gave earlier crucial testimony on direct examination. Such other related aspects of the witness's testimony need not be important in and of themselves but can be significant simply as a way of testing the grievant's perception or recollection. For example, in a case in which a witness testified on direct examination that he saw a coworker punch the time card of a fellow employee (in violation of the employer's rules), the cross-examiner might pose the following questions.

*UA:* Ms. Gomez, you testified that you saw Ms. Hernandez punch the time card of Mr. Agee on November 24, correct?

*W:* Yes.

*UA:* How far away from the time clock were you standing?

*W:* Approximately five feet.

*UA:* Could you read the name of Mr. Agee on the card Ms. Hernandez put into the time clock?

*W:* Yes, I could.

*UA:* You could read his full name on the card, is that true?

*W:* Yes.

*UA:* And what is Mr. Agee's middle initial, shown on the card?

*W:* I don't recall.

*UA:* Is it that you don't recall, or that you didn't see it?

*W:* I'm not sure. I think I saw it, but just don't recall it now.

*UA:* But you're not exactly sure whether your inability to tell us what that initial was is because you did not see it or simply because you forgot it, is that a fair statement?

*W:* Yes, I suppose that's correct.

*UA:* Can you tell us at this time whether Mr. Agee's middle initial was even shown on the card?

*W:* I'm really not sure.

In the above example the initial of Mr. Agee is not significant for any part of the case other than as a means of testing Ms. Gomez's powers of perception and recollection. Based on the course of this cross-examination, the strength of Ms. Gomez's testimony has been significantly weakened. To the extent that the cross-examiner can produce evidence that Mr. Agee's middle initial was not even printed on the card, the testimony will be further weakened.

A similar technique can be used to test the witness's powers of estimating quantifiable measures. For example, continuing with the same cross-examination described just above, the cross-examiner might proceed as follows.

UA: Ms. Gomez, it's your testimony that you were about five feet away from the time clock when you saw Ms. Hernandez punching Mr. Agee's time card, correct?

W: Yes.

UA: Any you feel pretty confident with that estimate, do you?

W: Yes, it might have been four or six feet, but I think five feet is pretty accurate.

UA: I'd like you to look at the corners of this room on the window side of the room—from the corner near the one set of drapes to the corner with the other set of drapes—and tell us the distance between the two corners.

W: [after a momentary pause and examination of the room by the witness] I'd say it was twenty feet.

UA: Would it surprise you that the actual distance is twenty-eight feet, or more than thirty-three percent greater than what you estimated? I will represent to you that I measured the distance this morning before the hearing began.

W: Well, it looks shorter to me than twenty-eight feet.

Another frequent estimate that a witness often needs to make is a time estimate, particularly time intervals (i.e., the amount of time that elapses between two or more events). Ordinary persons are often quite mistaken in gauging time intervals, usually overestimating the amount of time that passes between two significant events, such as the beginning and end of a conversation, the time elapsing from one action to another, and the time needed to move from one place to another. Cross-examiners can often do damage to a witness's testimony by testing the witness's powers of estimating time. For example:

UA: Mr. Diggins, you said that it was about 3:15 P.M. when you saw the grievant entering the shop, is that correct?

*W:* Yes.

*UA:* And you saw him get some tools from his tool box and then get something out of his locker, right?

*W:* That's right.

*UA:* About how long was it from the time he entered the shop until the time he left?

*W:* Oh, I'd say about ten minutes.

*UA:* Did you check your watch, or is that just an estimate you're making?

*W:* Just an estimate.

*UA:* I am going to ask you to estimate the amount of time that passes from the time I say ''start'' to the time I say ''stop,'' without looking at your watch. OK?

*W:* OK.

*UA:* Start. [allows twenty seconds to pass] Stop. How much time passed from the time I said ''start'' to the time I said ''stop''?

*W:* I'd say about a minute.

*UA:* Let the record show that twenty seconds elapsed from the time I said ''start'' to the time I said ''stop.'' Mr. Diggins's estimate was three times—or three hundred percent of what the actual time was.

Of course, in the various types of tests discussed just above, the cross-examining advocate takes a risk that the witness will be able to accurately guage the matters inquired about or estimate the quantities called for in the question. When this occurs, the credibility of the witness is enhanced significantly, not only with respect to those particular aspects of the witness's testimony, but to other aspects of his or her testimony as well. Consequently, the advocate should be very careful in using such tests. When the facts in the case are against the cross-examiner's side and there is not much to lose, such a risk is more prudent than in a close case or in one that already favors the cross-examiner's party. Also, when the witness has previously demonstrated a weakness of perception, recollection, or precision, the use of such a test may be a reasonable risk.

## DON'T: Ask the Witness about Recollections or for Approximations

Questions posed to a witness on cross-examination should call for direct and precise answers as to what happened or did not happen, rather than for the witness's recollection or remembrance about what happened. The following examples illustrate effective and ineffective ways of asking about past events or situations.

*Ineffective:* What is your recollection of the color of the box in which the goods were shipped?

*Effective:* What was the color of the box in which the goods were shipped?

*Ineffective:* What time do you remember arriving at work that day?

*Effective:* What time did you arrive at work that day?

*Ineffective:* Approximately how fast was the truck going when it entered the plant through the east gate?

*Effective:* How fast was the truck going when it went into the plant through the east gate?

The purpose of the cross-examination is to pin the witness down to specific times, places, events, and so on in order to lay a foundation for possible later impeachment. By asking for the witness's recollection, rather than specific occurrences, the witness may later be able to avoid impeachment by saying that it was only a recollection rather than a certainty. Consider which of the following two statements is more susceptible to impeachment:

"The box was blue."
"I recall that the box was blue."

Similarly, when the witness is asked only to approximate times, distances, and so on, it is easier for the witness to escape contradiction. Again the reader should note the value of answers relative to their impeachability.

"The truck was going 35 miles per hour."
"The truck was going approximately 35 miles per hour."

Of course, a well-prepared and/or astute witness will frequently supply his or her own qualifying words or phrases such as "to my best recollection" or "I would estimate," but it is quite another matter for the witness to add the qualifiers than to have the cross-examiner offer such qualifying words or phrases to the witness.

## DO: Challenge the Testimony of Witnesses Who Appear to Be Giving Rehearsed Testimony

During the course of direct examination of a witness, it will sometimes become apparent that a witness is following a script, that is, the witness has been rehearsed to the point where the words are coming from repeated practice and memorization rather than the witness's own recollections. Hopefully, that scripted testimony will be apparent to the arbitrator, and the testimony will be given little or no weight.

The advocate on the other side, however, cannot know whether the arbitrator is perceiving the witness in the same way, and therefore the cross-examination of that witness needs to be tailored in such a way as to disclose the artificial or rehearsed testimony. Rehearsed testimony is not necessarily untrue or insincere, but the fact that the witness has been schooled, or has to have memorized the answers, to the point where answers are from the script rather than from memory, gives the testimony an artificial quality on which the opposing advocate can capitalize.

Once the cross-examiner has spotted this tendency, it is usually best to begin by repeating some of the key questions asked on direct examination. If the witness truly has been over rehearsed, the answers on cross-examination will be identical, or nearly identical, to those given on direct. If the arbitrator did not spot the artificial quality on direct, it should begin to become apparent on cross-examination when the same words and phrases are used as on direct examination.

Next, the cross-examiner should vary and expand the questions somewhat, testing the witness's veracity and ability to supply supporting information that would be expected in light of the earlier testimony. The following interrogation will illustrate the point.

> [Witness testified on direct examination that when he was called at home for the purpose of reporting to work to handle an emergency problem, he had just awakened from a deep sleep and that he felt too ill to come to work.]

*EA:* Mr. Hingle, would you please relate to us once more just why you did not report for work on the night of October 21 when you were called to report for emergency work.

 *W:* I had gone to sleep about an hour earlier because I was not feeling well, and I awoke when the call came in, and I still was not feeling well, so I told my wife to tell the supervisor that I could not go to the plant that night.

*EA:* You said you were not feeling well. Are you saying you were actually sick?

 *W:* Yes.

*EA:* You wouldn't say that you had a disabling illness, would you?

 *W:* I don't know just what "disabling" means, but I know I didn't feel well enough to go to work.

*EA:* You weren't taking any medication, were you?

 *W:* Just aspirin.

*EA:* And you were able to come to work the next day, weren't you?

*W:* Yes, that's true.

*EA:* And you didn't see a doctor for your illness, did you?

*W:* No.

*EA:* And you haven't accepted any overtime work in the last twelve months, have you?

*W:* No, I don't like to work overtime.

*EA:* And you didn't want to work any overtime that night, did you?

*W:* That's not why I didn't come in. I was sick.

*EA:* But not too sick to work the next day.

*W:* No, not that sick.

*EA:* You were able to get up and walk around, weren't you?

*W:* A little bit, but I was pretty much out of it.

*EA:* And you were able to speak, weren't you?

*W:* Yes.

*EA:* And you could have told the supervisor yourself, rather than relying on you wife, why you were not coming in to work that night, correct?

*W:* Well, I felt pretty bad. I wanted to stay in bed.

Although the witness has not been completely destroyed by the cross-examination, his testimony has certainly been weakened. The rehearsed witness has had to fill in a number of details that were not part of the script and in doing so was forced to provide some less than persuasive answers by expanding on the earlier testimony.

Another technique used by many advocates is to ask a witness if his or her testimony has been rehearsed with the witness's advocate prior to the hearing. Many advocates alert their witnesses to anticipate such a question and instruct them to forthrightly respond, "Yes, Mr./Ms. [advocate] reviewed my testimony with me several days ago." Witnesses who have not been so schooled, however, may be troubled or embarrassed by such a question and either deny or dodge the question, believing that preparation of testimony is not proper. Of course, all arbitrators realize that such preparation is not only proper, but failure to do so is negligence on an advocate's part.

The stock question relating to witness preparation has special meaning for a witness who shows signs of actual rehearsal or memorization of answers. In these cases the cross-examining advocate may wish to pursue the issue to greater lengths by inquiring whether the witness has been given written answers to review or memorize, how many preparation sessions were held, and the like. Such detailed questions will certainly elicit objections from the opposing advocate, but the cross-examiner may rebut such objections on the basis of the apparent unnatural manner in which the witness is answering questions.

## DON'T: Allow the Opposing Advocate to Coach or Instruct the Witness

Some advocates believe it is necessary to give their witnesses some assistance in the course of cross-examination by supplying them with suggested answers in the form of objections and statements interjected during the cross-examination. Depending on the skill of the opposing advocate, such prompting of a witness may be either obvious to an arbitrator or not very evident.

When it is clear to the cross-examining advocate that the opposing advocate is giving suggested answers to his or her witness in the form of objections, no time should be lost in calling the advocate to task through a motion or request to the arbitrator to admonish the offending advocate from continuing such coaching. The following is an example of coaching of a witness and an appropriate response.

*UA:* Ms. Shultz, I now want to inquire about your participation in labor contract negotiations in 1994. You were a member of the employer bargaining committee, weren't you?

*W:* Yes, I was.

*UA:* And you recall, don't you, the discussions during negotiations concerning the inclusion of a cost of living clause in the labor contract?

*W:* Yes, most of them.

*UA:* You remember, don't you, when your management spokesperson, Mr. Wong, said that all increases from the COLA clause would be in addition to any increases you were negotiating in the general wage rates?

*EA:* Objection. This calls for parole evidence, and, besides, Mr. Wong previously testified that he did not make any references to general wage increases, and therefore this witness couldn't possibly have heard a such statement. Besides, the question calls for hearsay.

*UA:* Madam Arbitrator, the employer advocate is not merely making an evidentiary objection. He is blatantly coaching the witness. I would ask for a direction from you to the advocate that all such coaching of this witness, and of any other witnesses, cease. I further move that the objection be stricken from the record and the witness be instructed to answer the question posed.

A: I think there is merit in what the union advocate says. The objection is overruled and stricken from the record. The employer advocate is advised to merely state the objection and the reason therefor, and in doing so to refrain from characterizing other testimony and evidence.

Some coaching is not as blatant as exemplified above. Sometimes it is done by the simple interjection of the words "if he (she) knows" after a question. This is often a signal to the witness to claim lack of knowledge. For example:

EA: What was the standard procedure for correcting an error caused by a malfunction in the odometer?

UA: If the witness knows.

W: I don't know what the standard procedure was for correcting those errors.

If this tactic is used more than once, the cross-examiner should call it to the arbitrator's attention and ask for an instruction from the arbitrator that the practice cease. The following request is appropriate.

Mr. Arbitrator, the interjection by the advocate for the union (employer) of the words "if he knows" is not necessary and is disruptive of my cross-examination. If the witness does not know the answer to a question, the witness can so state. I would ask that this interjection be stopped.

Another tactic used by some advocates is to request a clarification, such as the following: "Madam Arbitrator, I would ask for a clarification of the phrase 'reverse seniority.' I don't think it's clear what that term means."

This is a veiled hint to the witness that the question contains a curve or that the witness's previous answers concerning the words "reverse seniority" were not very good from that party's standpoint. An alert witness will catch the signal, ask for an explanation of the words, and likely rephrase or correct a previous answer. Again, recourse against such tactics should be through the arbitrator.

## DON'T: Extend Cross-Examination
## Longer Than Necessary

There is a great temptation for cross-examiners to try to squeeze every possible admission or contradiction from a witness, causing the cross-examination to continue long after any worthwhile evidence is being elicited. The author confesses to having succumbed to such temptations from time to time. There is often a feeling that one or two more questions will cause the witness to reveal some evidence damaging to his or her case. This is occasionally true, but more often it simply causes the arbitrator to lose interest and to question the judgement of the cross-examining advocate.

Effective cross-examinations cover the necessary ground but do not extend beyond the point where the previous testimony is simply rehashed. As with so many aspects of life, "more is not necessarily better."

## TIPS ON IMPEACHING WITNESSES

As indicated earlier, the crowning achievement of a cross-examination is to impeach the testimony of a witness to the point where the essence of the opposing side's case is destroyed. It is the equivalent of the grand slam home run. In reality, though, it seldom occurs.

Although most impeachments of opposing witnesses will not necessarily lead to winning the case, no single aspect of the evidentiary portion of the case is more likely to contribute to a successful outcome than the destruction of a key adverse witness or the impeachment of some critical line of testimony of an adverse witness. A successful attack on a witness's credibility frequently taints the entire case being made by that party. The rewards of a successful impeaching cross-examination are so abundant that it behooves all advocates to prepare for and attempt to execute an effective cross-examination aimed at impeaching a witness and/or some aspect of his or her testimony.

## Specific Areas to Attack

In order to break down the credibility of a witness, it is not necessary to show that the witness is dishonest or not telling the truth as the witness understands it. All that the advocate needs to show is that the witness's testimony is erroneous, regardless of the reason. Once this objective is fully accepted by the cross-examining advocate, it becomes much easier to formulate an effective impeaching cross-examination.

### Veracity

The ideal way to impeach a witness is to show that he or she has not been truthful. This is most effectively done by showing that the witness has answered the same, or virtually the same, question during the hearing in a contradictory fashion, that the witness said one thing to one person and something very different to another, that the witness said one thing and acted completely contrary to that statement, and/or that the witness admitted to being untruthful. Regardless of the way in which the witness is shown to be untruthful, it is devastating to the other side to have one of its witnesses proven to be untrustworthy.

### Prejudice or Bias

Another way of impeaching a witness is to show that the witness has a history of untruthfulness or has taken a public position or has expressed sentiments that reflect a bias, prejudice, or interest in a particular outcome or in support of a particular person or idea to the point that he or she cannot be relied on. Thus, if it can be shown that a witness has such a close relationship with a key participant in the case that it would be extremely unlikely for the person to testify in any but a favorable way toward the participant, there is a good opportunity to impeach, or at least seriously weaken, the witness's testimony. This is shown in the following example.

> [The witness is a plant manager in a case in which one of the plant's supervisors, Mr. Groping, has been accused of sexual harassment by a female grievant, Ms. Vicktim, in his department. The employer advocate has called the plant manager to support the supervisor and vouch for his character. Following direct examination, the union advocate is cross-examining the plant manager.]

*UA:* Mr. Peterson, as plant manager, how long have you supervised Mr. Groping?

*W:* About fifteen years.

*UA:* During that time, it's a fact, isn't it, that you have been responsible for, or supported, the promotion of Mr. Groping in moving up the corporate ladder?

*W:* Yes, I recommended him for promotion to foreman, and about six years later I promoted him to supervisor of the galvanizing department.

*UA:* You believe he is a good supervisor, don't you?

*W:* Yes, I do.

*UA:* And you don't believe he would ever sexually harass a female employee, do you?

*W:* Certainly, I know that is not something he would ever do.

*UA:* How often does Mr. Groping come to your home for a social visit or a social occasion?

*W:* Oh, perhaps twice a year.

*UA:* In other words, he has been a guest in your home about thirty times?

*W:* That's about right.

*UA:* And you frequently have lunch with him don't you?

*W:* About once or twice a week.

*UA:* How many times has Ms. Vicktim been to your home for a social visit or on a social occasion?

*W:* I don't believe she has ever been to my home.

*UA:* And how many times have you had lunch with her?

*W:* I never have.

Note that the cross-examiner has not attempted to show that the witness has been untruthful. All that has been attempted (and achieved) is to show that the witness is likely to be biased in favor of the supervisor and is likely to give testimony that is favorable to the supervisor. Of course, most observers and the arbitrator would presume that a plant manager has a predisposition in favor of one of his supervisors. What the union advocate has succeeded in doing, however, is to show that the plant manager had much more than a normal motive to support a supervisor. Here the plant manager was instrumental, if not the key factor, in the accused supervisor being promoted into the supervisory/management ranks and also from there to a departmental supervisor. The plant manager has a personal interest in seeing that the supervisor succeeds, since that success reflects favorably on the plant manager (and, conversely, failure for any reason would reflect adversely on the plant manager). The union advocate will surely point out such personal motivations to the arbitrator in the argument phase of the hearing.

Likewise, the cross-examination has shown that the two men have a rather close social relationship. The union advocate will later state in the argument phase that the plant manager has a personal relationship with the supervisor and could not possibly be unbiased, or even reasonably objective, in a case involving the character and reputation of a personal friend.

### Character and Reputation

Another means of impeaching a witness is to show that his or her character is such that he or she is not likely to give truthful testimony.

This may come from records or other evidence of testimony given by the witness in other cases. It may also come from extended cross-examination in which the witness is shown to have a weak, unprincipled, or unreliable character. It may also come from the testimony of other witnesses, testifying about prior instances wherein the witness's poor character was demonstrated. This type of impeachment is extremely difficult to bring off, and, unless the advocate has rather solid evidence on which to rely, it is better not to attempt impeachment, at least not by means of a frontal attack.

### *Interest or Motive*

From time to time a witness will be called to testify in a case in which the interests of the witness are so allied or directly influenced by the outcome of the case that it is not reasonable to believe that the witness can be objective or unbiased in favor of (or against) the grievant or the grievance being arbitrated. The following is an example of such a cross-examination.

*EA:* Would you tell us what your position is?

*W:* Data entry clerk in the accounts receivable department.

*EA:* Did you file a grievance in this case?

*W:* No.

*EA:* Have you ever filed a grievance in the past that raised any of the issues raised in this case?

*W:* Well, about five years ago I filed a grievance against the company for requiring us to work through our lunch hour.

*EA:* Did you win your grievance?

*W:* We won the part alleging that we were not paid properly for the day in question, but the arbitrator did not uphold our claims for double time for the time we lost from our lunch period.

*EA:* If this case were to be decided in favor of the grievant, Ms. Kerect, you and other employees would gain the same benefits you sought in your earlier grievance, wouldn't you?

*W:* I suppose we would.

Here the employer advocate has effectively shown that the witness has a bias, not necessarily in favor of the particular grievant, but in favor of the issue or interest being arbitrated. Following such cross-examination, no arbitrator is likely to believe that the witness is testifying from a completely unbiased position.

Bias can also be shown when the witness has a history of testifying only for one side or the other (applicable to a third party such as an expert witness) or has a plausible reason to harm one side or the other. Any of these bases may provide a foundation from which an effective impeaching cross-examination may be launched.

### Recollection

Because witnesses testify, or are expected to testify, from their recollection, proof of poor or inaccurate recollection is a potential basis of impeachment. It is very difficult to prove that a witness has poor powers of recollection in general. It is much more feasible to challenge the witness's memory of the matters to which he or she has already testified and of the matters at issue in the case at hand. For example:

*EA:* Mr. Gaze, when you checked the log book that night, on what page was the last entry made?

*W:* Page 37 or 38.

*EA:* You feel pretty confident about that, do you?

*W:* Yes. I noted it because I thought someone might question it later on.

*EA:* And would you say you feel as sure of this as anything else you've testified to today.

*W:* Yes, I do.

*EA:* I'm going to hand you a copy of the log book, which I will mark for identification as Employer Exhibit 6, and ask you to turn to pages 37 and 38. Tell us what you see there.

*W:* [after turning the pages] Nothing. They are blank.

*EA:* Go through the log book and tell us the last page on which there is an entry.

*W:* On page 21.

In a few questions the employer advocate has planted a major seed of doubt about the accuracy and completeness of the witness's earlier testimony. It should be noted that the cross-examiner did not ask ''Do you recall...?'' but rather asked questions seeking direct information about the point at issue.

Questions concerning details associated with key aspects of the direct testimony can often trip up the most persuasive witnesses. Questions relating to time, sequence of events, and quotations of statements may be overlooked or forgotten by witnesses in favor of the main occurrence or situation about which the witness has testified. Failure to remember such details can erode a witness's credibility.

### Perception

Closely related to memory is perception. In fact, what may appear to be a failure of memory may simply be a failure of perception. The failure to notice an event, object, or situation interferes with the witness's ability to testify accurately about such matters, because it is impossible to recall something that one did not originally perceive. For example:

UA: Ms. Kopay, you testified that the man you saw that night entering the storeroom was wearing a red sweater and blue denim jeans, correct?

W: That's right.

UA: Was he wearing a hat?

W: I don't recall.

UA: Was he carrying anything in his hands?

W: I'm not sure; I don't believe so.

UA: Aside from the pants and sweater, you don't seem to remember much else about the grievant that morning, do you?

W: Well . . . .

UA: And I don't suppose you could tell us if he was wearing glasses or not?

W: No, not really.

Here again, the error may be one of perception or memory, but it matters little because the witness has been unable to give a complete description of who and what she saw that night, and, because she is not able to testify as to certain matters of perception, it is plausible that her perception of other matters was inaccurate. The arbitrator is likely to discredit or at least give less weight to the witness's perceptions on this and on other matters to which she testifies.

### Discrediting Conduct

Impeachment is generally thought of as an attack on the witness's statements made when testifying on direct examination. That is generally the case, but not the exclusive way in which a witness's credibility can be impeached. Sometimes actions taken or not taken and statements made or not made by the witness outside the hearing can reflect adversely on the witness's credibility. For example:

*EA:* Ms. Franz, you testified that during the office get-together to celebrate your birthday after work, your supervisor, Mr. Hanz, touched your breasts as you were exiting the women's restroom about 6 P.M., is that correct?

*W:* Correct.

*EA:* And you believe now, and you believed then, that this was a form of sexual harassment, right?

*W:* Yes, I do. And I did then.

*EA:* There will be testimony from another witness, one of your coworkers, that you were smiling just as you exited the restroom and as Mr. Hanz touched you. Do you admit that you were smiling while Mr. Hanz touched you?

*W:* Well, I may have been, but I was smiling for another reason. Someone told a joke about that time.

*EA:* Did you talk in a friendly manner with Mr. Hanz later during the party?

*W:* I don't specifically recall. . . . I might have.

*EA:* And these friendly conversations with Mr. Hanz occurred after you were, according to your testimony, sexually harassed by Mr. Hanz, correct?

*W:* Yes, but since he's my group leader, I didn't have any choice but be friendly.

Statements, actions, expressions, and failure to say or do something can raise doubts about the witness's credibility. The failure to include an important aspect of an event in a report of that event is likely to raise questions about whether the aspect ever occurred or was present. Implausible or irrational actions or statements create doubts about the witness's truthfulness or rationality. The cross-examiner should always ask in his or her own mind, "What would a reasonable person in the witness's shoes do or not do, say or not say, under the circumstances?" If the actual action or statements differ significantly from the expected, some basis for impeachment likely exists.

## STEPS TO IMPEACH

When an attempt is going to made to impeach a witness based on testimony given on direct examination, it is usually best to follow a three-step procedure.

1. Have the witness recommit to the earlier testimony.
2. Build the witness up for the planned impeachment.
3. Contrast the testimony given with the actual facts.

An example of these steps is shown in a case in which a supervisor has discharged an employee for lying about the reasons for an absence. The supervisor testified on direct examination that when he asked the employee in the final meeting before discharge about why the employee was absent, the employee said that she had to go to her brother-in-law's funeral. The supervisor's secretary kept notes of the meeting, but they were not introduced during direct examination.

> UA: Mr. Bacon [supervisor], you testified earlier that Ms. Peters [employee] told you that the reason she was absent on January 22 was that she had to go to the funeral for her brother-in-law, is that correct?
>
> W: Yes, that's what she said. [witness recommits]
>
> UA: And that's the reason you discharged her, correct?
>
> W: Yes. [further recommitment]
>
> UA: And you have a good recollection of that meeting, don't you?
>
> W: Yes, I would say so. [buildup]
>
> UA: And you believe Ms. Peters was lying because you later learned that that was not the reason she was absent that day, correct?
>
> *[further* buildup]
>
> W: Yes.
>
> UA: I am showing you a copy of the notes taken of that meeting that were made by your secretary, Ms. Shorthand, and I direct your attention to the last paragraph of page three. Please read it out loud.
>
> W: It says, "Ms. Peters says that she was too upset to go to work that day. Her brother-in-law in Cincinnati died the day before, and she couldn't come to work that day."
>
> *[contrast* and impeachment]

It is particularly important, when impeaching with a document, that the cross-examiner not show the witness the document until the witness has reconfirmed and recommitted to the earlier testimony. If the contrast between the testimony on direct and the document are not crystal clear, the cross-examining advocate should clear up any ambiguities before disclosing the document. Once the witness has seen the document and realizes the impeaching aspect of it, he or she will invariably conjure up some plausible or seemingly plausible reason to explain the inconsistency or contradiction. The witness needs to be pinned down before the impeaching evidence is shown.

## Summary of Impeachment Techniques

As indicated earlier, the opportunities for outright, clear-cut impeachments are relatively limited. When they occur, they can be very valuable, but advocates should not get so focused on impeaching the other party's witnesses that the overall case suffers. Cross-examination is but one part of a case, and failure to demolish opposing witnesses does not mean that the case will be lost. Above all, the advocate needs to be forthright and direct in examining the other side's witnesses. Tactics and techniques that appear designed simply to trick or embarrass the opposing party's witnesses will be poorly received by the arbitrator and will lose points for the cross-examining advocate's case.

# 13

# Redirect and Recross-Examinations and Rebuttal

This chapter might be entitled "The Comeback Case" or perhaps "Additional Bites at the Apple," in that it addresses those aspects of an arbitration hearing that call for a response, reaction, and/or rebuttal to what has just previously transpired in the hearing. Whether the contemplated actions are to ask additional questions of one's own witness (redirect examination), ask additional questions of the other side's witness (recross-examination), call back a previous witness, or call new witnesses (rebuttal case), the considerations are much the same.

Is it wise and prudent to pursue a line of inquiry or open a new line of inquiry in order to improve one's case or to salvage a witness or evidence that is in trouble? If the answer is yes, how extensive should the examination and rebuttal be and what techniques should be employed? Answering the first of theses questions requires a cost/benefit analysis— weighing the benefit of reopening or pursuing a line of inquiry or rehabilitating a witness against the danger that such pursuit will do more harm than good to that advocate's case. The answer to the second question requires a rapid evaluation of the advocate's case at that particular point in the hearing and an assessment of how the case can be improved.

Prior to dealing with the factors concerning each of these aspects, some time is devoted in this chapter to a tactic that is sometimes employed as an alternative or prelude to producing additional evidence: the motion to dismiss or motion for summary judgment.

# PREEMPTORY MOTIONS: MOTIONS TO DISMISS AND MOTIONS FOR SUMMARY JUDGMENT

In courts of law, once the plaintiff or the prosecution has completed the presentation of its case in chief, it is not uncommon for the defendant to make a motion to dismiss. A somewhat similar motion called a motion for summary judgment is also common, being filed by either side at almost any time in the proceeding, but most likely after each side has presented all of its evidence. Both of these motions request that the judge put a hasty end to the case on the basis that the other side has failed to allege or present sufficient facts or a sufficient legal foundation on which a court of law could uphold the side of the case against whom the motion was brought. Because these motions are made before the full hearing process has been exhausted, they are often called preemptory motions. Although the two motions are different, for purposes of labor arbitration hearings they can be discussed together.

In labor arbitration both of the preemptory motions are normally made by the party that does not carry the burden of proof or, more precisely, the burden of persuasion, that is, the employer in contract interpretation cases and the union in discipline and discharge cases. The basis of the motion to dismiss is that the other side (the one that has the burden of proof), after presenting its evidence, has not made a sufficiently strong case (usually termed a prima facie case) that it could win the arbitration *even if the other side presented no evidence to counter what was presented.* The basis for the motion for summary judgment is that even if the arbitrator were to find the facts to be just as they are alleged by the other side, the moving party bringing the motion claims that no relief may be granted because no contract violation could be found.

In essence, both motions say to the arbitrator, ''The other side has had an opportunity to present its evidence and to explain that a contract violation occurred. Based on what they have shown, there is no factual or contractual basis on which you could possibly decide in their favor even if we remain silent. Consequently, you should not require any more evidence or argument from us, and should rule immediately in our favor.''

## Procedure for Making a Preemptory Motion

Because these motions are infrequently made and even more infrequently granted, it is especially important for the advocate who plans to make them to fully explain the basis on which one or both of them are being made. For example, a union filed a grievance protesting the employer's decision to promote an employee with only three years seniority to the position of salaried supervisor. It presents two witnesses, including the grievant (who has ten years seniority) to testify in support of the contention that the employer's decision on the promotion was unfair. At the conclusion of the union's case the employer advocate makes a preemptory motion to dismiss the case, addressing the arbitrator as follows:

> Madam Arbitrator, the employer hereby makes a motion to dismiss this case and deny the grievance, or as an alternative, asks for summary judgment. The union has presented its evidence regarding the employer's decision to promote Ms. X to the position of supervisor of the hand lettering department. Joint Exhibit 1, the labor agreement between the parties, contains no provisions whatsoever relating to the promotion of bargaining unit employees to positions outside the bargaining unit, that is, to supervisory or management positions. The union has presented no evidence, in fact it hasn't even alleged, that this position falls within the bargaining unit. The employer submits that it had good and sufficient reasons to promote Ms. X to that position, but even if it didn't, the union cannot complain because it has no contractual basis on which to do so. The employer has not given up its unilateral right to choose its own supervisors—whether it hires them off the street or whether it promotes them from the bargaining unit. Consequently, the union has no contractual basis to challenge such a decision, and for that reason you should deny the grievance without further evidence or argument.

At this point the arbitrator is likely to turn to the union advocate and ask for a response. If there is nothing in the contract about promotion to supervisory positions, the union advocate may be hard pressed to respond effectively. He or she may point to some general provisions in the labor agreement regarding the importance of seniority or good faith and fair dealing between the parties. If seniority was a major factor in prior promotions to supervisory positions, past practice may be invoked.

Notwithstanding the absence of strong arguments by the union advocate in this example, the arbitrator is unlikely to grant the employer advocate's motions. The institutional needs of the union as well as the conceptual framework of arbitration (i.e., to provide an open, nontechnical forum for the hearing and resolution of disputes) is too strong to cut off the union's right to have the matter fully heard and decided after the presentation of evidence by both sides.

# Value of Preemptory Motions

In courts of law preemptory motions are granted with some frequency. In labor arbitration they practically never are. Why then, the reader is prompted to ask, are they made? Why is it even discussed in this book? The simple answer is that some advocates believe they achieve a tactical advantage by making the motion as a way of emphasizing to the arbitrator that the other side has a weak case. These advocates, almost invariably lawyers, tend to view labor arbitration hearings as minitrials, in which the rules of procedure more or less follow those utilized in courts of law.

The perspective of labor arbitrators is different, however. Few arbitrators are inclined to grant such preemptory motions. First, many arbitrators are not lawyers, are not conversant with such motions, and are not accustomed to deciding cases without a full presentation of evidence and arguments by both sides. Second, the principles underlying labor arbitration decision making are not so precise that it is safe to conclude, after hearing only a portion of the case, that there is no way one side or the other could possibly prevail. Third, and perhaps most important, there is a notion that one of the primary functions of labor arbitration is to give both sides their day in court, that is, a fair hearing. Terminating a case before both sides have had a full opportunity to present their evidence and arguments deprives them of their full day in court.

With extremely long, if not completely overwhelming, odds against having such a motion granted, an advocate may question the value of making such a motion. Indeed, it is not usually beneficial to make a motion that is virtually certain to be rejected. Nevertheless, there are some reasons why such a motion may be advisable. First, it is a good opportunity to make an argument attacking the other side's case before the time for full argument is at hand. It allows the advocate who makes the motion to point out flaws in the other side's case even before having to present its own side. Second, depending on the arguments made to support the motion, the arbitrator may be persuaded to reduce the amount of evidence that the moving party is required to present (on the basis of narrowing the issues). Third, it puts the opposing side on the defensive, requiring the opposing advocate to argue why the case should not be terminated immediately. Fourth, it is essentially a no-risk gambit. If the motion is granted, the case is over. If it is not granted, the moving party is no worse off than before. The only cost may be one of credibility, particularly if the motion is not well founded. For this reason advocates are strongly advised to make a motion to dismiss or for summary judgment only when it is very clear that the other side's facts and arguments cannot support a winning decision—regardless of what is presented in opposition.

## RECESS

After the opposing side has completed the examination of an important witness or after it has completed its case in chief, it is usually advisable to request a recess to prepare for the response. Such requests must be addressed to the arbitrator and are invariably granted. The length of the recess will be determined by the arbitrator but is usually no more than fifteen to twenty minutes, unless there are special circumstances (e.g., surprise witnesses or new evidence) that justify additional time. If the proceedings are approaching a normal break time, such as lunch or the end of the day, the advocate may request that the recess be scheduled to coincide with that break, giving the advocate a much longer period in which to prepare. It is preferable to leave the hearing room to conduct the recess preparation in a separate room or in another setting that provides an opportunity for discussion without eavesdropping by others.

The time during the recess should be used wisely. The use of this time is similar to that employed in preparation for cross-examination, as discussed in Chapter 12. An assessment should be made of the key points of evidence that were adduced by the other side. Witnesses and other members of the advocate's team should be polled to see what, if any, significant points were noted that were not detected by the advocate. Notes should be made of matters to be covered in the redirect or recross-examination or in the rebuttal case.

## REDIRECT EXAMINATION

### Damage Assessment

Once an advocate's witness has been cross-examined, an important decision needs to be made—and made quickly. Should any questions be asked of this witness on redirect examination? The answer must be based on a prompt assessment of how much, if any, damage has been done to this witness and the witness's testimony in the cross-examination. If little or no damage has been done, it is usually advisable to refrain from further questions and allow the witness to be excused. The reason is that further questioning by way of redirect examination will enable the opposing side to ask further questions on recross-examination, possibly causing damage that did not result from the initial cross-examination. A good advocate wants to minimize the exposure of his or her witnesses as much as possible from wounds that can be inflicted by the other side. The longer witnesses are in the witness chair and the more times the opposing advocate has to renew questioning of them, the greater will be their vulnerability to attack.

Beyond considering the repair of any damage that may have been done on cross-examination, the examining advocate needs to think about any key points that he or she may have neglected to cover on direct examination. If these points are essential or even very important to the advocate's case, it will be advisable to pose the neglected questions on redirect examination. Similarly, the cross-examination may not have inflicted harm on the witness but may have raised one or more issues that had not previously occurred to the examining advocate. This too may be good reason to conduct a redirect examination. The advocate should always realize, however, that some risk is being assumed each time a redirect examination is conducted, because the witness will be exposed once more to recross-examination, with the attendant risk of losing some ground.

## Damage Repair

If a witness has been damaged on cross-examination and if there is some basis for repairing the damage, there is little doubt that redirect examination should be initiated. The problem is to determine how best to repair the damage.

If the witness was impeached because of some confusion caused by the cross-examiner, the obvious solution is to ask questions to elicit the witness's understanding of the testimony that contained the erroneous information. For example:

> *UA:* Mr. Green, you were asked by the advocate from the company whether you had ever been terminated from a job, and you said yes. What do you understand the word "terminated" to mean?

> *W:* It means lose my job.

> *UA:* Do you believe that you have been terminated if you lose your job because of a layoff for lack of work?

> *W:* Yes.

> *UA:* Have you ever been discharged or fired from a job?

> *W:* No.

> *UA:* Have you ever been laid off for lack of work?

> *W:* Yes, twice.

> *UA:* When you answered "yes" to the question about termination, were they the layoffs that you were referring to?
>
> *W:* Yes.

If the impeachment was caused by an attack on the witness's ability to perceive or recollect, the repair is likely to be much more difficult. Nevertheless, it is often possible to rehabilitate the witness to one degree or another. For example:

> *UA:* Mr. Blue, you answered on cross-examination that you had never been fired from a job before now, yet there is now evidence to the effect that you left XYZ Company in 1987 because you had violated their sick leave policy. Can you explain this apparent discrepancy?
>
> *W:* Yes, I had worked for XYZ for two years. They had a rule that sick leave could be used only for illness of the employee. I took two days off because my wife was having a baby, although when I filled out the sick leave form I put on the sick leave slip "disability." When they found out the reasons for my absence they said I would be fired. The personnel manager said I could resign instead of being fired. Although I wanted to protest it, I had an opportunity for another and better job and decided to resign and take the other job. When counsel for the company asked me earlier if I had ever been fired, I said "no," because that is what I believed to be the truth—and I still do.

If a witness has been thoroughly prepared, the chances of an outright impeachment are greatly minimized, but there is always some chance that an advocate's witness may be shown to have misrepresented the facts. This presents a serious dilemma. Should the advocate attempt to rehabilitate the witness, or should the damage be left alone with the hope that it will not unduly impact the case? Unfortunately, there are no easy answers. If the evidence that was impeached can be repaired through the testimony of some other witness, that alternative should certainly be considered. If the impeachment was on a relatively minor matter, it is often advisable to simply ignore it.

When, however, the impeachment has been on a rather significant matter and has directly destroyed the witness's credibility, glossing over or ignoring the impeachment may be virtually impossible. The advocate may have no alternative but to face the problem directly and attempt to have the witness put the misrepresentation in the most favorable light possible. The following example illustrates one way that may be done.

> *EA:* Mr. White, you testified on direct examination that you were in the office reception area when the delivery person came into

the building and when he went to the reception desk. You later testified on cross-examination that you never saw the delivery person that day. This appears to be in conflict. Can you explain?

W: When you and I were reviewing the facts of this case two days ago, I had a definite recollection that I saw the delivery boy in the reception area that day. As I heard the testimony of Ms. Schmitz and Mr. Malden earlier in the hearing today, it caused me to rethink my recollection and to believe that I was mistaken. Shortly after, when I was being cross-examined, the chain of events became even clearer to me, and I realized that I hadn't seen him at all that day.

EA: Do you now have a good recollection of that day, and can you say with certainty that you did not see the delivery person in the reception area on the day in question?

W: Yes.

Although this type of rehabilitation will not completely salvage a witness's credibility, it is usually better than letting the contradiction stand and having the arbitrator conclude that the witness was simply lying. Such a conclusion can be devastating if the witness has testified about other key points in the case. If the arbitrator believes that the witness is not a truthful person, that belief will certainly transfer to other aspects of the witness's testimony. For this reason the advocate may wish to expand the rehabilitation to minimize the adverse impact on other testimony. Using the last example, the advocate may continue as follows.

EA: Mr. White, is there any other aspect of your testimony today in which other testimony or evidence has caused you to doubt the accuracy of your memory?

W: No.

EA: And you are absolutely certain that all other aspects of your testimony are consistent with what you saw and what you remember of those events?

W: Yes, there is no doubt about any other aspect of my testimony.

Of course, such questions should never be asked unless the advocate and the witness are absolutely certain no other possible contradictions exist. A repeat of the impeachment following such rehabilitation will nail the lid on the witness's coffin and most likely on the entire case.

## Routine Redirect Examination

There are other types of redirect examination besides damage control. From time to time there will be a need to clarify or elaborate on some aspect of a witness's testimony that will enhance the evidence previously presented by that witness on direct. When the anticipated benefit of the additional evidence appears to outweigh the potential danger of having the witness remain in the witness chair, the advocate should proceed. The same approach is advisable when cross-examination of the advocate's witness has brought out some additional points not covered on direct and when the witness's answers were not as clear or effective as they might have been. Some elaboration and/or clarification may be advisable.

It is important, however, that an advocate conducting redirect examination not merely repeat the questions asked earlier on direct examination. This is likely to trouble the arbitrator and elicit an objection from the opposing advocate that the questions have been asked and answered. The questions should be limited to those areas that need additional explanation or elaboration.

To discourage the opposing advocate from using the next opportunity for recross-examination to delve into new areas of inquiry, the advocate about to commence redirect examination may offer a preliminary phrase describing the limited scope of the redirect examination. For example, ''Mr. White, I am going to ask you just a few more questions, and they all relate to the events on the morning of August 3.'' If, after these questions are asked, the opposing advocate chooses to pursue recross-examination and attempts to open up new areas for questioning, it is advisable to point out to the arbitrator that the questions are outside the scope of the redirect examination and are therefore improper. Most arbitrators are not likely to enforce this technical rule of trial procedure, but it may serve to inhibit the cross-examining advocate and perhaps cause the arbitrator to impose some restraints that he or she otherwise might not.

## Covering Matters That Were Overlooked

From time to time an advocate who has completed direct or cross-examination will subsequently realize that one or more significant matters were forgotten, overlooked, or not previously considered. The witness is about to be excused, and the advocate must decide whether to delve into the matters not previously covered. In a court of law such matters would not usually be permissible on redirect or recross-examination because they are not within the scope of direct examination [or cross-examination]. This rule is seldom, however, applied in labor arbitration hearings, and therefore an advocate wishing to pursue such matters—however late in the game—is normally permitted to do so. The essential question from a strategic standpoint is whether it is advisable to do so.

The wisdom of opening up such issues will depend on how important they are in the case and how much value the evidence will have, notwithstanding its tardy presentation. There are no hard and fast guidelines that an advocate may consider in making such decisions, but if the advocate believes that the evidence not previously covered could have a significant influence on the arbitrator's decision, it is usually advisable to go forward with the overlooked questions. Less weight is likely to be given by the arbitrator to such afterthoughts, but one can never be sure what aspect of evidence is apt to be decisive in any particular case.

## RECROSS-EXAMINATION

When the other side's witness has been questioned by his or her own advocate on redirect examination, the cross-examining advocate has the option of asking the witness additional questions on recross-examination (i.e., the second round of questions on cross-examination). If the advocate was not able to land any punishing blows on the initial cross-examination, there is a strong urge on the part of most advocates to try again in the hope that some damage may be done to the witness. The more significant factor that should determine whether recross-examination should be conducted is the testimony given by the witness on redirect examination. If the witness enhanced the other side's case with the evidence provided on redirect examination, and if there appears to be some area of vulnerability that can be taken advantage of, the advocate is well advised to conduct recross-examination.

Sometimes witnesses will grow tired and irritable after being in the witness chair for an extended period of time. Their mental and emotional stamina may have deteriorated to the point that they give careless and obviously defensive answers. This provides a window of opportunity for the cross-examining advocate to probe areas in which there may be some vulnerability. Moreover, by answering additional questions from his or her advocate, the witness may have testified to a somewhat different, though not necessarily contradictory, version of the facts than were testified to earlier. This will give the cross-examining advocate an opportunity to attack the witness's credibility. For example:

> *EA:* Ms. Cannon, when you testified earlier about the events on the night of September 9 in the emergency room, you said that the room was full of waiting patients until 3 A.M. You later testified that the last patient waiting for treatment on your shift (that we understand ended at 4 A.M.) was seen by the E.R. doctor at 2:30 A.M. Obviously, both answers can't be true. Were you telling the truth the first time or the second time?

> *W:* I must have misspoken. The last patient was seen by Dr. Meyers at 2:30 A.M.

> *EA:* So your testimony about the waiting room being full until 3 A.M. wasn't true, was it?

> *W:* No, I was in error.

The cross-examining advocate needs, however, to be careful that such additional questioning does not take on the appearance of brow beating or taking advantage of a naive witness. If the tone of the recross-examination is that of attacking the witness over a matter that appears to be a simple oversight by the witness, the aggressive, challenging cross-examiner assumes the risk that pointed and accusatory questions will be interpreted as intimidation of the witness, and the witness may become the object of the arbitrator's sympathy. When, on the other hand, the witness has proven himself or herself to be contradictory on other matters as well, arbitrators are unlikely to bestow much sympathy on them, even if the cross-examining advocate is overreaching a bit.

The cross-examining advocate must acquire something of a sixth sense to know just how far to carry the recross-examination and how vigorously to carry it. There is a rather fine line between legitimate probing questions designed to uncover the truth and a strident and hostile series of questions that appear to be directed more at embarrassing the witness than in obtaining new evidence or clarifying existing evidence.


# THE REBUTTAL CASE

When the moving party (i.e., the union in a contract interpretation case and the employer in a discharge or discipline case) has completed its case in chief, and when the responding party (i.e., the employer in a contract interpretation case and the union in a discharge or discipline case) has completed its case in chief, the evidentiary portion of the hearing may be completed. What will keep it from being completed is if either side has any rebuttal, that is, any additional evidence to present that is intended to rebut evidence produced by the other side. The factors to be assessed in determining whether to present rebuttal evidence are much the same as those considered in determining whether to cross-examine an opposing side's witness or to conduct redirect examination of one's own witness.

## Damage Assessment and Damage Repair

The advocate who has observed the other side's evidence must decide whether it is possible to improve his or her case by presenting additional witnesses or other new evidence. This usually comes down to an evaluation of how much damage has been done by the other side and whether there is other evidence that can be produced that will overcome or weaken evidence produced by the other side. The advocate needs to consider these matters promptly, because there is very little time to evaluate all the relevant considerations.

## Sandbagging with New Evidence

Some advocates believe that they can achieve an advantage by not presenting important evidence as part of their case in chief and holding that evidence to present as part of their rebuttal case. The term for this practice is sandbagging. The idea is that if the other side does not learn of the evidence during the principal part of the case, they will not be prepared to cope with or counter it when it is presented late in the game. The difficulty with such new evidence becomes more pronounced when that evidence was never presented at any stage of the grievance procedure before arbitration.

For example, in a case involving the discharge of an employee for rudeness to a customer, an employer advocate presents the employee's supervisor as the principal witness during the case in chief, knowing that the customer herself is available to testify later in the case. The union presents the employee who disputes the evidence presented by the supervisor. It is one witness's testimony versus another. After both sides present their cases in chief, the employer calls as a witness the customer who was allegedly ill-treated by the employee. Now it is the testimony of two against one, and the union advocate has no time to come up with another witness to support the testimony of the employee. In some sense, the employer advocate has sandbagged (i.e., held back important evidence in order to gain a strategic advantage) his or her union counterpart.

Sandbagging carries a connotation of unfair or unethical advocacy. In some sense that may be exactly the case. If one side has probative evidence and withholds it until a point in the procedure when a strategic or tactical advantage can be obtained, it may very well be argued that such a practice is unethical, because the purpose of arbitration is to get a full presentation of the facts so that the arbitrator may make a fair, reasoned decision. On the other hand, there is nothing written in the canons of arbitration or in the rules of the American Arbitration Association that suggests that evidence has to be produced in any particular order. If evidence can be made more effective by being presented late in the hearing, why shouldn't that be permissible and ethical?

The author is loathe to set out any definitive judgments as to the ethics of sandbagging. One point of caution, however, to the advocate who blatantly attempts to do so: some arbitrators have a strict sense of fairness, and the specter of an advocate who holds back critical evidence from the other side until the very end of the case may cause them to sustain an objection by the other side on the basis that it is not truly rebuttal evidence because the evidence is not grounded simply on refuting evidence produced by the other side. An additional basis may be that, because one side or the other did not present the evidence during the grievance procedure, the other party did not have a full and fair opportunity to prepare its case for arbitration, and therefore the late-produced evidence should not be admitted. Although most arbitrators are not likely to uphold such a technical argument, they may give less weight to such late-produced evidence, unless there is some justification offered for the fact that the evidence was not produced earlier (e.g., the witness was en route to the hearing).

In most cases it is preferable that all important evidence be presented as part of the case in chief. When evidence is discovered later, or evidence that was known earlier, but was not fully appreciated, is recognized for its value and promises to enhance the case of the side proposing it, such evidence should certainly be offered. An explanation should be presented to the arbitrator, however, to show that sandbagging was not the advocate's intention, and that earlier presentation of such evidence was not feasible or prudent.

## The Witness in Waiting

As discussed above, some advocates hold back a witness or other evidence in the expectation that an advantage can be gained from late-produced evidence. There is another motivation, however, for holding back evidence from the case in chief, namely, that the evidence will not be necessary or that the source of the evidence (usually a witness) is not strong, and that it is best not to use it unless there is a real need for the evidence.

In preparing a case the perceptive advocate is usually able to discern which witnesses will be effective in the witness chair and which ones will not. When a choice exists (i.e., two or more witnesses are capable of testifying to key facts in the case), the more effective witness is the obvious choice. Unfortunately, such choices are not always available, and an advocate often has only one witness who can testify to relevant facts in the case. The dilemma is whether to put a weak witness in the witness chair with the potential for having the evidence presented in an ineffective fashion and exposing that witness to possibly damaging cross-examination or keeping the witness out of the witness chair and foregoing the advantage of that evidence. A compromise between these two positions is to refrain from offering the weak witness to testify as part of the case in chief and to hold that witness in reserve for rebuttal only if it becomes apparent that the evidence that witness can supply is necessary to win the case or is necessary to at least increases the odds of winning a case that might otherwise be lost. The decision of whether to use a weak witness is not an easy one, but the ability to make such a decision after one has heard all the evidence the other side has produced in its case in chief makes it significantly easier than if it was made in advance of the hearing.

## New Theories

Closely related to late-produced evidence are late-produced theories or grounds on which to argue a case. For example, an employee's grievance protesting a layoff out of seniority order is opposed by the employer throughout the grievance procedure and throughout the case in chief on the basis of the wording of the seniority section of the contract. During the rebuttal case the employer presents additional evidence for the first time that the grievance was filed too late according to the time limits for filing grievances as contained in the labor agreement. The union protests that no issue of timeliness had ever been raised during the grievance procedure nor as part of the employer's case in chief, and therefore the employer should be estopped (i.e., prevented) from making such an argument and from presenting evidence to support such an argument so late in the proceedings.

Some arbitrators will be inclined to reject such an objection but are likely to give such a tardily produced argument much less weight than if it had been presented during earlier stages of the grievance procedure or at least earlier in the arbitration proceedings. When the late-appearing theory goes to arbitrability (especially timeliness of filing), arbitrators are inclined to find a waiver by the party that did not raise the issue during the processing of the grievance.[1] When the late-appearing theory relates to an argument or explanation for a party's conduct, the weight of arbitral authority appears to be that new theories are permissible even if they first appear in the arbitration hearing.[2]

More often than not, the failure to raise an argument or a contractual theory earlier in the handling of a grievance is not because of sandbagging, but is merely a failure to realize the existence of a basis for advancing or defending a grievance. Those who handle grievances at the work place level are not generally lawyers, nor are they always skilled labor relations professionals. Consequently, they are apt to overlook certain technical or other bases for pursuing or defending a grievance. They should not be penalized for such failure. Experienced labor relations professionals and union representatives, however, are expected to spot all potential issues prior to commencing the hearing, and an advocate who introduces new issues (and especially issues related to arbitrability) for the first time in the arbitration hearing risks having them ignored by the arbitrator and loses credibility with the arbitrator.

## Calling Witnesses from the Other Side

In labor arbitration there are few rules governing which witnesses either side may call. Thus, either party may call witnesses who are allied with the other side (i.e., the union may call the plant manager and the employer may call the union shop steward). The sole exception to this general rule is the employer's calling of the grievant as its witness in a discharge or discipline. Some, but certainly not all, arbitrators adhere to the concept of the Fifth Amendment right to be protected from any possibility of self-incrimination and therefore preclude employers from calling a grievant who has been discharged or disciplined.[3] Otherwise, any witness is fair game and may be called by either side.

---

[1]Westvaco Corp., 99 LA 513 (Dugan, 1992); Liquid Transporters, 99 LA 217 (Witney, 1992); Teledyne Monarch Rubber Co., 97 LA 233 (Dworkin, 1991).
[2]AT&T Communications, 94 LA 1229 (Kaufman, 1990); Arkansas Power & Light Co., 89 LA 1028, 1032 (Woolf, 1987).
[3]See chapter 9, note 4.

When one side has been hurt by evidence produced by the other side, the possibility of calling the other side's witnesses is often considered. Although there was an earlier opportunity to fully cross-examine such witness, by the time rebuttal evidence is appropriate, the advocate may have more information on which to base an interrogation or may simply have more confidence that a more effective interrogation may be possible as part of the rebuttal case. The advocate should keep in mind that even though the witness is being called as one's own, the witness is an adversary witness, and the advocate is permitted to use leading questions as if it were cross-examination.

One of the advantages of calling the other side's witnesses as one's own as part of the rebuttal case is that it takes the witness somewhat out from under the protective wing of his or her own advocate. As in cross-examination, the witness is unaware of the questions to be posed and may be unsure of what the better answers are. Moreover, the fact that the witness is being called back to testify may impose some degree of uncertainty and trepidation that will cause the witness to give answers that are less supportive of his or her case than those given as part of the case in chief.

## Using a Stronger Witness and Other, More Persuasive Evidence

Occasionally, an advocate will be surprised with how weak and ineffective the testimony of one or more of his or her witnesses was during the advocate's case in chief. There may be a need to strengthen the evidence that the weak and/or ineffective witnesses attempted to provide. The rebuttal case may offer that opportunity. The advocate may have another witness available who could shore up the weak areas of testimony of the witnesses who testified as part of the case in chief. Likewise, there may have been documentary or other evidence that initially appeared persuasive but that, after cross-examination or closer scrutiny, proved to be unconvincing. The rebuttal case offers the advocate another bite at the apple by allowing the introduction of corroborating witnesses and/or evidence.

## Deciding When Enough is Enough

At some point each advocate has to decide when enough evidence has been produced and when it is time to let well enough alone. This usually carries with it a decision that there is no other evidence available that will enhance the advocate's case. Some advocates come to this realization earlier than others. One might admire an advocate who is so desirous of winning a case that he or she pursues the last full measure to find and present evidence that could win the case or at least increase the odds of winning. At the same time, one must fault the advocate who does not know when to quit and who tries the patience of the arbitrator by extending the hearing beyond the point at which any new and/or compelling evidence is being offered. The seasoned and competent advocate knows when that point has been reached. The novice must learn by trial and error.

# 14

# Closing Arguments

When all evidence has been presented by both parties, the last part of the hearing is the presentation by both sides of their arguments attempting to persuade the arbitrator to rule in their favor. Up to this point the case (except for some argument interspersed in the opening statement) has dealt with facts or alleged facts. Now it is time for the arbitrator to hear (or read) the reasons why both sides contend that the arbitrator should rule in their favor.

## ORAL ARGUMENT VS. WRITTEN BRIEFS

When the evidentiary portion of the case has been completed, the arbitrator typically will ask both advocates, "How do you wish to argue the case?" or "Do you wish to make oral argument or file written briefs?" The question is whether they wish to present their arguments orally at that time or to prepare written briefs and submit them to the arbitrator at a later date to be established.

### Strategy of Oral or Written Arguments

By long established practice, if either advocate requests to file a written brief, that will be the method chosen by the arbitrator. This leaves the other advocate with the option of also filing a written brief or arguing the case orally at the end of the hearing, but this is really not an option at all, because it would be foolhardy for one advocate to make an oral argument at the end of a hearing, knowing that the other side will be filing a written brief and taking into consideration the arguments made orally, without any opportunity for the other side to respond. Clearly, when one advocate requests to file a written brief, the other side should file its arguments in brief form as well. To do otherwise is to place one's case at a serious disadvantage.

In the majority of labor arbitration cases one or both of the advocates request to file written briefs, and therefore that is the method by which most labor arbitration cases are argued.[1] There are a number of reasons why that method is preferable. Among them are the following.

1. Both sides have a greater opportunity to consider and evaluate the evidence presented and to formulate their arguments in a more coherent and persuasive fashion.
2. If a transcript has been taken of the hearing, the transcript can be reviewed in preparation of the briefs and can be referred to in the briefs themselves.
3. The arbitrator can inform both sides as to the issues he or she considers most important and instruct them to specifically address them in the written briefs.
4. After having a full realization of the evidence and the issues at stake in the case, both sides can research reported arbitration cases and/or other applicable authorities and include citations in the briefs filed with the arbitrator.

The fact that most cases are argued in briefs does not mean that is the most advantageous for both sides. In some cases one side or the other may be able to achieve an advantage by making an oral argument. Of course, that advantage cannot be achieved if the other side simply requests to file a written brief. Consequently, it is usually advisable for an advocate who perceives an advantage by oral argument to broach the subject with the opposing advocate to see whether an agreement is possible. It may be possible to reach an agreement in advance of the hearing that oral arguments will be made. If so, that agreement can be communicated to the arbitrator at the outset of the hearing, precluding the other party from reneging later in the hearing.

The author seldom, if ever, has found an advantage in making oral arguments. Nevertheless, other advocates find one. The following factors should be taken into consideration in making such a decision.

---

[1]Federal Mediation and Conciliation Service, Arbitration Statistics, Fiscal Year 1994.

1. How complex is the case in terms of conflicts in evidence? How extensive is the evidence? The more complex, extensive, and contentious the evidence in the case, the more reason to file a brief.
2. How complex and uncertain are the contractual issues to be decided by the arbitrator? The more complex and uncertain they are, the greater the justification for filing written briefs.
3. What are the relative research and writing capabilities of the respective advocates?
4. To what extent is this case apt to set a precedent or standard for other cases? The greater the likelihood that it will, the more reason to file written briefs.
5. Was a transcript made of the hearing? If one was, all the more reason to file briefs (unless, of course, the other side is likely to make better use of the transcript).
6. Did the arbitrator display a good grasp of the facts and issues involved in the case? The less the arbitrator is fully conversant with the facts and issues, the greater the reason to file written briefs in order to better lead the arbitrator to a proper result (unless one side has a very weak case and wants to rely on the arbitrator's ignorance or incompetence in trying to win the case).
7. Does the union face the potential of a charge of failure to properly represent the grievant under the National Labor Relations Act? The greater the potential of such a charge, the more reason for the union to file a written brief.

## Opting for Oral Argument

Because written briefs have become such a common means of arguing labor arbitration cases, the question arises why and under what circumstances an advocate should seek to make an oral argument rather than file a brief. The reasons for requesting oral argument more or less track the considerations listed just above. Far and away the most important consideration from the advocate's perspective, however, are the comparative writing skills and anticipated quality of the briefs of the two advocates. If one advocate has superior writing skills and is willing and able to devote a significant amount of time to prepare a thorough and carefully written brief, and the other side is not likely to do so (or at least not to the same extent), that advocate is well advised to do so.

If, on the other hand, an advocate possesses excellent skills at extemporaneous speaking, has prepared some notes in advance of and during the hearing, and is less skilled as a writer, that advocate gains an advantage by being able to argue the case orally. This opportunity depends, of course, on the other side being willing to forego the right to file a brief. If the opposing advocate is aware of the relative writing skills and the amount of time each side is willing to devote to brief writing, one side or the other is likely to request a written brief, causing the arbitrator to order briefs. If, however, such information is not equally available, it is possible that both sides may agree to argue orally at the conclusion of the hearing.

An advocate who perceives, in advance of a hearing, an advantage to arguing orally may wish to communicate with the opposing advocate about the intended method of arguing the case. Such a discussion may open the door to a negotiation that will result in an agreement to argue orally. The opposing counsel may simply prefer oral argument, or there may be some other aspect of the hearing in dispute (e.g., the admissibility of certain evidence, the opportunity to obtain certain documents in advance of the hearing, etc.) that will provide a reasonable compromise leading to agreement to argue the case orally.

## Alternative Forms of Briefing

Occasionally an advocate will request the right to make oral argument and file a written brief. Most arbitrators will discourage, if not reject outright, such a request. It offers little or no advantage to either side or to the arbitrator.

Another possible option is to permit written briefs and reply briefs, whereby each side is given the opportunity to submit an initial brief and after reading the other side's brief, submit what amounts to a rebuttal brief. While this is not favored by most arbitrators, it is permitted by some, and if both parties jointly request the arbitrators to permit it, the request will often be granted, even by arbitrators who take a dim view of this practice. Such a practice is discouraged by those who see arbitration as a simple, inexpensive, and nontechnical means for resolving disputes. Permitting reply briefs extends, complicates, and makes more costly the process of labor arbitration. For those reasons alone it should be discouraged. Indeed, reply briefs are filed very infrequently.

## ORAL ARGUMENT

The major challenge to an advocate of making an effective oral argument is to have sufficient command of all pertinent evidence and contractual arguments to make a comprehensive and persuasive argument with very little preparation time. This calls for more extensive prehearing preparation, good note taking, assistance from others, and an ability to quickly assimilate facts and blend them with cogent arguments to form a persuasive closing argument. Even with such capabilities, most advocates can make more effective arguments in a written brief when there is adequate time to review the record, analyze the competing arguments, and formulate a thoughtful, well-articulated written brief. The key issue, however, may be not so much one of which mode is best, but which mode will give the advocate an advantage over the opposing advocate.

## Order of Oral Argument

One of the major differences between oral argument and written briefs is the order of presenting the arguments. When written briefs are filed, the most common practice is to have both advocates file simultaneous briefs with the arbitrator. When oral argument is to be made, the party carrying the burden of proof (actually, the burden of going forward) is first to present oral argument. The other side then presents its arguments. Sometimes arbitrators will permit rebuttal oral argument on certain issues.

## Preparation for Oral Argument

If an advocate knows there will be, or has good reason to believe that there will be, oral argument, it is extremely important, if not essential, that the advocate prepare an outline of the anticipated closing argument. While new and perhaps surprising evidence may be produced in the hearing that could not be anticipated, it is likely that most of the evidence will be known in advance based on the record of the grievance processing. In addition, it is even more likely that the contractual issues in the case will be well established before the hearing. Consequently, an advocate who anticipates making an oral argument usually has sufficient opportunity to anticipate and prepare for the oral argument in advance of the hearing.

It is not suggested that the advocate write a script for oral argument. For the same reasons given for not having a scripted opening statement, advocates are advised to prepare an outline of the key evidentiary and contractual issues that are likely to be presented during the hearing. Amendments to the outline may need to be made after the opening statements are made and after all the evidence has been presented. Nevertheless, the outline of oral argument will be invaluable. Even if the advocate who anticipates having the opportunity to make an oral closing argument finds that the other side will not agree, the prepared outline will still be invaluable in preparing the written brief following the hearing.

In order to be able to make an effective closing statement, it is useful to have someone on the advocate's arbitration team taking good notes (verbatim of key points, if possible) and pass them on to the arguing advocate in advance of closing statements.

## Carrying through the Theme of the Opening Statement

In Chapter 8 it was suggested that the opening statement have a theme that would set the tone for the case to be presented. That theme serves as a hook on which the various arguments can be hung. Periodically through the presentation of evidence, it is helpful if the opening theme can be woven into the testimony and other evidence. Equally important is the refrain of that theme in the closing argument. It encourages the arbitrator to see the evidence, emanating from many different sources, coming together as an integrated whole to form a picture that substantiates the position advocated by the side that advances the theme. Moreover, it adds credibility to the side presenting the theme, because it tacitly says to the arbitrator, ''We told you what this case was all about, and we were true to our word in presenting evidence to substantiate that theme.''

For example:

> Mr. Arbitrator, when we began this hearing earlier today we explained that this case is about the negligence of a self-centered employee who was so concerned about his physical comfort and leisure that he endangered the lives of his fellow workers and put at risk the employer's equipment that enables hundreds of workers in the Eastbank plant to earn a living. During the course of presenting our evidence we have been able to show repeated displays of the employee's negligence and callous self-absorption with his own welfare. In the first instance. . . .

## Organization of Oral Argument

The effectiveness of oral argument depends a great deal on the way in which the arguing advocate organizes the presentation. Keep in mind that the arbitrator has just heard a great deal of evidence (usually conflicting and often disjointed) and now has the task of putting it into some sort of rational order. The advocates need to understand the arbitrator's dilemma and help the arbitrator by presenting the facts and the contractual arguments in a fashion that assist the arbitrator to see the case as an integrated whole—in a way that favors each arguing advocate's case.

### Issue-Oriented Presentation

As with a written brief, oral argument may be organized in a number of ways. One way is to follow the traditional organization of written briefs, that is, organize by the issues. In other words, each issue is identified, and then each piece of evidence that supports one side's case is reviewed within the framework of that issue. Under this issue-by-issue method the contractual arguments are laid out, with the supporting evidence presented within the framework of each issue.

For example, in a case in which the union contends that the employer unilaterally changed the procedure by which overtime work is assigned, the advocate for the union might begin the closing argument as follows.

> Madam Arbitrator, there are three basic issues in this case. The first is whether the employer violated Article I, Section A, by not consulting with the union about a "basic condition of work," a commitment that the parties made as a central feature of their relationship and set forth in Article I. The second issue is whether the change in procedure of assigning overtime was done as a retaliatory measure against the employees in the fabric finishing department because of their protest, only three weeks earlier, against their supervisor. The third is whether the employer violated a long-standing and consistently applied past practice of assigning overtime according to departmental seniority. Let me enumerate all the pieces of the evidence that have been introduced today to support the union's position with respect to each of these issues. With regard to the first issue, you will recall the testimony of. . . .

Under this approach the advocate proceeds from one issue to the next and explains each piece of evidence that bears on that issue and how that evidence supports the arguments being made. Reason and logic are brought to bear to show in what way the evidence supports the contractual argument being made.

### Evidence-Oriented Presentation

Another form of organization is the witness-by-witness approach, whereby the advocate reviews the testimony of each witness and the documentary or other evidence produced through each witness. Once the evidence has been thoroughly reviewed, the advocate then proceeds to explain how each part supports his or her side of the case.

The following example is from a case in which an employee was discharged for theft. The employer's closing argument, based on an evidentiary-oriented presentation might begin as follows.

During the course of this case we heard the testimony of five witnesses. Let's briefly review the testimony of each of them to illustrate the mountain of evidence that proves that the grievant stole the goods as she has been charged and that her discharge was for just cause. The first witness was Mr. Roger Fry. You will recall that he testified that on the night of October 12, he was. . . . His testimony is entirely consistent with that of Susan Koenig, who described her observations that same day. . . .

## Dealing with Adverse Evidence and Arguments by the Other Side

It is vital in an effective closing argument to address and counter evidence that supports the other side's case and arguments that the opposing advocate has made or likely will make. An advocate's case will seldom, if ever, be so strong that it can carry the day without minimizing or defeating the arguments posed by the other side.

In terms of structuring the closing argument the advocate should consider the wisdom of addressing the other side's evidence and arguments in conjunction with his or her own or of dealing with them as a separate portion of the closing argument. The author prefers the latter option. If the other side's strong evidentiary points and arguments are interspersed with the advocate's affirmative arguments, the other side's points may detract from the advocate's arguments. For this reason the author prefers a presentation that lays out the basic evidence and arguments to support an advocate's case, then addresses the case made by the other side, knocking down (where possible) the other side's major points and then returning briefly to one's own major points while drawing to a conclusion. The transition from one's own case to the other side's might proceed as in the following example of a union's closing statement in which the union advocate is making the first closing argument.

And the testimony of Wilma Knight, along with the records of the purchases and sales of that day, can leave no doubt that the employer's assignment of work to Ms. Knight was clearly in violation of the labor agreement. Now, let's take a few minutes to address the evidence presented by the employer. Their first witness was Oscar Levant. He testified that his practice had always been to assign work according to seniority within the classification. On cross-examination, however, he could not name one specific date on which he had done so under the set of circumstances that existed in this case. In addition, his testimony was refuted by store manager Rhonda Fleming, who said that assignments to the checkout clerk desk were based on the seniority in that store. Mr. Levant's testimony is simply not to be believed. Then the employer attempted to show. . . .

## Advantage of the Party Arguing Last

As noted above, when written briefs are filed, the normal practice is to file them simultaneously, whereas with oral argument, one side (i.e., the party that presented its evidence first) makes its argument first and is then followed by the other. While the advocate who argues first usually has a reasonably good idea of what points the other side will make, it is not possible to know exactly what those arguments will be. The advocate arguing last, however, has a distinct advantage in having heard the other side's arguments before commencing his or her closing statement. This advantage should be maximized.

The advocate arguing last should make detailed notes of the opposing advocate's arguments, focusing particularly on how the evidence has been characterized and on the specific contractual arguments being advanced. In responding, the advocate arguing last may wish to begin by refuting the points made by the other side in the closing argument just completed. This is usually an effective way to begin because the arbitrator has those points well in mind and may give them considerable weight if they are not effectively refuted. By picking up immediately on the points made by the other side, refuting them, and then proceeding to the arguments that support that advocate's case, it is possible to achieve a strong closing argument with an initial defensive thrust and an offensive closing. The following example, given in this case by an employer advocate in a contract interpretation case, shows how such an argument might be structured.

> The union has just attempted to advance three basic arguments to support its position that the employer violated the labor contract by changing the procedure for assigning overtime. The first argument was that the change constituted a violation of Article I of the labor agreement. The contract language that the union relies on states, "The union and the employer agree to work together to establish basic working conditions for employees in the Eastbank plant that enable the employer to be competitive in its industry and that foster fair treatment and the general welfare of employees in the bargaining unit." Such general language cannot possibly be construed to limit the type of change made in this case. The quoted language does not preclude the employer from acting in any way, but merely supplies a homily that union and management should work together. Such language falls far short of anything that would require mutual agreement in instituting changes of matters that had never previously been a matter of agreement.

> Next, the union argues that the change in the overtime procedure was some form of retaliation against the employees in the fabric finishing department because of their earlier demonstration against their supervisor. Such an argument is absurd. Proof that it is absurd is overwhelming. First, evidence supplied by plant manager Alan Ladd shows that the decision to make

changes in the overtime procedure were made prior to the employees' demonstration. Moreover, employees demonstrated against supervisors in three separate departments, whereas the change in overtime procedures was made in only one of them. If the employer's motivation was retaliation, why weren't the overtime procedures in the other departments changed also?

The union's final argument is that the overtime procedures in effect prior to the change were part of a long-standing past practice. The argument simply does not stand the light of day. According to employer and union witnesses alike, the prior procedure had been in effect for only two years before the change. Previous to that, the procedure was the same as the employer has now adopted. Moreover, there is not a scintilla of evidence to show that the union ever negotiated any of the changes in the overtime procedures—regardless of which way they changed.

Now, let's turn to the employer's arguments. . . .

By attacking the other side's arguments and ending with one's own, the advocate who argues last has the distinct advantage of refuting each and every argument the other side has made, while finishing off with the strongest part of his or her case.

## Closing the Argument

Just as an effective salesperson ends his or her sale presentation "asking for the business," an advocate should state in no uncertain terms just what the arbitrator is being asked to do. When a union advocate seeks a reversal of a management decision regarding the application of the labor agreement, the message to the arbitrator should be loud and clear, "We ask that you grant the grievance, rule that a labor contract violation has occurred, and grant full back pay to the grievant." Similarly, a union advocate's request in the case of a discipline or discharge is that the arbitrator grant the grievance, reinstate the employee with full back pay and benefits and restoration of all seniority, and expunge the grievant's work record.

The employer's conclusion is typically simpler and more routine. The employer usually asks the arbitrator simply to deny the grievance. Regardless of the thrust of the final petition, the main point is for each advocate to make a clear and unequivocal statement of the award the arbitrator is being asked to grant.

# 15

# Posthearing Briefs

As indicated in the last chapter, the predominant method of presenting closing arguments is in the form of written briefs filed by the advocates after the close of the hearing. Such a procedure allows both parties to carefully review the record, research applicable cases, marshall the supporting facts, and effectively present their arguments. Only particularly articulate advocates are capable of making more effective oral arguments than those made in written form.

## ARRANGEMENTS FOR WRITTEN BRIEFS

Typically, at the close of the evidentiary portion of the hearing, the arbitrator will ask the parties how they wish to argue their respective cases. Upon learning that one side or the other desires to file a written brief, the arbitrator will invariably rule that both sides are to file briefs and will proceed to establish a date on which briefs are to be received by the arbitrator. A normal period of time is four to six weeks following the close of the hearing or, when a transcript has been made of the hearing, about thirty days following the receipt of copies of the transcript by the advocates. Different arbitrators will suggest different periods of time, and the personal calendars of the advocates will usually be taken into consideration by the arbitrator in setting the time for filing briefs.

Some arbitrators are less controlling and are willing to allow the advocates to establish by agreement the date on which briefs are to be filed. In such cases the arbitrator will state to the advocates, ''I will direct the parties to agree on a date on which briefs are due to be filed with me. Please notify me of the date you have set so that I may know when to expect them.''

## Reply Briefs

Occasionally, one party or the other will request the opportunity to file reply briefs, that is, a second set of briefs by each side responding to the arguments of the other side. Arbitrators are generally loathe to grant this right but will sometimes do it out of deference to the parties. When an advocate believes that his or her presentation of arguments will be enhanced by filing a second brief, the request should be accompanied by supporting arguments. The most persuasive supporting arguments will be based on one or more of the following reasons:

- The facts and/or contractual arguments in the case are so extensive and complex that a single set of briefs will be inadequate to give the arbitrator full argumentation of the parties.
- New or novel arguments are likely to emerge in the initial briefs, and it would be fairer to the parties to have an opportunity to respond.
- Arguments advanced in the grievance procedure were not fully explained, and additional time and articulation of arguments will be necessary in the briefs.
- The principles and potential liability (recovery) at stake in the case are so significant to the parties, that a very thorough briefing of the issues is warranted.

# PREPARING TO WRITE A BRIEF

A very important aspect of writing an effective brief is thorough preparation in advance of writing the brief. Summarizing the evidence, formulating the arguments, researching the authorities, and pulling all of this information together into a coherent package requires a substantial amount of time and effort.

## Reviewing the Transcript

The task of preparing a posthearing brief is significantly eased if a transcript of the hearing has been made. Not only have the advocate and the advocate's team been relieved of taking copious notes of the testimony during the hearing, but the advocate has a distinct advantage of having the entire body of evidence (verbatim and in the same order as presented in the hearing) available in one package. Of course, when a transcript has been prepared, both sides may order a copy, and there is no distinct advantage to either side. If one side ordered the reporter without the concurrence of the other, the ordering advocate will have a distinct advantage in preparing a brief, unless the opposing advocate changes his or her mind and decides to order a copy of the transcript (in which case the costs of the reporter's appearance and the production of a transcript normally would be shared equally). An advocate who does not avail himself or herself of the opportunity to have a transcript in order to prepare a brief when the transcript will be used by the other side and the arbitrator is putting his or her party at a distinct disadvantage.

The advocate should thoroughly review the transcript and make notes of all significant testimony and of all other significant evidence. Some advocates prefer to make notes on the transcript itself, whereas others prefer to keep a separate list of important pieces of evidence, noting the page number (and even the number of the line on the page) where the significant evidence appears. The author prefers the latter. In fact, the separate list of significant evidence can be made more useful by organizing the evidence on the basis of categories of evidence. A common manner of organizing evidence is to list the issues involved in the case, the transcript page number or the page and line numbers, and the witnesses or exhibits that revealed that evidence. The following is an example of the way in which this can be done

*Arbitrability*
45:22—Williams: never negotiated wage classification system
73:3—Filoberto: declined to discuss grievance at step 1
Er.Ex.5—letter from Filoberto to Beemis rejecting grievance

*Merits—Job didn't change*
101—Phillips: same duties
140:10—Senara: new equip. but same process
197—Waters: [adverse] comments by vendor re: new skills
222:3—Filoberto: descrip. of job overall and contrast

The purpose of taking notes of the transcript is to collect all pertinent points in the evidentiary case (whether favorable or unfavorable to the advocate's case) in such a manner as to be able to retrieve them promptly when drafting the brief.

## Organization of the Brief

The advocate embarking on writing a brief needs to determine just how it should be organized. Some advocates prefer to write the brief in much the same style as an oral argument, commencing with the issues to be decided and presenting the facts and arguments supporting the advocate's position on each issue. These advocates provide more or less a stream of consciousness argumentation. It is almost as if the advocate made an oral argument to the arbitrator, and this argument was transcribed into the form of a brief.

Other advocates prefer a style that mirrors that of a trial or appellate brief. This type of brief is much more organized, and presents the issues, arguments, and case authorities in a rather organized and logical sequence. Although the specific form of good briefs following this format varies somewhat among advocates, the major sections of a brief that are styled along the lines of an appellate brief are more or less as follows.

1. Introduction
2. Issues presented
3. Summary of facts
4. Pertinent contract provisions
5. Arguments (including case authority)
6. Conclusion

Each of these segments of the brief will be discussed, with examples, in the following sections of this chapter. The same case will be used to illustrate the various parts of a normal brief. The sample brief is one filed by a union representative and involves a case in which the employer did not fill a position for a period of a week during the vacation of the employee who normally occupied that position. It is based loosely on the facts of a case reported in *Labor Arbitration Reports.*[1]

### Cover Page

Although there is no requirement for a cover page on a brief, much less a specific format for the cover page, experienced advocates and labor lawyers typically use a stylized format for the cover page of a brief, an example of which is shown in Figure 15-1.

---

[1]Ladish Co., 100 LA 690 (Redel, 1992)

**Figure 15-1.**
**Sample Cover Page**

**Able N. Advocate**
**International Representative**
**Industrial Workers International Union**
**325 Solidarity Place**
**Unity, NY 12345**
**(212) 345-6789**

<br>

BEFORE THE HONORABLE SOLOMON WISDOM

Local 25, Industrial Workers International Union,      )
                                                    )
                                                    )
        and                                         )
                                                    )
                                                    )
                                                    )
Reliable Manufactured Products, Inc.--Topeka Plant     )
                                                    )
                                                    )
                                                    )
                                                    )
Re:   Grievance Concerning the Scheduling of a Bay 5    )
        Operator to Cover an Absence Due to Vacation    )
_____)

<br>

Post-Hearing Brief Filed On Behalf of
Industrial Workers International Union, Local 25

<br>

April 5, 1996

## Introduction

The essential purpose of the introduction is to set the scene for the arbitrator and to reorient him or her about the general nature of the case. The reader may question why the arbitrator, after sitting through the entire hearing and possibly taking notes, would need to be reoriented. It should be kept in mind that successful arbitrators hear scores of cases during the course of a year. Frequently, the time lapse from the close of the hearing to the reading of the briefs by the arbitrator can be two to three months. During that period the arbitrator may have heard dozens of other cases. The arbitrator is likely to have forgotten many aspects of the case and may likely confuse some aspects of the case with details of other cases he or she has heard. A succinct, simple summary of the nature and key aspects of the case will be very useful. The following is an example of such an introduction.

### INTRODUCTION

This arbitration comes before the Honorable Donald Wisdom, Arbitrator, and involves a dispute between Reliable Manufactured Products Incorporated (hereinafter "RMPI" or the "Company") and Industrial Workers Union, Local 25 (hereinafter "IWU" or the "Union"). This dispute arises under the parties' 1994–97 collective bargaining agreement (hereinafter the "Contract" or the "Agreement") (Jt. Exh. 1) and concerns the obligation of the Company to schedule employees to fill a vacancy in its Heat Treat Department to cover a job left vacant by an employee who was on vacation during the week of July 12–19, 1995. The Union relies on the plain meaning of the labor agreement, the past practice of the parties, the history of bargaining of the language at issue, and the safety and health interests of the employees involved.

## Issues Presented

An essential element in a labor arbitration case is a statement of the issues to be decided by the arbitrator. In Chapter 7 some attention was devoted to this aspect of the case. If the parties stipulated to the issues, the task is a simple one, that is, to merely reproduce in the brief the wording of the stipulation. If each side submitted different issues, leaving to the arbitrator to decide between them, then some time should be spent in this section arguing why the arbitrator should accept the advocate's version of the issue statement.

If at the time of writing a brief the issues have not been established, a significant error has been made by someone (likely the arbitrator, for it is the responsibility of the arbitrator to establish the issues prior to, or during, the hearing). In any event, if the issue(s) has not been established a significant task faces the brief writer. It will be necessary to set out in some detail the rationale of why the brief writer's version of the issue should be accepted. Typically, in a case of contract interpretation a statement of the issue begins with the phrase, ''Did the employer violate the labor agreement when it ...?'' In a discipline or discharge case the introductory phrase is ''Was the [discharge, suspension, reprimand, demotion] of (name of grievant) for just cause?'' Both of these types of issues should always be followed by the question, ''If yes [no in the case of just cause], what remedy should be granted?'' An advocate for the employer or the union who proposes issues phrased in this fashion will be on solid ground.

Applying this to the sample case used throughout this chapter, which involves the employer's decision not to fill a position that was unoccupied due to the vacation of the employee who held that position, the issue might be phrased in one of the following two ways:

> Did RMPI violate the labor agreement by not scheduling an employee as a Bay 5 Operator during the week of July 12–19 when the regular Bay 5 Operator was on vacation? If not, what remedy is appropriate?

or

> Is the Company obligated under the labor agreement and/or past practice to fill jobs that are left vacant due to employees who normally fill those positions being on vacation? If yes, what remedy is appropriate for failure to meet those obligations?

The reader should note the different approaches to the same issue. The first version limits the decision to a specific instance whereas the second version is much broader and would apply to a variety of situations in which jobs would be left unfilled due to a vacation. Employers would usually prefer the first version, whereas unions would usually prefer the second.

## *Summary of the Facts*

In order to set the framework for presenting arguments, it is useful to provide the arbitrator with a summary of the facts in the case as established through evidence adduced in the hearing. The challenging aspect of this portion of the brief is to present the facts in a manner that fairly sets forth all relevant evidence but that also lays a foundation for the arguments about to be made. In other words, all pertinent facts are reviewed but are arranged in such a way that they support the brief writer's case. The brief writer must be careful, however, not to slant the facts so much to support the arguments that the factual statements sound like the arguments. If the facts are presented in an obviously biased fashion and if pertinent facts that do not support the brief writer's arguments are omitted, the brief and its author will lose credibility.

Another challenge is to present enough of the facts to be complete
and persuasive, but not so many that the arbitrator gets bored or is
distracted from the main feature of the brief—the arguments. Nonessen-
tial details and overly long repetition of testimony is to be avoided. The
facts should be covered sufficiently to draw the arbitrator's attention to
the key elements in the case and should draw together disparate pieces of
evidence from different witnesses so that the arbitrator can see the thrust
of the arguments that are to follow. The statement of facts should be as
objective as possible and should avoid obvious argumentation. Whatever
arguments come through in this section should be subtle.

Particular thought and attention should be devoted to the organization of the statement of facts. In some cases an order that follows a
chronology of events (either the latest being first or the earliest being
first) is a logical one. In other cases it may be best to follow the order of
the evidence as it was presented in the hearing. In still others it may make
more sense to recount the most important evidence first, followed by that
of lesser import. It should always be kept in mind that the advocate wants
to simplify and clarify the facts as much as possible for the arbitrator,
without overlooking necessary details and complexities. The more the
arbitrator is able to understand the facts in the case, the greater likelihood
there is that he or she will accept the arguments made by the party that
presented the facts in the simpler and clearer fashion.

## Summary of the Facts

The facts in this case are quite simple and relatively undisputed.

The dispute occurred in the Heat Treat Department of the plant. This
department is responsible for heat treating steel rods to impart metallurgi-
cal properties that enhance their performance under stress. Bay 5 is the
most critical operation of that department (TR 16). Bay 5 is the final stage
of the heat treat process; errors at this stage of the operation can undo the
work of the prior three steps and can cause off-standard material to be
produced, which, if shipped to the customer, can create safety hazards and
result in costly claims (TR 17-18).

During the week of July 12–19 the regular Bay 5 Operator on the
swing shift, Mario Conte, was on vacation. Conte had scheduled that
vacation two months in advance (TR 23). During the week he was on
vacation the Company did not schedule, nor did it assign, any employee to
fill that position. During the week in question Bay 5 operations were
covered with a two-person, rather than the normal three-person, crew. (Un.
Exh. 3)

Production records admitted into evidence reveal that the amount of
production on the shift and week in question was within five percent of the
normal output of that operation (Un. Exhs. 4-6). There is also evidence in
the record from at least two witnesses that failure of Bay 5 to properly treat
materials sent to that department can affect the entire operations of the
plant (TR 44, 65, 72).

The employer in previous negotiations attempted to negotiate language in the labor agreement that would have given it sole discretion to determine staffing levels in the Heat Treat Department (Un. Exh. 9). It failed to obtain the union's agreement to that proposal, and settled for language that obligated it to staff with "a reasonable number of employees." It did not do so during the week in question.

There is testimony of reliable witnesses that failure to schedule a full crew creates significant safety hazards, and that the crew members on duty on swing shift on the nights in question were concerned that there might be a breakdown without sufficient staffing to correct the problem (TR 46, 63).

The record also reflects that there is a longstanding practice in the company's plant to schedule replacements for vacationing employees (TR 75-76). This practice also has been followed in the Heat Treat Department since at least 1988 (Tr 77).

The union filed a timely grievance to protest the company's failure to replace the vacationing Conte (Jt. Exh. 2), the matter was processed through all steps of the grievance procedure (Jt. Exhs. 3, 5), and the issue is properly before the arbitrator.

## Pertinent Contract Provisions

Some advocates routinely reproduce in their briefs the sections of the contract and/or side letters of agreement or other agreements that pertain to the case. Other advocates prefer to address the pertinent contract provisions in the course of making their arguments. The advantage of a separate listing of these provisions is that the arbitrator can easily refer to that section of the brief, rather than hunting for them in the argument section of the brief or going through the contract itself.

The following paragraphs illustrate the principal contract provisions that would apply in the case of the nonreplaced Bay 5 Heat Treat Operator, and the manner in which it would appear in the brief.

### Relevant Contract Provisions

The following provisions of the labor agreement (Jt. Exh. 1) are relevant to this case

#### ARTICLE II
#### PRINCIPLES UNDERLYING THIS AGREEMENT

... In addition, the parties to this agreement agree that they will cooperate to the fullest extent possible to achieve high quality production and a safe work environment, taking into account to the fullest extent possible the needs of the Company, the Union, and the Employees.

#### ARTICLE XV
#### HEAT TREAT DEPARTMENT

Section 6. Classifications will be structured as group bid and employees will be given primary assignments as defined below:
1. Heating Specialist
2. Building #2
3. Building #66

4. Bays 5 & 6
5. Bays 1, 2, & 3
6. Bay 4
7. Auxiliary

Employees holding primary assignments in 1 through 6 above will report to their primary assignment at the beginning of their shift unless notified by Heat Treat Supervision to report to the daily lineup.

Section 7. ... Each classification and primary assignment shall have manpower levels that provide a reasonable number of employees to safely and efficiently perform the tasks of the position and the department.

ARTICLE XX
VACATIONS

Section 10. Employees shall indicate their preference for vacation time off no less than thirty (30) days in advance of the vacation period requested in order that the Company will have sufficient time to schedule a replacement.

EXHIBIT A-JOB CLASSIFICATIONS AND WAGE RATES
HEAT TREAT DEPARTMENT

...
Bay 5
Operator            $14.50
Asst. Operator       12.87
Discharge Tender     10.05

## Arguments

The heart and soul of a brief is contained in the arguments section. This is where the advocate has the opportunity (and the obligation) to explain to the arbitrator why the decision should be in the brief writer's favor.

The author's preferred method of making arguments is to separate each argument or theory of the case from the others and to make each argument under a separate heading. The breakdown of arguments is usually somewhat arbitrary with most arguments overlapping one another. Nevertheless, by separating the arguments and differentiating the theories on which the case rests it is usually easier to catch the attention of the arbitrator and to make a more persuasive presentation.

Effective argumentation usually consists of the right blending of rational arguments, references to evidence in the case and references to language in the labor agreement, all of which should unite to support the basic positions being advanced. In some cases, arguments made by the other side can be refuted as part of the brief writer's own arguments, whereas in other cases such refutations need to be stated as independent arguments. Usually, when the other side has one or more particularly strong arguments, it is best to refute them as separate arguments. In refuting the other side's positions, however, arguments that are derogatory or demeaning of the other side should be avoided. It is always better to try to persuade an arbitrator by superior logic, facts, and arguments than by cavalierly berating the other side.

In our sample case some of the arguments in the union's brief would be made as follows

### ARGUMENTS

A. THE LABOR AGREEMENT CLEARLY OBLIGATES THE COMPANY TO FILL JOBS THAT ARE VACANT DUE TO EMPLOYEES GOING ON VACATION. THE JOB OF BAY 5 OPERATOR WAS NOT FILLED DURING THE WEEK OF JULY 12–19.

The labor agreement in Articles II, XV, and XX leave no doubt that the parties intended to require the filling of all jobs that are vacant when the employees filling those jobs go on vacation.

Article II establishes that. . . .

B. THE LONG-STANDING AND CONSISTENTLY FOLLOWED PRACTICE OF THE COMPANY IN FILLING JOBS LEFT VACANT BY EMPLOYEES ON VACATION CLARIFIES WHATEVER QUESTION THERE MIGHT BE IN THE CONTRACT.

Union witnesses Brady and Majeski testified that in their 30 combined years in the plant, the employer has always filled the jobs of those employees who went on vacation. Brady testified that in 1989 the company was about to let the job of Furnace Tender go unfilled when the employee holding that position was going on vacation. The company reversed its position, and filled the job (TR 88)....

C. THE HISTORY OF BARGAINING ON THE LANGUAGE OF ARTICLE XV-HEAT TREAT DEPARTMENT SHOWS THAT THE COMPANY UNSUCCESSFULLY ATTEMPTED TO GET LANGUAGE THAT WOULD HAVE GIVEN IT AN UNFETTERED RIGHT TO NOT FILL ALL JOBS. IT NOW ATTEMPTS TO GET IN ARBITRATION WHAT IT COULD NOT GET THROUGH NEGOTIATIONS.

The testimony of Joe Sparks, former President and Chief Negotiating Spokesman for Local 25, concerning the 1991 labor contract negotiations over the language at issue in this case leaves no doubt that the employer unsuccessfully sought to obtain a change that would have given it the right to not fill the Bay 5 Operator position as it did in this case (TR 102-104). Sparks credibly testified that...

D. FAILURE TO FILL THE JOB OF BAY 5 OPERATOR DURING THE WEEK OF JULY 12–19 CREATED A POTENTIAL SAFETY HAZARD THAT NOT ONLY VIOLATED THE LABOR AGREEMENT, BUT JEOPARDIZED THE SAFETY OF THE OTHER CREW MEMBERS OF BAY 5.

The Company has recognized that it takes three crew members to operate each Heat Treat Bay. This is evidenced by the fact that it has bid a three person crew for this work for more than twenty years. Now it argues that during a particular week when a crew member happens to be on vacation that it does not need the third crew member. Assistant Operator, Paul Ogden, testified without refutation that on the night of July 14 the Heat Treat generator overheated and caused a fire in the entry chamber of the Bay (TR 133-134). It was only the accidental presence of the Heat Treat Millwright at the time that prevented a major accident....

## Use of Reported Case Authorities

In the arguments section of the brief many advocates often refer to decisions in reported cases that support the arguments being made. These cases do not constitute precedent in any legal sense. They simply reflect the thinking of other arbitrators in similar factual settings and/or comparable contractual issues. References to other decisions is entirely proper, and in order to use them for argumentation it is not necessary for those decisions to have been introduced into evidence or even to have been mentioned in the hearing at all.

In the sample case of the Heat Treat job vacancy, references to case authority in the argument section of the brief might be handled as follows

> Reported arbitration cases in which employers have attempted to circumvent the labor agreement by staffing operations with less than the agreed upon number of crew members reveals that such actions have been in violation of the applicable labor agreements. *Cooper/T. Smith Stevedoring Co. and Longshoremen, ILA, Local 3033,* 99 LA 297 (Massey, 1992); *Bethlehem Steel Corp. and Steelworkers,* 92 L 553 (Witt, 1988); *Pacific Crown Distributors and Teamsters, Local 70,* 72 LA 1042 (Boner, 1979)

The weight likely to be given by the arbitrator to decisions in reported cases will vary significantly from one arbitrator to another, depending on the parties involved in the case from which the decision resulted, how similar the facts and contract language in the cited cases are to the case at hand, and the willingness of the particular arbitrator to consider other decisions. When the decision relied upon by the brief writer involves the same parties and same labor agreement, the arbitrator is likely to treat it with great deference, if not to treat it as binding precedent. When other parties were involved, but the facts and/or contract language at issue are the same or very similar, most arbitrators will give them some consideration, but certainly will not feel bound by such decisions. When the arbitrator rendering the cited decision is a well-known and respected person in the labor arbitration field, the decision is likely to be given more weight than one from a novice or otherwise unknown arbitrator.

Lawyers who have been schooled in the legal principle of stare decisis, that is, that legal principles established by higher courts in published opinions in the same jurisdiction in prior cases involving the same issues under similar facts must be followed, will find that this concept has little or no applicability to labor arbitration. Only a small proportion of arbitration decisions are ever published. Moreover, with the exception of cases involving the same parties, the same labor contract language, and the same issues, there is no higher authority that arbitrators are required to follow.[2] Consequently, with the exception noted in the previous sentence, each case may be judged on its own merits, irrespective of prior arbitration awards.

Notwithstanding the freedom arbitrators have to disregard other arbitration decisions, many arbitrators are willing to consider and be significantly influenced by other decisions. This is particularly true when the labor agreement is silent on the issues in the case and when the evidence adduced in the hearing is more or less evenly balanced. In such situations arbitrators are searching for guidance, for a standard, or for some rational basis on which to rest a conclusion. In such cases, other decisions can prove very useful. Not only may the result in the previous case be significant, but, often more important, the logic and rationale adopted by the arbitrator in the prior case can prove enlightening to the arbitrator.

## Conclusion

The conclusion of an arbitration brief is simply included to tie a ribbon around the package. It is usually relatively short, and highlights the major points made earlier in the brief.

Going back to Heat Treat case example, a typical conclusion in the union's brief might read as follows:

CONCLUSION

There could hardly be a clearer case of a contract violation. The Company made an ill-advised decision not to replace Mr. Conte during the week he was on vacation. The decision was obviously motivated by a desire to save the company money. The Company did not make a conscious decision that it did not need three employees to operate Bay 5 of the Heat Treat Department. Such a decision could not have been rationally made in light of the operating conditions that existed that week. The Company and the Union have entered into a labor agreement spelling out

---

[2]Arbitrators are generally free to apply their own interpretation and rationale to cases before them, with little or no obligation to follow precedent.

the staffing for the Bay 5 operating crew and stipulating that when employees go on vacation the Company must have sufficient notice to schedule a replacement. These agreements obligate the Company to schedule replacements when crew members go on vacation. The Company has revealed its understanding of that obligation by following that practice for years and years.

Additionally, the Company has agreed that it will staff positions with a reasonable number of employees to perform the work *safely*. Without question, the Company has entered into a contractual obligation to have a three person crew on Bay 5 of the Heat Treat Department whenever it operates. It did not do this during the week of July 12–19.

In summation, the Arbitrator should rule...

# ADDITIONAL POINTS TO REMEMBER IN WRITING BRIEFS

There are some additional points that advocates should keep in mind in preparing a written brief.

## Keep It as Brief as Possible

Perhaps the greatest misnomer in the practice of law and labor arbitration is the word "brief," because most briefs are exactly the opposite. Some advocates believe that the weight accorded to a brief by an arbitrator is directly proportional to the actual weight of the pages that comprise the brief. This is definitely not the case. What is usually most important is the clarity of the overall presentation of evidence and the persuasiveness of the arguments. This is not to suggest that important points should be left out in order to meet some predetermined page length. What is suggested is to make the points as succinctly as possible. An arbitrator who grows tired of reading a brief will lose interest and not fully absorb the points that the brief writer is attempting to make. Moreover, an extremely lengthy brief with but a few salient points may suggest to the arbitrator that the brief writer is simply blowing smoke, trying to mask the truth with a flurry of words. A reasonably short brief that makes the important points in a clear and convincing fashion has a distinct advantage over a lengthy brief in which the key points are lost in a plethora of words.

## Include Detailed References to Evidence and Case Authorities

In cases when the hearing has been transcribed and a transcript prepared it is usually effective to make references to the testimony of witnesses and to other information and documents admitted into evidence. Thus, when a particular aspect of a witness's testimony is being referred to in the brief, either by way of narrative or by a direct quotation, the reference should be followed by a specific citation, or reference to the portion of the record in which the evidence is contained. A common means of doing so is to include in parenthesis, immediately following the passage or description, an abbreviation of the transcript and a number indicating the page. A common abbreviation for transcript is "TR" followed by the page number. For example:

> Unrebutted evidence of Joe Sparks was that in the 1991 labor contract negotiations the Company's chief spokesman, Ralph Washington, stated on a number of occasions that the Company had no intention of trying to "save pennies in not filling jobs for short periods of time," but that it needed language in the labor agreement that would give it the right to make "crew readjustments" as it felt necessary (TR 89-90).

Some advocates prefer to provide the arbitrator with more precise direction to the referenced evidence and include reference to the lines of the page in which the evidence begins and ends. They commonly do this by listing the line number following the page number and separating them by a colon. Thus, the above quoted passage from the transcript would read as follows:

> but it needed language in the labor agreement that would give it the right to make "crew readjustments" as it felt necessary (TR 89:16–90:22).

When the reference is to an exhibit in the case, the brief writer should insert, immediately following the reference to that evidence, the number of the exhibit (and if a transcript has been made, the number of the page on which the exhibit was entered into evidence). For example:

> It cannot be reasonably disputed that the Company was fully aware of the Union's opposition to leaving jobs unfilled during vacations, particularly when it involved a safety-sensitive positions. (Un.Exhs. 3 and 5)

If reported arbitration decisions are being relied on as persuasive authority, the transcript should include the names of the parties and a citation to the volume and page number of the reporting service, the arbitrator issuing the award, and the year in which the award was handed down. For example:

> The rule applied consistently by labor arbitrators is that when a labor agreement provides that a specific number of employees are to be assigned to an operation, it is a contract violation to employ less. *Cooper/T. Smith Stevedoring Co. and Longshoremen, ILA, Local 3033,* 99 LA 297 (Massey, 1992)

When there is a list of several case citations, it is proper form to list the most recent cases first.

If there are not too many decisions cited in the brief, it is a good idea to include a photocopy of each case relied on and to include those cases in an appendix to the brief or in a separate bound packet properly labeled and/or indexed to assist the arbitrator in reading them. If the decisions cited are too numerous to copy and include with the brief, it is advisable to include copies of the most important decisions. In either event, the full case title and citation should be included in the text of the brief and, if a copy is included, a reference as to where the photocopy may be found in the brief (e.g., Appendix A-3).

## Include Selected Reproductions of Recorded Testimony

There are times when a description of a witness's testimony by the brief writer cannot adequately capture the essence of the importance and impact of the evidence. This is particularly true when a witness has given contradictory testimony, has stated facts in a particularly forceful way, or has revealed a particular intention or state of mind that is important in the case. To say that a witness made an admission against the interest of the party for whom he or she was testifying is not nearly as persuasive as to reproduce the damaging testimony verbatim. In order to do this most effectively, it is necessary for a transcript of the hearing to have been made. For example [union brief]:

> The inequity and error of the Company's decision to not fill the Heat Treat Operator vacancy was verified by the testimony of its Bay 4-5 Supervisor, Henry Mancusco. He testified on cross-examination as follows:
>
> *Q.* Therefore, is it fair to say that nothing was different about the operations, and the manpower needs, in Bay 5 during the week of July 12–19 than there was during the previous week or, for that matter, during any other week that year other than the fact that there was a two person crew rather than a three person crew?
>
> *A.* I suppose that's true.
>
> *Q.* Do you think that's fair?
>
> *Er. Adv.* Objection, asks for an opinion, and is argumentative.
>
> *Arb.* Objection overruled.
>
> *A.* I can't say it's fair, but that's what management decided.
>
> (TR 93: 6–22)

When such testimony is reproduced verbatim it is typically single spaced and indented, and it is advisable to include a reference to the transcript, preferably showing the beginning and ending line numbers (of the page of the transcript) from which the quote was extracted. Quoting specific portions of a witness's testimony can be particularly effective where that witness has given contradicting testimony. For example, "Initially, the witness said '. . .'. Later, however, the witness testified testified '. . .'." The witness is not to be believed.

The brief writer should take care not to reproduce testimony too frequently in a brief. It should be assumed that the arbitrator has read the transcript, and the purpose of the reproduced testimony is simply to draw the arbitrator's attention to particularly significant portions of testimony. The more it is done, the less likely it is that the arbitrator will be impressed by the quoted testimony. Similarly, the shorter the reproduced testimony the better. It is usually disadvantageous to reproduce lengthy excerpts of testimony. Arbitrators tend to lose interest unless the passage is particularly engrossing.

When quoting particularly significant passages from a witness's testimony, it is often useful to italicize or underline particular words and phrases. When this is done, it is necessary to add a brief phrase to alert the arbitrator that the emphasis was added by the brief writer, not the speaker or the hearing reporter. The phrase "emphasis added" or "emphasis supplied" is usually employed for this purpose. For example:

> A. *I can't say it's fair,* but that's what management decided.
> (TR 110:7-12; emphasis supplied)

## Organize Evidence to Enhance Understanding and Persuasiveness

In many cases evidence is admitted in a haphazard and disjointed fashion (not necessarily by any fault of the advocates). In such cases it is frequently in a sequence that does not lead to easy analysis or persuasive argument. The advocate needs to organize and clarify throughout the brief. This often means organizing facts in a chronological or other systematic order. It may mean making lists or preparing charts or graphs that display evidence in an orderly, logical, and effective way. This should be accompanied by a similarly logical presentation of arguments. In so doing, the brief writer must be careful not to add evidence, but merely to organize and present it in a different and more understandable way.

In assembling and organizing the facts and arguments in such a manner, the brief writer needs to have command of the evidence and the issues, and needs to put himself or herself in the position of the arbitrator. What aspects of the case may be confusing or poorly understood by the arbitrator? What manner of presentation of evidence will be most persuasive to the arbitrator? What are the factors on which the arbitrator is most likely to focus? When these have been identified, they can be woven into a tight, systematic, and persuasive fabric. This is the essence of a winning brief.

## If a Brief is Lengthy, Prepare a Table of Contents

Advocates need to be sensitive to the time pressures on an arbitrator and the fact that deliberation on and preparation of an opinion and award may be done over an extended period of time and be subject to many interruptions. Consequently, arbitrators often need a road map to lead them through the brief and the evidence in the case. By preparing a table of contents of the brief, including the main and supporting arguments, the brief writer can assist the arbitrator in finding key points in the brief. The following is an example of such a table of contents in our job vacancy example:

| *Section of the Brief* | *Page* |
|---|---|
| I.    INTRODUCTION | 1 |
| II.   ISSUES PRESENTED | 3 |
| III.  FACTS | 5 |
| IV.   RELEVANT CONTRACT PROVISIONS | 8 |
| V.    ARGUMENTS | |
| A.    THE LABOR AGREEMENT CLEARLY OBLIGATES THE COMPANY TO FILL JOBS THAT ARE LEFT VACANT DUE TO EMPLOYEES GOING ON VACATION. THE JOB OF BAY 5 OPERATOR WAS NOT FILLED DURING THE WEEK OF JULY 12–19. | 11 |
| B.    THE LONG-STANDING AND CONSISTENTLY FOLLOWED PRACTICE OF FILLING BEHIND VACATIONING EMPLOYEES CLARIFIES WHATEVER QUESTION THERE MIGHT BE IN THE CONTRACT. | 16 |
| C.    THE HISTORY OF BARGAINING ON THE LANGUAGE OF ARTICLE XV-HEAT TREAT DEPARTMENT, ... | 21 |
| VI.   CONCLUSION | 32 |

## Stress Equity and Fairness, Not Just Facts and Contract Language

Arbitrators are required to abide by the labor agreement and to decide issues based on the language of the agreement as applied to a particular set of facts. Nevertheless, arbitrators are human beings, and, other things being equal, they prefer to decide cases in favor of the most deserving party. In doing so they must nevertheless follow the labor agreement's provisions. The lesson in this for the brief writer is to show the arbitrator not only where the language of the agreement favors the advocate's side, but where the equities favor the same result. A frequently overlooked skill in brief writing is moving the arbitrator's heart as well as his or her mind.

This means that all of the rational arguments in favor of the brief writer's position should be laid out first. Following this, the brief writer should marshal all the logical, ethical, moral, humanitarian and equitable reasons supporting a decision in his or her favor. The thrust is to show the arbitrator that a ruling in the writer's favor is mandated by common sense, fairness, and the labor agreement.

## Stress the Burden of Proof Where Possible

Brief writers should not overlook which party has the burden of proof in any particular case and should show (when possible) how that burden favors their side. In a contract interpretation case the union (if it filed the grievance) carries the burden of proof. Consequently, in writing a brief, employer advocates should stress that the union carries the burden of proof that the labor agreement has been violated. Similarly, union advocates need to emphasize that in discipline and discharge cases employers bear the burden of proof.[3] Moreover, the advocate should address the quantum of proof argument in a way that best favors its case. For example, union advocates should argue for the highest quantum of proof (i.e., beyond a reasonable doubt) in discharge cases when that is credible, and employer advocates should stress the lowest quantum of proof (i.e., substantial evidence or preponderance of the evidence) in such cases. Of course, the advocate should be prepared to substantiate, through case references as well as reasoning, why such a quantum of proof is appropriate in that case.

Burden of proof and quantum of proof arguments may be lost on arbitrators who do not have a legal background. For this reason, spending some time to cite cases or learned authorities may be necessary to orient the arbitrator on the significance of the appropriate party carrying its burden of proof and the weight of that proof. Because so many cases are so evenly balanced on the amount of evidence on both sides, an arbitrator who is torn between both sides may very well be persuaded by burden of proof and quantum of proof arguments.

---

[3] It is also important in discharge and discipline cases for union advocates to indicate the level of the burden that should be met such as ''proof beyond a reasonable doubt,'' ''a preponderance of the evidence,'' etc.

## Address Remedy

As discussed under the segment above dealing with oral argument, it is vital that brief writers address the remedy sought. Too often, advocates become so enmeshed in the facts in the case and the thought of winning or losing that they overlook the important aspect of the relief sought in the case. The party bringing the grievance is the one seeking a remedy, and this is invariably the union. The relief or remedy sought in the case should be fully laid out in the brief. Not only should the language of, and experience under, the labor agreement be used as a basis for awarding a complete remedy, but the brief writer should set out all the reasons why the relief sought is justified in terms of a fair means of correcting the damage that has been done by the violation of the labor agreement.

Sometimes employer advocates are reluctant to address the question of an appropriate remedy for fear of being thought to have conceded a violation of the labor agreement. In other words, because the employer has argued vehemently that no labor contract violation has occurred and that any discussion of remedy is therefore moot, they sometimes feel that addressing remedy in a brief may be interpreted by the arbitrator as a concession of the possibility that a contract violation may have occurred. That fear should be cast aside, for failure to address remedy in the written argument could, in the event of a decision adverse to the employer, result in the imposition of a remedy that goes far beyond anything that the employer could have anticipated.

The way for a responding party to avoid the discomfort of addressing remedy without making any concessions on the merits is to take a "what if," "assuming for the sake of argument," *(assuming arguendo)* approach. The following is an example of this approach in a hypothetical case of discharge for theft of the employer's property in which the union's defense is that the employee did not realize that removal of goods was against the rules because he had seen so many other employees do the same without adverse consequences.

[From the Employer's brief]

As has just been outlined in great detail above, the weight of testimony and other evidence produced in this case prove conclusively that the grievant, Nick O. Teen, stole or misappropriated company property and, furthermore, covered up his acts with a series of lies to his supervisor. Despite the overwhelming and uncontroverted evidence establishing the guilt of the grievant in this case, the union argues that discharge is not appropriate and that the arbitrator should reinstate him with full back pay.

Assuming solely for the sake of argument, and solely for the completeness of argumentation, that the arbitrator were to find that Mr.

Teen had not stolen the property for which he has been charged, it is still contended by the employer that reinstatement with back pay is completely inappropriate. There is no conflict whatsoever in the evidence presented by both parties that Mr. Teen lied to his supervisor at least twice in connection with this incident. Even if the arbitrator were to find that the grievant had not violated the labor contract by theft, the most liberal remedy that should be provided is reinstatement with no back pay. The failure of the grievant to be forthright with his supervisor and his thwarting of the investigation of this matter should not be rewarded with back pay in any amount.

Having made this argument, the employer nevertheless insists that a remedy in this case is a moot issue since there is no plausible or comprehensible way to find that the grievant was not terminated for just cause.

## PROCEDURES FOR FILING BRIEFS

Arrangements for filing briefs are usually made at the close of the hearing. The arbitrator will either issue instructions to the parties on how and when briefs are to be filed or, more commonly, discuss with them their preferred arrangements and make a decision on the arrangements after hearing from the respective advocates.

When both parties (and/or both advocates) regularly appear in arbitration cases together, they usually have a mutually acceptable procedure that they follow regarding submission of briefs. Unless that procedure is totally unacceptable to the arbitrator, it will usually be followed. When such an ongoing relationship does not exist, the arbitrator typically will invite the advocates to state their preferences and then direct them on how to proceed, based on common labor arbitration practices. These will now be outlined.

### Length and Format

Usually, there is no specified limit on the length of a brief. Each party risks losing the interest of the arbitrator by filing an unusually long brief, and therefore there is somewhat of a self-policing mechanism at work. Similarly, there is no commonly required format, although the style illustrated in this chapter is widely used. In some cases, the arbitrator may request letter briefs, meaning written arguments in the form of a letter. Rather than adherence to a common business letter (e.g., salutation, body, complementary close), that phrase usually means that the arbitrator is attempting to avoid an unduly long and legalistic brief. If the advocates nevertheless submit a brief in a legal format, the arbitrator will not reject it and will normally not penalize the advocate for submitting arguments in a formal brief format.

## Order and Means of Submission

There are several means by which briefs are customarily submitted to an arbitrator. In most cases each party is limited to filing one brief and both sides are directed to submit them on the same day. Some arbitrators may agree to the parties' desires to file reply briefs, which allow each to submit a second brief after having reviewed the other party's initial brief. The practice of allowing reply briefs is, however, relatively rare in arbitration practice. Reply briefs are used most often in complex cases or when a great deal is at stake. The normal procedure is for one brief to be submitted by each side and dispatched to the arbitrator on the same day.

Filing a brief is usually done by mail (or, frequently, by messenger, overnight, or other expedited delivery) and follows a pattern of delivery of the original to the arbitrator with a copy sent to the opposing side. Some arbitrators direct that briefs in duplicate be sent to the arbitrator, who then forwards a copy to each of the parties following receipt of both briefs. The advantage of having the arbitrator perform the exchange of briefs is to avoid the problem created when one party is early or late in filing its brief, giving the other side an advantage of seeing the other side's brief before sending its own.

In cases held under the auspices of the American Arbitration Association, the briefs are to be filed with the AAA, which takes the responsibility of forwarding them to the arbitrator and to the parties.

An issue that should be addressed by the arbitrator and the advocates is the permissibility of filing briefs via facsimile (fax) transmission. Arbitration advocates are notorious procrastinators and often do not complete the brief writing until the last day. Because fax transmissions are so common in business and law practice, the use of this technology for filing briefs should be addressed. Many arbitrators prohibit the use of fax transmission because the quality of some machines is not high, making for more difficult reading. A possible compromise is to permit a fax transmission to be filed on the due date, with the original to be received the following day by expedited delivery. Whatever arrangements are worked out, it is important that the question of transmission of briefs be addressed at the close of the hearing.

## Time of Submission

One of the key arrangements for filing briefs is the due date. When a transcript of the hearing has been made, it is necessary to get a date or an estimated date from the reporter as to when the transcript will be delivered to the advocates. The period of time for filing is then usually reckoned from the date the transcripts are received by the advocates. In some cases the arbitrator will set a specific date for filing transcripts (on the presumption that the finished transcript will be delivered to the advocates within a specified time period), whereas in other cases the due date is set in reference to the date on which the transcripts are received by the parties (e.g., ''briefs will be due 30 days from receipt of transcripts''). In this case the reporter should be directed by the arbitrator to note on the face of the transcript, or in the cover letter transmitting the transcript, the official date of receipt by the parties, which will then also establish the due date for submission of briefs. Of course, when no transcript has been made of the hearing, a definite filing date can easily be established at the close of the hearing.

### *Meaning of Filing Date*

It is important for the arbitrator to indicate whether the filing date is the day on which the briefs are to be received by the arbitrator or the date on which they are to be dispatched by the advocates (e.g., ''briefs must be received by the arbitrator by x date or ''briefs must be postmarked or sent via overnight delivery by x date''). While this may not appear to be a crucial distinction, it is a potential source of conflict, and one that is easily avoided by a simple clarification.

Some arbitrators are content to allow the advocates themselves to establish the date for filing briefs by simply instructing them to agree on a date for filing briefs after they have each received the transcript. Such a direction is usually accompanied by an instruction to notify the arbitrator in writing of the date they have selected. The problem with this approach is that, in leaving the matter to mutual agreement, one party or the other can forestall the filing date by claiming to have schedule or workload problems. This can give one side or the other an advantage of delaying the arbitrator's decision. When the parties have an ongoing, reasonably amicable relationship, the mutual agreement means of setting a filing date usually works satisfactorily. When that is not the case, it is generally preferable for the arbitrator to establish a firm filing date.

## *Extensions of Time*

Another issue concerning time for filing briefs is that of extensions of time. More often than not, one side or the other encounters a problem that precludes or imposes a hardship in meeting the original filing date. The normal means for obtaining an extension is for the advocate needing the extension to contact the other advocate and seek his or her agreement on a postponement of the submission date. If an agreement is reached, the parties advise the arbitrator of the agreement and seek the arbitrator's concurrence. It is invariably given, unless the arbitrator believes that some third party not represented by either advocate will be seriously disadvantaged by the delay (a possibility that seldom exists). Some arbitrators advise the parties that the arbitrator's concurrence will not be necessary for extensions and that the advocates' agreement to extend the filing date is all that is necessary, provided the arbitrator is advised of the new filing date.

A problem with extensions can occur when one advocate will not agree to the other's request. In such cases the advocate needing the additional time must petition the arbitrator (usually in writing), giving all the reasons why an extension is necessary. The arbitrator will usually allow the advocate opposing the extension to state the reasons for opposition before making a decision on the request. Advocates who oppose requests from the other side for extensions of time are, except in the most compelling situations, being short-sighted. More often than not advocates who are unyielding in agreeing to an extension at one time will find themselves in need of an extension at another time. Their failure to agree in the earlier instance is likely to come back to haunt them.

# 16

# Posthearing Matters

Once the case is submitted, that is, all evidence has been received and all arguments made (either by closing statements or in the form of written briefs), there is *apparently* little to be done except await the arbitrator's decision. The word "apparently" is emphasized, because there are several tasks that should be undertaken between the time when the case is fully submitted and when a decision and award are rendered. This chapter addresses those tasks.

## REVIEWING THE OPPOSING PARTY'S BRIEF

When the parties argue the case in the form of written briefs, the briefs are usually submitted simultaneously. Consequently, neither side has the advantage of reading the other party's brief until its own has been filed. In most cases an advocate's brief has just been sent when the other party's arrives.

### An Untimely Filed Brief

In the rare event the other side is late in its filing, a troublesome problem presents itself. Did the tardy advocate have an opportunity to review the timely advocate's brief before submitting his or her own brief? What was the reason for the tardiness? Has this occurred previously with that particular advocate? In all cases encountered by the

447

author the problem was created by an emergency, a faulty delivery service, or some reason other than an opposing advocate's attempt to gain an advantage. An advocate who encounters a late-filed brief should, nevertheless, determine the cause and ascertain whether the other side gained any advantage from the late filing of a brief. In the unlikely event that it was intentional, that fact should usually be brought to the arbitrator's attention. There is little recourse for the arbitrator other than to disregard the brief in deciding the case. Unless there is no plausible excuse for the late filing, arbitrators are unlikely to sanction the late-filing party.

## Improper Inclusions in a Brief

When the other party's brief arrives, the advocate should read it carefully to determine whether there are any portions of the brief that rely on evidence that was not admitted into the case.[1] Such evidence may have been discovered after the hearing or was available prior to it but was overlooked or disregarded for one reason or another. Sometimes an advocate will rely, intentionally or inadvertently, on evidence that was offered but not admitted into the record. A similar, but distinctly different, problem is presented by a blatant misrepresentation in a brief of the facts as presented in the case. Any of these situations raises an important issue for the advocate who discovers them in the other side's brief: should the new evidence or the blatant misrepresentation be brought to the arbitrator's attention and challenged? That question is not easily answered.

As to new or unadmitted evidence or a blatant misrepresentation, the advocate first needs to assess the damage that could be caused if the arbitrator were to give it some credence. If the matter is minor, does not go to the key issues in the case, and is unlikely to influence a decision, it is usually advisable to ignore the evidence or misrepresentation. Most labor arbitrators are sufficiently sophisticated to detect such inappropriate matters and give them no weight—or even react negatively toward the party that raised them. When, however, the evidence or misrepresentation is not so benign or obvious, it may be necessary to challenge the improper inclusions in the brief.

---

[1] If the brief makes reference to evidence that was offered but not admitted and correctly characterizes the evidence as not admitted, there is little room for objection, because that offer and exclusion are in the record. The problem arises when the brief relies on evidence that was not admitted and does not acknowledge that the evidence was never entered into the record.

### Challenging Evidence that Was Not Admitted

If the problem is evidence that, without question, was not admitted in the case, it is quite appropriate to notify the arbitrator of that fact and request that the arbitrator give no consideration to it. There are several means to carry this out. The first recommended step is for the challenging advocate to contact the opposing advocate, point out the portion of the brief being challenged, and request that the advocate voluntarily withdraw that portion of the brief by requesting the arbitrator in writing to disregard or strike it.

It is unlikely that the advocate will agree to do so, but in the discussion the opposing advocate will likely set forth his or her rationale to justify its inclusion. If the challenging advocate has made a mistake (e.g., a piece of evidence thought to be excluded was actually admitted), this will be a good opportunity to discover the mistake without embarrassment or reprimand by the arbitrator. If the rationale provided by the opposing advocate does not justify the inclusion, the challenging advocate should then write to the arbitrator, with a copy to the opposing side, explaining the inappropriate evidence and moving to have it stricken and given no consideration by the arbitrator. That communication should include a description of the steps the challenging advocate has taken to have the other side correct the problem and the unwillingness of the opposing advocate to cooperate. If the opposing advocate does not respond (which is highly unlikely), the arbitrator will undoubtedly invite the opposing advocate to provide a written response. If the evidence was not entered into the record, either because it was never offered or because it was offered and rejected by the arbitrator, it should be disregarded by the arbitrator in evaluating the merits of the case.

### Challenging a Blatant Misrepresentation

A much different situation is encountered with a brief that contains one or more blatant misrepresentations. If the misrepresentation concerns evidence that was not admitted, the problem is more or less the same as the one described just above, and the same corrective procedure is recommended. If, however, the misrepresentation deals with the manner in which testimony has been characterized, for example, "The employer's plant manager said that he went home early" (when the actual testimony was that he said he went home at 7 P.M.) or misstating facts in the record, such as, "The parties' initial labor contract was negotiated in 1979" (when the record clearly shows it was 1968), it is not usually necessary to bring such matters to the arbitrator's attention. The reason is that such misstatements are so intertwined with argumentation or obviously off base that a challenging advocate may appear to be splitting hairs, reopening the argument, or stating the obvious by a challenge of the other side's veracity. Here again, one must have some confidence in the acuity of the arbitrator and his or her ability to spot such blatant errors or misrepresentations.

Notwithstanding such a recommendation, there may be cases in which the misrepresentation is so significant in its potential impact on the case, and yet so subtle that it may not be spotted by the arbitrator, that an advocate must notify the arbitrator of the misrepresentation. As a general rule, the more subtle the misrepresentation and the greater the impact on the case, the more reason to bring it to the attention of the arbitrator. As with the misstatements regarding evidence, it is advisable to first contact the opposing advocate, point out the error, and request the opposing advocate to correct the error voluntarily. Failing such cooperation, a written communication should be sent to the arbitrator.

## SENDING THE OPPOSING SIDE'S BRIEF TO THE PRINCIPALS

Just as the advocate was advised earlier to send a copy of his or her brief to the principals in the case (i.e., in the case of the union, the grievant, the union shop steward, and perhaps other union representatives, and in the case of the employer, to the supervisors, managers, labor relations representative, or other principal management representative in the case). It is important for them to see what arguments are being made by the other side. In most cases, it will cause them to realize that the case is perhaps not as one-sided and as clear cut as they might have believed. It will also help them to better understand the decision when it is issued.

## DEBRIEFING WITNESSES AND OBSERVERS

### Educational Value to Witnesses and Observers

Most labor arbitration advocates fail to appreciate the educational value of labor arbitration hearings to those who participate. Virtually everything that occurs during a hearing is familiar to the advocate but is usually new and strange to most participants and observers. Witnesses and observers are usually surprised at the thoroughness with which examination and cross-examination are conducted. Matters they thought were fairly obvious or inconsequential often occupy a significant amount of time and interrogation in a hearing. They invariably come to realize the importance of making written records of events and details, rather than committing them to memory.

Advocates should take some time as soon as practicable following a hearing to review with their principals and other observers what occurred in the hearing, the way certain witnesses testified, the importance of certain testimony (as well as the insignificance of other testimony), which strategies and tactics worked well, and which did not. A personnel manager with whom the author worked on numerous arbitration cases would frequently invite to labor arbitration hearings supervisors who had no connection with the grievances being arbitrated, solely as an educational experience. He found that they improved their documentation and perception skills simply from observing how important those skills became when a grievance went before an arbitrator.

## Special Value of Debriefing Witnesses

It is also useful to debrief witnesses following their testimony. Ascertaining from the witnesses which questions, on both direct and cross-examination, they found easy to handle and those that gave them difficulty is a useful way to improve the advocate's own skills. Witnesses also appreciate feedback from the advocate as to what aspects of their testimony were effective and which were not. It is especially important for advocates to thank and congratulate their witnesses immediately following the hearing. Most witnesses are apprehensive about how well they did and sincerely appreciate acknowledgment and appreciation from the advocate.

If this debriefing occurs before the posthearing briefs are filed (and it normally should, because the debriefing is seldom effective if it is delayed more than a few hours, or at most a few days following the end of the hearing), it can also be useful for the advocate to gather additional ideas for preparing the brief. Occasionally, a witness or observer will bring to light or remind an advocate of a fact, piece of evidence, or potential argument that the advocate may have overlooked.

The debriefing is also helpful in correcting any misunderstandings or misperceptions that the witnesses may have about issues in the case, how the arbitrator ruled on certain matters, or other aspects of the case. Correcting such misunderstandings will be useful when the witnesses return to the work place and discuss the case with others. This debriefing can be of real value to the witnesses if and when they are called to testify in another case.

## Correcting Practices or Contract Interpretations

Sometimes matters are brought to light in an arbitration hearing that were unknown or overlooked in the normal day-to-day functioning of the work place. For example, a manager might discover that employees in one department are being required to follow certain procedures that are different than in all other departments, with no rational reason for the difference. Similarly, a union representative may learn that union members are routinely being denied certain privileges to which they are entitled under the labor agreement. Either side might discover a side letter of agreement it did not know existed that could influence the way the labor agreement is interpreted.

This type of information may necessitate changes in the way business is conducted, irrespective of the immediate grievance that has just been heard by the arbitrator. The employer may change some of its practices, forms, or ways of supervising. The union may see avenues for future grievances, documentation that should be kept, and areas for shop steward monitoring. Both sides may discover the need for changes in the labor contract, which they will want to negotiate in the next labor contract negotiations.

The value of a debriefing shortly following the hearing is to raise these issues while they are still fresh in everyone's mind and to take corrective action on a timely basis.

## DEALING WITH NEWLY DISCOVERED EVIDENCE

It is rather well established in labor arbitration that once the evidentiary record in a case has been closed, neither side may introduce any additional evidence. As discussed above, it is improper for a party to attempt to bring in new evidence in a written brief. A dilemma occurs, however, when one party discovers evidence following the close of the evidentiary record, but prior to filing briefs, believes that the evidence could influence the outcome of the case, and wants to have the record reopened for the purpose of having the newly discovered evidence admitted into the record. The question presented is whether there is any exception to the general rule that will permit entering this new evidence into the record after the closing of the case.

## Evaluating Importance and Value of Evidence

An advocate who discovers new evidence following the close of the record first needs to evaluate the evidence in terms of its potential influence on the case. If the evidence is not clearly decisive or likely to affect the outcome of the case, it is not worth undertaking efforts to have it included in the case. Because it is so exceptional for arbitrators to permit such late-discovered evidence into a case, it is only in those situations where the evidence is vitally important to the case that the extraordinary efforts to get it admitted are worth the work.

## Reason for Late Discovery

Assuming that the evidence is sufficiently important and valuable to the advocate's case, the next step is to determine the reason why the evidence was not presented during the hearing. If the cause of the nonproduction of evidence in the hearing was the fault of the party attempting to have it included (e.g., failed to interrogate a possible witness or did not request certain documents from the other side), the chances of getting it admitted will be slim. If, however, the fault lies with the other side (e.g., failure to produce documents that were previously requested, intentional destruction or disguising of evidence), the chances of getting it admitted will be considerably enhanced.

If neither party is at fault (e.g., a witness whose identity or whose possible testimony was not known and could not have reasonably been known by either party at the time of the hearing), the reason for the nonproduction will not be held against the party seeking to have it admitted into evidence. The fact that the nonproduction will not be held against a party does not, however, mean that it will necessarily be admitted. More will normally have to be shown. The most important factors that will persuade an arbitrator to admit it will be its relevance to the case and the reasons why it was not presented earlier. Consequently, a piece of evidence that could turn the tide in a case but was excluded because the opposing side actively thwarted its disclosure prior to the hearing will have a reasonably good chance of being admitted. Anything short of such a compelling reason will likely be met with rejection.

## Relevance and Importance of Evidence

It will be incumbent on the party seeking to include the new evidence to show that it is relevant to the case,[2] that it's omission would seriously prejudice the party seeking its admission (e.g., a neutral witness who can corroborate the testimony of an employee who was fired for misconduct), and that its production will not prejudice the other side (e.g., it will not require the other side to search for additional contradic-

---

[2]United States Potash, 30 LA 1039 (Abernethy, 1958).

tory evidence or be unable to argue about the new evidence without an opportunity for cross-examination).

## Means of Incorporating New Testimony

One of the types of new evidence sometimes sought to be introduced following the close of a hearing is the testimony of a witness whose identity or possession of relevant information was not known at the time of the hearing or of a witness who was not available to testify at the hearing. Assuming that the testimony could be decisive, the question arises as to how such testimony could be entered into the record without completely reopening the hearing.

Some advocates request permission to file affidavits (i.e., written, sworn statements) by the missing or unavailable witness. The obvious problem with affidavits is that the opposing advocate cannot cross-examine the person giving the affidavit. Another means of obtaining such evidence is to schedule a deposition (i.e., an interrogation of a witness by both advocates in the presence of a court reporter). Such a device does not require the presence of the arbitrator or any other witnesses, but, the arbitrator is not available to rule on any evidentiary objections or observe the demeanor of the witness, nor can the arbitrator ask the witness any questions. This problem can be mitigated somewhat if the arbitrator can be available via telephone conference to hear the witness's testimony and rule on objections. A third technique is to reopen the record with testimony given over a telephone conference call with perhaps the witness, the advocates, and the arbitrator all in separate locations. While this allows the arbitrator to rule on objections and to ask questions of the witness, it does not permit him or her to observe the witness first-hand. This last deficiency can be cured by using video conferencing, which in recent years has become much more available and cost effective.

Under all of these techniques testimony by the witness can raise issues that legitimately prompt the opposing advocate to seek to present rebuttal testimony from other witnesses, further prolonging a final disposition of the case.

## Unlikelihood of Reopening the Case

Notwithstanding the showing of one or more of the factors in favor of considering new evidence, the chances of having new evidence admitted into a record are very slim. Arbitrators are loathe to reopen the record once it has been closed. If such new evidence were permitted, it is almost certain that the opposing party would seek to offer additional evidence in rebuttal of the new evidence, resulting in the necessity of reopening the entire hearing. Arbitration's distinct advantages of simplicity and economy are significantly impaired by allowing new evidence after the close of the record. For these reasons an advocate who attempts to have new evidence admitted after the record has been closed has a distinct uphill battle.

## THE DELIBERATIVE PROCESS— BOARDS OF ARBITRATION

The way in which cases are considered and decided varies a great deal from one arbitrator to another. The speed with which cases are decided will obviously be influenced by the complexity of the case and the size of the record and will be significantly influenced by the work habits and caseload of the arbitrator.

The manner and timing of decision making will be distinctly different if the case is heard by a board of arbitration rather than by a single arbitrator. Although a neutral arbitrator on a board of arbitration, that is, the chair of the board, will ultimately decide the case, neutral arbitrators are typically solicitous of input by the partisan members of the board, usually resulting in a longer time from closing the case to issuance of a decision. In addition, the language in the decision and award may be different than in a case heard by a single arbitrator.

The typical practice of a neutral arbitrator on an arbitration board is to prepare a draft decision and award and submit it to the partisan members of the board for review and comment. The neutral realizes that the partisan member of the board who represents the losing party will likely oppose the decision and attempt to have the arbitrator change his or her mind. Similarly, an experienced partisan member realizes that the neutral will not, absent very extraordinary (almost nonexistent) circumstances, change the final outcome. Nevertheless, both realize that there is some leeway for changing the language of the decision to give some consolation or face-saving language to the losing party. What often transpires in such circumstances is a mininegotiation among the partisan arbitrators and the neutral. It is in this process that advocates can sometimes influence the outcome of a case after the close of the hearing and the submission of all arguments.

At least a potential ethical issue arises as to whether it is proper for an advocate to communicate with a partisan member of a board of arbitration while the case is under deliberation. Keeping in mind that partisan members of a board are usually closely allied with, if not actual representatives of, the party that has selected them, there is no illusion by anyone (least of all the arbitrator) that such members seek only one result—a decision in the favor of the side selecting them. There is no pretense of objectivity. Partisan board members are often regarded as extensions of the advocates. Consequently, communications between a partisan member of an arbitration board and the advocate who represents that party should not be regarded as improper.

Similarly, it is not improper for advocates to work with the partisan members in order to influence the language of the decision and award that the board will issue. Of course, advocates cannot speak in lieu of the partisan members in discussions with the arbitrator, but they can coach the partisan members and draft, on their behalf, correspondence to the neutral arbitrator and prepare suggested wording for the decision and award. Experienced arbitrators are aware of this practice. Of course, any direct unilateral communications between an advocate and a sole arbitrator or a neutral member of a board of arbitration regarding the merits of a case would be highly improper.

## DELAYS IN ISSUANCE OF AN AWARD

Most arbitrators usually issue a decision and award within about sixty days following the full submission (including briefs) of a case. Where the labor agreement mandates a shorter period, an arbitrator must follow such a mandate unless the parties agree to waive or extend the period for issuance of an award. Some arbitrators are notorious for issuing awards many months following full submission of the case, and other arbitrators occasionally get behind in their cases and therefore issue late decisions. An advocate encountering such a tardy decision needs to assess what, if any, actions should be taken under these circumstances.

### Impact of Delay

The threshold question is whether or not the advocate's principals are prejudiced by the delay. Because unions are usually the moving parties in labor arbitration cases and are the ones seeking relief from the arbitrator, they are the ones most likely to be disadvantaged by an inordinate delay. A decision on a grievance challenging an employer's interpretation of the labor agreement or an improper work practice that is delayed by the arbitrator permits additional instances of the erroneous interpretation or improper work practices. Even though grievances may be filed for each such additional instance, the harm created by the employer's actions (e.g., employee inconvenience, discomfort, or unfair treatment) may not be susceptible to relief other than with a cease-and-desist order from the arbitrator. When the relief sought is not in the form of monetary damages or restoration of seniority, the harm caused by a delay may not be remedied. In discharge cases, delays in issuing an award usually work to the detriment of the grievant/dischargee. First, the grievant lives in a state of uncertainty, not knowing for sure whether he or she will be able to return to the former employer. Second, many arbitrators who decide to reinstate dischargees are reluctant to issue full back pay when the return to work was delayed for a long time—even when the delay is largely attributable to the arbitrator's tardiness. Consequently, the arbitrator may award partial back pay (frequently on the theory that the discharged employee was partially at fault in the discharge), meaning that the employee suffers monetarily from the delay.

Employers can also be disadvantaged by the tardiness of an award. This is particularly true in seniority cases and discharge cases when back pay is accrued while another employee is receiving the pay that would have been earned by the grievant. If there is a back pay award, the employer usually winds up having paid two employees for the same period of time.

## Protesting Delays in Issuing Awards

Advocates are often reluctant to prod or file a protest with an arbitrator when an unusually long delay is encountered in the issuance of an award. The fear is that the arbitrator will somehow be offended by the action and that such offense will influence the way the case is decided. Consequently, advocates seldom seek to have arbitrators issue more prompt (or at least less tardy) decisions. The author is aware of cases that have been under submission to arbitrators for more than one year.

The advocates' fear of incurring the wrath of an arbitrator by trying to get an award issued is greatly lessened, if not eliminated, if both advocates jointly make a request to the arbitrator. This is usually difficult to arrange, however, because the disadvantage to one party of a delay is usually an advantage to the other. When it is not, or when the party achieving an advantage by the delay is willing to cooperate, there is no reason to refrain from some level of joint prodding or protest.

When a joint request cannot be negotiated, there may be good cause for one party to unilaterally seek prompt issuance of an award. By describing in writing, politely yet firmly, to the arbitrator, with a copy to the opposing advocate, the adverse effect of the delay on the parties and the collective bargaining relationship, an arbitrator may be stimulated to issue an award and decision sooner than he or she otherwise would.

## RECEIVING AND REVIEWING
## THE DECISION AND AWARD

In due course the decision and award will be issued by the arbitrator. Contrary to awards in real estate, commercial disputes, and other types of arbitration cases, awards in labor arbitration cases are almost always accompanied by an opinion or decision that sets forth in some detail the rationale and basis for the arbitrator's award. It is not unusual for such decisions to fill dozens of pages. Frequently, they include an extensive recapitulation of the facts, the arguments made by both sides, and an elaborate explanation of the arbitrator's analysis of the facts, interpretation of the labor contract language, and reasons for the conclusions reached. The important task of the advocate at this point is to carefully read and analyze the decision.

## Analysis of Decision and Award

The tendency of many advocates on receiving an arbitrator's decision is to turn to the last page to see which party won the case. Allowing for such natural inclinations, advocates need to thoroughly pour over the decision and award and assess the following factors:

1. Is the award clear as to what was decided? If the grievance was granted wholly or in part, is it clear what relief was awarded? Is the remedy appropriate with respect to the decision reached and the rationale on which it is based?
2. Is the statement of facts accurate? If there are errors, do they appear to have influenced the decision reached?
3. If labor contract provisions are cited, are they accurately quoted or described? Were any essential labor contract provisions ignored? Was past practice relied on, and, if so, was it supported by evidence in the record? Were side bar agreements part of the basis for the decision, and, if so, where they valid agreements and correctly interpreted?

4. What is the rationale and analysis used by the arbitrator to reach the conclusion? Do the facts and/or the labor contract reasonably or plausibly support that conclusion?
5. Did the arbitrator rely on any facts not contained in the record? Did the arbitrator rely on any law, oral agreement, or provisions outside the labor agreement? If so, on what did he or she rely, and how strong is the factual or quasi-contractual basis for such reliance?

It might be supposed that the advocate of the winning party need not raise the questions enumerated above, because the decision is in favor of that advocate's party. That can sometimes be a false sense of security, because answers to some of those questions by the opposing advocate may open the door to legal challenges to the award. The winning side will want to be prepared in the event of a motion for reconsideration or an attempt to obtain, through a court of law, vacature of the decision and award, or a rehearing of the case. Nevertheless, it is the advocate for the losing party who needs to read the decision more carefully and pose the above-listed questions with greater zeal, because it is the losing party that will seek to take advantage from a critical flaw in the award.

## Compliance with the Award

One of the more frequent problems encountered in the issuance of labor arbitration decisions and awards is implementation of the remedies provided in an award in which a contract violation has been found by the arbitrator. The types of problems range from uncertainty in calculating the amount of back pay to the complexities of readjusting seniority dates and direction of job assignments resulting from grievances over the application of seniority sections of the labor agreement. Although it is the employer who normally has the obligation of complying with an award, the union needs to ensure that the compliance meets each and every aspect of the remedy ordered by the arbitrator. Consequently, both parties have the task of seeing that the implementation carries out the dictates of the award.

### Back Pay Awards

When the arbitrator decides that a grievant has been discharged or suspended without good cause; an employee other than the rightful employee has been promoted, assigned work, or awarded overtime; an employee other than the correct employee has been laid off; or work has been improperly outsourced, the usual remedy is an award of back pay. In legal parlance the aggrieved employee is to be "made whole" for all wages and benefits lost as a result of the contract violation.

Although the concept of determining and paying an employee for the compensation lost as a result of a contract violation seems relatively simple, a number of questions arise in almost any back pay remedy that is awarded. For example:

1. Should the calculation of back pay include only pay for normal work hours, or should it also include lost earnings from overtime that might also have been worked and paid for? If so, how is it to be determined how much overtime the grievant would have worked during the applicable period of back pay?
2. Are there any deductions from the amount of back pay for wages earned from employment with another employer or unemployment compensation benefits? If so, how are those amounts to be determined? If the grievant did not receive other earnings during the period of termination or suspension, was there any obligation on the part of the grievant to make reasonable efforts to seek other employment in order to mitigate damages? If so, who has the burden of showing that the employee did or did not make such reasonable efforts?
3. If an employee suffered damages other than loss of earnings (e.g., repossession of an automobile or medical bills not covered by insurance) as a result of unemployment because of the contract violation, does the employer have any obligation to make the employee whole for such damages? What is the basis, if any, for such "consequential damages?"
4. Is there any interest due on the back pay award, particularly if the employee has been off work for a considerable period of time?

These are just some examples of the types of issues that arise in determining the correct amount of an award of back pay. Analagous problems arise with respect to other remedies.

### Other Types of Make-Whole Remedies

In some cases in which an arbitrator has found a contract violation, no loss of pay was suffered by the grievant, but other adverse consequences may have been encountered. A common situation is one in which an employee is reprimanded for violating the employer's rules and is given a written notice with a copy placed in his or her file. If the reprimand was not for just cause, the obvious remedy is to have the notice removed from the employee's file.

## Work Out of Classification

Another common situation is one in which an employee in a particular job classification has been assigned work outside that classification. The employee assigned the work, or the employee who would have otherwise performed that work, is likely to be the grievant. In many cases no monetary damage has been incurred because the grievant has been fully employed and compensated at a pay rate equal to, or higher, than the work in dispute. The grievance was likely filed to protect the work jurisdiction or to avoid diluting the work content of a particular classification. Because the work will have already been completed, there is really no true make-whole remedy possible, because history cannot be changed. Usually the most that an arbitrator can accomplish is to issue a declaration that such an assignment is in violation of the labor agreement. In some cases, an arbitrator will presume that the misassigned work would have been done by an employee in the proper classification (which may or may not have been the grievant) on an overtime basis and award back pay at the overtime rate to the employee who would most likely have performed that work.

## Operation Closure, Relocation, or Sale

Serious issues of compliance arise when the employer has made major decisions concerning the operation of its business that have been found to be in violation of the labor agreement. One of the most serious is the sale or closure of an employer's facility covered by the labor agreement. If the sale or closure was found by the arbitrator to have been in violation of the agreement, a logical make-whole remedy would be to rescind the sale or reopen the facility. The burden and difficulty of compliance in such cases are obvious. That does not mean that compliance is excused, but simply that the obligation of carrying out the arbitrator's award may be formidable—for employer and union alike.

## Fashioning the Remedy

The task of fashioning an appropriate award falls to the arbitrator, although the party filing the grievance (usually the union) has the opportunity, if not the obligation, to point out to the arbitrator what remedy it feels is appropriate. This should be done during the arbitration hearing, or at least during final argument (or brief in lieu thereof). The test of a proper remedy is usually, "What would have happened, and who would have received the benefit (or absence of burden), had the labor agreement not been violated?" The followup question is how that benefit or absence of burden is to be measured.

When an arbitration award is not clear as to how compliance is to be achieved, either or both parties should seek clarification from the arbitrator.

### Cease-and-Desist Orders

In cases in which no monetary loss has been suffered because of a contract violation, but in which the action or decision that constituted the violation is likely to be repeated, the appropriate remedy may be an order for the employer to cease and desist from engaging in the prohibited conduct (e.g., calling employees at home for mandatory overtime) or an affirmative order to comply with a contractual obligation (e.g., giving the union advance notice of intended layoffs). There may be some question as to the enforceablilty, if not the validity, of such future obligations, but because most arbitrators will honor prior arbitration awards, the enforceability usually comes by virtue of a subsequent grievance.

### Punitive Damages

As a general and consistently applied rule, labor arbitrators do not have the authority to issue punitive damages.[3] Only when the employer has engaged in obviously egregious conduct or has blatantly disregarded prior arbitration awards have punitive awards been issued.[4]

### Awards with General Directives and Retained Jurisdiction

Because of the difficulties addressed above involving back pay calculations and implementation of make-whole remedies, some arbitrators refrain from issuing detailed implementation instructions in their decisions and rely primarily on the parties themselves to work out the details of compliance. Such arbitrators set forth their rationale for the decision and the general aspects of the award and then direct the parties to agree on the specific means of compliance. In such situations the arbitrator typically retains jurisdiction to adjudicate any disputes concerning the correct implementation. For example, such an award would be phrased as follows.

---

[3]Great Atlantic & Pacific Tea Co., 88 LA 430 (Lipson, 1986); Hill and Sinicropi, *Remedies in Arbitration,* (BNA Books, 1991), 436–49.
[4]John Morrell & Co., 69 LA 264, 281 (Conway, 1977); Acme Paper Co., 47 LA 238, 242 (Hilpert, 1966).

## AWARD

The arbitrator finds that the employer violated the labor agreement when it contracted out fabrication work on the Phase II sequence of X-202 module modification. The employer is directed to cease and desist from such outsourcing of this work and to pay back wages (and restoration of any contractual benefits lost as a result of the work loss) to all employees who would have performed such work but for the improper contracting. The parties shall seek to determine and agree on the amounts obligated under this award and the employees to whom such payments are to be made. If no such agreement is reached within thirty days following issuance of this award, either party may petition the arbitrator to determine the amounts due and/or the persons entitled to back pay. The arbitrator hereby retains jurisdiction to ensure full compliance with this award.

A variation of this approach (appropriate in cases with complex implementation requirements) is for the arbitrator to issue a decision and a preliminary award and include in that award an order to both parties to submit to the arbitrator (within a short period of time, such as fourteen days) their respective proposed forms of compliance orders that spell out in specific terms how the award should be implemented. The arbitrator can retain jurisdiction for a limited period to receive such proposed orders and utilize the proposals in issuing a single compliance order in a final award.

# 17

# Challenging the Award

One of the features of labor arbitration treasured by unions and employers alike is its finality. Unlike litigation in courts of law, there is no general right of appeal. This treasured feature, however, is not without exception, and, in fact, there are avenues, albeit narrow, for losing parties to reverse (the more appropriate term is "to vacate" or "to seek vacatur of") adverse decisions and awards.

A party on the losing end of an arbitration decision has essentially only four options. The first is to comply with the award as it is written. The second is to petition the arbitrator to reconsider, or modify, the award. The third is to decline to abide by it. The fourth is to seek to have the award vacated by a court.

Because winning parties are seldom content to allow the losing parties to ignore awards, the third option (i.e., not complying with an award) usually results in the winning party taking the matter to court to have the award confirmed. Not abiding by an award and having the winning party sue to confirm that award presents more or less the same considerations as the losing party suing to vacate the award. Both options bring the arbitrator's decision before a court of law. Therefore, both options will be discussed in this chapter as one, that is, as attempts to avoid or vacate an award.

This chapter addresses the strategic decision making and consideration of alternatives that should procede any attempt to vacate an arbitrator's decision, the procedures available through the courts for making and defending against such an attempt, and the legal grounds for vacating an award.

The author has reservations about detailing such matters out of fear that it may in some way encourage readers to attempt to overturn arbitration awards or otherwise diminish in their eyes the finality of labor arbitration that has made this process such an efficient and effective means of resolving labor disputes. Nevertheless, the existence of such recourse is a reality, and to ignore it would render this volume incomplete and unrealistic. Moreover, a party favored by an arbitrator's award needs to be aware of the potential for losing the benefit of an award and the means to seek to preserve it.

## LEGAL AUTHORITY TO VACATE AN ARBITRATOR'S DECISION

The mechanism by which losing parties seek to vacate arbitration awards is a lawsuit filed normally under Section 301 of the National Labor Relations Act (NLRA). That section provides that suits for violation of contracts between employers and unions may be brought in any federal district court having jurisdiction of the parties. Such suits may also be brought in state courts, although the defendant may "remove" the case to federal court.[1]

In addition, certain types of cases may be brought under state law as well as federal law in those states that have a statute governing arbitration.[2] In every case filed in state or federal court in those states that have an arbitration statute, lawyers should rely on both state and federal law in order to maximize the bases on which they may rely to overturn an arbitration award.

The time within which such a suit must be brought will vary depending on the state in which the lawsuit is brought. Even in cases brought in federal court, most courts will look to the state statute of limitations applicable to suits for breach of contract.[3] As of this writing, however, two federal circuits (3d and 9th) apply the six-month statute of

---

[1]Keystone Printed Specialties Co. v. Printing Pressmen Local 119, 386 F. Supp. 416, 87 LRRM 3191 (M.D. Pa. 1974) *aff'd,* 517 F.2d 1398, 90 LRRM 2889 (3d Cir. 1975).
[2]The following states have arbitration statutes that prohibit fraud and corruption and provide at least some basis for overturning arbitrators' awards: Alaska, Arizona, Arkansas, California, Colorado, Delaware, Florida, Georgia, Hawaii, Idaho, Illinois, Indiana, Iowa, Kansas, Maine, Massachusetts, Minnesota, Mississippi, Missouri, Montana, Nevada, New Hampshire, New Jersey, New Mexico, North Carolina, North Dakota, Virginia, West Virginia, Wisconsin, and Wyoming. SCHOONHAVEN, ed., FAIRWEATHER'S PRACTICE AND PROCEDURE IN LABOR ARBITRATION, 448.
[3]Automobile Workers v. Hoosier Cardinal Corp., 383 U.S. 696, 61 LRRM 2545 (1966).

limitations applicable to unfair labor practice charges under the NLRA, rather than the appropriate state statute of limitations.[4]

There is little question that courts of law have the authority to reverse labor arbitration awards, to order a different result, or to remand the case for decision by the same or a different arbitrator. The grounds on which this occurs have been drawn very narrowly by the courts. Moreover, there are important strategic reasons why such an effort may be inadvisable. The following sections address the considerations that should precede any decision to attempt to vacate an arbitration award.

# DECIDING TO CHALLENGE

Prior to embarking on a quest to vacate an award, the advocate contemplating such action should carefully analyze a number of factors. Regardless of the outcome of the effort, there are likely to be significant consequences resulting simply from the attempt.

## Assessing the Impact of the Decision and Award

The driving force behind any attempt to vacate an arbitration award is, of course, the effect of an adverse decision and award. Winning parties do not seek to nullify arbitration decisions, except perhaps in extremely rare instances where an award is in their favor but the decision contains harmful language that could have long-term adverse effects on contract interpretation or employment practices in the future. Losing parties, therefore, are the ones that consider attempts to vacate awards, and it is they who need to fully assess the likely consequences of an adverse award.

There are three principal reasons why unions and employers seek to vacate awards. They are as follows:

1. The decision and award violate one or more strongly held principles.
2. The award imposes a substantial cost or other heavy burden on the losing party.
3. The decision and award establish an undesirable precedent for the future.

---

[4]Teamsters Local 315 v. Great W. Chem. Co., 781 F.2d 764, 121 LRRM 2666 (9th Cir. 1986); Westinghouse Indep. Salaried Unions v. Westinghouse Elec. Corp., 736 F.2d 896, 116 LRRM 2732 (3d Cir. 1984).

In assessing these impacts the losing party should probe each reason and ask itself a series of penetrating questions. Because the consequences of challenging an award, with respect to cost and interference with the collective bargaining relationship, are significant, it is useful to ask questions that will test the validity of the initial notions favoring a challenge. Decisions to challenge arbitration awards are often made out of initial disappointment and emotion and are not always inspected under the microscope of rationality. For this reason, a calm, analytical, and objective examination should be made.

With respect to the first reason, that is, violation of a strongly held principle, the following questions are useful in analyzing a decision to seek vacatur:

- What exactly is the principle that has been violated?
- Does this principle go to the essence of the organization challenging the award, or is it one that, while perhaps important, is more peripheral?
- When was the principle established, and has it been consistently honored in all contexts?
- To what extent was the principle now sought to be protected compromised when the contract language at issue in the case was negotiated or compromised sometime during intervening years?
- Did the conduct of the challenging party's representatives contribute substantially to the compromising of the principle?

Considering the second reason, that is, imposition of excessive or unmanageable costs or other burdens, the following questions are suggested:

- What is the true cost of the award? Has a thorough cost estimate been prepared based on realistic assumptions? Has the estimate been reviewed and analyzed from several different perspectives?
- What is the true cost measured on a unit basis (e.g., per work hour or per unit of production)?
- Is there some reasonable means for offsetting the cost of the award? Can it be amortized over a period of time?
- Aside from cost, what other burdens are imposed by the award? Is it clear that the anticipated burdens will actually be borne by the losing party?
- To what extent is it possible to avoid or circumvent the costs or other onerous burdens of the award by changing practices, procedures, or other variables?

Addressing the third reason for seeking vacatur, that is, establishing an undesirable precedent for the future, the following questions are appropriate:

- Is the language of the decision and award so broad that it is likely to apply to many future situations? To what extent does the arbitrator's analysis and reasoning depend on the facts in this case so that it might not apply to other cases where the facts are different?
- About how frequently do the facts, contract language, and issues involved in this case occur? Can changes be made that will cause them to occur less frequently?
- Is it feasible to negotiate changes in the labor agreement to overcome the adverse effect of this decision on other cases? Will concessions be necessary to achieve such a change? If so, how extensive and expensive might those concessions have to be?

## Strategic Issues to Consider

Assuming that the answers to the questions listed above lead to the conclusion that an attempt to vacate the decision and award is worth the effort, there are still some additional factors that should be considered.

### Impact on Union-Management Relationship

Language commonly found in a labor agreement's arbitration clause provides that the arbitrator's decision is "final and binding on the parties." Even without such explicit phrasing, the tacit understanding of negotiating parties is that the arbitrator's decision will govern the dispute without further recourse. Consequently, when one of the parties challenges an award, there is a substantial risk that the other party will feel betrayed and will conclude that the spirit of the labor agreement is being violated.

There are some collective bargaining relationships that are so adversarial that such a breach of the spirit of a labor agreement is no surprise (often because such spirit does not exist) and confirms the other party's perception of the challenging party's lack of good faith. Other relationships are more amicable, and in such relationships an attempt to vacate an arbitration award may be viewed as a genuine breach of trust. In the latter situation, the advocate (or his or her principals) should carefully evaluate the adverse influence such a challenge is likely to have on the union-management relationship. If, notwithstanding such evaluation, the decision is made to go forward, the moving party is well advised to meet with the other party's counterparts to provide notice of the decision and an explanation of the rationale for doing so. This will not cause the other party to accept the decision but may soften the negative impact on the relationship.

### *Influence on the Moving Party-Arbitrator Relationship*

Another relationship that may be affected by a decision to vacate an arbitrator's award is that between the party challenging the award and the arbitrator. Where the arbitrator is an *ad hoc* arbitrator (i.e., scheduled to hear single cases) and where the arbitrator does not regularly hear cases involving the moving party, the decision to challenge is not likely to adversely impact an existing or future relationship with the arbitrator. Where, however, the arbitrator is a permanent arbitrator or on a panel of arbitrators that regularly hears cases involving that party, the impact of a challenge should be assessed.

There are three likely responses of an arbitrator whose decision is challenged by a party for whom he or she regularly or periodically hears cases:

- No significant adverse reaction.
- Negative or hostile reaction; feels personally challenged; desires to retaliate against the party that challenged his or her authority.
- Intimidated; fears that future decisions may also be challenged; adopts cautious approach in future cases, or anticipates that he or she will not be selected again to hear cases for that party.

The party contemplating an action to vacate will find it difficult to estimate which of the three listed alternatives is most likely. To the extent that the second reaction, that is, retaliation, seems likely and if there is no way to avoid having the arbitrator hear future cases (e.g., this is a permanent arbitrator named in the labor agreement), the party contemplating a challenge may want to reassess the decision to challenge. Usually, however, the need to use the same arbitrator in future cases is so uncertain and the ability to anticipate the arbitrator's reaction is so imprecise that neither of these factors is likely to dissuade a party from challenging an award.

## Assessing the Chances of Success

One of the major factors, if not *the* major factor, in deciding whether to challenge an arbitration award is the chance of success. If the grounds for attacking the award are narrow, and therefore the likelihood of having a court of law overturn the arbitrator is slim, the losing party has little reason to move forward. Even under the best of circumstances, the chances of success in reversing any arbitrator's award are relatively low. Although some cases present more favorable opportunities for vacatur than others, in general, a party that attempts to overturn a labor arbitration decision faces a fierce uphill battle.

Later in this chapter, the grounds for having a labor arbitration award vacated are reviewed in detail.

## Alternatives to Court Action

A party dissatisfied with an arbitration decision and award should be aware that there are possible alternatives to court action to avoid the burdens imposed by an adverse decision. Although they do not offer optimistic opportunities for relief, they should nevertheless be evaluated prior to initiating court action.

### Buy-Out of Award

Labor negotiators are fond of saying, "everything is negotiable." This holds true for many arbitration awards. The party favored by the award may be willing to sacrifice all or part of the award's benefit in exchange for something it values more highly. Some arbitration awards and decisions that concern personal and/or nonmonetary considerations, for example, restoration of seniority, may not be susceptible to negotiation, but most awards can be translated into dollars and cents or are susceptible to other trade-offs. Consequently, a losing party should at least consider what matters are valued by the opposing party and evaluate the chances of washing out an adverse award, or at least the most onerous aspects of such an award.

A variation of this approach is to make the results of the arbitration a subject of negotiation at the next reopening of the labor agreement. The opportunities for trading are likely to be much more favorable at that time, since many other issues are likely to be on the table. Of course, by that time it is almost certain that the remedy imposed by the award itself will have been implemented. For decisions and awards that impose a continuing burden on a losing party, however, correction through a subsequent labor contract negotiation is sometimes a viable solution.

### Modification/Correction of Award by the Arbitrator

The chances of having an arbitrator reverse his or her own decision and award are about as great as having an umpire reverse a call of safe or out in a baseball game. It virtually never happens. What may be possible, however, is to have the arbitrator modify or correct some aspect of the decision and award to mitigate one or more harmful aspects of the case. For example, in reinstating a grievant following a discharge, the remedy may be modified from one of returning the employee to the last position held (causing the displacement of another employee) to one of a position of like pay and status. Similarly, an arbitrator's decision to interpret a seniority clause in a way that differs significantly from the past practice may be mitigated if it is modified to apply only to future situations that are identical to the one involved in the case, rather than to all job movements controlled or effected by the past practice.

Any attempt to obtain a modification or correction of an arbitrator's award must, if it is to be successful, be accompanied by abundant evidence of the justice and fairness of the modification or correction and should be supported by compelling arguments as to why such a change is justified under the labor agreement. If an arbitrator is willing to consider such a change, he or she will offer the opposing party an opportunity to respond and make counterarguments. Anticipating such arguments and preparing counterarguments to them is an important aspect of an attempt to modify or correct an award.

The possibility of obtaining relief of an adverse decision and award in this manner is remote, but so too is the likelihood of having a court of law do so. Certainly, the time, effort, and cost of seeking a voluntary modification by the arbitrator are substantially less than litigation.

## GROUNDS FOR VACATING AN ARBITRATION AWARD

Far and away the most important factor that should influence a party in its decision whether to seek to vacate an arbitration award are the grounds for establishing a viable legal basis on which such an effort will be premised. Was the proceeding conducted in a biased or inequitable manner that precluded a just decision? Was the reasoning and analysis underlying the decision so improbable that it bears no rational relationship to the contract on which it is premised? Did the arbitrator have some relationship with one of the parties that influenced, or reasonably could have influenced, his or her decision? Does the decision and award directly conflict with a law, clearly enunciated public policy, or decision of some other tribunal? The material that follows in this chapter is an attempt to provide an overview of the bases for vacatur of arbitration awards and the means to seek and defend against vacatur.

There are five fundamental bases for vacating an award. The first concerns the issues of fraud and undue influence on or by the arbitrator; the second relates to whether the arbitrator exceeded his or her authority under the labor agreement or under the submission agreement presented to the arbitrator; the third is whether there were any procedural errors in the manner in which the case was heard and considered; the fourth concerns the substance of the decision and award and whether they "drew their essence from the agreement"; and the fifth addresses whether the decision and award conformed with applicable law or a clearly enunciated public policy or whether it was in conflict with a decision of another tribunal.

In covering each of these bases, some attention will be focused on the party attempting to defend against vacatur and the strategy and rationale it might employ to support its position that the award should stand as rendered.

## Fraud and Undue Influence

A bedrock tenet of labor arbitration is that an arbitrator have no personal interest in, or close relationship with, either of the parties to the dispute nor the matters at issue in the case. The arbitrator should be truly neutral. Thus, where there is any evidence of bias, courts may vacate an award.[5] Evidence of actual bias must, however, be reasonably established, and mere opportunity for being influenced to favor one side or the other is not sufficient.[6]

### *Bases for Fraud and Undue Influence*

The types of situations in which bias has been found to taint an award sufficiently to justify vacatur include the following:

---

[5]Commonwealth Coating Corp. v. Continental Casualty Co., 393 U.S. 145; Stereotypers Local 18 v. Newark Morning Ledger Co., 397 F.2d 594, 599, 68 LRRM 2561 (3rd Cir.) *cert. denied.* 393 U.S. 954, 69 LRRM 2653 (1968).
[6]Firefighters Local 1296 v. City of Kennewick, 542 P.2d 1252, 92 LRRM 2118 (Wash. 1975) [arbitrator had drinks with one of the union members]; Brewery Workers Joint Local Executive Bd. of New Jersey v. P. Ballentine & Sons, 83 LRRM 2712 (D. N.J. 1973) [arbitrator's relative purchased major asset from employer shortly following the decision]; Teamsters Local 560 v. Bergen-Hudson Roofing Supply Co., 98 LRRM 3059 (N.J. Sup. Ct., 1978) [arbitrator was an attorney who had previously represented one of the parties].

- A father-son relationship between the arbitrator and the president of an international union that was a parent of the union participating in the arbitration.[7]
- Evident predisposition of arbitrator who upheld termination of an employee who was engaged in decertification activities by the grievant.[8]
- Arbitrator's permission of nonparty union to attend hearing and his private communications with nonparty union officials between hearings in the case.[9]

The obvious question that arises in situations where there is a relationship between the arbitrator and one of the parties is why the arbitrator did not disclose it prior to commencing the arbitration. The arbitrator may not have appreciated the significance of the relationship, may not have recalled a previous relationship far in the past, or in some cases the relationship with the real parties in interest may not have been known to the arbitrator, such as in the case where the employer party is a minor subsidiary to a corporation in which the arbitrator had some interest.

The other major occasion for bias is where there is some contact between the arbitrator and a representative or principal of one of the parties under circumstances that would suggest undue influence or inappropriate communications. For example, certain limited types of ex parte (unilateral) communications between the arbitrator and a representative of one of the parties may be grounds for vacating an award. Such communications must be rather egregious, however, and mere socializing or casual discourse between arbitrator and advocate are not grounds for reversing a decision and award.[10]

Suffice it to say that evidence of undue influence on an arbitrator must be compelling, and mere opportunity for bias normally will be insufficient to justify vacating an arbitrator's award. For example, the party seeking to vacate the award must prove more than the appearance of impropriety, but also facts that create a "reasonable impression of

[7]Morelite Constr. Corp. v. Carpenters Benefit Fund, New York City District Council, 748 F. 79, 117 LRRM 3009 (2nd Cir. 1984).
[8]Allen v. Allied Plant Maintenance Co. of Tennessee Inc., 881 F.2d 291, 132 LRRM 2021 (6th Cir. 1989).
[9]Food & Commercial Workers, Local 50N v. SIPCO Inc. d/b/a Monfort Park, 8 F.3d 10, 144 LRRM 2577 (8th Cir. 1993).
[10]Firefighters v. City of Kennewick, 542 P.2d 1252, 92 LRRM 2118 (Wash. 1975); Journal Times v. Typographical Union No. 23, 409 F. Supp. 24, 92 LRRM 2818 (E.D. Wis. 1976).

partiality."[11] Even an attorney-client relationship between the arbitrator and one of the counsel who appears before the NLRB (National Labor Relations Board) on behalf of the employer represented by one of the advocates does not create the "evident partiality" required under the U.S. Arbitration Act.[12]

### *Defending Against an Attempt to Vacate for Fraud or Undue Influence*

A party intending to defend an award against a challenge based on fraud or undue influence should consider whether the challenging party knew or should have known at the outset of the hearing of the improper relationship or compromising situation on which the challenge is based. If such knowledge or the opportunity for such knowledge existed at the time formal proceedings began, the defense would be based on waiver.[13] Why didn't the challenging party raise the alleged fraud or undue influence at the time of the hearing? Was it because that party wanted to await the decision to see who won the case, in order to decide whether a challenge was necessary? Such defenses have proven to be effective.[14]

## Decision and Award Exceeds the Arbitrator's Authority

Another key rationale for vacating an arbitrator's award is that it exceeds the authority granted to the arbitrator by the labor agreement or the submission agreement under which the case was presented to the arbitrator. Although some court decisions vacating arbitration awards clearly set forth facts and rationale that establish a convincing basis for determining that the arbitrator exceeded his or her authority, others appear to use this rationale to reverse awards that appear flawed not by the authority that they usurp, but rather by the paucity of logic and good judgment in the decision. In other words, courts sometimes appear to vacate decisions they consider ill advised on the premise that the

---

[11]Toyota of Berkeley v. Automobile Salesmen's Union, Local 1095, 834 F.2d 751, 127 LRRM 2112 (9th Cir. 1987); Sheet Metal Workers Int'l Assn. Local 420 v. Kinney Air Cond. Co., 756 F.2d 742, 118 LRRM 3398 (9th Cir. 1985).
[12]Sanford Home for Adults v. Health Professionals, Local 6, 665 F. Supp 312, 126 LRRM 3149 (S.D. N.Y. 1987).
[13]Kodiak Oil Field Haulers, Inc. v. Teamsters Local No. 959, 611 F.2d 1286, 103 LRRM 2288 (9th Cir. 1990); Sheet Metal Workers Local 206 v. West Coast Sheet Metal Co., 660 F. Supp. 1500, 137 LRRM 2843 (S.D. Cal. 1987).
[14]Anderson v. Fleet Carrier Corp., 879 F.2d 1344, 131 LRRM 3079 (6th Cir. 1989); Early v. Early Transfer 699 F.2d 552, 112 LRRM 3381 (1st Cir. 1983).

arbitrator went beyond the confines of his or her authority under the labor agreement or the submission agreement of the parties.

### Examples of Rulings of Arbitrators Exceeding Their Authority

The following are examples of types of cases that have been vacated based on arbitrators exceeding their authority.

- Arbitrator ignored oral agreement between an employer and a union concerning the wearing of safety protective gear by employees and reinstated an employee who refused to wear such equipment.[15]
- Employees not covered by a trial incentive pay plan were granted "punitive" damages by an arbitrator for the employer's contract violation, even though such damages were not authorized under the labor agreement.[16]
- Arbitrator determined that a nonunit employee should have been laid off prior to a union-represented grievant under a standard of "reasonableness" without properly evaluating the employer's reasons for taking the action it did.[17]
- Award covered a period of time before the labor agreement was in effect.[18]
- Arbitrator ruled that the labor agreement did not expire on the date set forth in the labor agreement, but rolled over and became effective for another year because of employer's violation of a section of the NLRA.[19]
- Award provided back pay for a period beyond the contract expiration date for subcontracting of work in violation of the labor agreement.[20]

---

[15]Shop 'N Save Warehouse Foods, Inc. v. Commercial Workers Local 88, 864 F. Supp. 113, 147 LRRM 2591 (E.D. Mo. 1994).
[16]Georgia Power Co. v. Elec. Workers, IBEW Local 84, 995 F.2d 1030, 143 LRRM 2987 (11th Cir. 1993).
[17]United Inter-Mountain Tel Co. v. Communication Workers Local 387, 662 F. Supp. 82, 126 LRRM 2124 (E.D. Tenn. 1987); *aff'd* 845 F.2d 327, 129 LRRM 3144 (6th Cir. 1988).
[18]Dorado Beach Hotel Corp. v. Union De Trabajadores De La Industria Gastronomica De Puerto Rico Local 610, 811 F. Supp. 41, 143 LRRM 2337 (D.P.R. 1993).
[19]Roadmaster Corp. v. Laborers Local 504, 655 F. Supp. 1460, 125 LRRM 3059 (S.D. Ill. 1987); *aff'd* 851 F.2d 886, 129 LRRM 2449 (7th Cir. 1988).
[20]Polk Bros. Inc. v. Chicago Truck Drivers, 973 F.2d 593, 141 LRRM 2172 (7th Cir. 1992).

- Arbitrator decided an issue in an arbitration hearing that had been withdrawn previously by the union and that was not included in the submission agreement.[21]
- Arbitrator issued award of back pay, where the issue submitted did not specify that a remedy was to be decided.[22]

What to some eyes appear to be examples of merely poor arbitral judgment are sometimes viewed by courts of law as an arbitrator "exceeding the authority" granted under the labor agreement or going beyond the issues submitted for decision.

## Defending Against Attack Based on Exceeding Authority

A party facing the possible loss of a favorable award because of a challenge based on the arbitrator's having exceeded his or her authority must, at the outset, closely examine the record in the case to see what, if any, evidence there is that the issues decided by the arbitrator are the ones submitted by the parties and/or that were encompassed within the grievance or the grievance processing leading up to the arbitration. Prearbitration correspondence, preliminary statements by the parties during the arbitration hearing, past practice of submitting prior arbitration cases without technical niceties, and the like may all be persuasive in convincing a court of law that there was no overstepping of bounds of the arbitrator's authority.

In facing attacks aimed at the remedy portion of an award, advocates should determine whether the main portion of the award may be salvaged, even though one or more aspects of the vacatur case are upheld. For example, in a case where an employer was found to have violated the labor agreement in discharging an employee, the union was assessed back pay because of its complicity in the discharge. The arbitrator ordered the union to reimburse the employer for the back pay due. Such a directive was held to be beyond the arbitrator's authority, but rather than vacate the entire award, the court struck only that portion concerning the union's obligation to reimburse the employer for the back pay.[23]

---

[21]Champion Int'l Corp. v. Paperworkers Local 37, 779 F.2d 328, 121 LRRM 2449 (6th Cir. 1985).

[22]Retail Clerks Local 782 v. Sav-On Groceries, 508 F.2d 500, 88 LRRM 3205 (10th Cir. 1975).

[23]Carpenters Local 1027, Mill Cabinet-Indus. Div. v. Lee Lumber & Building Material Corp., 2 F.3d 796, 144 LRRM 2199 (7th Cir. 1993).

## Procedural Errors

The typical absence of procedural rules for arbitration in labor agreements and the lack of governmental regulation of labor arbitration mean that the opportunity to challenge arbitration awards on the basis of procedural error is quite small. Nevertheless, there are certain types of conduct by an arbitrator that are likely to open the door to vacatur.

### *Means of Selecting and Appointing the Arbitrator*

Where the arbitrator is not selected or appointed in accordance with the provisions of the labor agreement, the award may be declared null and void. Thus, where an arbitrator was not chosen by the union and employer representatives as specified in the labor agreement, the resulting decision and award was vacated.[24] Similarly, where a labor agreement stipulated that each party was to appoint one arbitrator to a panel, and the other party disregarded this procedure and unilaterally initiated arbitration, a court held the award to be ineffective.[25]

### *Lateness of Award*

It is rather common for arbitration clauses in labor agreements to set forth the time within which an arbitrator must render a decision. Thirty days is often specified in such clauses. Given the heavy calendars of many arbitrators, such time limits are often unrealistic. Careful arbitrators often seek a stipulation by the parties at the close of a hearing that the time limits may be extended by the arbitrator, provided that the arbitrator notifies the parties that more time will be necessary. This practice is not, however, universally followed.

Where a decision and award are not issued within the time limit established by a labor agreement, grounds for vacatur may exist.[26] A number of courts have held, however, that late awards are not invalid unless there is some showing of prejudice caused by the late award or unless the labor agreement specifies that an award issued after the deadline is invalid.[27] The length of the delay will, however, strongly

[24]Hod Carriers Local 227 v. Sullivan, 221 F. Supp. 696, 54 LRRM 2548 (E.D. Ill. 1963).
[25]Food Handlers Local 425 v. Pluss Poultry, 260 F.2d 835, 43 LRRM 2090 (8th Cir. 1958).
[26]Givens, *The Validity of Delayed Awards under Section 301 Taft-Hartley Act,* 16 ARB. J. 161 (1961).
[27]Hill v. Norfolk & Western Ry., 814 F.2d 220, 71 LRRM 3205 (7th Cir. 1987); Machinists West Rock Lodge 2120 v. Geometric Tool Co. Div., 406 F.2d 284, 70 LRRM 2228 (2d Cir. 1968); Elec. Workers IBEW Local 2 v. Gerstner Elec. Inc., 614 F. Supp. 874, 124 LRRM 2627 (E.D. Mo. 1985); Elec. Workers IBEW Local 272 v. Pennsylvania Power Co., 645 F. Supp. 138, 123 LRRM 3271 (W.D. Pa. 1986).

influence whether a court will overlook a delay when an award is challenged. Thus, even though a court ruled that a late award would not normally justify vacatur, an award issued 14 months after the close of a hearing where the labor agreement had a 15-day period for issuance of an award was vacated.[28]

## Improper Procedures in the Hearing

Although issues concerning the type and treatment of burdens of proof, admission of evidence, and other aspects of the hearing are not generally bases on which a court will vacate an arbitration award, there are some exceptions to that general rule. The following are examples of hearing procedural irregularities that were grounds for vacatur.

- An arbitrator's award was vacated where the arbitrator established a burden of ''beyond a reasonable doubt'' rather than ''preponderance of the evidence'' in a discharge case.[29]
- Where a union and employer agreed to forgo witnesses and submit the entire case in the form of briefs, an award issued by an arbitrator who neglected to read the employer's brief was vacated.[30]
- An award was vacated where the arbitrator permitted the attendance of an interested nonparty throughout the course of the hearing and actively solicited ex parte evidence and consultations.[31]
- An award that was based on a decision by the arbitrator to give collateral-estoppel effect based on a prior arbitration award under a different labor agreement was vacated and remanded.[32]
- An arbitrator's exclusion from a hearing of a potential witness's husband, causing the witness to refuse to testify, was held to be grounds for vacatur of an award.[33]
- One party was foreclosed from presenting its case in a hearing after it previously had refrained from presenting evidence in the prior hearing because of assurances that it would have another opportunity to present its case.[34]

---

[28]Jones v. St. Louis-San Francisco Ry., 728 F.2d 257, 115 LRRM 2905 (6th Cir. 1984).
[29]Square Plus Operating Corp. v. Teamsters Local 917, 140 LRRM 2389, 123 LC 10, 440 (S.D. N.Y. 1992).
[30]Green-Wood Cemetery v. Cemetery Workers, 82 LRRM 2894 (S.D. N.Y. 1973).
[31]Food & Commercial Workers Local 50N v. SIPCO d/b/a Montfort Pork Inc., 8 F.3d 10, 144 LRRM 2577 (8th Cir. 1993).
[32]Westvaco Corp. v. Paperworkers Local 579, 139 LRRM 2877 (D. Mass. 1992).
[33]Hoteles Condado Beach v. Local 901 Union de Tronquistas, 588 F. Supp. 679, 116 LRRM 2901 (D.P.R. 1984); *aff'd* 763 F.2d 34, 119 LRRM 2659 (1st Cir. 1985).
[34]Teamsters v. Clapp, 551 F. Supp. 570, 97 LC 10, 250 (N.D. N.Y. 1982).

*Defending Against Attempted Vacatur Based on Procedural Errors*

When a party seeks to overturn an arbitration award because of some procedural defect, whether the defect was challenged in the hearing or prior to the issuance of the award is significant. Failure to raise the defect as an issue when it was first known and to delay it until after an unfavorable decision and award are rendered may be grounds for rejecting the vacatur attempt. Not raising the defect before issuance of the decision and award gives the appearance that the objecting party was merely waiting to see how the arbitrator decided the case before entering the challenge. Waiver can easily be implied.

Thus, no protest of a late award being advanced until after a decision was issued was found to be a waiver of the untimely award.[35] Similarly, an employer's failure to contest a proceeding while it was in progress because the employer did not have a representative constituted a waiver and precluded vacatur.[36] An employer's failure to contest the composition of a joint arbitration committee at the time the members were appointed was held to be a waiver to a challenge lodged following an adverse award.[37]

Consequently, a party seeking to keep in effect a favorable arbitration decision in the face of an attempt to vacate because of procedural error should closely examine when the procedural defect was alleged to have been made and whether the party challenging the award was aware, or through due diligence could have been aware, of the defect prior to the issuance of the award. If such knowledge can be shown (and it often can), a defense of waiver should always be registered on the record and strongly argued.

# Decision Did Not Draw Its Essence from the Labor Agreement

A leading principle of valid labor arbitration awards and a source of security from vacatur, is the degree to which the decision and award are faithful to the terms of the labor agreement on which they are based. In the nomenclature of the leading court case on this point, the award *must*

---

[35]McKesson Corp. v. Local 150 IBT, 969 F.2d 831, 140 LRRM 2974 (9th Cir. 1992); West Rock Lodge No. 2120 v. Geometric Tool Co., 406 F.2d 284, 70 LRRM 2228 (2d Cir. 1968).
[36]Walters Sheet Metal Corp. v. Sheet Metal Workers Local 18, 910 F.2d 1565, 135 LRRM 2097 (7th Cir. 1990).
[37]Elec. Workers IBEW Local 2 v. Gerstner Elec. Inc., 614 F. Supp. 874, 124 LRRM 2627 (E.D. Mo. 1985).

*draw its essence from the labor agreement.* The U.S. Supreme Court in *Steelworkers v. Enterprise Wheel & Car Corp.* held as follows:

> [An] arbitrator is confined to interpretation and application of the collective bargaining agreement; he does not sit to dispense his own brand of industrial justice. He may of course look for guidance from many sources, yet his award is legitimate *only so long as it draws its essence from the collective bargaining agreement.* When the arbitrator's words manifest an infidelity to this obligation, courts have no choice but to refuse enforcement of the award.[38] (emphasis added)

The choice of words employed by the court to set the standard is instructive. The words, "drawing essence," suggest that the decision need not be correct, adequately reasoned, or strictly according to the contract provisions. Subsequent decisions have refined the term and make clear that the award need not be the correct one, but merely be plausibly, remotely, or in one way or another connected with the labor agreement on which it is based. While presumably not intending to give lower courts a tool with which to overturn arbitrators' decisions, judges have frequently relied on the language quoted above to reverse arbitration decisions where the result reached or the rationale employed by the arbitrator did not meet the court's judgment of what the particular court thought the labor agreement meant under a particular set of facts.

The following are representative samples of the types of cases in which courts have held that arbitration decisions did not draw their essence from the labor agreements on which they were based.

- An arbitrator granted pensions to employees who did not meet the contractually established minimum age and service requirements for a pension.[39]
- Despite the absence of any such benefit in the labor agreement, employees who left work to vote in a national election were awarded paid time off based on an alleged past practice.[40]
- Arbitrator's award found a contract violation in an employer's unilateral discontinuance of a 30-minute lunch break that resulted in 30 minutes of overtime pay each day.[41]

---

[38]363 U.S. 593, 597, 46 LRRM 2423, 2425 (1960).
[39]H.K. Porter Co. v. Saw, File & Steel Prod. Workers 333 F.2d 596, 56 LRRM 2537 (3d Cir. 1964).
[40]Torrington Co. v. Auto. Workers, Metal Prod. Workers Local 1645, 361 F.2d 677, 62 LRRM 2495 (2d Cir. 1966).
[41]Woodworkers v. Weyerhaeuser Co., 7 F.3d 133, 144 LRRM 2471 (8th Cir. 1993).

- Arbitrator disregarded "last chance" agreement between employer and employee (signed by employee following his union's recommendation) in reversing employee's discharge.[42]
- Arbitrator's award reinstated discharged employee with back pay, obligating union to reimburse employer for amount of back pay.[43]
- Obligation placed on employer to return all striking employees to work in seniority order or pay for time lost by more senior employees who were not returned to work before junior employees.[44]
- An employee who was discharged for theft for not returning the full amount of cash found in a wallet was reinstated where the labor contract permitted summary discharge for dishonesty.[45]
- Arbitrator merged seniority lists based on "guiding principle of equity" rather than express contract provision about how seniority lists were to be merged.[46]
- In finding that the employer did not have just cause for discharging two employees for the same rule infraction, the arbitrator reinstated one employee, but not the other.[47]

When one examines the types of cases that courts have found did not draw their essence from the labor agreements on which they were based, it is often difficult to discern in what way the decisions failed to draw their essence from the agreement as opposed to simply being incorrectly decided. Contrasted with the cases listed just above, the following are examples of cases in which a factual error critical to a decision was unquestionably made, but the court nevertheless declined to vacate.

- Decision upholding an employee's discharge, which was based on absenteeism on certain days, was not vacated, even though the employee was legitimately absent from work because of an industrial injury.[48]

---

[42]Coca-Cola Bottling Co. v. Teamsters Local 688, 959 F.2d 1438, 139 LRRM 2899 (8th Cir. 1992).

[43]Carpenters Local 1027, Mill Cabinet-Indus. Div. v. Lee Lumber & Building Material Corp., 2 F.3d 796, 144 LRRM 2199 (7th Cir. 1993).

[44]Iowa Mold Tooling Co. v. Teamsters Local 828, 16 F.3d 311, 145 LRRM 2449 (8th Cir. 1994).

[45]Browning-Ferris Indus. of Tennessee Inc., Memphis District v. Teamsters Local 984, 785 F. Supp. 104, 141 LRRM 2978 (W.D. Tenn. 1990).

[46]In re Marine Pollution Serv., 857 F.2d 91, 129 LRRM 2472 (2d Cir. 1988).

[47]HMC Management Corp. v. Carpenters Dist. Council, 750 F.2d 1302, 118 LRRM 2425 (5th Cir. 1985).

[48]Grimm v. Copperweld Steel Co., 139 LRRM 2934, 121 LC 10, 091 (N.D. Ohio 1991).

- Arbitrator ruled that an agreement providing a 40-hour work week entitled employees to three days' pay for time not worked when the employer unilaterally changed paydays, resulting in employees receiving less than 40 hours pay in the week of the changeover.[49]
- In upholding discharge for trafficking in marijuana, arbitrator rested decision on mistaken belief that the employer relied on employee's guilty plea in court when guilty plea was entered after discharge, and therefore employer could not have relied on that fact.[50]
- Arbitrator rendered two directly conflicting decisions on the same issue.[51]

The U.S. Supreme Court in *Paperworkers v. Misco, Inc.*, a key decision affecting the scope of review courts are to apply to arbitrators' decisions, held that courts may not review alleged factual or legal errors in the manner in which appellate courts review decisions of lower courts. The court said,

> As long as the arbitrator is even arguably construing or applying the contract and acting within the scope of his authority, that a court is convinced he committed serious error does not suffice to overturn his decision.[52]

Notwithstanding the clear and unequivocal mandate of the U.S. Supreme Court in *Misco* that courts not substitute their judgment for that of an arbitrator, a number of cases after *Misco* have been decided on grounds that appear to be little more than judicial second-guessing of arbitration decisions.[53]

# Decision is Against Public Policy or Contrary to Law

The final category for vacating arbitration awards is that the decision and award (1) violate public policy or (2) contravene some

---

[49]Safeway Stores v. Bakery & Confectionery Workers Local 111, 390 F.2d 79, 67 LRRM 2646 (1968).

[50]Laborers v. Postal Serv., 751 F.2d 834, 118 LRRM 2216 (6th Cir. 1985).

[51]Hotel Employees Local 878 v. Cullop d/b/a Harbor Inn, 146 LRRM 3086 (D.C. Alaska 1994).

[52]484 U.S. 29, 126 LRRM 3113 (1987).

[53]Leed Architectural Prod., Inc. v. Steelworkers Local 6674, 916 F.2d 63, 135 LRRM 2766 (2d Cir. 1990); S.D. Warren v. United Papermakers and Paperworkers, 815 F.2d 178, 125 LRRM 2086 (1st Cir. 1987); Cement Div., Nat'l Gypsum Co. v. Steelworkers Local 135, 793 F.2d 759, 123 LRRM 2015 (6th Cir. 1986); Machinists District 72 v. Teter Tool & Die Inc., 630 F. Supp. 732, 121 LRRM 3270 (N.D. Ind. 1986).

established law or decision of another forum. Although similar in orientation, these two bases differ somewhat in the way courts apply them, and they will be discussed separately.

### Against Public Policy

There is no codification of what constitutes "public policy." As with beauty, it lies in the eyes of the beholder (who in this case is a state or federal court judge). A review of the cases in which courts have vacated arbitration decisions because they violate public policy shows that the courts have found the awards to impinge on such sacrosanct matters as personal or public safety, constitutionally protected rights, and the rendering of necessary services or functions for the welfare of the public. The majority of these cases involve challenges to discharge actions that were based on conduct that had grave consequences, or the potential for such consequences, to significant numbers of people because of health or safety risks, but that were reversed by the arbitrator with the discharged employees being reinstated to their former employment. The following are examples of arbitration awards that courts have held to have violated public policy and were therefore vacated.

- Arbitrator reinstated employee who sexually harassed a co-worker, because the victim of the harassment failed to file a written complaint and made merely an oral complaint.[54]
- Employee who was discharged for testing positive for drugs following an oil tanker accident was reinstated by the arbitrator because the arbitrator believed the discharge was "excessive" on the basis that the grievant was not impaired and did not deal in drugs.[55]
- Reinstatement of a letter carrier who unlawfully delayed mail on grounds that the conduct was not purposeful nor undertaken for self-enrichment.[56]
- Arbitrator who, despite a finding of employee wrongdoing, reinstated a discharged licensed practical nurse who was negligent in administering cardiac medication based on the arbitrator's conclusion that the discharge was premised on a violation of a previously established probation rather than the failure to give medications.[57]

---

[54]Transp. Union v. Burlington N. R.R. Co., 864 F. Supp. 138, 147 LRRM 2325 (D. Ore. 1994).
[55]Exxon Shipping Co. v. Exxon Seamen's Union, 788 F. Supp. 829, 140 LRRM 2096 (D. N.J. 1992).
[56]U.S. Postal Serv. v. Letter Carriers, 631 F. Supp. 599, 121 LRRM 3501 (D. D.C. 1986).
[57]Russell Memorial Hosp. Ass'n v. Steelworkers, 720 F. Supp. 583, 132 LRRM 2642 (E.D. Mich. 1989).

- A nuclear power plant control room operator who was discharged for violation of plant rules in defeating an interlock system controlling the doors of a secondary containment area was overturned because of the arbitrator's finding of less serious consequences than the employer contended and the employer's failure to provide adequate training.[58]
- Arbitrator ordered reinstatement of a postal worker who shot two bullets through the window of a supervisor's unoccupied car following a shouting match with the supervisor, even though the employee pleaded guilty to criminal mischief charges in court for the same conduct.[59]
- An auto mechanic who, following previous warnings of failure to properly tighten bolts on customers' automobiles, was reinstated from discharge for repetition of the same type of negligence based on the arbitrator's evaluation that loss of employment was excessive for the infraction.[60]
- An airline pilot was reinstated by an arbitrator following discharge for flying commercial aircraft while intoxicated.[61]

### Contrary to Laws and/or Decisions of Courts or Administrative Agencies

Closely related, but somewhat different in rationale than the straight public policy situations, are those cases in which arbitrators' decisions have been reversed by the courts because the award and decision were contrary to some specific statute, body of decisional law, or a decision of a court of law or administrative agency (most commonly the National Labor Relations Board). Examples of awards that have been vacated for these reasons are as follows.

- Arbitrator awarded back pay for work claimed by two competing unions to members of the roofers union although the NLRB had previously awarded that same work to the laborers' union.[62]
- Professional football players were ordered by an arbitrator to pay union dues notwithstanding a right-to-work statute in the state in

---

[58]Iowa Elec. Light & Power Co. v. Elec. Workers IBEW Local 204, 834 F.2d 1424, 127 LRRM 2049 (8th Cir. 1987).

[59]U.S. Postal Serv. v. Letter Carriers, 663 F. Supp. 118, 125 LRRM 3190 (W.D. Pa. 1987).

[60]Stead Motors of Walnut Creek v. Machinists Lodge 1173, 843 F.2d 357, 127 LRRM 3213 (9th Cir. 1988).

[61]Delta Air Lines v. Air Line Pilots Ass'n, 861 F.2d 665, 130 LRRM 2014 (11th Cir. 1988).

[62]Roofers Local 30 v. Gundle Lining Constr. Corp., 1 F.3d 1429, 144 LRRM 2049 (3d Cir. 1993).

which players resided, which statute precluded mandatory union membership.[63]

- Arbitration award permitted trustees of joint union-management pension and welfare funds to increase unilaterally the rates of employer contributions to such funds in the face of labor contract language that required that wages and benefit changes be negotiated betweed the employer and the union.[64]
- Employee who was discharged for participating in an illegal strike was reinstated by arbitrator notwithstanding contrary settlement agreement between employer and union and despite public policy against such strikes enunciated in Sections 8(d) and (g) of the National Labor Relations Act, as amended.[65]
- Arbitrator's award required employer to commence contributions to a pension plan immediately following its entry into sponsorship of the pension plan despite a waiver of the annual minimum pension funding requirement during the first year of participation as provided in the controlling statute (ERISA).[66]
- Arbitration award required employer to reinstate a process technician who tested positive for cocaine where the arbitrator based the reinstatement decision on postdischarge conduct.[67]
- Award granted work jurisdiction to a union despite the fact that the NLRB had previously granted such work to another union.[68]

## SUMMARY OF CHALLENGES TO AWARDS

Arbitration was designed as a means of resolving disputes during the term of a labor contract in a prompt, inexpensive, and final manner. It has met those goals with astounding success. Occasionally, arbitrators have rendered decisions that appear, at least on their face, to be contrary

---

[63]Nat'l Football League Players Ass'n v. Pro-Football Inc. d/b/a Washington Redskins, 857 F. Supp. 71, 146 LRRM 2302 (D. D.C. 1994).

[64]Professional Adm'rs Ltd. v. Kopper-Glo Fuel Inc., 819 F.2d 639, 125 LRRM 3010 (6th Cir. 1987).

[65]Shelby County Health Care Corp. d/b/a Regional Medical Ctr. at Memphis v. State, County & Municipal Employees Local 1733, 756 F. Supp. 349, 137 LRRM 2565 (W.D. Tenn. 1991).

[66]Auto Workers v. Keystone Consol. Indus., 782 F.2d 1400, 121 LRRM 2702 (7th Cir. 1986).

[67]Gulf Coast Indus. Workers v. Exxon Co., USA, 991 F.2d 244, 143 LRRM 2375 (5th Cir. 1993).

[68]Eichleay Corp. v. Iron Workers, 944 F.2d 1047, 137 LRRM 2781 (3d Cir. 1991).

to the intent and meaning of the labor agreements on which they are based or appear to violate a well-established public policy, law, or decision of a judicial or administrative tribunal. More rarely, decisions have been rendered by arbitrators who appear to be biased or have an interest in the parties or issues in the case.

In such cases, the courts have carved out exceptions to the general rule disfavoring reversal of labor arbitration awards. Many of the exceptions appear to be little more than disagreement of judges with the result reached by the arbitrator. Other reversals seem to be based on more solid and established judicial bases. Nevertheless, the number of labor arbitration decisions that have been vacated (or not enforced) are so small as a percentage of all arbitration cases taken to court that any advocate or party to a labor contract contemplating a challenge to an award should give long and thoughtful consideration to the action. The unlikely chances of success, coupled with the deleterious effect on the collective bargaining relationship, are so persuasive against a challenge that such a move should be undertaken only in the most compelling of cases. Even then it should not be undertaken until all alternative solutions have been explored.

# APPENDIX A

## American Arbitration Association
## Labor Arbitration Rules

### (Including Expedited Labor Arbitration Procedures)

# Labor Arbitration Rules

## 1. Agreement of Parties

The parties shall be deemed to have made these rules a part of their arbitration agreement whenever, in a collective bargaining agreement or submission, they have provided for arbitration by the American Arbitration Association (hereinafter the AAA) or under its rules. These rules and any amendment thereof shall apply in the form obtaining when the arbitration is initiated. The parties, by written agreement, may vary the procedures set forth in these rules.

## 2. Name of Tribunal

Any tribunal constituted by the parties under these rules shall be called the Labor Arbitration Tribunal.

## 3. Administrator

When parties agree to arbitrate under these rules and an arbitration is instituted thereunder, they thereby authorize the AAA to administer the arbitration. The authority and obligations of the administrator are as provided in the agreement of the parties and in these rules.

## 4. Delegation of Duties

The duties of the AAA may be carried out through such representatives or committees as the AAA may direct.

## 5. Panel of Labor Arbitrators

The AAA shall establish and maintain a Panel of Labor Arbitrators and shall appoint arbitrators therefrom as hereinafter provided.

## 6. Office of Tribunal

The general office of the Labor Arbitration Tribunal is the headquarters of the AAA, which may, however, assign the administration of an arbitration to any of its regional offices.

## 7. Initiation under an Arbitration Clause in a Collective Bargaining Agreement

Arbitration under an arbitration clause in a collective bargaining agreement under these rules may be initiated by either party in the following manner—

(a) by giving written notice to the other party of its intention to arbitrate (demand), which notice shall contain a statement setting forth the nature of the dispute and the remedy sought, and

(b) by filing at any regional office of the AAA three copies of the notice, together with a copy of the collective bargaining agreement or such parts thereof as relate to the dispute, including the arbitration provisions. After the arbitrator is appointed, no new or different claim may be submitted except with the consent of the arbitrator and all other parties.

## 8. Answer

The party upon whom the demand for arbitration is made may file an answering statement with the AAA within ten days after notice from the AAA, simultaneously sending a copy to the other party. If no answer is filed within the stated time, it will be treated as a denial of the claim. Failure to file an answer shall not operate to delay the arbitration.

## 9. Initiation under a Submission

Parties to any collective bargaining agreement may initiate an arbitration under these rules by filing at any regional office of the AAA two copies of a written agreement to arbitrate under these rules (submission), signed by the parties and setting forth the nature of the dispute and the remedy sought.

## 10. Fixing of Locale

The parties may mutually agree on the locale where the arbitration is to be held. If the locale is not designated in the collective bargaining agreement or submission, and if there is a dispute as to the appropriate locale, the AAA shall have the power to determine the locale and its decision shall be binding.

## 11. Qualifications of Arbitrator

Any neutral arbitrator appointed pursuant to Section 12, 13, or 14 or selected by mutual choice of the parties or their appointees, shall be subject to disqualification for the reasons specified in Section 17. If the parties specifically so agree in writing, the arbitrator shall not be subject to disqualification for those reasons.

Unless the parties agree otherwise, an arbitrator selected unilaterally by one party is a party-appointed arbitrator and is not subject to disqualification pursuant to Section 17.

The term "arbitrator" in these rules refers to the arbitration panel, whether composed of one or more arbitrators and whether the arbitrators are neutral or party appointed.

## 12. Appointment from Panel

If the parties have not appointed an arbitrator and have not provided any other method of appointment, the arbitrator shall be appointed in the following manner: immediately after the filing of the demand or submission, the AAA shall submit simultaneously to each party an identical list of names of persons chosen from the Panel of Labor Arbitrators. Each party shall have ten days from the mailing date in which to strike any name to which it objects, number the remaining names to indicate the order of preference, and return the list to the AAA.

If a party does not return the list within the time specified, all persons named therein shall be deemed acceptable.

From among the persons who have been approved on both lists, and in accordance with the designated order of mutual preference, the AAA shall invite the acceptance of an arbitrator to serve. If the parties fail to agree upon any of the persons named, if those named decline or are unable to act, or if for any other reason the appointment cannot be made from the submitted lists, the administrator shall have the power to make the appointment from among other members of the panel without the submission of any additional list.

## 13. Direct Appointment by Parties

If the agreement of the parties names an arbitrator or specifies a method of appointing an arbitrator, that designation or method shall be followed. The

notice of appointment, with the name and address of the arbitrator, shall be filed with the AAA by the appointing party. Upon the request of any appointing party, the AAA shall submit a list of members of the panel from which the party may, if it so desires, make the appointment.

If the agreement specifies a period of time within which an arbitrator shall be appointed and any party fails to make an appointment within that period, the AAA may make the appointment.

If no period of time is specified in the agreement, the AAA shall notify the parties to make the appointment and if within ten days thereafter such arbitrator has not been so appointed, the AAA shall make the appointment.

## 14. Appointment of Neutral Arbitrator by Party-Appointed Arbitrators

If the parties have appointed their arbitrators or if either or both of them have been appointed as provided in Section 13, and have authorized those arbitrators to appoint a neutral arbitrator within a specified time and no appointment is made within that time or any agreed extension thereof, the AAA may appoint a neutral arbitrator who shall act as chairperson.

If no period of time is specified for appointment of the neutral arbitrator and the parties do not make the appointment within ten days from the date of the appointment of the last party-appointed arbitrator, the AAA shall appoint a neutral arbitrator who shall act as chairperson.

If the parties have agreed that the arbitrators shall appoint the neutral arbitrator from the panel, the AAA shall furnish to the party-appointed arbitrators, in the manner prescribed in Section 12, a list selected from the panel, and the appointment of the neutral arbitrator shall be made as prescribed in that section.

## 15. Number of Arbitrators

If the arbitration agreement does not specify the number of arbitrators, the dispute shall be heard and determined by one arbitrator, unless the parties otherwise agree.

## 16. Notice to Arbitrator of Appointment

Notice of the appointment of the neutral arbitrator shall be mailed to the arbitrator by the AAA and the signed acceptance of the arbitrator shall be filed with the AAA prior to the opening of the first hearing.

## 17. Disclosure and Challenge Procedure

No person shall serve as a neutral arbitrator in any arbitration under these rules in which that person has any financial or personal interest in the result of the arbitration. Any prospective or designated neutral arbitrator shall immediately disclose any circumstance likely to affect impartiality, including any bias or financial or personal interest in the result of the arbitration. Upon receipt of this information from the arbitrator or another source, the AAA shall communicate the information to the parties and, if it deems it appropriate to do so, to the arbitrator. Upon objection of a party to the continued service of a neutral arbitrator, the AAA, after consultation with the parties and the arbitrator, shall determine whether the arbitrator should be disqualified and shall inform the parties of its decision, which shall be conclusive.

## 18. Vacancies

If any arbitrator should resign, die, or otherwise be unable to perform the duties of the office, the AAA shall, on proof satisfactory to it, declare the office vacant. Vacancies shall be filled in the same manner as that governing the making of the original appointment, and the matter shall be reheard by the new arbitrator.

## 19. Date, Time, and Place of Hearing

The arbitrator shall fix the date, time, and place for each hearing. At least five days prior thereto, the AAA shall mail notice of the date, time, and place of hearing to each party, unless the parties otherwise agree.

## 20. Representation

Any party may be represented by counsel or other authorized representative.

## 21. Stenographic Record and Interpreters

Any party wishing a stenographic record shall make arrangements directly with a stenographer and shall notify the other parties of such arrangements in advance of the hearing. The requesting party or parties shall pay the cost of the record. If the transcript is agreed by the parties to be or, in appropriate cases, determined by the arbitrator to be the official record of the proceeding, it must be made available to the arbitrator and to the other party for inspection, at a time and place determined by the arbitrator.

Any party wishing an interpreter shall make all arrangements directly with the interpreter and shall assume the costs of the service.

## 22. Attendance at Hearings

Persons having a direct interest in the arbitration are entitled to attend hearings. The arbitrator shall have the power to require the retirement of any witness or witnesses during the testimony of other witnesses. It shall be discretionary with the arbitrator to determine the propriety of the attendance of any other person.

## 23. Postponements

The arbitrator for good cause shown may postpone the hearing upon the request of a party or upon his or her own initiative and shall postpone when all of the parties agree thereto.

## 24. Oaths

Before proceeding with the first hearing, each arbitrator may take an oath of office and, if required by law, shall do so. The arbitrator may require witnesses to testify under oath administered by any duly qualified person and, if required by law or requested by either party, shall do so.

## 25. Majority Decision

Whenever there is more than one arbitrator, all decisions of the arbitrators shall be by majority vote. The award shall also be made by majority vote unless the concurrence of all is expressly required.

## 26. Order of Proceedings

A hearing shall be opened by the filing of the oath of the arbitrator, where required; by the recording of the date, time, and place of the hearing and the presence of the arbitrator, the parties, and counsel, if any; and by the receipt by the arbitrator of the demand and answer, if any, or the submission.

Exhibits may, when offered by either party, be received in evidence by the arbitrator. The names and addresses of all witnesses and exhibits in order received shall be made a part of the record.

The arbitrator may vary the normal procedure under which the initiating party first presents its claim, but in any case shall afford full and equal opportunity to all parties for the presentation of relevant proofs.

## 27. Arbitration in the Absence of a Party or Representative

Unless the law provides to the contrary, the arbitration may proceed in the absence of any party or representative who, after due notice, fails to be present or fails to obtain a postponement. An award shall not be made solely on the default of a party. The arbitrator shall require the other party to submit such evidence as may be required for the making of an award.

## 28. Evidence

The parties may offer such evidence as is relevant and material to the dispute, and shall produce such additional evidence as the arbitrator may deem necessary to an understanding and determination of the dispute. An arbitrator authorized by law to subpoena witnesses and documents may do so independently or upon the request of any party. The arbitrator shall be the judge of the relevance and materiality of the evidence offered and conformity to legal rules of evidence shall not be necessary. All evidence shall be taken in the presence of all of the arbitrators and all of the parties except where any of the parties is absent in default or has waived the right to be present.

### 29. Evidence by Affidavit and Filing of Documents
The arbitrator may receive and consider the evidence of witnesses by affidavit, giving it only such weight as seems proper after consideration of any objection made to its admission.

All documents that are not filed with the arbitrator at the hearing, but arranged at the hearing or subsequently by agreement of the parties to be submitted, shall be filed with the AAA for transmission to the arbitrator. All parties shall be afforded opportunity to examine such documents.

### 30. Inspection
Whenever the arbitrator deems it necessary, he or she may make an inspection in connection with the subject matter of the dispute after written notice to the parties, who may, if they so desire, be present at the inspection.

### 31. Closing of Hearings
The arbitrator shall inquire of all parties whether they have any further proof to offer or witness to be heard. Upon receiving negative replies or if satisfied that the record is complete, the arbitrator shall declare the hearings closed and a minute thereof shall be recorded. If briefs or other documents are to be filed, the hearings shall be declared closed as of the final date set by the arbitrator for filing with the AAA. If documents are to be filed as provided in Section 29 and the date for their receipt is later than the date set for the receipt of briefs, the later date shall be the date of closing the hearing. The time limit within which the arbitrator is required to make an award shall commence to run, in the absence of another agreement by the parties, upon the closing of the hearings.

### 32. Reopening of Hearings
The hearings may for good cause shown be reopened by the arbitrator at will or on the motion of either party at any time before the award is made but, if the reopening of the hearings would prevent the making of the award within the specific time agreed

upon by the parties in the contract out of which the controversy has arisen, the matter may not be reopened unless both parties agree to extend the time. When no specific date is fixed in the contract, the arbitrator may reopen the hearings and shall have thirty days from the closing of the reopened hearings within which to make an award.

### 33. Waiver of Oral Hearings
The parties may provide, by written agreement, for the waiver of oral hearings. If the parties are unable to agree as to the procedure, the AAA shall specify a fair and equitable procedure.

### 34. Waiver of Rules
Any party who proceeds with the arbitration after knowledge that any provision or requirement of these rules has not been complied with and who fails to state an objection thereto in writing shall be deemed to have waived the right to object.

### 35. Extensions of Time
The parties may modify any period of time by mutual agreement. The AAA or the arbitrator may for good cause extend any period of time established by these rules, except the time for making the award. The AAA shall notify the parties of any such extension of time and its reason therefor.

### 36. Serving of Notice
Each party to a submission or other agreement that provides for arbitration under these rules shall be deemed to have consented and shall consent that any papers, notices, or process necessary or proper for the initiation or continuation of an arbitration under these rules; for any court action in connection therewith; or for the entry of judgment on an award made thereunder may be served upon the party by mail addressed to the party or its representative at the last known address or by personal service, in or outside the state where the arbitration is to be held.

The AAA and the parties may also use facsimile transmission, telex, telegram, or other written forms of electronic communication to give the notices required by these rules.

### 37. Time of Award
The award shall be rendered promptly by the arbitrator and, unless otherwise agreed by the parties or specified by law, no later than thirty days from the date of closing the hearings, with five additional days for mailing if briefs are to be filed.

If oral hearings have been waived, the award shall be rendered no later than thirty days from the date of transmitting the final statements and proofs to the arbitrator.

## 38. Form of Award

The award shall be in writing and shall be signed either by the neutral arbitrator or by a concurring majority if there is more than one arbitrator. The parties shall advise the AAA whenever they do not require the arbitrator to accompany the award with an opinion.

## 39. Award upon Settlement

If the parties settle their dispute during the course of the arbitration, the arbitrator may, upon their request, set forth the terms of the agreed settlement in an award.

## 40. Delivery of Award to Parties

Parties shall accept as legal delivery of the award the placing of the award or a true copy thereof in the mail by the AAA, addressed to the party at its last known address or to its representative; personal service of the award; or the filing of the award in any other manner that is permitted by law.

## 41. Release of Documents for Judicial Proceedings

The AAA shall, upon the written request of a party, furnish to such party, at its expense, certified facsimiles of any papers in the AAA's possession that may be required in judicial proceedings relating to the arbitration.

## 42. Judicial Proceedings and Exclusion of Liability

(a) Neither the AAA nor any arbitrator in a proceeding under these rules is a necessary party in judicial proceedings relating to the arbitration.

(b) Neither the AAA nor any arbitrator shall be liable to any party for any act or omission in connection with any arbitration conducted under these rules.

## 43. Administrative Fees

As a not-for-profit organization, the AAA shall prescribe an administrative fee schedule to compensate it for the cost of providing administrative services. The schedule in effect at the time of filing shall be applicable.

## 44. Expenses

The expenses of witnesses for either side shall be paid by the party producing such witnesses.

Expenses of the arbitration, other than the cost of the stenographic record, including required traveling and other expenses of the arbitrator and of AAA representatives and the expenses of any witness or the cost of any proof produced at the direct request of the arbitrator, shall be borne equally by the parties, unless they agree otherwise, or unless the arbitrator, in the award, assesses such expenses or any part thereof against any specified party or parties.

## 45. Communication with Arbitrator

There shall be no communication between the parties and a neutral arbitrator other than at oral hearings, unless the parties and the arbitrator agree otherwise. Any other oral or written communication from the parties to the arbitrator shall be directed to the AAA for transmittal to the arbitrator.

## 46. Interpretation and Application of Rules

The arbitrator shall interpret and apply these rules insofar as they relate to the arbitrator's powers and duties. When there is more than one arbitrator and a difference arises among them concerning the meaning or application of any such rule, it shall be decided by a majority vote. If that is unobtainable, the arbitrator or either party may refer the question to the AAA for final decision. All other rules shall be interpreted and applied by the AAA.

*Administrative Fees*

### Initial Administrative Fee

The initial administrative fee is $150 for each party, due and payable at the time of filing. No refund of the initial fee is made when a matter is withdrawn or settled after the filing of the demand for arbitration or submission.

### Arbitrator Compensation

Unless mutually agreed otherwise, the arbitrator's compensation shall be borne equally by the parties, in accordance with the fee structure disclosed in the arbitrator's biographical profile submitted to the parties.

### Additional Hearing Fees

A fee of $50 is payable by each party for each hearing held after the first hearing.

### Hearing Room Rental

Hearing rooms for second and subsequent hearings are available on a rental basis at AAA offices. Check with your local office for specific availability and rates.

### Postponement Fees

A fee of $50 is payable by a party causing a postponement of any scheduled hearing.

# Expedited Labor Arbitration Procedures

In response to the concern of parties over rising costs and delays in grievance arbitration, the American Arbitration Association has established expedited procedures under which cases are scheduled promptly and awards rendered no later than seven days after the hearings. In return for giving up certain features of traditional labor arbitration, such as transcripts, briefs, and extensive opinions, the parties using these simplified procedures can get quick decisions and realize certain cost savings.

Leading labor arbitrators have indicated a willingness to offer their services under these procedures, and the Association makes every effort to assign the best possible arbitrators with early available hearing dates. Since the establishment of these procedures, an ever increasing number of parties has taken advantage of them.

## E1. Agreement of Parties

These procedures shall apply whenever the parties have agreed to arbitrate under them, the Streamlined Labor Arbitration Rules, or the Expedited Labor Arbitration Rules of the American Arbitration Association, in the form obtaining when the arbitration is initiated.

These procedures shall be applied as set forth below, in addition to any other portion of the Labor Arbitration Rules that is not in conflict with these expedited procedures.

## E2. Appointment of Neutral Arbitrator

The AAA shall appoint a single neutral arbitrator from its Panel of Labor Arbitrators, who shall hear and determine the case promptly.

## E3. Qualifications of Neutral Arbitrator

No person shall serve as a neutral arbitrator in any arbitration in which that person has any financial or personal interest in the result of the arbitration. Prior to accepting an appointment, the prospective arbitrator shall disclose any circumstance likely to prevent a prompt hearing or to create a presumption of bias. Upon receipt of such information, the AAA shall immediately replace that arbitrator or communicate the information to the parties.

## E4. Vacancies

The AAA is authorized to substitute another arbitrator if a vacancy occurs or if an appointed arbitrator is unable to serve promptly.

## E5. Date, Time, and Place of Hearing

The arbitrator shall fix the date, time, and place of the hearing, notice of which must be given at least 24 hours in advance. Such notice may be given orally or by facsimile.

## E6. No Stenographic Record

There shall be no stenographic record of the proceedings.

## E7. Proceedings

The hearing shall be conducted by the arbitrator in whatever manner will most expeditiously permit full presentation of the evidence and arguments of the parties. The arbitrator shall make an appropriate minute of the proceedings. Normally, the hearing shall be completed within one day. In unusual circumstances and for good cause shown, the arbitrator may schedule an additional hearing to be held within seven days.

## E8. Posthearing Briefs

There shall be no posthearing briefs.

## E9. Time of Award

The award shall be rendered promptly by the arbitrator and, unless otherwise agreed by the parties, no later than seven days from the date of the closing of the hearing.

## E10. Form of Award

The award shall be in writing and shall be signed by the arbitrator. If the arbitrator determines that an opinion is necessary, it shall be in summary form.

## Administrative Fees

### Initial Administrative Fee

The initial administrative fee is $75 for each party, due and payable at the time of filing. No refund of the initial fee is made when a matter is withdrawn or settled after the filing of the demand for arbitration or submission.

### Arbitrator Compensation

Unless mutually agreed otherwise, the arbitrator's compensation shall be borne equally by the parties, in accordance with the fee structure disclosed in the arbitrator's biographical profile sumitted to the parties.

## Additional Hearing Fees

A fee of $50 is payable by each party for each hearing held after the first hearing.

## Hearing Room Rental

Hearing rooms for second and subsequent hearings are available on a rental basis at AAA offices. Check with your local office for specific availability and rates.

## Postponement Fees

A fee of $50 is payable by a party causing a postponement of any scheduled hearing.

*Source:* American Arbitration Association.

# APPENDIX B

## Federal Mediation and Conciliation Service
## Office of Arbitration Services

# Policies, Functions, and Procedures

## Subpart A: Arbitration Policy; Administration of Roster

### 1404.1 Scope and Authority

This chapter is issued by the Federal Mediation and Conciliation Service (FMCS) under Title II of the Labor Management Relations Act of 1947 (Public Law 80-101) as amended in 1959 (Public Law 86-257) and 1974 (Public Law 93-360). The chapter applies to all arbitrators listed on the FMCS Roster of Arbitrators, to all applicants for listing on the Roster, and to all persons or parties seeking to obtain from FMCS either names or panels of names of arbitrators listed on the Roster in connection with disputes which are to be submitted to arbitration or fact-finding.

### 1404.2 Policy

The labor policy of the United States is designed to promote the settlement of issues between employers and represented employees through the processes of collective bargaining and voluntary arbitration. This policy encourages the use of voluntary arbitration to resolve disputes over the interpretation or application of collective bargaining agreements. Voluntary arbitration and fact-finding in disputes and disagreements over establishment or modification of contract terms are important features of constructive labor-management relations, as alternatives to economic strife in the settlement of labor disputes.

### 1404.3 Administrative Responsibilities

(a) *Director.* The Director of FMCS has ultimate responsibility for all aspects of FMCS arbitration activities and is the final agency authority on all questions concerning the Roster or FMCS arbitration procedures.

(b) *Office of Arbitration Services.* The Office of Arbitration Services (OAS) maintains a Roster of Arbitrators (the "Roster"); administers Subpart C of these Regulations (Procedures for Arbitration Services); assists, promotes, and cooperates in the establishment of programs for training and developing new arbitrators; collects information and statistics concerning the arbitration function, and performs other tasks in connection with the function that may be assigned by the Director.

(c) *Arbitrator Review Board.* The Arbitrator Review Board (the "Board") shall consist of a presiding officer and such members and alternate members as the Director may appoint, and who shall serve at the Director's pleasure and may be removed at any time. The Board shall be composed entirely of full-time officers or employees of the Federal Government. The Board shall establish its own procedures for carrying out its duties.

(1) *Duties of the Board.* The Board shall:

(i) Review the qualifications of all applicants for listing on the Roster, interpreting and applying the criteria set forth in subsection 1404.5 of this part;
(ii) Review the status of all persons whose continued eligibility for listing on the Roster has been questioned under subsection 1404.5 of this part;
(iii) Make recommendations to the Director regarding acceptance or rejection of applicants for listing on the Roster, or regarding withdrawal of listing on the Roster for any of the reasons set forth herein.

## Subpart B: Roster of Arbitrators; Admission and Retention

### 1404.4 Roster and Status of Members

(a) *The Roster.* The FMCS shall maintain a Roster of labor arbitrators consisting of persons who meet the criteria for listing contained in subsection 1404.5 of this part and whose names have not been removed from the Roster in accordance with subsection 1404.5(d).

497

(b) *Adherence to Standards and Requirements.* Persons listed on the Roster shall comply with the FMCS rules and regulations pertaining to arbitration and with such guidelines and procedures as may be issued by OAS pursuant to Subpart C hereof. Arbitrators are also expected to conform to the ethical standards and procedures set forth in the Code of Professional Responsibility for Arbitrators of Labor Management Disputes, as approved by the Joint Steering Committee of the National Academy of Arbitrators.

(c) *Status of Arbitrators.* Persons who are listed on the Roster and are selected or appointed to hear arbitration matters or to serve as factfinders do not become employees of the Federal Government by virtue of their selection or appointment. Following selection or appointment, the arbitrator's relationship is solely with the parties to the dispute, except that arbitrators are subject to certain reporting requirements and to standards of conduct as set forth in this Part.

(d) *Role of FMCS.* FMCS has no power to:

(1) Compel parties to arbitrate or agree to arbitration;
(2) Enforce an agreement to arbitrate;
(3) Compel parties to agree to a particular arbitrator;
(4) Influence, alter or set aside decisions of arbitrators listed on the Roster;
(5) Compel, deny or modify payment of compensation to an arbitrator.

(e) *Nominations and Panels.* On request of the parties to an agreement to arbitrate or engage in fact-finding, or where arbitration or fact-finding may be provided for by statute, OAS will provide names or panels of names without charge. Procedures for obtaining these services are contained in Subpart C. Neither the submission of a nomination or panel nor the appointment of an arbitrator constitutes a determination by FMCS that an agreement to arbitrate or enter fact-finding proceedings exists; nor does such action constitute a ruling that the matter in controversy is arbitrable under any agreement.

(f) *Rights of Persons Listed on the Roster.* No person shall have any right to be listed or to remain listed on the Roster. FMCS retains the authority and responsibility to assure that the needs of the parties using its facilities are served. To accomplish this purpose it may establish procedures for the preparation of panels or the appointment of arbitrators or factfinders which include consideration of such factors as background and experience, availability, acceptability, geographical location and the expressed preferences of the parties.

## 1404.5 Listing on the Roster; Criteria for Listing and Retention

Persons seeking to be listed on the Roster must complete and submit an application form which may be obtained from the Office of Arbitration Services. Upon receipt of an executed form, OAS will review the application, assure that it is complete, make such inquiries as are necessary, and submit the application to the Arbitrator Review Board. The Board will review the completed applications under the criteria set forth in subsections (a), (b) and (c) of this Section, and will forward to the Director its recommendation on each applicant. The Director makes all final decisions as to whether an applicant may be listed. Each applicant shall be notified in writing of the Director's decision and the reasons therefore.

(a) *General Criteria.* Applicants for the Roster will be listed on the Roster upon a determination that they:

(1) Are experienced, competent and acceptable in decision-making roles in the resolution of labor relations disputes; or
(2) Have extensive experience in relevant positions in collective bargaining; and
(3) Are capable of conducting an orderly hearing, can analyze testimony and exhibits and can prepare clear and concise findings and awards within reasonable time limits.

(b) *Proof of Qualifications.* The qualifications listed in (a) above are preferably demonstrated by the submission of actual arbitration awards prepared by the applicant while serving as an impartial arbitrator chosen by the parties to disputes. Equivalent experience acquired in training, internship or other development programs, or experience such as that acquired as a hearing officer or judge in labor relations controversies may also be considered by the Board.

(c) *Advocacy.*

(1) Definition. An advocate is a person who represents employers, labor organizations, or individuals as an employee, attorney or consultant, in matters of labor relations, including but not limited to the subjects of union representation and recognition matters, collective bargaining, arbitration, unfair labor practices, equal employment opportunity and other areas generally recognized as constituting labor relations. The definition includes representatives of employers or employees in individual cases or controversies involving workmen's compensation, occupational health or safety, minimum wage or other labor standards matters.

The definition of advocate also includes a person who is directly associated with an advocate in a business or professional relationship as, for example, partners or employees of a law firm.

(2) Eligibility. Except in the case of persons listed on the Roster before November 17, 1976, no person who is an advocate, as defined above, may be listed. No person who was listed on the Roster at any time who was not an advocate when listed or who did not divulge advocacy at the time of listing may continue to be listed after becoming an advocate or after the fact of advocacy is revealed.

(d) *Duration of Listing, Retention.* Initial listing may be for a period not to exceed three years, and may be renewed thereafter for periods not to exceed two years, provided upon review that this listing is not cancelled by the Director as set forth below. Notice of cancellation may be given to the member whenever the member;

(1) No longer meets the criteria for admission;

(2) Has been repeatedly and flagrantly delinquent in submitting awards;

(3) Has refused to make reasonable and periodic reports to FMCS, as required in Subpart C, concerning activities pertaining to arbitration;

(4) Has been the subject of complaints by parties who use FMCS facilities, and the Director, after appropriate inquiry, concludes that just cause for cancellation has been shown;

(5) Is determined by the Director to be unacceptable to the parties who use FMCS arbitration facilities; the Director may base a determination of unacceptability on FMCS records showing the number of times the arbitrator's name has been proposed to the parties and the number of times it has been selected.

No listing may be cancelled without at least sixty days notice of the reasons for the proposed removal, unless the Director determines that the FMCS or the parties will be harmed by continued listing. In such cases an arbitrator's listing may be suspended without notice or delay pending final determination in accordance with these procedures. The member shall in either case have an opportunity to submit a written response showing why the listing should not be cancelled. The Director may, at his discretion, appoint a hearing officer to conduct an inquiry into the facts of any proposed cancellation and to make recommendations to the Director.

**1404.6 Freedom of Choice**

Nothing contained herein should be construed to limit the rights of parties who use FMCS arbitration facilities to select jointly any arbitrator or arbitration procedure acceptable to them.

**Subpart C: Procedures for Arbitration Services**

**1404.10 Procedures for Requesting Arbitration Panels**

The Office of Arbitration Services has been delegated the responsibility for administering all requests for arbitration services under these regulations.

(a) The Service will refer a panel of arbitrators to the parties upon request. The Service prefers to act upon a joint request which should be addressed to the Federal Mediation and Conciliation Service, Washington, D.C. 20427, Attention: Office of Arbitration Services. In the event that the request is made by only one party, the Service will submit a panel; however, any submission of a panel should not be construed as anything more than compliance with a request and does not necessarily reflect the contractual requirements of the parties.

(b) The parties are urged to use the Request for Arbitration Panel form (R-43) which has been prepared by the Service and is available in quantity at all FMCS regional offices and field stations or upon request to the Federal Mediation and Conciliation Service, Office of Arbitration Services, Washington, D.C. 20427. The form R-43 is reproduced herein for the purpose of identification.

(c) A brief statement of the issues in dispute should accompany the request and enable the Service to submit the names of arbitrators qualified for the issues involved. The request should also include a current copy of the arbitration section of the collective bargaining agreement or stipulation to arbitrate.

(d) If form R-43 is not utilized, the parties may request a panel by letter which must include the names, addresses, and phone numbers of the parties, the location of the contemplated hearing, the issue in dispute, the number of names desired on the panel, the industry involved and any special qualifications of the panel or special requirement desired.

**1404.11 Arbitrability**

Where either party claims that a dispute is not subject to arbitration, the Service will not decide the merits of such claim.

Copy No. 1, Original - To Federal Mediation and Conciliation Service

## 1404.12 Nominations of Arbitrators

(a) When the parties have been unable to agree on an arbitrator, the Service will submit to the parties on request the names of seven arbitrators unless the applicable collective bargaining agreement provides for a different number, or unless the parties themselves request a different number. Together with the submission of a panel of arbitrators, the Service will furnish a biographical sketch for each member of the panel. This sketch states the background, qualifications, experience, and per diem fee established by the arbitrator. It states the existence, if any, of other fees such as cancellation, postponement, rescheduling or administrative fees.

(b) When a panel is submitted, an FMCS control case number is assigned. All future communications between the parties and the Service should refer to the case number.

(c) The Service considers many factors when selecting names for inclusion on a panel, but the agreed-upon wishes of the parties are paramount. Special qualifications of arbitrators experienced in certain issues or industries, or possessing certain backgrounds, may be identified for purposes of submitting panels to accommodate the parties. The Service may also consider such things as general acceptability, geographical location, general experience, availability, size of fee, and the need to expose new arbitrators to the selection process in preparing panels. The Service has no obligation to put an individual on any given panel, or on a minimum number of panels in any fixed period, such as a month or a year.

(1) If at any time both parties request, for valid reasons, that a name or names be omitted from a panel, such name or names will be omitted, unless they are excessive in number.

(2) If at any time both parties request that a name or names be included on a panel, such name or names will be included.

(3) If only one party requests that a name or names be omitted from a panel, or that specific individuals be added to the panel, such request shall not be honored.

(4) If the issue described in the request appears to require special technical experience or qualifications, arbitrators who possess such qualifications will, where possible, be included on the panel submitted to the parties.

(5) In almost all cases, an arbitrator is chosen from one panel. However, if either party requests another panel, the Service shall comply with the request providing that an additional panel is permissible under the terms of the agreement or the other party so agrees. Requests for more than two panels must be accompanied by a statement of explanation and will be considered on a case-by-case basis.

## 1404.13 Selection and Appointment of Arbitrators

(a) The parties should notify the OAS of their selection of an arbitrator. The arbitrator, upon notification by the parties, shall notify the OAS of his selection and willingness to serve. Upon notification of the parties' selection of an arbitrator, the Service will make a formal appointment of the arbitrator.

(b) Where the contract is silent on the manner of selecting arbitrators, the parties may wish to consider one of the following methods for selection of an arbitrator from a panel:

(1) Each party alternately strikes a name from the submitted panel until one remains.

(2) Each party advises the Service of its order of preference by numbering each name on the panel and submitting the numbered list in writing to OAS. The name on the panel that has the lowest accumulated numerical number will be appointed.

(3) Informal agreement of the parties by whatever method they choose.

(c) The Service will, on joint or unilateral request of the parties, submit a panel or, when the applicable collective bargaining agreement authorizes, will make a direct appointment of an arbitrator. Submission of a panel or name signifies nothing more than compliance with a request and in no way constitutes a determination by the Service that the parties are obligated to arbitrate the dispute in question. Resolution of disputes as to the propriety of such a submission or appointment rests solely with the parties.

(d) The arbitrator, upon notification of appointment, is required to communicate with the parties immediately to arrange for preliminary matters, such as date and place of hearing.

### 1404.14 Conduct of Hearings

(a) All proceedings conducted by the arbitrator shall be in conformity with the contractual obligations of the parties. The arbitrator is also expected to conduct all proceedings in conformity with Section 1404.4(b). The conduct of the arbitration proceeding is under the arbitrator's jurisdiction and control and the arbitrator's decision is to be based upon the evidence and testimony presented at the hearing or otherwise incorporated in the record of the proceeding. The arbitrator may, unless prohibited by law, proceed in the absence of any party who, after due notice, fails to be present or to obtain a postponement. An award rendered in an *ex parte* proceeding of this nature must be based upon evidence presented to the arbitrator.

### 1404.15 Decision and Award

(a) Arbitrators are encouraged to render awards not later than 60 days from the date of the closing of the record as determined by the arbitrator, unless otherwise agreed upon by the parties or specified by law. A failure to render timely awards reflects upon the performance of an arbitrator and may lead to his removal from the FMCS Roster.

(b) The parties should inform the OAS whenever a decision is unduly delayed. The arbitrator shall notify the OAS if and when the arbitrator (1) cannot schedule, hear and determine issues promptly, or; (2) learns a dispute has been settled by the parties prior to the decision.

(c) After an award has been submitted to the parties, the arbitrator is required to submit a Fee and Award Statement, form R-19 showing a breakdown of the fee and expense charges so that the Service may be in a position to review conformance with stated charges under Section 1404.12(a). Filing the Statement within 15 days after rendering an award is required of all arbitrators. The Statements are not used for the purpose of compelling payment of fees.

(d) The Service encourages the publication of arbitration awards. However, the Service expects arbitrators it has nominated or appointed not to give publicity to awards they issue if objected to by one of the parties.

### 1404.16. Fees and Charges of Arbitrators

(a) No administrative or filing fee is charged by the Service. The current policy of the Service permits each of its nominees or appointees to charge a per diem fee and other predetermined fees for services, the amount of which has been certified in advance to the Service. Each arbitrator's maximum per diem fee and the existence of other predetermined fees, if any, are set forth on a biographical sketch which is sent to the parties when panels are submitted and are the controlling fees. The arbitrator shall not change any fee or add charges without giving at least 30 days advance notice to the Service.

(b) In cases involving unusual amounts of time and expenses relative to pre-hearing and post-hearing administration of a particular case, an administrative charge may be made by the arbitrator.

(c) All charges other than those specified by 1404.16(a) shall be divulged to and agreement obtained by the arbitrator with the parties immediately after appointment.

(d) The Service requests that it be notified of any arbitrator's deviation from the policies expressed herein. However, the Service will not attempt to resolve any fee dispute.

### 1404.17 Reports and Biographical Sketches

(a) Arbitrators listed on the Roster shall execute and return all documents, forms and reports required by the Service. They shall also keep the Service informed of changes of address, telephone number, availability, and of any business of other connection or relationship which involves labor-management relations, or which creates or gives the appearance of advocacy as defined in Section 1404.4(c)(1).

(b) The Service may require each arbitrator listed on the Roster to prepare at the time of initial listing, and to revise, biographical information in accordance with a format to be provided by the Service at the time of initial listing or biennial review. Arbitrators may also request revision of biographical information at other times to reflect changes in fees, the existence of additional charges, address, experience or background, or other relevant data. The Service reserves the right to decide and approve the format and content of biographical sketches.

*Source:* 29. C.F.R. § 1404.

# APPENDIX C

# FEDERAL RULES OF EVIDENCE

## (as amended through December 1, 1993)

[Author's Note: As discussed in Chapter 10, rules of evidence are applied very loosely, if at all, in labor arbitration hearings. Nevertheless, they appear to be applied more frequently as more and more cases are presented by lawyers, and as more lawyers are serving as arbitrators. The Federal Rules of Evidence are included in this Appendix as a reference for those advocates and arbitrators who find themselves facing significant evidentiary issues, and who wish to consult the most universal set of evidentiary rules in the United States. Certain rules relating solely to civil or criminal cases in the courts which have no relevance to labor arbitration have been deleted. In such cases the subject of the rule is retained, but the content has been deleted.]

## TABLE OF CONTENTS

## ARTICLE V.   PRIVILEGES

## ARTICLE VI.   WITNESSES

## ARTICLE VII.   OPINIONS AND EXPERT TESTIMONY

# RULES OF EVIDENCE FOR UNITED STATES COURTS AND MAGISTRATES

## ARTICLE I.  GENERAL PROVISIONS

### Rule 101.  Scope

These rules govern proceedings in the courts of the United States and before the United States bankruptcy judges and United States magistrate judges, to the extent and with the exceptions stated in rule 1101.

### Rule 102.  Purpose and construction

These rules shall be construed to secure fairness in administration, elimination of unjustifiable expense and delay, and promotion of growth and development of the law of evidence to the end that the truth may be ascertained and proceedings justly determined.

### Rule 103.  Rulings on evidence

**(a) Effect of erroneous ruling.**   Error may not be predicated upon a ruling which admits or excludes evidence unless a substantial right of the party is affected, and

**(1) Objection.**   In the case the ruling is one admitting evidence, a timely objection or motion to strike appears of record, stating the specific ground of objection, if the specific ground was not apparent from the context; or

**(2) Offer of proof.**   In case the ruling is one excluding evidence, the substance of the evidence was made known to the court by offer or was apparent from the context within which questions were asked.

**(b) Record of offer and ruling.**   The court may add any other or further statement which shows the character of the evidence, the form in which it was offered, the objection made, and the ruling thereon. It may direct the making of an offer in question and answer form.

**(c) Hearing of jury.**   In jury cases, proceedings shall be conducted, to the extent practicable, so as to prevent inadmissible evidence from being suggested to the jury by any means, such as making statements or offers of proof or asking questions in the hearing of the jury.

**(d) Plain error.**   Nothing in this rule precludes taking notice of plain errors affecting substantial rights although they were not brought to the attention of the court.

## Rule 104. Preliminary questions

(a) **Questions of admissibility generally.** Preliminary questions concerning the qualification of a person to be a witness, the existence of a privilege, or the admissibility of evidence shall be determined by the court, subject to the provisions of subdivision (b). In making its determination, it is not bound by the rules of evidence except those with respect to privileges.

(b) **Relevancy conditioned on fact.** When the relevancy of evidence depends upon the fulfillment of a condition of fact, the court shall admit it upon, or subject to, the introduction of evidence sufficient to support a finding of the fulfillment of the condition.

(c) **Hearing of jury.** Hearings on the admissibility of confessions shall in all cases be conducted out of the hearing of the jury. Hearings on other preliminary matters shall be so conducted when the interests of justice require or when an accused is a witness and so requests.

(d) **Testimony by accused.** The accused does not, by testifying upon a preliminary matter, become subject to cross-examination as to other issues in the case.

(e) **Weight and credibility.** This rule does not limit the right of a party to introduce before the jury evidence relevant to weight or credibility.

## Rule 105. Limited admissibility

When evidence which is admissible as to one party or for one purpose but not admissible as to another party or for another purpose is admitted, the court, upon request, shall restrict the evidence to its proper scope and instruct the jury accordingly.

## Rule 106. Remainder of or related writings or recorded statements

When a writing or recorded statement or part thereof is introduced by a party, an adverse party may require the introduction at that time of any other part or any other writing or recorded statement which ought in fairness to be considered contemporaneously with it.

## ARTICLE II. JUDICIAL NOTICE

## Rule 201. Judicial notice of adjudicative facts

(a) **Scope of rule.** This rule governs only judicial notice of adjudicative facts.

**(b) Kinds of facts.** A judicially noticed fact must be one not subject to reasonable dispute in that it is either (1) generally known within the territorial jurisdiction of the trial court or (2) capable of accurate and ready determination by resort to sources whose accuracy cannot reasonably be questioned.

**(c) When discretionary.** A court may take judicial notice, whether requested or not.

**(d) When mandatory.** A court shall take judicial notice if requested by a party and supplied with the necessary information.

**(e) Opportunity to be heard.** A party is entitled upon timely request to an opportunity to be heard as to the propriety of taking judicial notice and the tenor of the matter noticed. In the absence of prior notification, the request may be made after judicial notice has been taken.

**(f) Time of taking notice.** Judicial notice may be taken at any stage of the proceeding.

**(g) Instructing jury.** In a civil action or proceeding, the court shall instruct the jury to accept as conclusive any fact judicially noticed. In a criminal case, the court shall instruct the jury that it may, but is not required to, accept as conclusive any fact judicially noticed.

## ARTICLE III. PRESUMPTIONS IN CIVIL ACTIONS AND PROCEEDINGS

### Rule 301. Presumptions in general civil actions and proceedings

In all civil actions and proceedings, not otherwise provided for by Act of Congress or by these rules, a presumption imposes on the party against whom it is directed the burden of going forward with evidence to rebut or meet the presumption, but does not shift to such party the burden of proof in the sense of the risk of nonpersuasion, which remains throughout the trial upon the party on whom it was originally cast.

### Rule 302. Applicability of state law in civil actions and proceedings [deleted]

## ARTICLE IV. RELEVANCY AND ITS LIMITS

### Rule 401. Definition of "relevant evidence"

"Relevant evidence" means evidence having any tendency to make the existence of any fact that is of consequence to the determination of the action more probable or less probable than it would be without the evidence.

## Rule 402.  Relevant evidence generally admissible; irrelevant evidence inadmissible

All relevant evidence is admissible, except as otherwise provided by the Constitution of the United States, by Act of Congress, by these rules, or by other rules prescribed by the Supreme Court pursuant to statutory authority. Evidence which is not relevant is not admissible.

## Rule 403.  Exclusion of relevant evidence on grounds of prejudice, confusion, or waste of time

Although relevant, evidence may be excluded if its probative value is substantially outweighed by the danger of unfair prejudice, confusion of the issues, or misleading the jury, or by consideration of undue delay, waste of time, or needless presentation of cumulative evidence.

## Rule 404.  Character evidence not admissible to prove conduct; exceptions; other crimes

(a) Character evidence generally.   Evidence of a person's character or a trait of character is not admissible for the purpose of proving action in conformity therewith on a particular occasion, except:
(1) Character of accused.   Evidence of a pertinent trait of character offered by an accused, or by the prosecution to rebut the same;
(2) Character of victim.   Evidence of a pertinent trait of character of the victim of the crime offered by an accused, or by the prosecution to rebut the same, or evidence of a character trait of peacefulness of the victim offered by the prosecution in a homicide case to rebut evidence that the victim was the first aggressor;
(3) Character of witness.   Evidence of the character of a witness, as provided in rules 607, 608, and 609.
(b) Other crimes, wrongs, or acts.   Evidence of other crimes, wrongs, or acts is not admissible to prove the character of a person in order to show action in conformity therewith. It may, however, be admissible for other purposes, such as proof of motive, opportunity, intent, preparation, plan, knowledge, identity, or absence of mistake or accident, provided that upon request by the accused, the prosecution in a criminal case shall provide reasonable notice in advance of trial, or during trial if the court excuses pretrial notice on good cause shown, of the general nature of any such evidence it intends to introduce at trial.

## Rule 405.  Methods of proving character

**(a) Reputation or opinion.**   In all cases in which evidence of character or a trait of character of a person is admissible, proof may be made by testimony as to reputation or by testimony in the form of an opinion. On cross-examination, inquiry is allowable into relevant specific instances of conduct.

**(b) Specific instances of conduct.**   In cases in which character or a trait of character of a person is an essential element of a charge, claim, or defense, proof may also be made of specific instances of that person's conduct.

## Rule 406.   Habit; routine practice

Evidence of the habit of a person or of the routine practice of an organization, whether corroborated or not and regardless of the presence of eyewitnesses, is relevant to prove that the conduct of the person or organization on a particular occasion was in conformity with the habit or routine practice.

## Rule 407.   Subsequent remedial measures

When, after an event, measures are taken which, if taken previously, would have made the event less likely to occur, evidence of the subsequent measures is not admissible to prove negligence or culpable conduct in connection with the event. This rule does not require the exclusion of evidence of subsequent measures when offered for another purpose, such as proving ownership, control, or feasibility of precautionary measures, if controverted, or impeachment.

## Rule 408.   Compromise and offers to compromise

Evidence of (1) furnishing or offering or promising to furnish, or (2) accepting or offering or promising to accept, a valuable consideration in compromising or attempting to compromise a claim which was disputed as to either validity or amount, is not admissible to prove liability for or invalidity of the claim or its amount. Evidence of conduct or statements made in compromise negotiations is likewise not admissible. This rule does not require the exclusion of any evidence otherwise discoverable merely because it is presented in the course of compromise negotiations. This rule also does not require exclusion when the evidence is offered for another purpose, such as proving bias or prejudice of a witness, negativing a contention of undue delay, or proving an effort to obstruct a criminal investigation or prosecution.

## Rule 409.   Payment of medical and similar expenses

Evidence of furnishing or offering or promising to pay medical, hospital, or similar expenses occasioned by an injury is not admissible to prove liability for the injury.

## Rule 410.   Inadmissibility of pleas, offers of pleas, and related statements

Except as otherwise provided in this rule, evidence of a plea of guilty, later withdrawn, or a plea of nolo contendere, or of an offer to plead guilty or nolo contendere to the crime charged or any other crime or of statements made in connection with, and relevant to, any of the foregoing pleas or offers, is not admissible in any civil or criminal proceeding against the person who made the plea or offer. However, evidence of a statement made in connection with, and relevant to, a plea of guilty, later withdrawn, a plea of nolo contendere, or an offer to plead guilty or nolo contendere to the crime charged or any other crime, is admissible in a criminal proceeding for perjury or false statement if the statement was made by the defendant under oath, on the record, and in the presence of counsel.

## Rule 411.   Liability insurance

Evidence that a person was or was not insured against liability is not admissible upon the issue whether the person acted negligently or otherwise wrongfully. This rule does not require the exclusion of evidence of insurance against liability when offered for another purpose, such as proof of agency, ownership, or control, or bias or prejudice of a witness.

## Rule 412.   Rape cases; relevance of victim's past behavior [deleted]

## ARTICLE V.   PRIVILEGES

## Rule 501.   General rule

Except as otherwise required by the Constitution of the United States or provided by Act of Congress or in rules prescribed by the Supreme Court pursuant to statutory authority, the privilege of a witness, person, government,

State, or political subdivision thereof shall be governed by the principles of the common law as they may be interpreted by the courts of the United States in the light of reason and experience. However, in civil actions and proceedings, with respect to an element of a claim or defense as to which State law supplies the rule of decision, the privilege of a witness, person, government, State, or political subdivision thereof shall be determined in accordance with State law.

## ARTICLE VI.   WITNESSES

### Rule 601.   General rule of competency

Every person is competent to be a witness except as otherwise provided in these rules. However, in civil actions and proceedings, with respect to an element of a claim or defense as to which State law supplies the rule of decision, the competency of a witness shall be determined in accordance with State law.

### Rule 602.   Lack of personal knowledge

A witness may not testify to a matter unless evidence is introduced sufficient to support a finding that the witness has personal knowledge of the matter. Evidence to prove personal knowledge may, but need not, consist of the witness' own testimony. This rule is subject to the provisions of rule 703, relating to opinion testimony by expert witnesses.

### Rule 603.   Oath or affirmation

Before testifying, every witness shall be required to declare that the witness will testify truthfully, by oath or affirmation administered in a form calculated to awaken the witness' conscience and impress the witness' mind with the duty to do so.

### Rule 604.   Interpreters

An interpreter is subject to the provisions of these rules relating to qualification as an expert and the administration of an oath or affirmation to make a true translation.

### Rule 605.   Competency of judge as witness

The judge presiding at the trial may not testify in that trial as a witness. No objection need be made in order to preserve the point.

### Rule 606.   Competency of juror as witness [deleted]

### Rule 607.   Who may impeach

The credibility of a witness may be attacked by any party, including the party calling the witness.

### Rule 608.   Evidence of character and conduct of witness

**(a) Opinion and reputation evidence of character.**   The credibility of a witness may be attacked or supported by evidence in the form of opinion or reputation, but subject to these limitations: (1) the evidence may refer only to character for truthfulness or untruthfulness, and (2) evidence of truthful character is admissible only after the character of the witness for truthfulness has been attacked by opinion or reputation evidence or otherwise.

**(b) Specific instances of conduct.**   Specific instances of the conduct of a witness, for the purpose of attacking or supporting the witness' credibility, other than conviction of crime as provided in rule 609, may not be proved by extrinsic evidence. They may, however, in the discretion of the court, if probative of truthfulness or untruthfulness, be inquired into on cross-examination of the witness (1) concerning the witness' character for truthfulness or untruthfulness, or (2) concerning the character for truthfulness or untruthfulness of another witness as to which character the witness being cross-examined has testified.

The giving of testimony, whether by an accused or by any other witness, does not operate as a waiver of the accused's or the witness' privilege against self-incrimination when examined with respect to matters which relate only to credibility.

### Rule 609.   Impeachment by evidence of conviction of crime [deleted]

### Rule 610.   Religious beliefs or opinions

Evidence of the beliefs or opinions of a witness on matters of religion is not admissible for the purpose of showing that by reason of their nature the witness' credibility is impaired or enhanced.

### Rule 611.   Mode and order of interrogation and presentation

**(a) Control by court.**   The court shall exercise reasonable control over the mode and order of interrogating witnesses and presenting evidence so as to (1) make the interrogation and presentation effective for the ascertainment of the truth, (2) avoid needless consumption of time, and (3) protect witnesses from harassment or undue embarrassment.

**(b) Scope of cross-examination.** Cross-examination should be limited to the subject matter of the direct examination and matters affecting the credibility of the witness. The court may, in the exercise of discretion, permit inquiry into additional matters as if on direct examination.

**(c) Leading questions.** Leading questions should not be used on the direct examination of a witness except as may be necessary to develop the witness' testimony. Ordinarily leading questions should be permitted on cross-examination. When a party calls a hostile witness, an adverse party, or a witness identified with an adverse party, interrogation may be by leading questions.

### Rule 612.   Writing used to refresh memory

Except as otherwise provided in criminal proceedings by section 3500 of title 18, United States Code, if a witness uses a writing to refresh memory for the purpose of testifying, either—

(1) while testifying, or

(2) before testifying, if the court in its discretion determines it is necessary in the interests of justice,

an adverse party is entitled to have the writing produced at the hearing, to inspect it, to cross-examine the witness thereon, and to introduce in evidence those portions which relate to the testimony of the witness. If it is claimed that the writing contains matters not related to the subject matter of the testimony the court shall examine the writing in camera, excise any portions not so related, and order delivery of the remainder to the party entitled thereto. Any portion withheld over objections shall be preserved and made available to the appellate court in the event of an appeal. If a writing is not produced or delivered pursuant to order under this rule, the court shall make any order justice requires, except that in criminal cases when the prosecution elects not to comply, the order shall be one striking the testimony or, if the court in its discretion determines that the interests of justice so require, declaring a mistrial.

### Rule 613.   Prior statements of witnesses

**(a) Examining witness concerning prior statement.** In examining a witness concerning a prior statement made by the witness, whether written or not, the statement need not be shown nor its contents disclosed to the witness at that time, but on request the same shall be shown or disclosed to opposing counsel.

**(b) Extrinsic evidence of prior inconsistent statement of witness.** Extrinsic evidence of a prior inconsistent statement by a witness is not admissible unless the witness is afforded an opportunity to explain or deny the same and the opposite party is afforded an opportunity to interrogate the witness thereon, or the interests of justice otherwise require. This provision does not apply to admissions of a party-opponent as defined in rule 801(d)(2).

### Rule 614.  Calling and interrogation of witnesses by court

**(a) Calling by court.**  The court may, on its own motion or at the suggestion of a party, call witnesses, and all parties are entitled to cross-examine witnesses thus called.

**(b) Interrogation by court.**  The court may interrogate witnesses, whether called by itself or by a party.

**(c) Objections.**  Objections to the calling of witnesses by the court or to interrogation by it may be made at the time or at the next available opportunity when the jury is not present.

### Rule 615.  Exclusion of witnesses

At the request of a party the court shall order witnesses excluded so that they cannot hear the testimony of other witnesses and it may make the order of its own motion. This rule does not authorize exclusion of (1) a party who is a natural person, or (2) an officer or employee of a party which is not a natural person designated as its representative by its attorney, or (3) a person whose presence is shown by a party to be essential to the presentation of the party's cause.

### ARTICLE VII.  OPINIONS AND EXPERT TESTIMONY

### Rule 701.  Opinion testimony by lay witnesses

If the witness is not testifying as an expert, the witness' testimony in the form of opinions or inferences is limited to those opinions or inferences which are (a) rationally based on the perception of the witness and (b) helpful to a clear understanding of the witness' testimony or the determination of a fact in issue.

## Rule 702.   Testimony by experts

If scientific, technical, or other specialized knowledge will assist the trier of fact to understand the evidence or to determine a fact in issue, a witness qualified as an expert by knowledge, skill, experience, training, or education, may testify thereto in the form of an opinion or otherwise.

## Rule 703.   Bases of opinion testimony by experts

The facts or data in the particular case upon which an expert bases an opinion or inference may be those perceived by or made known to the expert at or before the hearing. If of a type reasonably relied upon by experts in the particular field in forming opinions or inferences upon the subject, the facts or data need not be admissible in evidence.

## Rule 704.   Opinion on ultimate issue

(a) Except as provided in subdivision (b), testimony in the form of an opinion or inference otherwise admissible is not objectionable because it embraces an ultimate issue to be decided by the trier of fact.

(b) No expert witness testifying with respect to the mental state or condition of a defendant in a criminal case may state an opinion or inference as to whether the defendant did or did not have the mental state or condition constituting an element of the crime charged or of a defense thereto. Such ultimate issues are matters for the trier of fact alone.

## Rule 705.   Disclosure of facts or data underlying expert opinion

The expert may testify in terms of opinion or inference and give reasons therefor without first testifying to the underlying facts or data, unless the court requires otherwise. The expert may in any event be required to disclose the underlying facts or data on cross-examination.

## Rule 706.   Court appointed experts

(a) Appointment.   The court may on its own motion or on the motion of any party enter an order to show cause why expert witnesses should not be appointed, and may request the parties to submit nominations. The court may appoint any expert witnesses agreed upon by the parties, and may appoint expert witnesses of its own selection. An expert witness shall not be appointed by the court unless the witness consents to act. A witness so appointed shall be informed of the witness' duties by the court in writing, a copy of which shall be filed with the clerk, or at a conference in which the parties shall have opportunity to participate. A witness so appointed shall advise the parties of the witness' findings, if any; the witness' deposition may be taken by any party; and the witness may be called to testify by the court or any party. The witness shall be subject to cross-examination by each party, including a party calling the witness.

**(b) Compensation.** Expert witnesses so appointed are entitled to reasonable compensation in whatever sum the court may allow. The compensation thus fixed is payable from funds which may be provided by law in criminal cases and civil actions and proceedings involving just compensation under the fifth amendment. In other civil actions and proceedings the compensation shall be paid by the parties in such proportion and at such time as the court directs, and thereafter charged in like manner as other costs.

**(c) Disclosure of appointment.** In the exercise of its discretion, the court may authorize disclosure to the jury of the fact that the court appointed the expert witness.

**(d) Parties' experts of own selection.** Nothing in this rule limits the parties in calling expert witnesses of their own selection.

## ARTICLE VIII. HEARSAY

### Rule 801. Definitions

The following definitions apply under this article:

**(a) Statement.** A "statement" is (1) an oral or written assertion or (2) nonverbal conduct of a person, if it is intended by the person as an assertion.

**(b) Declarant.** A "declarant" is a person who makes a statement.

**(c) Hearsay.** "Hearsay" is a statement, other than one made by the declarant while testifying at the trial or hearing, offered in evidence to prove the truth of the matter asserted.

**(d) Statements which are not hearsay.** A statement is not hearsay if—

**(1) Prior statement by witness.** The declarant testifies at the trial or hearing and is subject to cross-examination concerning the statement, and the statement is (A) inconsistent with the declarant's testimony, and was given under oath subject to the penalty of perjury at a trial, hearing, or other proceeding, or in a deposition, or (B) consistent with the declarant's testimony and is offered to rebut an express or implied charge against the declarant of recent fabrication or improper influence or motive, or (C) one of identification of a person after perceiving the person; or

**(2) Admission by party-opponent.**    The statement is offered against a party and is (A) the party's own statement, in either an individual or a representative capacity, or (B) a statement of which the party has manifested an adoption or belief in its truth, or (C) a statement by a person authorized by the party to make a statement concerning the subject, or (D) a statement by the party's agent or servant concerning a matter within the scope of the agency or employment, made during the existence of the relationship, or (E) a statement by a coconspirator of a party during the course and in furtherance of the conspiracy.

### Rule 802.    Hearsay rule

Hearsay is not admissible except as provided by these rules or by other rules prescribed by the Supreme Court pursuant to statutory authority or by Act of Congress.

### Rule 803.    Hearsay exceptions; availability of declarant immaterial

The following are not excluded by the hearsay rule, even though the declarant is available as a witness:

**(1) Present sense impression.**    A statement describing or explaining an event or condition made while the declarant was perceiving the event or condition, or immediately thereafter.

**(2) Excited utterance.**    A statement relating to a startling event or condition made while the declarant was under the stress of excitement caused by the event or condition.

**(3) Then existing mental, emotional, or physical condition.**    A statement of the declarant's then existing state of mind, emotion, sensation, or physical condition (such as intent, plan, motive, design, mental feeling, pain, and bodily health), but not including a statement of memory or belief to prove the fact remembered or believed unless it relates to the execution, revocation, identification, or terms of declarant's will.

**(4) Statements for purposes of medical diagnosis or treatment.**    Statements made for purposes of medical diagnosis or treatment and describing medical history, or past or present symptoms, pain, or sensations, or the inception or general character of the cause or external source thereof insofar as reasonably pertinent to diagnosis or treatment.

**(5) Recorded recollection.**    A memorandum or record concerning a matter about which a witness once had knowledge but now has insufficient recollection to enable the witness to testify fully and accurately, shown to have been made or adopted by the witness when the matter was fresh in the witness' memory and to reflect that knowledge correctly. If admitted, the memorandum or record may be read into evidence but may not itself be received as an exhibit unless offered by an adverse party.

**(6) Records of regularly conducted activity.** A memorandum, report, record, or data compilation, in any form, of acts, events, conditions, opinions, or diagnoses, made at or near the time by, or from information transmitted by, a person with knowledge, if kept in the course of a regularly conducted business activity, and if it was the regular practice of that business activity to make the memorandum, report, record, or data compilation, all as shown by the testimony of the custodian or other qualified witness, unless the source of information or the method or circumstances of preparation indicate lack of trustworthiness. The term "business" as used in this paragraph includes business, institution, association, profession, occupation, and calling of every kind, whether or not conducted for profit.

**(7) Absence of entry in records kept in accordance with the provisions of paragraph (6).** Evidence that a matter is not included in the memoranda reports, records, or data compilations, in any form, kept in accordance with the provisions of paragraph (6), to prove the nonoccurrence or nonexistence of the matter, if the matter was of a kind of which a memorandum, report, record, or data compilation was regularly made and preserved, unless the sources of information or other circumstances indicate lack of trustworthiness.

**(8) Public records and reports.** Records, reports, statements, or data compilations, in any form, of public offices or agencies, setting forth (A) the activities of the office or agency, or (B) matters observed pursuant to duty imposed by law as to which matters there was a duty to report, excluding, however, in criminal cases matters observed by police officers and other law enforcement personnel, or (C) in civil actions and proceedings and against the Government in criminal cases, factual findings resulting from an investigation made pursuant to authority granted by law, unless the sources of information or other circumstances indicate lack of trustworthiness.

**(9) Records of vital statistics.** Records or data compilations, in any form, of births, fetal deaths, deaths, or marriages, if the report thereof was made to a public office pursuant to requirements of law.

**(10) Absence of public record or entry.** To prove the absence of a record, report, statement, or data compilation, in any form, or the nonoccurrence or nonexistence of a matter of which a record, report, statement, or data compilation, in any form, was regularly made and preserved by a public office or agency, evidence in the form of a certification in accordance with rule 902, or testimony, that diligent search failed to disclose the record, report, statement, or data compilation, or entry.

**(11) Records of religious organizations.** Statements of births, marriages, divorces, deaths, legitimacy, ancestry, relationship by blood or marriage, or other similar facts of personal or family history, contained in a regularly kept record of a religious organization.

**(12) Marriage, baptismal, and similar certificates.** Statements of fact contained in a certificate that the maker performed a marriage or other ceremony or administered a sacrament, made by a clergyman, public official, or other person authorized by the rules or practices of a religious organization or by law to perform the act certified, and purporting to have been issued at the time of the act or within a reasonable time thereafter.

**(13) Family records.** Statements of fact concerning personal or family history contained in family Bibles, genealogies, charts, engravings on rings, inscriptions on family portraits, engravings on urns, crypts, or tombstones, or the like.

**(14) Records of documents affecting an interest in property.** The record of a document purporting to establish or affect an interest in property, as proof of the content of the original recorded document and its execution and delivery by each person by whom it purports to have been executed, if the record is a record of a public office and an applicable statute authorizes the recording of documents of that kind in that office.

**(15) Statements in documents affecting an interest in property.** A statement contained in a document purporting to establish or affect an interest in property if the matter stated was relevant to the purpose of the document, unless dealings with the property since the document was made have been inconsistent with the truth of the statement or the purport of the document.

**(16) Statements in ancient documents.** Statements in a document in existence twenty years or more the authenticity of which is established.

**(17) Market reports, commercial publications.** Market quotations, tabulations, lists, directories, or other published compilations, generally used and relied upon by the public or by persons in particular occupations.

**(18) Learned treatises.** To the extent called to the attention of an expert witness upon cross-examination or relied upon by the expert witness in direct examination, statements contained in published treatises, periodicals, or pamphlets on a subject of history, medicine, or other science or art, established as a reliable authority by the testimony or admission of the witness or by other expert testimony or by judicial notice. If admitted, the statements may be read into evidence but may not be received as exhibits.

**(19) Reputation concerning personal or family history.** Reputation among members of a person's family by blood, adoption, or marriage, or among a person's associates, or in the community, concerning a person's birth, adoption, marriage, divorce, death, legitimacy, relationship by blood, adoption, or marriage, ancestry, or other similar fact of his personal or family history.

**(20) Reputation concerning boundaries or general history.** Reputation in a community, arising before the controversy, as to boundaries of or customs affecting lands in the community, and reputation as to events of general history important to the community or State or nation in which located.

**(21) Reputation as to character.** Reputation of a person's character among associates or in the community.

**(22) Judgment of previous conviction.** Evidence of a final judgment, entered after a trial or upon a plea of guilty (but not upon a plea of nolo contendere), adjudging a person guilty of a crime punishable by death or imprisonment in excess of one year, to prove any fact essential to sustain the judgment, but not including, when offered by the Government in a criminal prosecution for purposes other than impeachment, judgments against persons other than the accused. The pendency of an appeal may be shown but does not affect admissibility.

**(23) Judgment as to personal, family, or general history, or boundaries.** Judgments as proof of matters of personal, family or general history, or boundaries, essential to the judgment, if the same would be provable by evidence of reputation.

**(24) Other exceptions.** A statement not specifically covered by any of the foregoing exceptions but having equivalent circumstantial guarantees of trustworthiness, if the court determines that (A) the statement is offered as evidence of a material fact; (B) the statement is more probative on the point for which it is offered than any other evidence which the proponent can procure through reasonable efforts; and (C) the general purposes of these rules and the interests of justice will best be served by admission of the statement into evidence. However, a statement may not be admitted under this exception unless the proponent of it makes known to the adverse party sufficiently in advance of the trial or hearing to provide the adverse party with a fair opportunity to prepare to meet it, the proponent's intention to offer the statement and particulars of it, including the name and address of the declarant.

### Rule 804. Hearsay exceptions; declarant unavailable

**(a) Definition of unavailability.** ''Unavailability as a witness'' includes situations in which the declarant—

(1) is exempted by ruling of the court on the ground of privilege from testifying concerning the subject matter of the declarant's statement or

(2) persists in refusing to testify concerning the subject matter of the declarant's statement despite an order of the court to do so; or

(3) testifies to a lack of memory of the subject matter of the declarant's statement; or

(4) is unable to be present or to testify at the hearing because of death or then existing physical or mental illness or infirmity; or

(5) is absent from the hearing and the proponent of a statement has been unable to procure the declarant's attendance (or in the case of a hearsay

exception under subdivision (b)(2), (3), or (4), the declarant's attendance or testimony) by process or other reasonable means.
A declarant is not unavailable as a witness if exemption, refusal, claim of lack of memory, inability, or absence is due to the procurement or wrongdoing of the proponent of a statement for the purpose of preventing the witness from attending or testifying.

**(b) Hearsay exceptions.**    The following are not excluded by the hearsay rule if the declarant is unavailable as a witness:

**(1) Former testimony.**    Testimony given as a witness at another hearing of the same or a different proceeding, or in a deposition taken in compliance with law in the course of the same or another proceeding, if the party against whom the testimony is now offered, or, in a civil action or proceeding, a predecessor in interest, had an opportunity and similar motive to develop the testimony by direct, cross, or redirect examination.

**(2) Statement under belief of impending death.**    In a prosecution for homicide or in a civil action or proceeding, a statement made by a declarant while believing that the declarant's death was imminent, concerning the cause or circumstances of what the declarant believed to be impending death.

**(3) Statement against interest.**    A statement which was at the time of its making so far contrary to the declarant's pecuniary to proprietary interest, or so far tended to subject the declarant to civil or criminal liability, or to render invalid a claim by the declarant against another, that a reasonable person in the declarant's position would not have made the statement unless believing it to be true. A statement tending to expose the declarant to criminal liability and offered to exculpate the accused is not admissible unless corroborating circumstances clearly indicate the trustworthiness of the statement.

**(4) Statement of personal or family history.**    (A) A statement concerning the declarant's own birth, adoption, marriage, divorce, legitimacy, relationship by blood, adoption, or marriage, ancestry, or other similar fact of personal or family history, even though declarant had no means of acquiring personal knowledge of the matter stated; or (B) a statement concerning the foregoing matters, and death also, of another person, if the declarant was related to the other by blood, adoption, or marriage or was so intimately associated with the other's family as to be likely to have accurate information concerning the matter declared.

**(5) Other exceptions.**    A statement not specifically covered by any of the foregoing exceptions but having equivalent circumstantial guarantees of trustworthiness, if the court determines that (A) the statement is offered as evidence of a material fact; (B) the statement is more probative on the point for which it is offered than any other evidence which the proponent can procure through reasonable efforts; and (C) the general purposes of these rules and the interests of justice will best be served by admission of the statement into evidence. However, a statement may not be admitted under this exception unless the proponent of it makes known to the adverse party sufficiently in advance of the trial or hearing to provide the adverse party with a fair opportunity to prepare to meet it, the proponent's intention to offer the statement and the particulars of it, including the name and address of the declarant.

### Rule 805. Hearsay within hearsay

Hearsay included within hearsay is not excluded under the hearsay rule if each part of the combined statements conforms with an exception to the hearsay rule provided in these rules.

### Rule 806. Attacking and supporting credibility of declarant

When a hearsay statement, or a statement defined in Rule 801(d)(2), (C), (D), or (E), has been admitted in evidence, the credibility of the declarant may be attacked, and if attacked may be supported, by any evidence which would be admissible for those purposes if declarant had testified as a witness. Evidence of a statement or conduct by the declarant at any time, inconsistent with the declarant's hearsay statement, is not subject to any requirement that the declarant may have been afforded an opportunity to deny or explain. If the party against whom a hearsay statement has been admitted calls the declarant as a witness, the party is entitled to examine the declarant on the statement as if under cross-examination.

### ARTICLE IX. AUTHENTICATION AND IDENTIFICATION

### Rule 901. Requirement of authentication or identification

(a) **General provision.** The requirement of authentication or identification as a condition precedent to admissibility is satisfied by evidence sufficient to support a finding that the matter in question is what its proponent claims.

(b) **Illustrations.** By way of illustration only, and not by way of limitation, the following are examples of authentication or identification conforming with the requirements of this rule:

(1) **Testimony of witness with knowledge.** Testimony that a matter is what it is claimed to be.

**(2) Nonexpert opinion on handwriting.**    Nonexpert opinion as to the genuineness of handwriting, based upon familiarity not acquired for purposes of the litigation.

**(3) Comparison by trier or expert witness.**    Comparison by the trier of fact or by expert witnesses with specimens which have been authenticated.

**(4) Distinctive characteristics and the like.**    Appearance, contents, substance, internal patterns, or other distinctive characteristics, taken in conjunction with circumstances.

**(5) Voice identification.**    Identification of a voice, whether heard firsthand or through mechanical or electronic transmission or recording, by opinion based upon hearing the voice at any time under circumstances connecting it with the alleged speaker.

**(6) Telephone conversations.**    Telephone conversations, by evidence that a call was made to the number assigned at the time by the telephone company to a particular person or business, if (A) in the case of a person, circumstances, including self-identification, show the person answering to be the one called, or (B) in the case of a business, the call was made to a place of business and the conversation related to business reasonably transacted over the telephone.

**(7) Public records or reports.**    Evidence that a writing authorized by law to be recorded or filed and in fact recorded or filed in a public office, or a purported public record, report, statement, or data compilation, in any form, is from the public office where items of this nature are kept.

**(8) Ancient documents or data compilation.**    Evidence that a document or data compilation, in any form, (A) is in such condition as to create no suspicion concerning its authenticity, (B) was in a place where it, if authentic, would likely be, and (C) has been in existence 20 years or more at the time it is offered.

**(9) Process or system.**    Evidence describing a process or system used to produce a result and showing that the process or system produces an accurate result.

**(10) Methods provided by statute or rule.**    Any method of authentication or identification provided by Act of Congress or by other rules prescribed by the Supreme Court pursuant to statutory authority.

### Rule 902.    Self-authentication

Extrinsic evidence of authenticity as a condition precedent to admissibility is not required with respect to the following:

**(1) Domestic public documents under seal.**    A document bearing a seal purporting to be that of the United States, or of any State, district, Commonwealth, territory, or insular possession thereof, or the Panama Canal Zone, or the Trust Territory of the Pacific Islands, or of a political subdivision, department, officer, or agency thereof, and a signature purporting to be an attestation or execution.

**(2) Domestic public documents not under seal.** A document purporting to bear the signature in the official capacity of an officer or employee of any entity included in paragraph (1) hereof, having no seal, if a public officer having a seal and having official duties in the district or political subdivision of the officer or employee certifies under seal that the signer has the official capacity and that the signature is genuine.

**(3) Foreign public documents.** A document purporting to be executed or attested in an official capacity by a person authorized by the laws of a foreign country to make the execution or attestation, and accompanied by a final certification as to the genuineness of the signature and official position (A) of the executing or attesting person, or (B) of any foreign official whose certificate of genuineness of signature and official position relates to the execution or attestation or is in a chain of certificates of genuineness of signature and official position relating to the execution or attestation. A final certification may be made by a secretary of embassy or legation, consul general, consul, vice consul, or consular agent of the United States, or a diplomatic or consular official of the foreign country assigned or accredited to the United States. If reasonable opportunity has been given to all parties to investigate the authenticity and accuracy of official documents, the court may, for good cause shown, order that they be treated as presumptively authentic without final certification or permit them to be evidenced by an attested summary with or without final certification.

**(4) Certified copies of public records.** A copy of an official record or report or entry therein, or of a document authorized by law to be recorded or filed and actually recorded or filed in a public office, including data compilations in any form, certified as correct by the custodian or other person authorized to make the certification, by certificate complying with paragraph (1), (2), or (3) of this rule or complying with any Act of Congress or rule prescribed by the Supreme Court pursuant to statutory authority.

**(5) Official publications.** Books, pamphlets, or other publications purporting to be issued by public authority.

**(6) Newspapers and periodicals.** Printed materials purporting to be newspapers or periodicals.

**(7) Trade inscriptions and the like.** Inscriptions, signs, tags, or labels purporting to have been affixed in the course of business and indicating ownership, control, or origin.

**(8) Acknowledged documents.** Documents accompanied by a certificate of acknowledgment executed in the manner provided by law by a notary public or other officer authorized by law to take acknowledgments.

**(9) Commercial paper and related documents.**   Commercial paper, signatures thereon, and documents relating thereto to the extent provided by general commercial law.

**(10) Presumptions under Acts of Congress.**   Any signature, document, or other matter declared by Act of Congress to be presumptively or prima facie genuine or authentic.

### Rule 903.   Subscribing Witness' Testimony Unnecessary

The testimony of a subscribing witness is not necessary to authenticate a writing unless required by the laws of the jurisdiction whose laws govern the validity of the writing.

### ARTICLE X.   CONTENTS OF WRITINGS, RECORDINGS, AND PHOTOGRAPHS

### Rule 1001.   Definitions

For purposes of this article the following definitions are applicable:

**(1) Writings and recordings.**   "Writings" and "recordings" consist of letters, words, or numbers, or their equivalent, set down by handwriting, typewriting, printing, photostating, photographing, magnetic impulse, mechanical or electronic recording, or other form of data compilation.

**(2) Photographs.**   "Photographs" include still photographs, X-ray films, video tapes, and motion pictures.

**(3) Original.**   An "original" of a writing or recording is the writing or recording itself or any counterpart intended to have the same effect by a person executing or issuing it. An "original" of a photograph includes the negative or any print therefrom. If data are stored in a computer or similar device, any printout or other output readable by sight, shown to reflect the data accurately, is an "original."

**(4) Duplicate.**   A "duplicate" is a counterpart produced by the same impression as the original, or from the same matrix, or by means of photography, including enlargements and miniatures, or by mechanical or electronic re-recording, or by chemical reproduction, or by other equivalent techniques which accurately reproduce the original.

## Rule 1002. Requirement of original

To prove the content of a writing, recording, or photograph, the original writing, recording, or photograph is required, except as otherwise provided in these rules by Act of Congress.

## Rule 1003. Admissibility of duplicates

A duplicate is admissible to the same extent as an original unless (1) a genuine question is raised as to the authenticity of the original or (2) in the circumstances it would be unfair to admit the duplicate in lieu of the original.

## Rule 1004. Admissibility of other evidence of contents

The original is not required, and other evidence of the contents of a writing, recording, or photograph is admissible if—

**(1) Originals lost or destroyed.** All originals are lost or have been destroyed, unless the proponent lost or destroyed them in bad faith; or

**(2) Original not obtainable.** No original can be obtained by any available judicial process or procedure; or

**(3) Original in possession of opponent.** At a time when an original was under the control of the party against whom offered, that party was put on notice, by the pleadings or otherwise, that the contents would be a subject of proof at the hearing, and that party does not produce the original at the hearing; or

**(4) Collateral matters.** The writing, recording, or photograph is not closely related to a controlling issue.

## Rule 1005. Public records

The contents of an official record, or of a document authorized to be recorded or filed and actually recorded or filed, including data compilations in any form, if otherwise admissible, may be proved by copy, certified as correct in accordance with rule 902 or testified to be correct by a witness who has compared it with the original. If a copy which complies with the foregoing cannot be obtained by the exercise of reasonable diligence, then other evidence of the contents may be given.

## Rule 1006.   Summaries

The contents of voluminous writings, recordings, or photographs which cannot conveniently be examined in court may be presented in the form of a chart, summary, or calculation. The originals, or duplicates, shall be made available for examination or copying, or both, by other parties at reasonable time and place. The court may order that they be produced in court.

## Rule 1007.   Testimony or written admission of party

Contents of writings, recordings, or photographs may be proved by the testimony or deposition of the party against whom offered or by that party's written admission, without accounting for the nonproduction of the original.

## Rule 1008.   Functions of court and jury

When the admissibility of other evidence of contents of writings, recordings, or photographs under these rules depends upon the fulfillment of a condition of fact, the question whether the condition has been fulfilled is ordinarily for the court to determine in accordance with the provisions of rule 104. However, when an issue is raised (a) whether the asserted writing ever existed, or (b) whether another writing, recording, or photograph produced at the trial is the original, or (c) whether other evidence of contents correctly reflects the contents, the issue is for the trier of fact to determine as in the case of other issues of fact.

## ARTICLE XI.   MISCELLANEOUS RULES [DELETED]

*Source:* 28 C.F.R. § 18.

# OTHER READINGS ON LABOR ARBITRATION AND ADVOCACY SKILLS

## Overview of Labor Arbitration Process

Brodia, Peter B. *A Guide to Federal Labor Relations Authority Law & Practice* (Arlington: Dewey Publications, Inc., 1994)

Coulson, Robert. *Labor Arbitration—What You Need to Know, 3rd ed.* (New York: American Arbitration Association, 1986)

Elkouri, Frank and Edna Asper Elkouri. *How Arbitration Works, 4th ed.* (Washington, D.C.: BNA Books, 1985)

Hayford, Stephen. "The Coming Third Era of Labor Arbitration" *Arbitration Journal*, Sept. 1993

LaCugna, Charles. *Introduction to Labor Arbitration* (Westport: Praeger, 1988)

Nolan, Dennis R. *Labor Arbitration Law and Practice in a Nutshell* (St. Paul: West, 1979)

Schoonhoven. *Fairweather's Practice and Procedure in Labor Arbitration, 3rd ed.* (Washington, D.C.: BNA Books, 1991)

Volz, Marlin. "Labor Arbitration and the Law of Collective Bargaining Agreements" *Labor Lawyer,* Summer, 1989

Volz, Marlin and Edward Groggin. *Supplement to How Arbitration Works* (Washington, D.C.: BNA Books, 1991)

Zack, Arnold. *Grievance Arbitration* (New York: Lexington Books, 1989)

## General Advocacy Skills and Techniques

Aron, Roberto and Jonathan Rosner. *How to Prepare Witnesses for Trial* (Colorado Springs: Shepard's/McGraw-Hill, 1985)

Brandschain, Joseph. "Preparation and Trial of a Labor Arbitration Case" 18:7 *Practical Lawyer* (1972), 17–42

Celmer, Al and Robert Creo. *Federal Arbitration Advocate's Handbook* (Horsham, PA: LRP Publications, 1991)

Givens, Richard A. *Advocacy: The Art of Pleading A Cause* (Colorado Springs: Shepard's/McGraw-Hill, 1992)

Harrison, Allan J. *Preparing and Presenting Your Arbitration Case: A Manual for Union and Management Representatives* (Washington, D.C.: BNA Books, 1979)

Hart, Jacob P. "A Practical Guide to Grievance Arbitration." 25:2 *Practical Lawyer* (1979), 33:56

Jeans, James W. *Trial Advocacy* (St. Paul: West, 1975)

Kagel, Sam. *Anatomy of a Labor Arbitration, 2nd ed.* (Washington, D.C.: BNA Books, 1986)

Levin, Edward and Donald Grody, *Witnesses in Arbitration: Selection, Preparation, and Presentation* (Washington, D.C.: BNA Books, 1987)

Mauet, Thomas A. *Fundamentals of Trial Techniques* (Boston: Little, Brown, 1992)

Sands, John E. "How to Handle Arbitrations in New York State and Federal Courts" *Litigation and Administrative Practice Course Handbook Series* (Philadelphia: Practising Law Institute, 1993)

Sonsteng, John O., Roger S. Haydock and James J. Boyd. *The Trial Handbook* (St. Paul: West, 1984)

Zack, Arnold M. *A Handbook for Grievance Arbitration; Procedural and Ethical Issues* (New York: Lexington Books, 1992)

Zimny, Max et.al., *Labor Arbitration: A Practical Guide for Advocates* (Washington, D.C.: BNA Books, 1990)

## Evidence, Examination and Cross-Examination

Aron, Roberto, Kevin T. Duffy and Jonathan L. Rosner. *Cross-Examination of Witnesses: The Litigator's Puzzle* (Colorado Springs: Shepard's/McGraw-Hill, 1989)

Aron, Roberto, Kevin T. Duffy and Jonathan L. Rosner. *Impeachment of Witnesses: The Cross-Examiner's Art* (Colorado Springs: Shepard's/McGraw-Hill, 1990)

Binder, David F. *Hearsay Handbook* (Colorado Springs: Shepard's/McGraw-Hill, 1991)

Hill, Marvin F. and Anthony V. Sinicropi. *Evidence in Arbitration* (Washington, D.C.: BNA Books, 1987)

Kestler, Jeffrey L. *Questioning Techniques and Tactics* (Colorado Springs: Shepard's/McGraw-Hill, 1992)

Loftus, Elizabeth F. *Eyewitness Testimony* (Cambridge: Harvard Univ. Press, 1979)

Park, Roger C. *Trial Objections Handbook and Quick Reference Guide to Trial Objections* (Colorado Springs: Shepard's/McGraw-Hill, 1993)

Scheinman, Martin F. *Evidence and Proof in Arbitration* (Ithaca: ILR Press, 1977)

Stone, Scott N. and Robert K. Taylor. *Testimonial Privileges* (Colorado Springs: Shepard's/McGraw-Hill, 1993)

Wellman, Francis L. *The Art of Cross Examination, 4th ed.* (New York: Collier, 1962)

## Substantive Labor Arbitration Issues

Coulson, Robert. *Alcohol, Drugs, and Arbitration* (New York: American Arbitration Association, 1987)

Denenberg, Tia Schneider and R.V. Denenberg. *Alcohol and Other Drugs: Issues in Arbitration* (Washington, D.C.: BNA Books, 1991)

Elkouri, Frank and Edna Asper Elkouri. *Resolving Drug Issues* (Washington, D.C.: BNA Books, 1993)

Hill, Marvin F. and Anthony V. Sinicropi. *Remedies in Arbitration* (Washington, D.C.: BNA Books, 1991)

Hill, Marvin F. and Anthony V. Sinicropi. *Management Rights: A Legal and Arbitral Analysis* (Washington, D.C.: BNA Books, 1986)

Hill, Marvin F. and James A. Wright. *Employee Lifestyle and Off-Duty Conduct Regulation* (Washington, D.C.: BNA Books, 1993)

Howan, Lillian T. "The Prospective Effect of Arbitration" *Industrial Relations Law Journal*, 1985

Koven, Adolph M. and Susan L. Smith. *Just Cause: The Seven Tests* (Washington, D.C.: BNA Books, 1992)

Panken, Peter M. et al. *Arbitrating Collectively Bargained Benefit Claims Reality or Illusion* (New York: American Law Institute, 1992)

Perritt, Henry H. *Employee Dismissal Law and Practice, 3rd ed* (New York: John Wiley & Sons, 1992)

Rubin, Pamela G. "Immigrants as Grievants: Protecting the Rights of Non-English-Speaking Union Members in Labor Arbitration" *Georgetown Immigration Law Journal*, Fall, 1994

Stern, James L. and Barbara D. Dennis. "Truth, Lie Detectors, and Other Problems in Labor Arbitration" *Proceedings of the Thirty-First Annual Meeting, National Academy of Arbitrators* (Washington, D.C.: BNA Books, 1979)

Thatcher, Sharon. "Grievance Arbitration Awards: Where is the Interest in Interest" *Labor Lawyer*, Spring, 1992

Volz, Marlin M. "Labor Arbitration and the Law of Collective Bargaining Agreements" *Labor Lawyer*, Summer, 1989

Zack, Arnold M. and Richard I. Bloch. *Labor Agreement in Negotiation and Arbitration, 2nd ed.* (Washington, D.C.: BNA Books, 1995)

## Labor Arbitration Awards–Judicial Review and NLRB Jurisdiction

Berger, Mark. "Judicial Review of Labor Arbitration Awards: Practices, Policies and Sanctions," *Hofstra Labor Law Journal*, Fall, 1992

Greenfield, Patricia A. "How Do Arbitrators Treat External Law" *Industrial and Labor Relations Review*, July, 1992

Hayford, Stephen L. and Anthony V. Sinicropi. "The Labor Contract and External Law: Revisiting the Arbitrator's Scope of Authority" *Journal of Dispute Resolution*, 1993

LeRoy, Michael H. and Peter Feuille. "The Steelworkers Trilogy and Griev-
ance Arbitration Appeals: How the Federal Courts Respond" *Industrial
Relations Law Journal*, 1991
Vacura, Julie R. "Arbitration and NLRB Deferral: From Spielberg to Suburban
Motor Freight and Beyond" *Willamette Law Review*, Fall, 1984
Werner, Charles S. "Clarification of Arbitration Awards" *Labor Lawyer*,
Winter, 1987

## Labor Arbitrators Functions and Development

Barreca, Christopher A., Anne Harmon Miller, and Max Zimny. *Labor Arbitra-
tor Development: A Handbook* (Washington, D.C.: BNA Books, 1983)
Bricker, Timothy R. "A Labor Arbitrator's Ability to Modify a Termination
Order Based on Employer Violations of the Grievance Procedure" *Ohio
State Journal on Dispute Resolution*, 1994
Fleming, Robin. "Reflections on Labor Arbitration" *Proceedings of the Thirty-
Seventh Annual Meeting, National Academy of Arbitrators* (Washington,
D.C.: BNA Books, 1984)
Gruenberg, Gladus W., "The Labor Arbitrator's Role" *Dispute Resolution
Journal*, Sept., 1994
Loewenberg, Joseph J. "The Neutral and Public Interests in Resolving Disputes
in the United States" *Comparative Labor Law Journal*, Summer, 1992
Schmedemann, Deborah A. "Reconciling Differences: The Theory and Law of
Mediating Labor Grievances" *Industrial Relations Law Journal*, 1987
Stone, Morris. *Labor Grievances and Decisions* (New York: American Arbitra-
tion Association, 1970)
Zack, Arnold M. *Arbitration in Practice* (Ithaca: ILR Press, 1984)
Zack, Arnold M. and Richard I. Bloch. *The Arbitration of Discipline Cases:
Concepts and Questions* (New York: American Arbitration Association,
1979)

# Index

[Alphabetization is word-by-word (e.g., Back pay precedes Background facts). References are to page numbers.]

# About the Author

Charles Loughran is an Assistant Circuit Executive for Human Resources for the Ninth Circuit Federal Courts in San Francisco. He has held that position since March, 1994.

Prior to joining the Ninth Circuit, he was President of Seahurst Associates, a human resources consulting firm in Seattle, Washington. He is a former Vice President of Human Resources for Alaska Airlines. Previously, he held executive management positions in labor and employee relations with Louisiana-Pacific Corporation, Trans World Airlines, and U.S. Steel Corporation. He was also associated with the law firm of Pettit & Martin in San Francisco where he specialized in labor and employment law.

Mr. Loughran was a member of the adjunct faculty of the University of Washington Graduate School of Business in Seattle and the University of Michigan Executive Management School in Ann Arbor, Michigan. He has written and lectured extensively, and is the author of *Negotiating a Labor Contract: A Management Handbook* (2nd Ed., BNA Books, 1992). He has written articles for such publications as the *Wall Street Journal* and *Directors and Boards*.

He has a B.A. from The Johns Hopkins University in Baltimore, an M.A. from the University of California (Berkeley), and a J.D. from Golden Gate University Law School in San Francisco. He is a member of the California Bar. He is married and has four children, and is a native of Pittsburgh, Pennsylvania.